D1177589

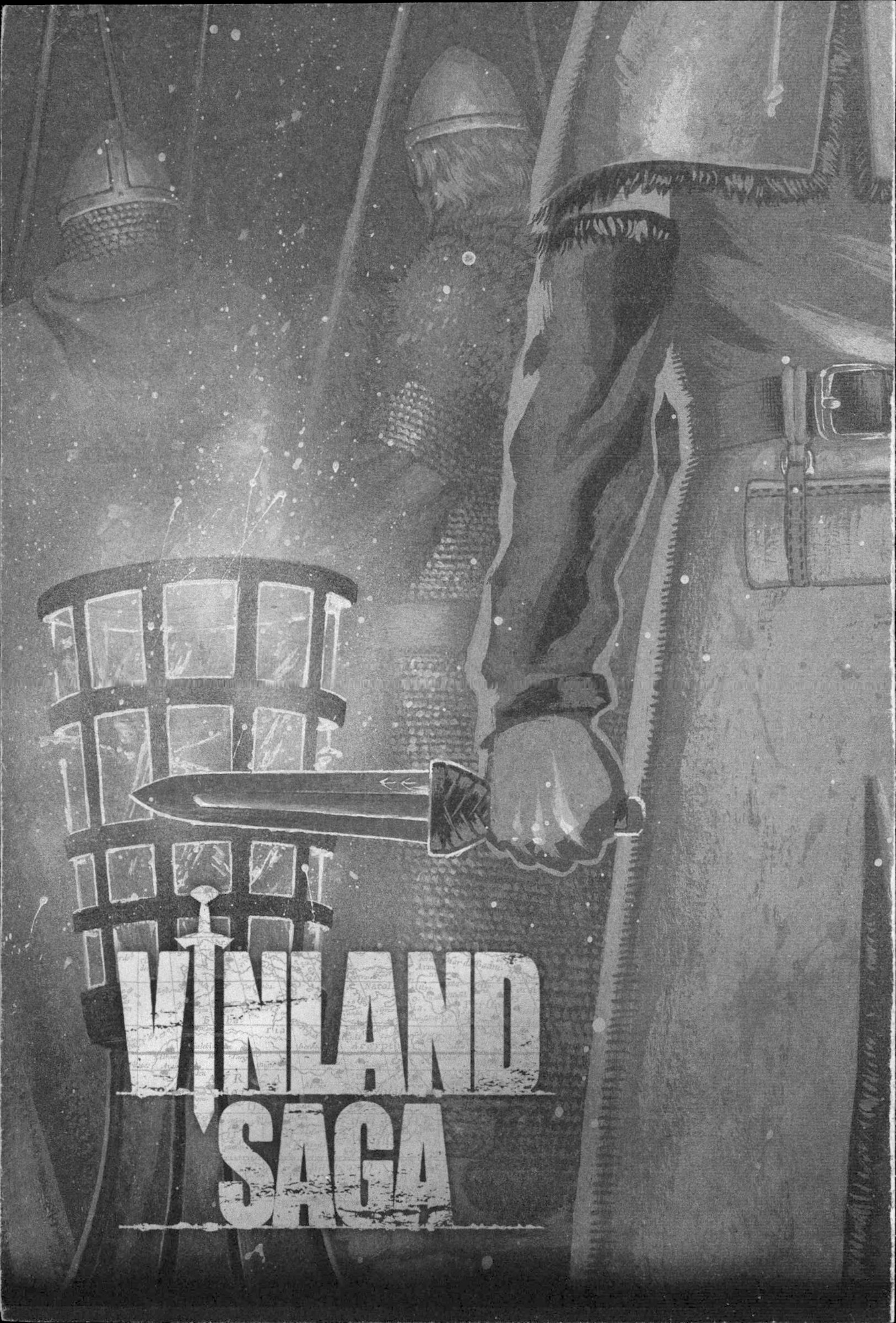
VINLAND
SAGA

# TABLE OF CONTENTS

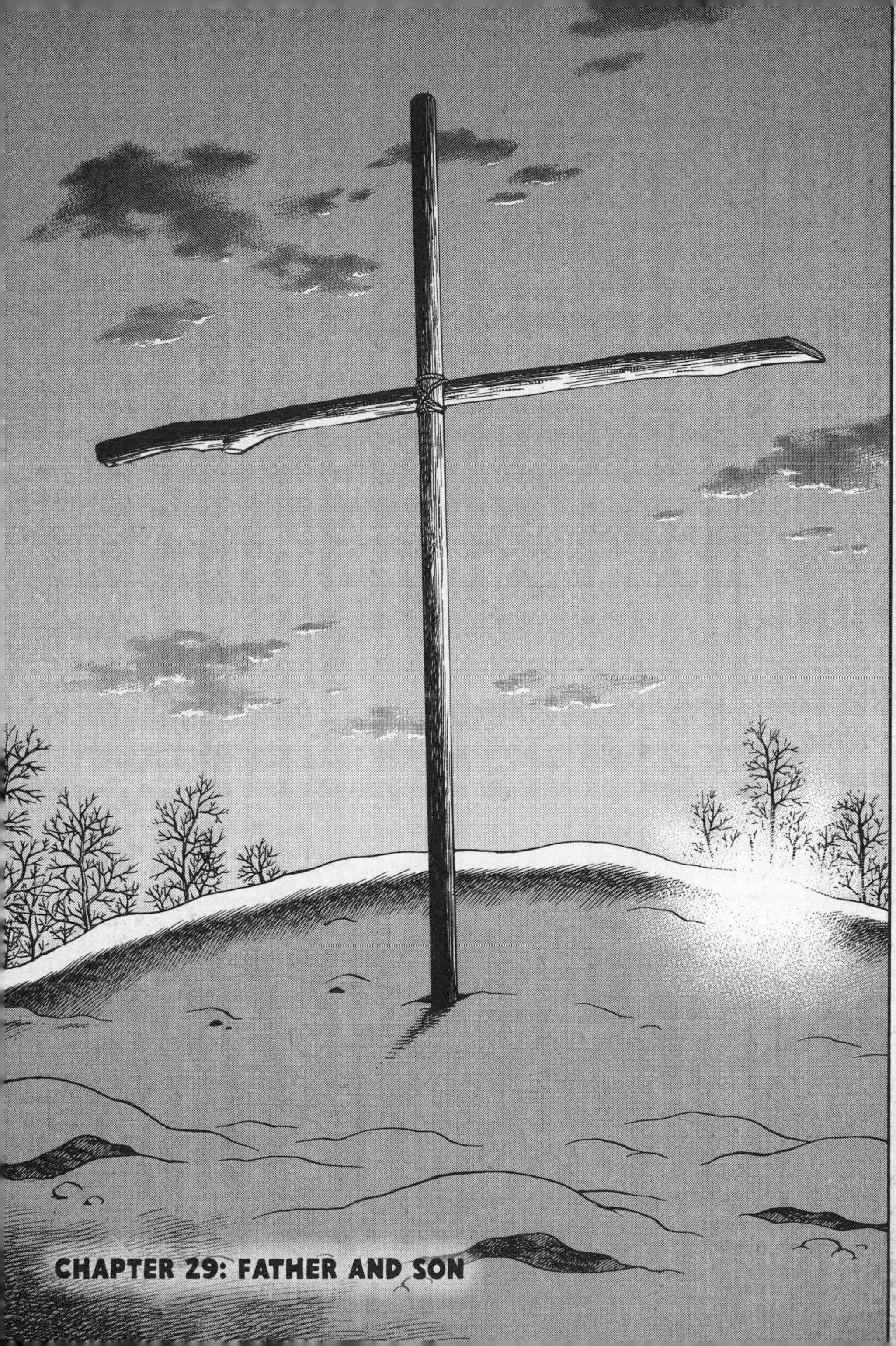

# CHAPTER 29: FATHER AND SON

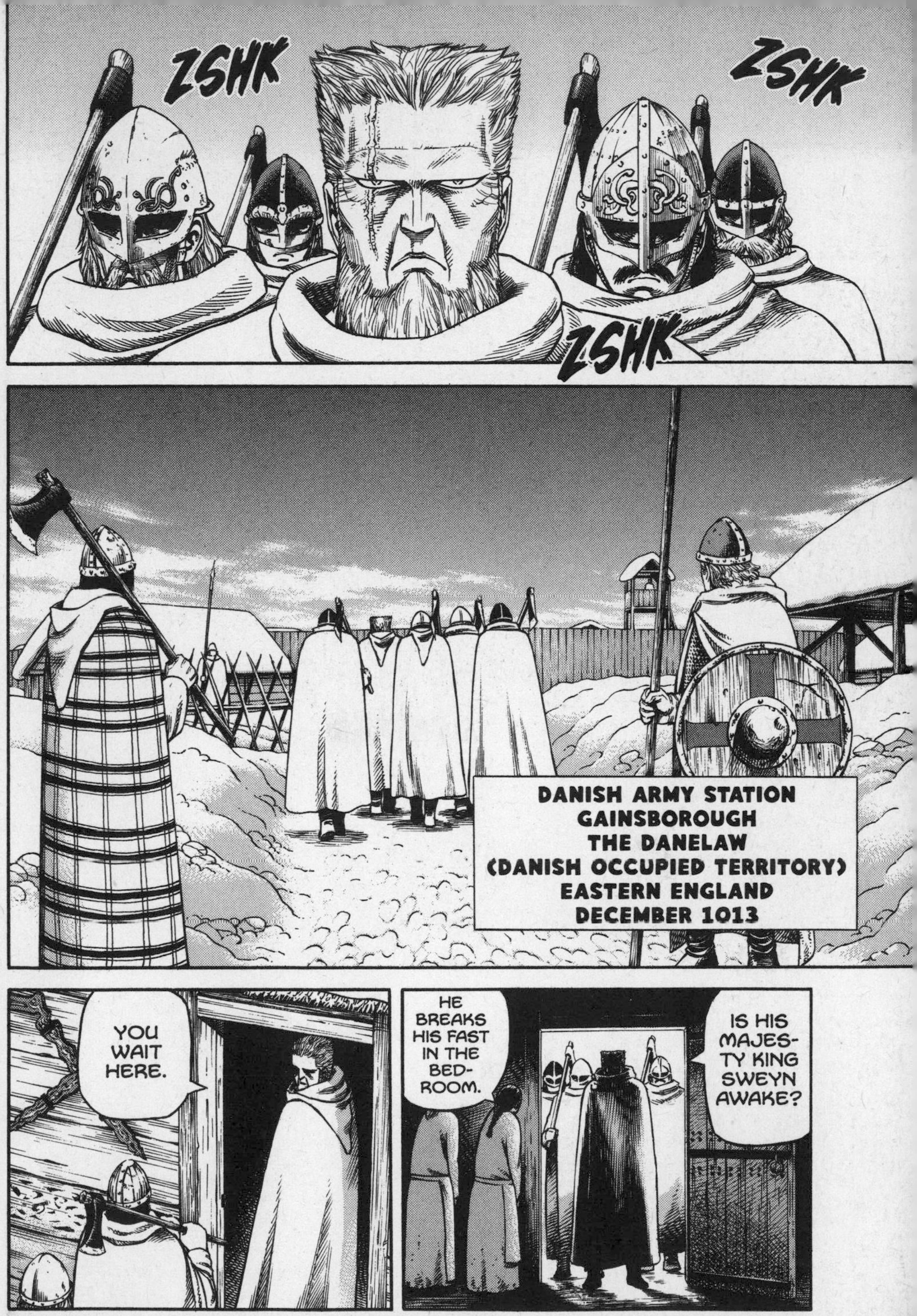
ZSHK
ZSHK
ZSHK
DANISH ARMY STATION GAINSBOROUGH THE DANELAW (DANISH OCCUPIED TERRITORY) EASTERN ENGLAND DECEMBER 1013
IS HIS MAJESTY KING SWEYN AWAKE?
HE BREAKS HIS FAST IN THE BEDROOM.
YOU WAIT HERE.

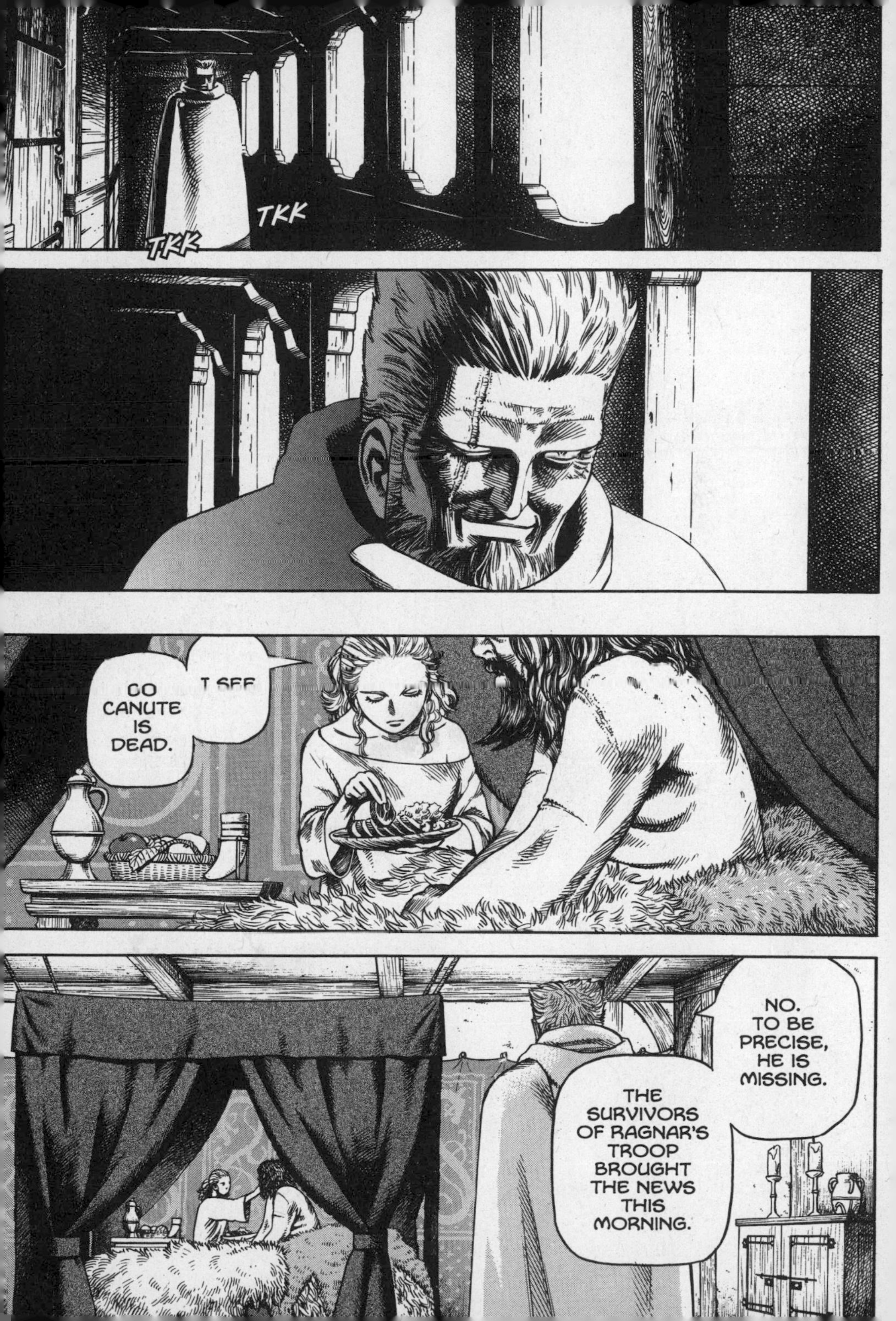
TKK
TKK
I SEE
SO CANUTE IS DEAD.
NO. TO BE PRECISE, HE IS MISSING.
THE SURVIVORS OF RAGNAR'S TROOP BROUGHT THE NEWS THIS MORNING.

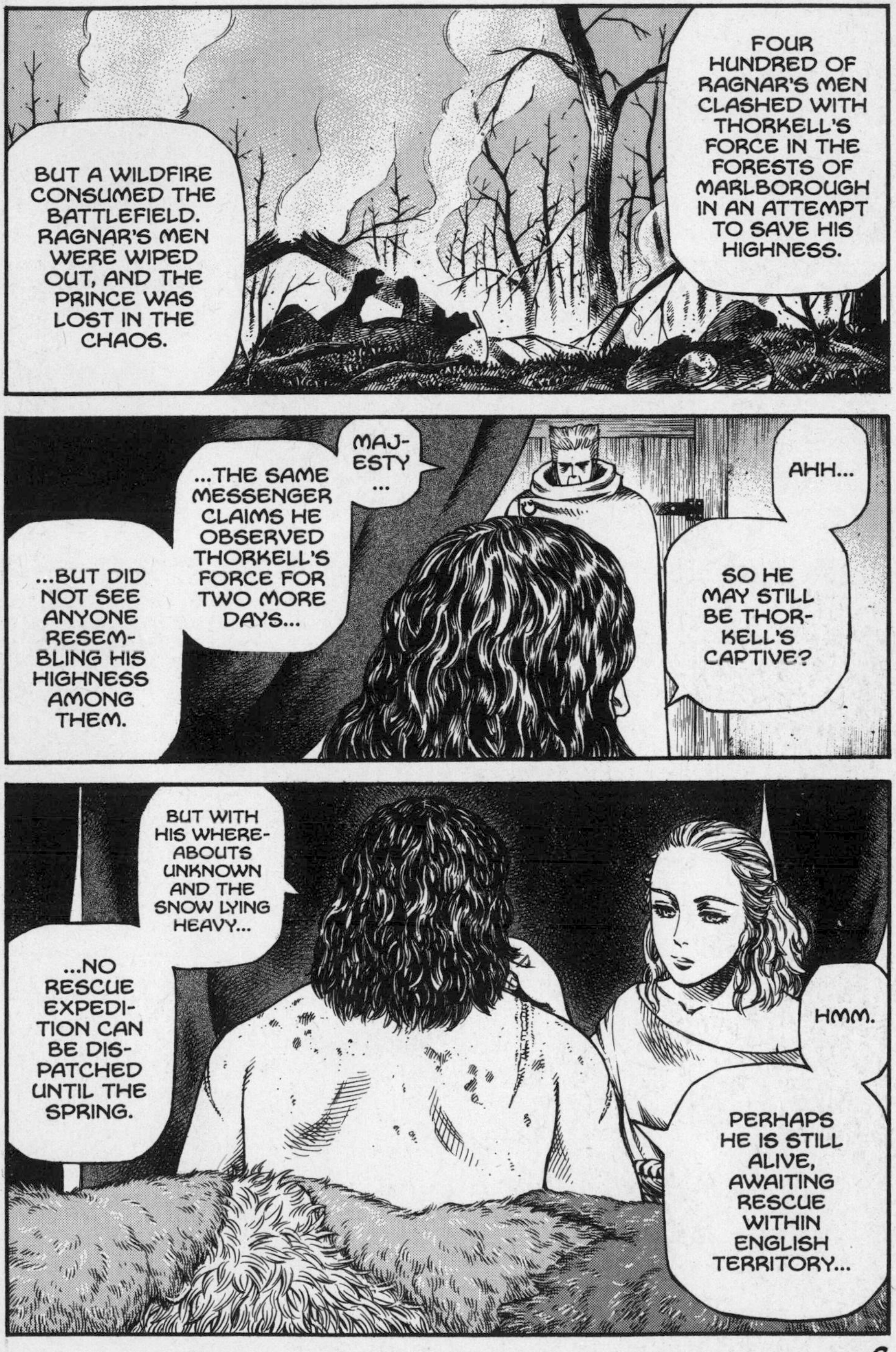

FOUR HUNDRED OF RAGNAR'S MEN CLASHED WITH THORKELL'S FORCE IN THE FORESTS OF MARLBOROUGH IN AN ATTEMPT TO SAVE HIS HIGHNESS.
BUT A WILDFIRE CONSUMED THE BATTLEFIELD. RAGNAR'S MEN WERE WIPED OUT, AND THE PRINCE WAS LOST IN THE CHAOS.
AHH...
SO HE MAY STILL BE THOR-KELL'S CAPTIVE?
MAJ-ESTY ...
...THE SAME MESSENGER CLAIMS HE OBSERVED THORKELL'S FORCE FOR TWO MORE DAYS...
...BUT DID NOT SEE ANYONE RESEM-BLING HIS HIGHNESS AMONG THEM.
HMM.
PERHAPS HE IS STILL ALIVE, AWAITING RESCUE WITHIN ENGLISH TERRITORY...
BUT WITH HIS WHERE-ABOUTS UNKNOWN AND THE SNOW LYING HEAVY...
...NO RESCUE EXPEDI-TION CAN BE DIS-PATCHED UNTIL THE SPRING.

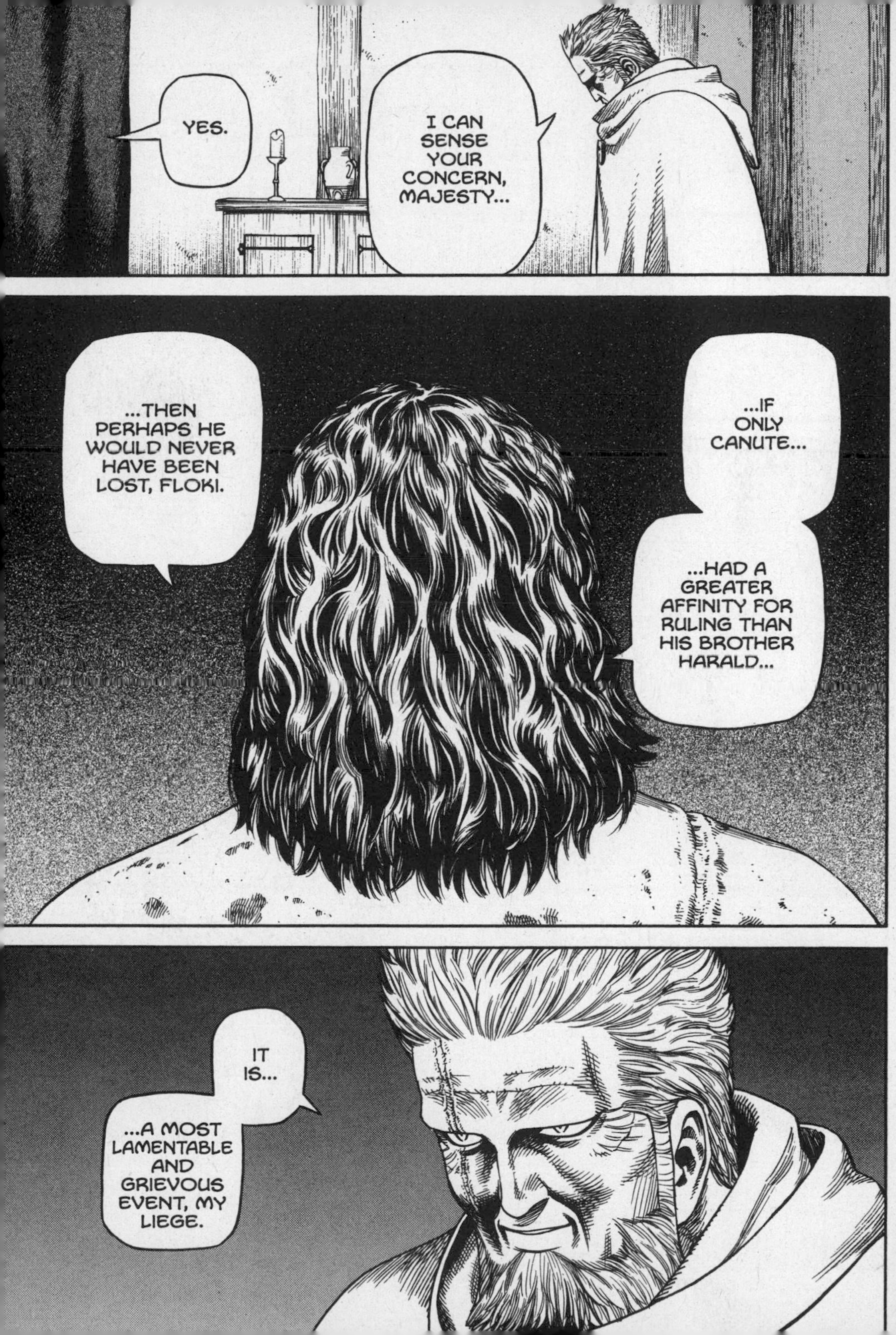
I CAN SENSE YOUR CONCERN, MAJESTY...
YES.
...IF ONLY CANUTE...
...HAD A GREATER AFFINITY FOR RULING THAN HIS BROTHER HARALD...
...THEN PERHAPS HE WOULD NEVER HAVE BEEN LOST, FLOKI.
IT IS...
...A MOST LAMENTABLE AND GRIEVOUS EVENT, MY LIEGE.

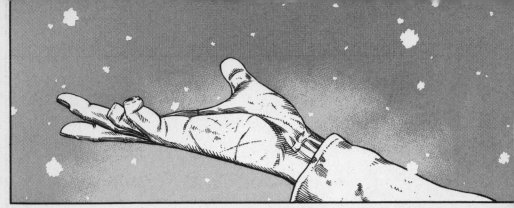

HERE COMES THE SNOW...

AND THERE GOES THE WAR...

HUFF...

AWW...

DEAR WINTER...

IT'S SO SAD...

OH WINTER... MUST YOU EVEN FREEZE THE HEARTS OF WARRIORS?

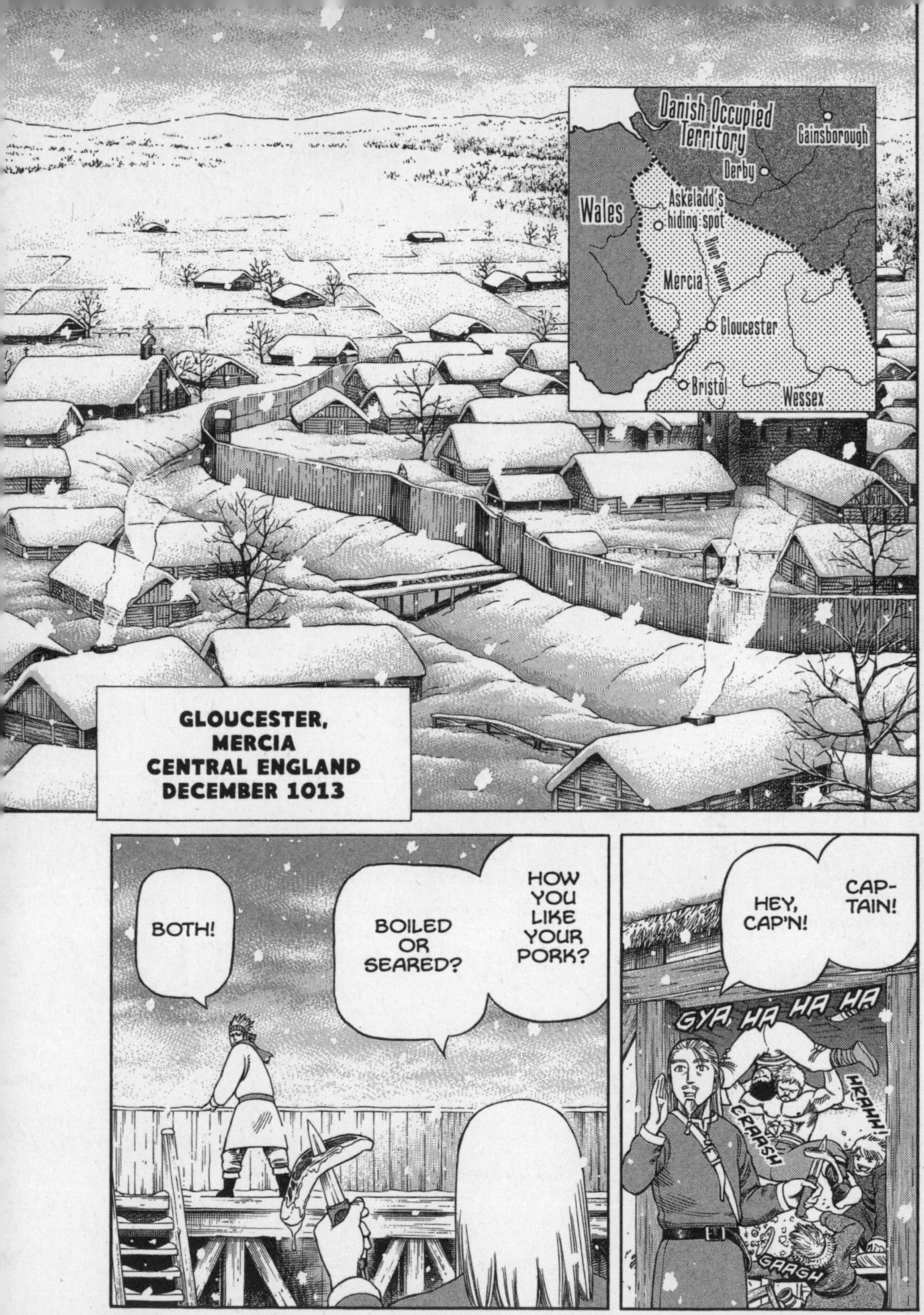
Danish Occupied Territory
Gainsborough
Derby
Wales
Askeladd's hiding spot
River Severn
Mercia
Gloucester
Bristol
Wessex
GLOUCESTER, MERCIA
CENTRAL ENGLAND
DECEMBER 1013
CAP-TAIN!
HEY, CAP'N!
GYA HA HA HA
HRAHH!
CRAASH
GAAGH
HOW YOU LIKE YOUR PORK?
BOILED OR SEARED?
BOTH!

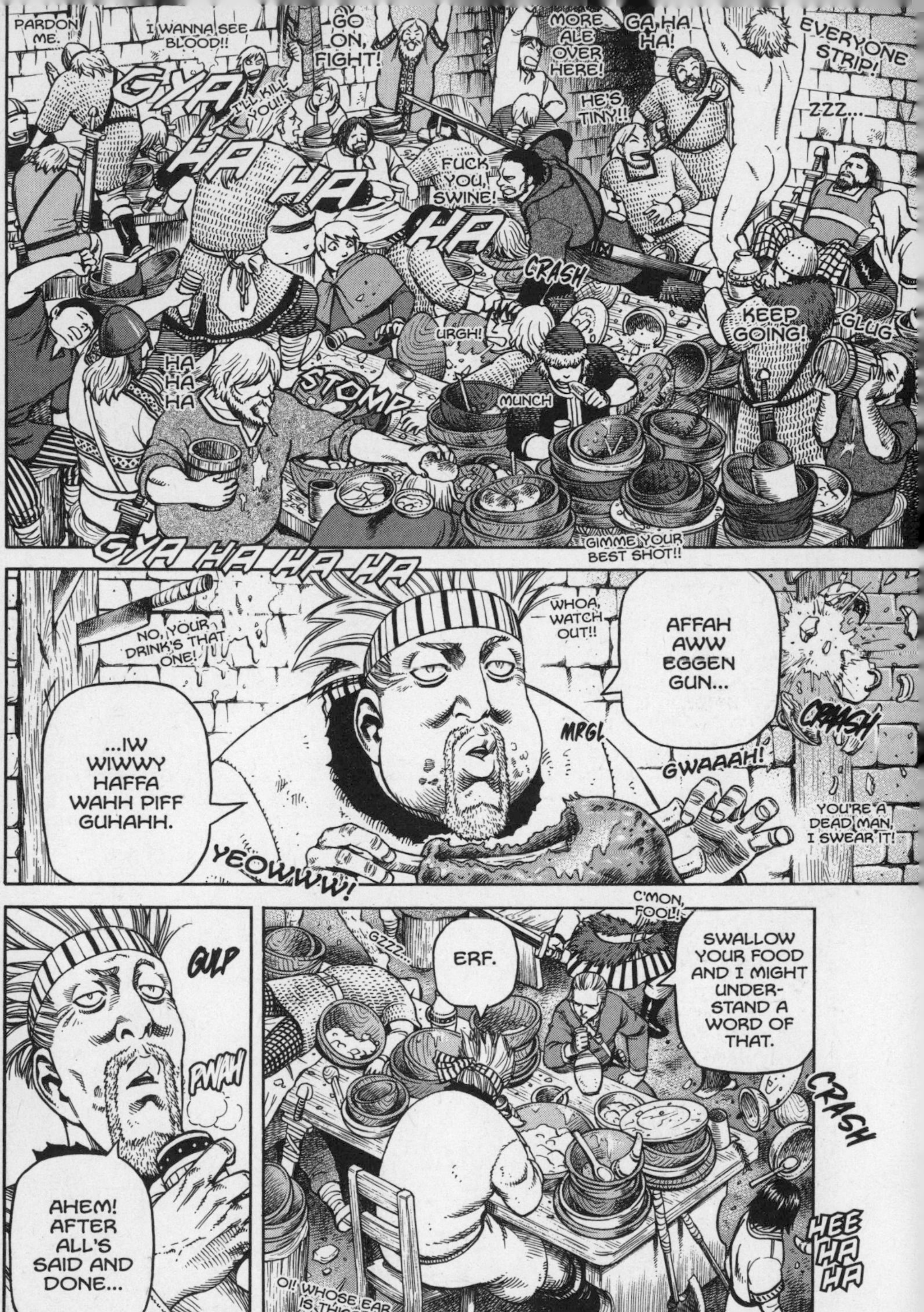
EVERYONE STRIP!!
GA HA HA!
MORE ALE OVER HERE!
GO ON, FIGHT!
I WANNA SEE BLOOD!!
PARDON ME.
ZZZ...
HE'S TINY!!
I'LL KILL YOU!!
GYA HA HA HA
FUCK YOU, SWINE!
CRASH
KEEP GOING!
GLUG
URGH!
MUNCH
STOMP
HA HA HA
GIMME YOUR BEST SHOT!!
GYA HA HA HA
CRASH
YOU'RE A DEAD MAN, I SWEAR IT!
AFFAH AWW EGGEN GUN...
WHOA, WATCH OUT!!
GWAAAH!
MRGL
NO, YOUR DRINK'S THAT ONE!
...IW WIWWY HAFFA WAHH PIFF GUHAHH.
YEOWWWW!
C'MON, FOOL!!
SWALLOW YOUR FOOD AND I MIGHT UNDER-STAND A WORD OF THAT.
ERF.
GZZZ...
CRASH
HEE HA HA HA
OI! WHOSE EAR IS THIS?
GULP
PWAH
AHEM! AFTER ALL'S SAID AND DONE...

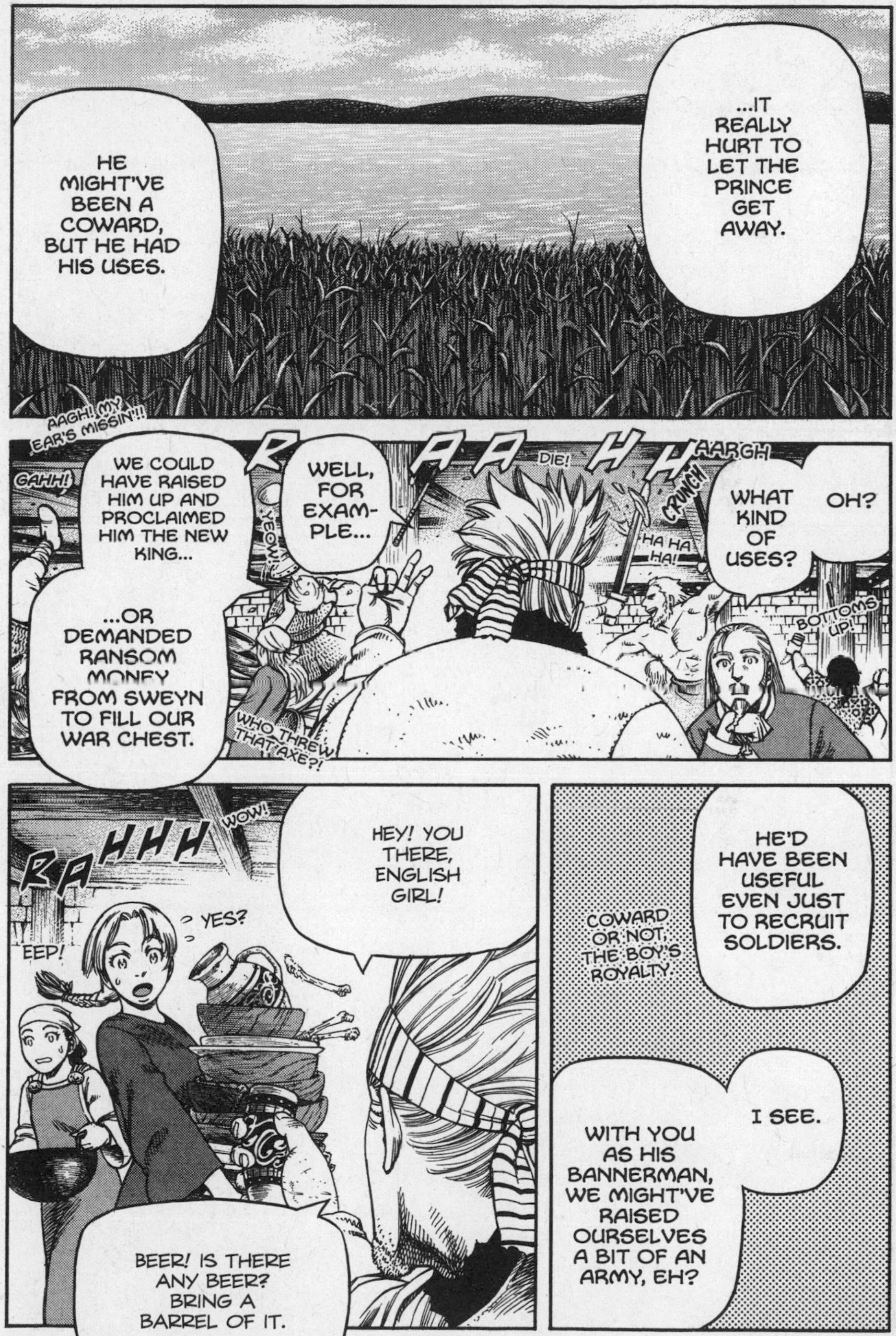
...IT REALLY HURT TO LET THE PRINCE GET AWAY.
HE MIGHT'VE BEEN A COWARD, BUT HE HAD HIS USES.
OH?
WHAT KIND OF USES?
BOTTOMS UP!
AARGH
CRUNCH
HA HA HA!
DIE!
RAAHH
WELL, FOR EXAMPLE...
YEOW!
WE COULD HAVE RAISED HIM UP AND PROCLAIMED HIM THE NEW KING...
AAGH! MY EAR'S MISSIN'!!
GAHH!
...OR DEMANDED RANSOM MONEY FROM SWEYN TO FILL OUR WAR CHEST.
WHO THREW THAT AXE?!
HE'D HAVE BEEN USEFUL EVEN JUST TO RECRUIT SOLDIERS.
COWARD OR NOT, THE BOY'S ROYALTY.
I SEE.
WITH YOU AS HIS BANNERMAN, WE MIGHT'VE RAISED OURSELVES A BIT OF AN ARMY, EH?
HEY! YOU THERE, ENGLISH GIRL!
WOW!
RAHHH
YES?
EEP!
BEER! IS THERE ANY BEER? BRING A BARREL OF IT.

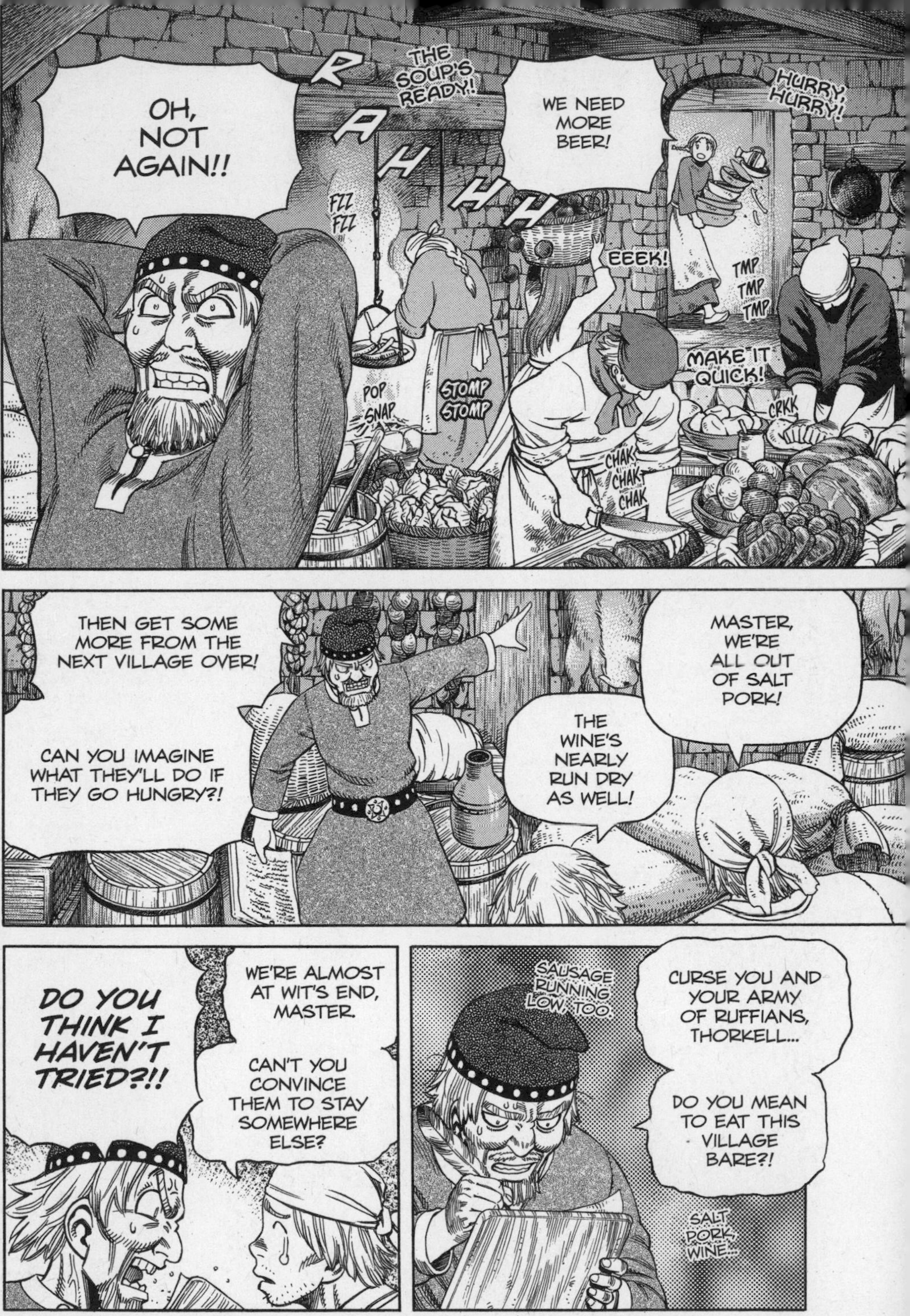
HURRY, HURRY!
WE NEED MORE BEER!
THE SOUP'S READY!!
RAHHH
OH, NOT AGAIN!!
FZZ FZZ
EEEK!
TMP TMP TMP
MAKE IT QUICK!
CRKK
STOMP STOMP
POP SNAP
CHAK CHAK CHAK
MASTER, WE'RE ALL OUT OF SALT PORK!
THE WINE'S NEARLY RUN DRY AS WELL!
THEN GET SOME MORE FROM THE NEXT VILLAGE OVER!
CAN YOU IMAGINE WHAT THEY'LL DO IF THEY GO HUNGRY?!
SAUSAGE RUNNING LOW, TOO.
CURSE YOU AND YOUR ARMY OF RUFFIANS, THORKELL...
DO YOU MEAN TO EAT THIS VILLAGE BARE?!
SALT PORK, WINE...
WE'RE ALMOST AT WIT'S END, MASTER.
CAN'T YOU CONVINCE THEM TO STAY SOMEWHERE ELSE?
*DO YOU THINK I HAVEN'T TRIED?!!*

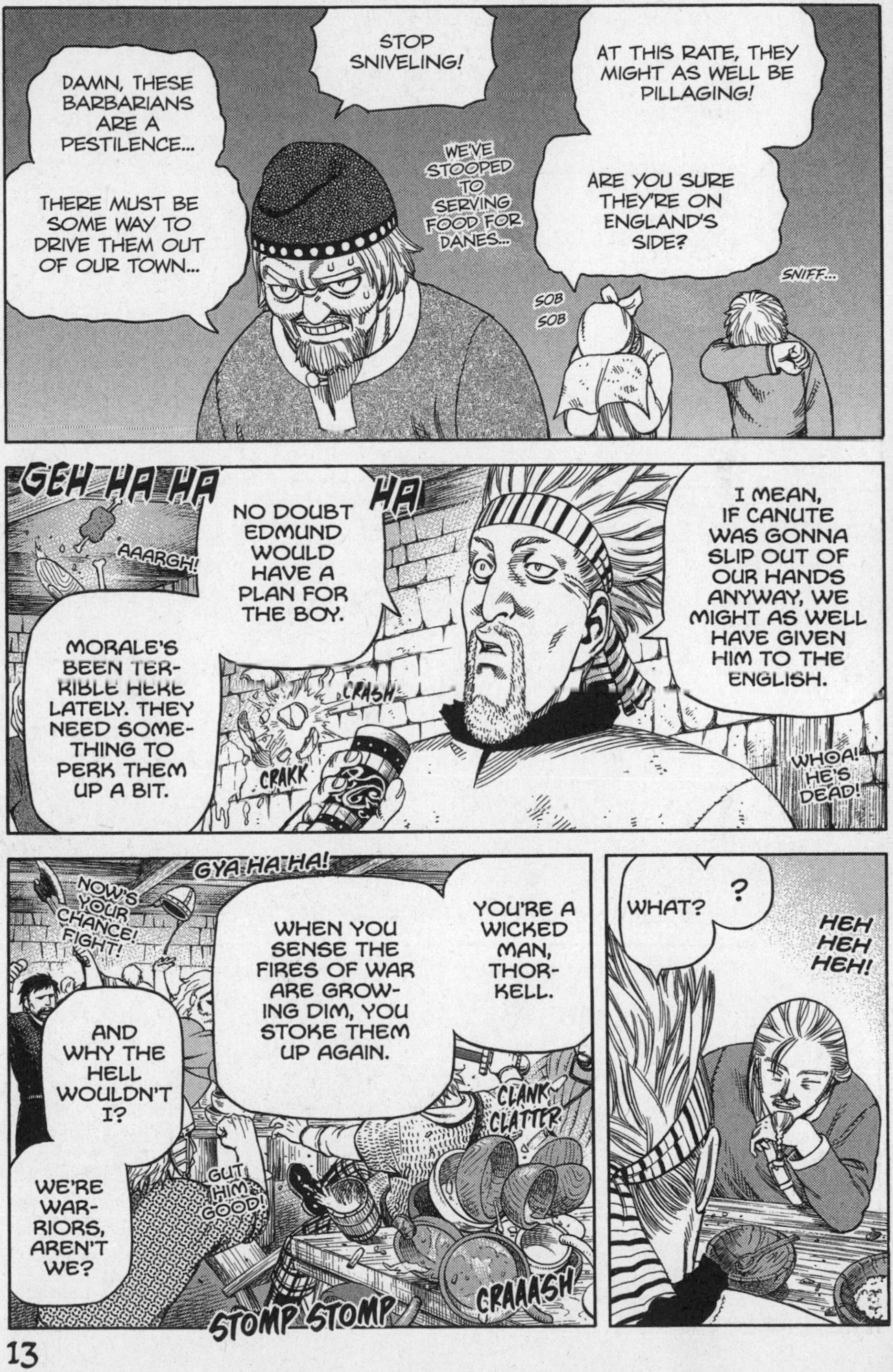
AT THIS RATE, THEY MIGHT AS WELL BE PILLAGING!
ARE YOU SURE THEY'RE ON ENGLAND'S SIDE?
SNIFF...
STOP SNIVELING!
WE'VE STOOPED TO SERVING FOOD FOR DANES...
SOB SOB
DAMN, THESE BARBARIANS ARE A PESTILENCE...
THERE MUST BE SOME WAY TO DRIVE THEM OUT OF OUR TOWN...
I MEAN, IF CANUTE WAS GONNA SLIP OUT OF OUR HANDS ANYWAY, WE MIGHT AS WELL HAVE GIVEN HIM TO THE ENGLISH.
WHOA! HE'S DEAD!
GEH HA HA HA
NO DOUBT EDMUND WOULD HAVE A PLAN FOR THE BOY.
AAARGH!
MORALE'S BEEN TERRIBLE HERE LATELY. THEY NEED SOMETHING TO PERK THEM UP A BIT.
CRASH
CRAKK
?
WHAT?
HEH HEH HEH!
YOU'RE A WICKED MAN, THORKELL.
WHEN YOU SENSE THE FIRES OF WAR ARE GROWING DIM, YOU STOKE THEM UP AGAIN.
GYA HA HA!
NOW'S YOUR CHANCE! FIGHT!
AND WHY THE HELL WOULDN'T I?
CLANK CLATTER
GUT HIM GOOD!
WE'RE WARRIORS, AREN'T WE?
CRAAASH
STOMP STOMP

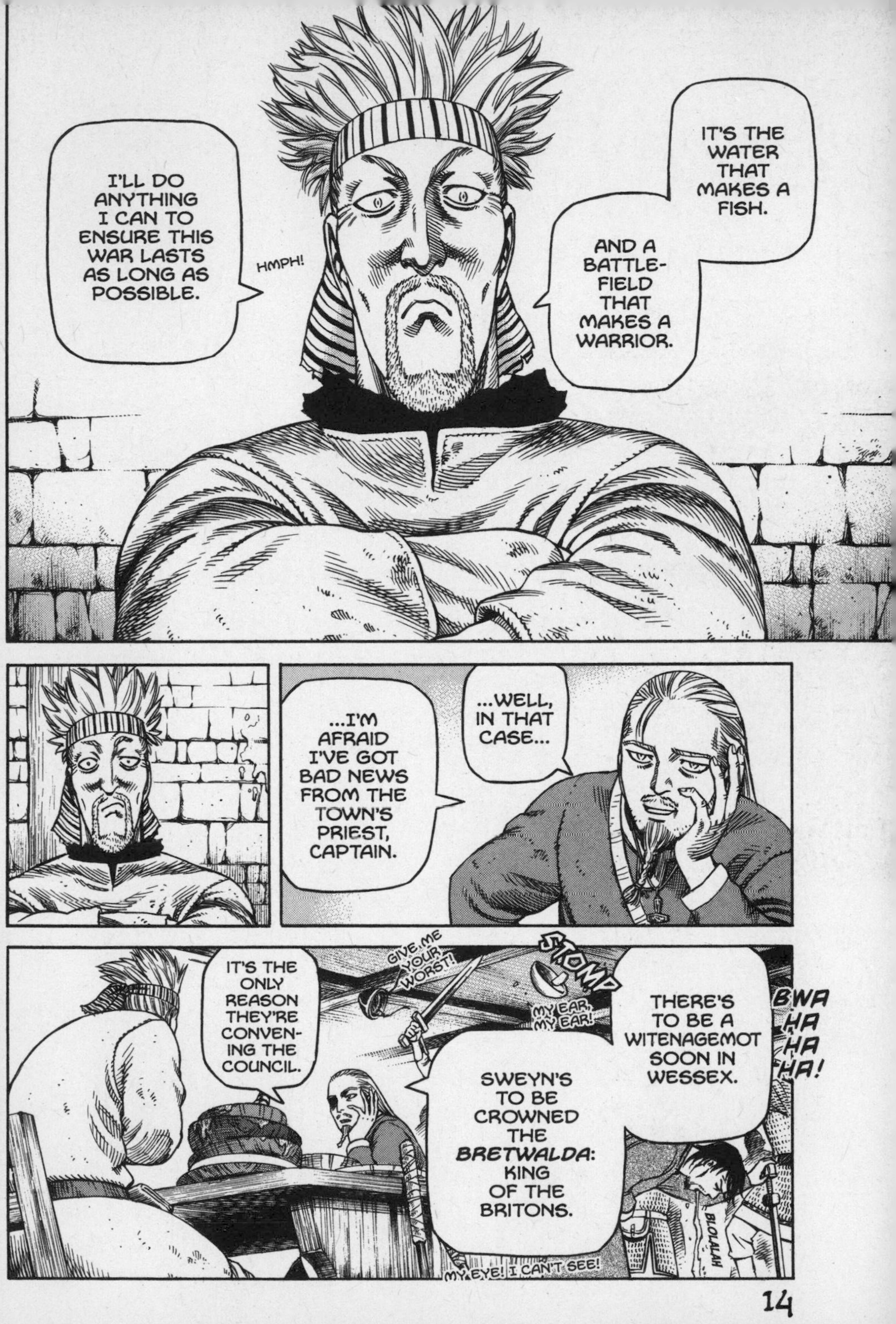
IT'S THE WATER THAT MAKES A FISH.
AND A BATTLE-FIELD THAT MAKES A WARRIOR.
HMPH!
I'LL DO ANYTHING I CAN TO ENSURE THIS WAR LASTS AS LONG AS POSSIBLE.
...WELL, IN THAT CASE...
...I'M AFRAID I'VE GOT BAD NEWS FROM THE TOWN'S PRIEST, CAPTAIN.
BWA HA HA HA!
STOMP
GIVE ME YOUR WORST!
MY EAR, MY EAR!
THERE'S TO BE A WITENAGEMOT SOON IN WESSEX.
SWEYN'S TO BE CROWNED THE *BRETWALDA*: KING OF THE BRITONS.
BLOLALAH
MY EYE! I CAN'T SEE!
IT'S THE ONLY REASON THEY'RE CONVEN-ING THE COUNCIL.

HUH?

...HUH?

...WHA? BUT... THAT'S UNCONDI-TIONAL SURRENDER!

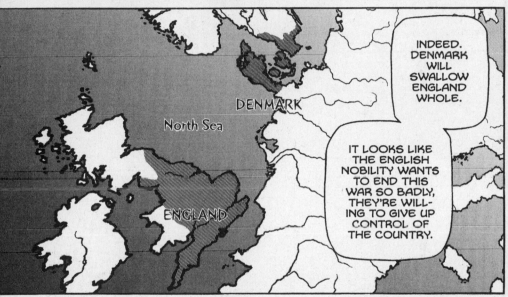

DENMARK

North Sea

ENGLAND

INDEED. DENMARK WILL SWALLOW ENGLAND WHOLE.

IT LOOKS LIKE THE ENGLISH NOBILITY WANTS TO END THIS WAR SO BADLY, THEY'RE WILLING TO GIVE UP CONTROL OF THE COUNTRY.

CREAK...

AAAGH...

WHY DO MY WORST FEELINGS ALWAYS COME TRUE?

OHH BOY.

...WA... ...ER... WOW.

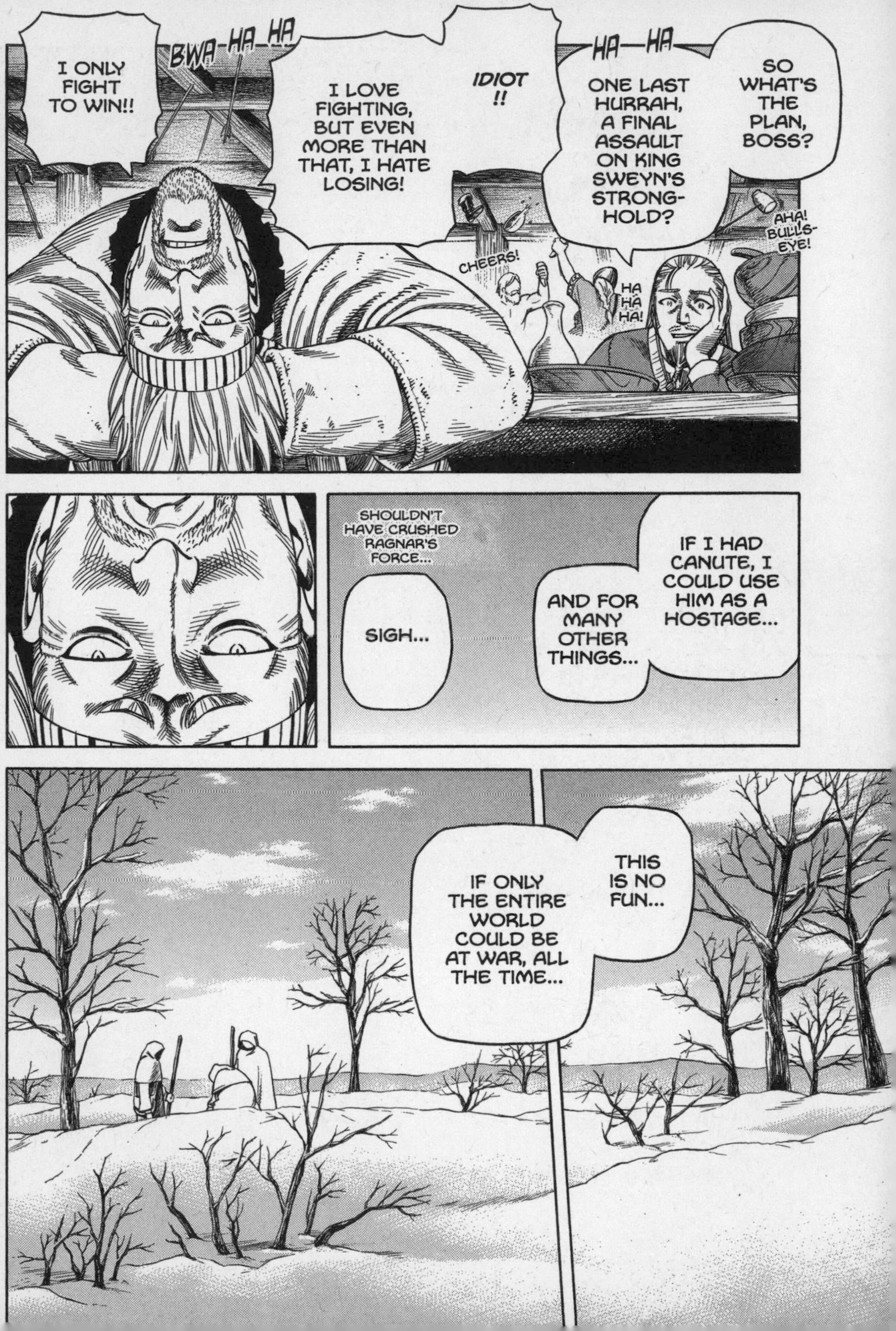
SO WHAT'S THE PLAN, BOSS?
HA—HA
ONE LAST HURRAH, A FINAL ASSAULT ON KING SWEYN'S STRONGHOLD?
AHA! BULL'S-EYE!
HA HA HA!
IDIOT !!
CHEERS!
I LOVE FIGHTING, BUT EVEN MORE THAN THAT, I HATE LOSING!
BWA-HA-HA
I ONLY FIGHT TO WIN!!
IF I HAD CANUTE, I COULD USE HIM AS A HOSTAGE...
AND FOR MANY OTHER THINGS...
SHOULDN'T HAVE CRUSHED RAGNAR'S FORCE...
SIGH...
THIS IS NO FUN...
IF ONLY THE ENTIRE WORLD COULD BE AT WAR, ALL THE TIME...

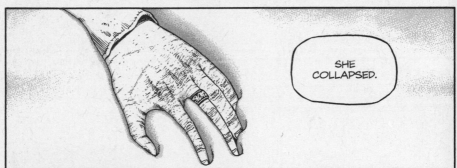

SHE COLLAPSED.

SHE'S GOT A RING.

MIGHT ACTUALLY BE OF NOBLE BIRTH.

THE POOR THING...

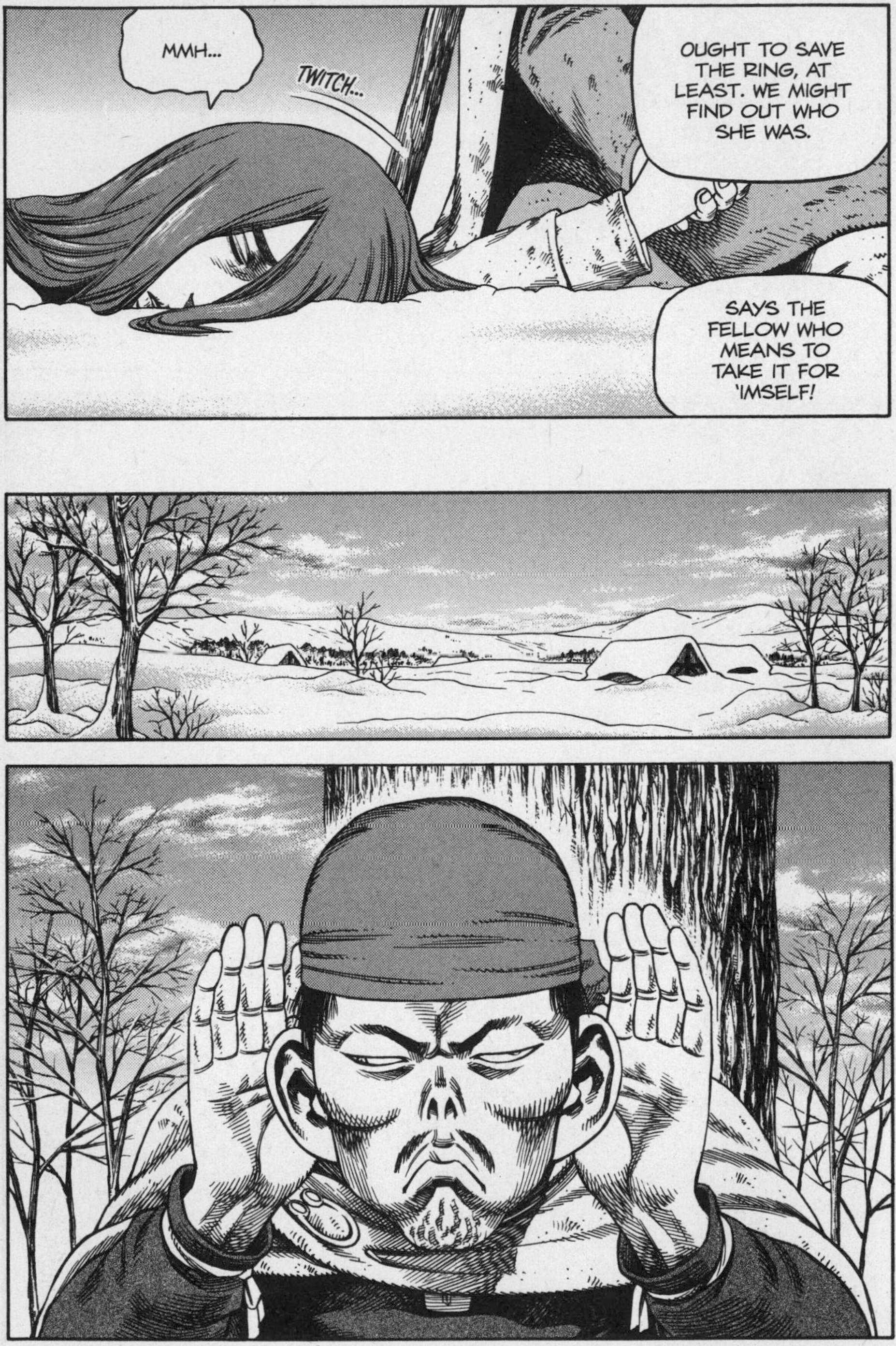
OUGHT TO SAVE THE RING, AT LEAST. WE MIGHT FIND OUT WHO SHE WAS.
SAYS THE FELLOW WHO MEANS TO TAKE IT FOR 'IMSELF!
MMH...
TWITCH...

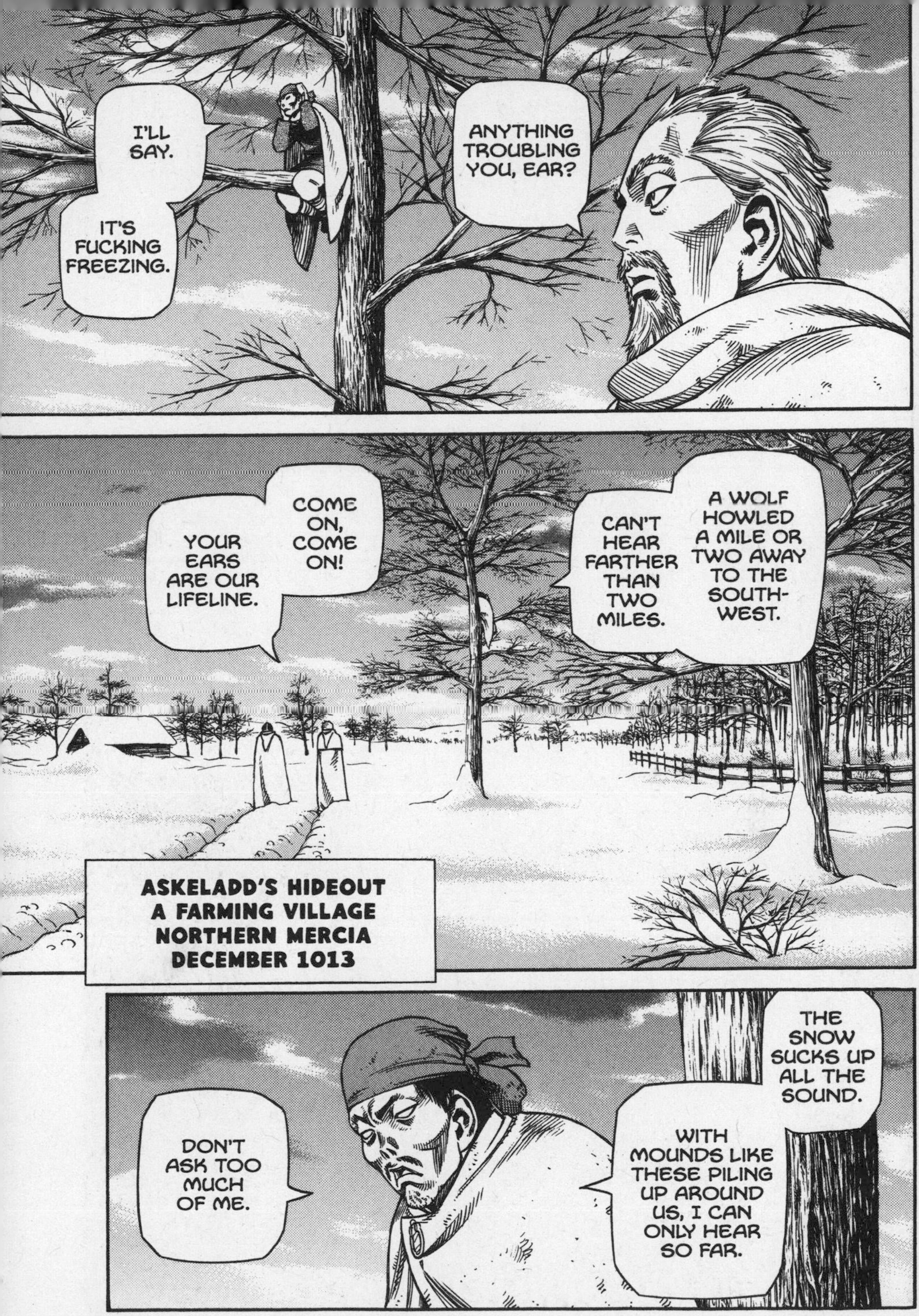
ANYTHING TROUBLING YOU, EAR?
I'LL SAY.
IT'S FUCKING FREEZING.
A WOLF HOWLED A MILE OR TWO AWAY TO THE SOUTH-WEST.
CAN'T HEAR FARTHER THAN TWO MILES.
COME ON, COME ON!
YOUR EARS ARE OUR LIFELINE.
ASKELADD'S HIDEOUT A FARMING VILLAGE NORTHERN MERCIA DECEMBER 1013
THE SNOW SUCKS UP ALL THE SOUND.
WITH MOUNDS LIKE THESE PILING UP AROUND US, I CAN ONLY HEAR SO FAR.
DON'T ASK TOO MUCH OF ME.

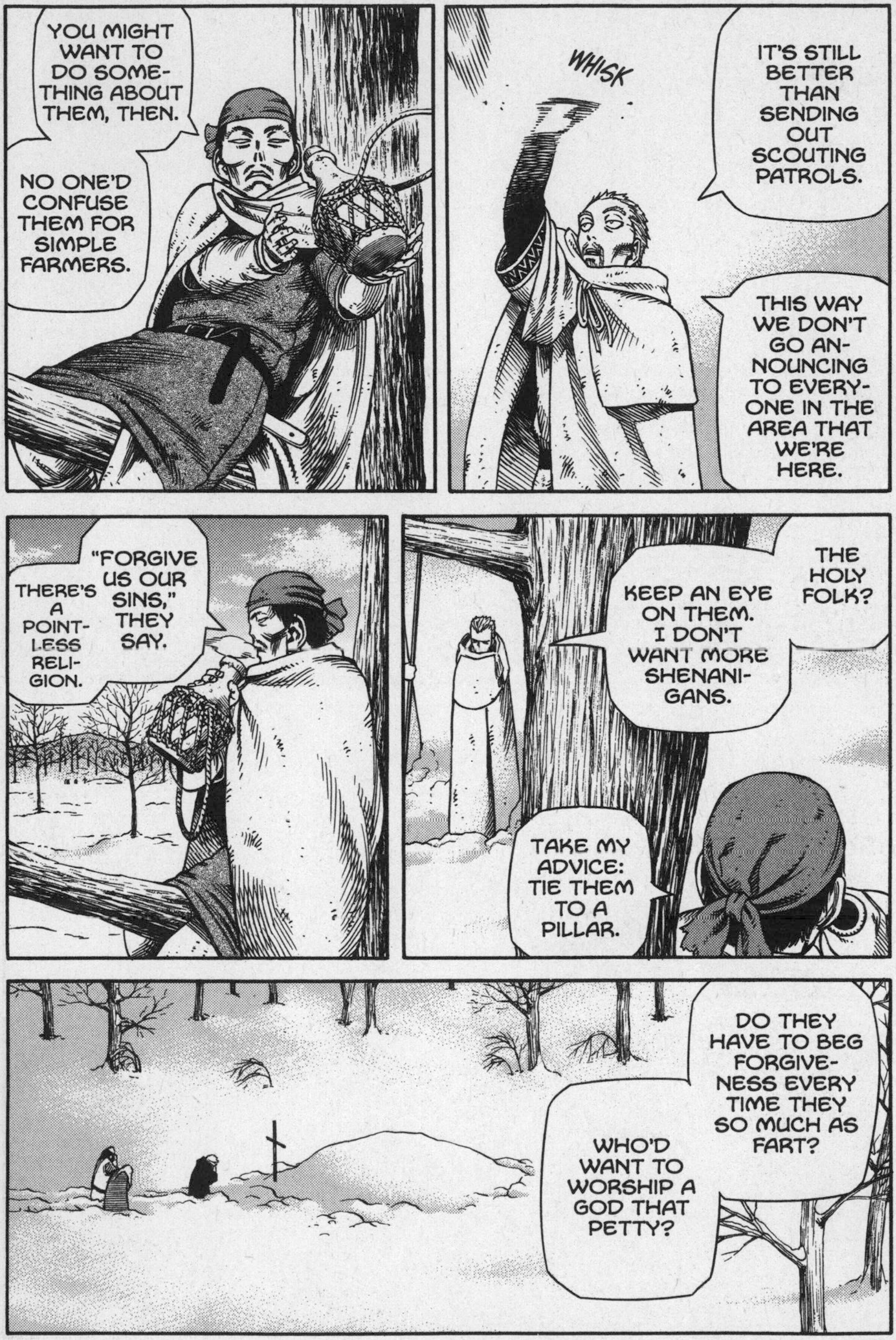
WHISK
IT'S STILL BETTER THAN SENDING OUT SCOUTING PATROLS.
THIS WAY WE DON'T GO ANNOUNCING TO EVERYONE IN THE AREA THAT WE'RE HERE.
YOU MIGHT WANT TO DO SOMETHING ABOUT THEM, THEN.
NO ONE'D CONFUSE THEM FOR SIMPLE FARMERS.
THE HOLY FOLK?
KEEP AN EYE ON THEM. I DON'T WANT MORE SHENANIGANS.
TAKE MY ADVICE: TIE THEM TO A PILLAR.
"FORGIVE US OUR SINS," THEY SAY.
THERE'S A POINTLESS RELIGION.
DO THEY HAVE TO BEG FORGIVENESS EVERY TIME THEY SO MUCH AS FART?
WHO'D WANT TO WORSHIP A GOD THAT PETTY?

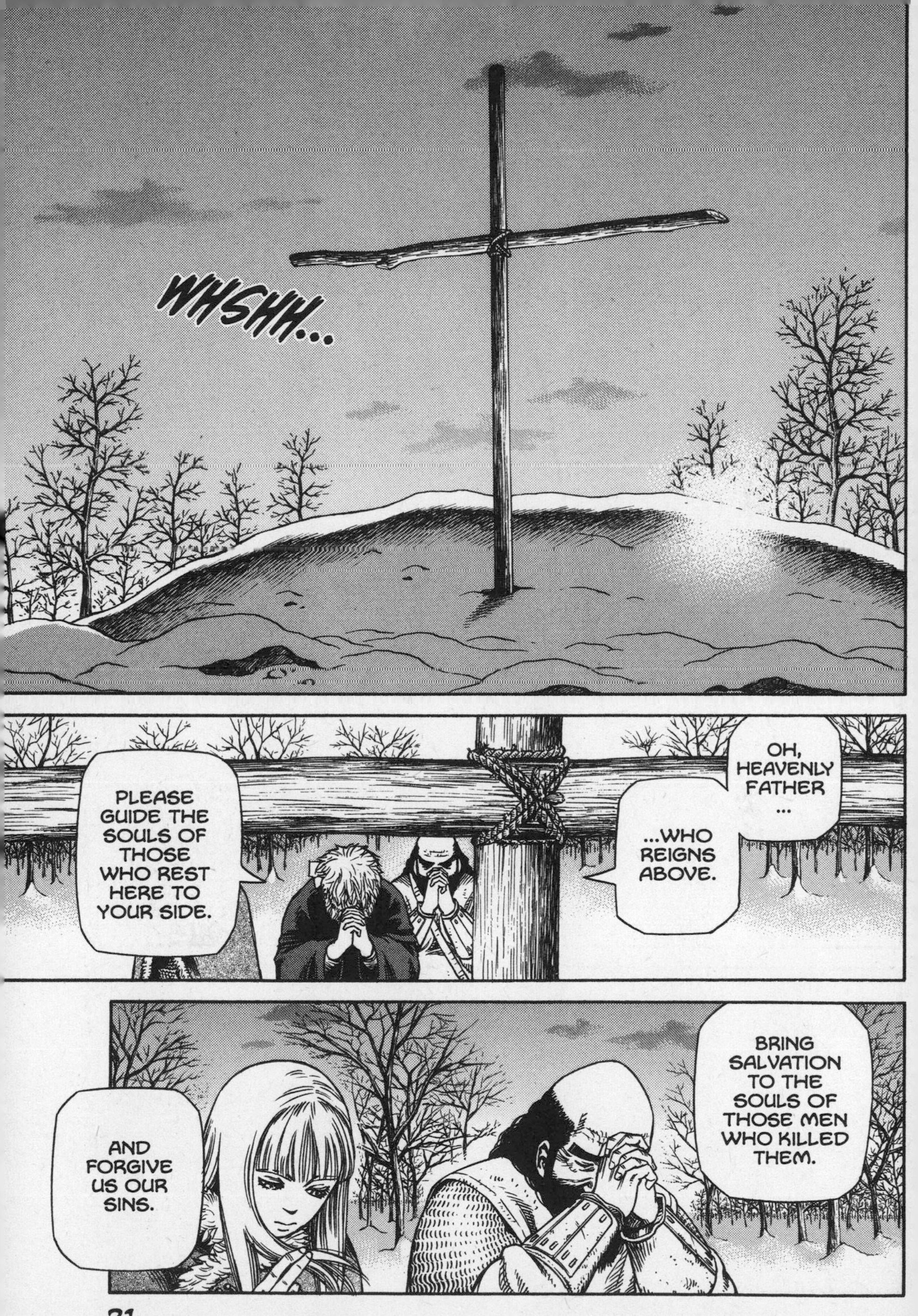
WHSHH...
OH, HEAVENLY FATHER ...
...WHO REIGNS ABOVE.
PLEASE GUIDE THE SOULS OF THOSE WHO REST HERE TO YOUR SIDE.
BRING SALVATION TO THE SOULS OF THOSE MEN WHO KILLED THEM.
AND FORGIVE US OUR SINS.

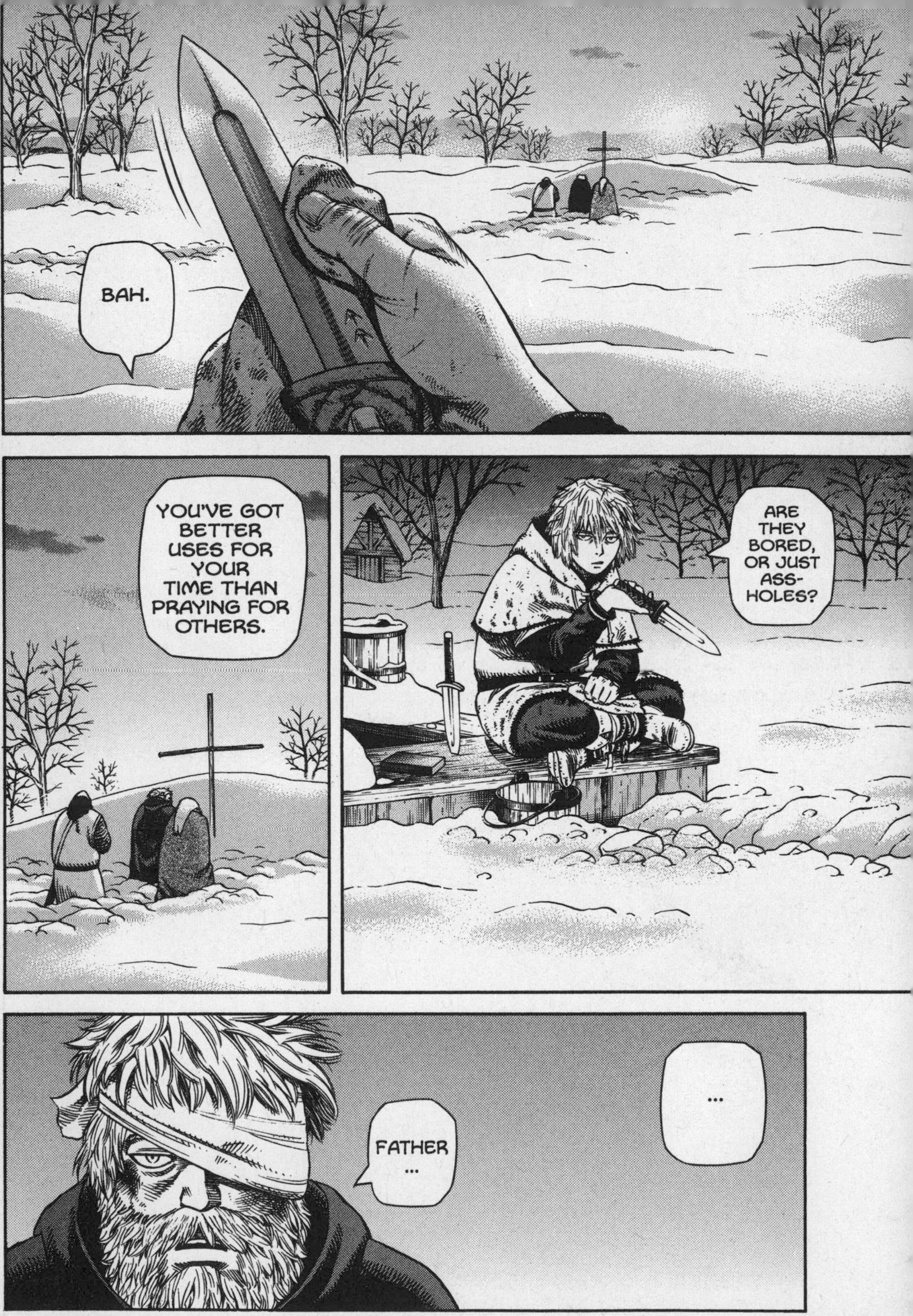
BAH.
ARE THEY BORED, OR JUST ASS-HOLES?
YOU'VE GOT BETTER USES FOR YOUR TIME THAN PRAYING FOR OTHERS.
...
FATHER ...

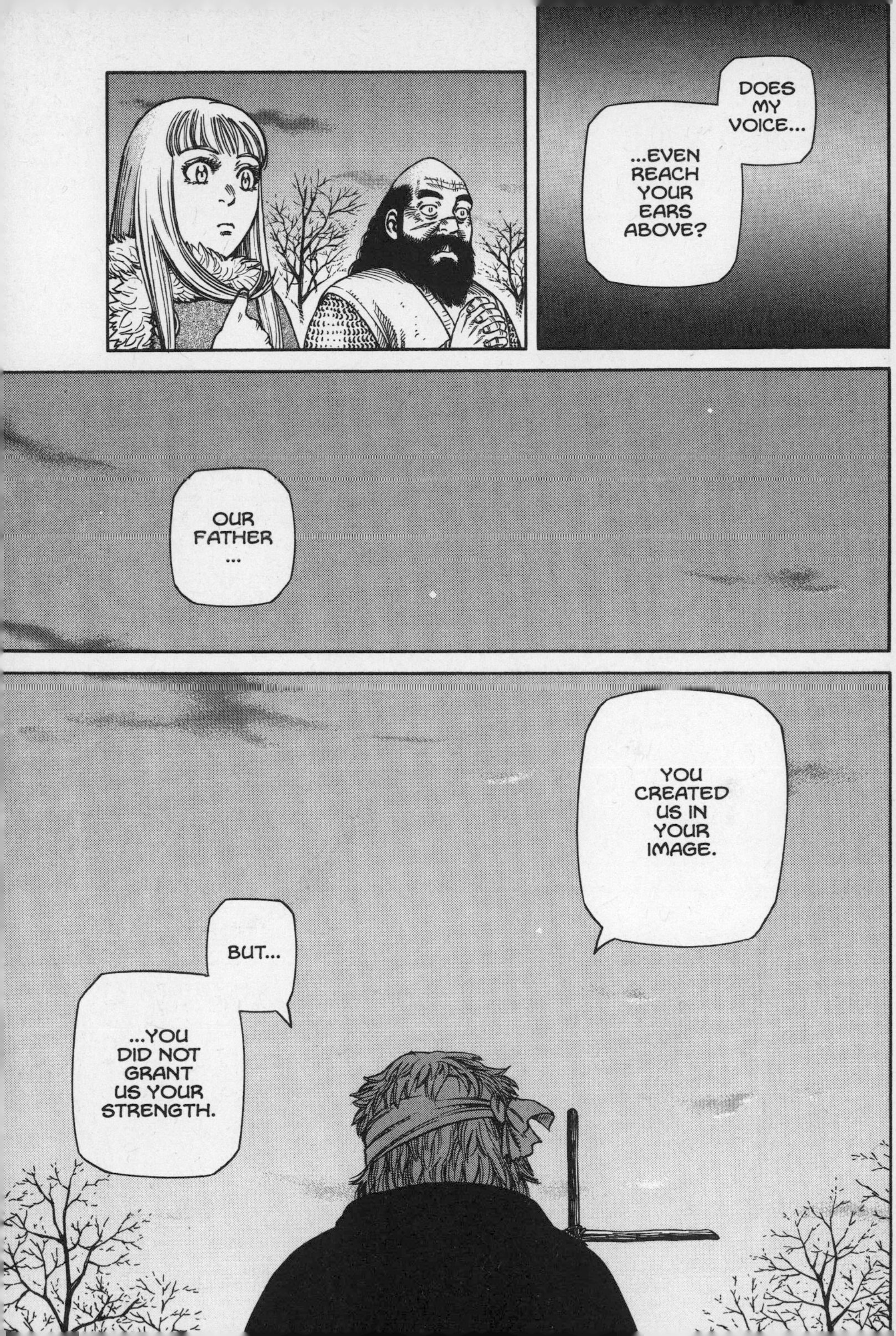
DOES MY VOICE...
...EVEN REACH YOUR EARS ABOVE?
OUR FATHER ...
YOU CREATED US IN YOUR IMAGE.
BUT...
...YOU DID NOT GRANT US YOUR STRENGTH.

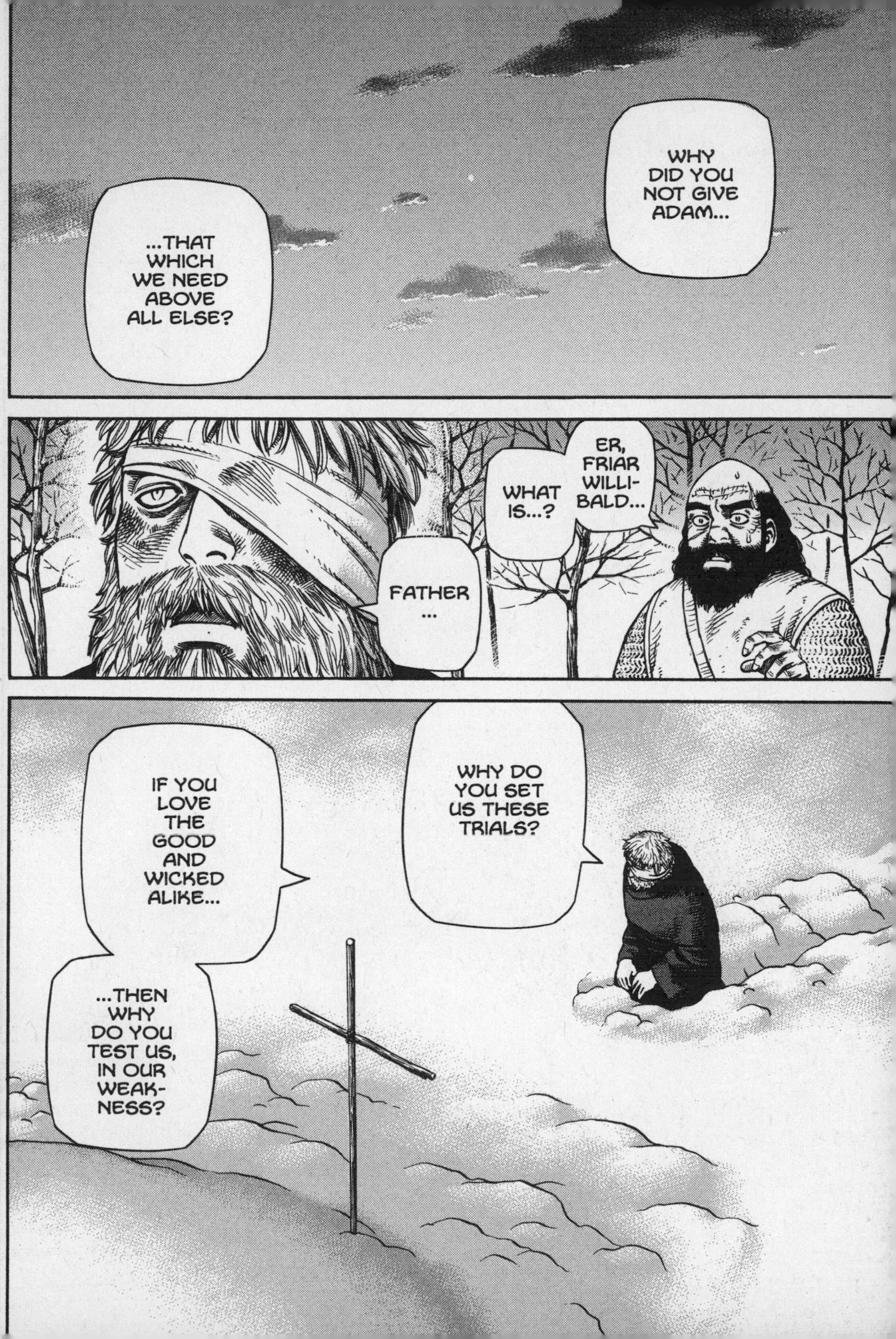
WHY DID YOU NOT GIVE ADAM...
...THAT WHICH WE NEED ABOVE ALL ELSE?
ER, FRIAR WILLI-BALD...
WHAT IS...?
FATHER ...
WHY DO YOU SET US THESE TRIALS?
IF YOU LOVE THE GOOD AND WICKED ALIKE...
...THEN WHY DO YOU TEST US, IN OUR WEAK-NESS?

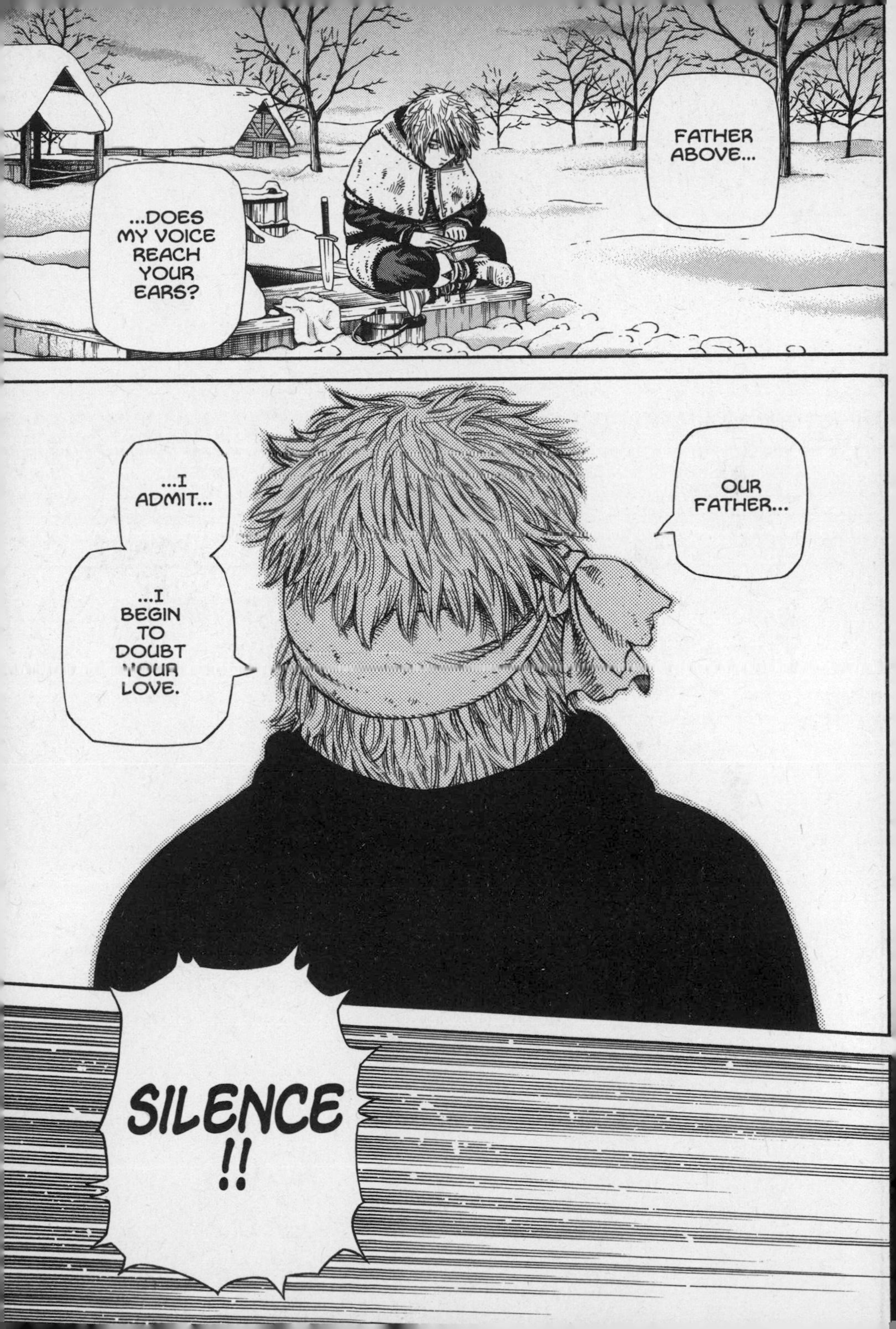
FATHER ABOVE...
...DOES MY VOICE REACH YOUR EARS?
OUR FATHER...
...I ADMIT...
...I BEGIN TO DOUBT YOUR LOVE.
SILENCE !!

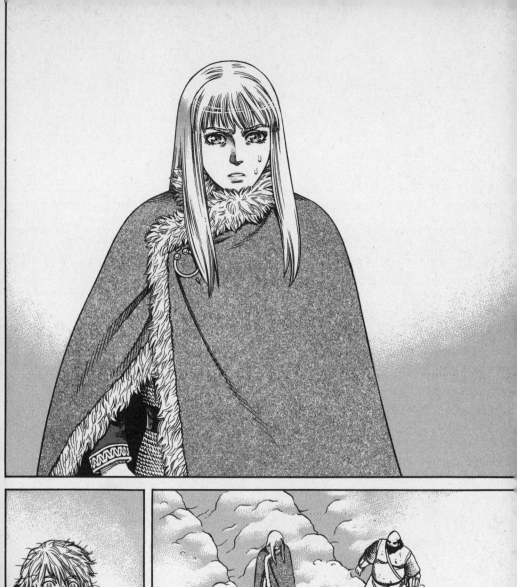

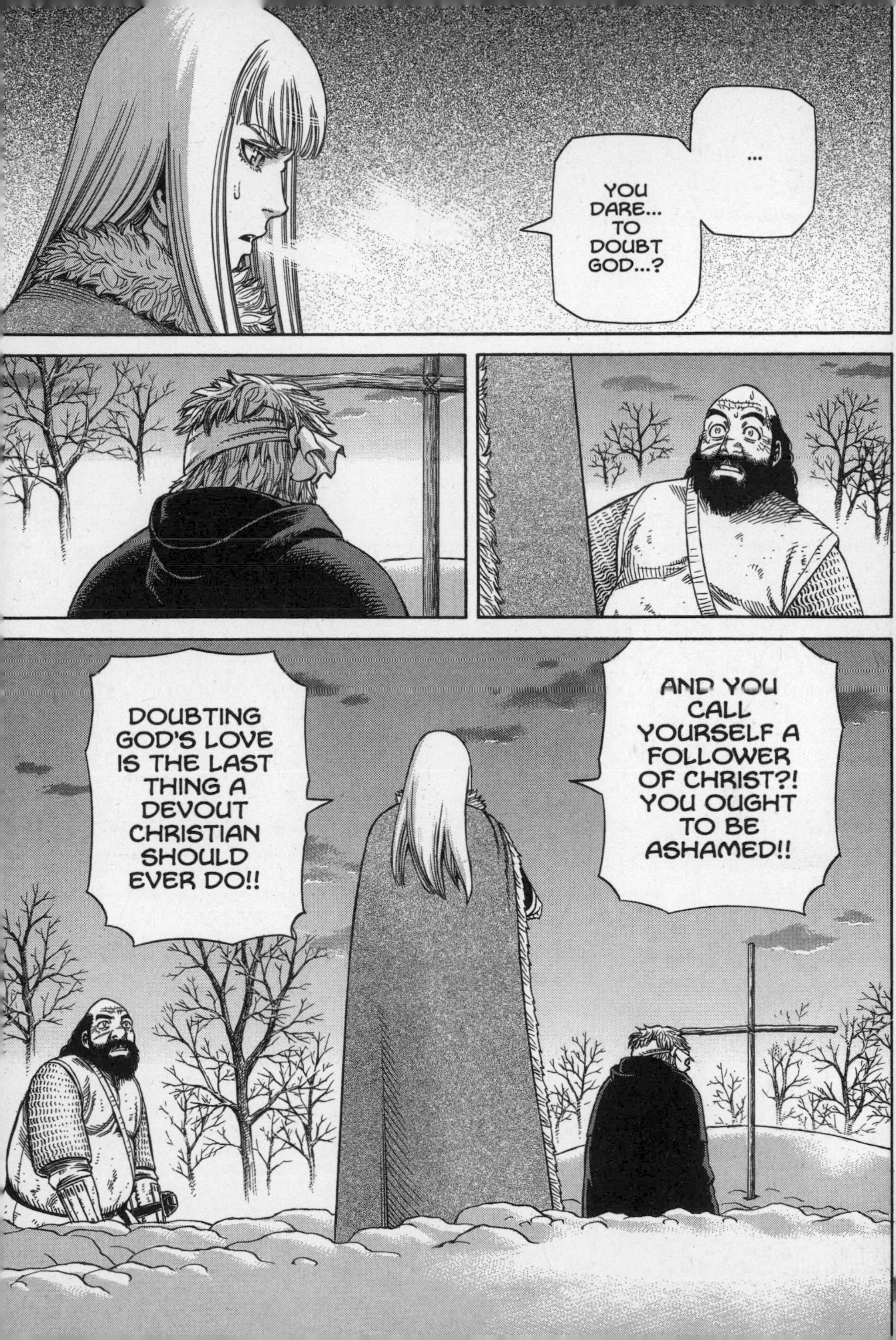
...
YOU DARE... TO DOUBT GOD...?
AND YOU CALL YOURSELF A FOLLOWER OF CHRIST?! YOU OUGHT TO BE ASHAMED!!
DOUBTING GOD'S LOVE IS THE LAST THING A DEVOUT CHRISTIAN SHOULD EVER DO!!

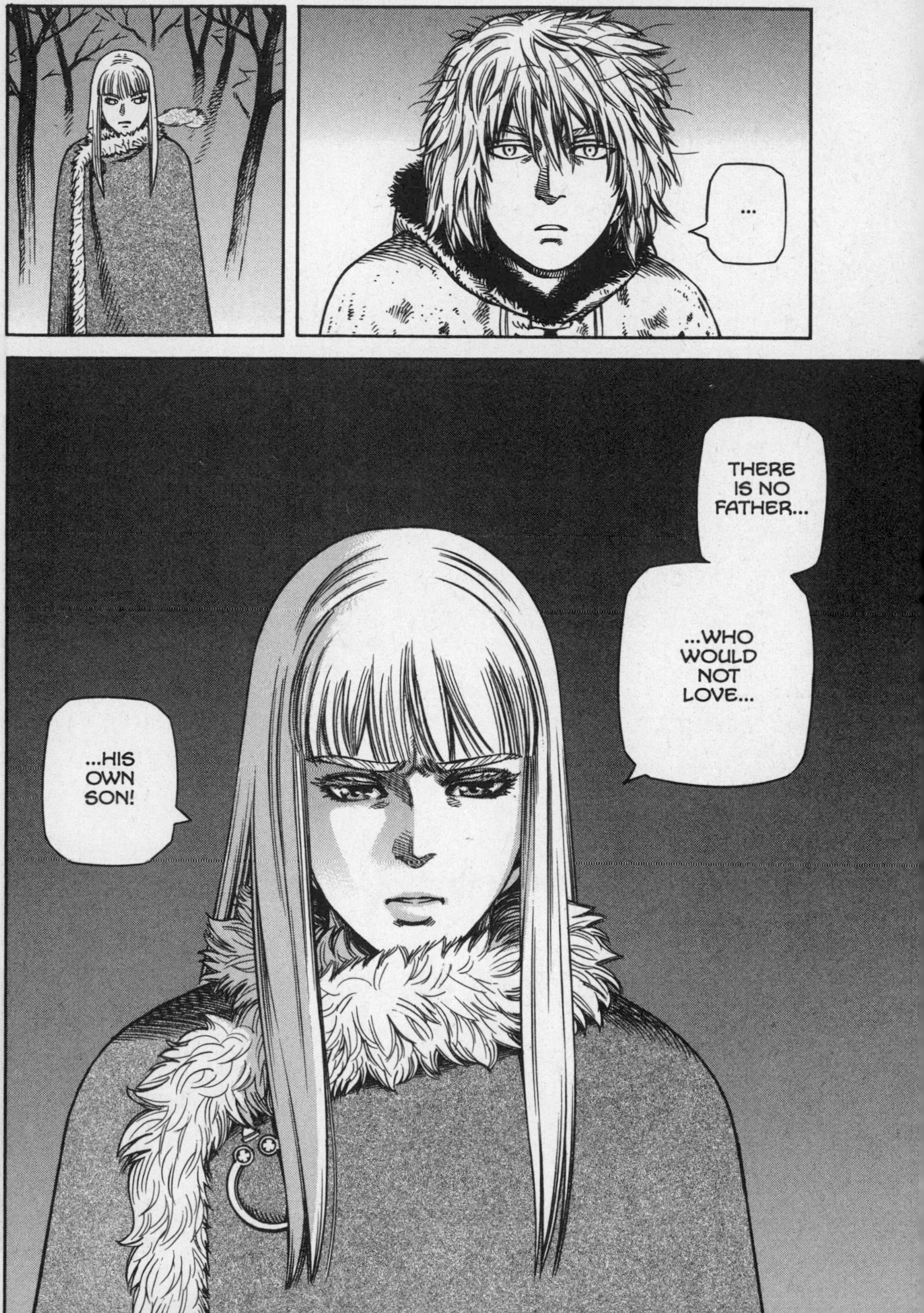
...
THERE IS NO FATHER...
...WHO WOULD NOT LOVE...
...HIS OWN SON!

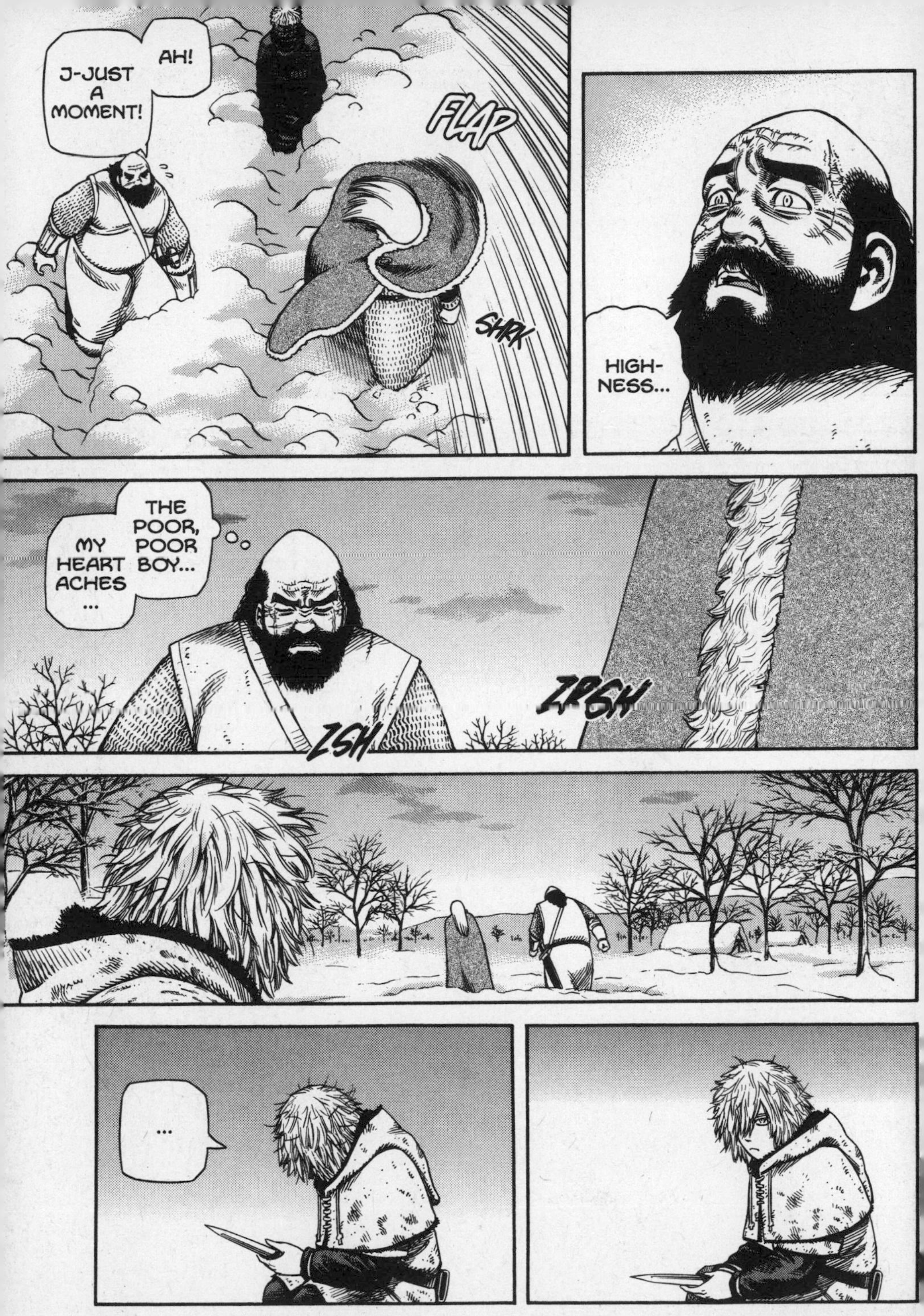
HIGH-
NESS...
FLAP
AH! J-JUST A MOMENT!
SHRK
THE POOR, POOR BOY...
MY HEART ACHES ...
ZPGH
ZSH
...

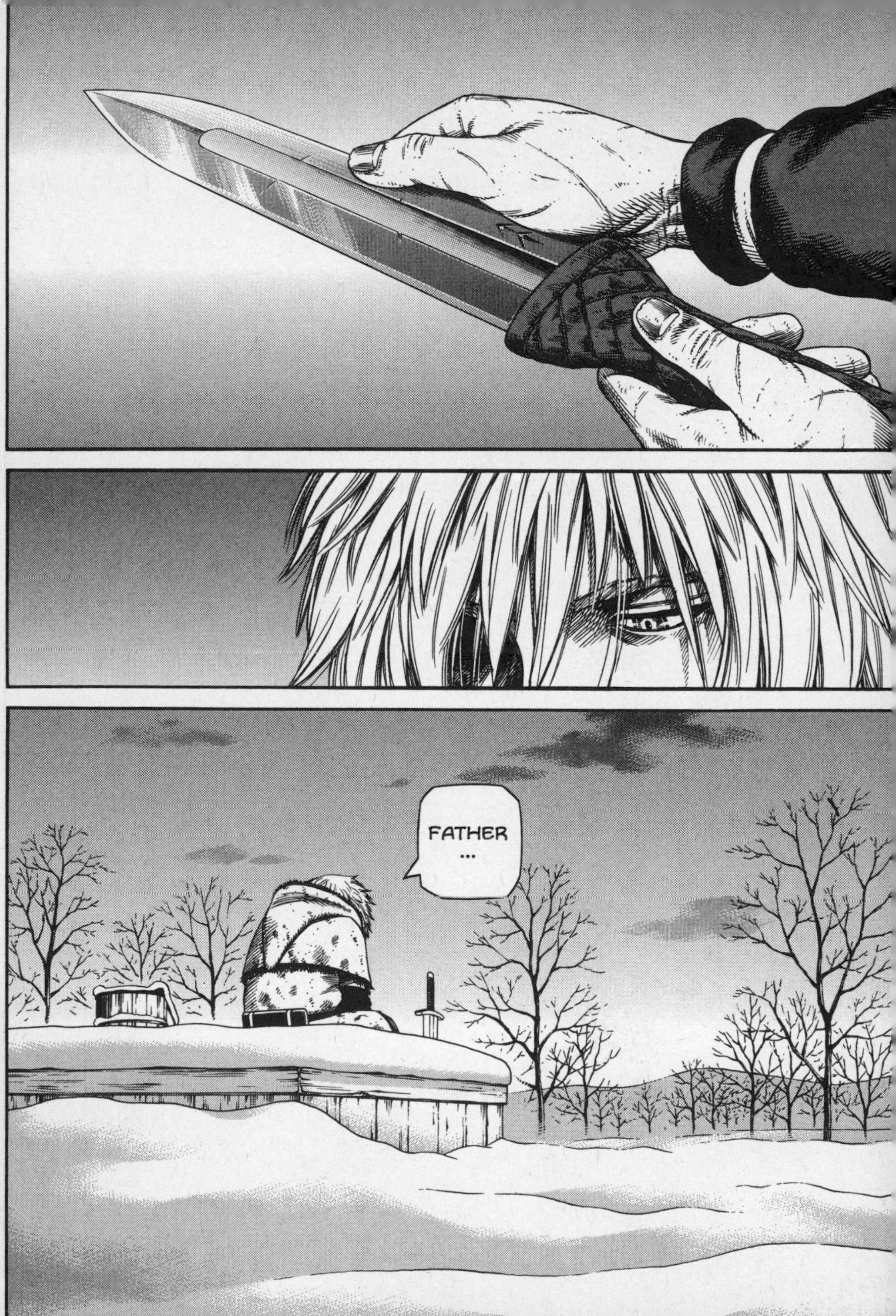
FATHER
...

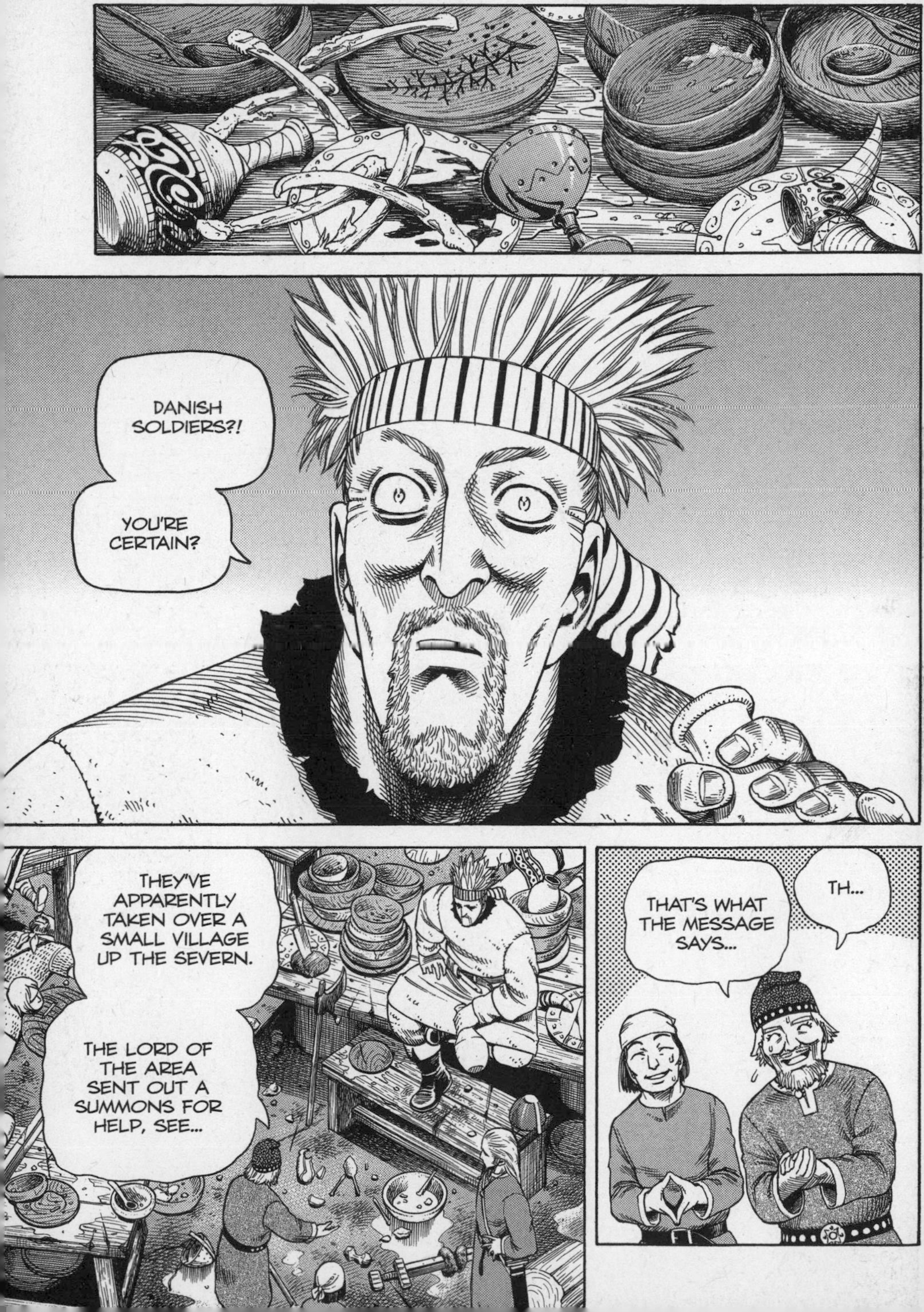
DANISH SOLDIERS?!
YOU'RE CERTAIN?
TH...
THAT'S WHAT THE MESSAGE SAYS...
THEY'VE APPARENTLY TAKEN OVER A SMALL VILLAGE UP THE SEVERN.
THE LORD OF THE AREA SENT OUT A SUMMONS FOR HELP, SEE...

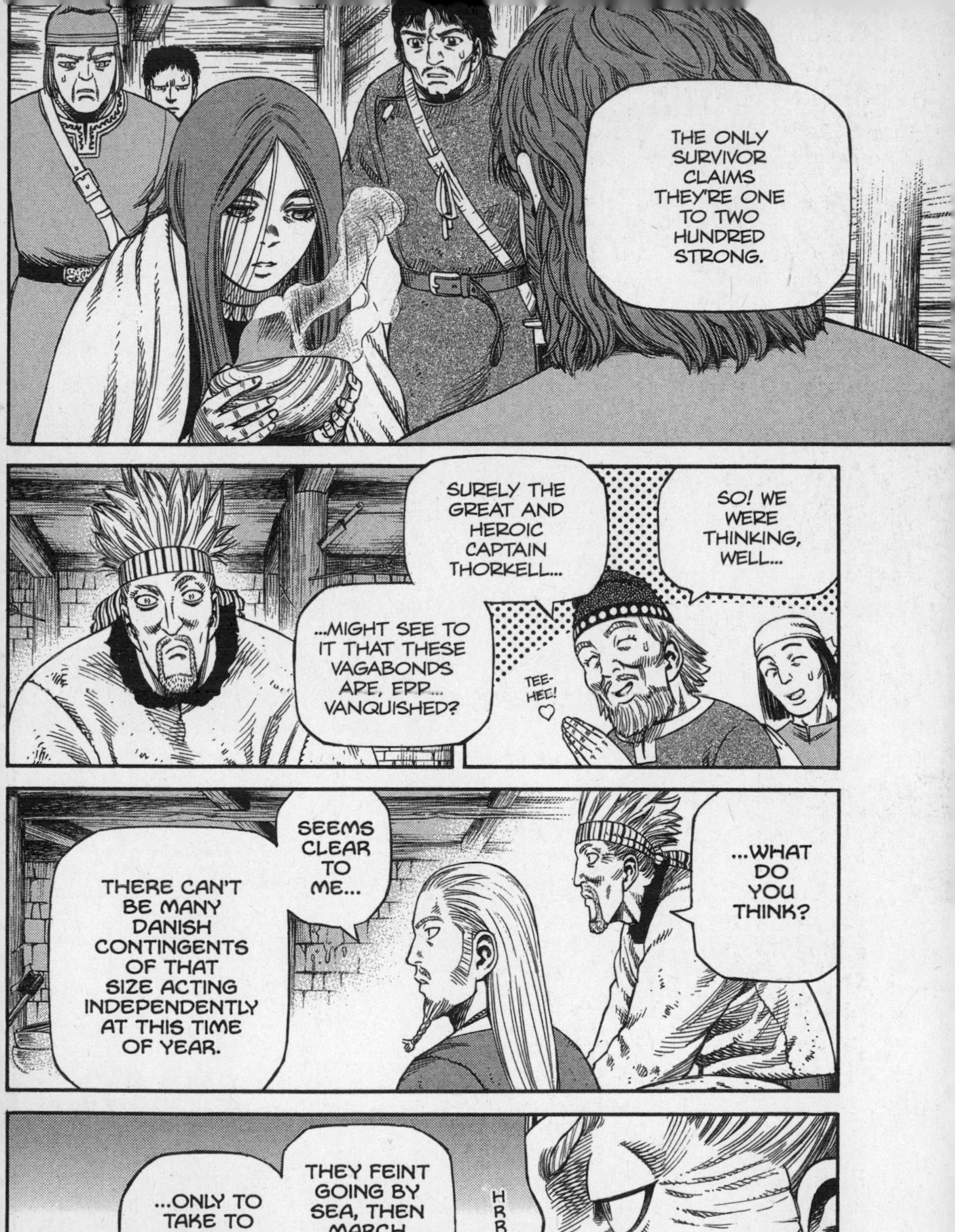
THE ONLY SURVIVOR CLAIMS THEY'RE ONE TO TWO HUNDRED STRONG.
SO! WE WERE THINKING, WELL...
SURELY THE GREAT AND HEROIC CAPTAIN THORKELL...
TEE-HEE! ♡
...MIGHT SEE TO IT THAT THESE VAGABONDS APE, EPP... VANQUISHED?
...WHAT DO YOU THINK?
SEEMS CLEAR TO ME...
THERE CAN'T BE MANY DANISH CONTINGENTS OF THAT SIZE ACTING INDEPENDENTLY AT THIS TIME OF YEAR.
HRRRM
THEY FEINT GOING BY SEA, THEN MARCH OVER LAND TO GAINS-BOROUGH...
...ONLY TO TAKE TO HIBERNA-TION WHEN THE SNOW TRAPS THEM?

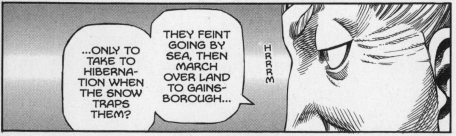

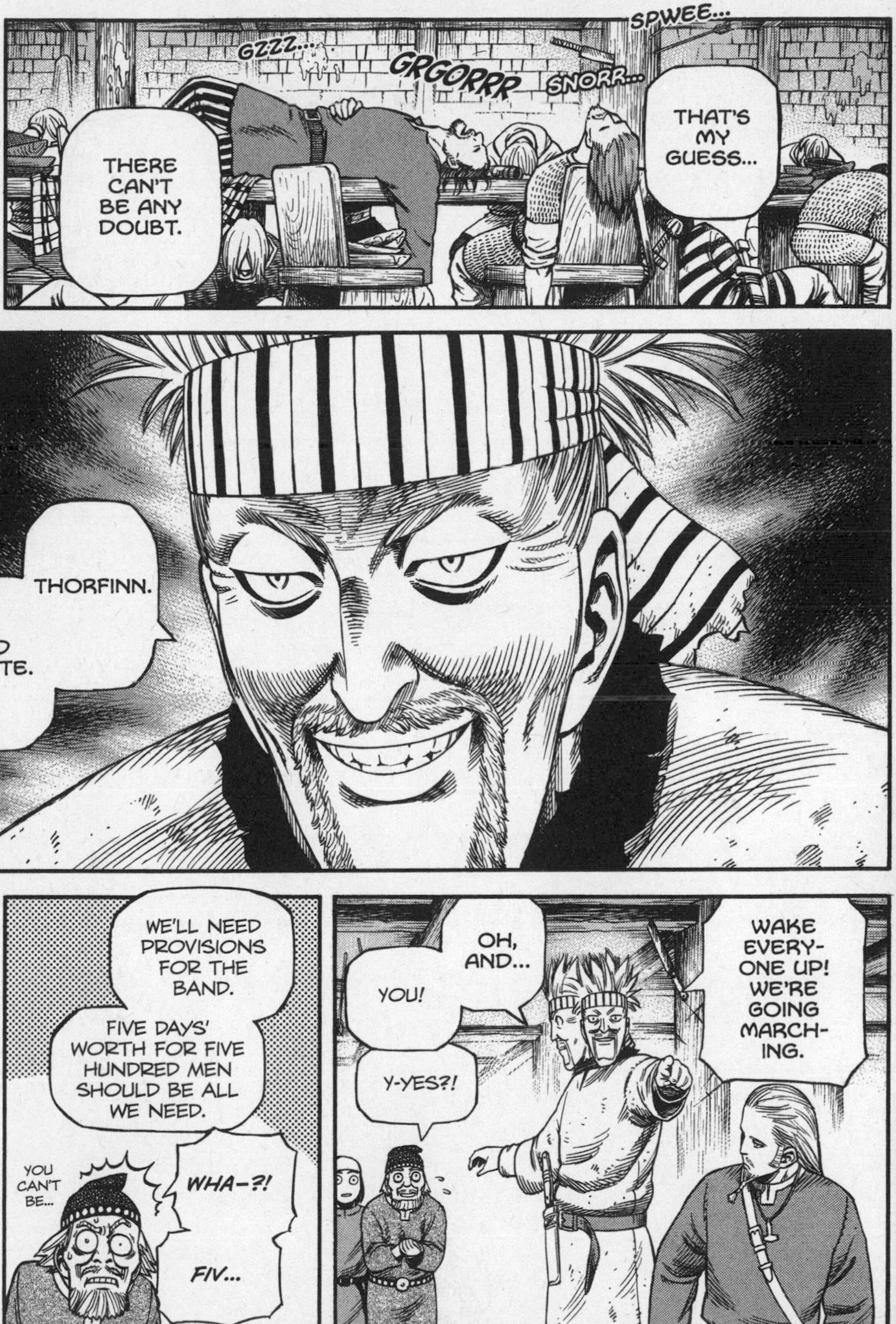
SPWEE...
SNORR...
THAT'S MY GUESS...
GRGORRR
GZZZ...
THERE CAN'T BE ANY DOUBT.
THORFINN.
AND CANUTE.
WAKE EVERY-ONE UP! WE'RE GOING MARCH-ING.
OH, AND...
YOU!
Y-YES?!
WE'LL NEED PROVISIONS FOR THE BAND.
FIVE DAYS' WORTH FOR FIVE HUNDRED MEN SHOULD BE ALL WE NEED.
WHA-?!
FIV...
YOU CAN'T BE...

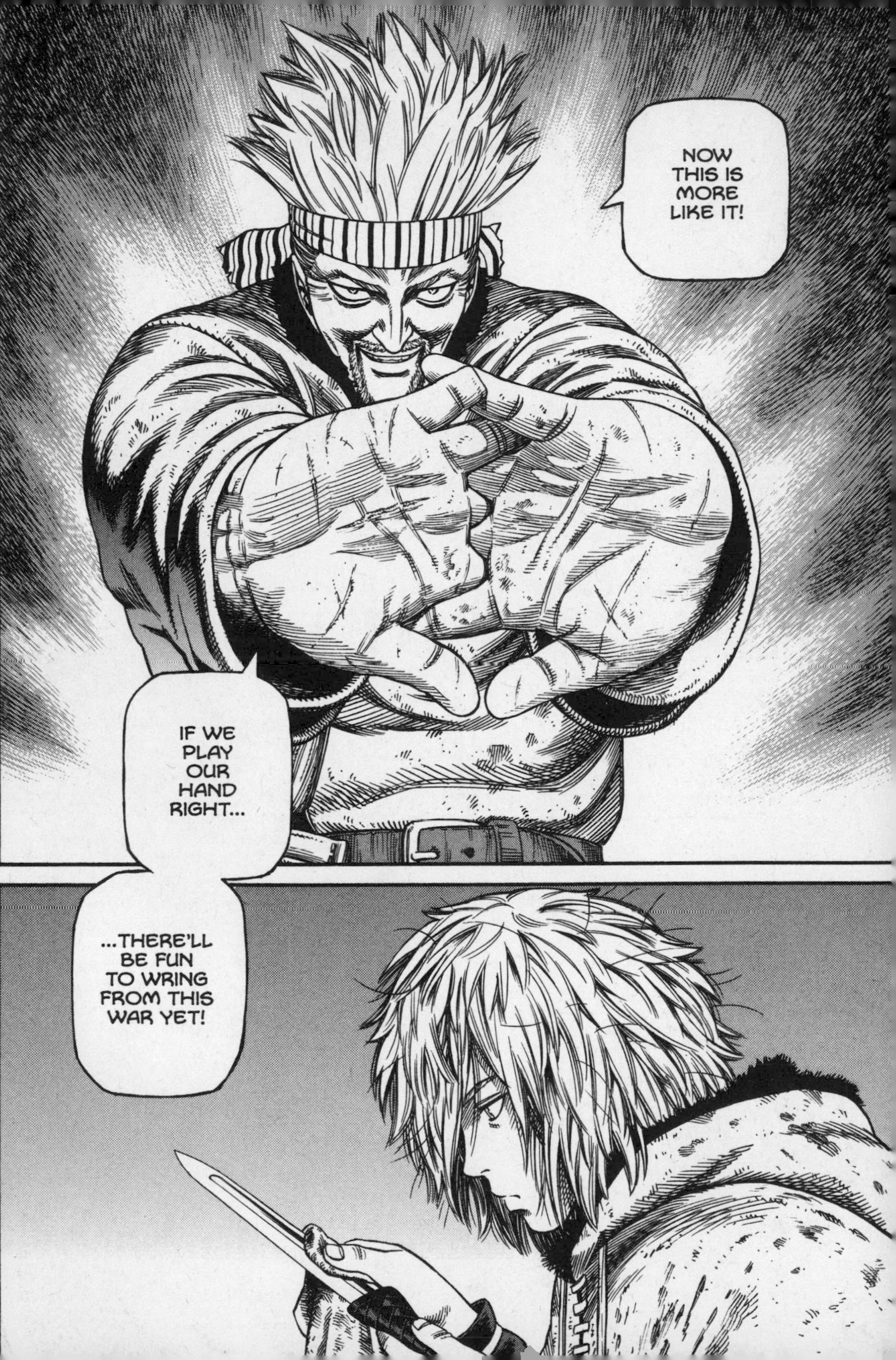
NOW THIS IS MORE LIKE IT!
IF WE PLAY OUR HAND RIGHT...
...THERE'LL BE FUN TO WRING FROM THIS WAR YET!

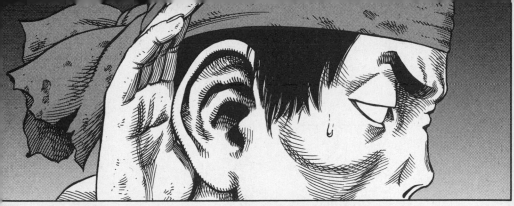

...

...TSK.

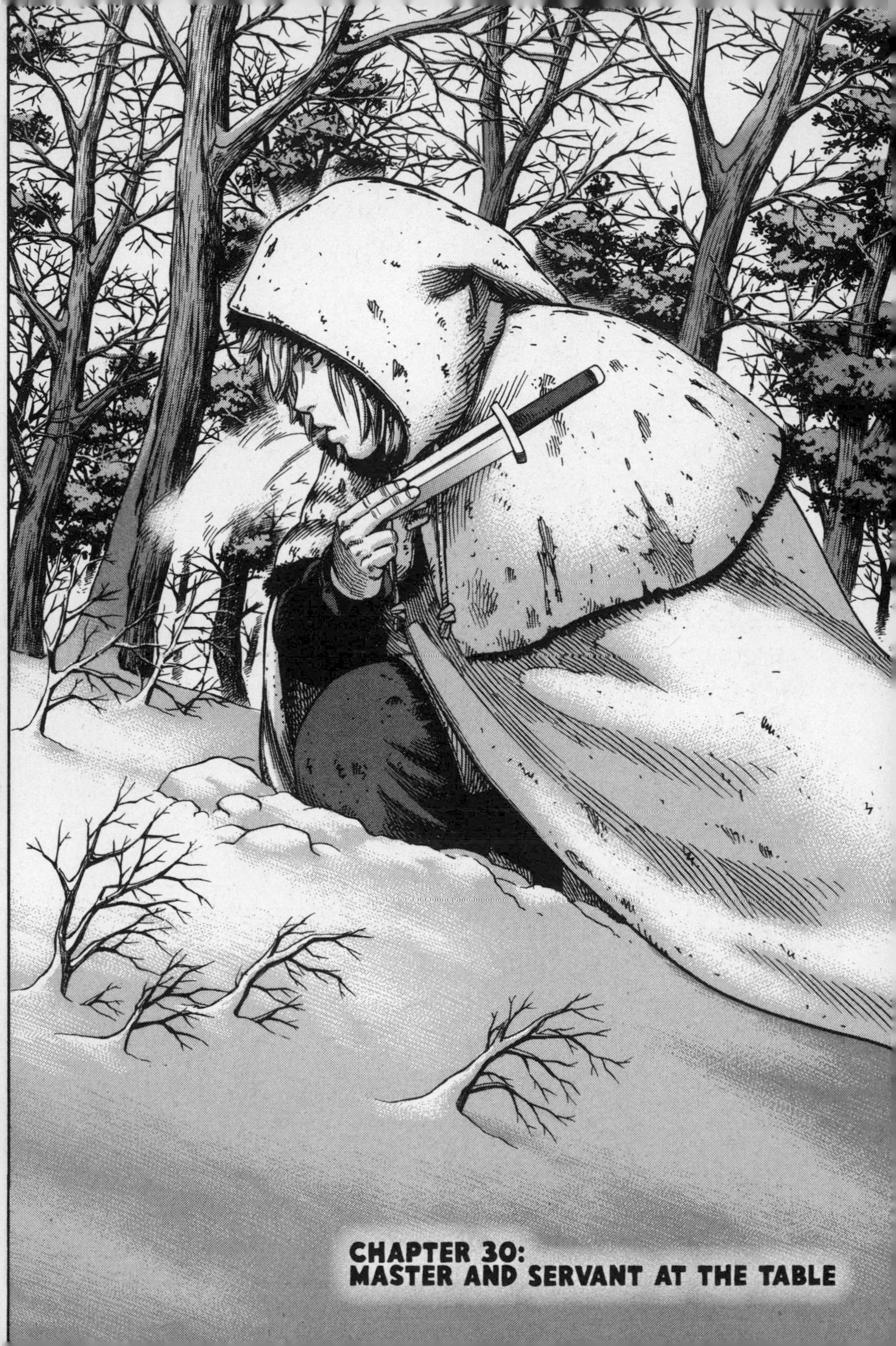

## CHAPTER 30: MASTER AND SERVANT AT THE TABLE

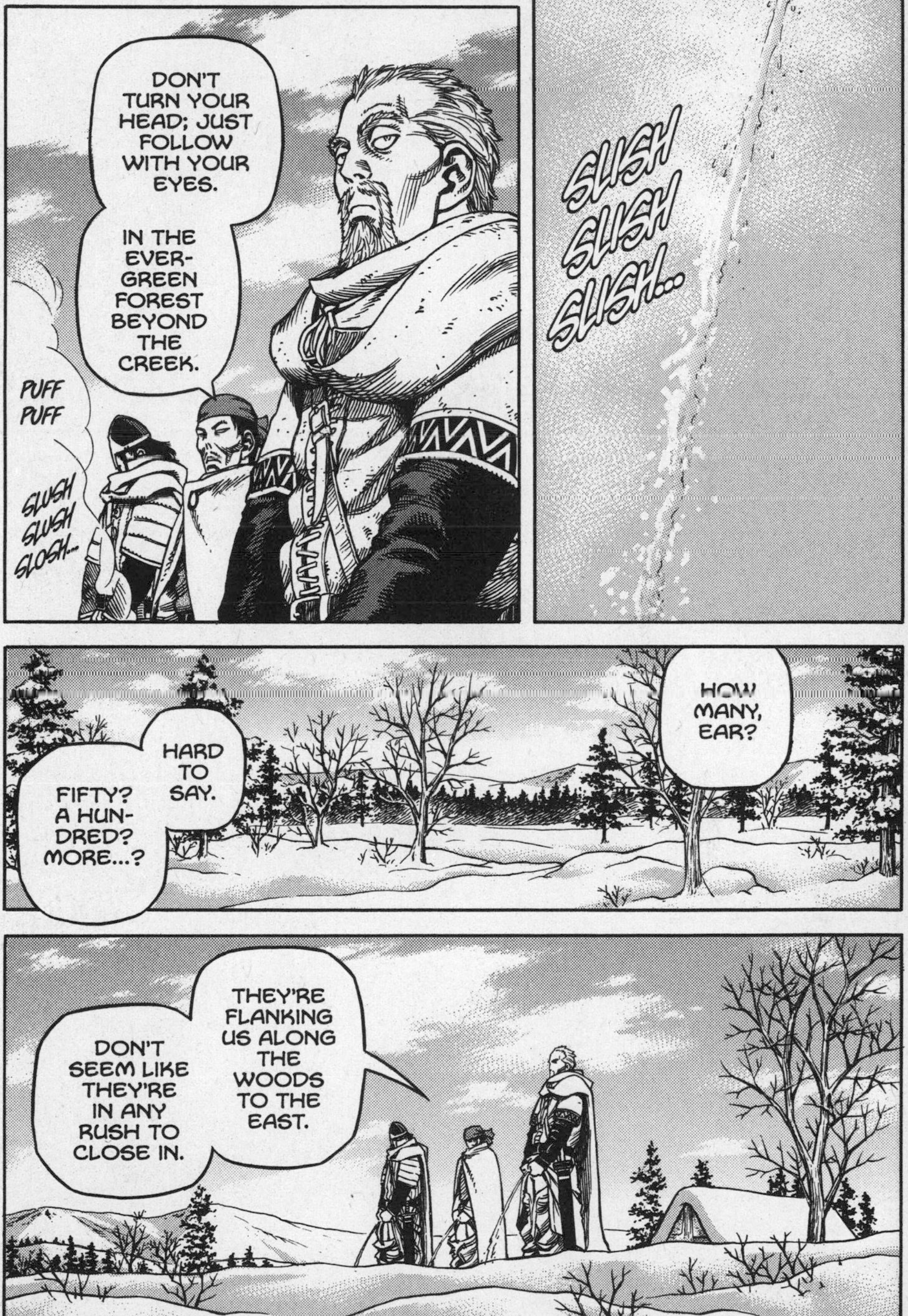
SLUSH SLUSH SLUSH...
DON'T TURN YOUR HEAD; JUST FOLLOW WITH YOUR EYES.
IN THE EVER-GREEN FOREST BEYOND THE CREEK.
PUFF PUFF
SLUSH SLUSH SLOSH...
HOW MANY, EAR?
HARD TO SAY.
FIFTY? A HUN-DRED? MORE...?
THEY'RE FLANKING US ALONG THE WOODS TO THE EAST.
DON'T SEEM LIKE THEY'RE IN ANY RUSH TO CLOSE IN.

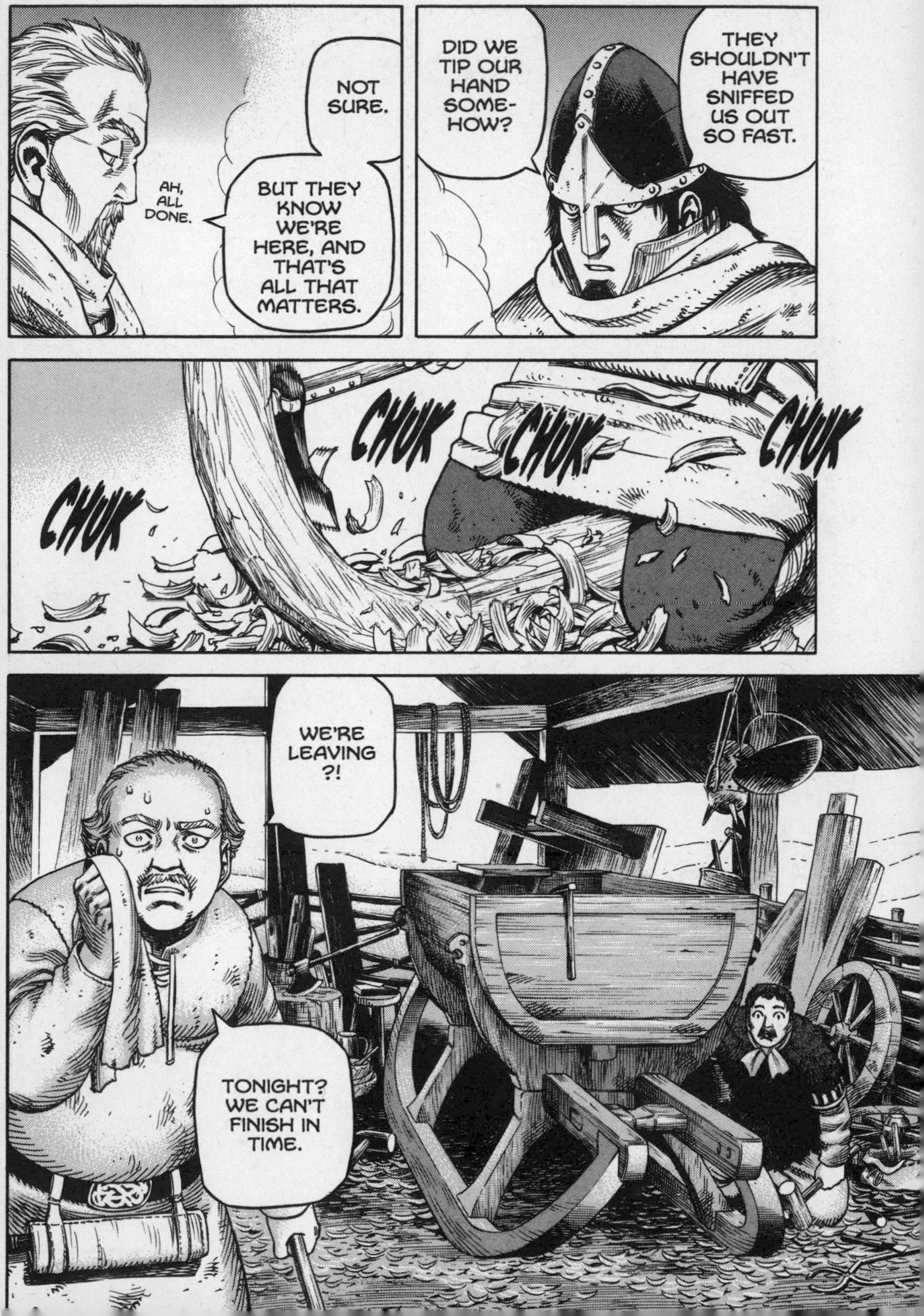
THEY SHOULDN'T HAVE SNIFFED US OUT SO FAST.
DID WE TIP OUR HAND SOME-HOW?
NOT SURE.
BUT THEY KNOW WE'RE HERE, AND THAT'S ALL THAT MATTERS.
AH, ALL DONE.
CHUK
CHUK
CHUK
CHUK
WE'RE LEAVING ?!
TONIGHT? WE CAN'T FINISH IN TIME.

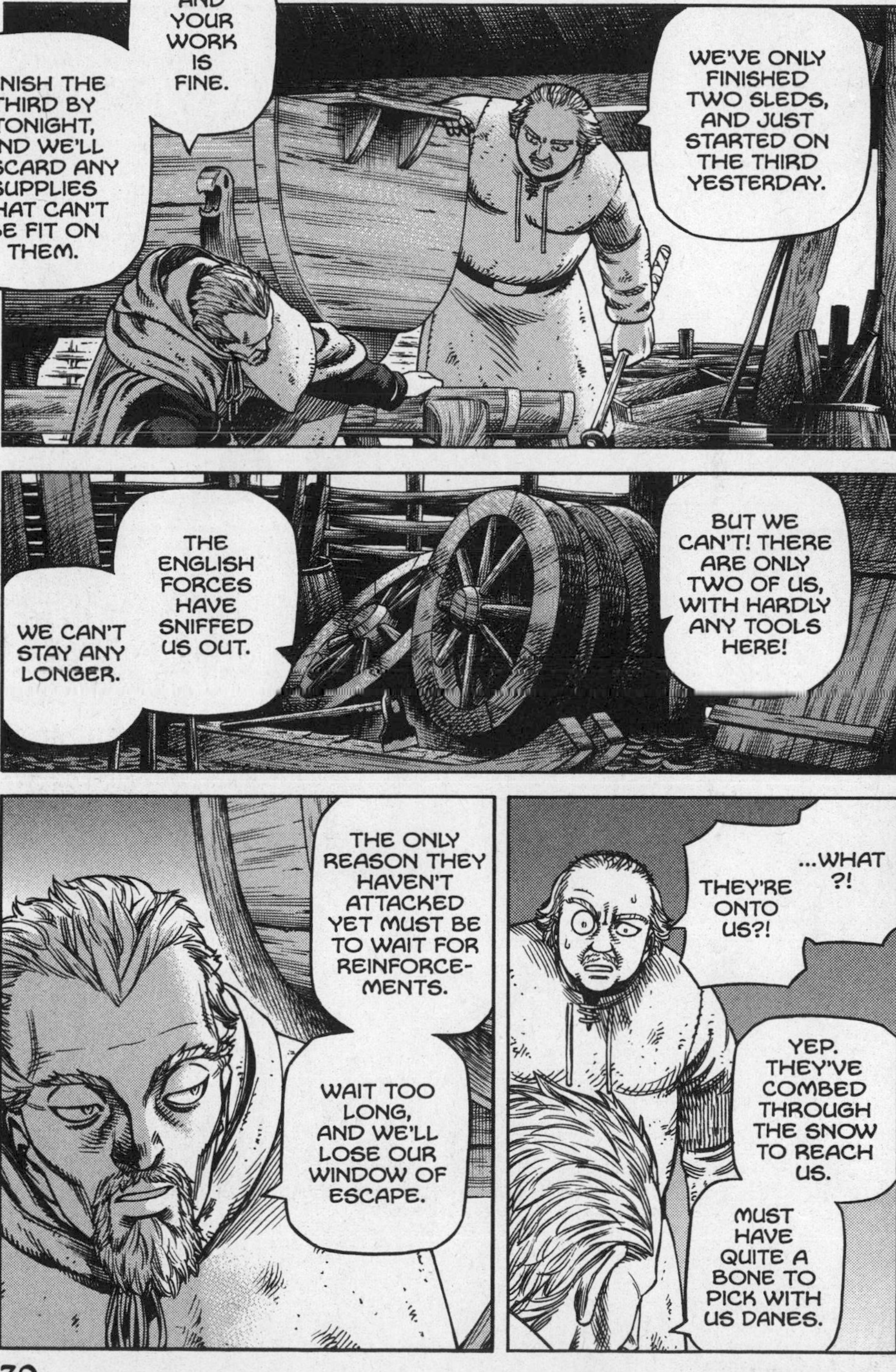
WE'VE ONLY FINISHED TWO SLEDS, AND JUST STARTED ON THE THIRD YESTERDAY.
AND YOUR WORK IS FINE.
FINISH THE THIRD BY TONIGHT, AND WE'LL DISCARD ANY SUPPLIES THAT CAN'T BE FIT ON THEM.
BUT WE CAN'T! THERE ARE ONLY TWO OF US, WITH HARDLY ANY TOOLS HERE!
THE ENGLISH FORCES HAVE SNIFFED US OUT.
WE CAN'T STAY ANY LONGER.
...WHAT ?!
THEY'RE ONTO US?!
YEP. THEY'VE COMBED THROUGH THE SNOW TO REACH US.
MUST HAVE QUITE A BONE TO PICK WITH US DANES.
THE ONLY REASON THEY HAVEN'T ATTACKED YET MUST BE TO WAIT FOR REINFORCE-MENTS.
WAIT TOO LONG, AND WE'LL LOSE OUR WINDOW OF ESCAPE.

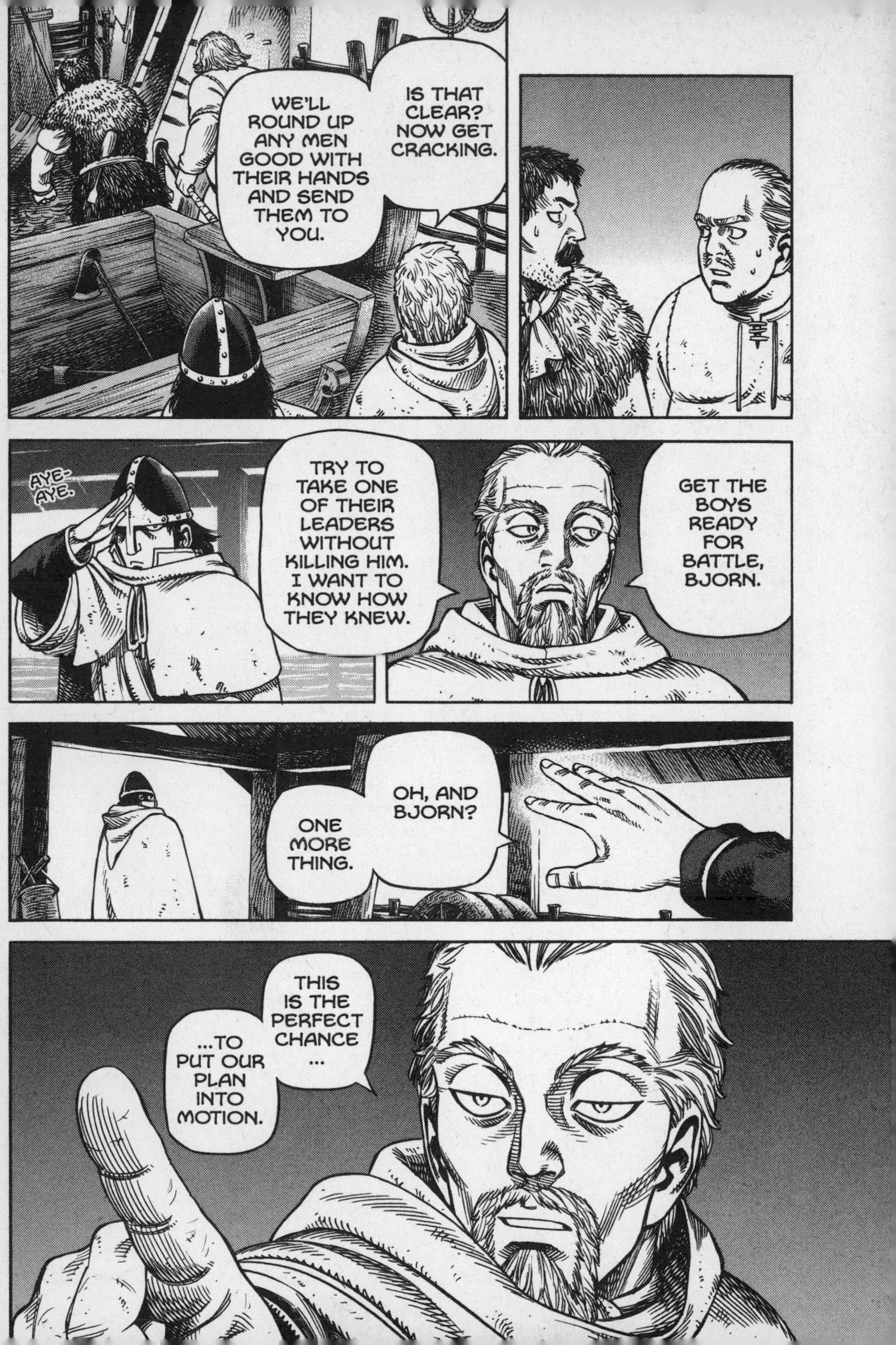
IS THAT CLEAR? NOW GET CRACKING.
WE'LL ROUND UP ANY MEN GOOD WITH THEIR HANDS AND SEND THEM TO YOU.
GET THE BOYS READY FOR BATTLE, BJORN.
TRY TO TAKE ONE OF THEIR LEADERS WITHOUT KILLING HIM. I WANT TO KNOW HOW THEY KNEW.
AYE-AYE.
OH, AND BJORN?
ONE MORE THING.
THIS IS THE PERFECT CHANCE ...
...TO PUT OUR PLAN INTO MOTION.

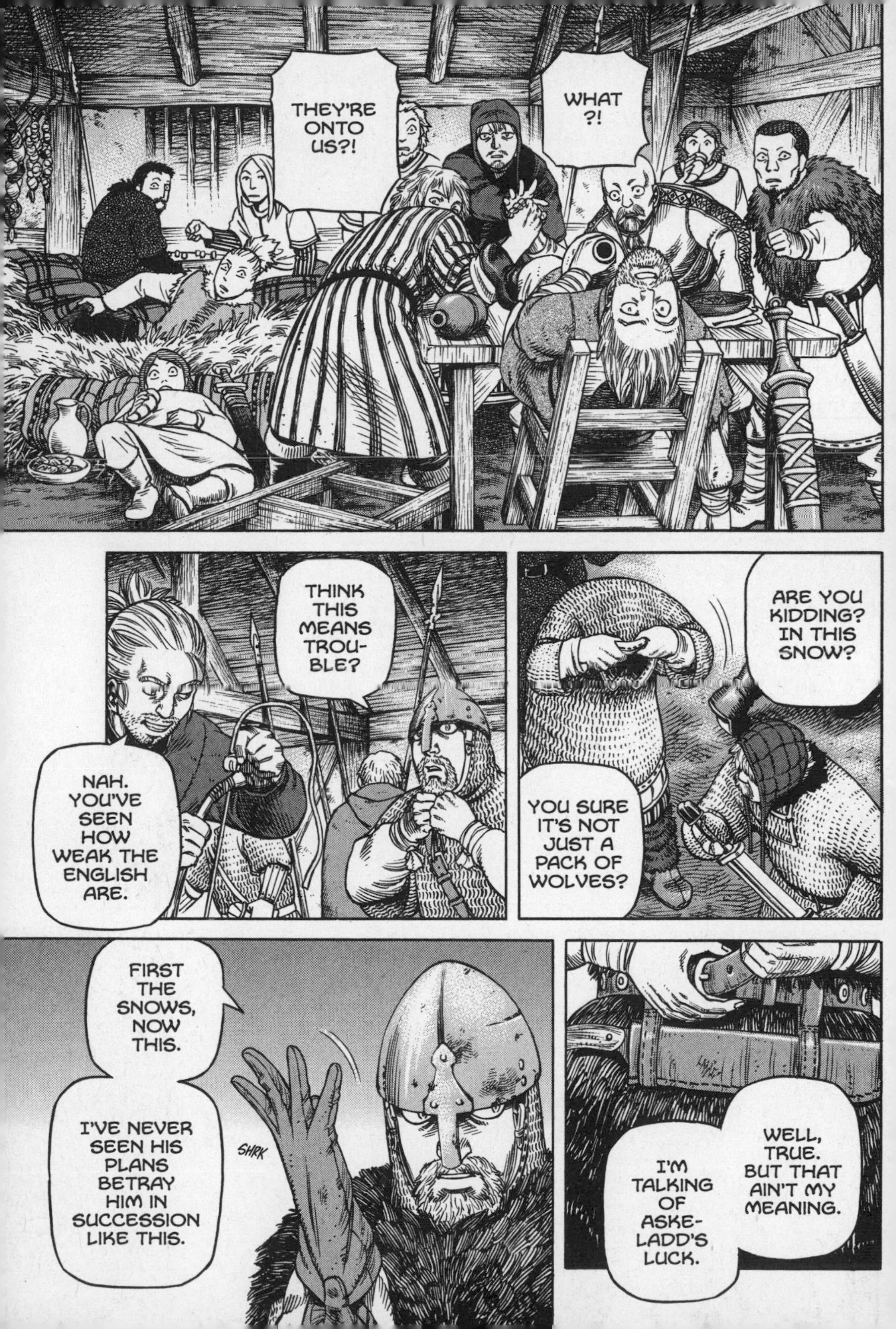
WHAT ?!
THEY'RE ONTO US?!
ARE YOU KIDDING? IN THIS SNOW?
YOU SURE IT'S NOT JUST A PACK OF WOLVES?
THINK THIS MEANS TROUBLE?
NAH. YOU'VE SEEN HOW WEAK THE ENGLISH ARE.
WELL, TRUE. BUT THAT AIN'T MY MEANING.
I'M TALKING OF ASKELADD'S LUCK.
FIRST THE SNOWS, NOW THIS.
I'VE NEVER SEEN HIS PLANS BETRAY HIM IN SUCCESSION LIKE THIS.
SHRK

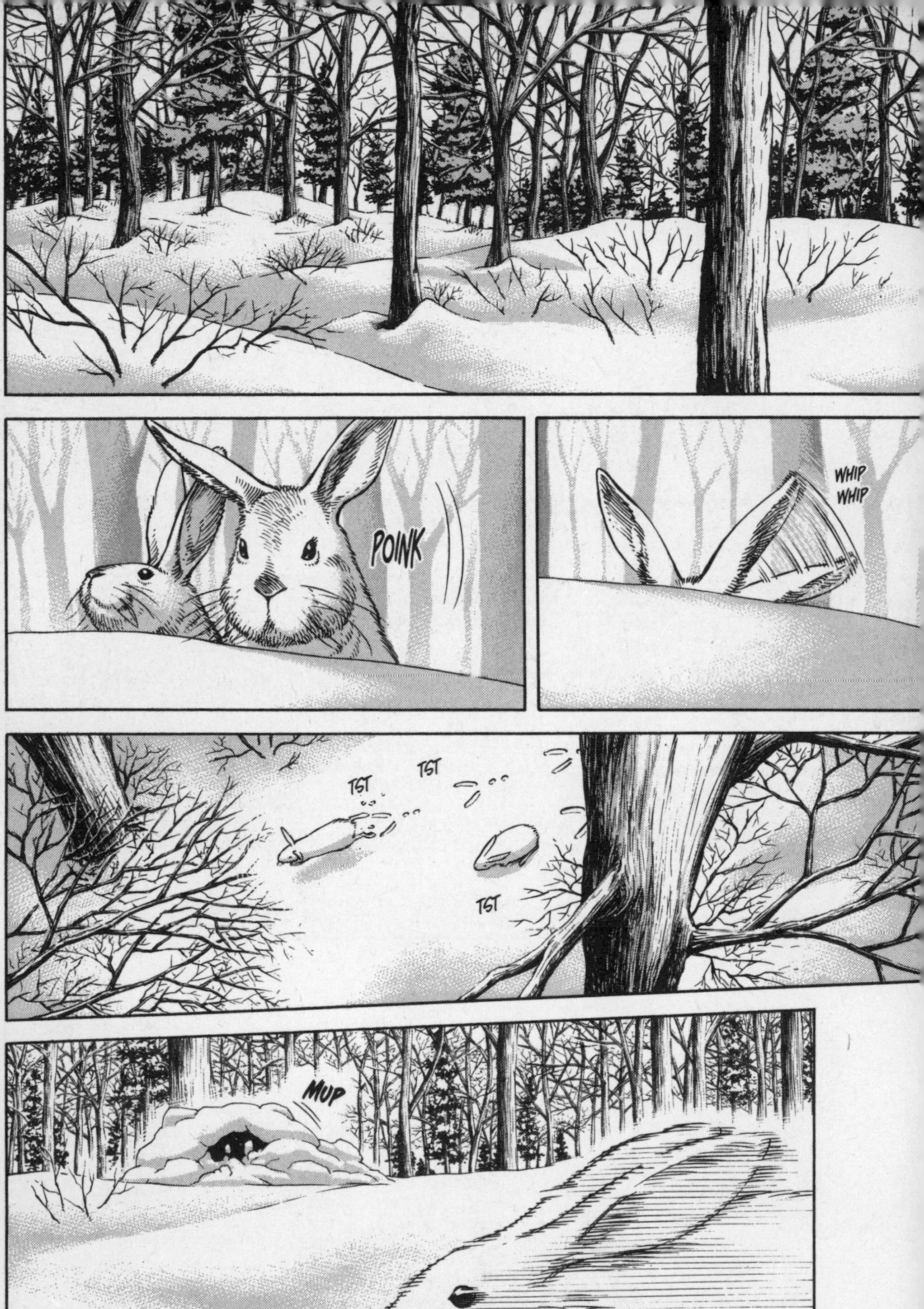
WHIP
WHIP
POINK
TST
TST
TST
MUP

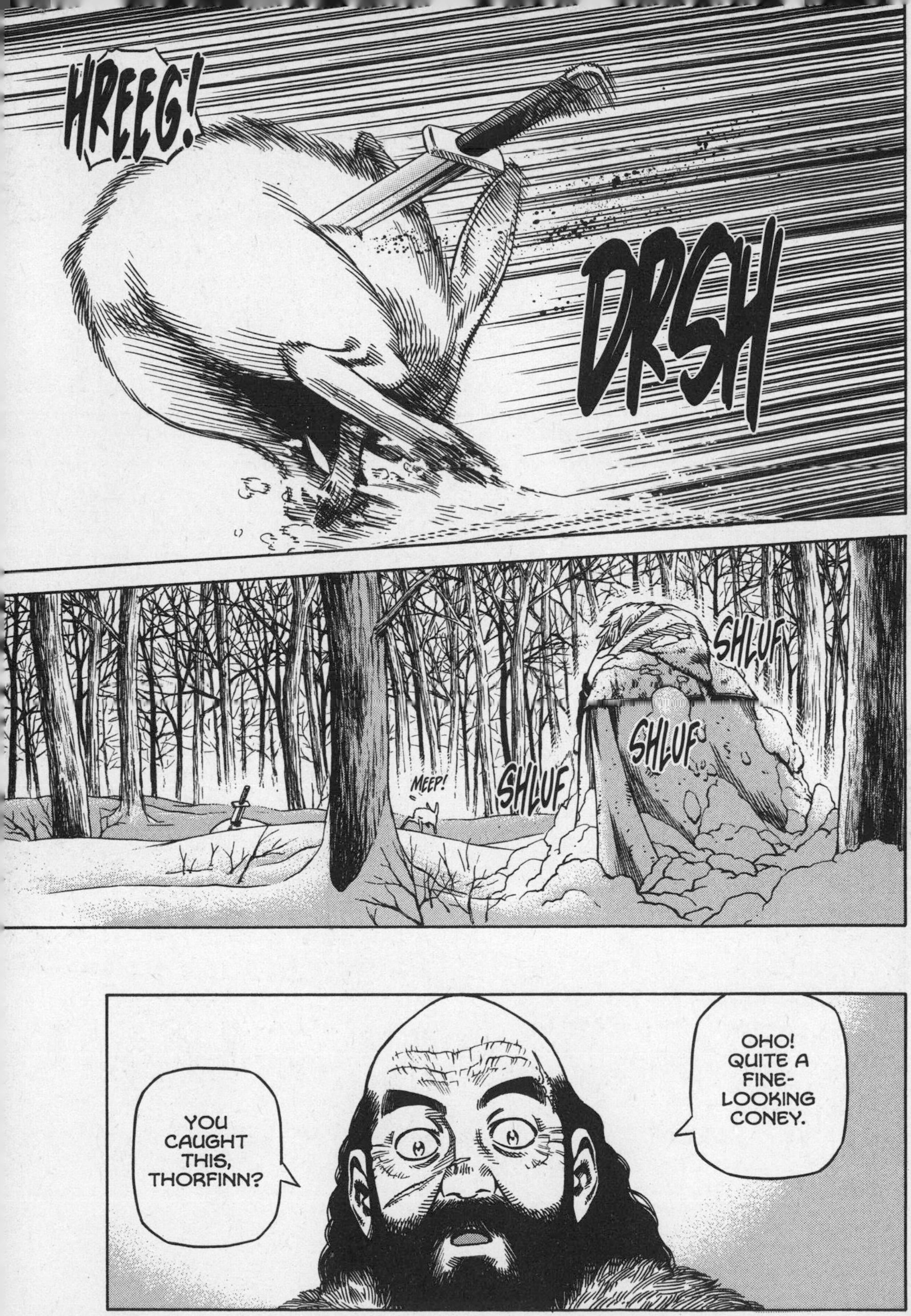
HREEG!
DRSH
SHLUF
SHLUF
SHLUF
MEEP!
OHO! QUITE A FINE-LOOKING CONEY.
YOU CAUGHT THIS, THORFINN?

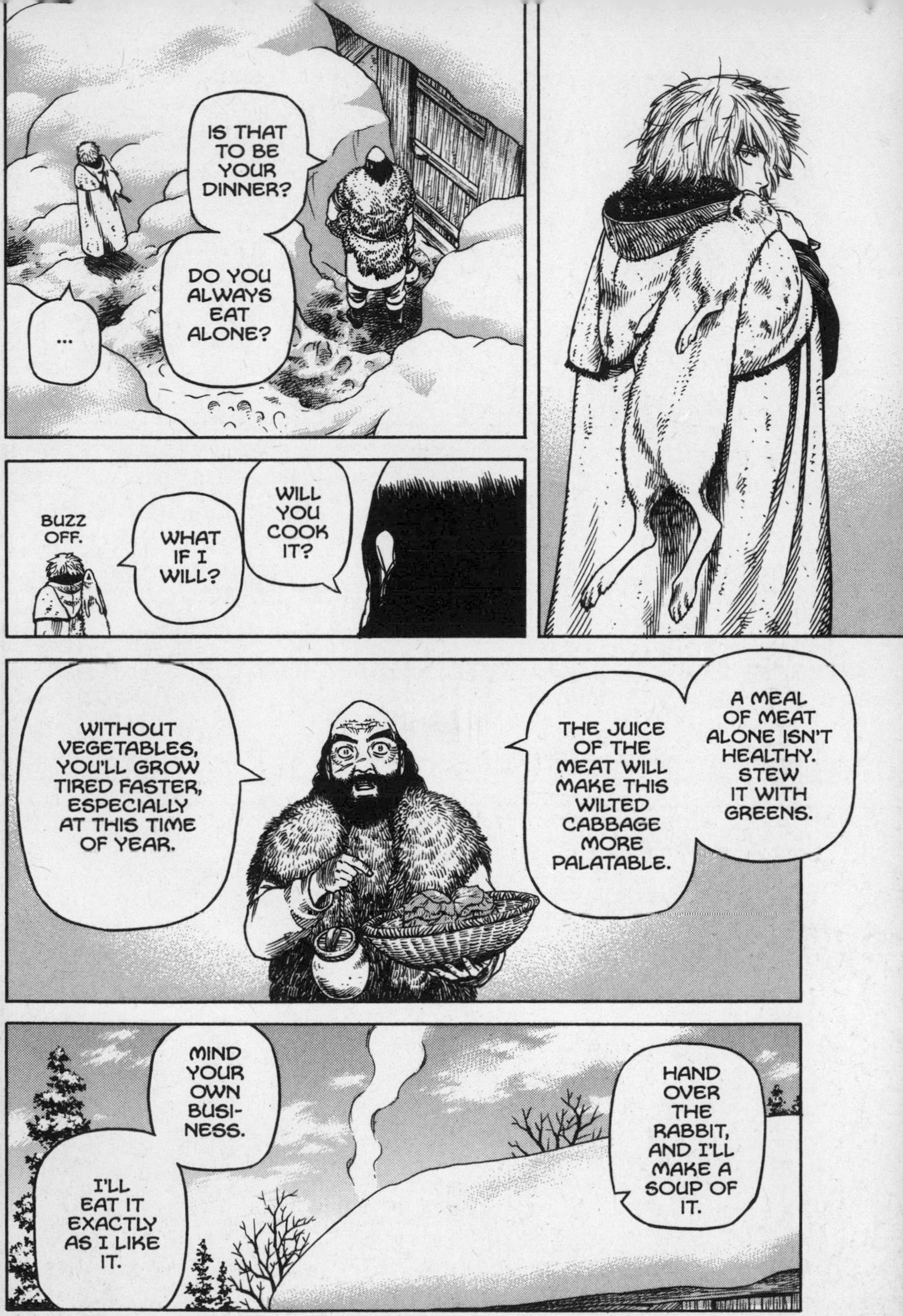
IS THAT TO BE YOUR DINNER?
DO YOU ALWAYS EAT ALONE?
...
WILL YOU COOK IT?
WHAT IF I WILL?
BUZZ OFF.
A MEAL OF MEAT ALONE ISN'T HEALTHY. STEW IT WITH GREENS.
THE JUICE OF THE MEAT WILL MAKE THIS WILTED CABBAGE MORE PALATABLE.
WITHOUT VEGETABLES, YOU'LL GROW TIRED FASTER, ESPECIALLY AT THIS TIME OF YEAR.
HAND OVER THE RABBIT, AND I'LL MAKE A SOUP OF IT.
MIND YOUR OWN BUSI-NESS.
I'LL EAT IT EXACTLY AS I LIKE IT.

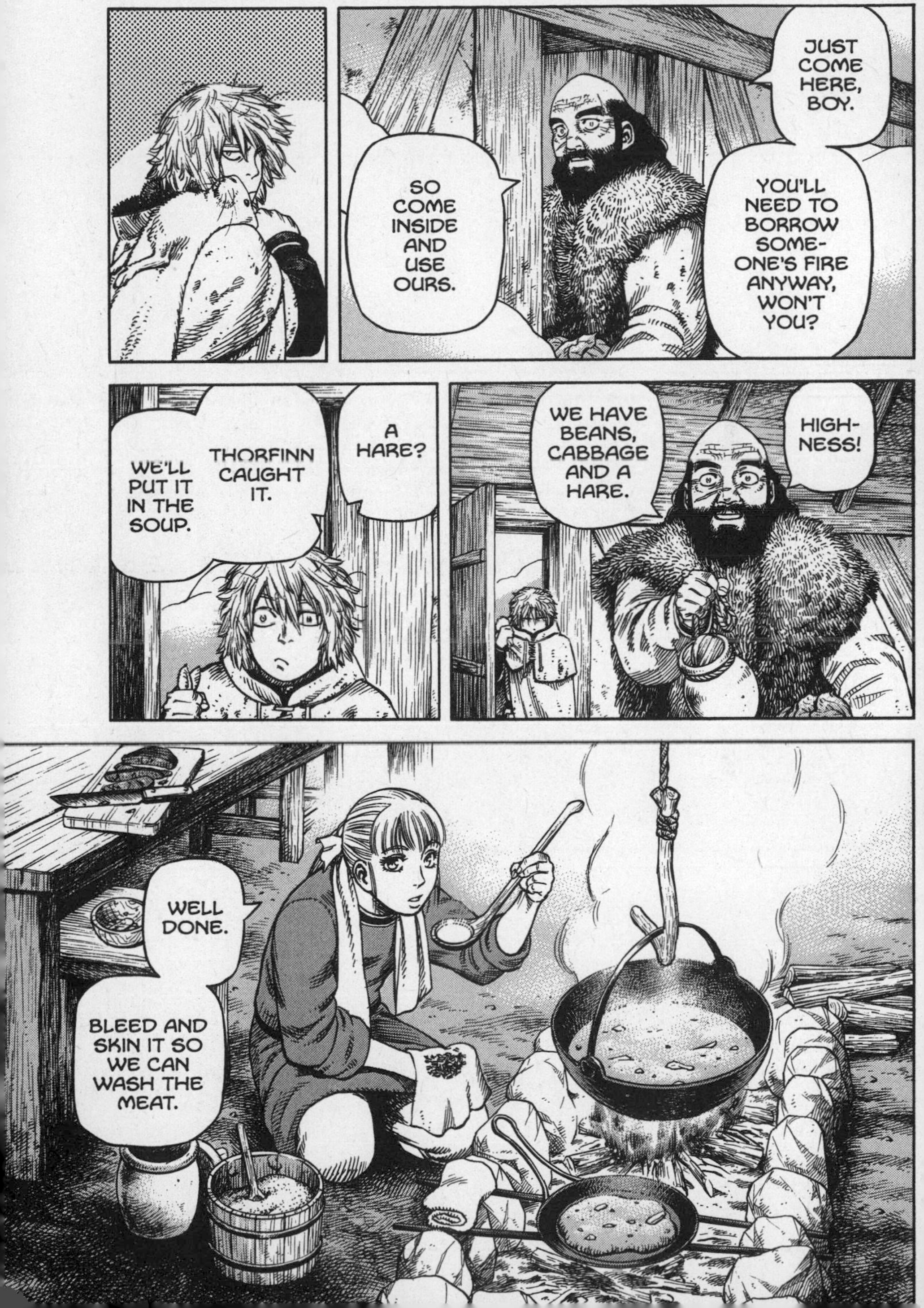
JUST COME HERE, BOY.
YOU'LL NEED TO BORROW SOME-ONE'S FIRE ANYWAY, WON'T YOU?
SO COME INSIDE AND USE OURS.
HIGH-NESS!
WE HAVE BEANS, CABBAGE AND A HARE.
A HARE?
THORFINN CAUGHT IT.
WE'LL PUT IT IN THE SOUP.
WELL DONE.
BLEED AND SKIN IT SO WE CAN WASH THE MEAT.

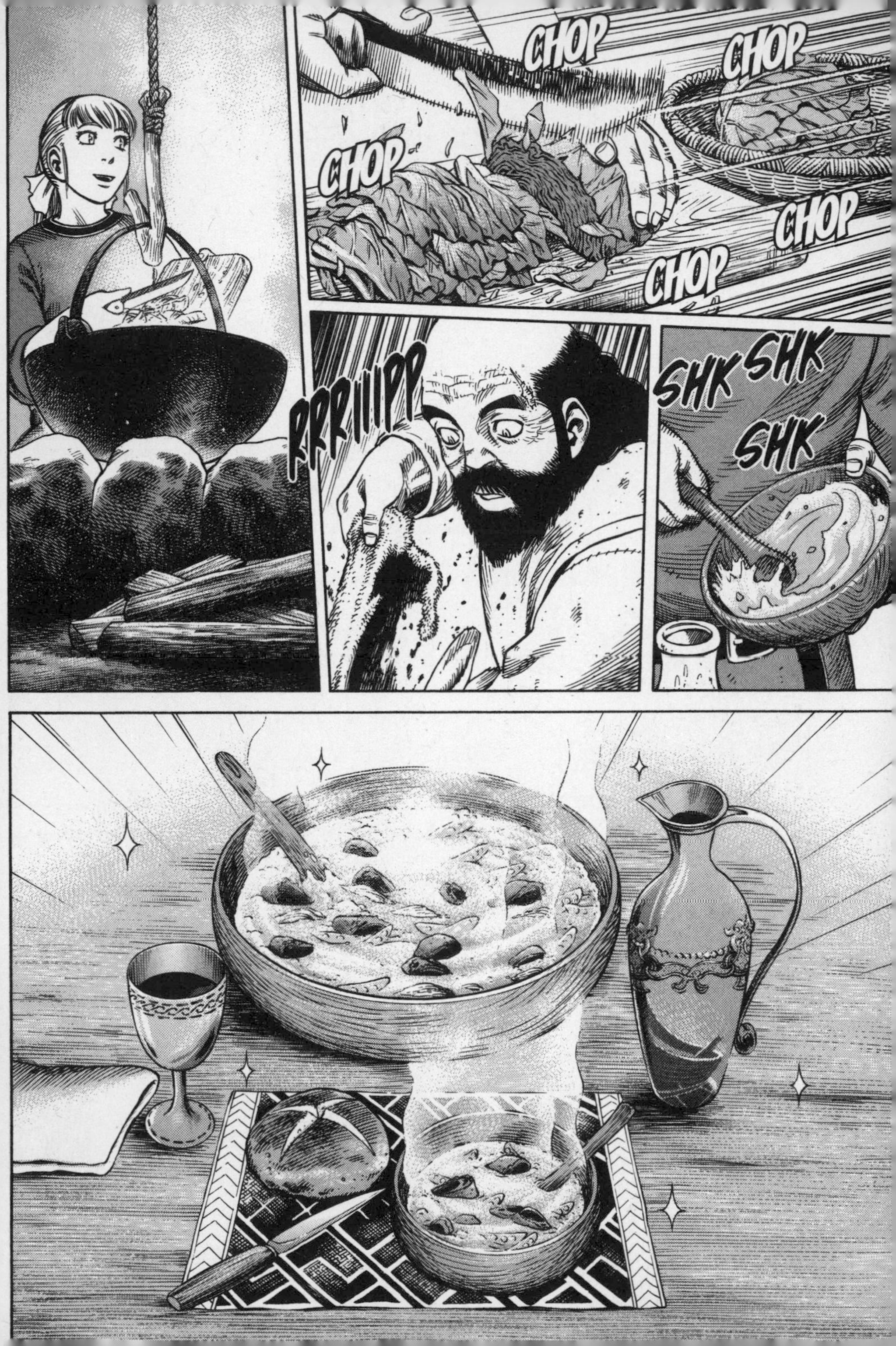
CHOP
CHOP
CHOP
CHOP
CHOP
SHK SHK
SHK
RRRIIIPP

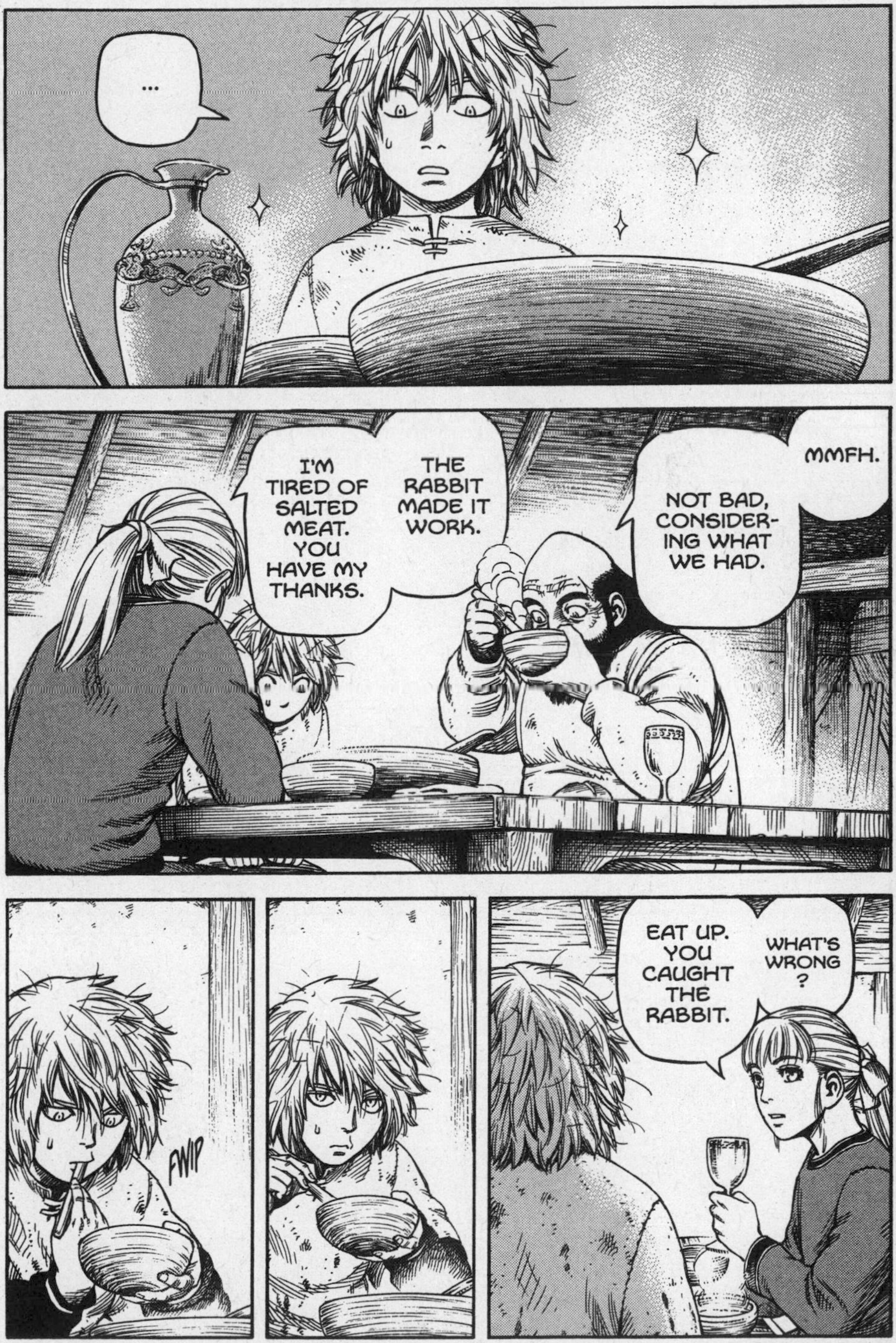
...
MMFH.
NOT BAD, CONSIDERING WHAT WE HAD.
THE RABBIT MADE IT WORK.
I'M TIRED OF SALTED MEAT. YOU HAVE MY THANKS.
WHAT'S WRONG?
EAT UP. YOU CAUGHT THE RABBIT.
FWIP

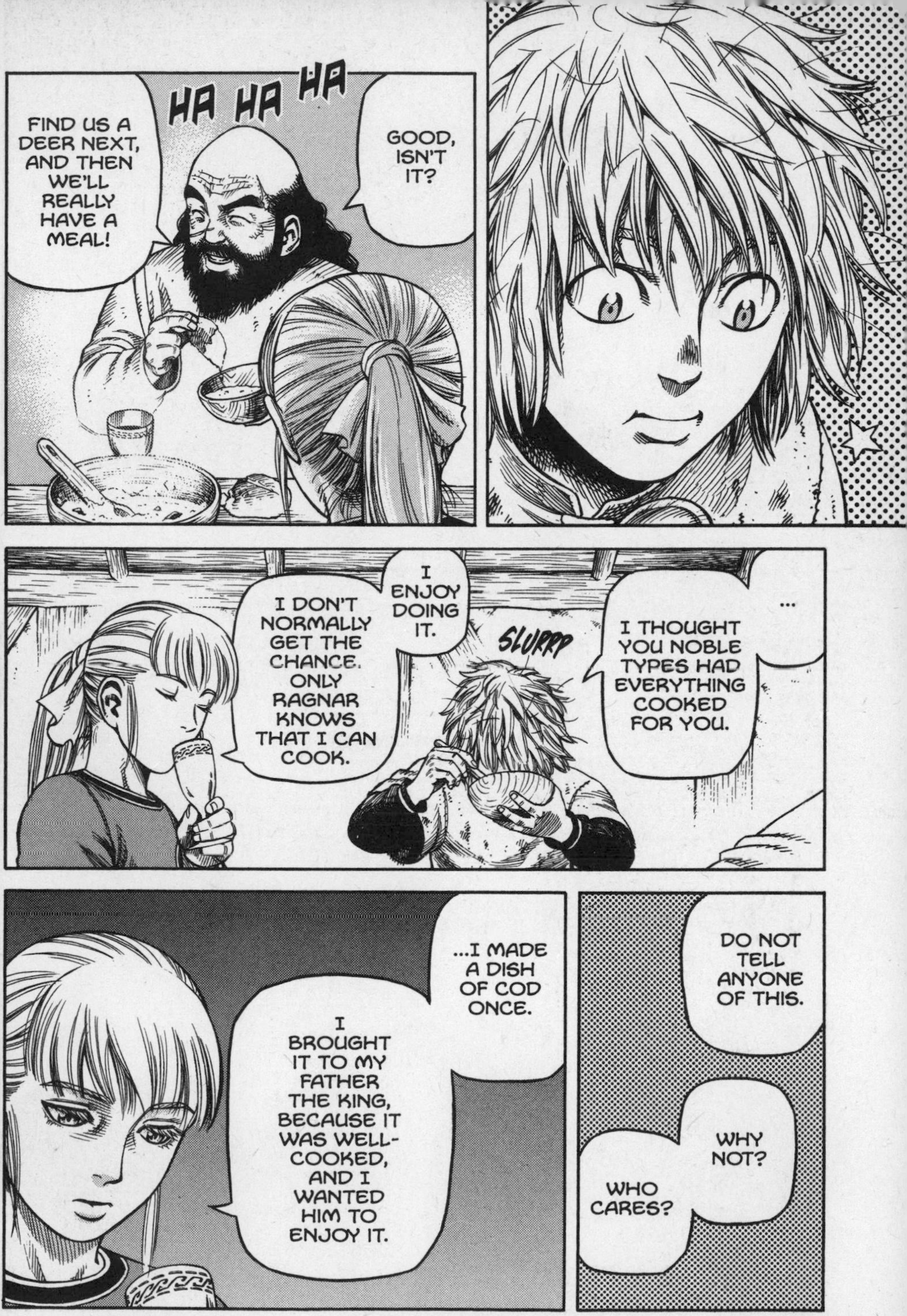
HA HA HA
GOOD, ISN'T IT?
FIND US A DEER NEXT, AND THEN WE'LL REALLY HAVE A MEAL!
...
I THOUGHT YOU NOBLE TYPES HAD EVERYTHING COOKED FOR YOU.
SLURRP
I ENJOY DOING IT.
I DON'T NORMALLY GET THE CHANCE. ONLY RAGNAR KNOWS THAT I CAN COOK.
DO NOT TELL ANYONE OF THIS.
WHY NOT?
WHO CARES?
...I MADE A DISH OF COD ONCE.
I BROUGHT IT TO MY FATHER THE KING, BECAUSE IT WAS WELL-COOKED, AND I WANTED HIM TO ENJOY IT.

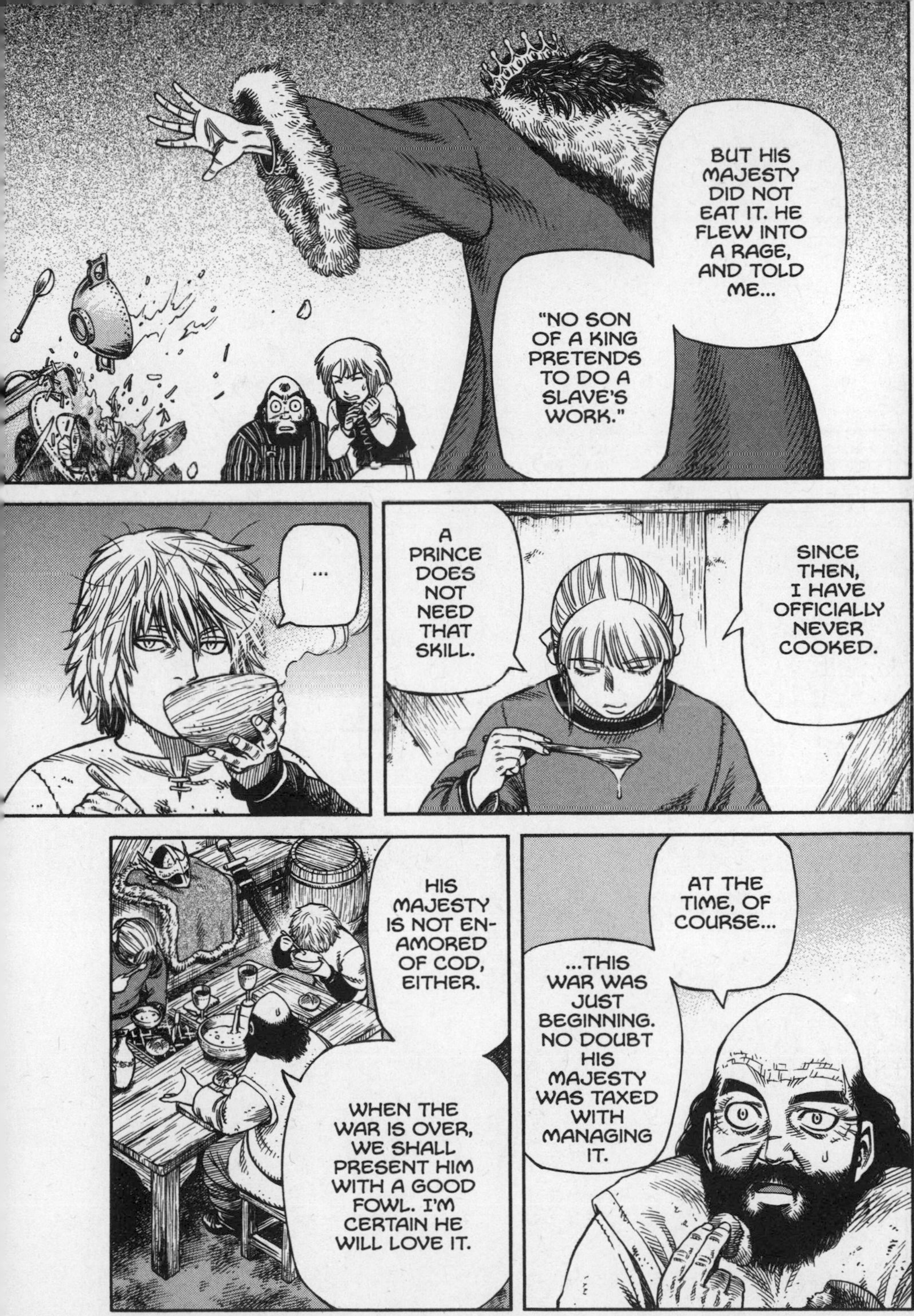
BUT HIS MAJESTY DID NOT EAT IT. HE FLEW INTO A RAGE, AND TOLD ME...
"NO SON OF A KING PRETENDS TO DO A SLAVE'S WORK."
SINCE THEN, I HAVE OFFICIALLY NEVER COOKED.
A PRINCE DOES NOT NEED THAT SKILL.
...
AT THE TIME, OF COURSE...
...THIS WAR WAS JUST BEGINNING. NO DOUBT HIS MAJESTY WAS TAXED WITH MANAGING IT.
HIS MAJESTY IS NOT EN-AMORED OF COD, EITHER.
WHEN THE WAR IS OVER, WE SHALL PRESENT HIM WITH A GOOD FOWL. I'M CERTAIN HE WILL LOVE IT.

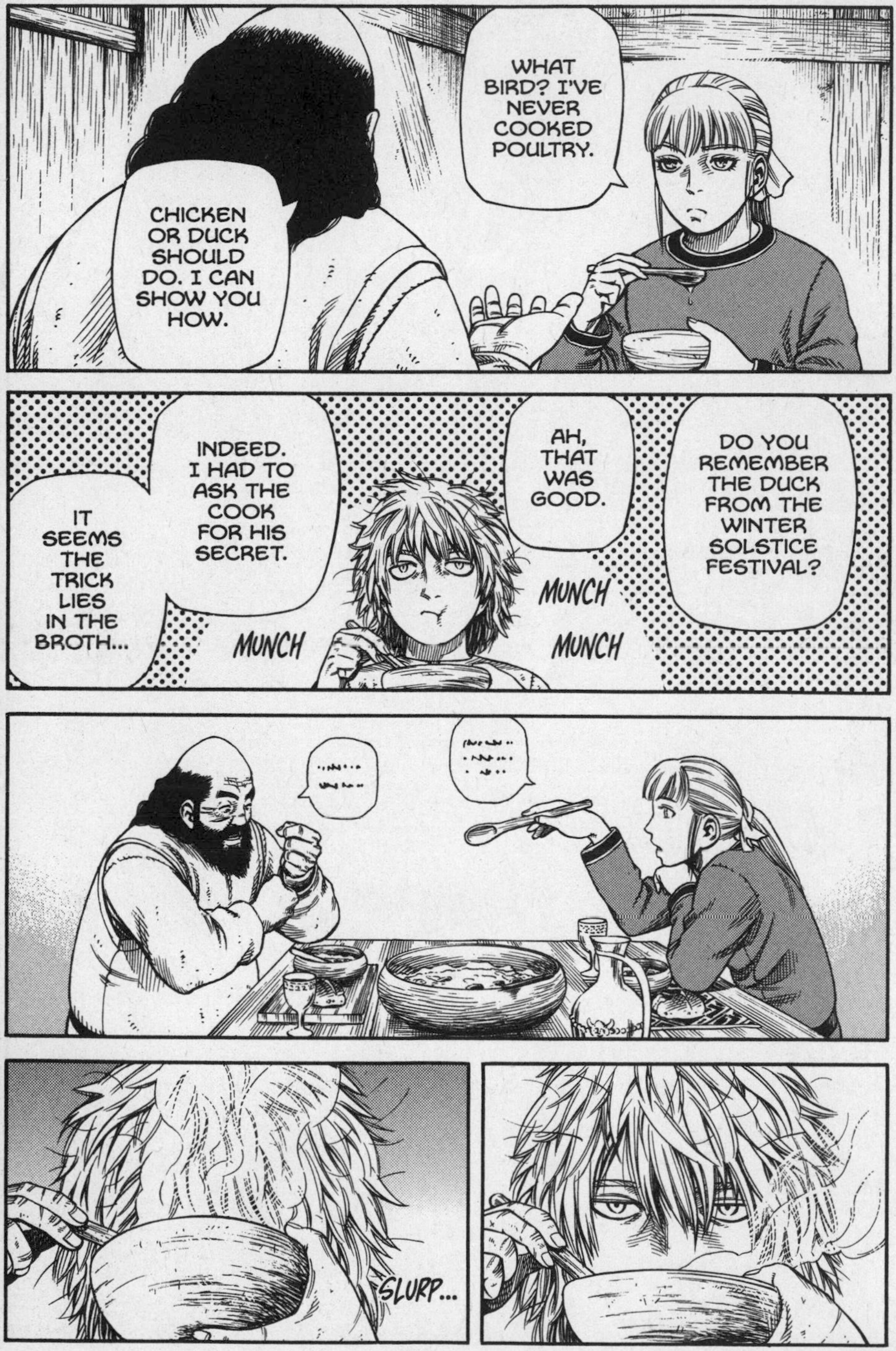
WHAT BIRD? I'VE NEVER COOKED POULTRY.
CHICKEN OR DUCK SHOULD DO. I CAN SHOW YOU HOW.
DO YOU REMEMBER THE DUCK FROM THE WINTER SOLSTICE FESTIVAL?
AH, THAT WAS GOOD.
MUNCH
MUNCH
INDEED. I HAD TO ASK THE COOK FOR HIS SECRET.
IT SEEMS THE TRICK LIES IN THE BROTH...
MUNCH
SLURP...

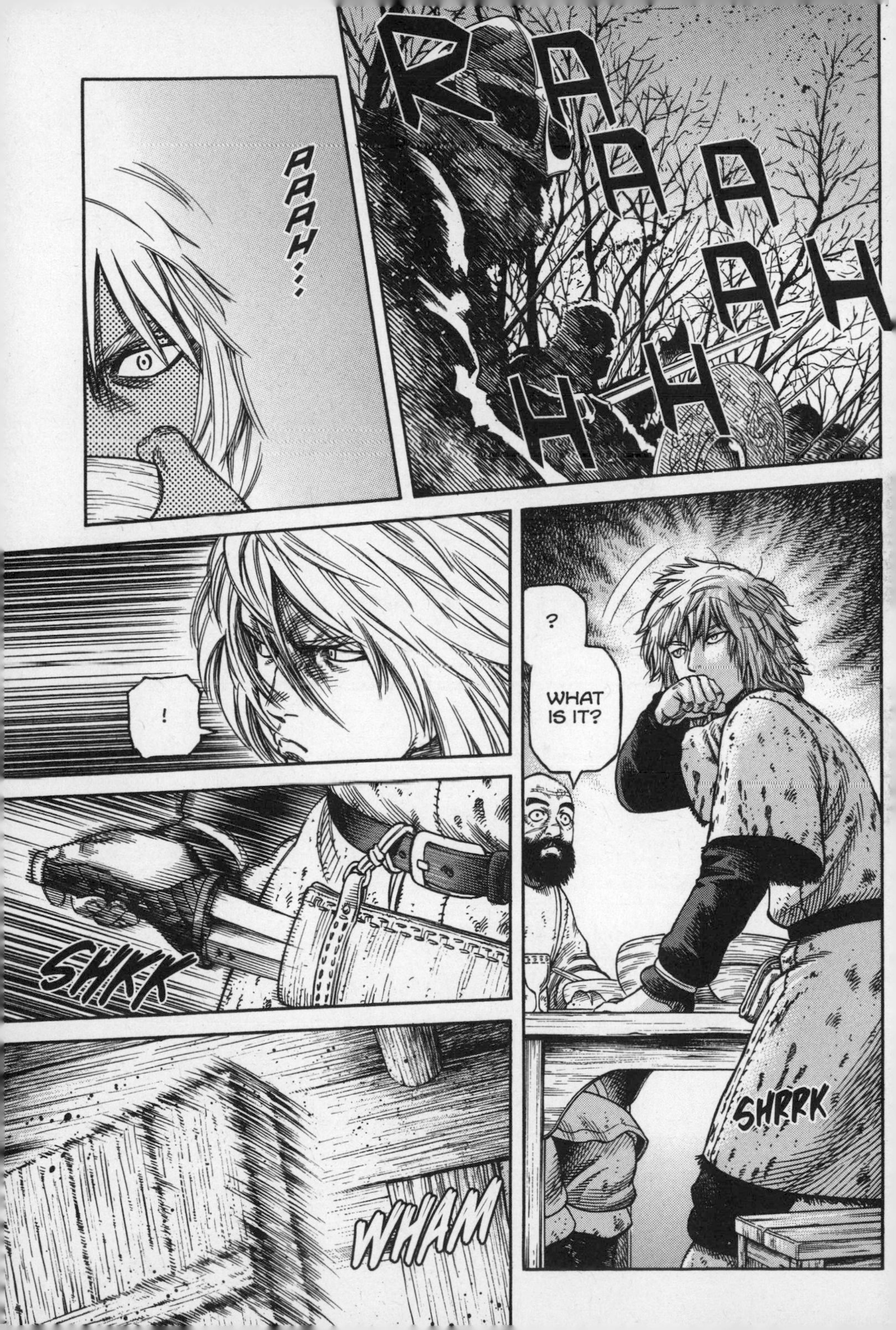
RAAAAHHH
AAAAH...
?
WHAT IS IT?
SHRRK
!
SHKK
WHAM

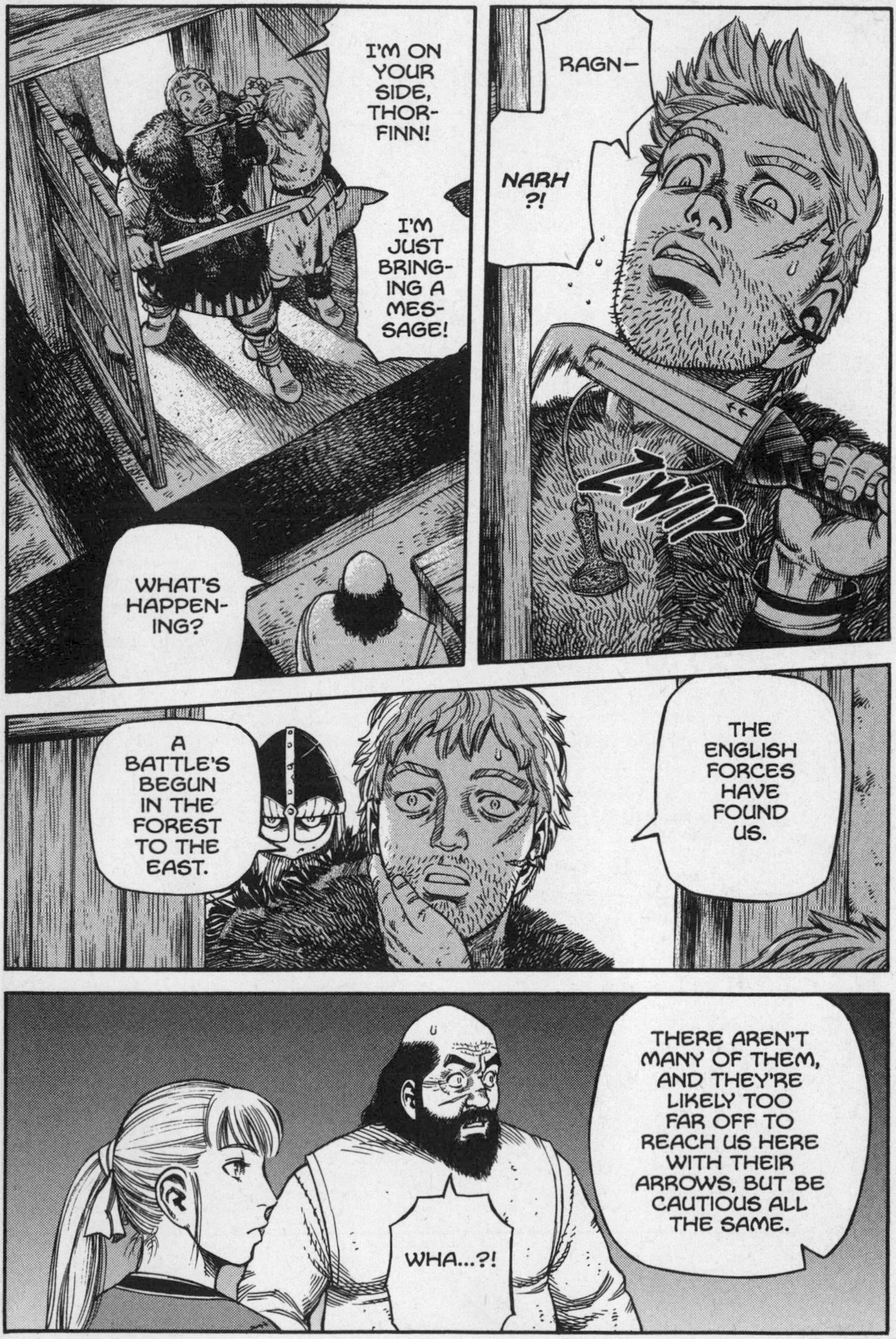

RAGN—
NARH?!
ZWIP
I'M ON YOUR SIDE, THORFINN!
I'M JUST BRINGING A MESSAGE!
WHAT'S HAPPENING?
THE ENGLISH FORCES HAVE FOUND US.
A BATTLE'S BEGUN IN THE FOREST TO THE EAST.
THERE AREN'T MANY OF THEM, AND THEY'RE LIKELY TOO FAR OFF TO REACH US HERE WITH THEIR ARROWS, BUT BE CAUTIOUS ALL THE SAME.
WHA...?!

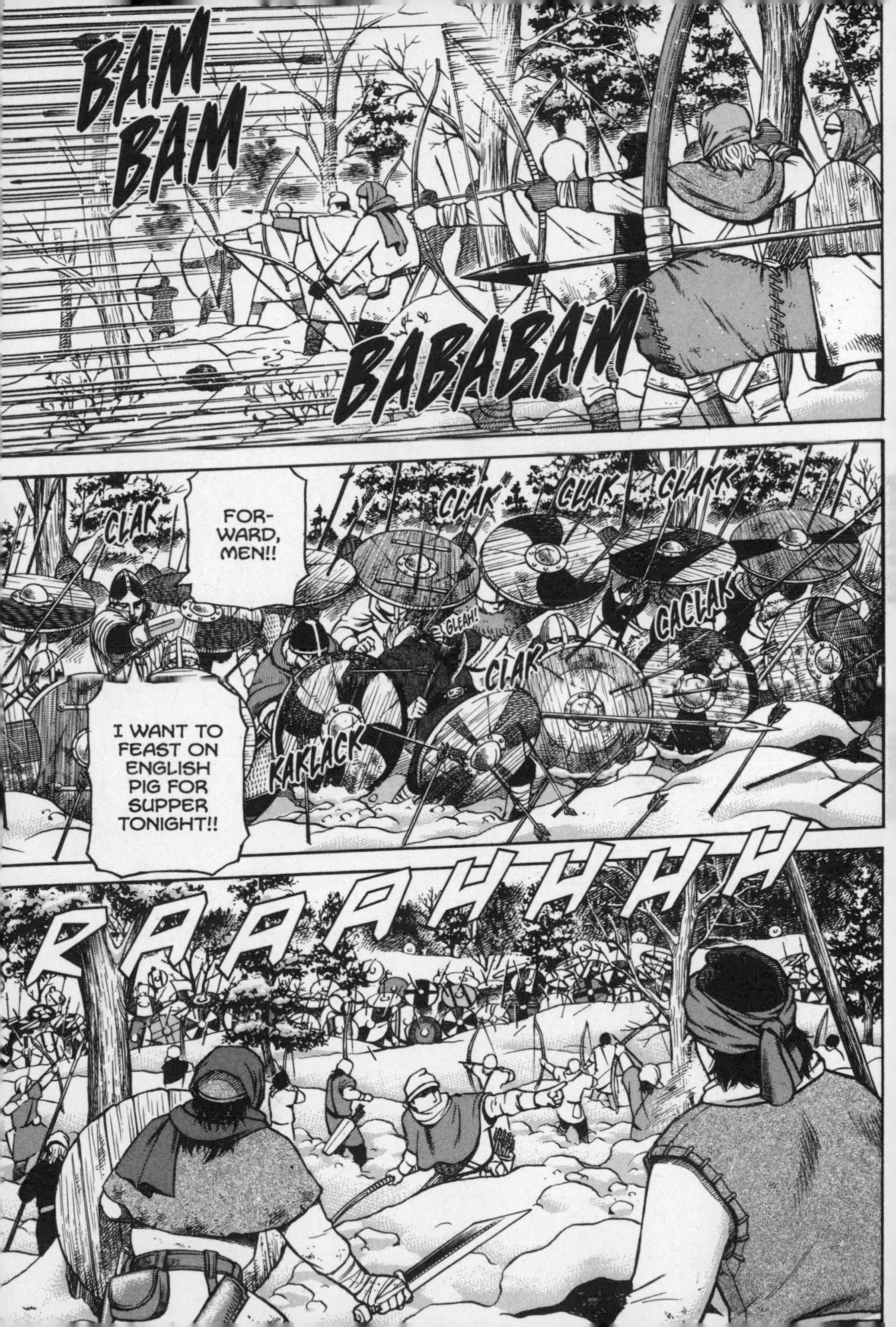
BAM
BAM
BABABAM
CLAKK
CLAK
CLAK
CACLAK
FOR-WARD, MEN!!
CLAK
GLEAH!
CLAK
I WANT TO FEAST ON ENGLISH PIG FOR SUPPER TONIGHT!!
KAKLACK
RAAAHHHHH

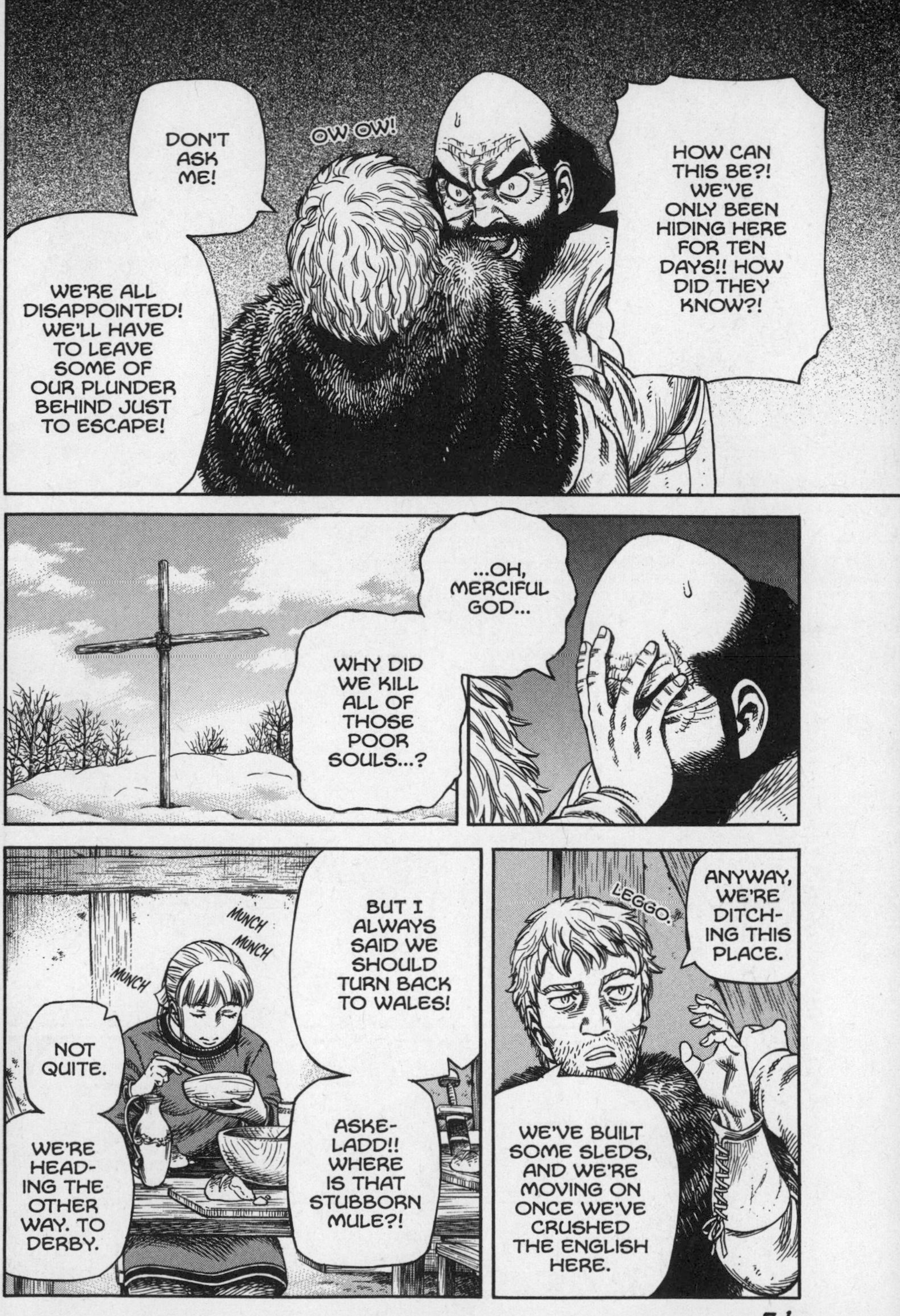
HOW CAN THIS BE?! WE'VE ONLY BEEN HIDING HERE FOR TEN DAYS!! HOW DID THEY KNOW?!
OW OW!
DON'T ASK ME!
WE'RE ALL DISAPPOINTED! WE'LL HAVE TO LEAVE SOME OF OUR PLUNDER BEHIND JUST TO ESCAPE!
...OH, MERCIFUL GOD...
WHY DID WE KILL ALL OF THOSE POOR SOULS...?
LEGGO.
ANYWAY, WE'RE DITCHING THIS PLACE.
WE'VE BUILT SOME SLEDS, AND WE'RE MOVING ON ONCE WE'VE CRUSHED THE ENGLISH HERE.
BUT I ALWAYS SAID WE SHOULD TURN BACK TO WALES!
MUNCH MUNCH MUNCH
ASKE-LADD!! WHERE IS THAT STUBBORN MULE?!
NOT QUITE.
WE'RE HEAD-ING THE OTHER WAY. TO DERBY.

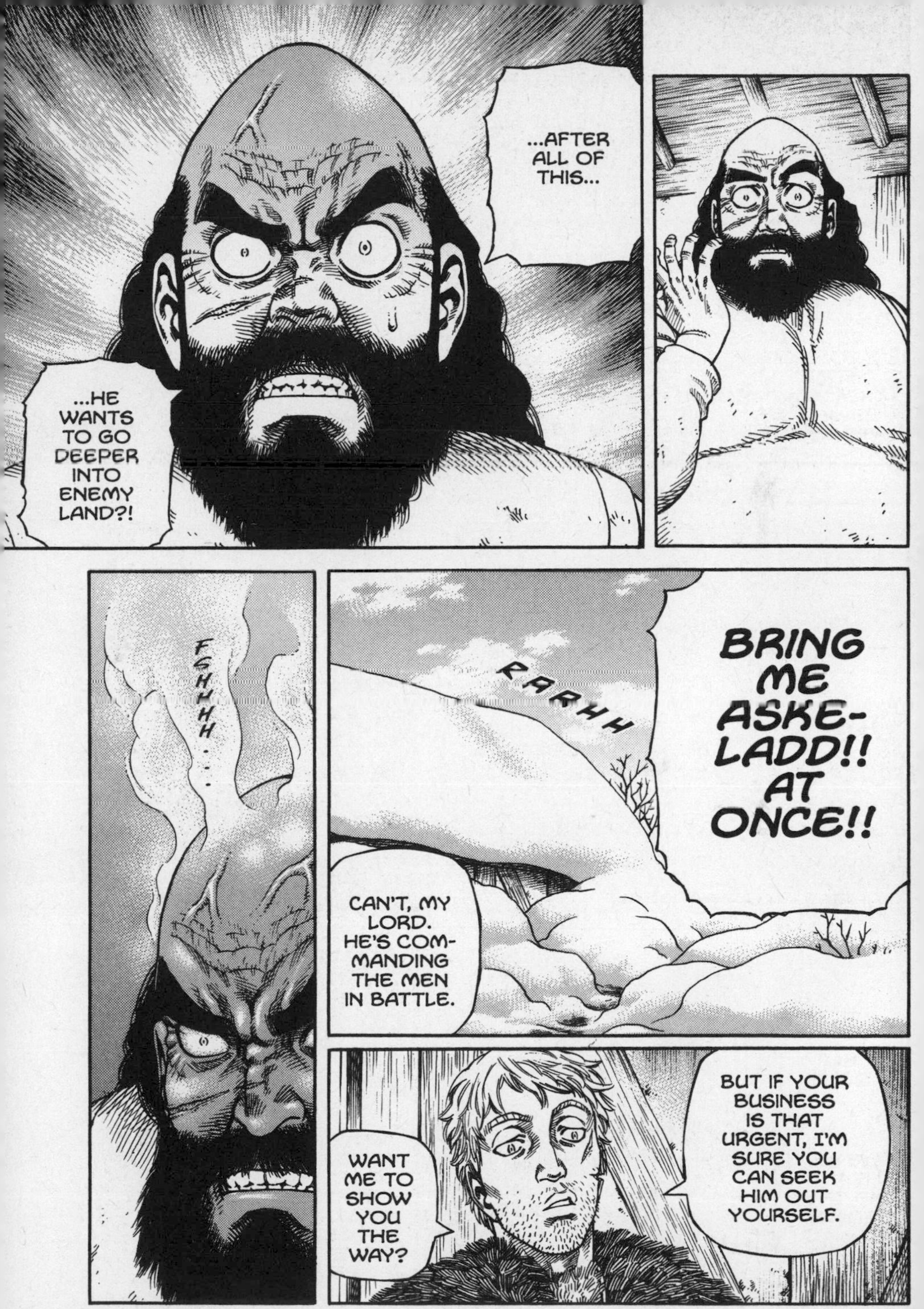
...AFTER ALL OF THIS...
...HE WANTS TO GO DEEPER INTO ENEMY LAND?!
BRING ME ASKE-LADD!! AT ONCE!!
RAAHH
CAN'T, MY LORD. HE'S COM-MANDING THE MEN IN BATTLE.
BUT IF YOUR BUSINESS IS THAT URGENT, I'M SURE YOU CAN SEEK HIM OUT YOURSELF.
WANT ME TO SHOW YOU THE WAY?
FSHHHH...

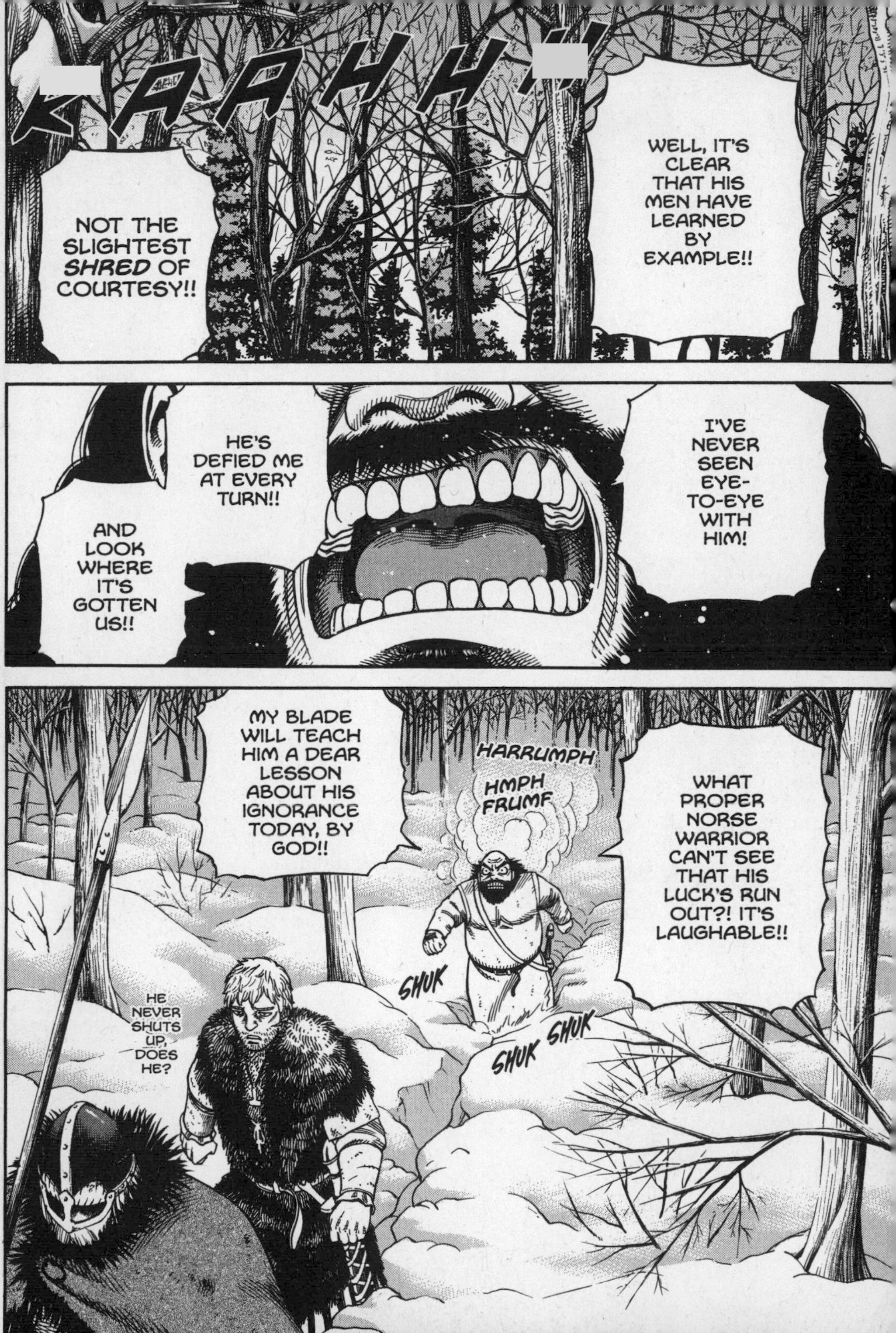
KRAAHH!!
WELL, IT'S CLEAR THAT HIS MEN HAVE LEARNED BY EXAMPLE!!
NOT THE SLIGHTEST SHRED OF COURTESY!!
I'VE NEVER SEEN EYE-TO-EYE WITH HIM!
HE'S DEFIED ME AT EVERY TURN!!
AND LOOK WHERE IT'S GOTTEN US!!
WHAT PROPER NORSE WARRIOR CAN'T SEE THAT HIS LUCK'S RUN OUT?! IT'S LAUGHABLE!!
HARRUMPH
HMPH FRUMF
MY BLADE WILL TEACH HIM A DEAR LESSON ABOUT HIS IGNORANCE TODAY, BY GOD!!
SHUK
SHUK SHUK
SHUK
HE NEVER SHUTS UP, DOES HE?

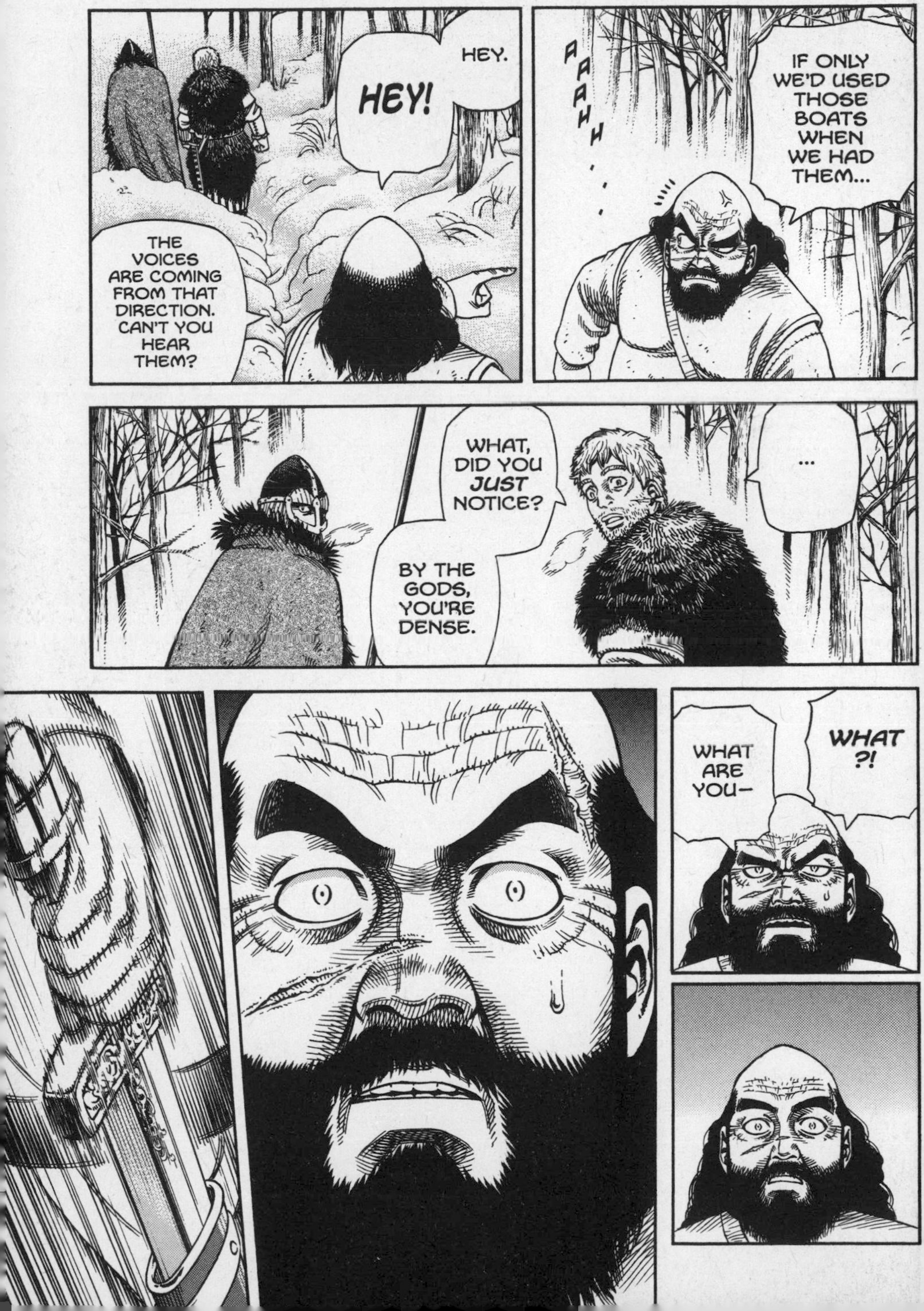
AAAHH...
IF ONLY WE'D USED THOSE BOATS WHEN WE HAD THEM...
HEY.
HEY!
THE VOICES ARE COMING FROM THAT DIRECTION. CAN'T YOU HEAR THEM?
...
WHAT, DID YOU JUST NOTICE?
BY THE GODS, YOU'RE DENSE.
WHAT ?!
WHAT ARE YOU—

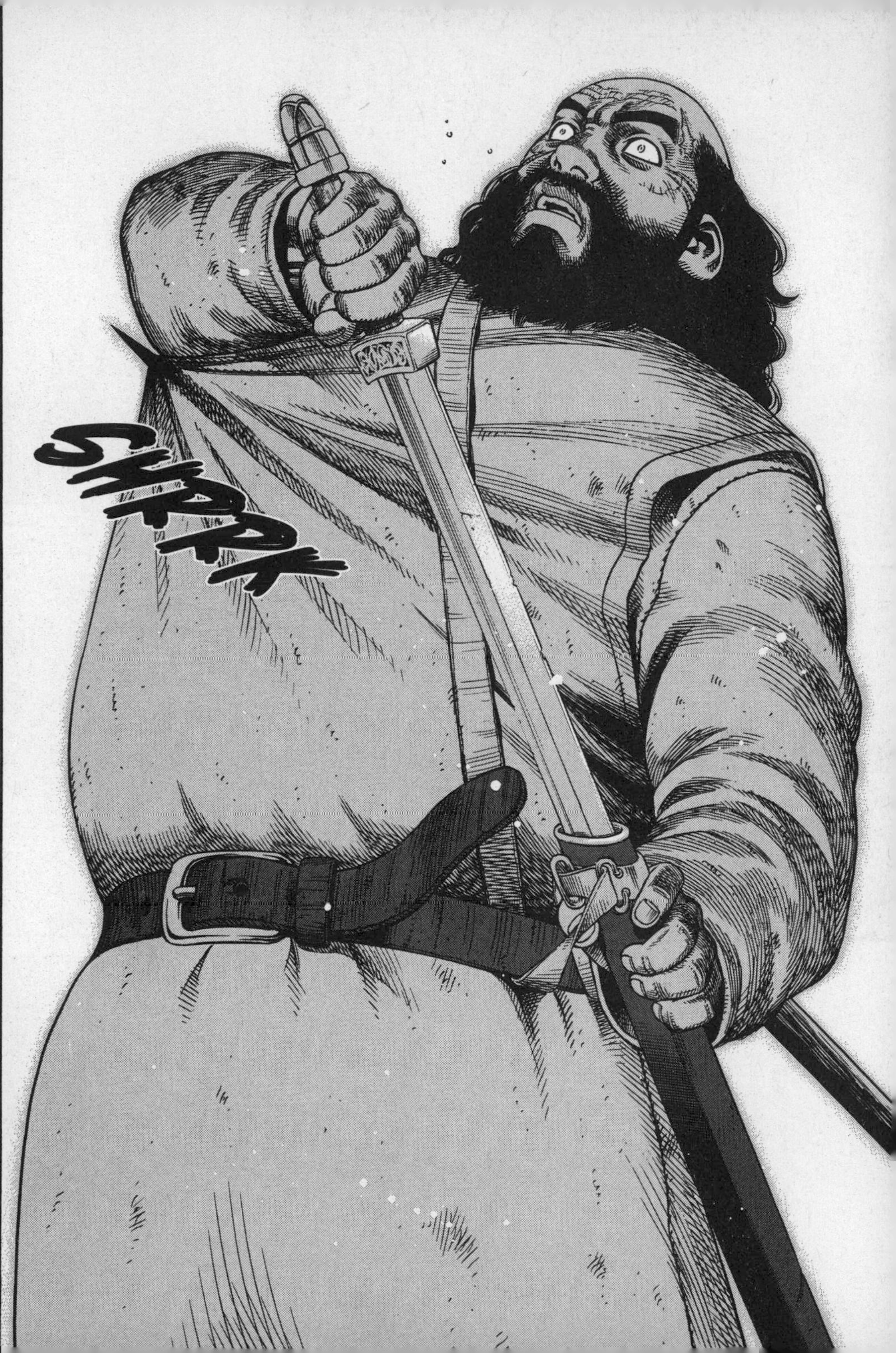
SHRRK

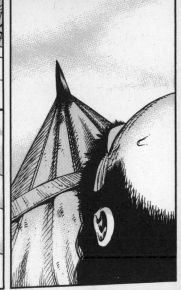

...YOU...
TRAITORS...

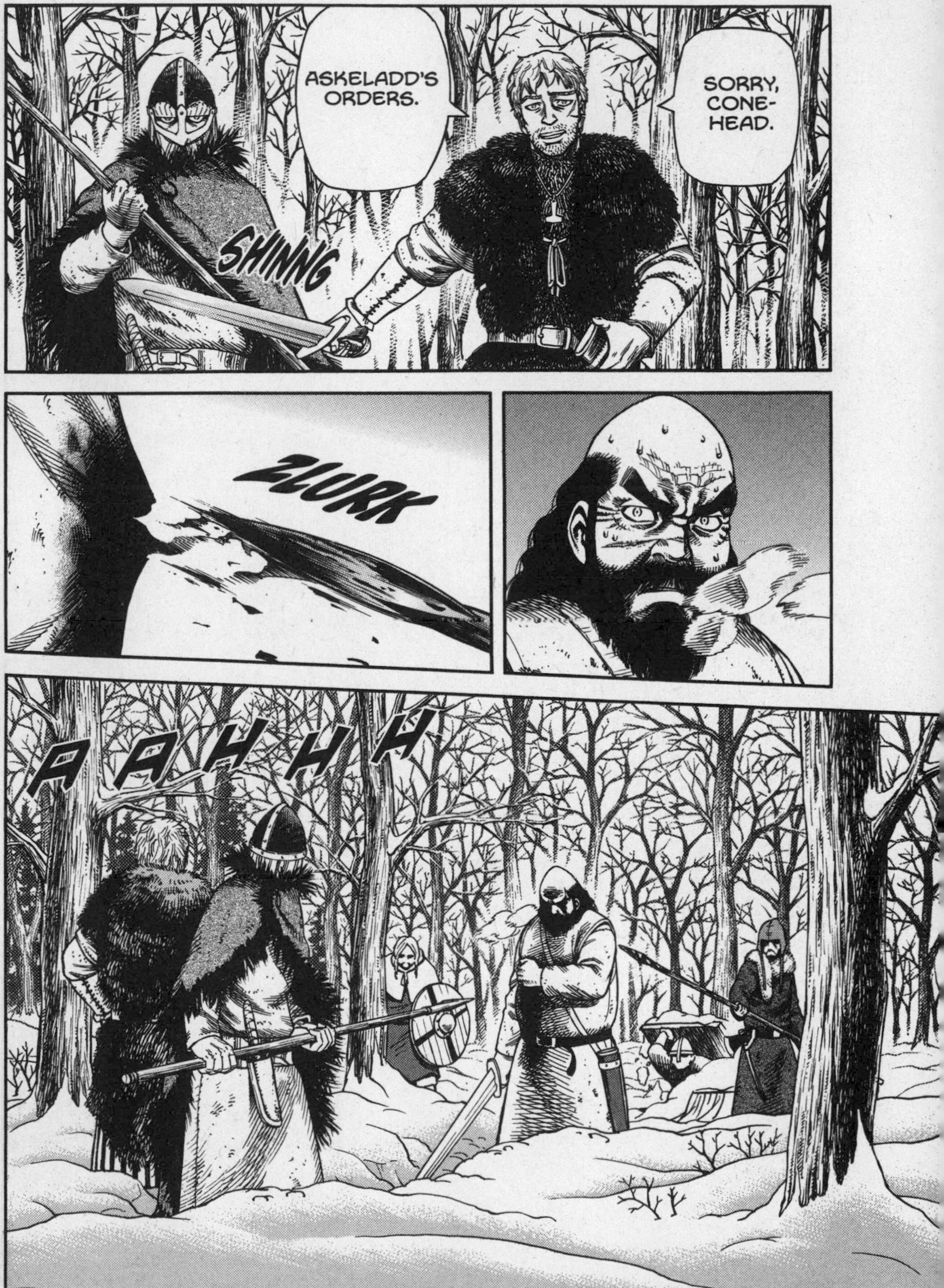
SORRY, CONE-HEAD.
ASKELADD'S ORDERS.
SHINNG
ZLURK
AAHHH

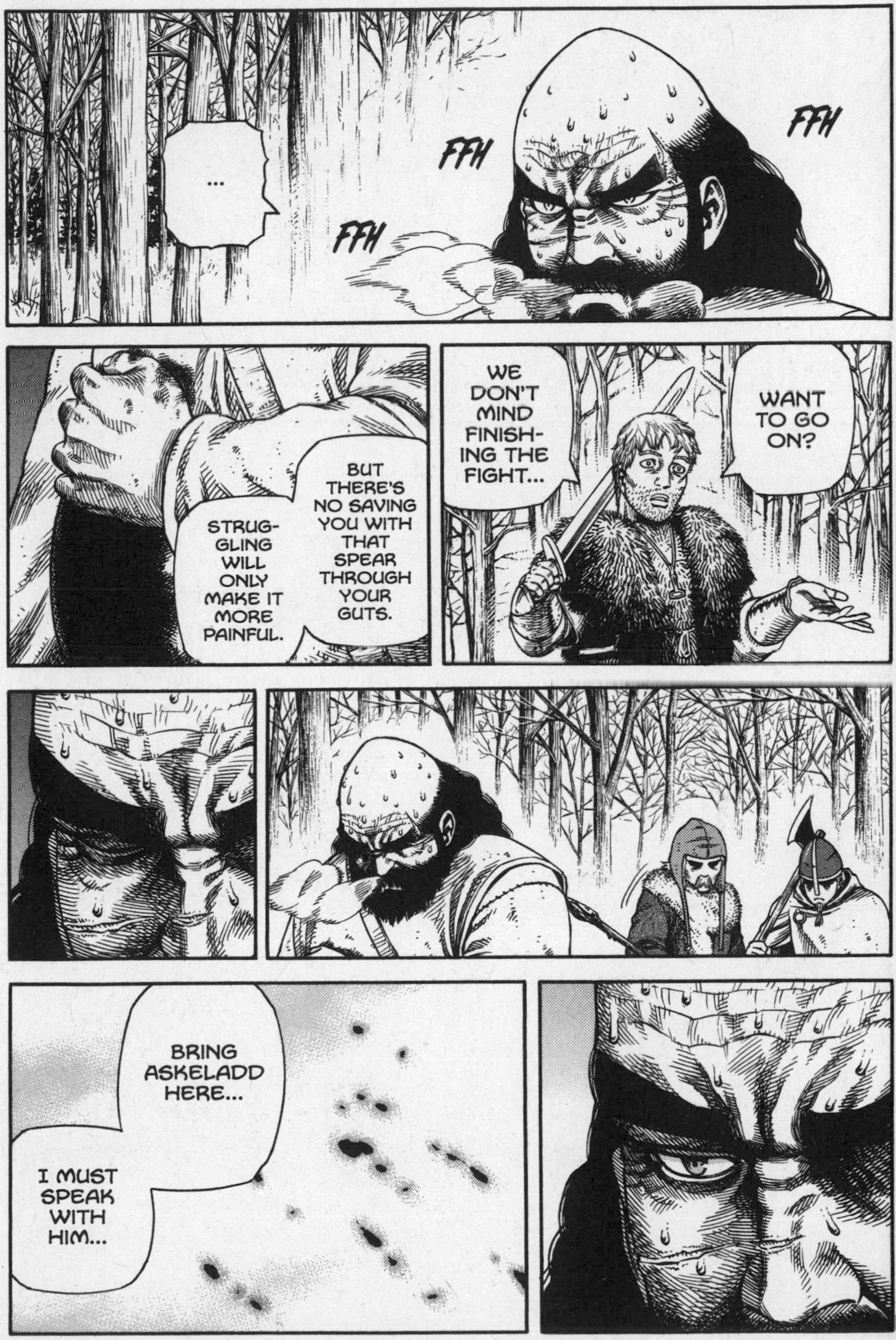
FFH
FFH
...
FFH
WANT TO GO ON?
WE DON'T MIND FINISHING THE FIGHT...
BUT THERE'S NO SAVING YOU WITH THAT SPEAR THROUGH YOUR GUTS.
STRUGGLING WILL ONLY MAKE IT MORE PAINFUL.
BRING ASKELADD HERE...
I MUST SPEAK WITH HIM...

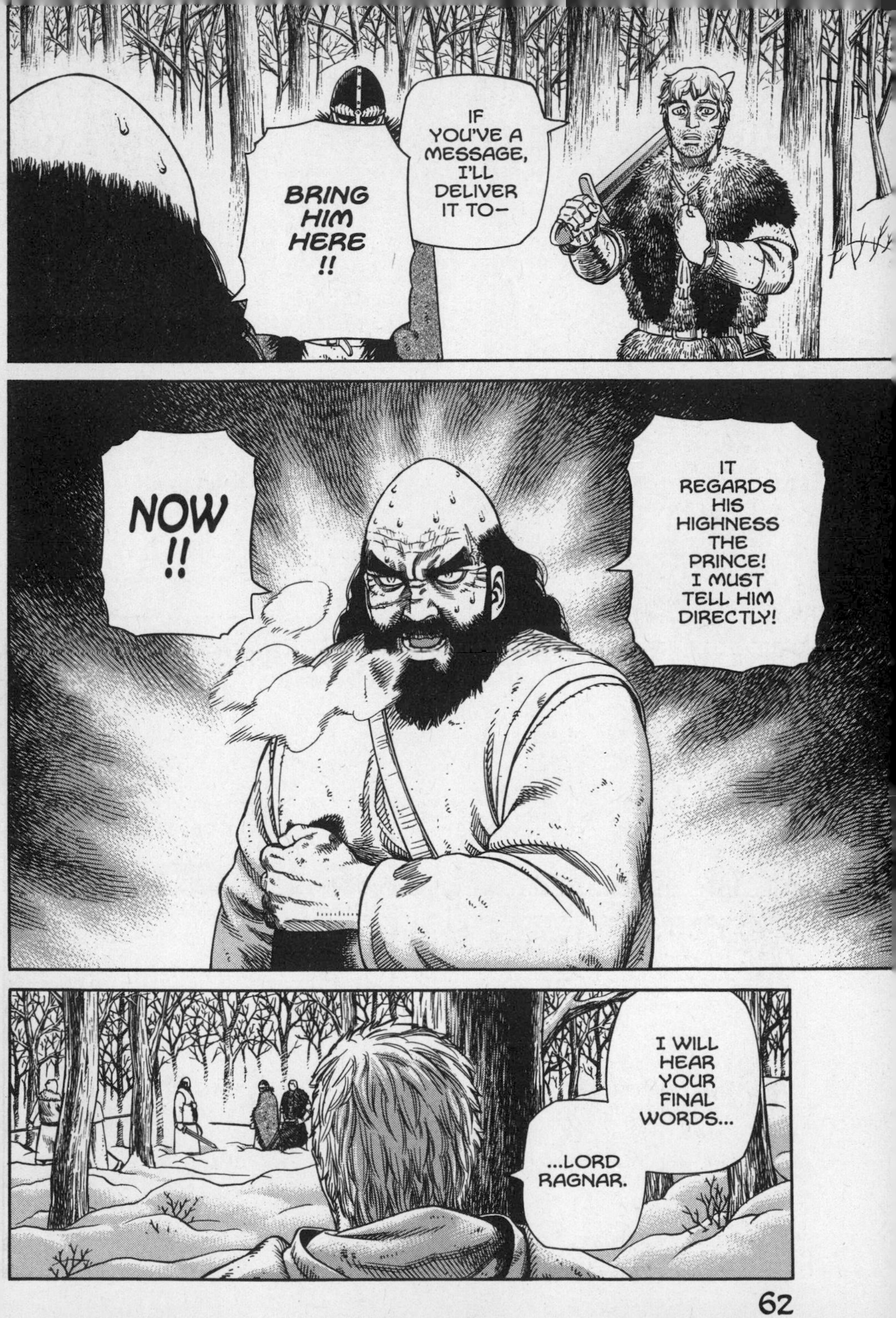
IF YOU'VE A MESSAGE, I'LL DELIVER IT TO–
BRING HIM HERE !!
IT REGARDS HIS HIGHNESS THE PRINCE! I MUST TELL HIM DIRECTLY!
NOW !!
I WILL HEAR YOUR FINAL WORDS...
...LORD RAGNAR.

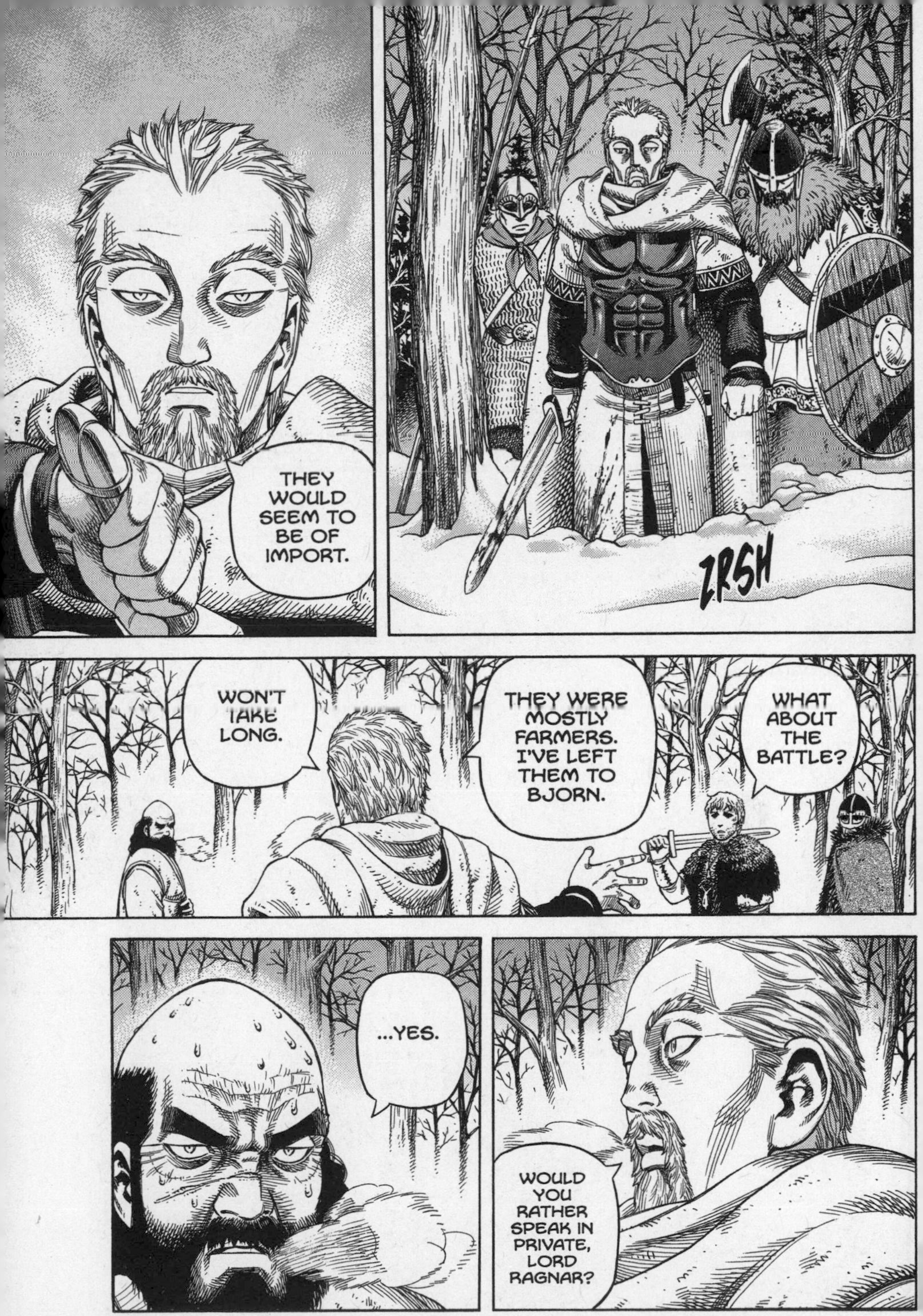
ZRSH
THEY WOULD SEEM TO BE OF IMPORT.
WHAT ABOUT THE BATTLE?
THEY WERE MOSTLY FARMERS. I'VE LEFT THEM TO BJORN.
WON'T TAKE LONG.
WOULD YOU RATHER SPEAK IN PRIVATE, LORD RAGNAR?
...YES.

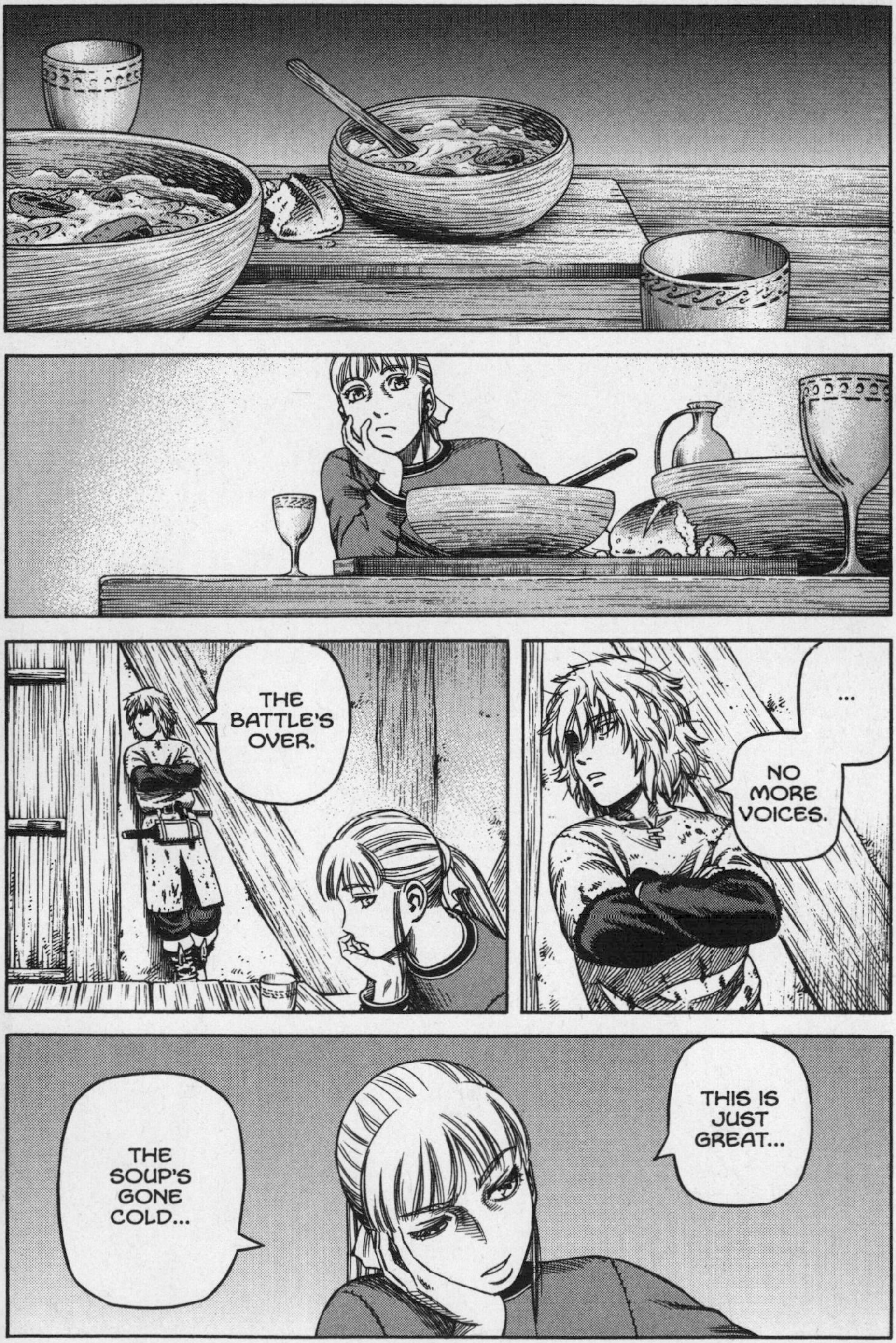
...
NO MORE VOICES.
THE BATTLE'S OVER.
THIS IS JUST GREAT...
THE SOUP'S GONE COLD...

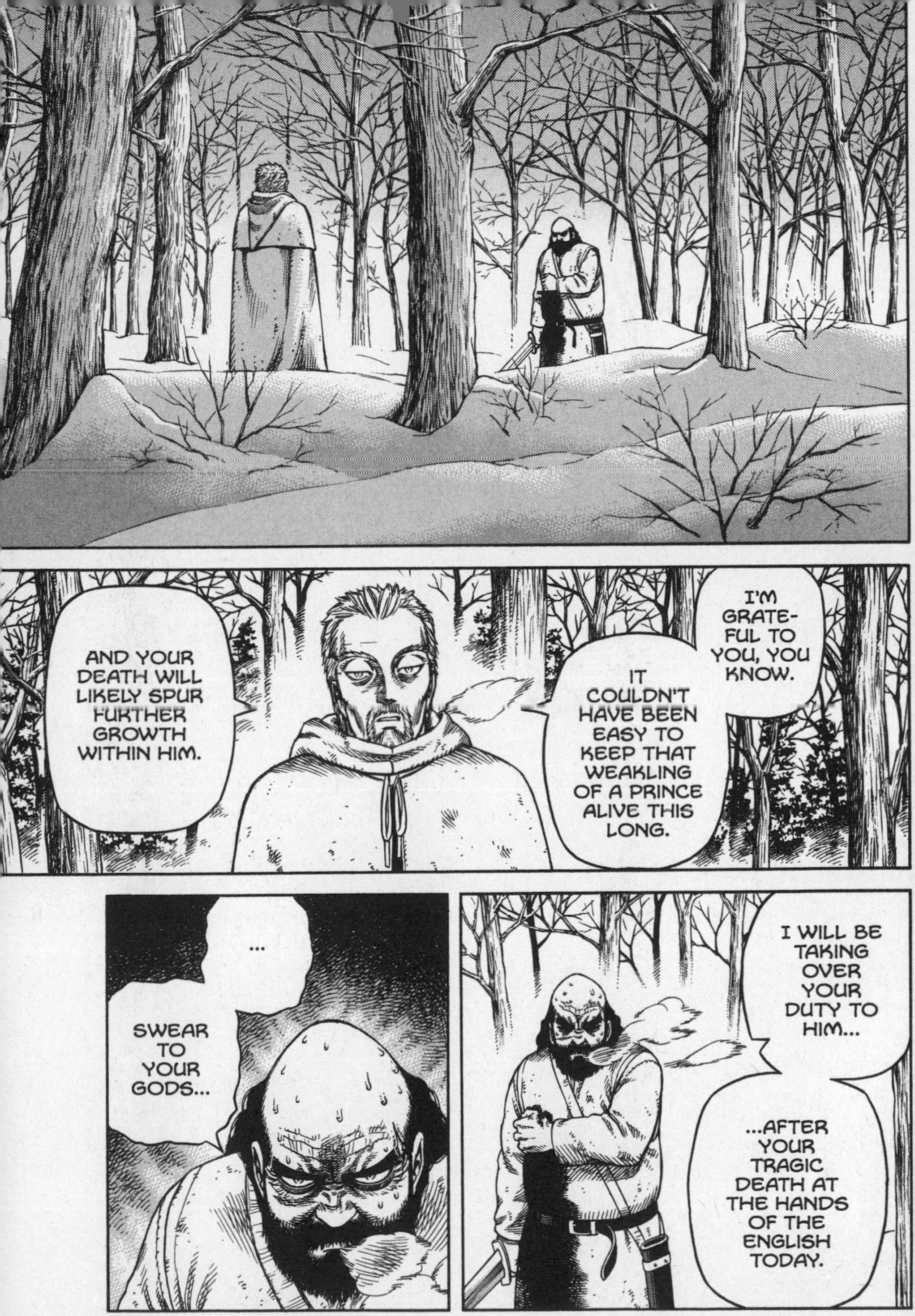
I'M GRATE-FUL TO YOU, YOU KNOW.
IT COULDN'T HAVE BEEN EASY TO KEEP THAT WEAKLING OF A PRINCE ALIVE THIS LONG.
AND YOUR DEATH WILL LIKELY SPUR FURTHER GROWTH WITHIN HIM.
I WILL BE TAKING OVER YOUR DUTY TO HIM...
...AFTER YOUR TRAGIC DEATH AT THE HANDS OF THE ENGLISH TODAY.
...
SWEAR TO YOUR GODS...

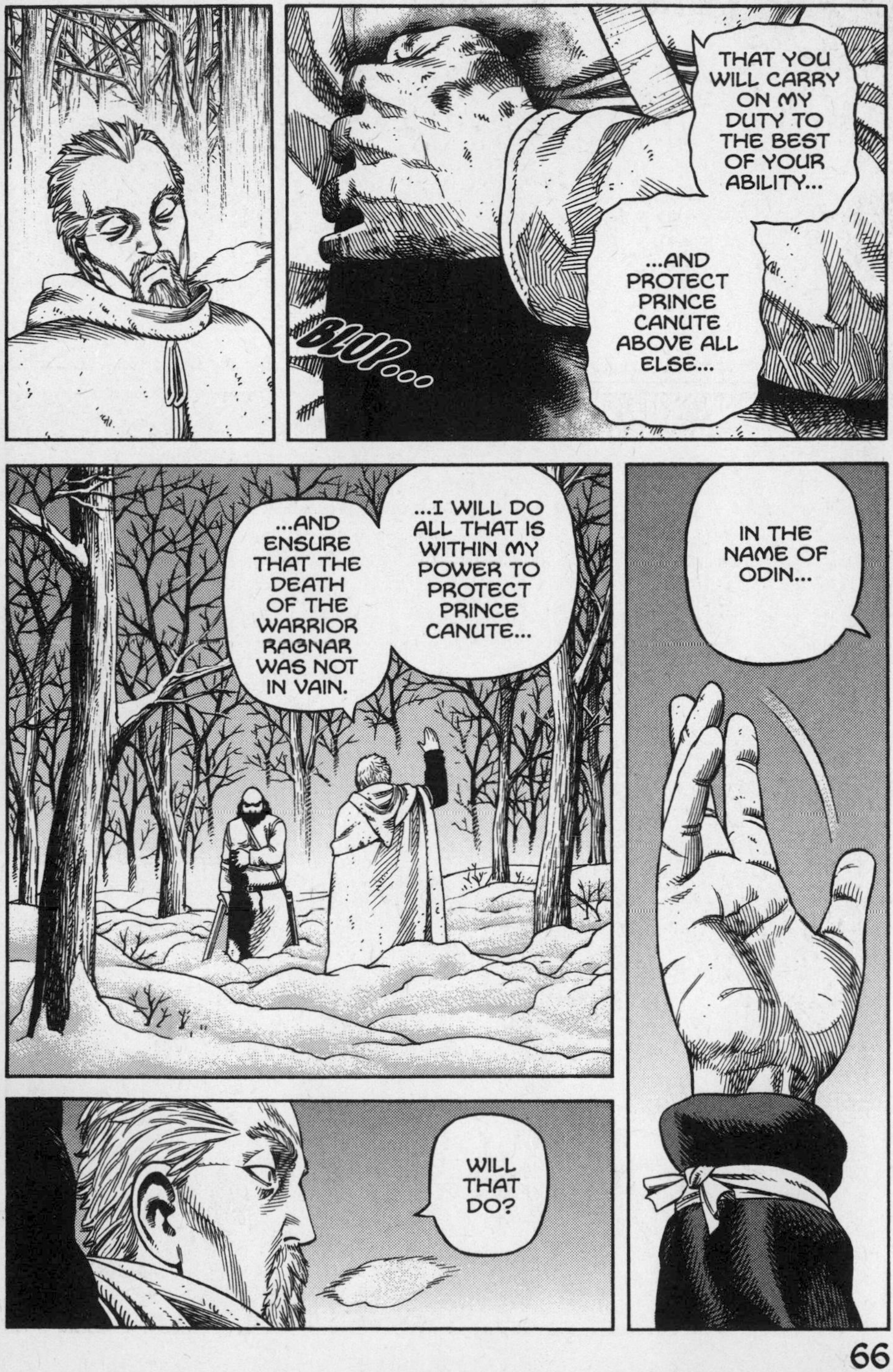
THAT YOU WILL CARRY ON MY DUTY TO THE BEST OF YOUR ABILITY...
...AND PROTECT PRINCE CANUTE ABOVE ALL ELSE...
BLUP...
IN THE NAME OF ODIN...
...I WILL DO ALL THAT IS WITHIN MY POWER TO PROTECT PRINCE CANUTE...
...AND ENSURE THAT THE DEATH OF THE WARRIOR RAGNAR WAS NOT IN VAIN.
WILL THAT DO?

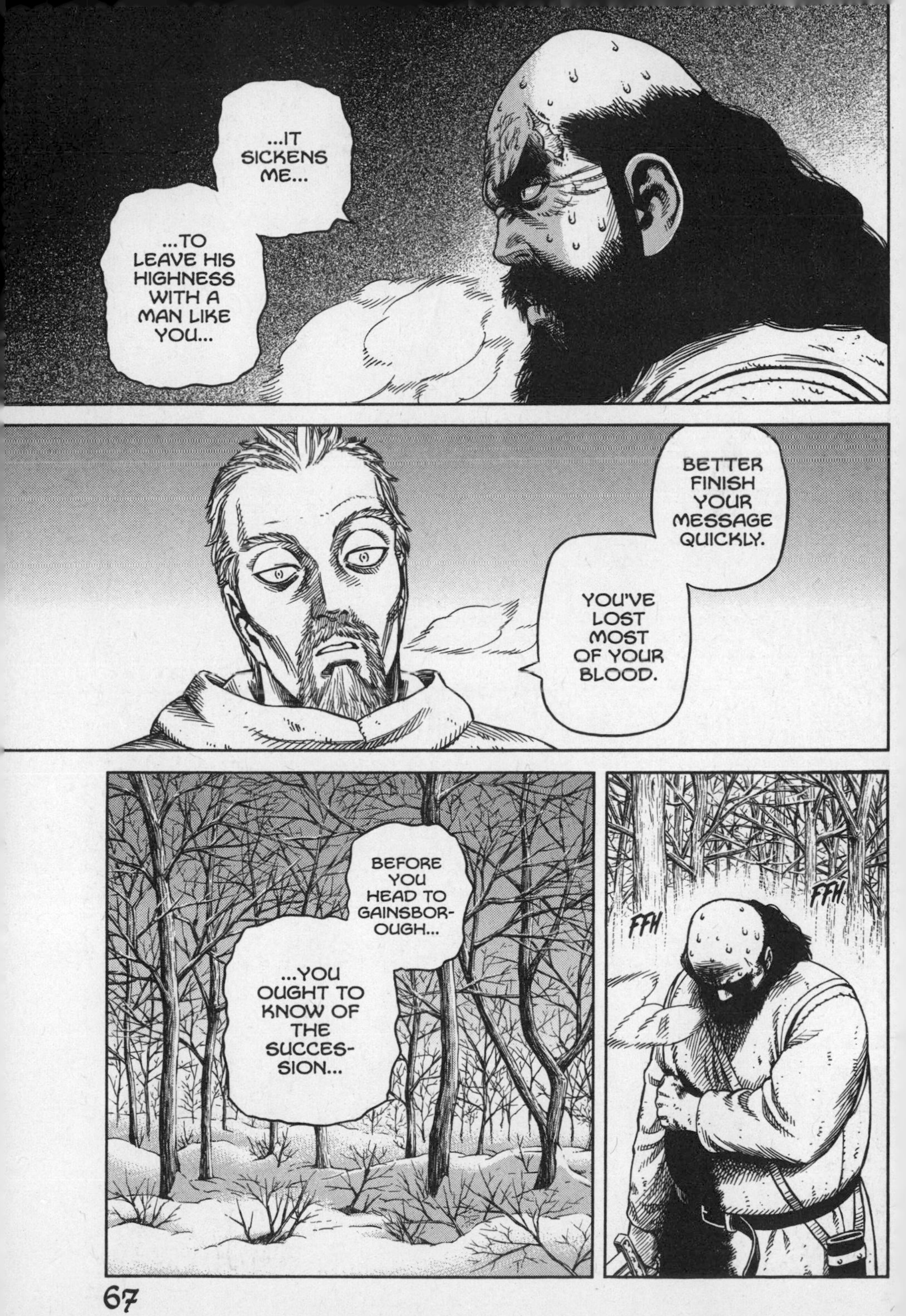
...IT SICKENS ME...
...TO LEAVE HIS HIGHNESS WITH A MAN LIKE YOU...
BETTER FINISH YOUR MESSAGE QUICKLY.
YOU'VE LOST MOST OF YOUR BLOOD.
FFH
FFH
BEFORE YOU HEAD TO GAINSBOROUGH...
...YOU OUGHT TO KNOW OF THE SUCCESSION...

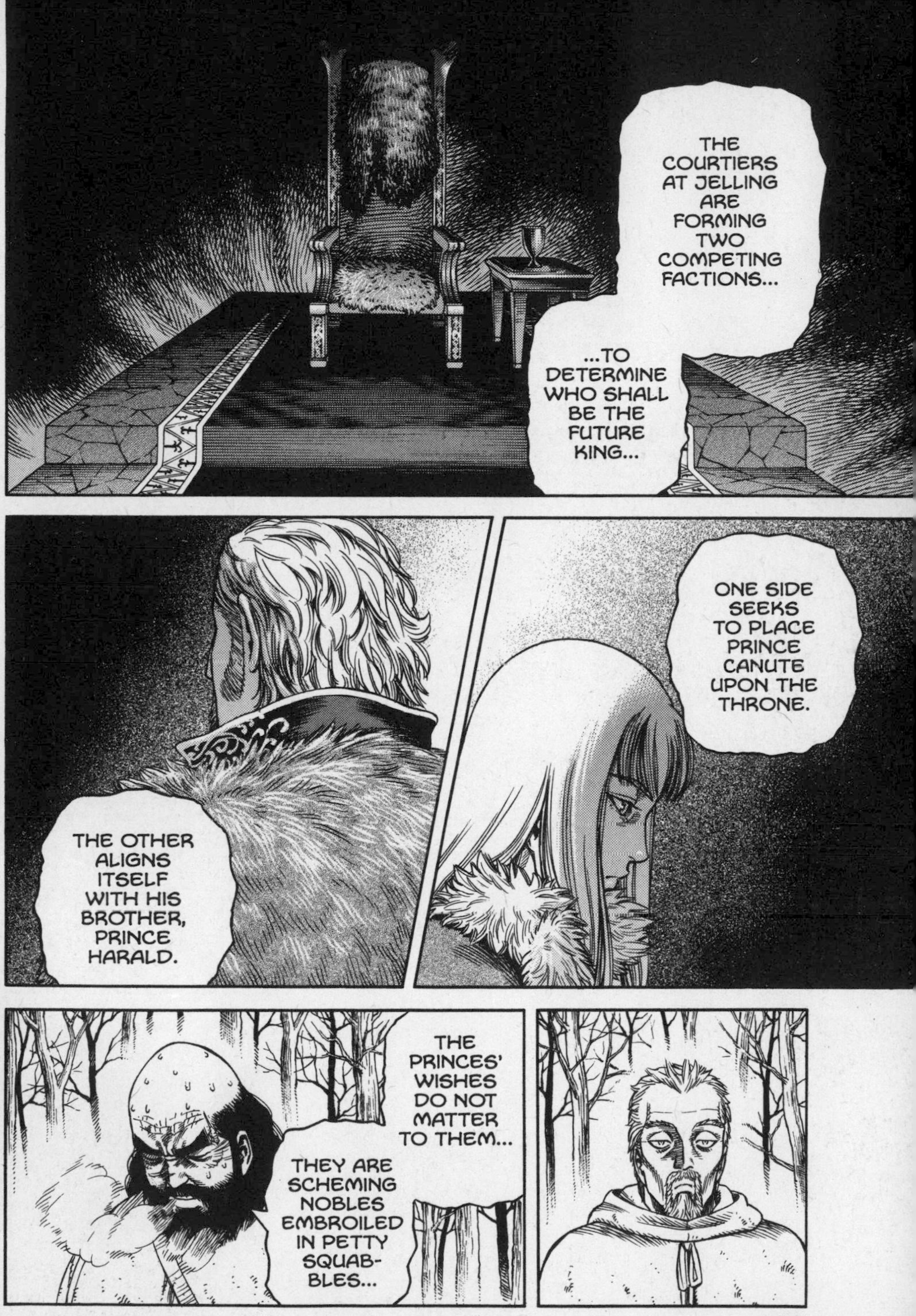
THE COURTIERS AT JELLING ARE FORMING TWO COMPETING FACTIONS...
...TO DETERMINE WHO SHALL BE THE FUTURE KING...
ONE SIDE SEEKS TO PLACE PRINCE CANUTE UPON THE THRONE.
THE OTHER ALIGNS ITSELF WITH HIS BROTHER, PRINCE HARALD.
THE PRINCES' WISHES DO NOT MATTER TO THEM...
THEY ARE SCHEMING NOBLES EMBROILED IN PETTY SQUAB-BLES...

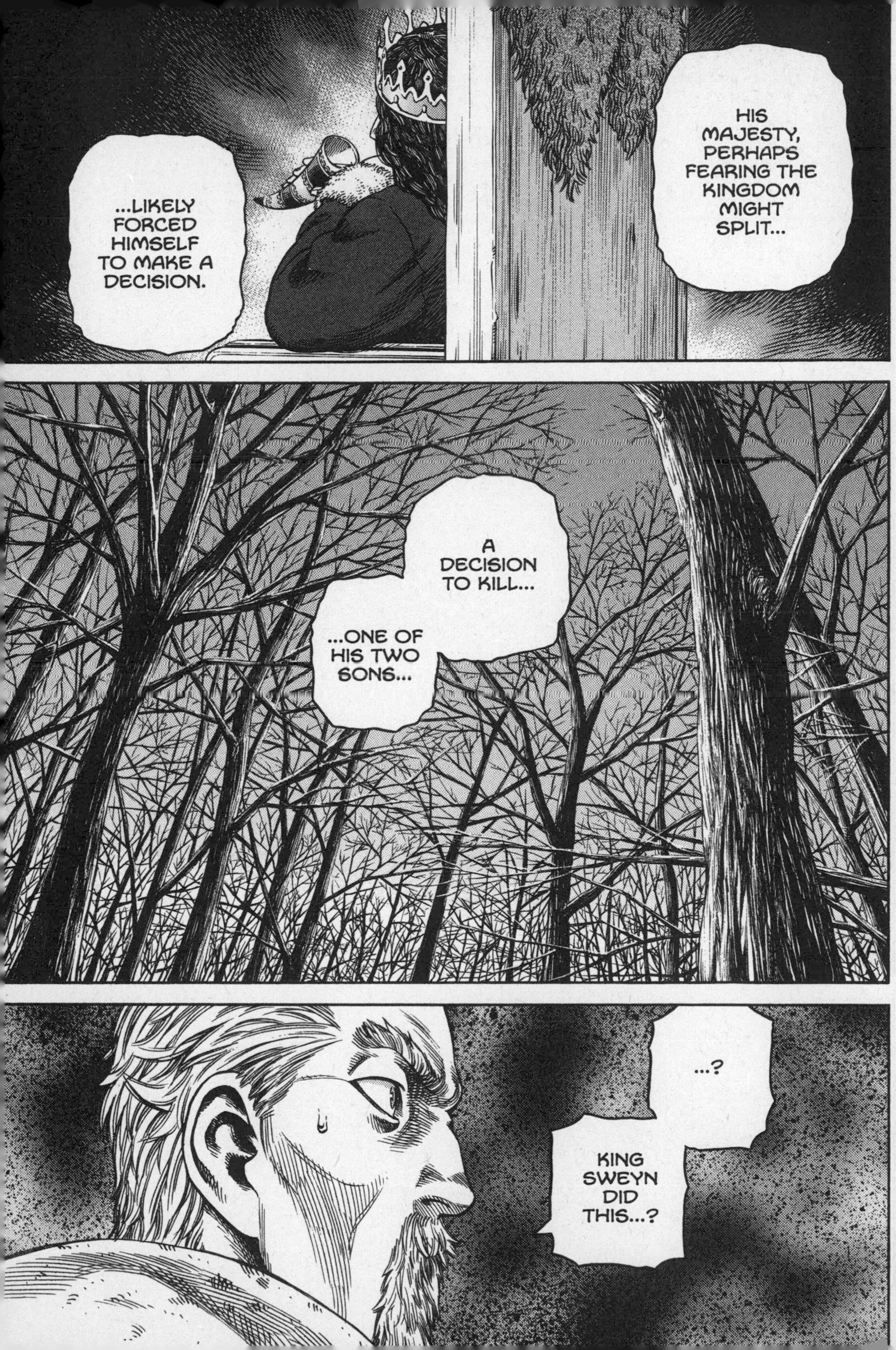
HIS MAJESTY, PERHAPS FEARING THE KINGDOM MIGHT SPLIT...
...LIKELY FORCED HIMSELF TO MAKE A DECISION.
A DECISION TO KILL...
...ONE OF HIS TWO SONS...
...?
KING SWEYN DID THIS...?

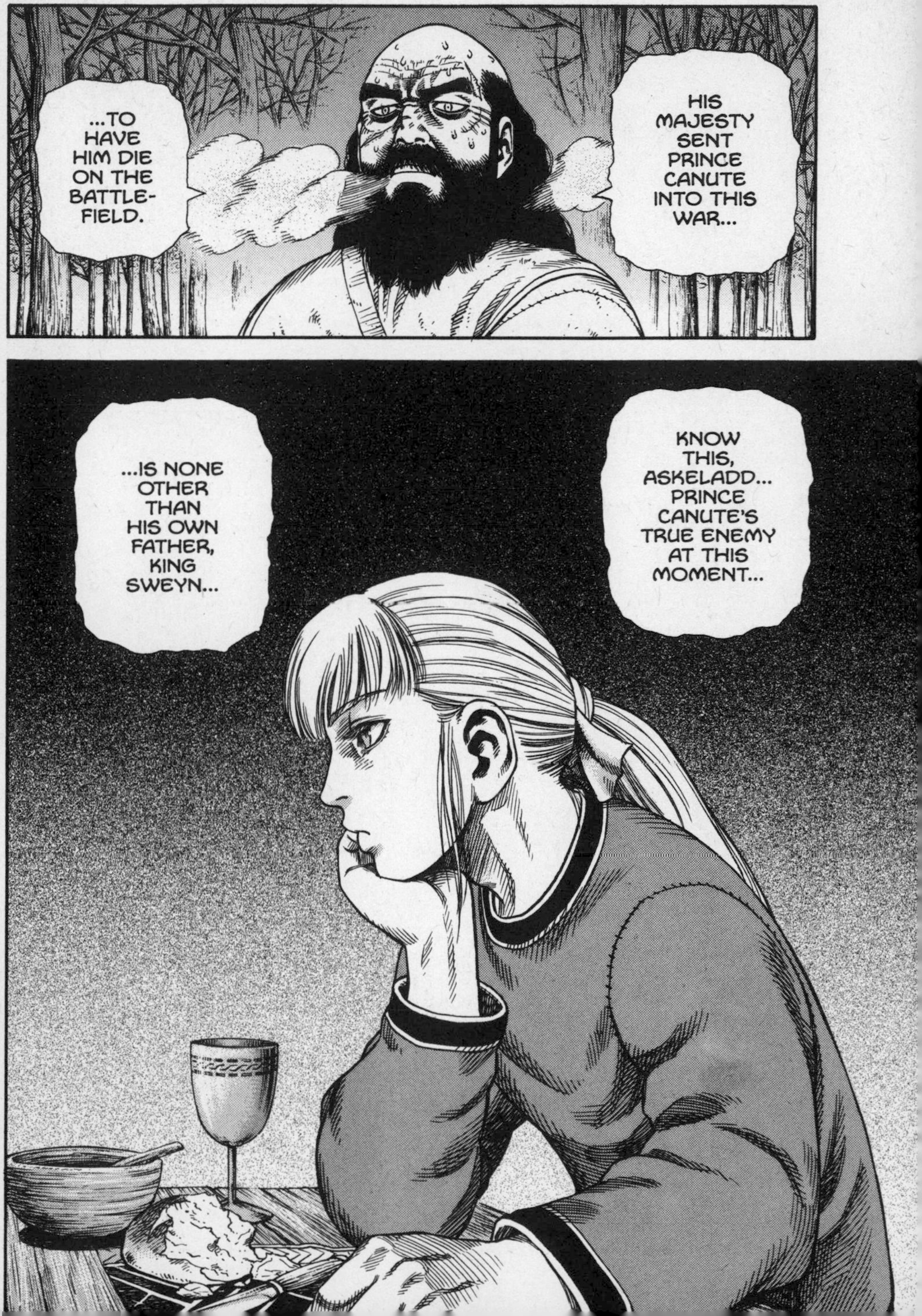
HIS MAJESTY SENT PRINCE CANUTE INTO THIS WAR...
...TO HAVE HIM DIE ON THE BATTLE-FIELD.
KNOW THIS, ASKELADD... PRINCE CANUTE'S TRUE ENEMY AT THIS MOMENT...
...IS NONE OTHER THAN HIS OWN FATHER, KING SWEYN...

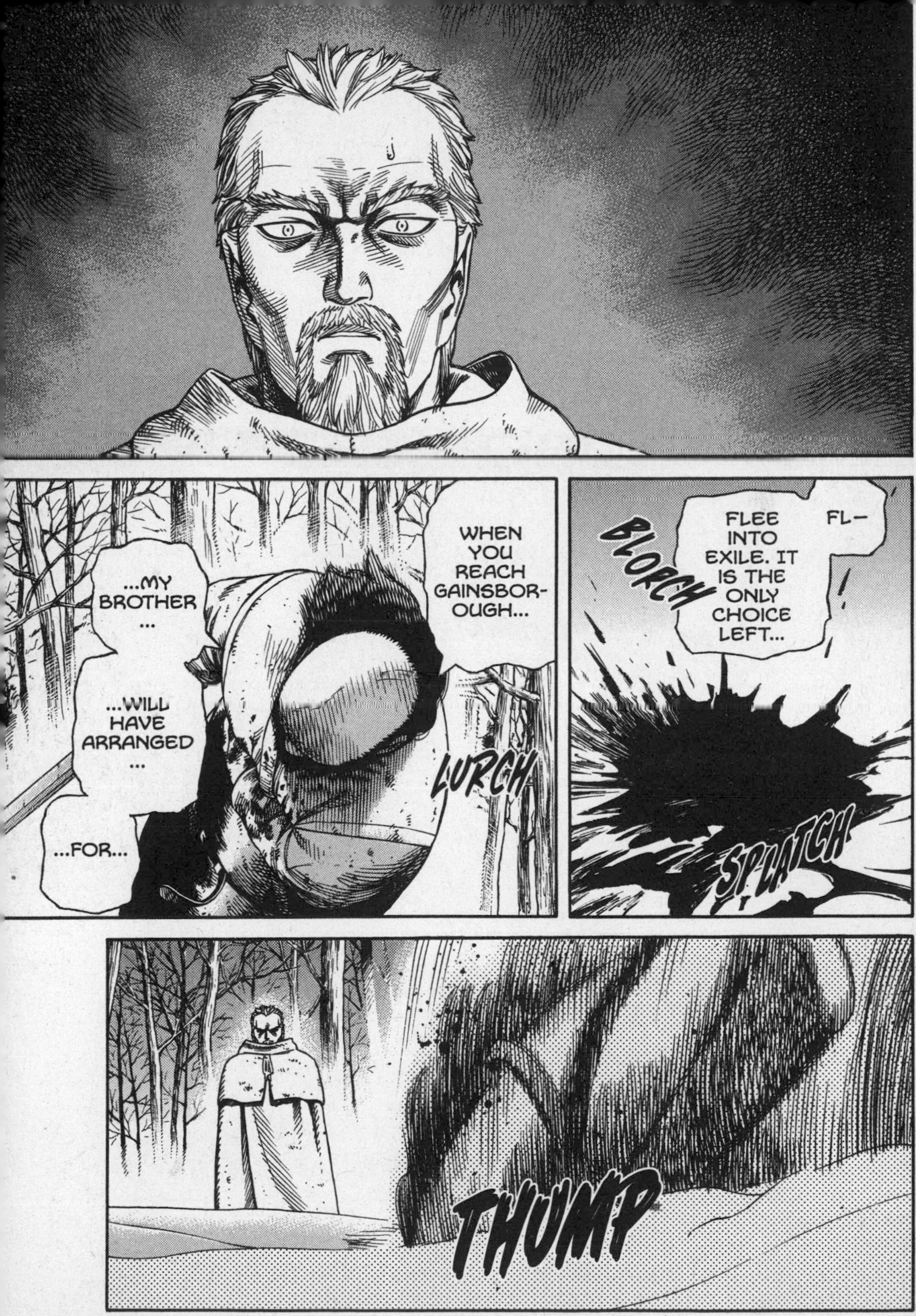
FL—
FLEE INTO EXILE. IT IS THE ONLY CHOICE LEFT...
BLORCH
SPLATCH
WHEN YOU REACH GAINSBOROUGH...
...MY BROTHER ...
...WILL HAVE ARRANGED ...
LURCH
...FOR...
THUMP

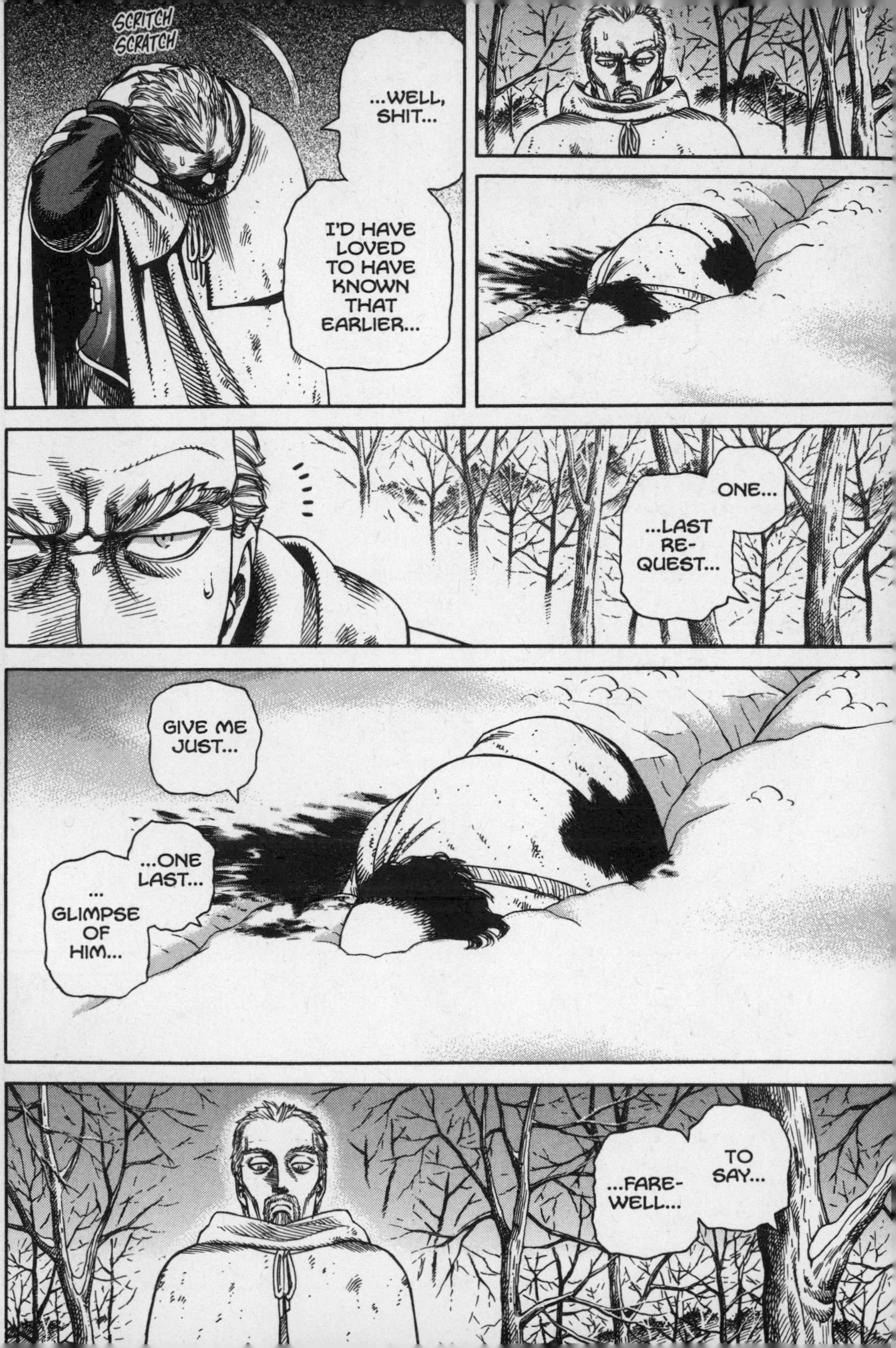
SCRITCH SCRATCH
...WELL, SHIT...
I'D HAVE LOVED TO HAVE KNOWN THAT EARLIER...
ONE... ...LAST RE-QUEST...
GIVE ME JUST...
...ONE LAST... ... GLIMPSE OF HIM...
TO SAY...
...FARE-WELL...

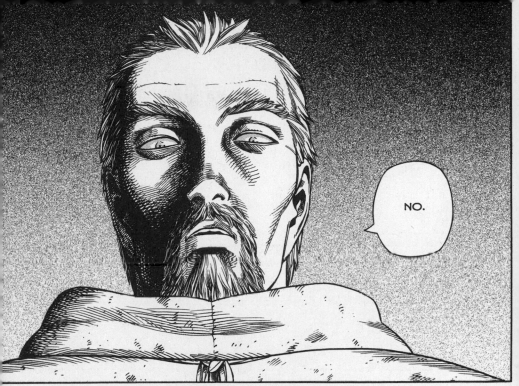

NO.

HIGH-
NESS...

WHEN
THIS
WAR... IS
OVER...

...WE'LL
COOK A
BIRD...

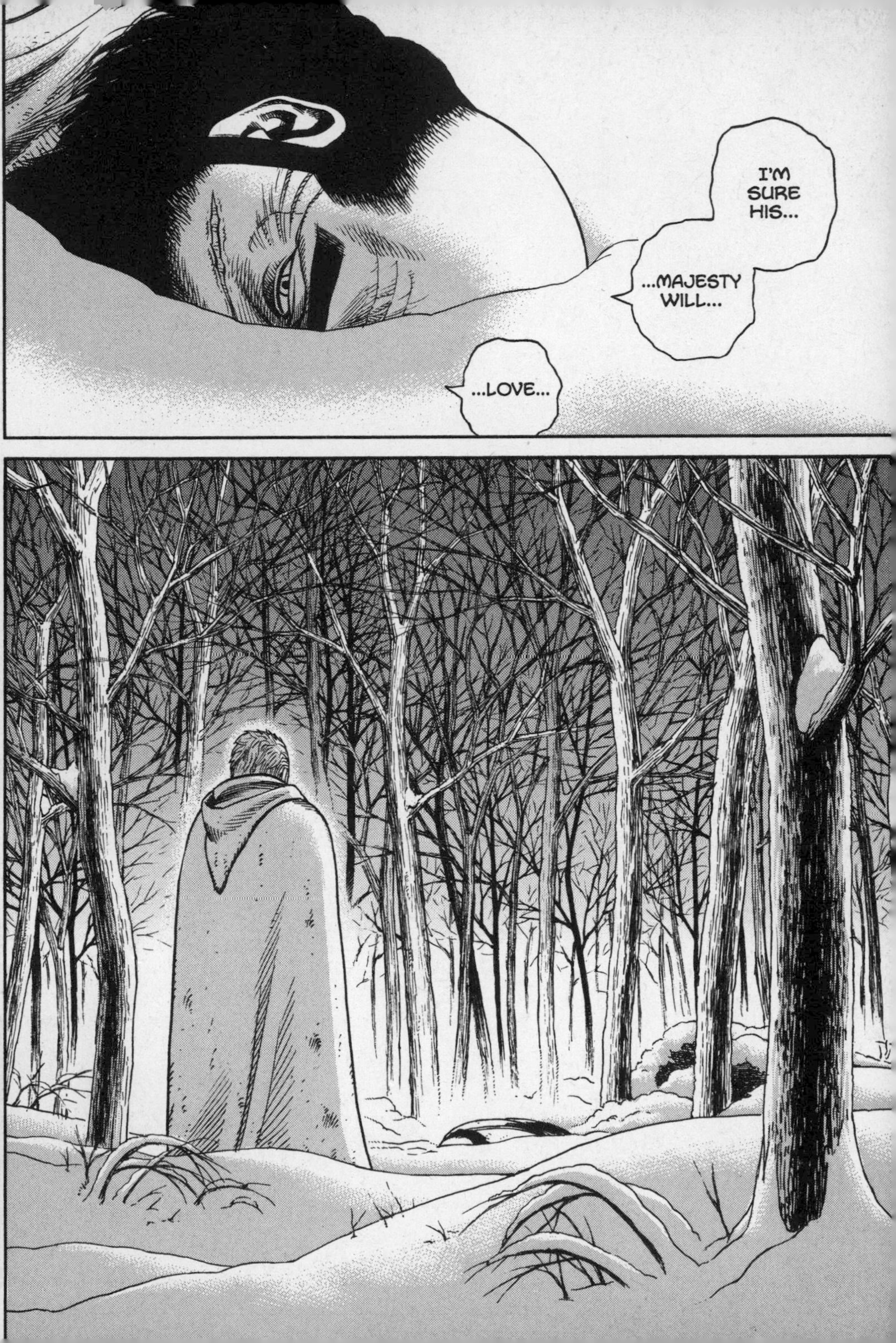
I'M SURE HIS...
...MAJESTY WILL...
...LOVE...

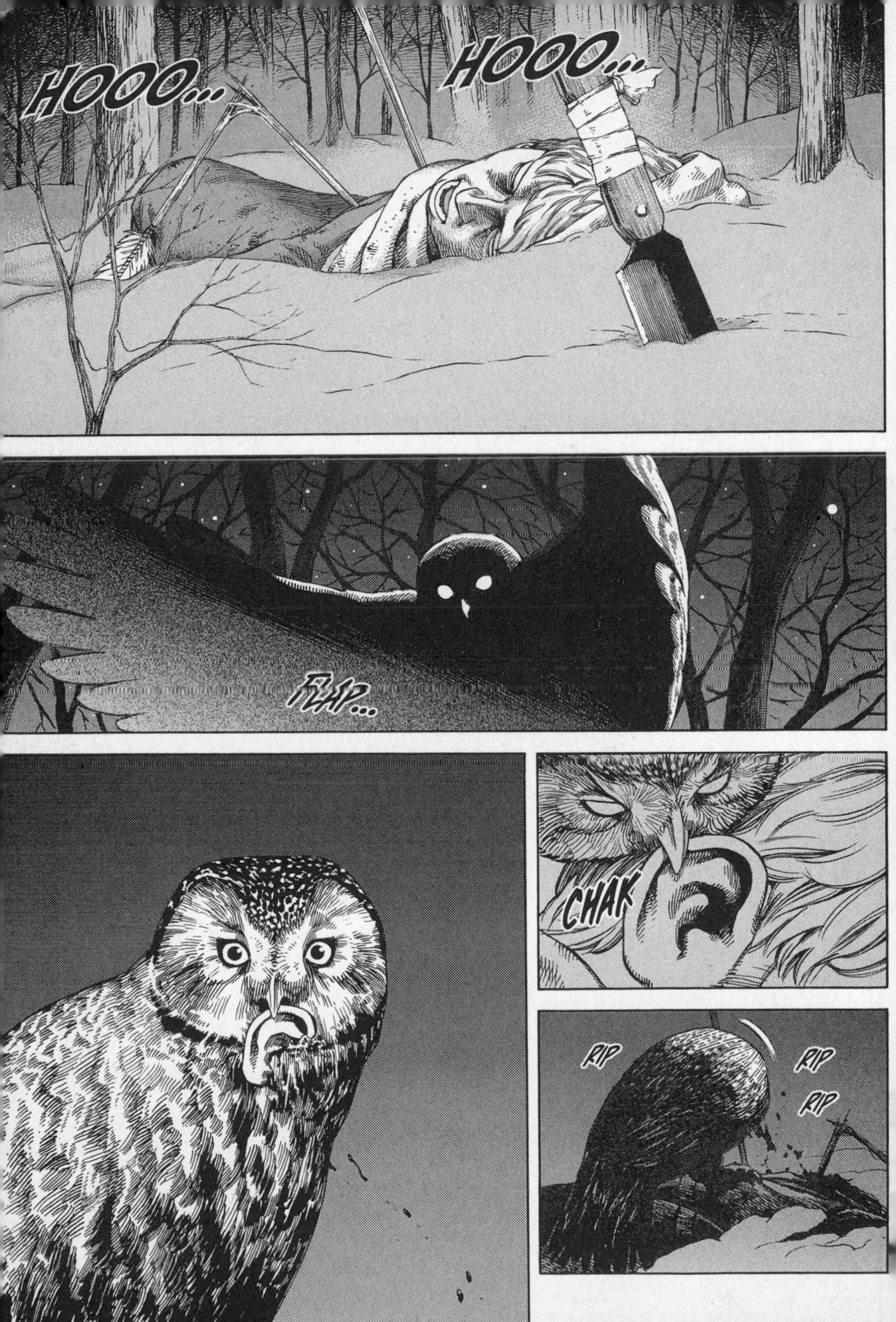
HOOO...
HOOO...
FLAP...
CHAK
RIP
RIP
RIP

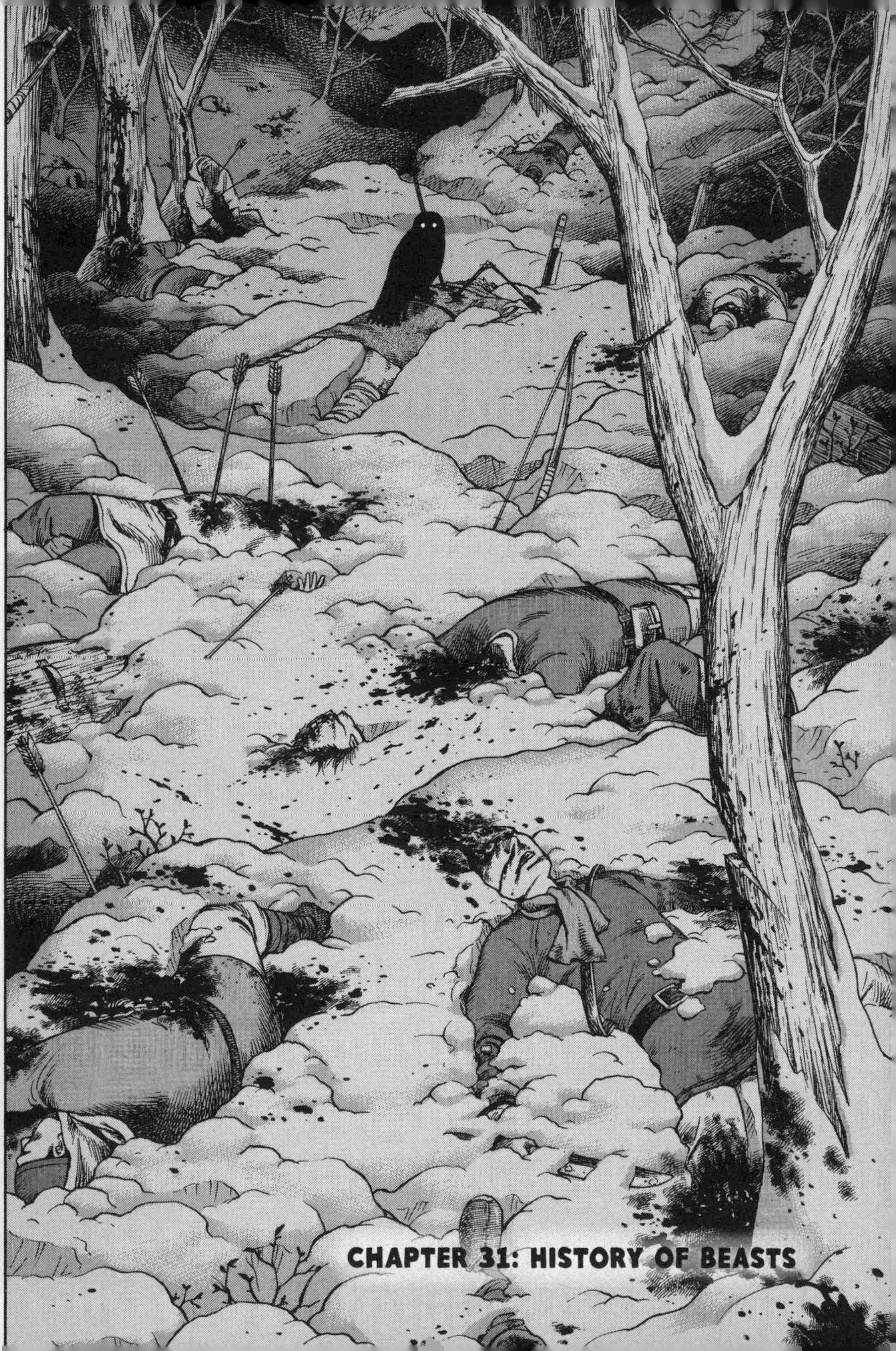
CHAPTER 31: HISTORY OF BEASTS

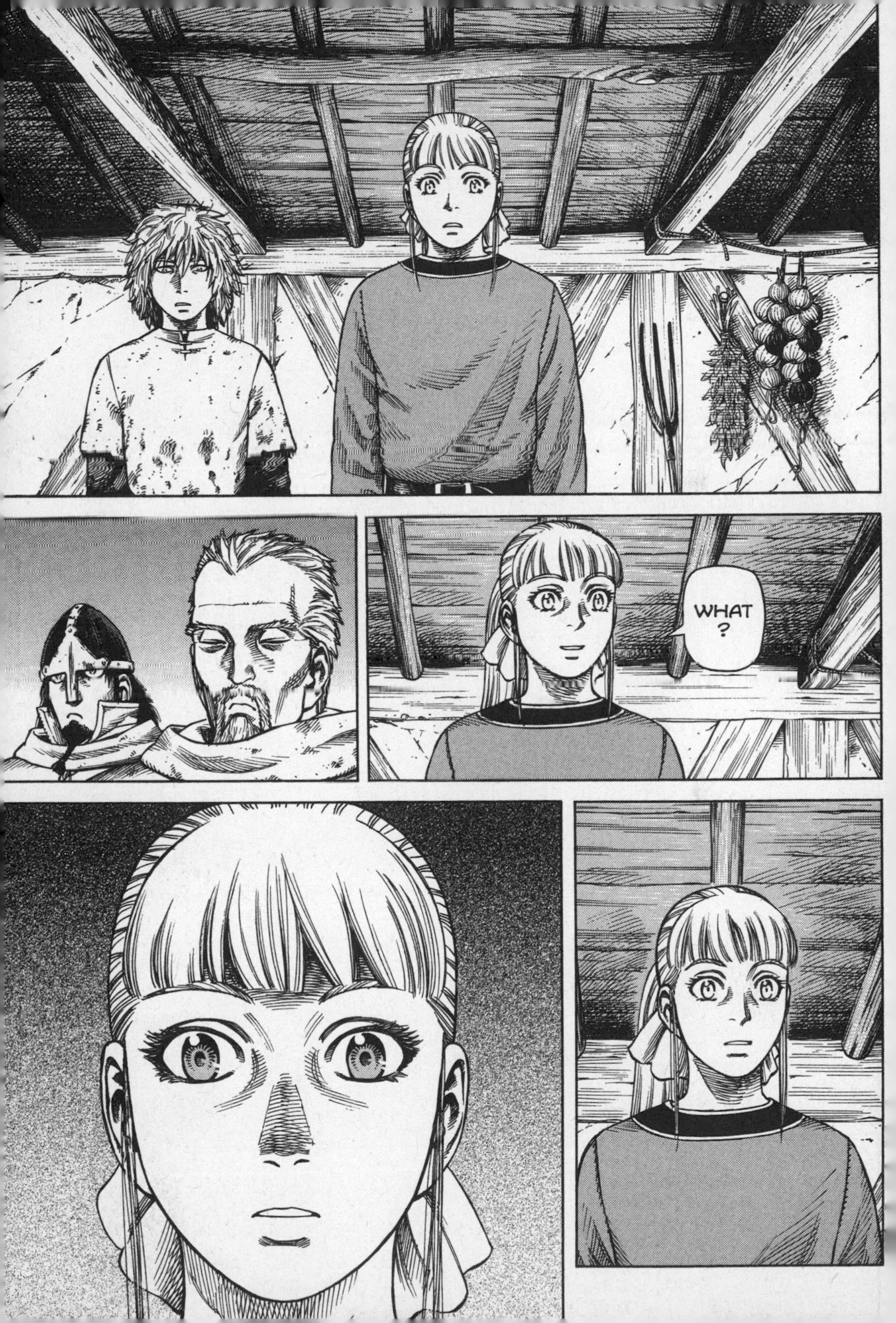
WHAT
?

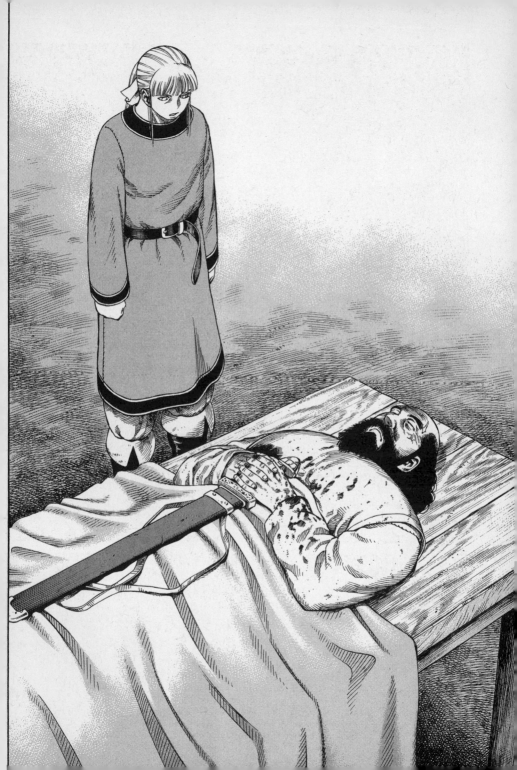

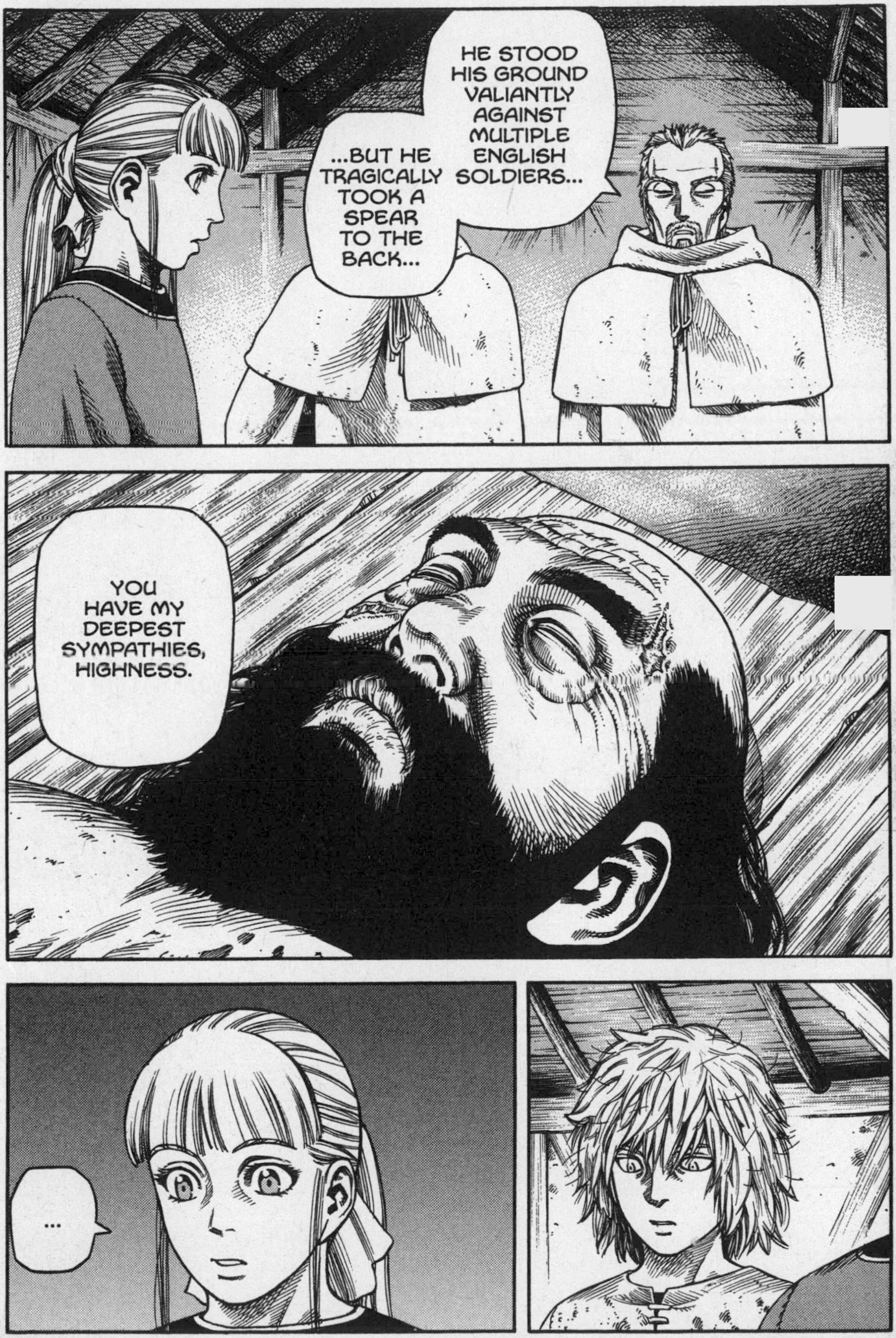
HE STOOD HIS GROUND VALIANTLY AGAINST MULTIPLE ENGLISH SOLDIERS...
...BUT HE TRAGICALLY TOOK A SPEAR TO THE BACK...
YOU HAVE MY DEEPEST SYMPATHIES, HIGHNESS.
...

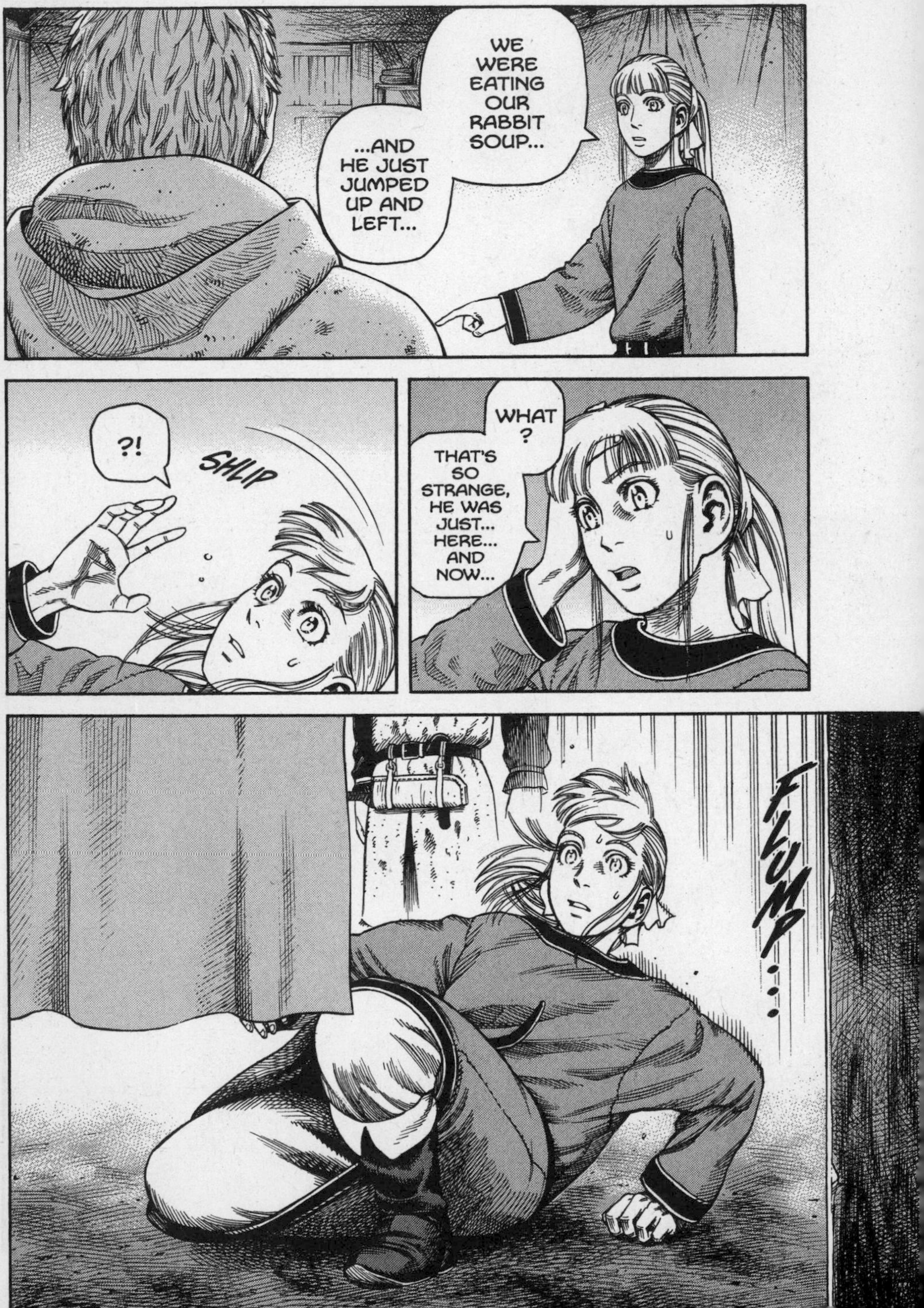
WE WERE EATING OUR RABBIT SOUP...
...AND HE JUST JUMPED UP AND LEFT...
WHAT?
THAT'S SO STRANGE, HE WAS JUST... HERE... AND NOW...
?!
SHLIP
FLUMP...

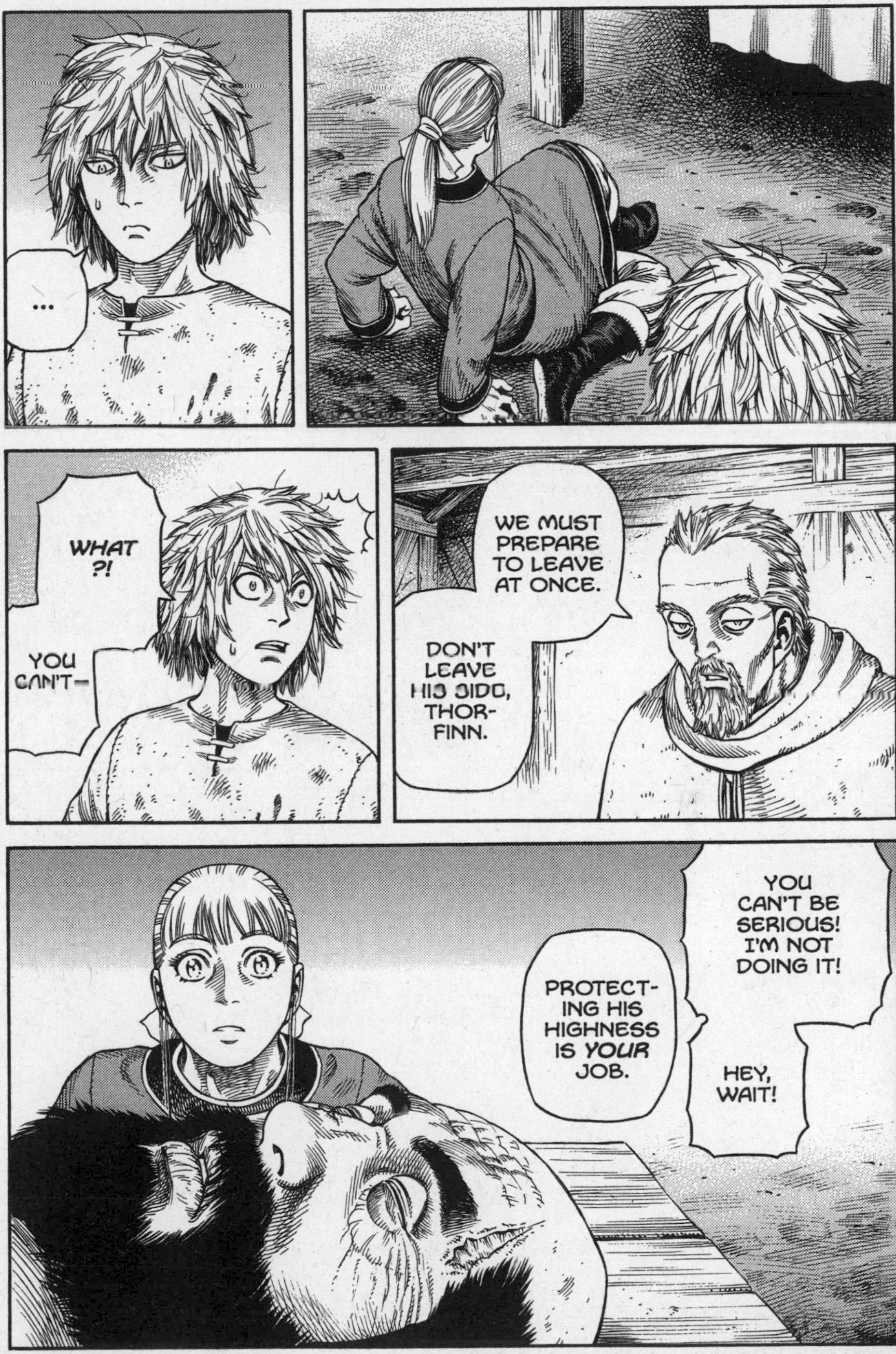
...
WE MUST PREPARE TO LEAVE AT ONCE.
DON'T LEAVE HIS SIDE, THORFINN.
WHAT ?!
YOU CAN'T—
YOU CAN'T BE SERIOUS! I'M NOT DOING IT!
PROTECTING HIS HIGHNESS IS *YOUR* JOB.
HEY, WAIT!

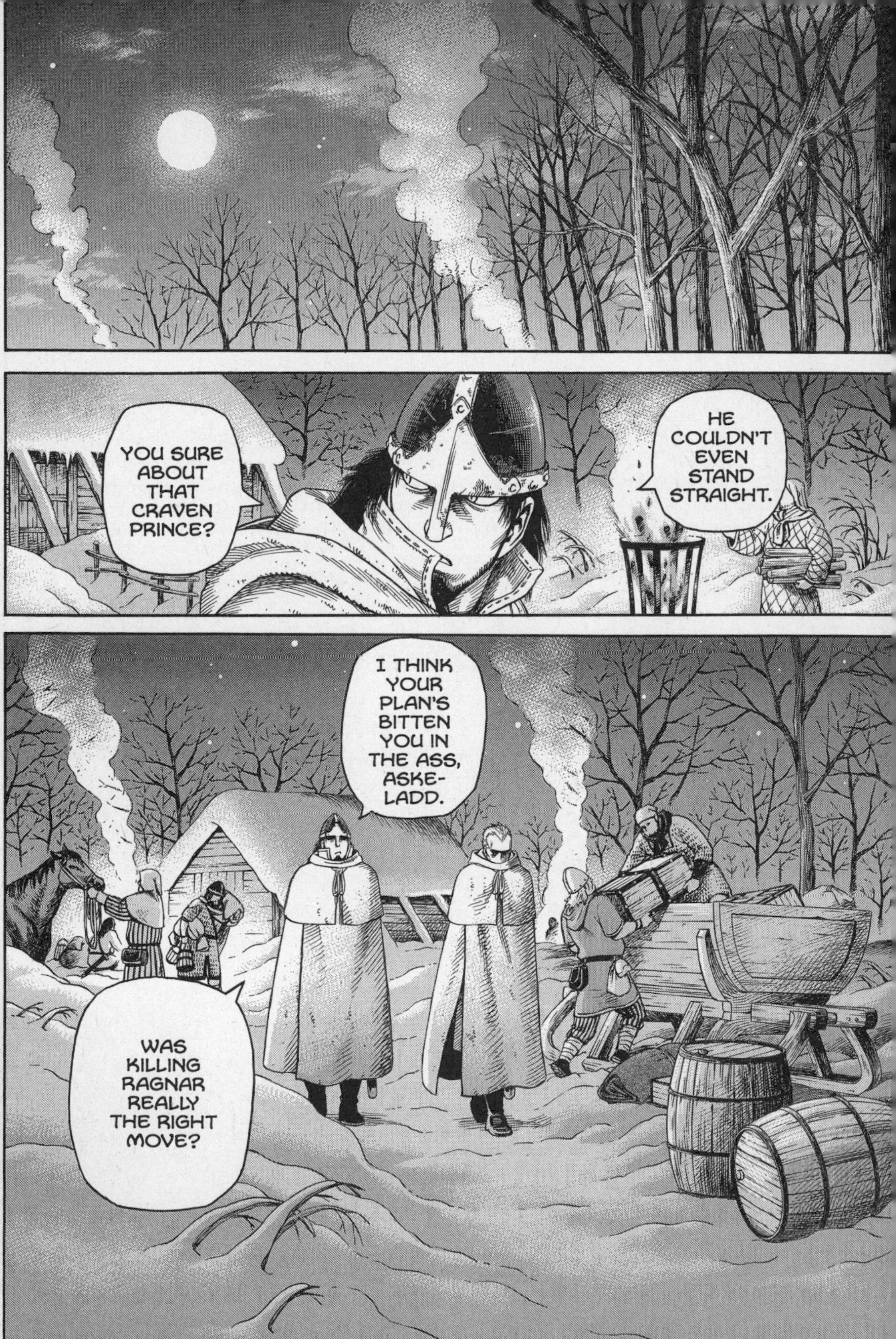
HE COULDN'T EVEN STAND STRAIGHT.
YOU SURE ABOUT THAT CRAVEN PRINCE?
I THINK YOUR PLAN'S BITTEN YOU IN THE ASS, ASKE-LADD.
WAS KILLING RAGNAR REALLY THE RIGHT MOVE?

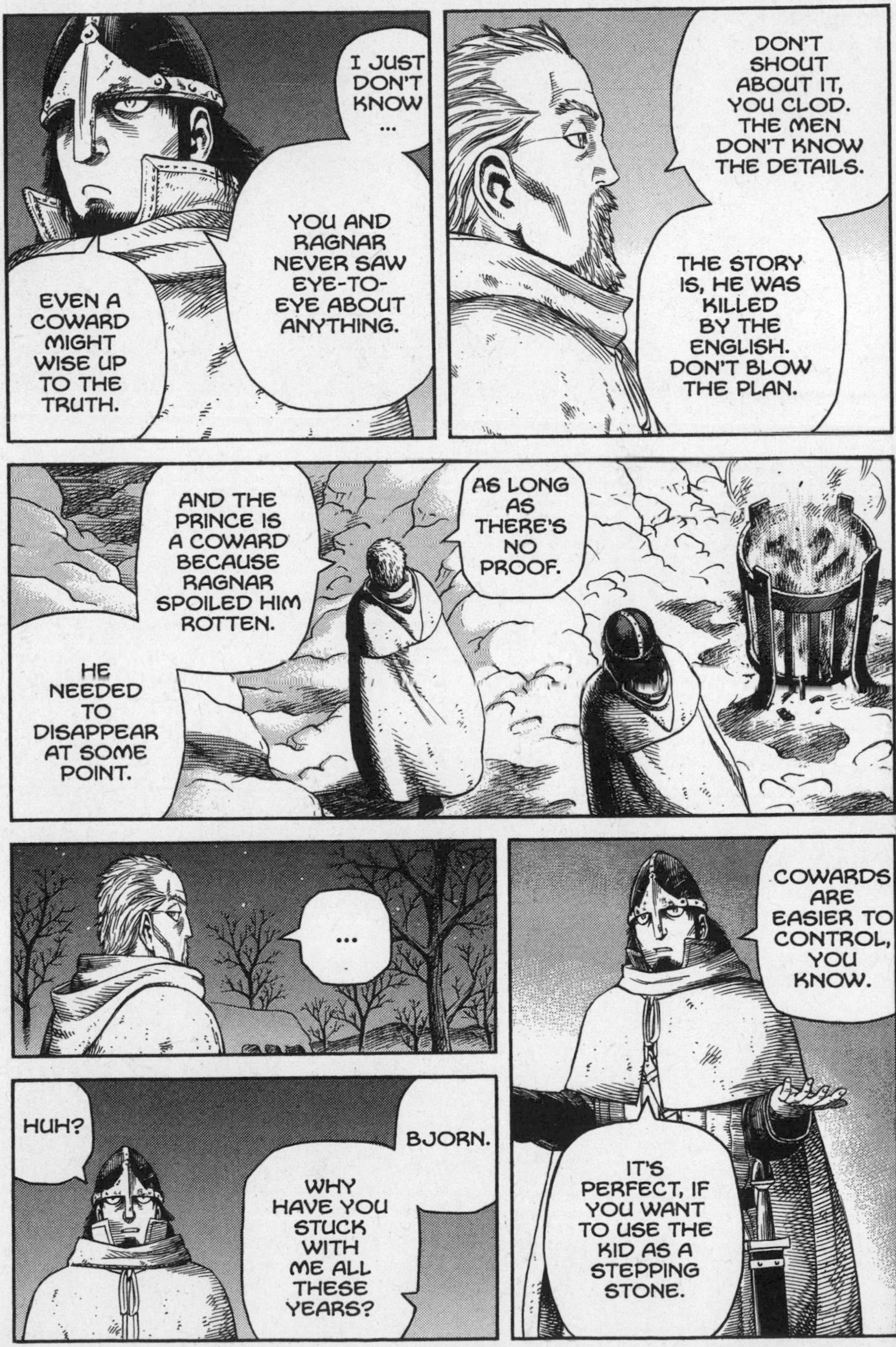
DON'T SHOUT ABOUT IT, YOU CLOD. THE MEN DON'T KNOW THE DETAILS.
THE STORY IS, HE WAS KILLED BY THE ENGLISH. DON'T BLOW THE PLAN.
I JUST DON'T KNOW ...
YOU AND RAGNAR NEVER SAW EYE-TO-EYE ABOUT ANYTHING.
EVEN A COWARD MIGHT WISE UP TO THE TRUTH.
AS LONG AS THERE'S NO PROOF.
AND THE PRINCE IS A COWARD BECAUSE RAGNAR SPOILED HIM ROTTEN.
HE NEEDED TO DISAPPEAR AT SOME POINT.
COWARDS ARE EASIER TO CONTROL, YOU KNOW.
IT'S PERFECT, IF YOU WANT TO USE THE KID AS A STEPPING STONE.
...
BJORN.
WHY HAVE YOU STUCK WITH ME ALL THESE YEARS?
HUH?

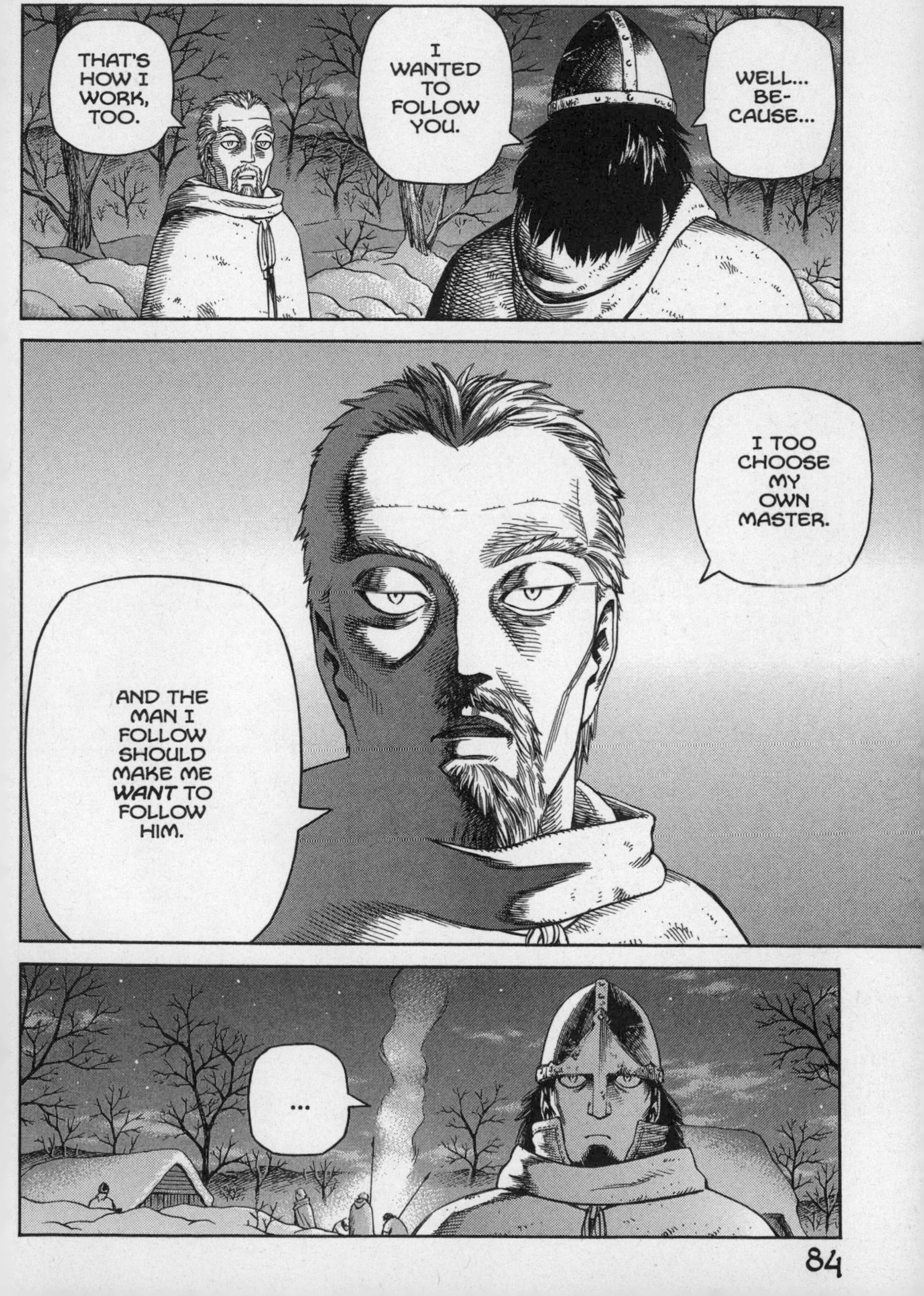
WELL... BE-CAUSE...
I WANTED TO FOLLOW YOU.
THAT'S HOW I WORK, TOO.
I TOO CHOOSE MY OWN MASTER.
AND THE MAN I FOLLOW SHOULD MAKE ME *WANT* TO FOLLOW HIM.
...

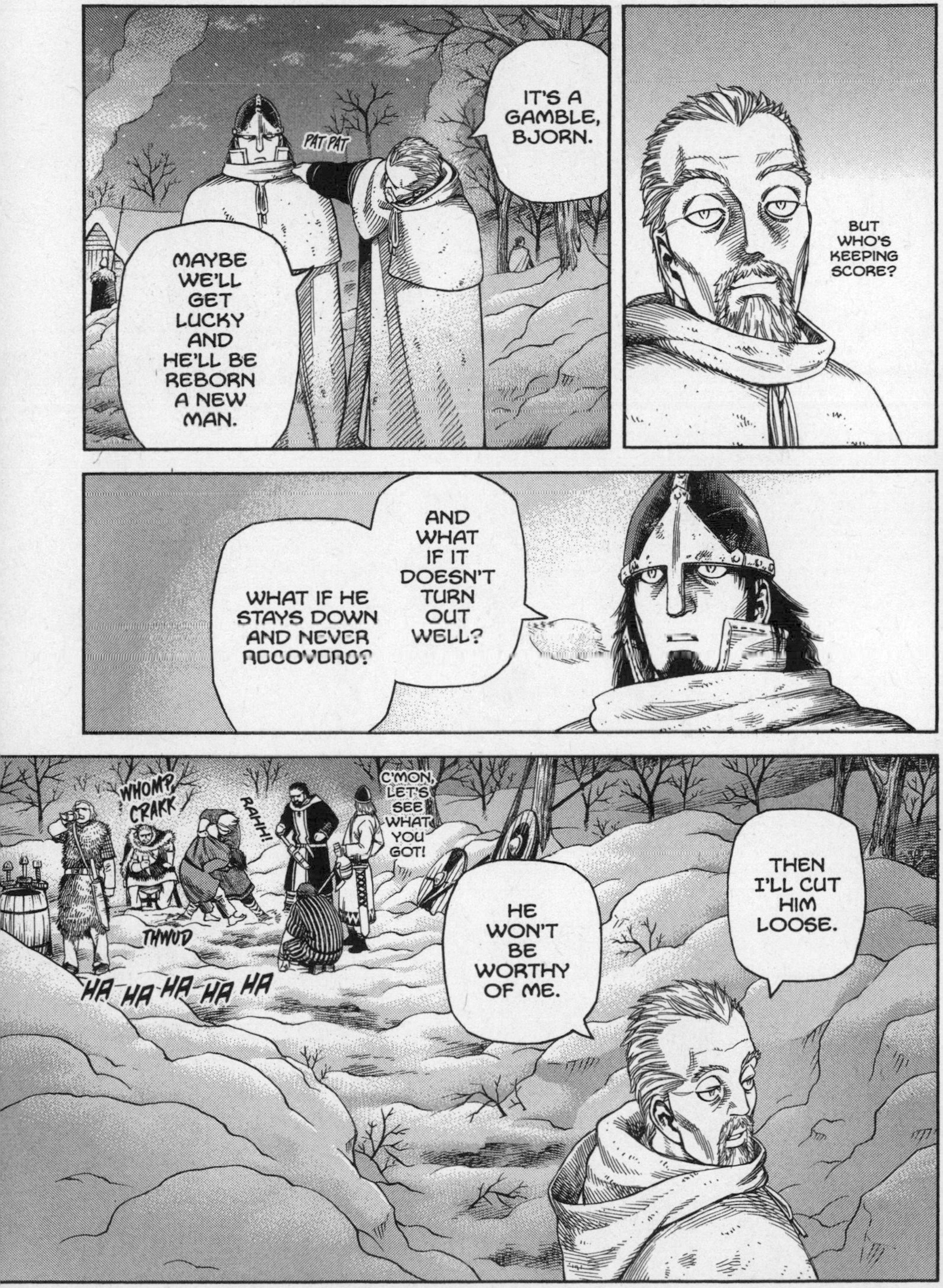
BUT WHO'S KEEPING SCORE?
IT'S A GAMBLE, BJORN.
PAT PAT
MAYBE WE'LL GET LUCKY AND HE'LL BE REBORN A NEW MAN.
AND WHAT IF IT DOESN'T TURN OUT WELL?
WHAT IF HE STAYS DOWN AND NEVER RECOVERS?
THEN I'LL CUT HIM LOOSE.
HE WON'T BE WORTHY OF ME.
C'MON, LET'S SEE WHAT YOU GOT!
RAHH!
WHOMP, CRAKK
THWUD
HA HA HA HA HA

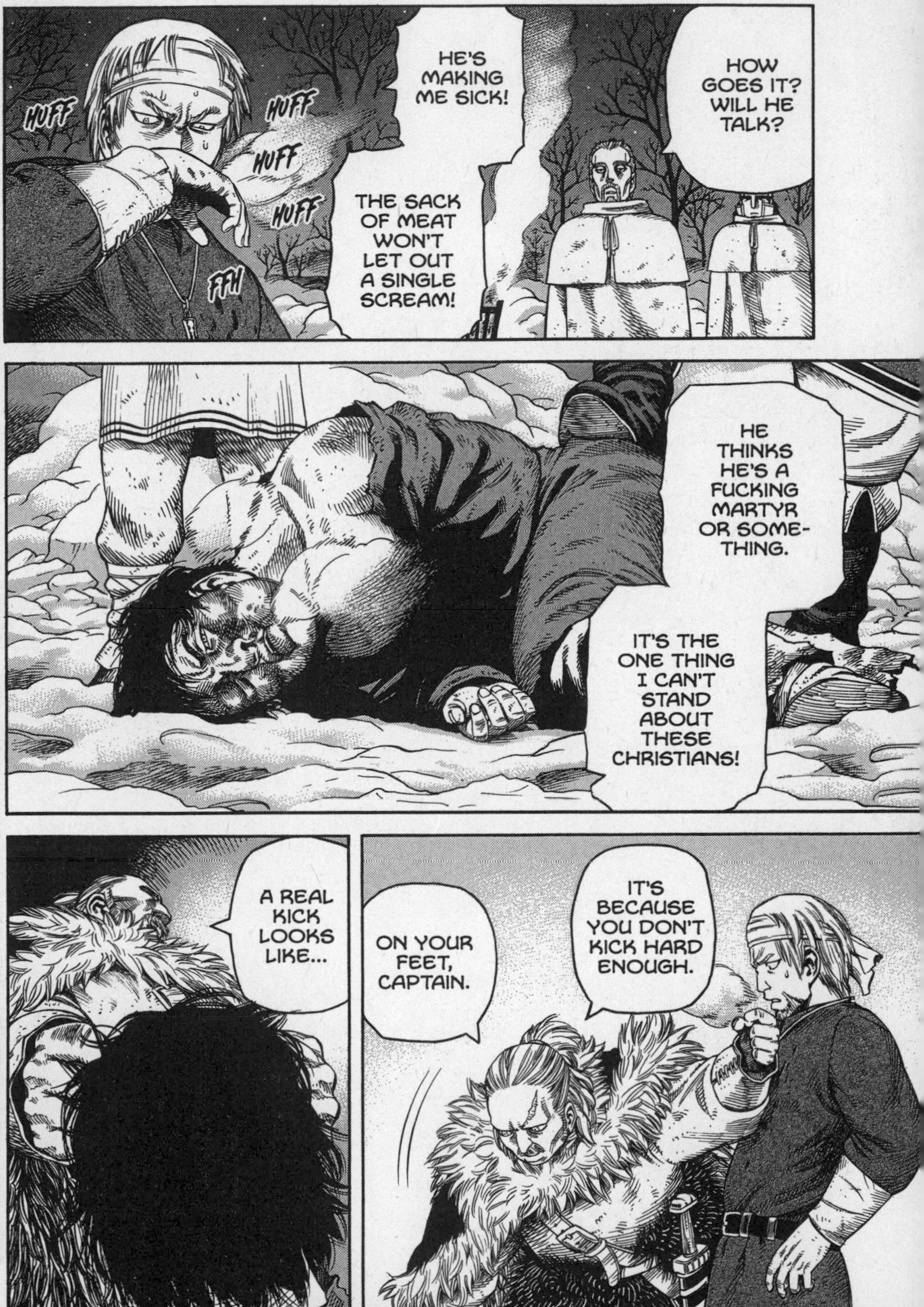
HOW GOES IT? WILL HE TALK?
HE'S MAKING ME SICK!
THE SACK OF MEAT WON'T LET OUT A SINGLE SCREAM!
HUFF
HUFF
HUFF
HUFF
FFH
HE THINKS HE'S A FUCKING MARTYR OR SOME-THING.
IT'S THE ONE THING I CAN'T STAND ABOUT THESE CHRISTIANS!
IT'S BECAUSE YOU DON'T KICK HARD ENOUGH.
ON YOUR FEET, CAPTAIN.
A REAL KICK LOOKS LIKE...

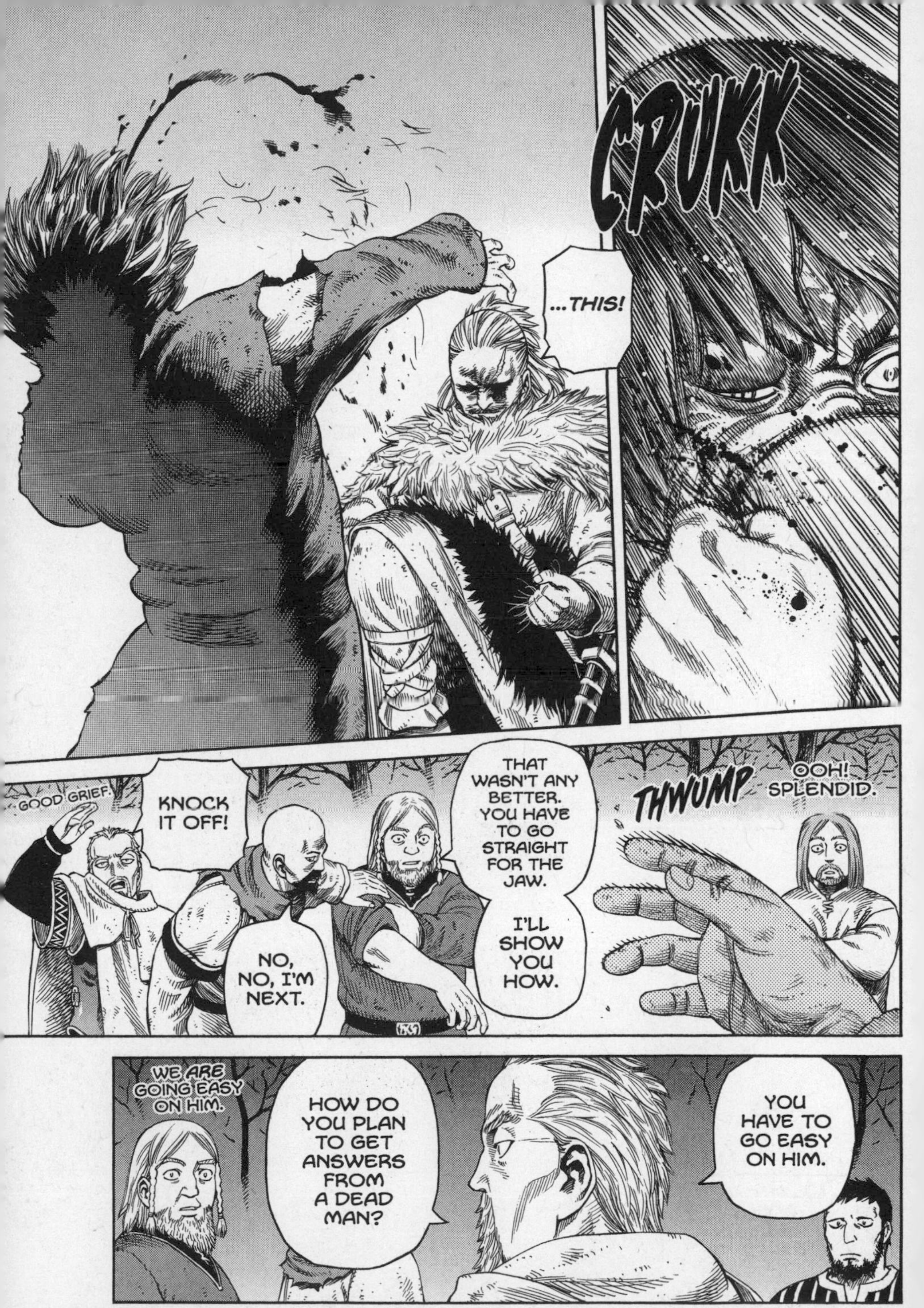
CRUKK
...THIS!
OOH! SPLENDID.
THWUMP
THAT WASN'T ANY BETTER. YOU HAVE TO GO STRAIGHT FOR THE JAW.
I'LL SHOW YOU HOW.
NO, NO, I'M NEXT.
KNOCK IT OFF!
GOOD GRIEF.
YOU HAVE TO GO EASY ON HIM.
HOW DO YOU PLAN TO GET ANSWERS FROM A DEAD MAN?
WE ARE GOING EASY ON HIM.

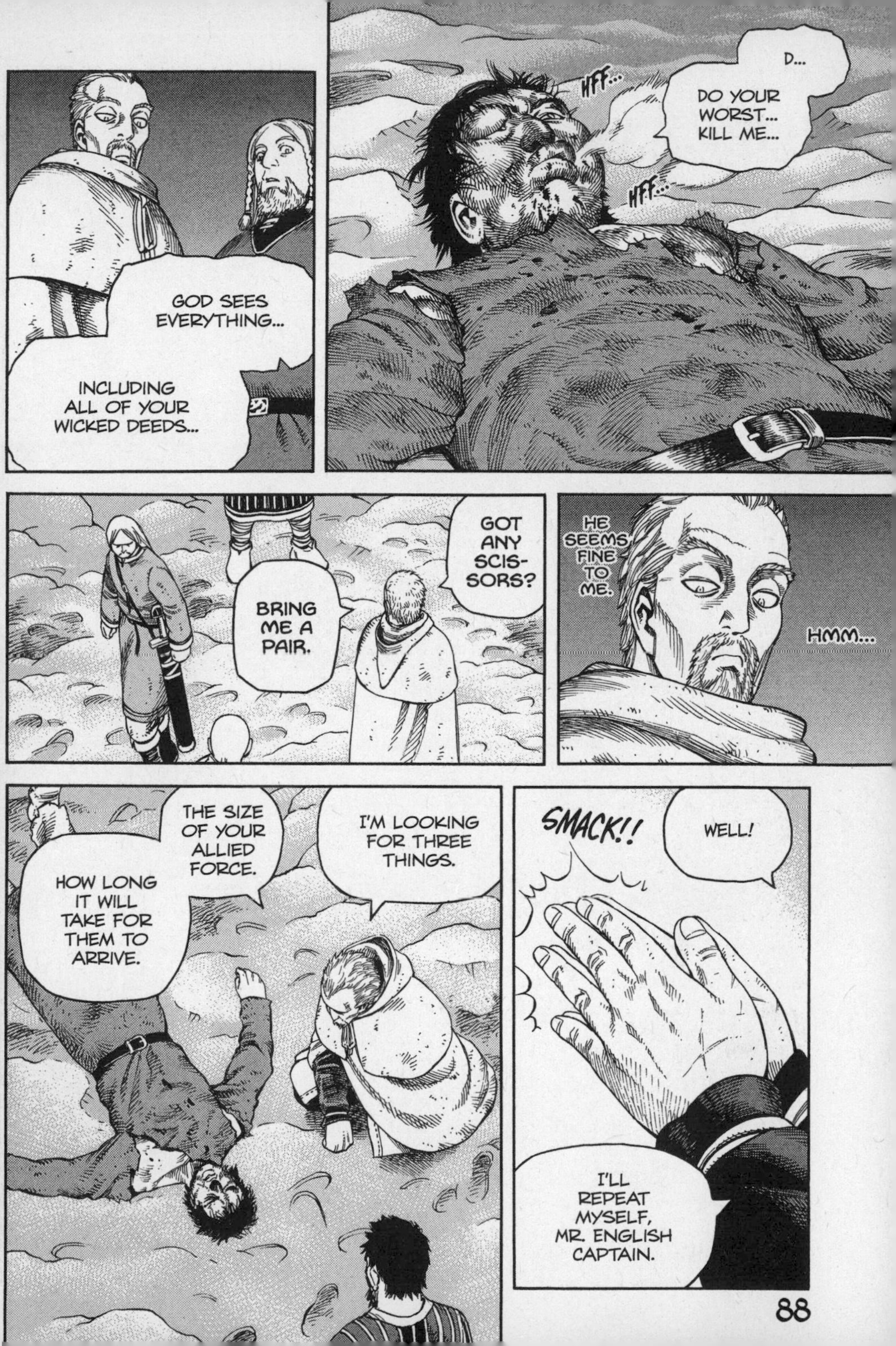
HFF...
D...
DO YOUR WORST... KILL ME...
HFF...
GOD SEES EVERYTHING...
INCLUDING ALL OF YOUR WICKED DEEDS...
HE SEEMS FINE TO ME.
HMM...
GOT ANY SCIS-SORS?
BRING ME A PAIR.
WELL!
SMACK!!
I'LL REPEAT MYSELF, MR. ENGLISH CAPTAIN.
I'M LOOKING FOR THREE THINGS.
THE SIZE OF YOUR ALLIED FORCE.
HOW LONG IT WILL TAKE FOR THEM TO ARRIVE.

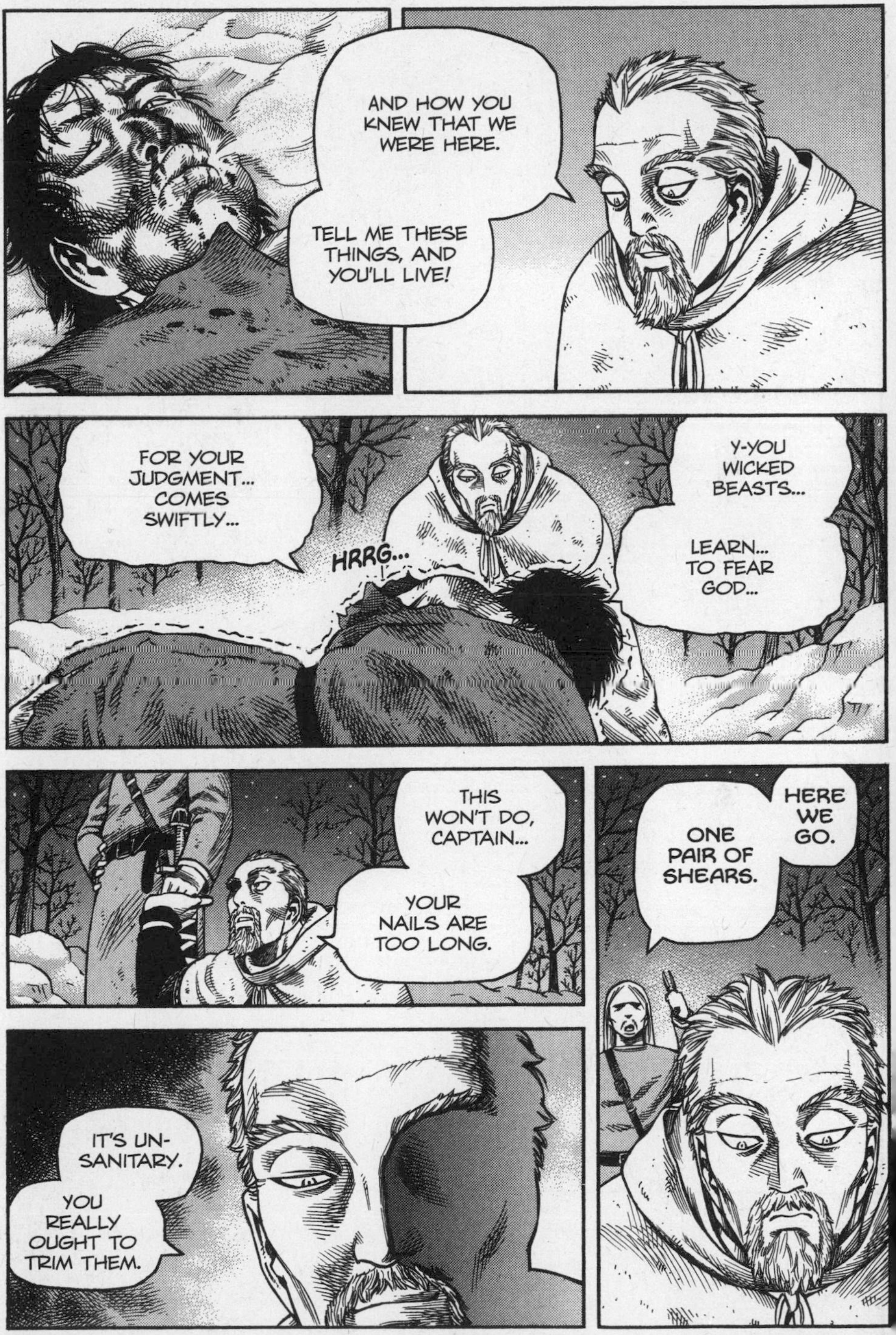
AND HOW YOU KNEW THAT WE WERE HERE.
TELL ME THESE THINGS, AND YOU'LL LIVE!
Y-YOU WICKED BEASTS...
LEARN... TO FEAR GOD...
FOR YOUR JUDGMENT... COMES SWIFTLY...
HRRG...
HERE WE GO.
ONE PAIR OF SHEARS.
THIS WON'T DO, CAPTAIN...
YOUR NAILS ARE TOO LONG.
IT'S UN-SANITARY.
YOU REALLY OUGHT TO TRIM THEM.

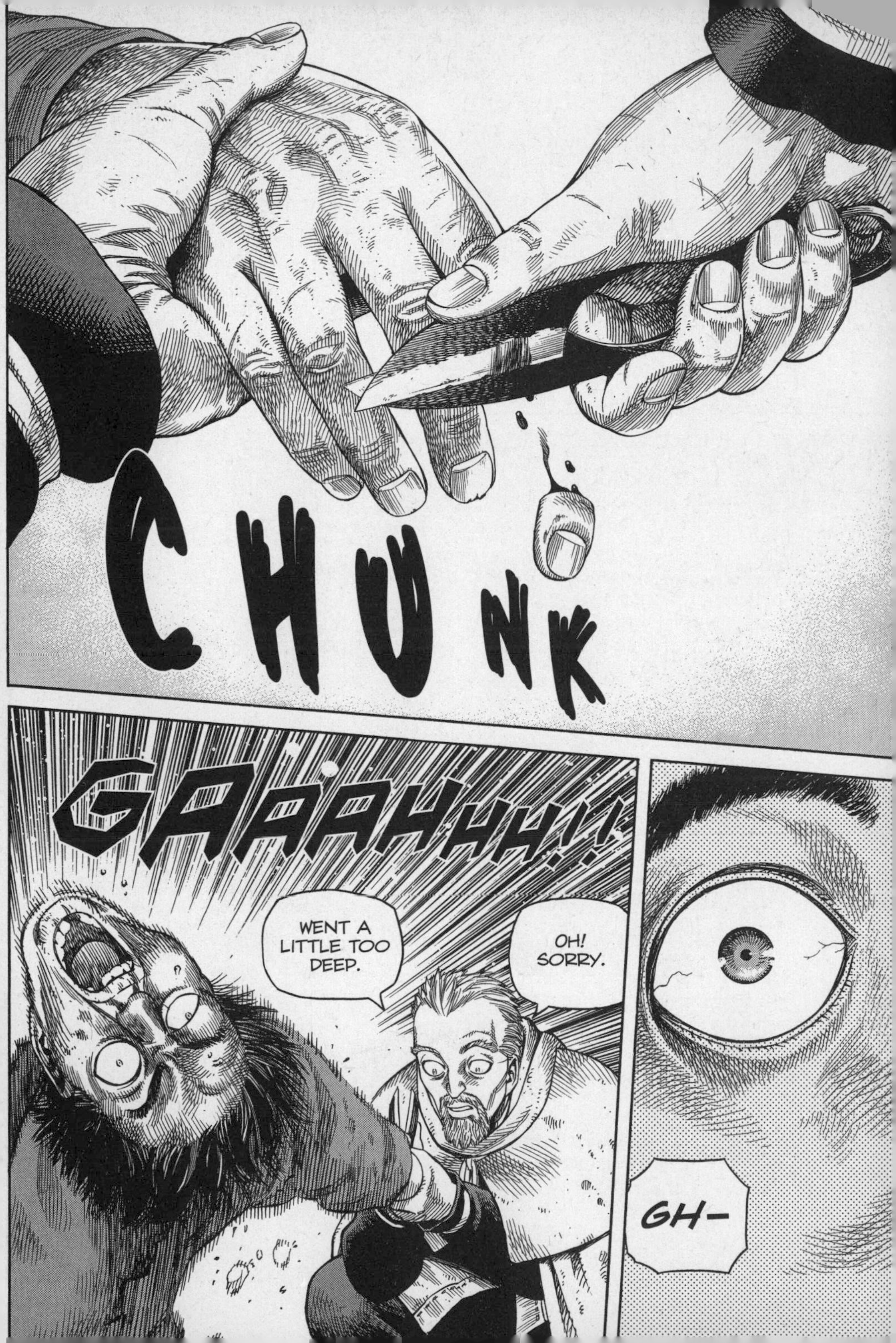
CHUNK
GH-
GAAAHHH!!
OH! SORRY.
WENT A LITTLE TOO DEEP.

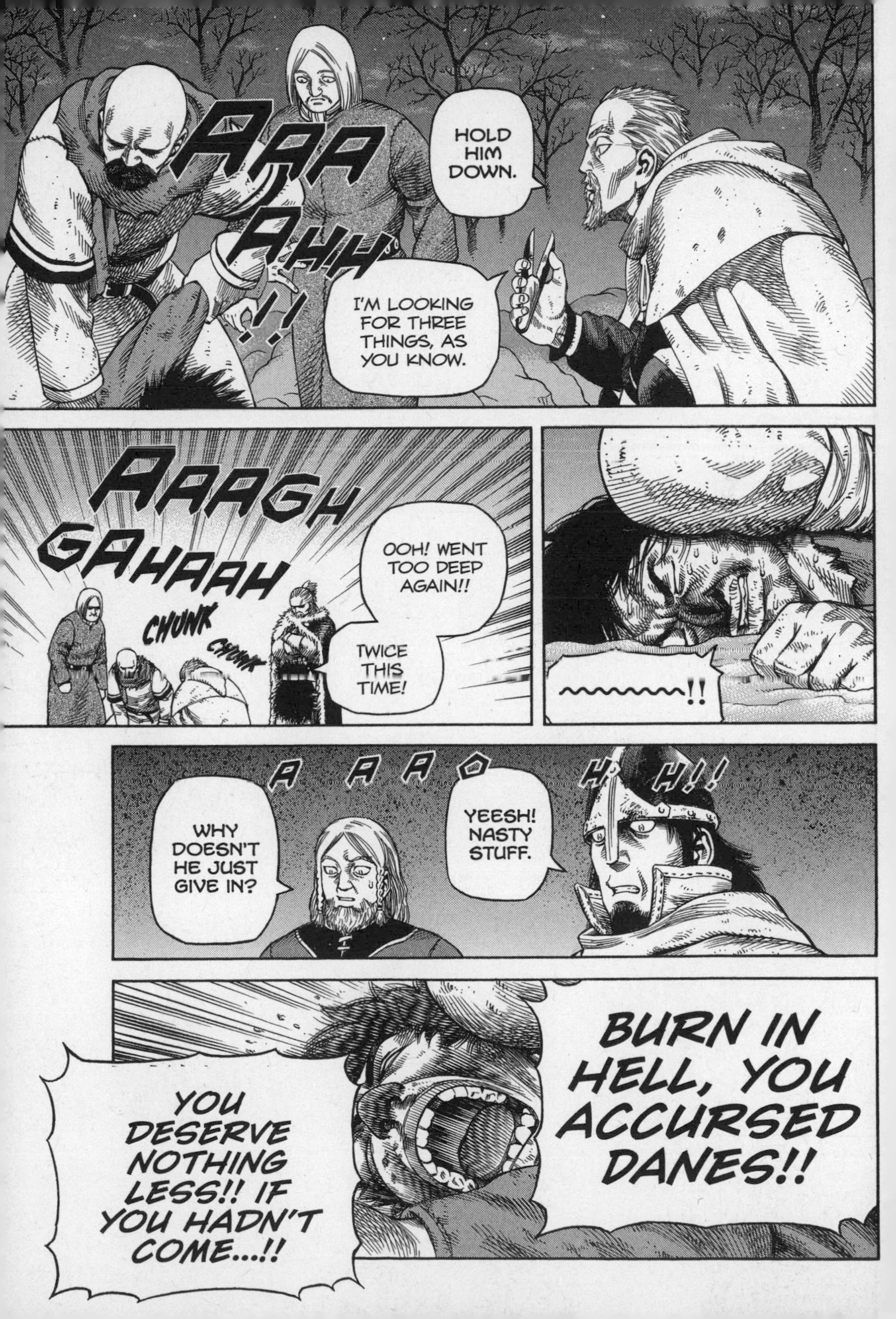
HOLD HIM DOWN.
AAAAHH!!
I'M LOOKING FOR THREE THINGS, AS YOU KNOW.
~~~~~~~~!!
AAAGH GAHAAH
OOH! WENT TOO DEEP AGAIN!!
CHUNK CHUNK
TWICE THIS TIME!
AAAAOHH!!
YEESH! NASTY STUFF.
WHY DOESN'T HE JUST GIVE IN?
BURN IN HELL, YOU ACCURSED DANES!!
YOU DESERVE NOTHING LESS!! IF YOU HADN'T COME...!!
~~~~~~~~

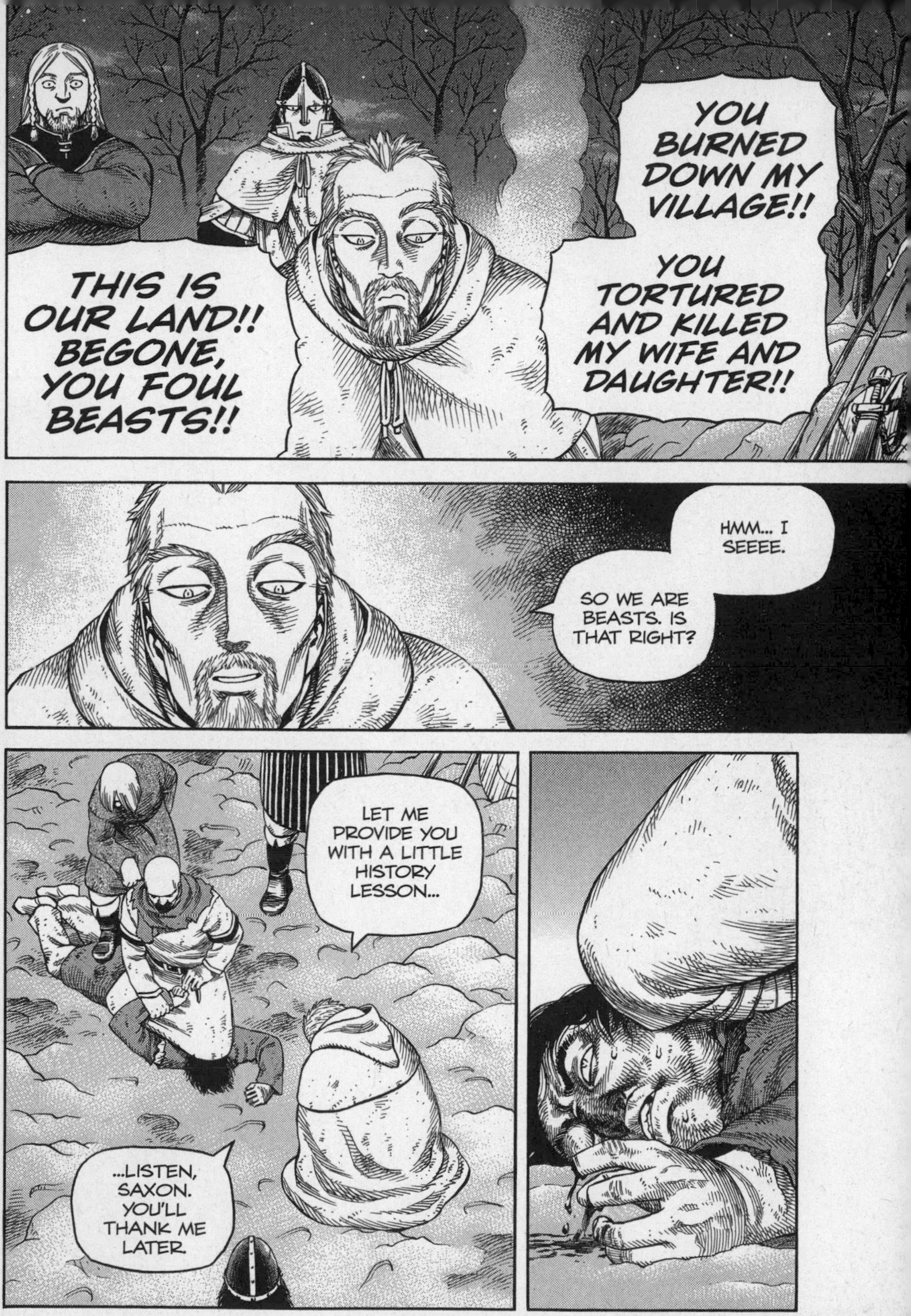
YOU BURNED DOWN MY VILLAGE!!
YOU TORTURED AND KILLED MY WIFE AND DAUGHTER!!
THIS IS OUR LAND!! BEGONE, YOU FOUL BEASTS!!
HMM... I SEEEE.
SO WE ARE BEASTS. IS THAT RIGHT?
LET ME PROVIDE YOU WITH A LITTLE HISTORY LESSON...
...LISTEN, SAXON. YOU'LL THANK ME LATER.

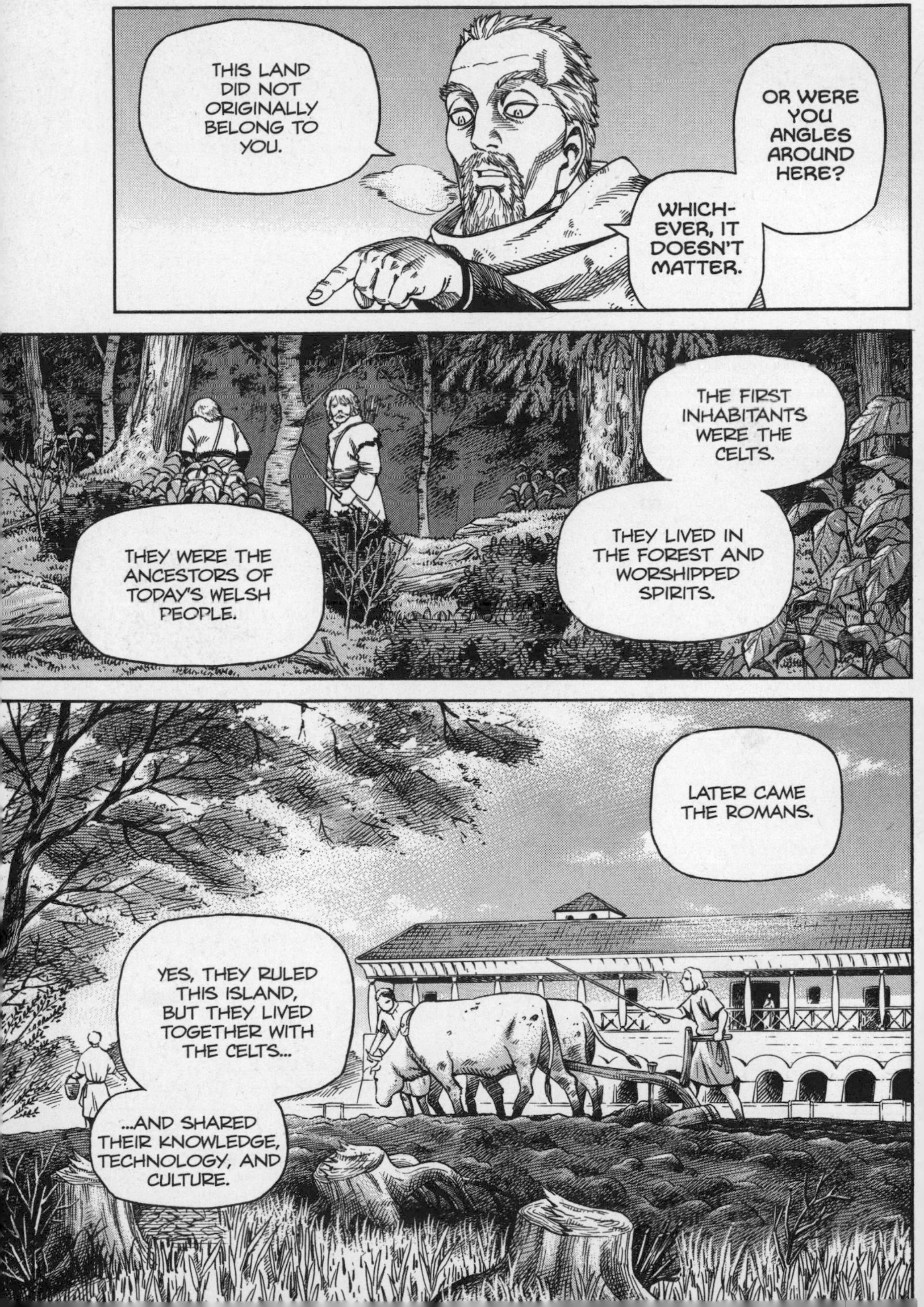
OR WERE YOU ANGLES AROUND HERE?
WHICH-EVER, IT DOESN'T MATTER.
THIS LAND DID NOT ORIGINALLY BELONG TO YOU.
THE FIRST INHABITANTS WERE THE CELTS.
THEY LIVED IN THE FOREST AND WORSHIPPED SPIRITS.
THEY WERE THE ANCESTORS OF TODAY'S WELSH PEOPLE.
LATER CAME THE ROMANS.
YES, THEY RULED THIS ISLAND, BUT THEY LIVED TOGETHER WITH THE CELTS...
...AND SHARED THEIR KNOWLEDGE, TECHNOLOGY, AND CULTURE.

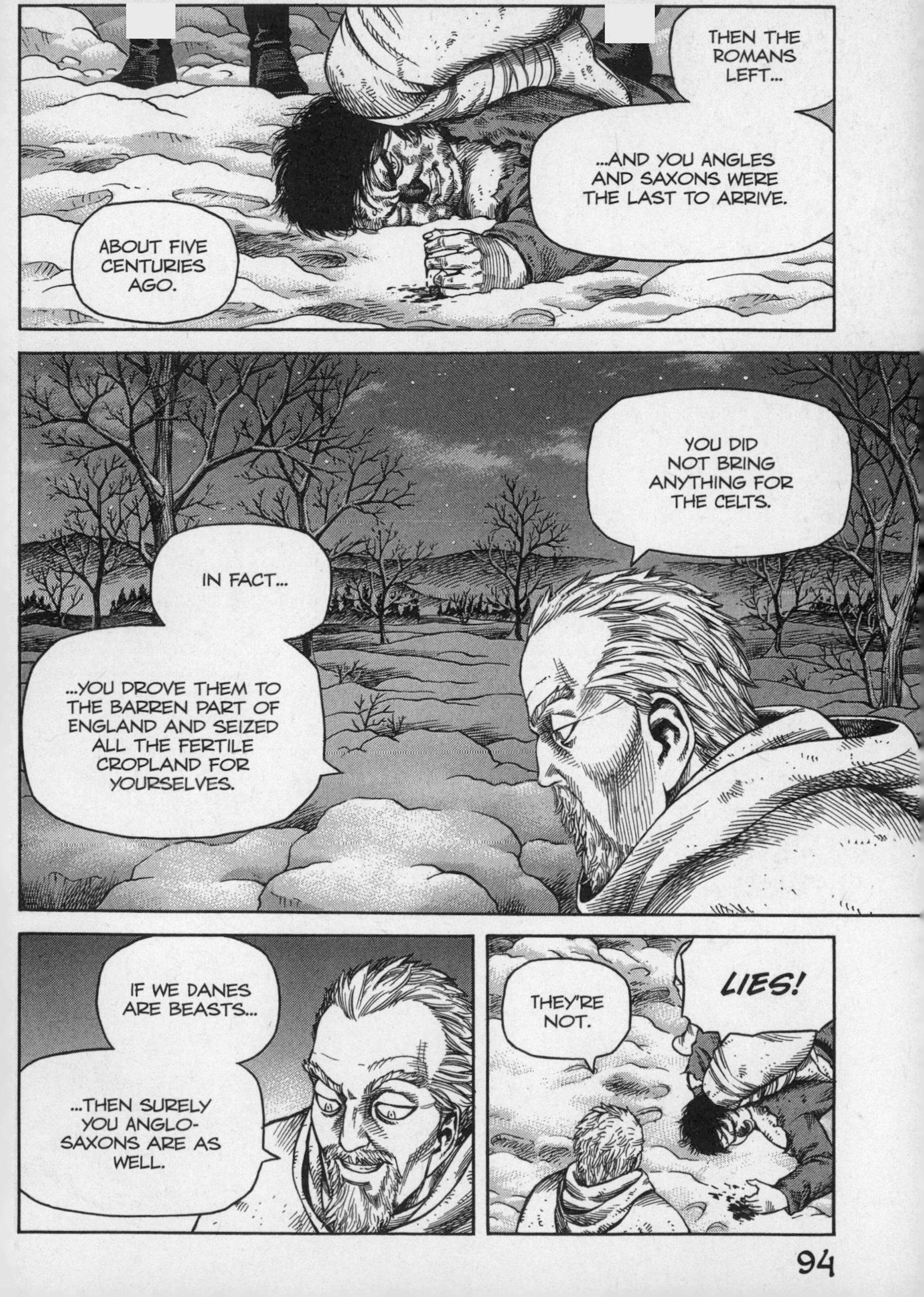
THEN THE ROMANS LEFT...
...AND YOU ANGLES AND SAXONS WERE THE LAST TO ARRIVE.
ABOUT FIVE CENTURIES AGO.
YOU DID NOT BRING ANYTHING FOR THE CELTS.
IN FACT...
...YOU DROVE THEM TO THE BARREN PART OF ENGLAND AND SEIZED ALL THE FERTILE CROPLAND FOR YOURSELVES.
LIES!
THEY'RE NOT.
IF WE DANES ARE BEASTS...
...THEN SURELY YOU ANGLO-SAXONS ARE AS WELL.

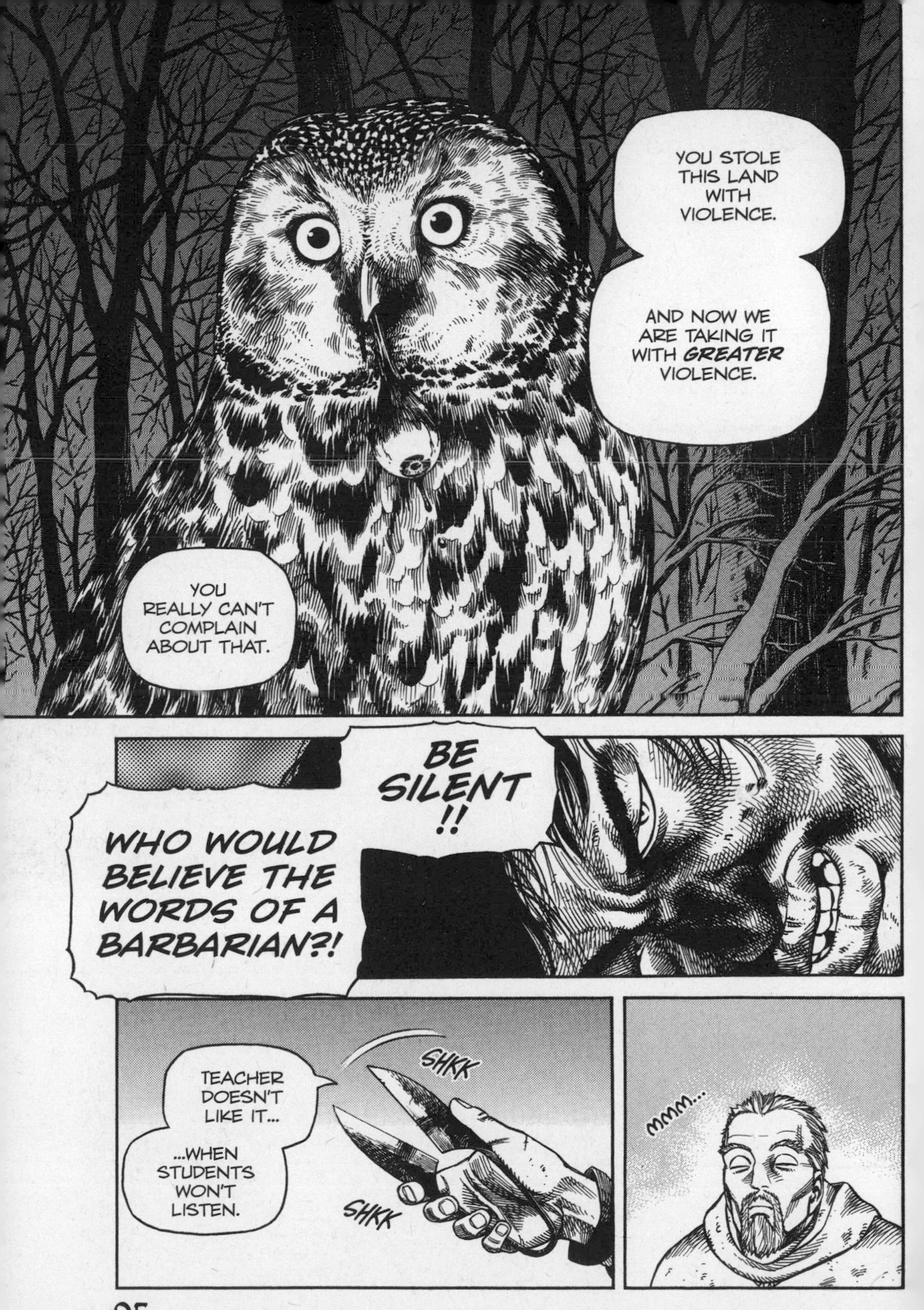
YOU STOLE THIS LAND WITH VIOLENCE.
AND NOW WE ARE TAKING IT WITH GREATER VIOLENCE.
YOU REALLY CAN'T COMPLAIN ABOUT THAT.
BE SILENT!!
WHO WOULD BELIEVE THE WORDS OF A BARBARIAN?!
mmm...
SHKK
TEACHER DOESN'T LIKE IT...
...WHEN STUDENTS WON'T LISTEN.
SHKK

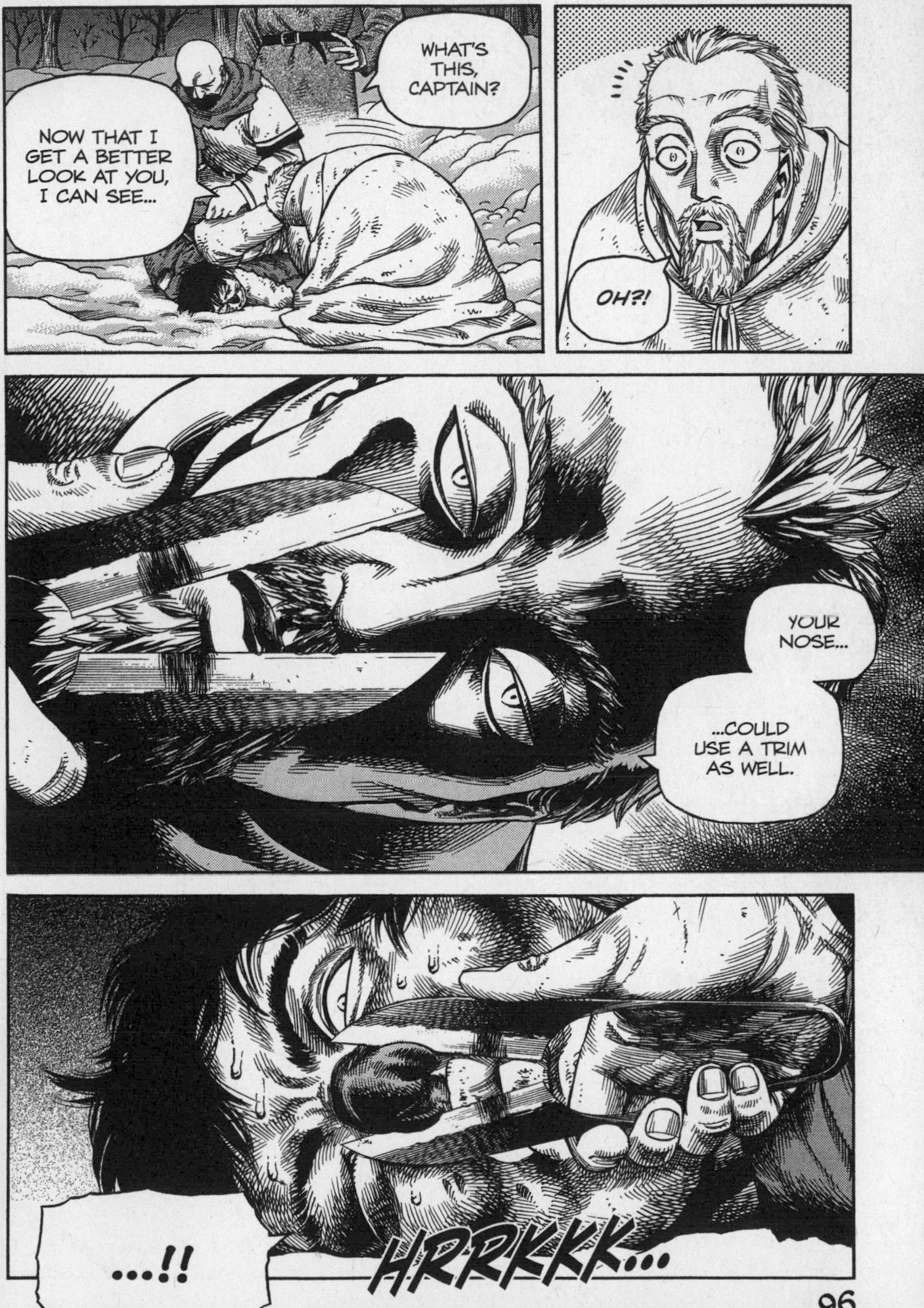
OH?!
WHAT'S THIS, CAPTAIN?
NOW THAT I GET A BETTER LOOK AT YOU, I CAN SEE...
YOUR NOSE...
...COULD USE A TRIM AS WELL.
HRRKKK...
...!!

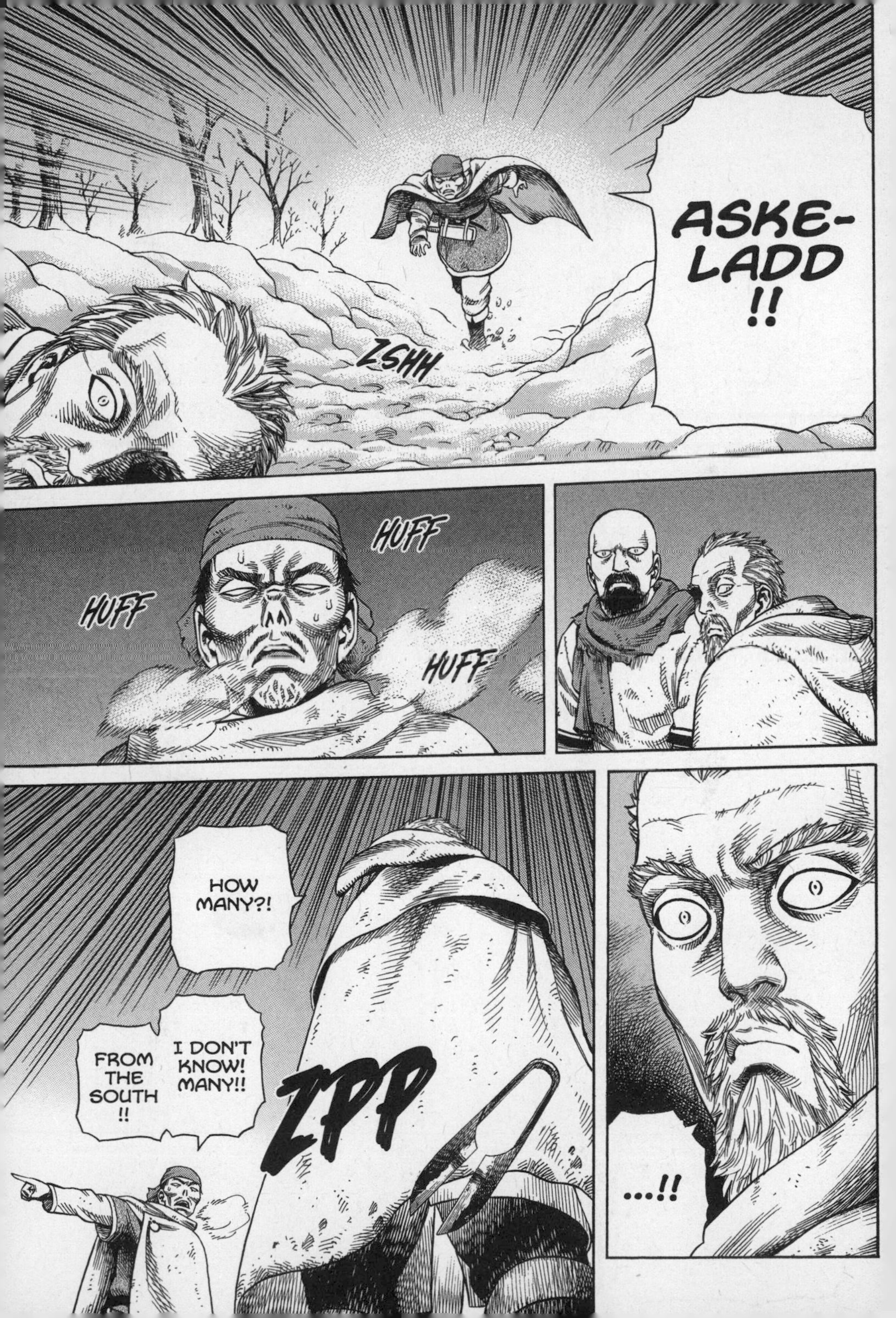
ASKE-LADD !!
ZSHH
HUFF
HUFF
HUFF
...!!
HOW MANY?!
I DON'T KNOW! MANY!!
FROM THE SOUTH !!
ZPP

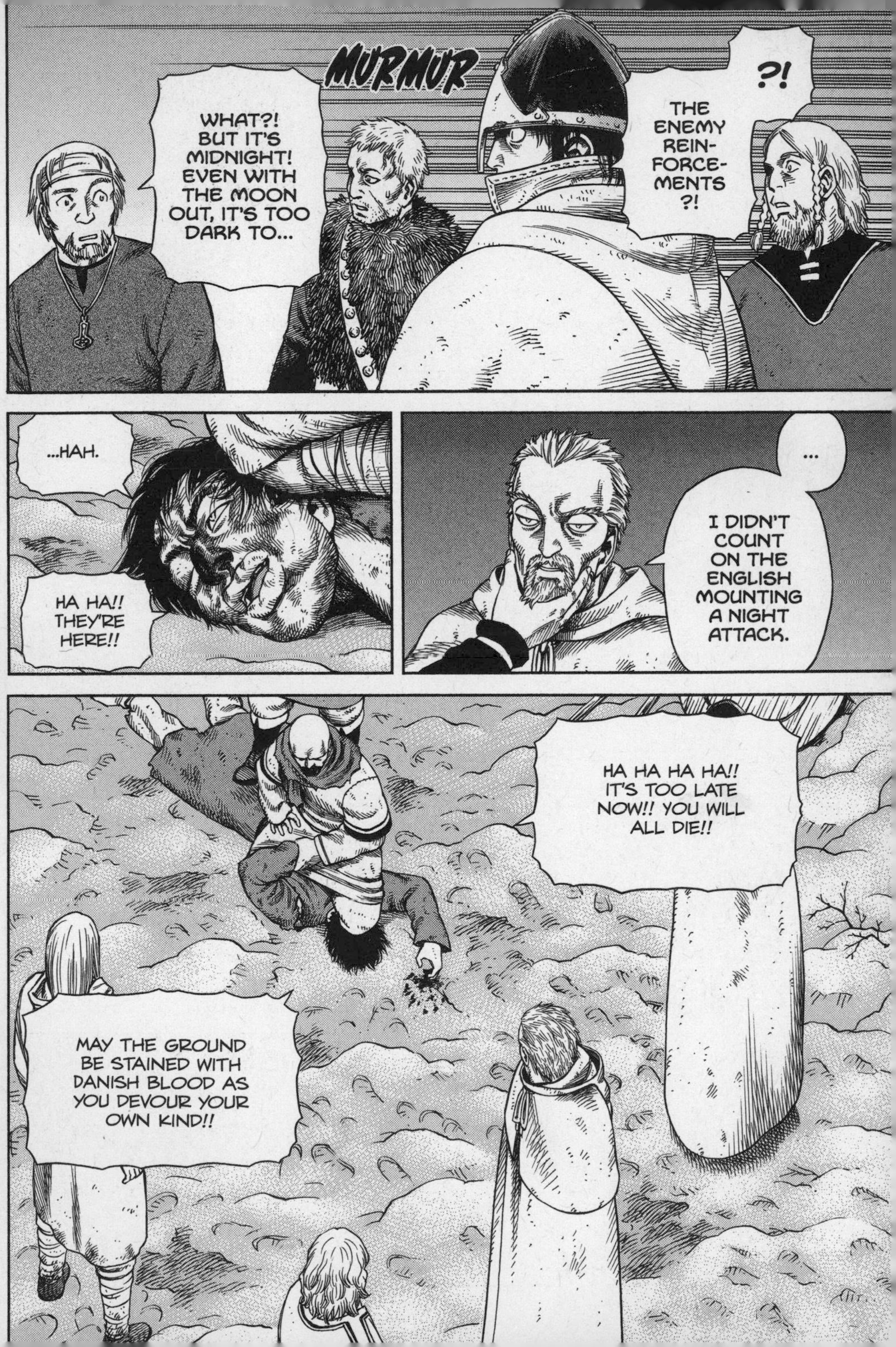
?!
THE ENEMY REIN-FORCE-MENTS?!
MURMUR
WHAT?! BUT IT'S MIDNIGHT! EVEN WITH THE MOON OUT, IT'S TOO DARK TO...
...
I DIDN'T COUNT ON THE ENGLISH MOUNTING A NIGHT ATTACK.
...HAH.
HA HA!! THEY'RE HERE!!
HA HA HA HA!! IT'S TOO LATE NOW!! YOU WILL ALL DIE!!
MAY THE GROUND BE STAINED WITH DANISH BLOOD AS YOU DEVOUR YOUR OWN KIND!!

?!

OTHER DANES?!

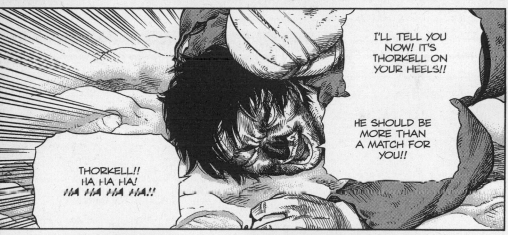

I'LL TELL YOU NOW! IT'S THORKELL ON YOUR HEELS!!

HE SHOULD BE MORE THAN A MATCH FOR YOU!!

THORKELL!! HA HA HA! HA HA HA HA!!

D-DUN-NO...

UH... DID HE JUST SAY "THOR-KELL"?

MAYBE HE DID, MAYBE HE DIDN'T...

HA HA HA HA HA HA HA HA HA HA

...TSK...

REALLY?!

THOR-KELL?!

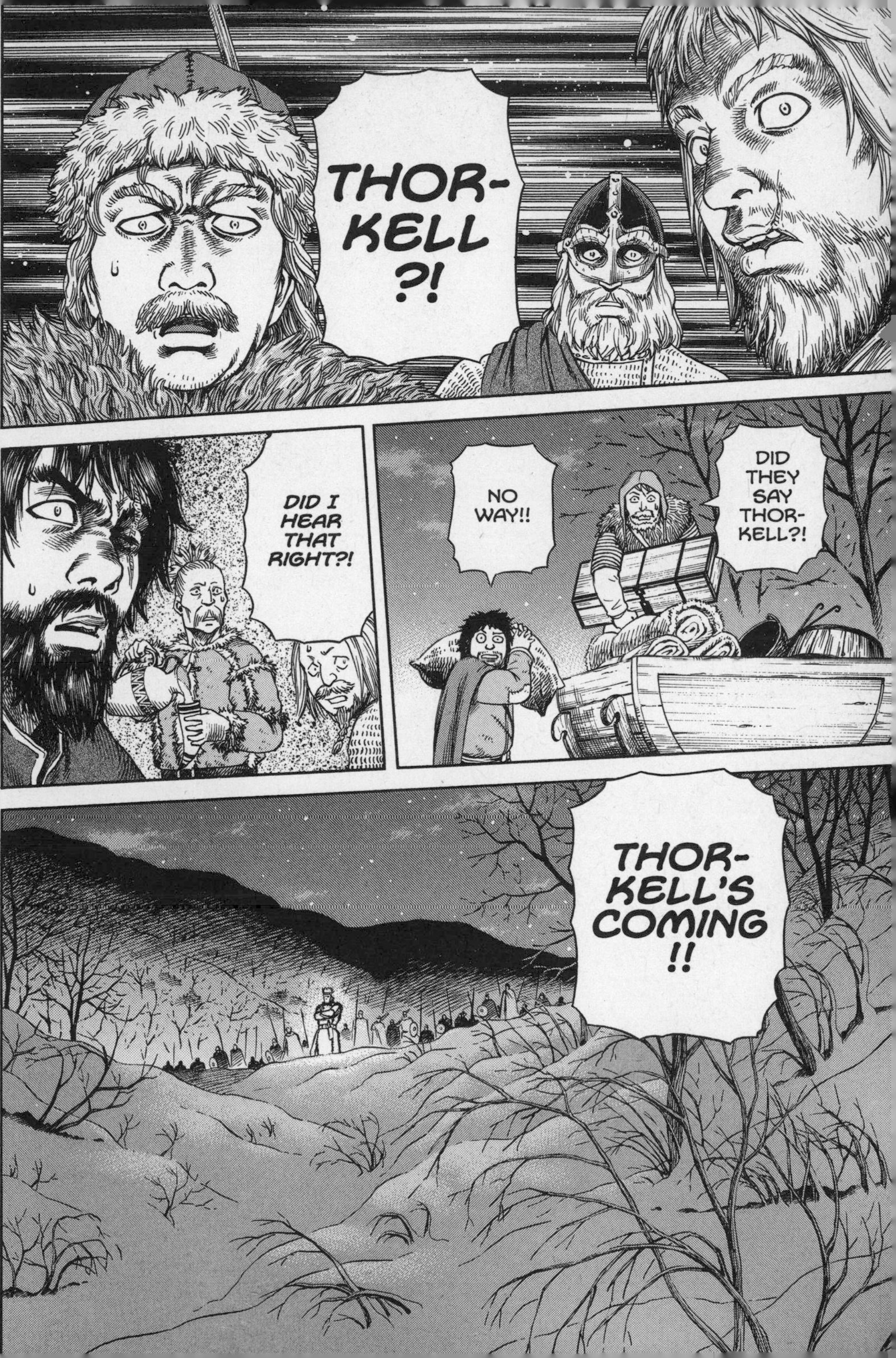
THOR-
KELL
?!
DID THEY SAY THOR-KELL?!
NO WAY!!
DID I HEAR THAT RIGHT?!
THOR-
KELL'S
COMING
!!

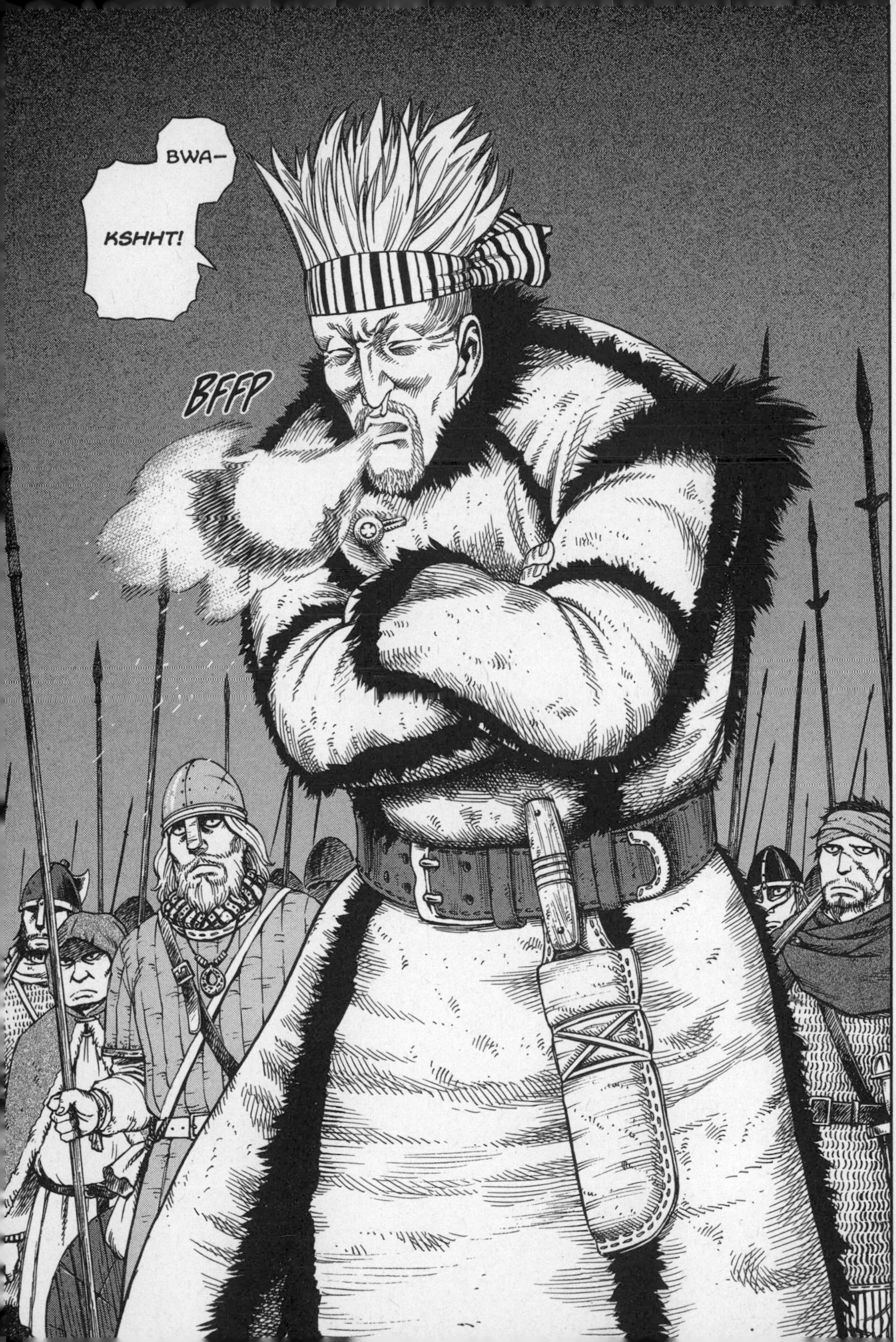
BWA-
KSHHT!
BFFP

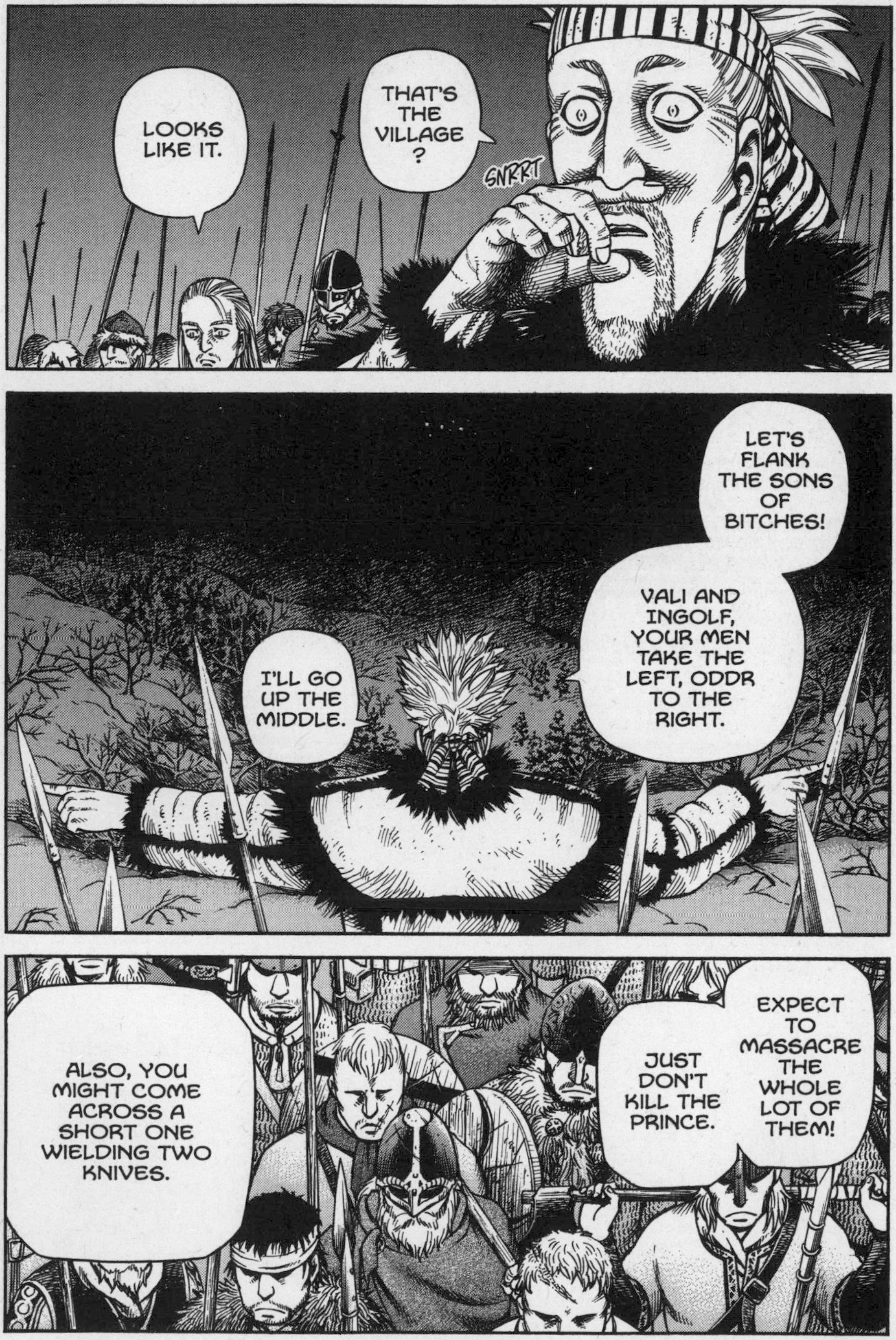
THAT'S THE VILLAGE?
SNRKT
LOOKS LIKE IT.
LET'S FLANK THE SONS OF BITCHES!
VALI AND INGOLF, YOUR MEN TAKE THE LEFT, ODDR TO THE RIGHT.
I'LL GO UP THE MIDDLE.
EXPECT TO MASSACRE THE WHOLE LOT OF THEM!
JUST DON'T KILL THE PRINCE.
ALSO, YOU MIGHT COME ACROSS A SHORT ONE WIELDING TWO KNIVES.

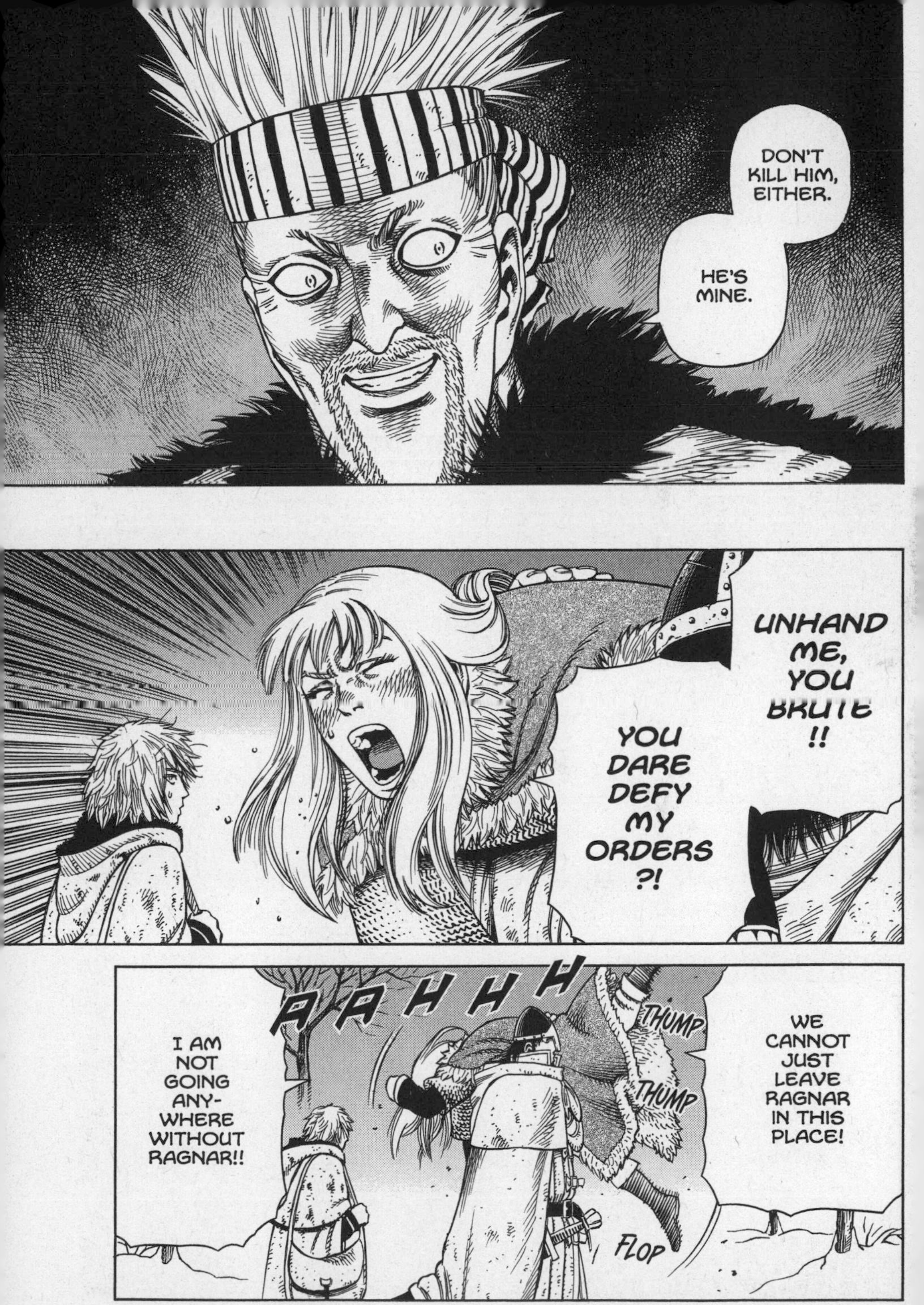
DON'T KILL HIM, EITHER.
HE'S MINE.
UNHAND ME, YOU BRUTE!!
YOU DARE DEFY MY ORDERS?!
WE CANNOT JUST LEAVE RAGNAR IN THIS PLACE!
AAHHHH
THUMP
THUMP
I AM NOT GOING ANY-WHERE WITHOUT RAGNAR!!
FLOP

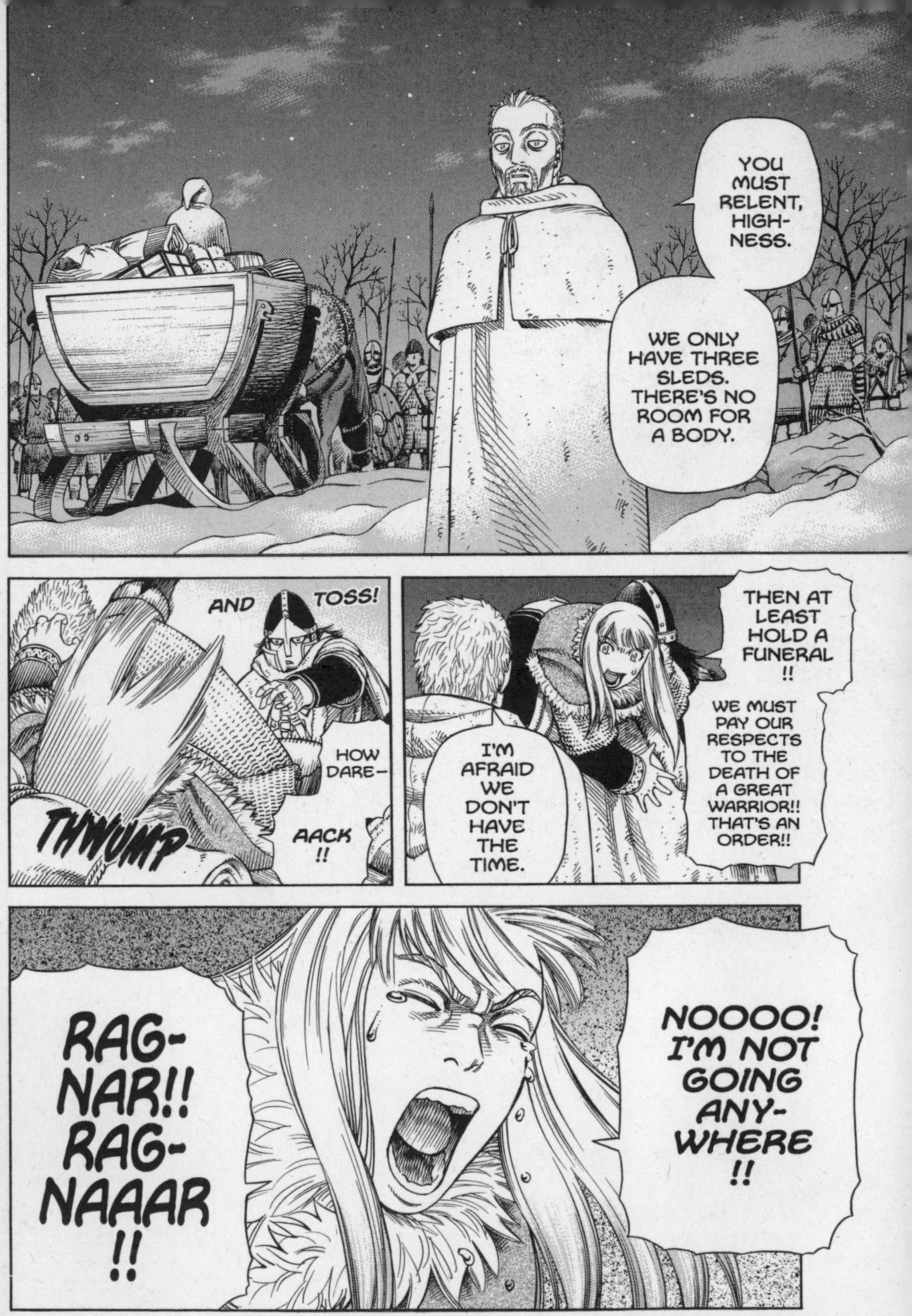
YOU MUST RELENT, HIGHNESS.
WE ONLY HAVE THREE SLEDS. THERE'S NO ROOM FOR A BODY.
THEN AT LEAST HOLD A FUNERAL!!
WE MUST PAY OUR RESPECTS TO THE DEATH OF A GREAT WARRIOR!! THAT'S AN ORDER!!
I'M AFRAID WE DON'T HAVE THE TIME.
AND TOSS!
HOW DARE—
AACK!!
THWUMP
NOOOO! I'M NOT GOING ANYWHERE!!
RAGNAR!! RAGNAAAR!!

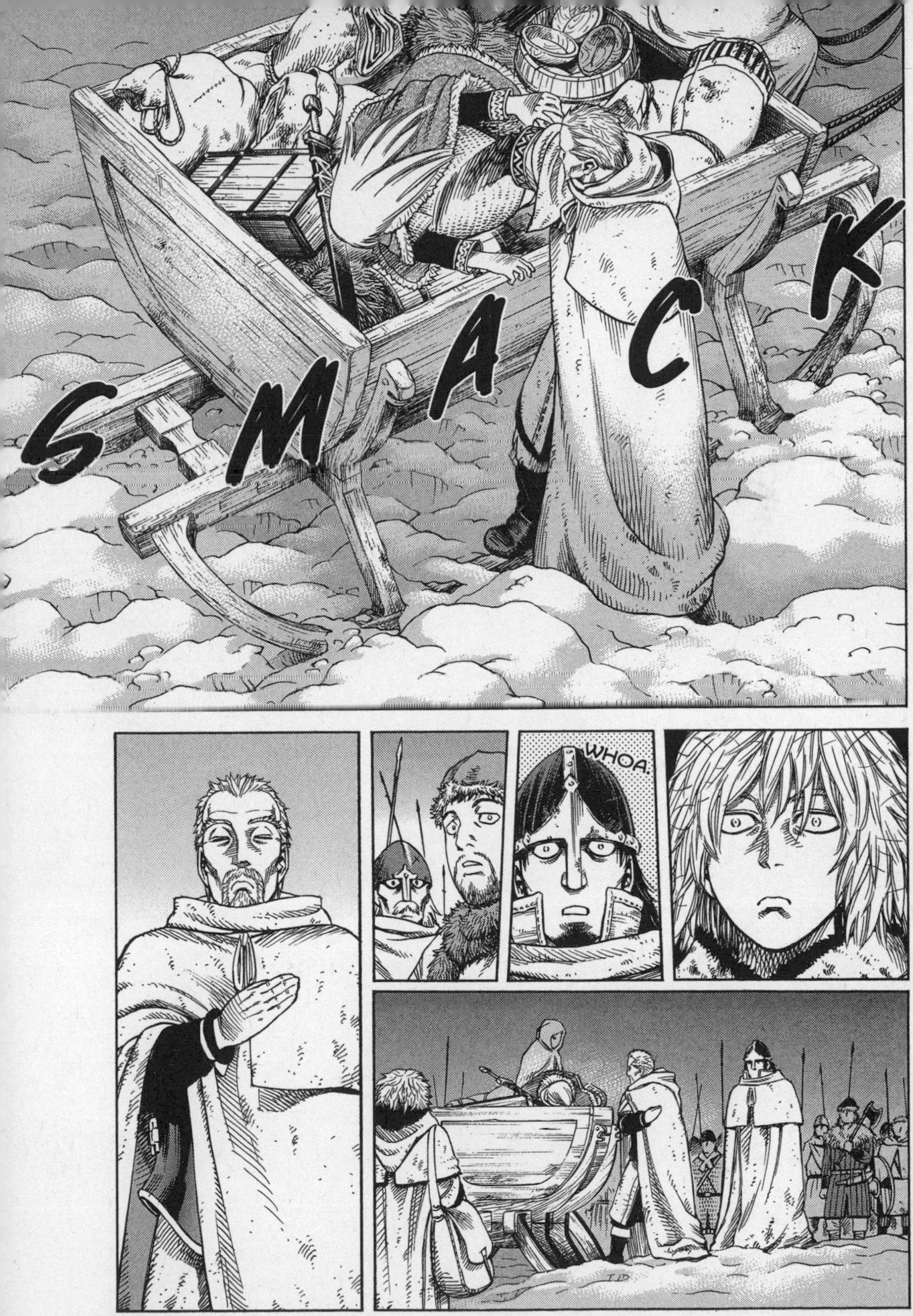
SMACK
WHOA.

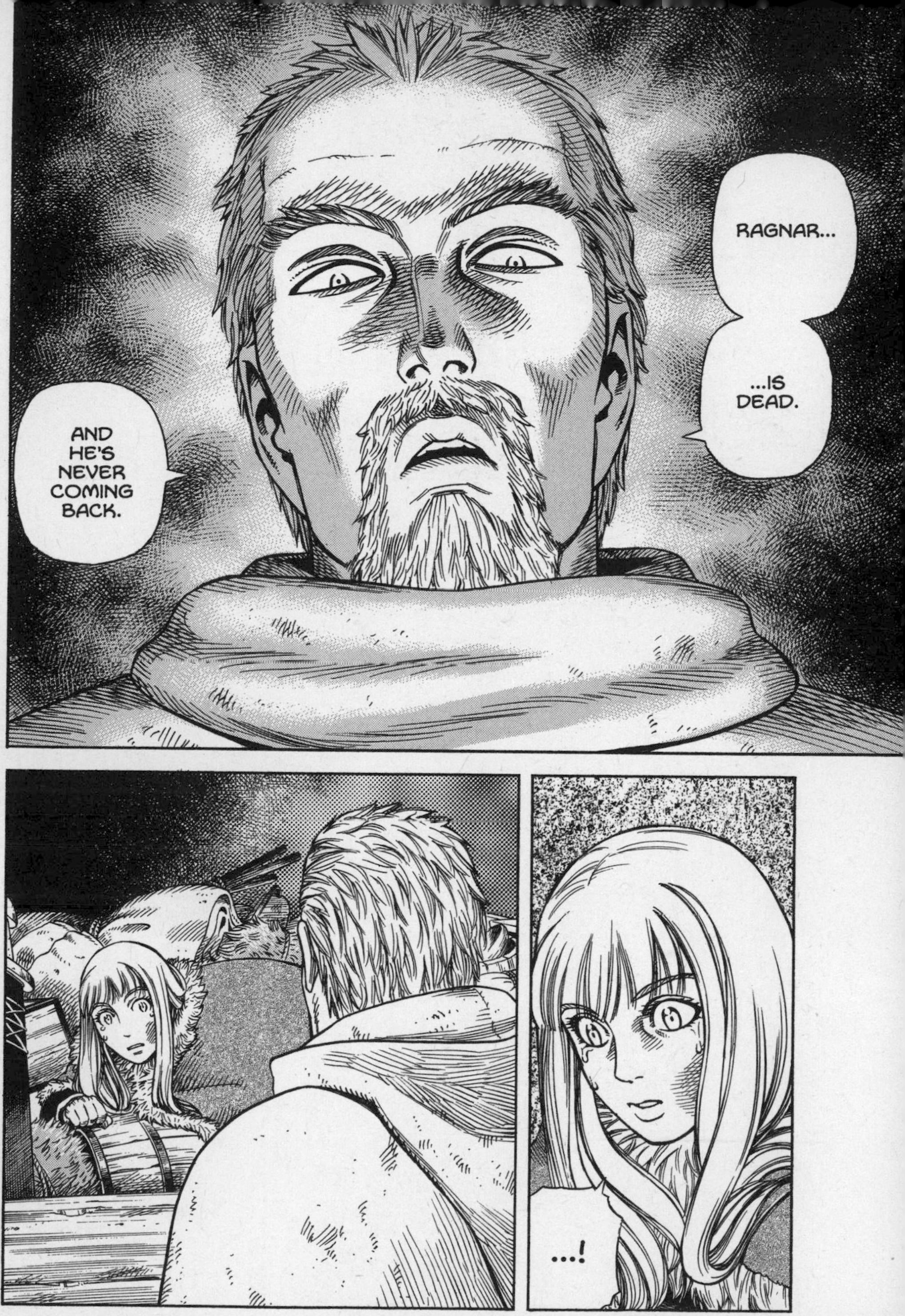
RAGNAR...
...IS DEAD.
AND HE'S NEVER COMING BACK.
...!

ASKE-LADD!!

GET MARCHING, CURSE YOU!!

...YOU...

THUD

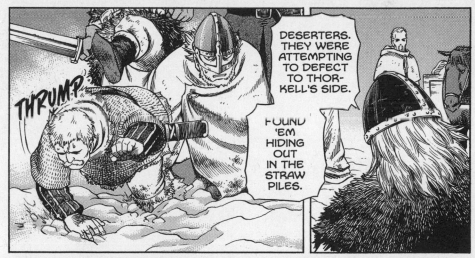

DESERTERS. THEY WERE ATTEMPTING TO DEFECT TO THOR-KELL'S SIDE.

FOUND 'EM HIDING OUT IN THE STRAW PILES.

THRUMP

R...

RAGNAR WAS RIGHT. FORTUNE HAS FORSAKEN YOU, ASKELADD...

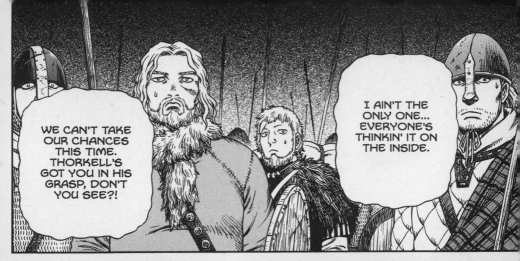

I AIN'T THE ONLY ONE... EVERYONE'S THINKIN' IT ON THE INSIDE.
WE CAN'T TAKE OUR CHANCES THIS TIME. THORKELL'S GOT YOU IN HIS GRASP, DON'T YOU SEE?!
ZSHH...
AAH...
?!
ZSH
ZUSHH

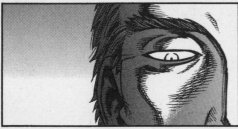

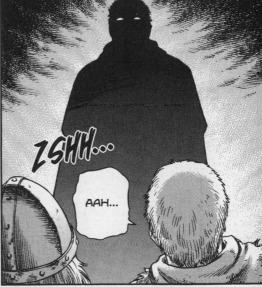

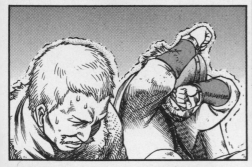

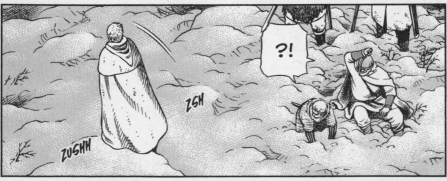

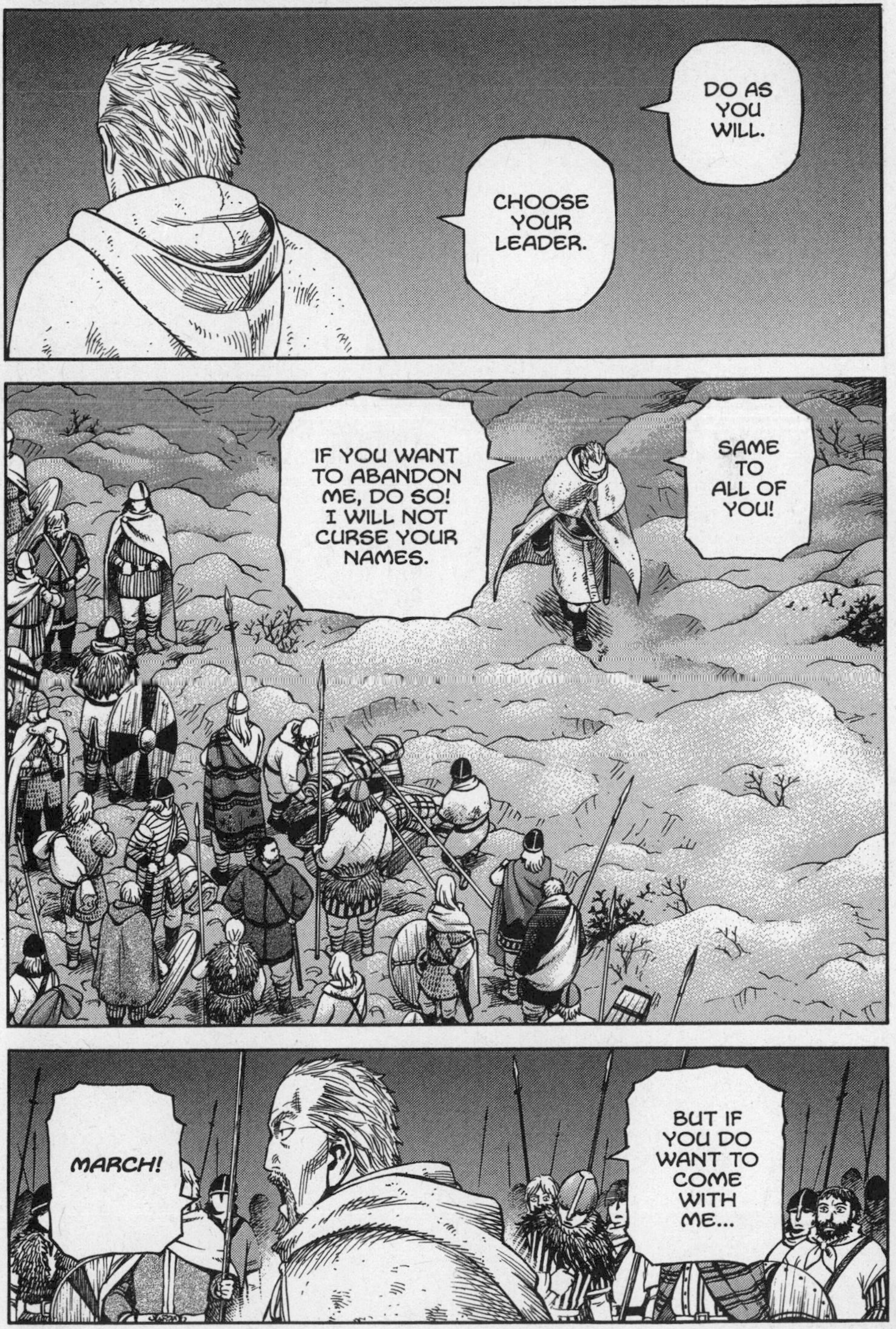
DO AS YOU WILL.
CHOOSE YOUR LEADER.
SAME TO ALL OF YOU!
IF YOU WANT TO ABANDON ME, DO SO! I WILL NOT CURSE YOUR NAMES.
BUT IF YOU DO WANT TO COME WITH ME...
MARCH!

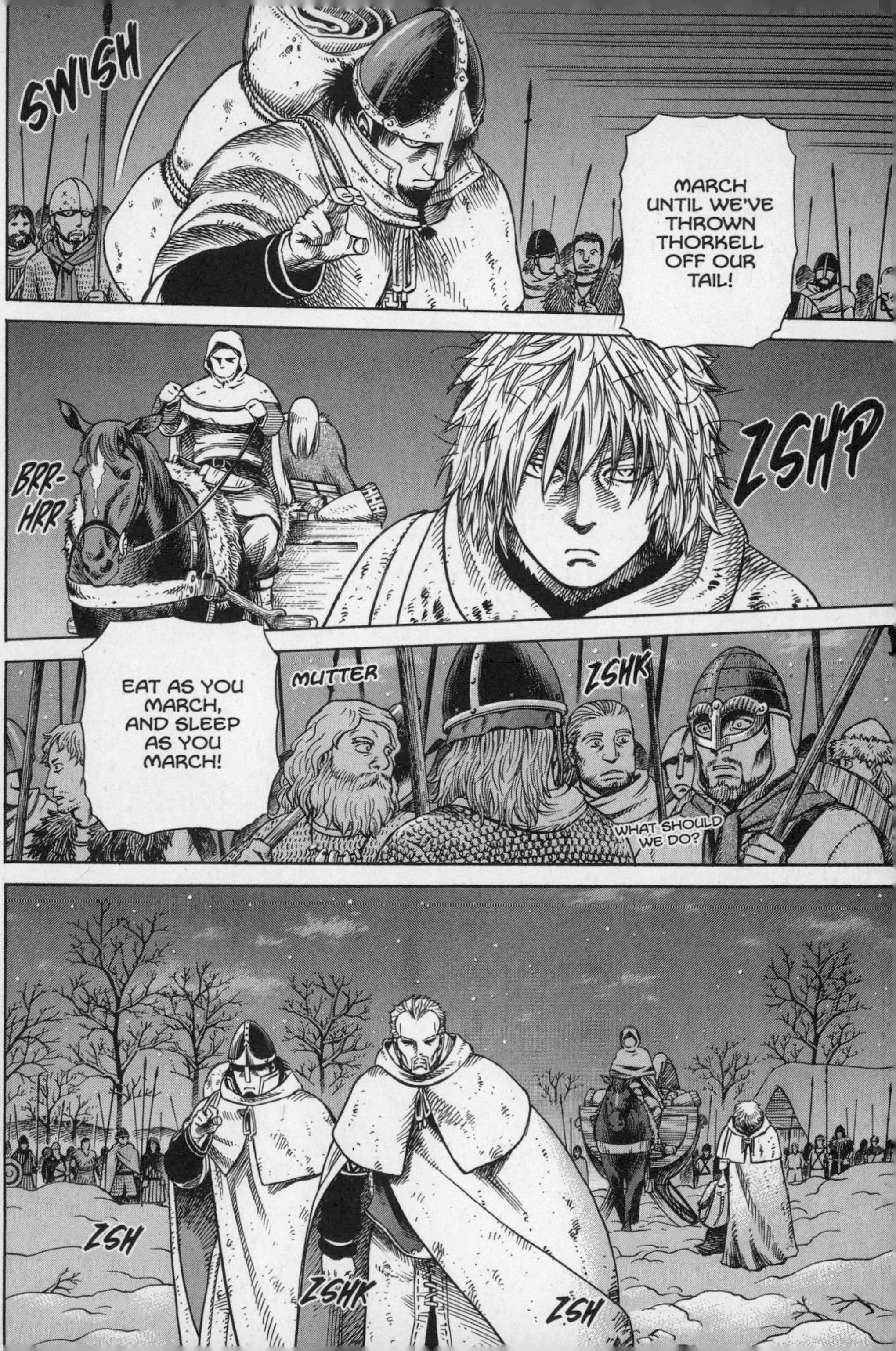
MARCH UNTIL WE'VE THROWN THORKELL OFF OUR TAIL!
SWISH
ZSHP
BRR-HRR
ZSHK
MUTTER
EAT AS YOU MARCH, AND SLEEP AS YOU MARCH!
WHAT SHOULD WE DO?
ZSH
ZSHK
ZSH

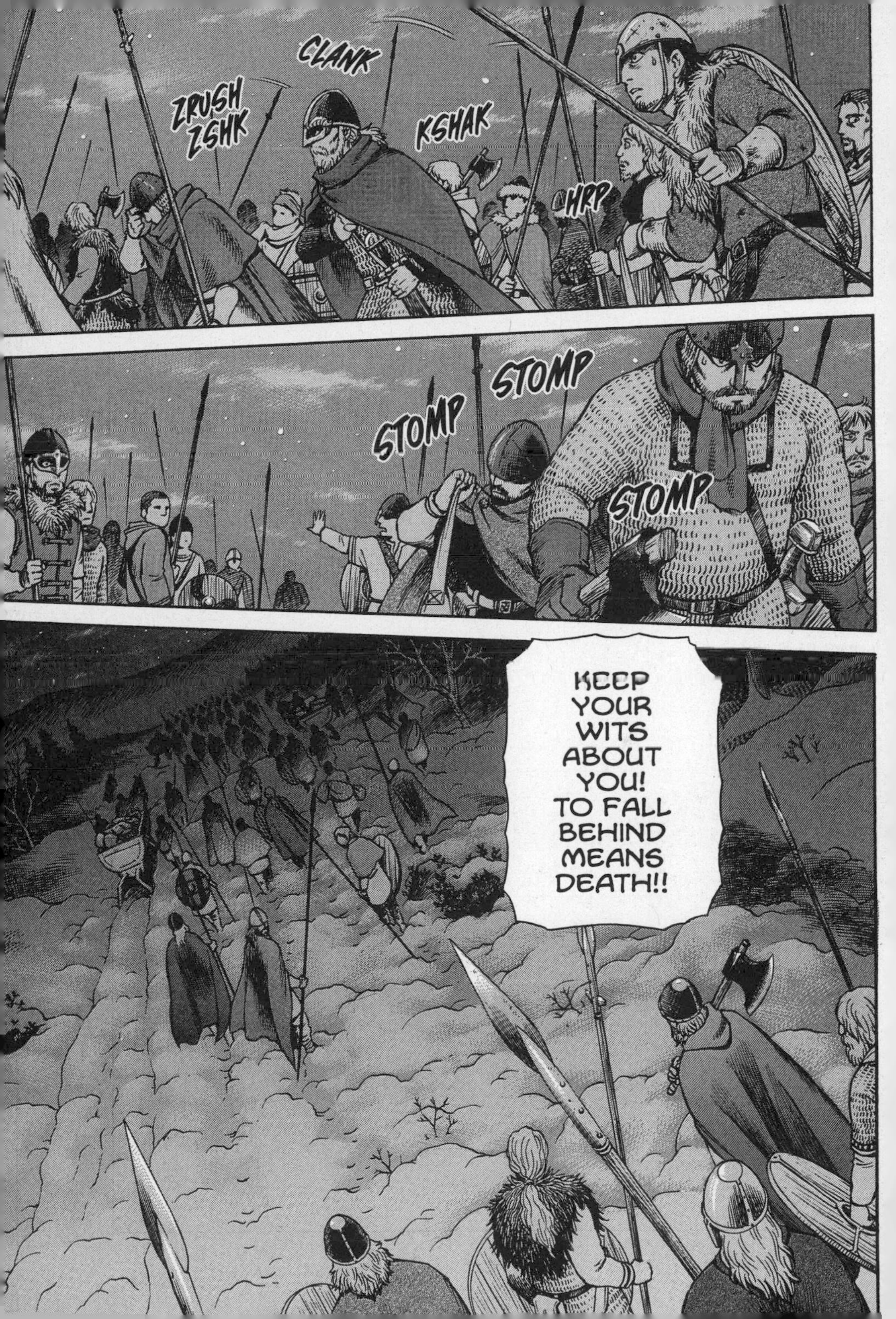
HRP
KSHAK
CLANK
ZRUSH ZSHK
STOMP
STOMP
STOMP
KEEP YOUR WITS ABOUT YOU! TO FALL BEHIND MEANS DEATH!!

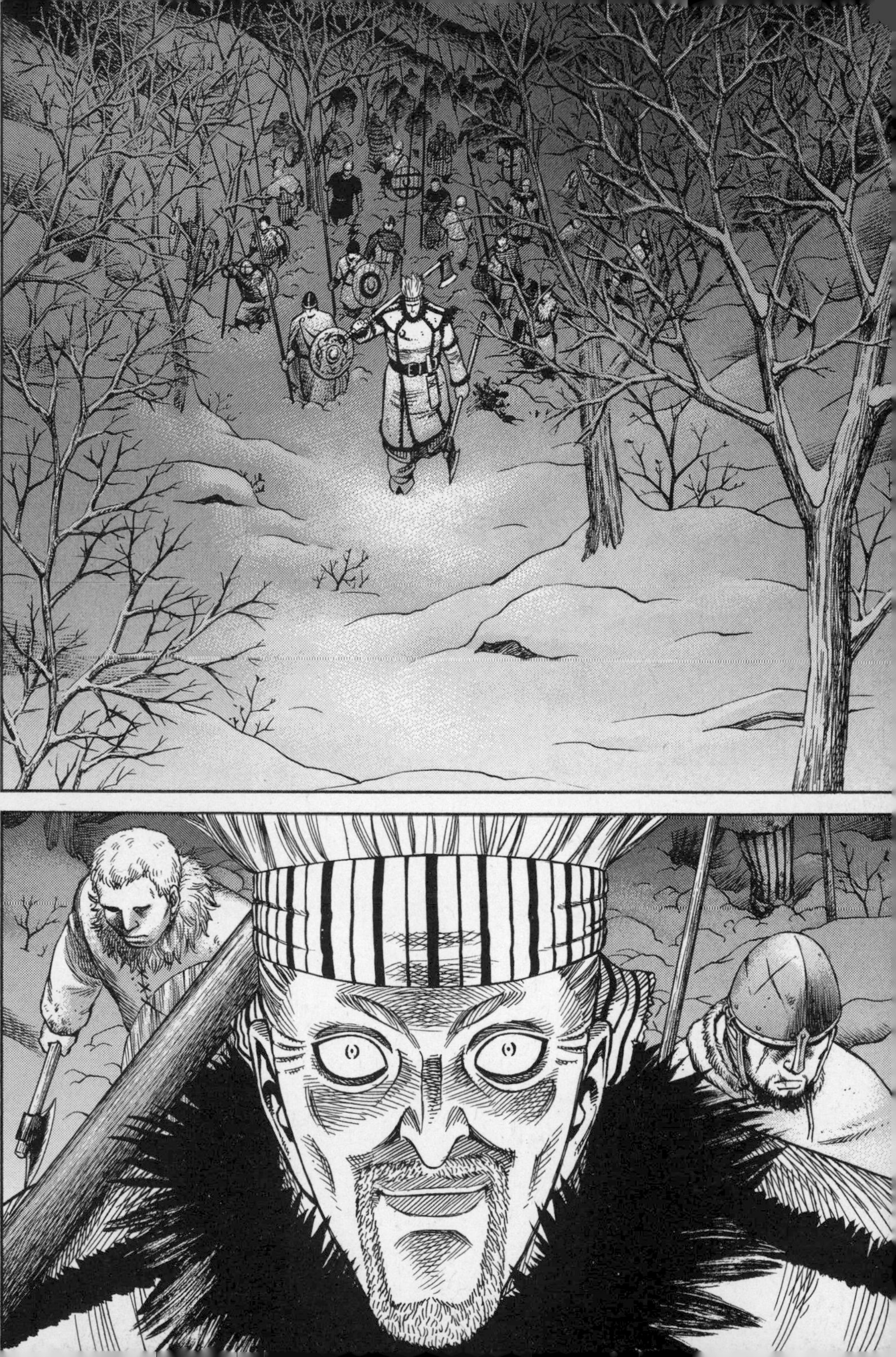

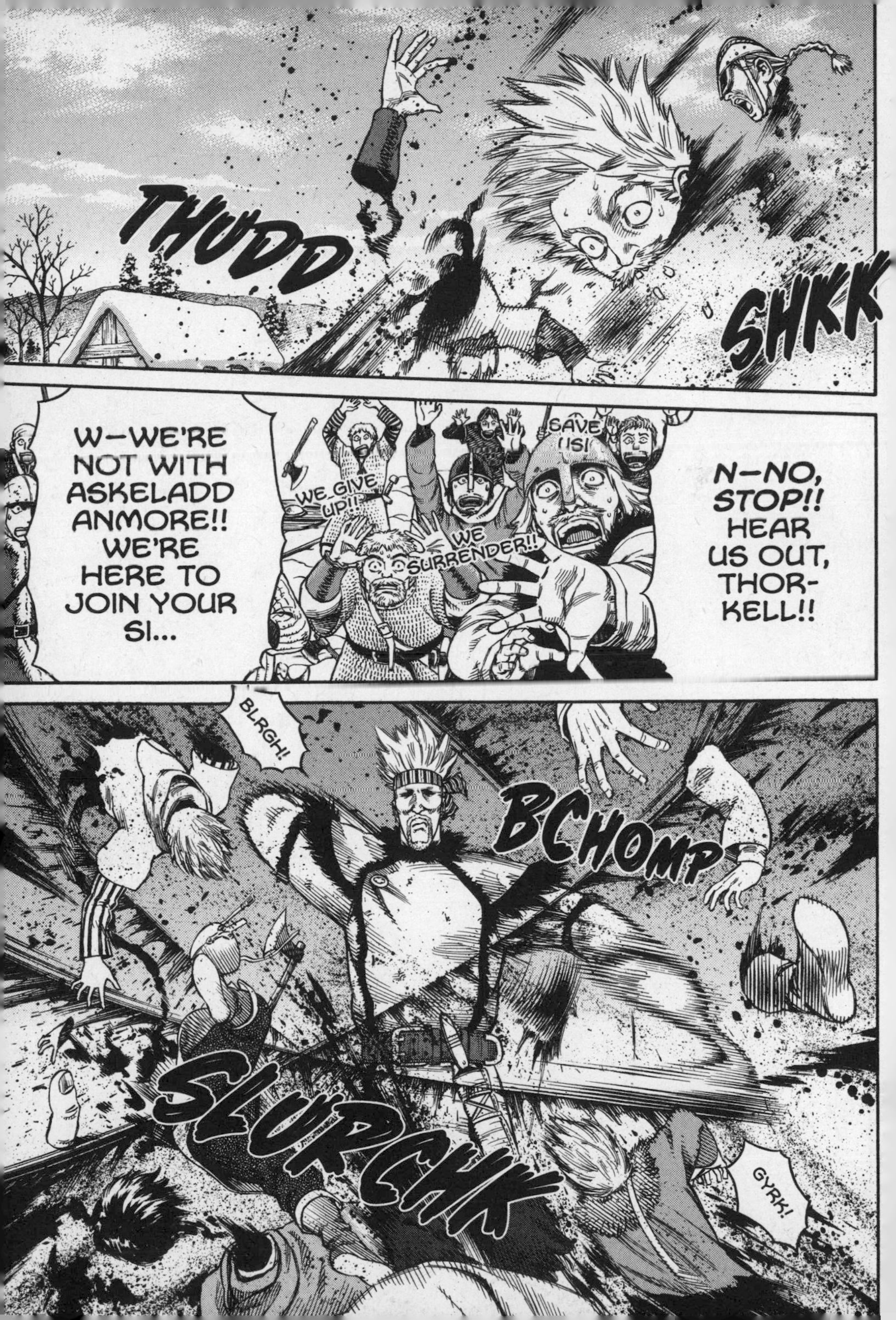
SHKK
THUDD
N-NO, STOP!! HEAR US OUT, THOR-KELL!!
SAVE US!
WE GIVE UP!!
WE SURRENDER!!
W-WE'RE NOT WITH ASKELADD ANMORE!! WE'RE HERE TO JOIN YOUR SI...
BLRGH!!
BCHOMP
GYRK!
SLURCHK

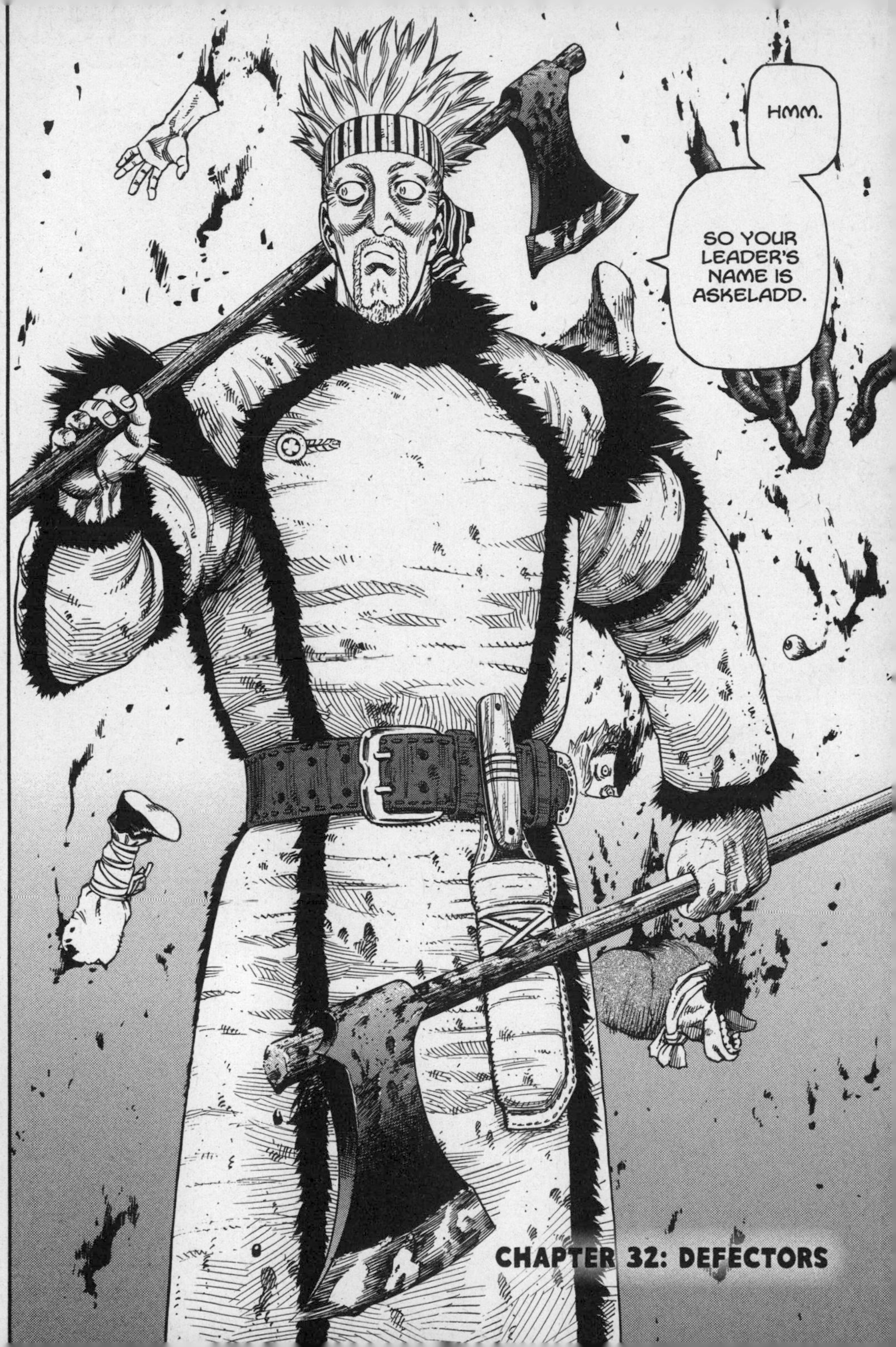
HMM.
SO YOUR LEADER'S NAME IS ASKELADD.

## CHAPTER 32: DEFECTORS

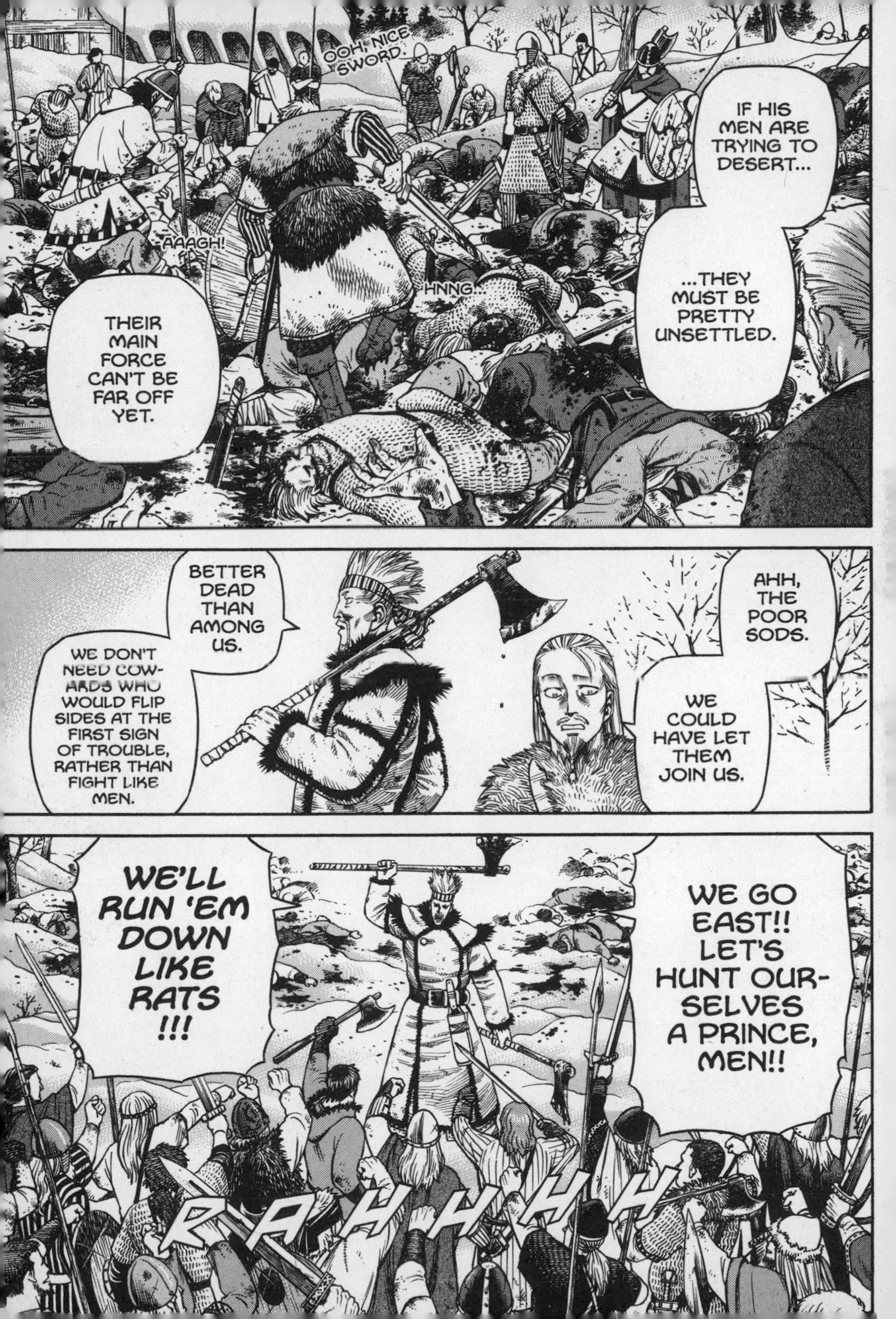
IF HIS MEN ARE TRYING TO DESERT...
...THEY MUST BE PRETTY UNSETTLED.
OOH, NICE SWORD.
AAAGH!
HNNG..
THEIR MAIN FORCE CAN'T BE FAR OFF YET.
AHH, THE POOR SODS.
WE COULD HAVE LET THEM JOIN US.
BETTER DEAD THAN AMONG US.
WE DON'T NEED COW-ARDS WHO WOULD FLIP SIDES AT THE FIRST SIGN OF TROUBLE, RATHER THAN FIGHT LIKE MEN.
WE GO EAST!! LET'S HUNT OUR-SELVES A PRINCE, MEN!!
WE'LL RUN 'EM DOWN LIKE RATS!!!
RAHHHH

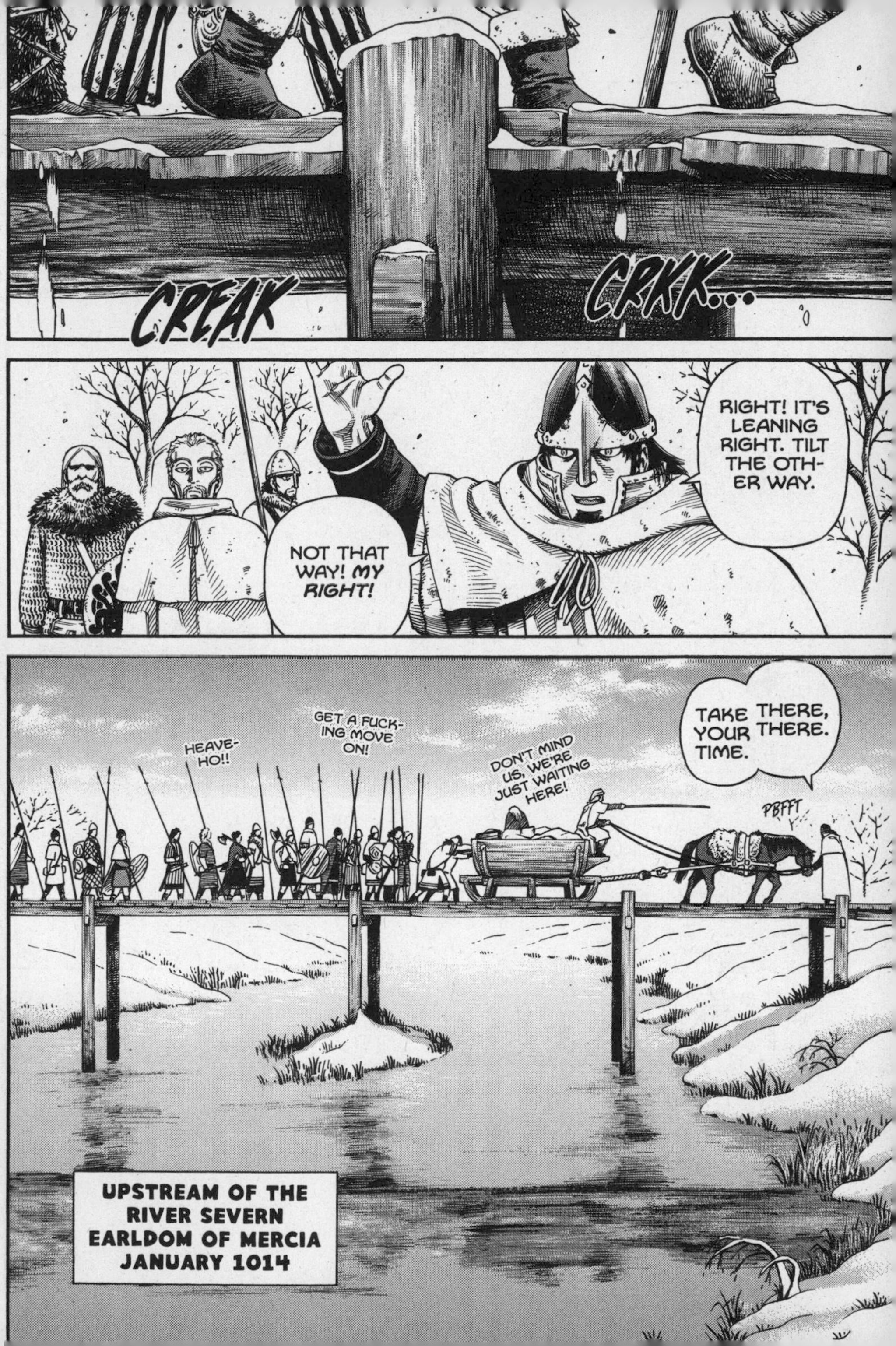
CRKK...
CREAK
RIGHT! IT'S LEANING RIGHT. TILT THE OTHER WAY.
NOT THAT WAY! MY RIGHT!
THERE, THERE. TAKE YOUR TIME.
PBFFT
DON'T MIND US, WE'RE JUST WAITING HERE!
GET A FUCKING MOVE ON!
HEAVE-HO!!
UPSTREAM OF THE RIVER SEVERN
EARLDOM OF MERCIA
JANUARY 1014

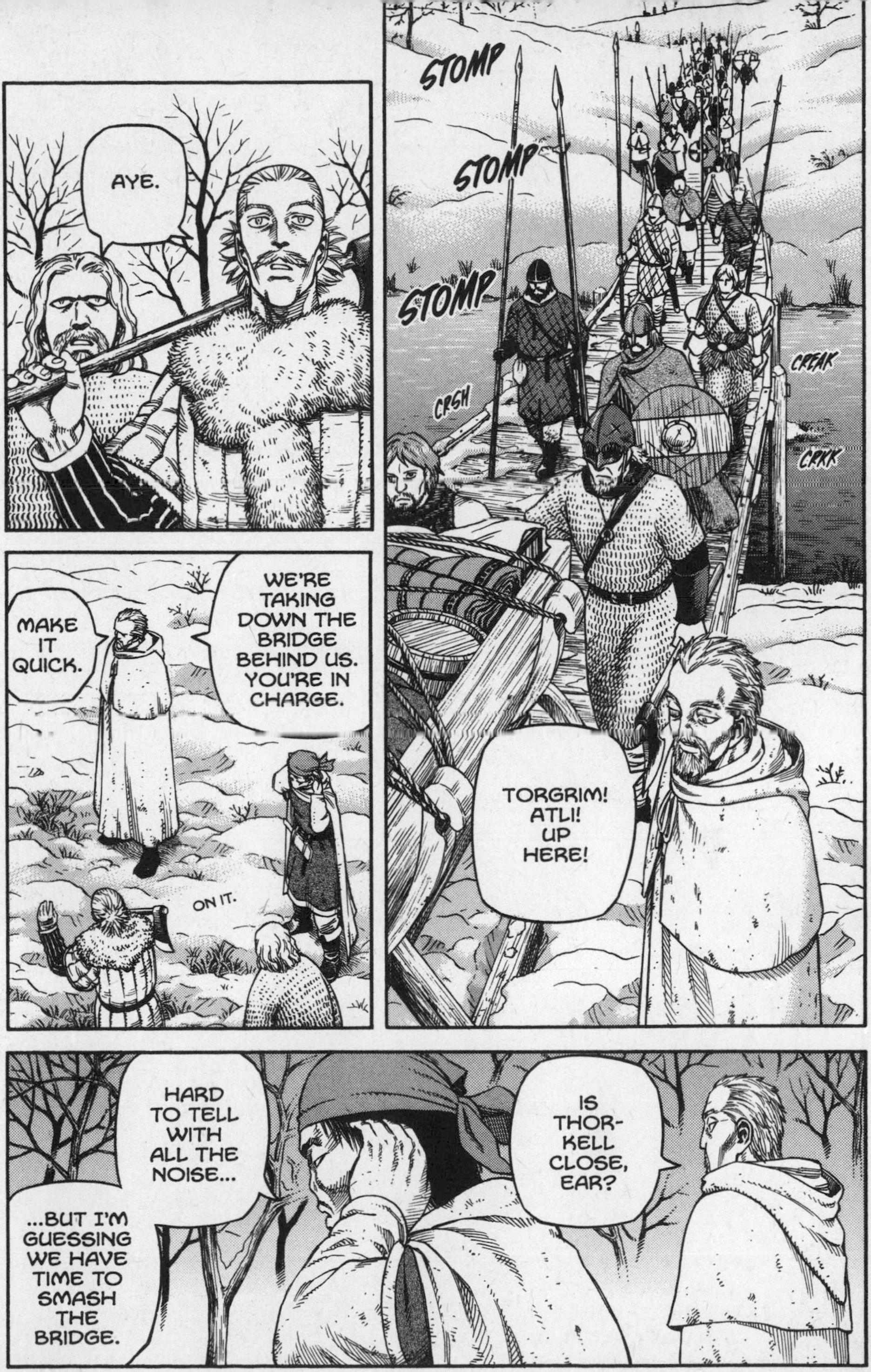
STOMP
STOMP
STOMP
CREAK
CRSH
CRKK
TORGRIM! ATLI! UP HERE!
AYE.
WE'RE TAKING DOWN THE BRIDGE BEHIND US. YOU'RE IN CHARGE.
MAKE IT QUICK.
ON IT.
IS THOR-KELL CLOSE, EAR?
HARD TO TELL WITH ALL THE NOISE...
...BUT I'M GUESSING WE HAVE TIME TO SMASH THE BRIDGE.

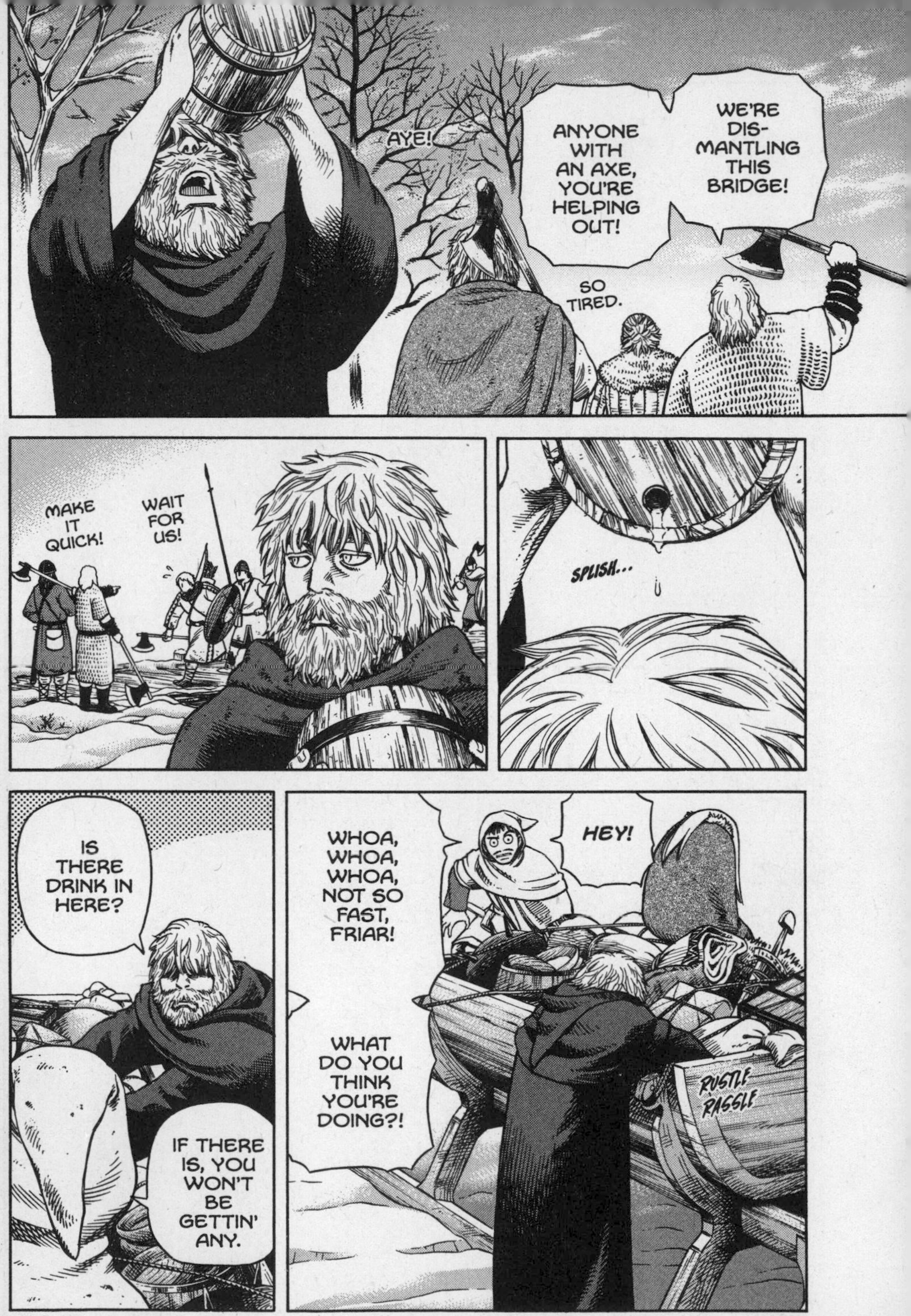
WE'RE DIS-MANTLING THIS BRIDGE!
ANYONE WITH AN AXE, YOU'RE HELPING OUT!
SO TIRED.
AYE!
SPLISH...
WAIT FOR US!
MAKE IT QUICK!
HEY!
WHOA, WHOA, WHOA, NOT SO FAST, FRIAR!
RUSTLE RASSLE
WHAT DO YOU THINK YOU'RE DOING?!
IS THERE DRINK IN HERE?
IF THERE IS, YOU WON'T BE GETTIN' ANY.

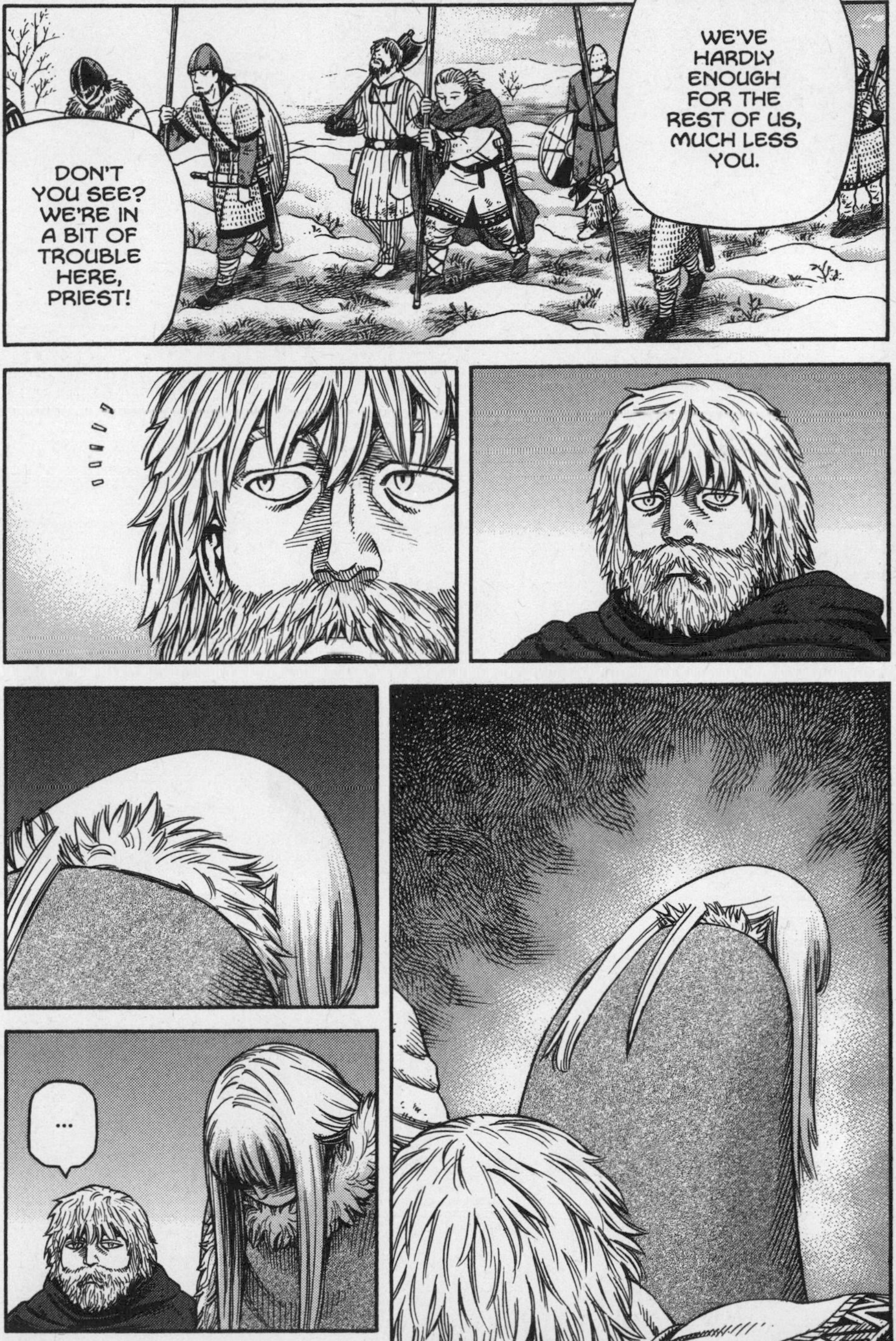
WE'VE HARDLY ENOUGH FOR THE REST OF US, MUCH LESS YOU.
DON'T YOU SEE? WE'RE IN A BIT OF TROUBLE HERE, PRIEST!
...

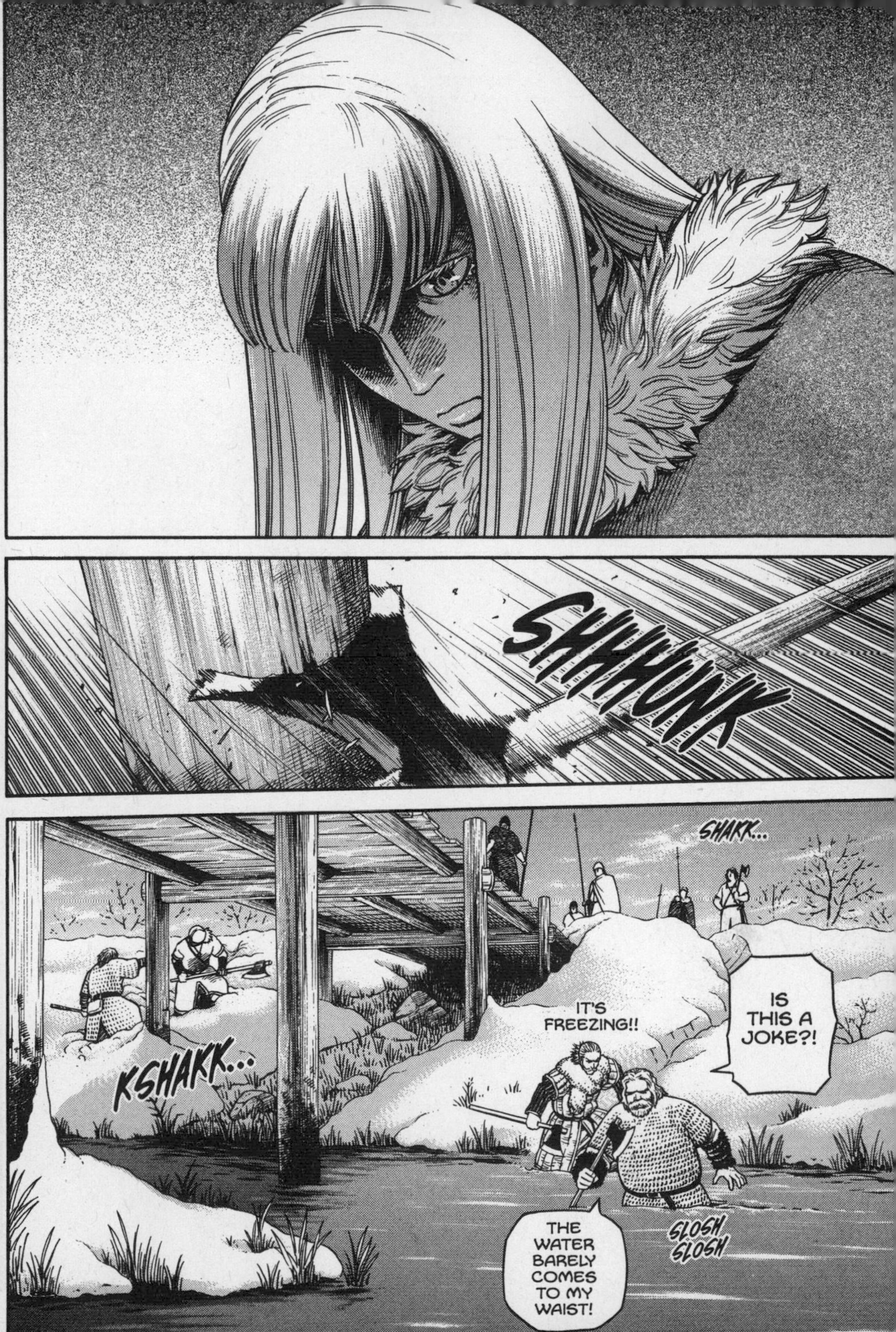
SHHHUNK
SHAKK...
IS THIS A JOKE?!
IT'S FREEZING!!
KSHAKK...
SLOSH SLOSH
THE WATER BARELY COMES TO MY WAIST!

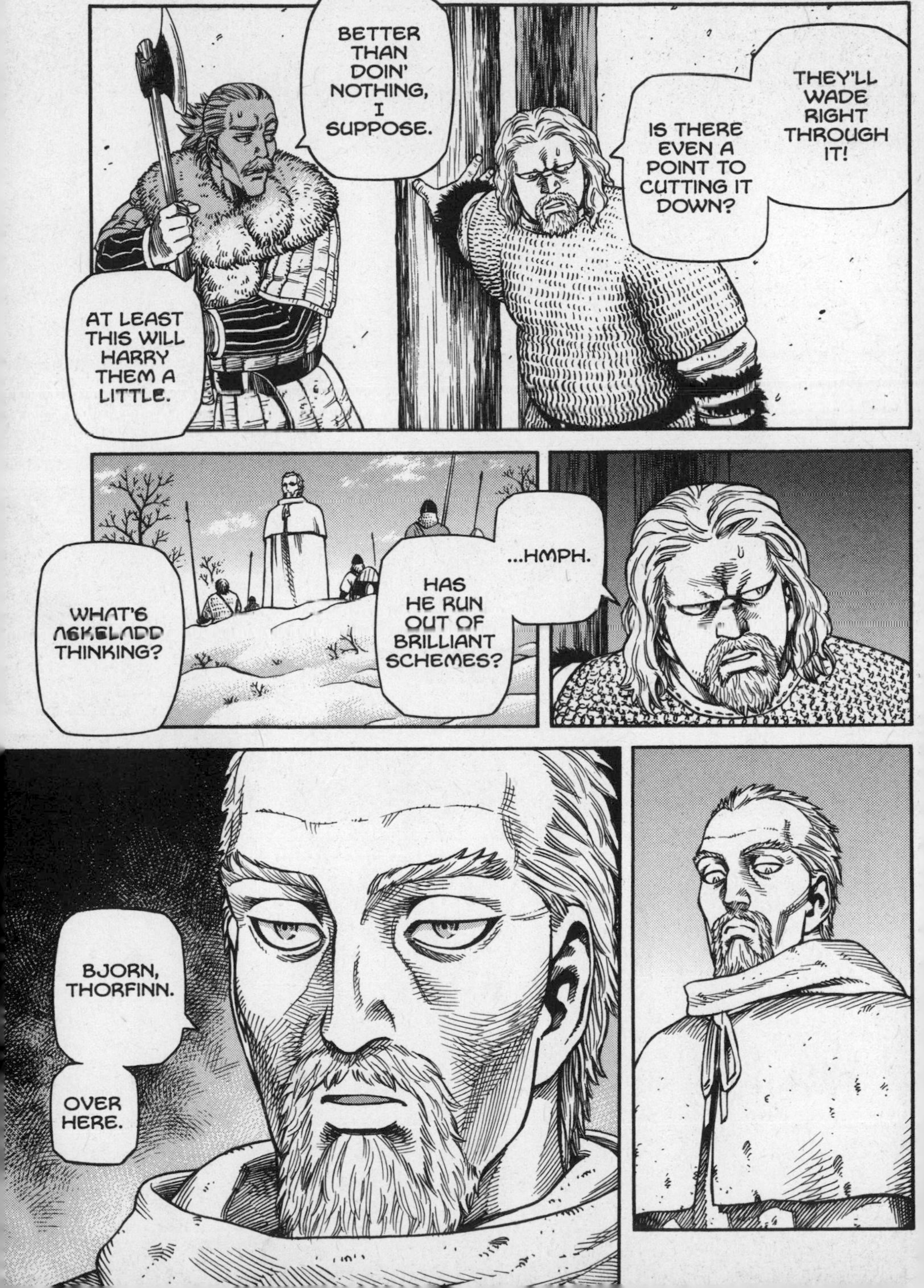
THEY'LL WADE RIGHT THROUGH IT!
IS THERE EVEN A POINT TO CUTTING IT DOWN?
BETTER THAN DOIN' NOTHING, I SUPPOSE.
AT LEAST THIS WILL HARRY THEM A LITTLE.
...HMPH.
HAS HE RUN OUT OF BRILLIANT SCHEMES?
WHAT'S ASKELADD THINKING?
BJORN, THORFINN.
OVER HERE.

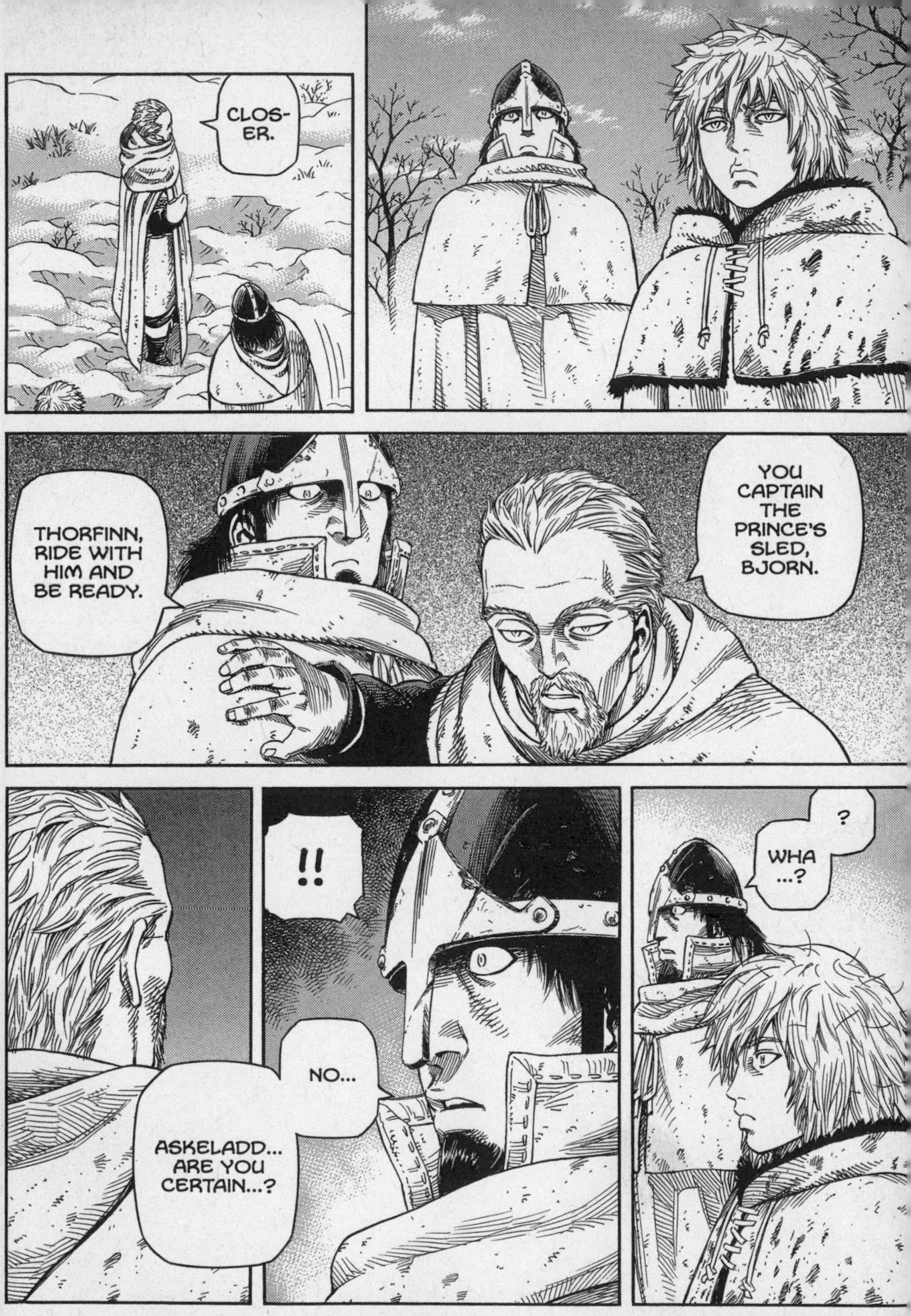
CLOS-ER.
YOU CAPTAIN THE PRINCE'S SLED, BJORN.
THORFINN, RIDE WITH HIM AND BE READY.
?
WHA ...?
!!
NO...
ASKELADD... ARE YOU CERTAIN...?

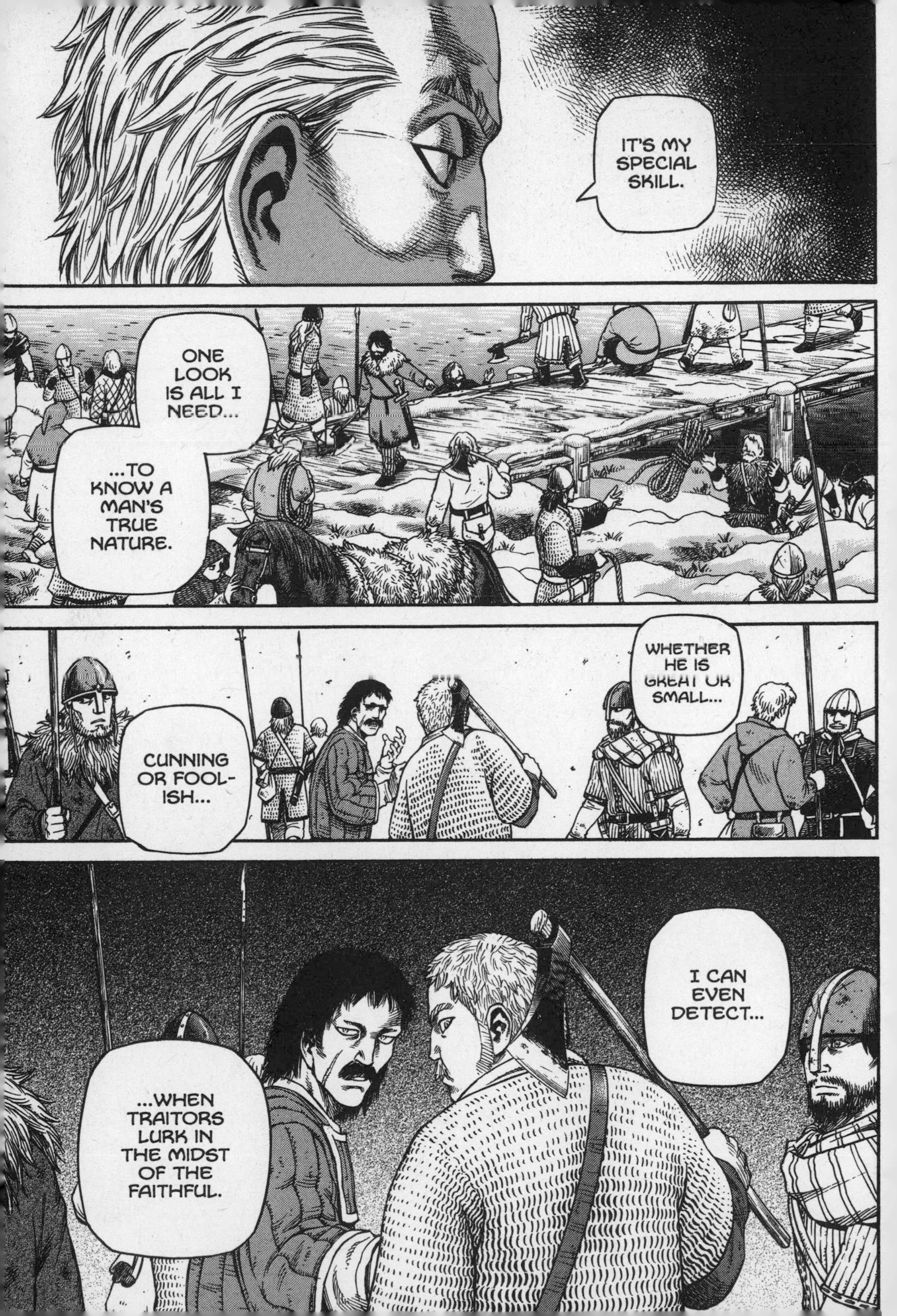
IT'S MY SPECIAL SKILL.
ONE LOOK IS ALL I NEED...
...TO KNOW A MAN'S TRUE NATURE.
WHETHER HE IS GREAT OR SMALL...
CUNNING OR FOOL-ISH...
I CAN EVEN DETECT...
...WHEN TRAITORS LURK IN THE MIDST OF THE FAITHFUL.

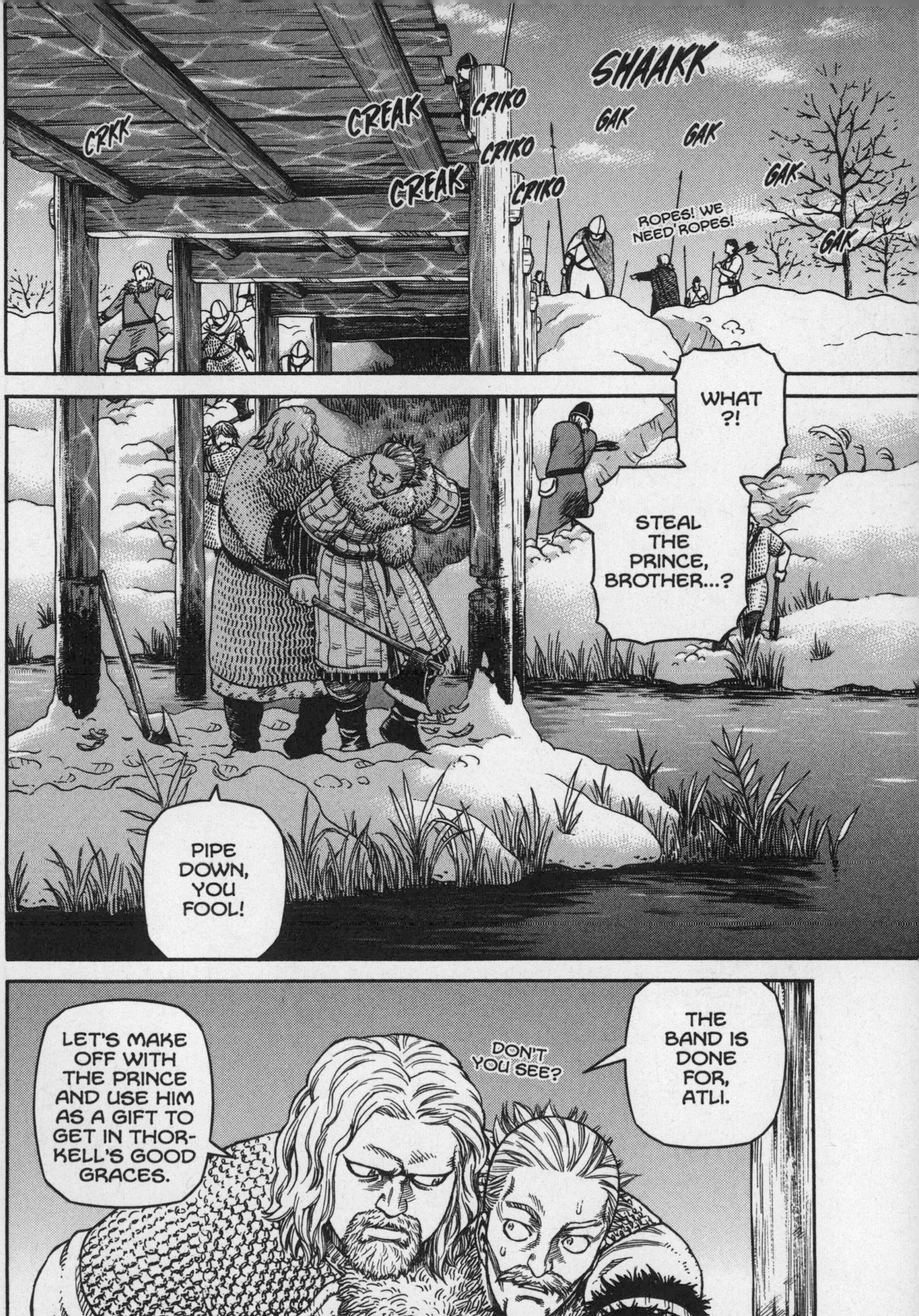
SHAAKK
GAK
GAK
GAK
GAK
ROPES! WE NEED ROPES!
CRIKO
CRIKO
CRIKO
CREAK
CREAK
CRKK
WHAT?!
STEAL THE PRINCE, BROTHER...?
PIPE DOWN, YOU FOOL!
THE BAND IS DONE FOR, ATLI.
DON'T YOU SEE?
LET'S MAKE OFF WITH THE PRINCE AND USE HIM AS A GIFT TO GET IN THORKELL'S GOOD GRACES.

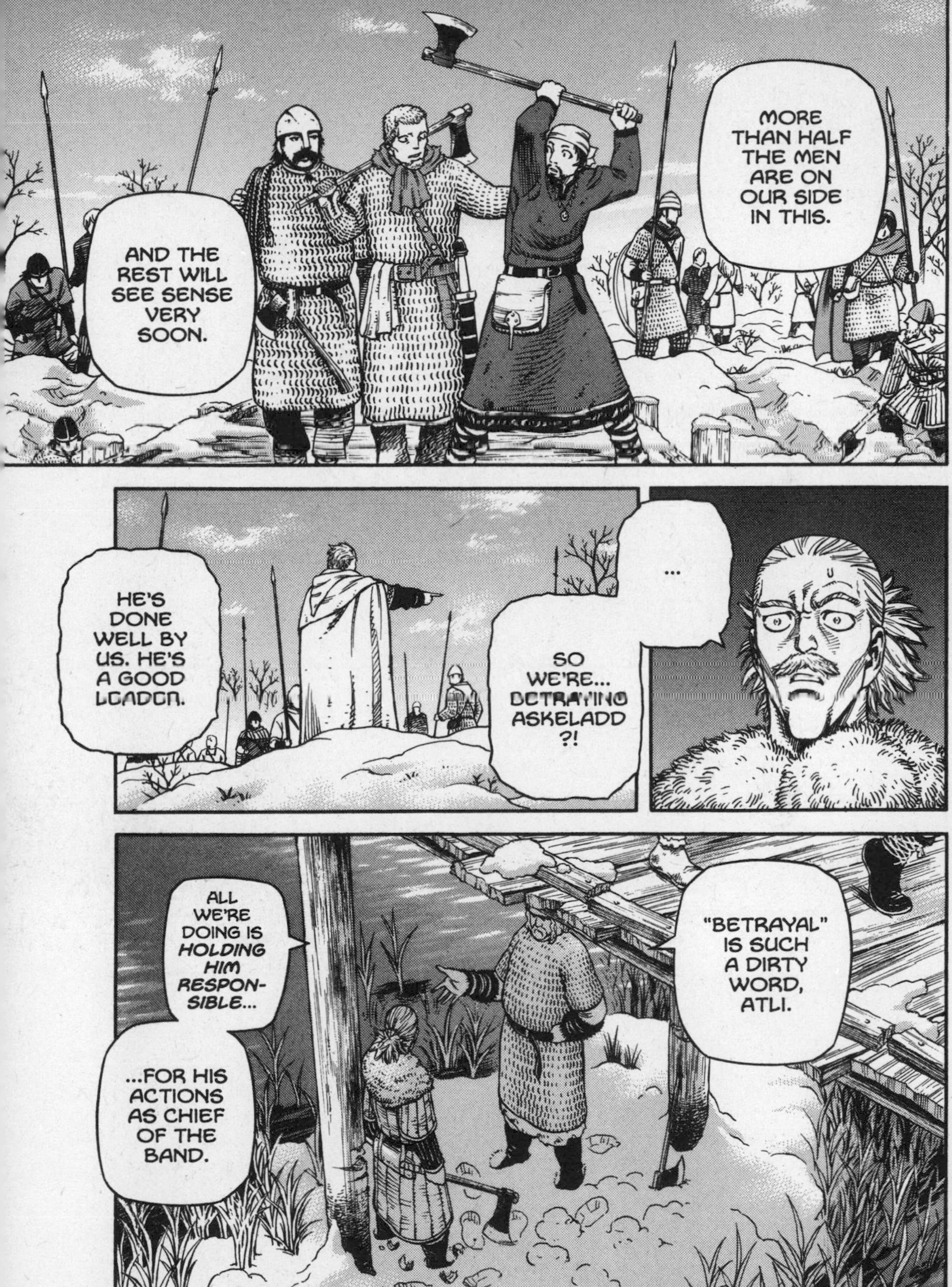
MORE THAN HALF THE MEN ARE ON OUR SIDE IN THIS.
AND THE REST WILL SEE SENSE VERY SOON.
...
SO WE'RE... BETRAYING ASKELADD?!
HE'S DONE WELL BY US. HE'S A GOOD LEADER.
"BETRAYAL" IS SUCH A DIRTY WORD, ATLI.
ALL WE'RE DOING IS *HOLDING HIM RESPONSIBLE*...
...FOR HIS ACTIONS AS CHIEF OF THE BAND.

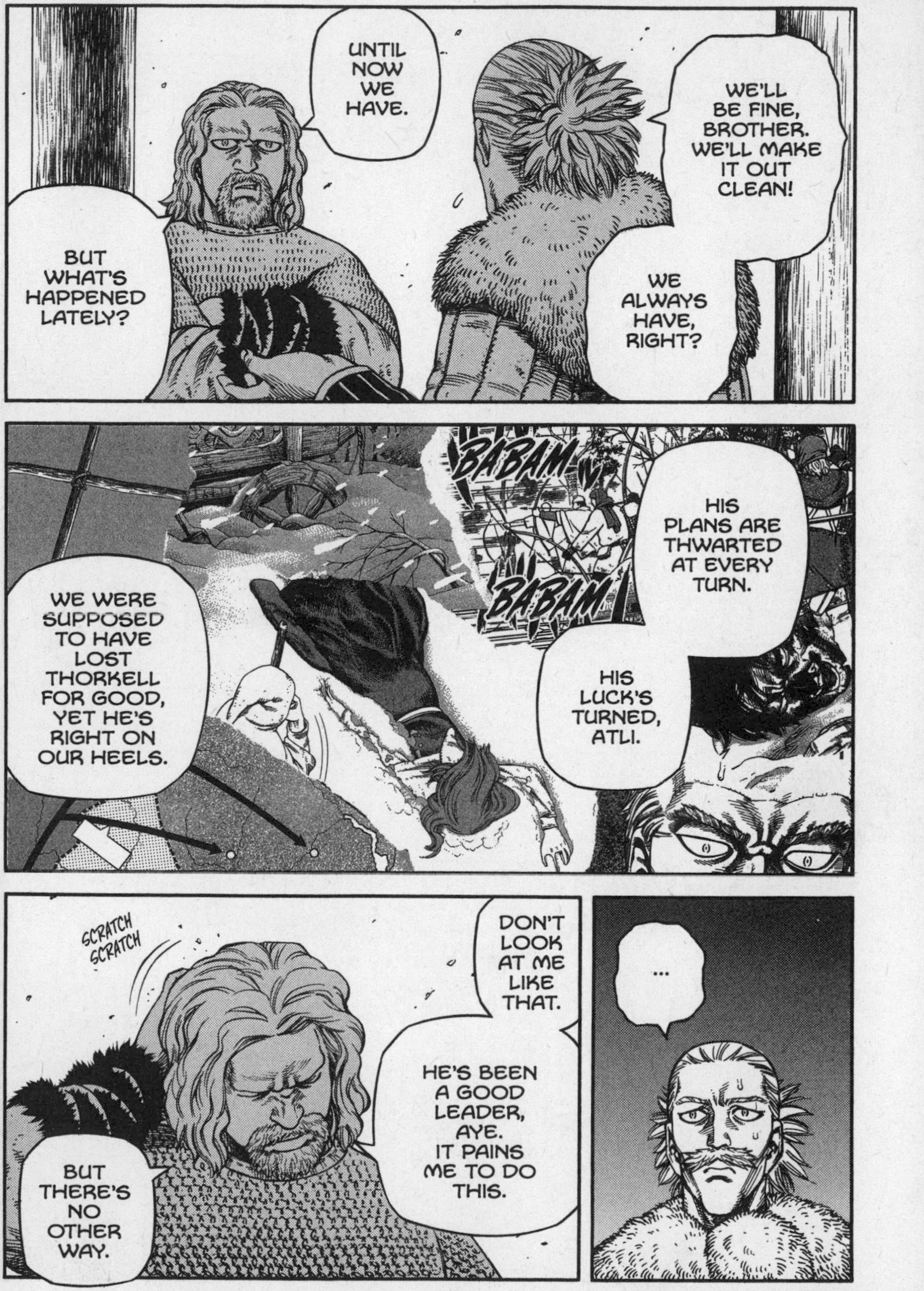

WE'LL BE FINE, BROTHER. WE'LL MAKE IT OUT CLEAN!
WE ALWAYS HAVE, RIGHT?
UNTIL NOW WE HAVE.
BUT WHAT'S HAPPENED LATELY?
HIS PLANS ARE THWARTED AT EVERY TURN.
BABAM
BABAM
HIS LUCK'S TURNED, ATLI.
WE WERE SUPPOSED TO HAVE LOST THORKELL FOR GOOD, YET HE'S RIGHT ON OUR HEELS.
...
DON'T LOOK AT ME LIKE THAT.
SCRATCH SCRATCH
HE'S BEEN A GOOD LEADER, AYE. IT PAINS ME TO DO THIS.
BUT THERE'S NO OTHER WAY.

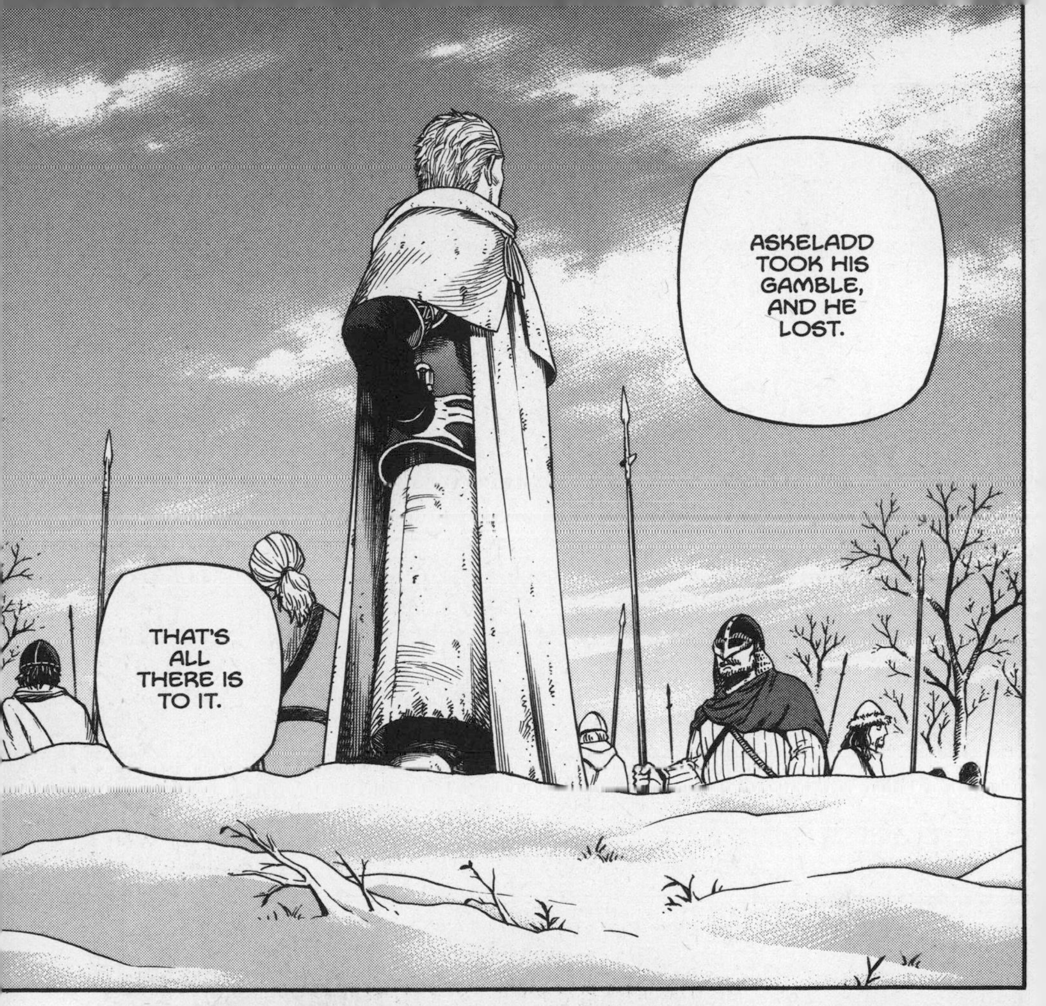
ASKELADD TOOK HIS GAMBLE, AND HE LOST.
THAT'S ALL THERE IS TO IT.

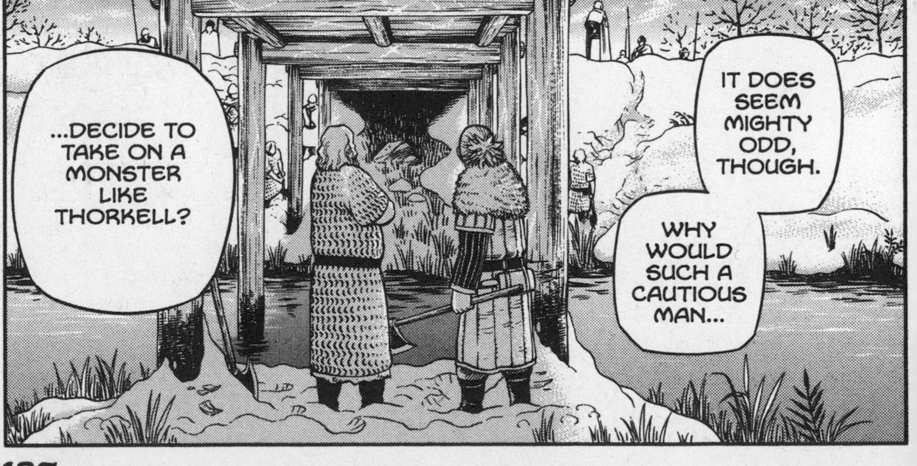
IT DOES SEEM MIGHTY ODD, THOUGH.
WHY WOULD SUCH A CAUTIOUS MAN...
...DECIDE TO TAKE ON A MONSTER LIKE THORKELL?

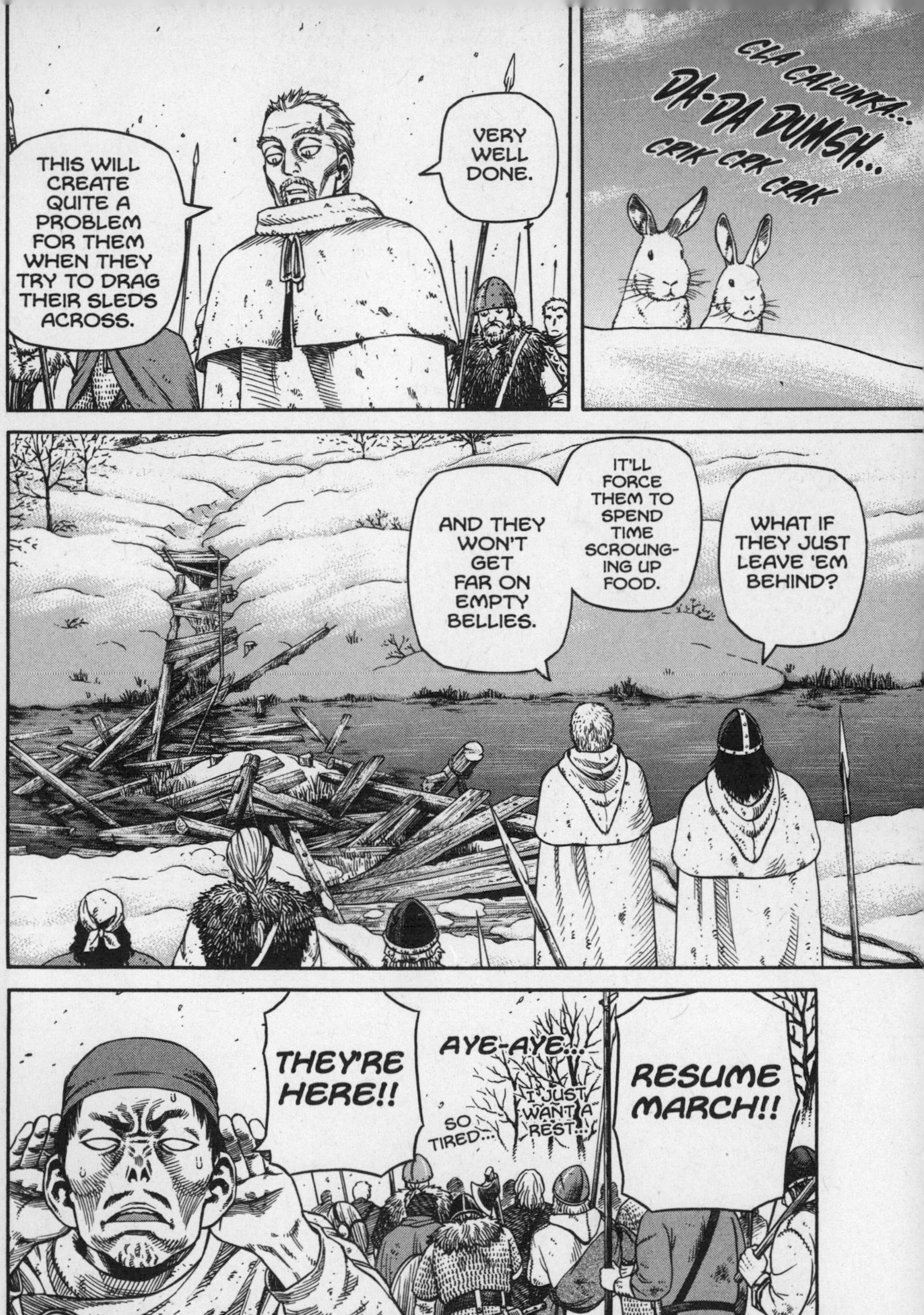
CLA CALUNKA...
DA-DA DUMSH...
CRIK CRK CRAK
VERY WELL DONE.
THIS WILL CREATE QUITE A PROBLEM FOR THEM WHEN THEY TRY TO DRAG THEIR SLEDS ACROSS.
WHAT IF THEY JUST LEAVE 'EM BEHIND?
IT'LL FORCE THEM TO SPEND TIME SCROUNGING UP FOOD.
AND THEY WON'T GET FAR ON EMPTY BELLIES.
RESUME MARCH!!
I JUST WANT A REST...
AYE-AYE...
SO TIRED...
THEY'RE HERE!!

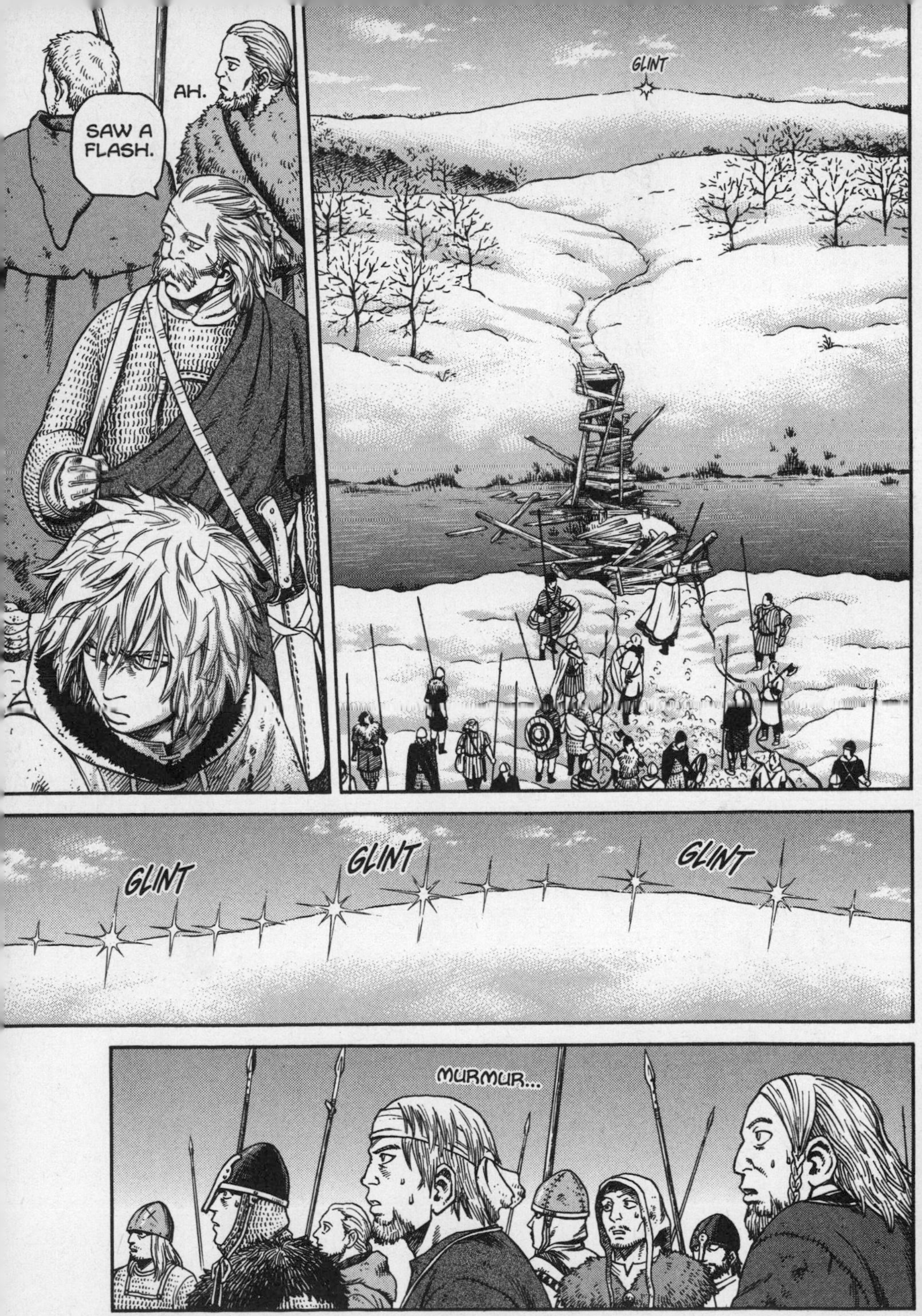
GLINT
AH.
SAW A FLASH.
GLINT
GLINT
GLINT
MURMUR...

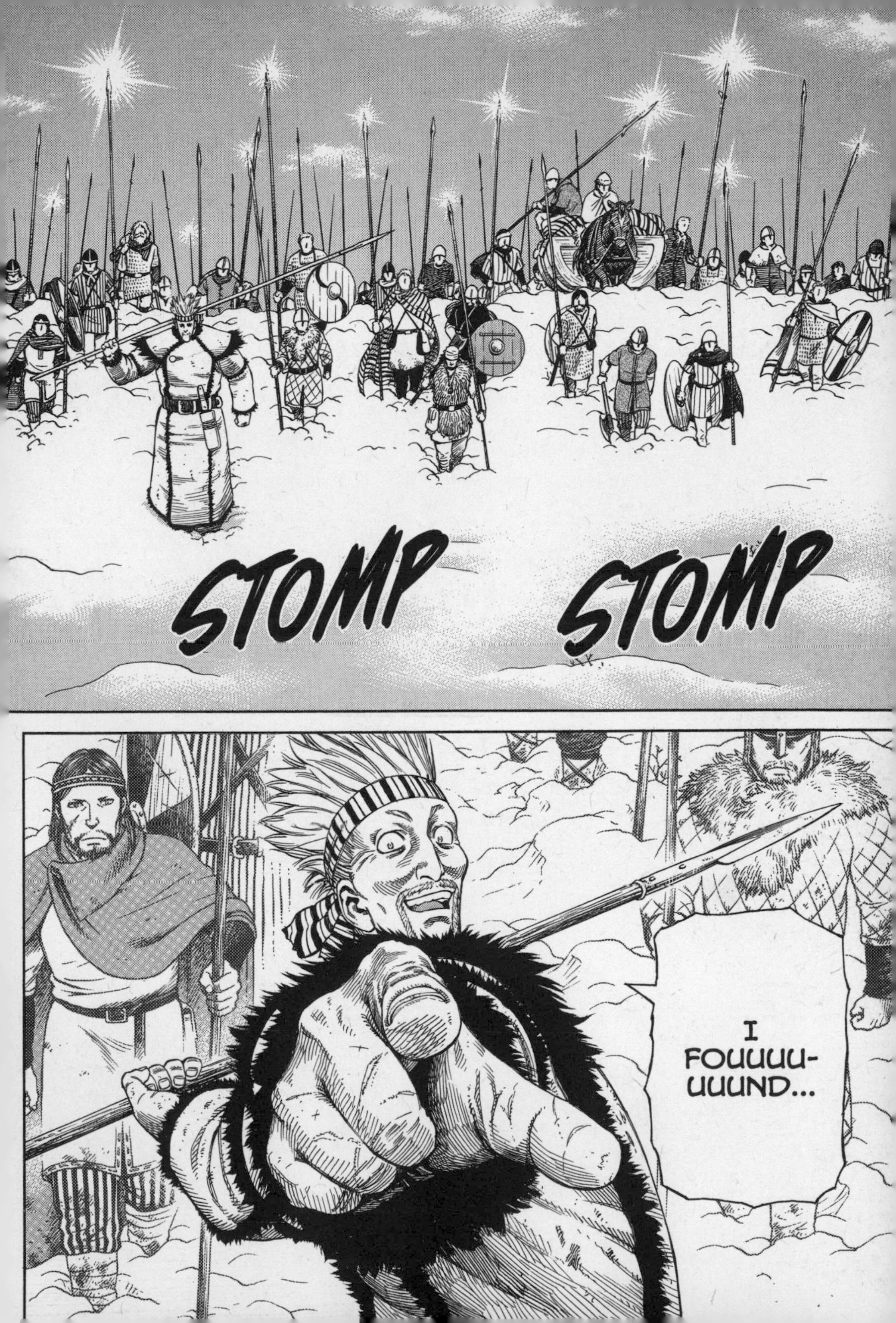
STOMP STOMP
I FOUUUU-UUUND...

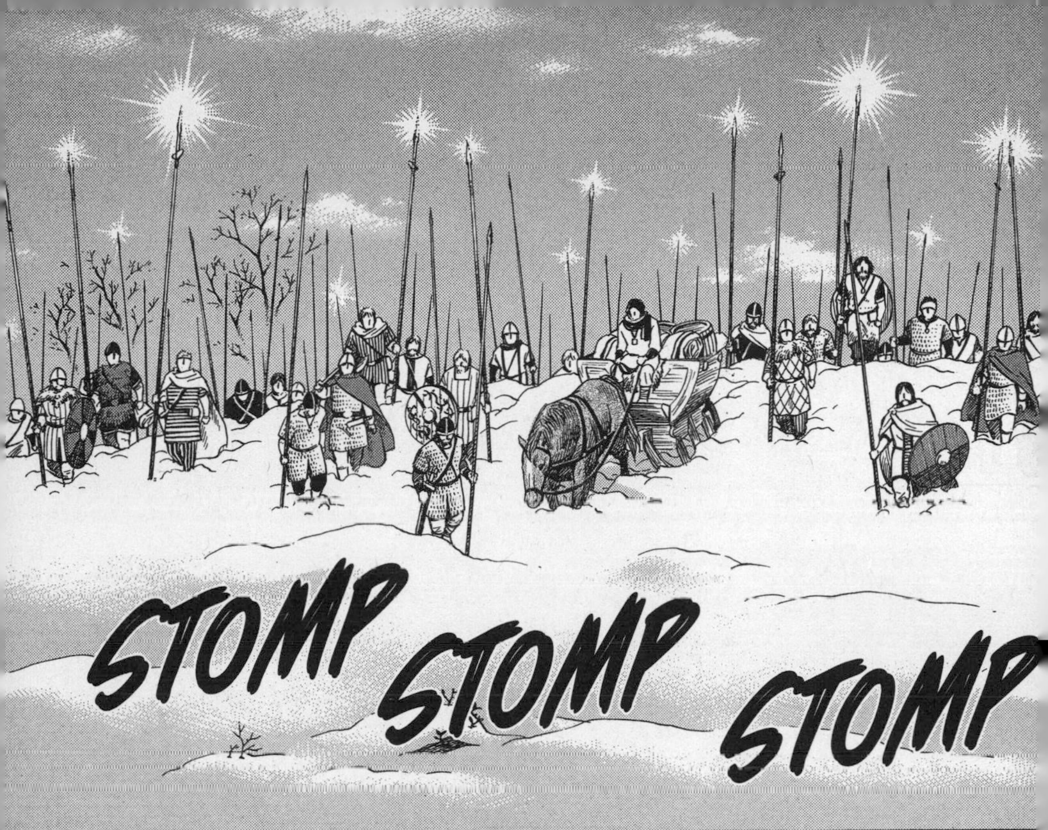
STOMP STOMP STOMP

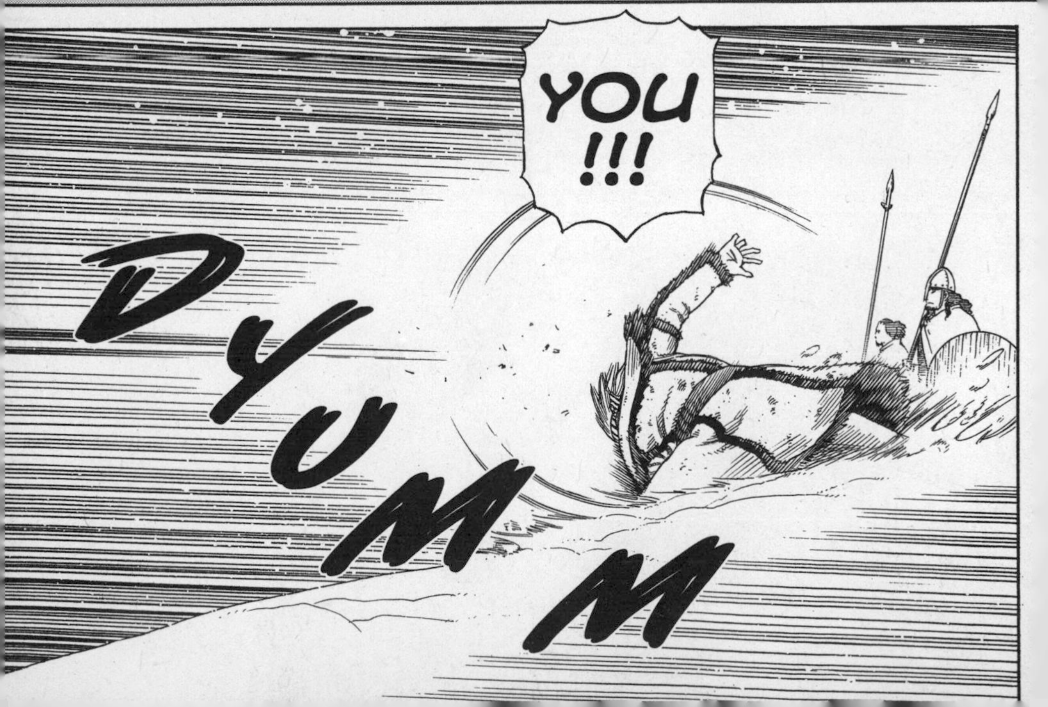
YOU
!!!
DYUMM

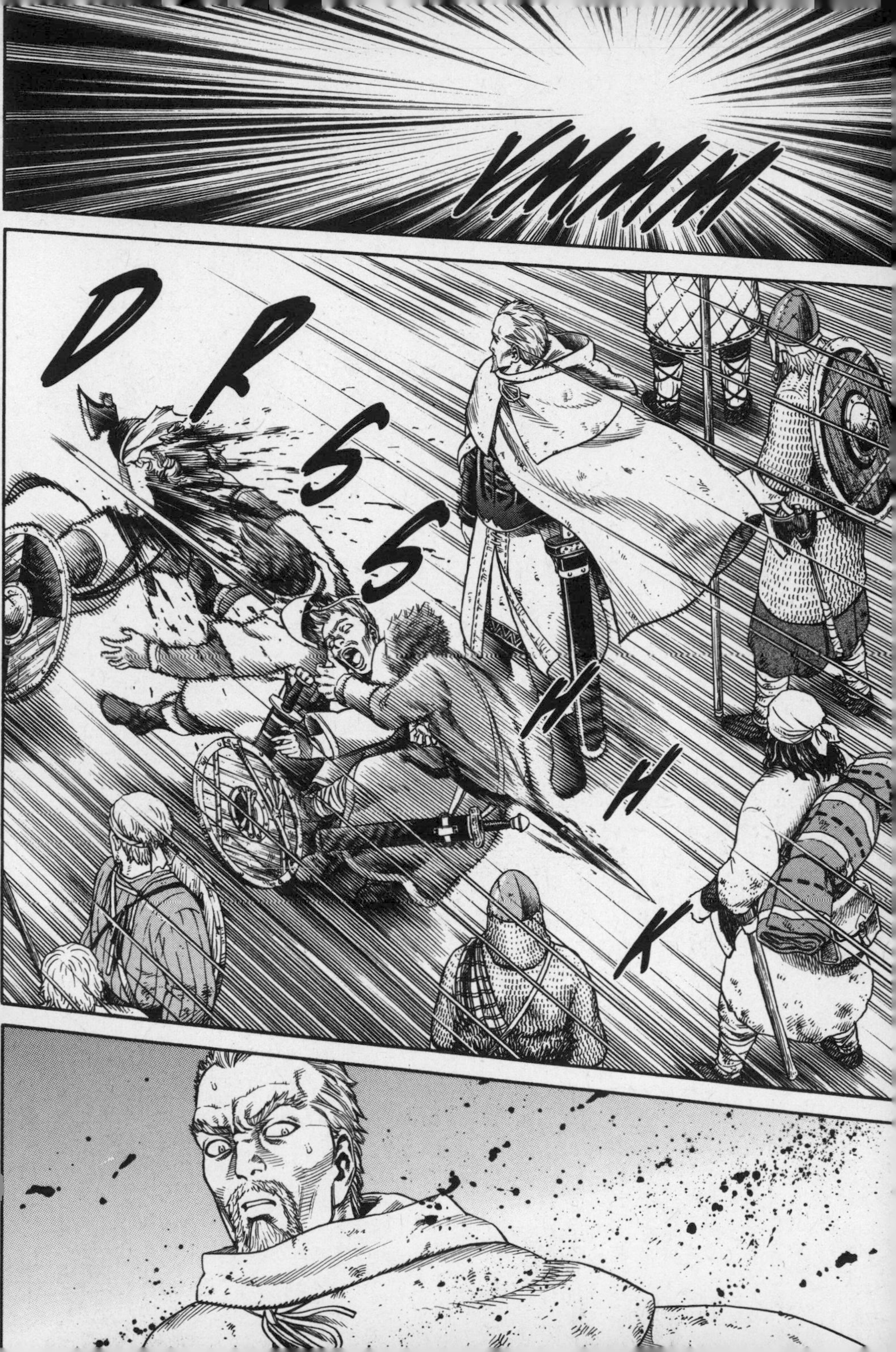
VMMMM
DPSSHHK

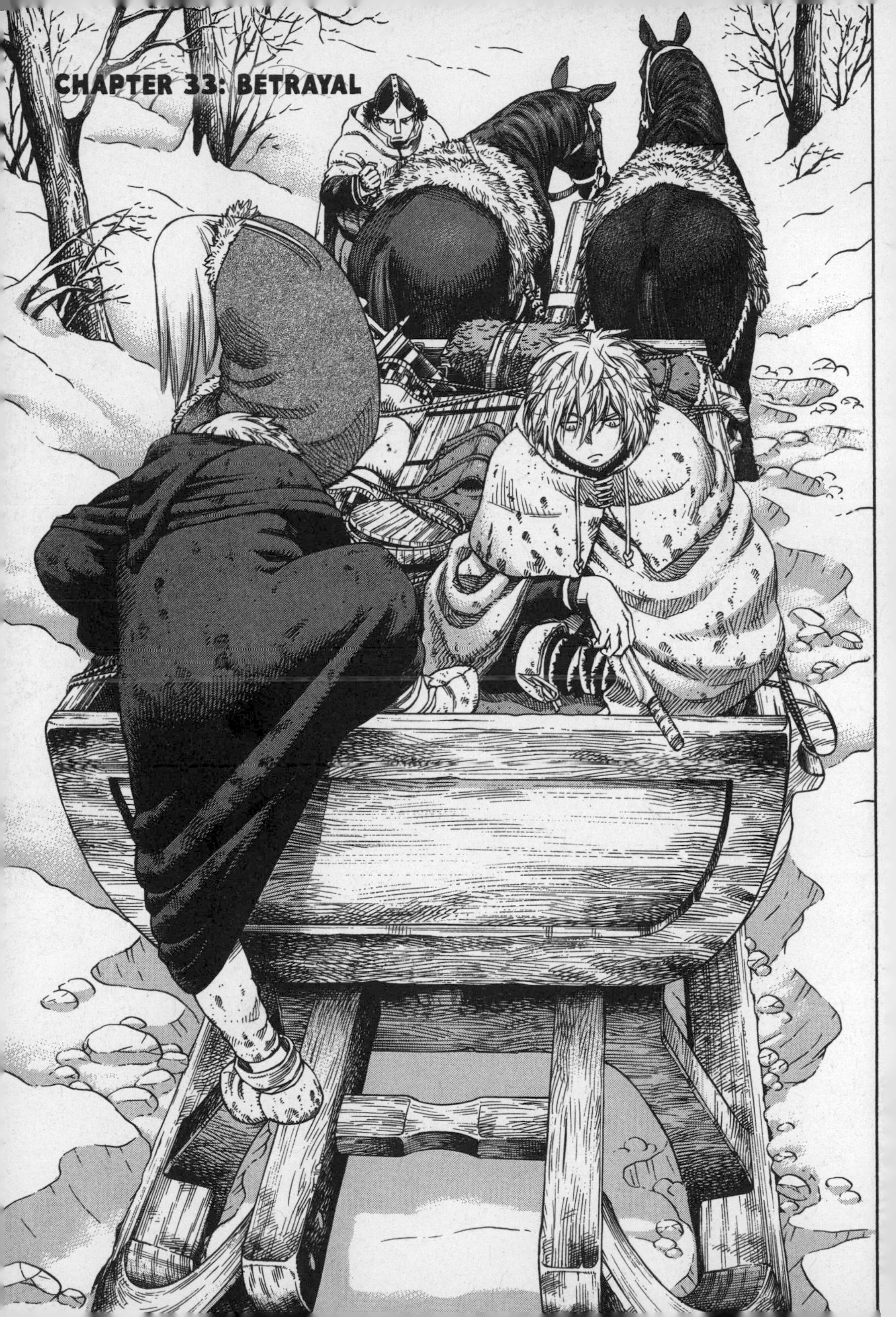
CHAPTER 33: BETRAYAL

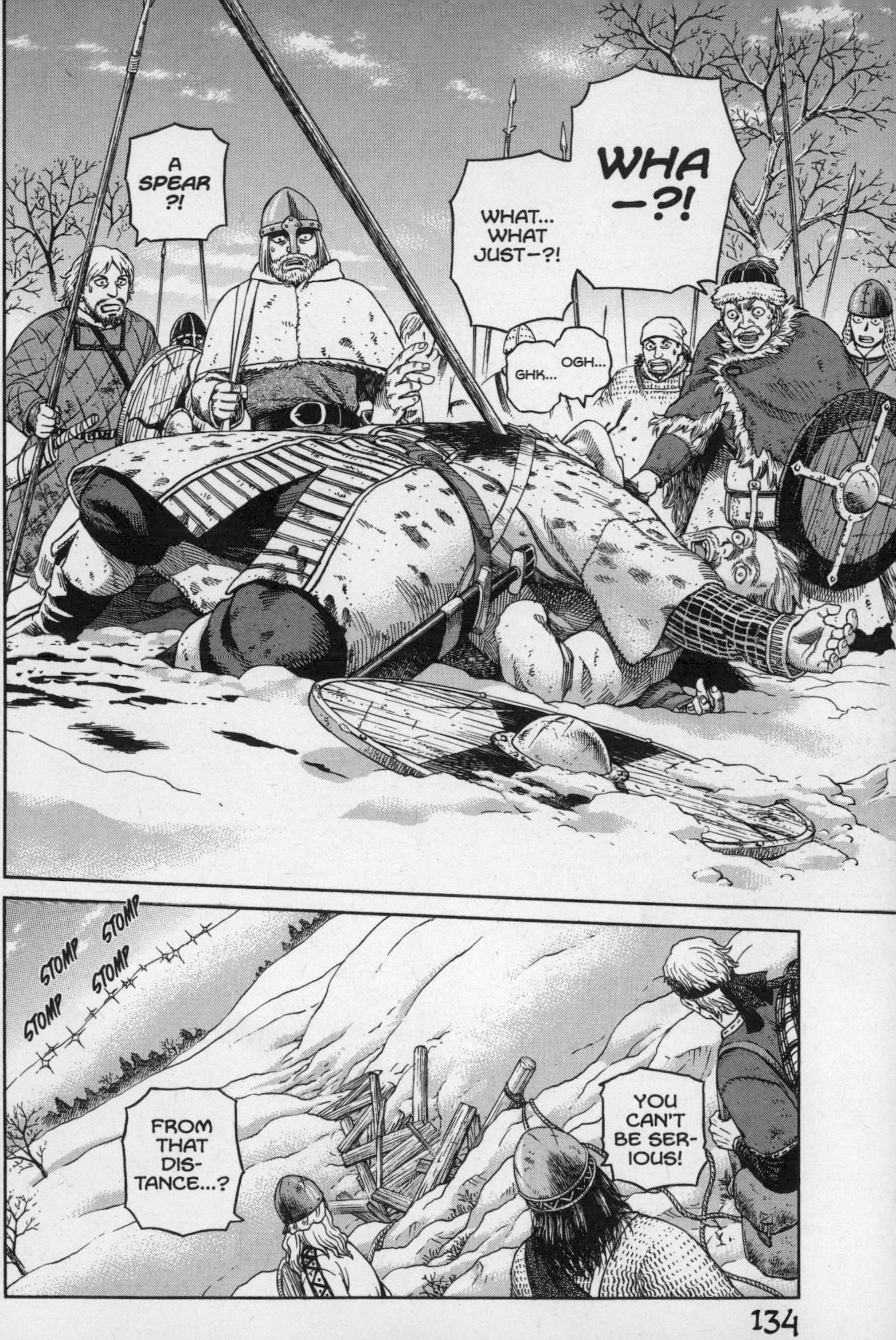
WHA—?!
WHAT... WHAT JUST—?!
OGH... GHK...
A SPEAR ?!
YOU CAN'T BE SERIOUS!
STOMP STOMP STOMP STOMP
FROM THAT DISTANCE...?

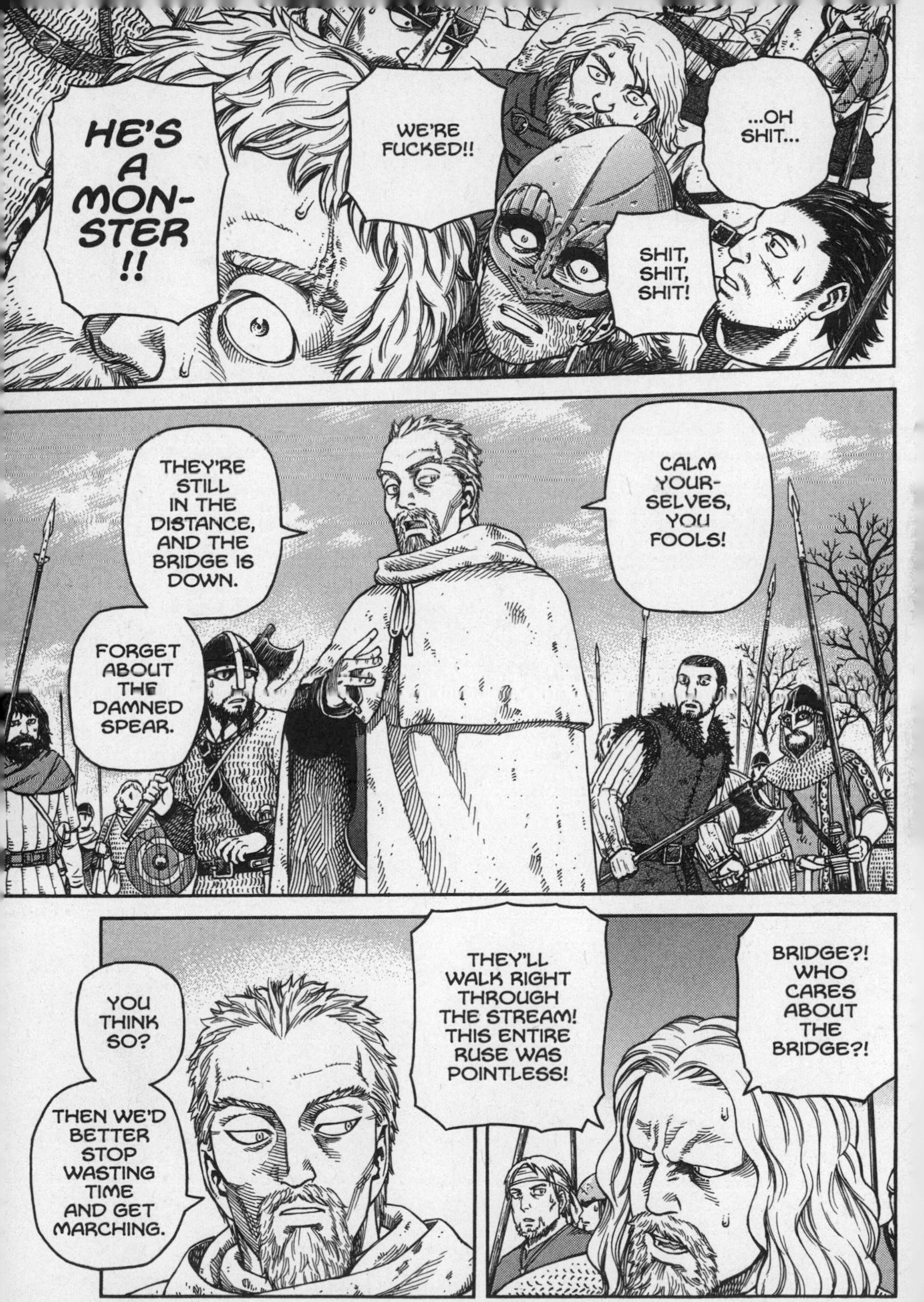
...OH SHIT...
SHIT, SHIT, SHIT!
WE'RE FUCKED!!
HE'S A MON-STER!!
CALM YOUR-SELVES, YOU FOOLS!
THEY'RE STILL IN THE DISTANCE, AND THE BRIDGE IS DOWN.
FORGET ABOUT THE DAMNED SPEAR.
BRIDGE?! WHO CARES ABOUT THE BRIDGE?!
THEY'LL WALK RIGHT THROUGH THE STREAM! THIS ENTIRE RUSE WAS POINTLESS!
YOU THINK SO?
THEN WE'D BETTER STOP WASTING TIME AND GET MARCHING.

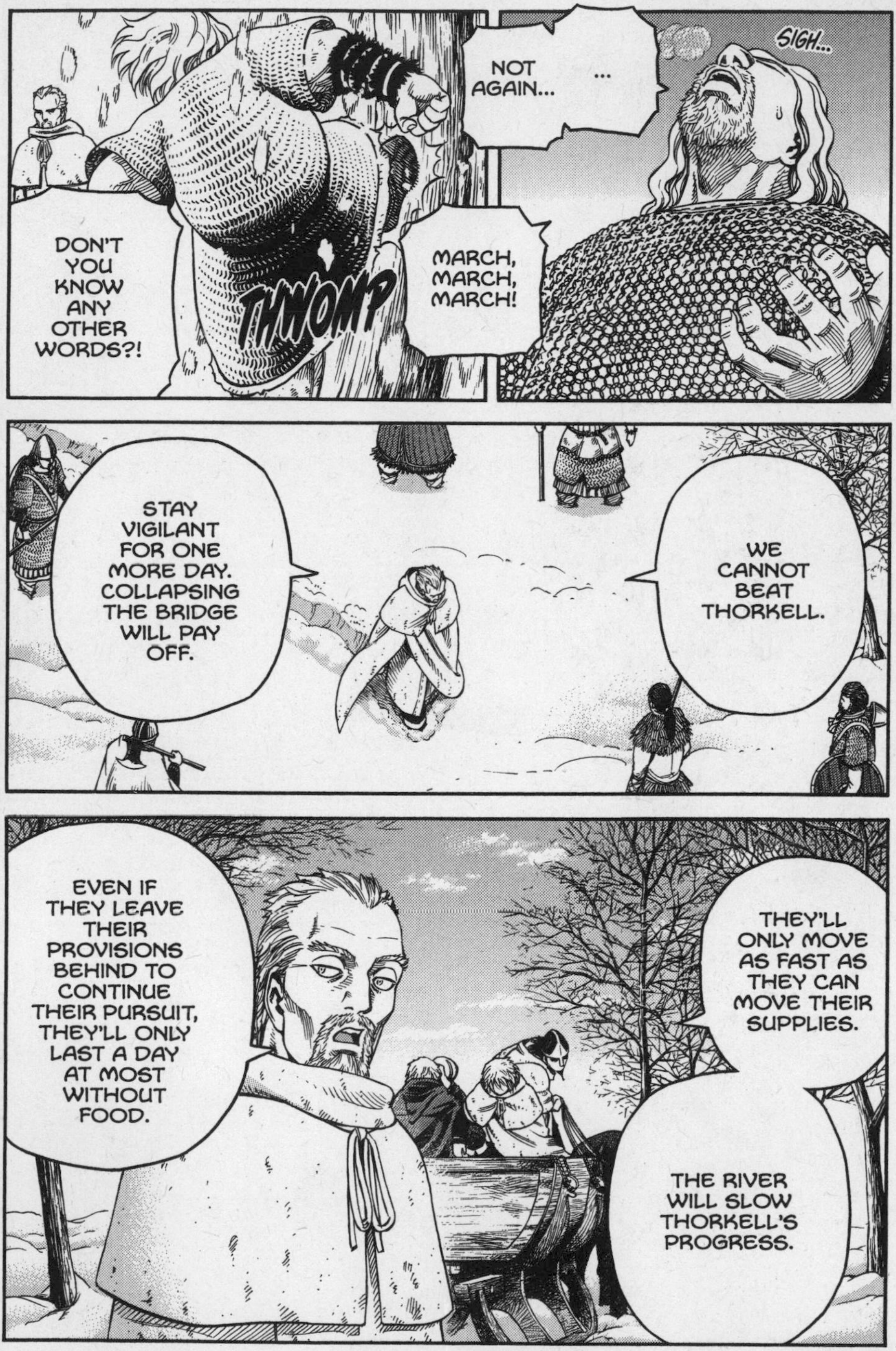
SIGH...
NOT AGAIN... ...
MARCH, MARCH, MARCH!
THWOMP
DON'T YOU KNOW ANY OTHER WORDS?!
WE CANNOT BEAT THORKELL.
STAY VIGILANT FOR ONE MORE DAY. COLLAPSING THE BRIDGE WILL PAY OFF.
THEY'LL ONLY MOVE AS FAST AS THEY CAN MOVE THEIR SUPPLIES.
THE RIVER WILL SLOW THORKELL'S PROGRESS.
EVEN IF THEY LEAVE THEIR PROVISIONS BEHIND TO CONTINUE THEIR PURSUIT, THEY'LL ONLY LAST A DAY AT MOST WITHOUT FOOD.

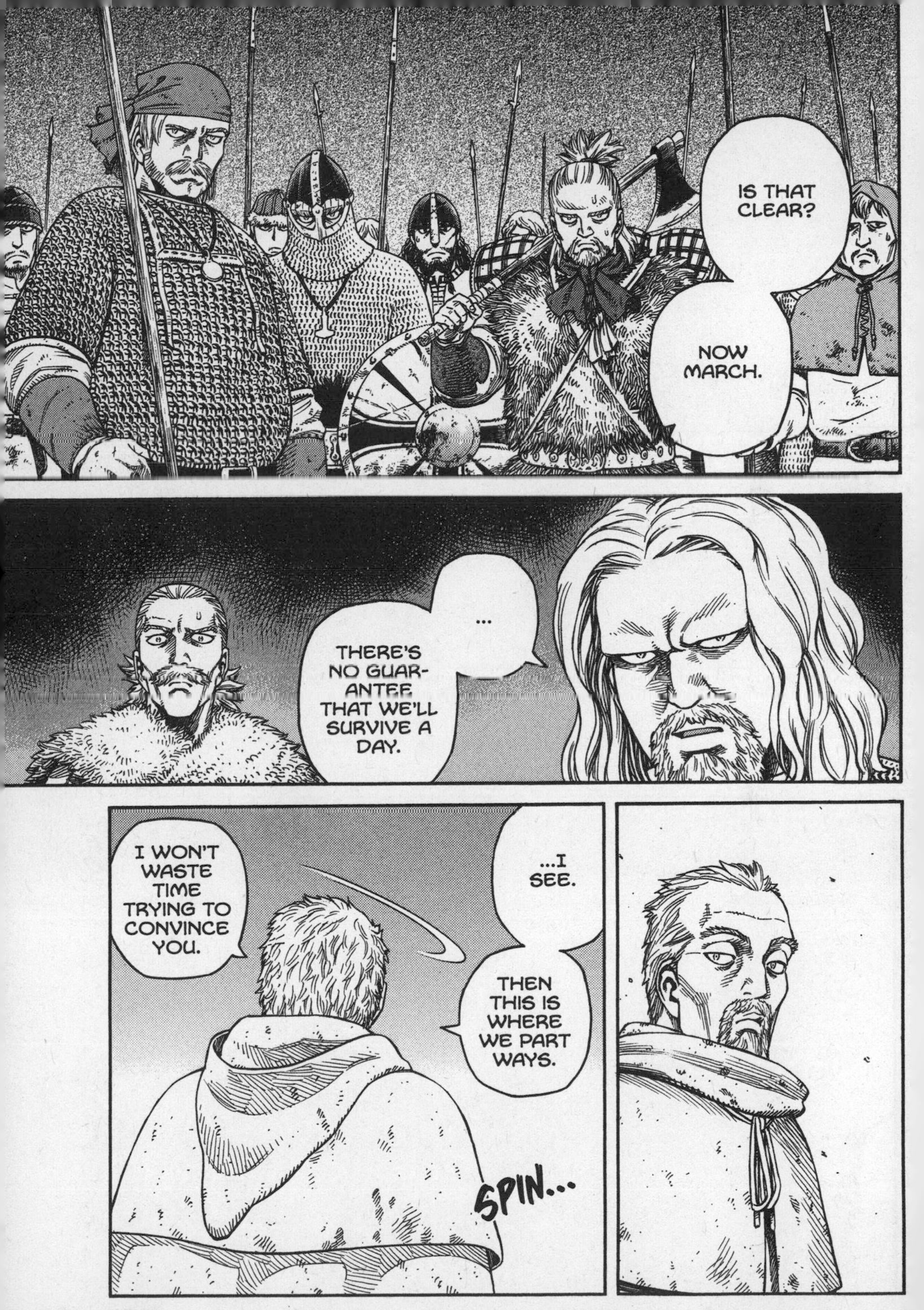
IS THAT CLEAR?
NOW MARCH.
...
THERE'S NO GUARANTEE THAT WE'LL SURVIVE A DAY.
...I SEE.
I WON'T WASTE TIME TRYING TO CONVINCE YOU.
THEN THIS IS WHERE WE PART WAYS.
SPIN...

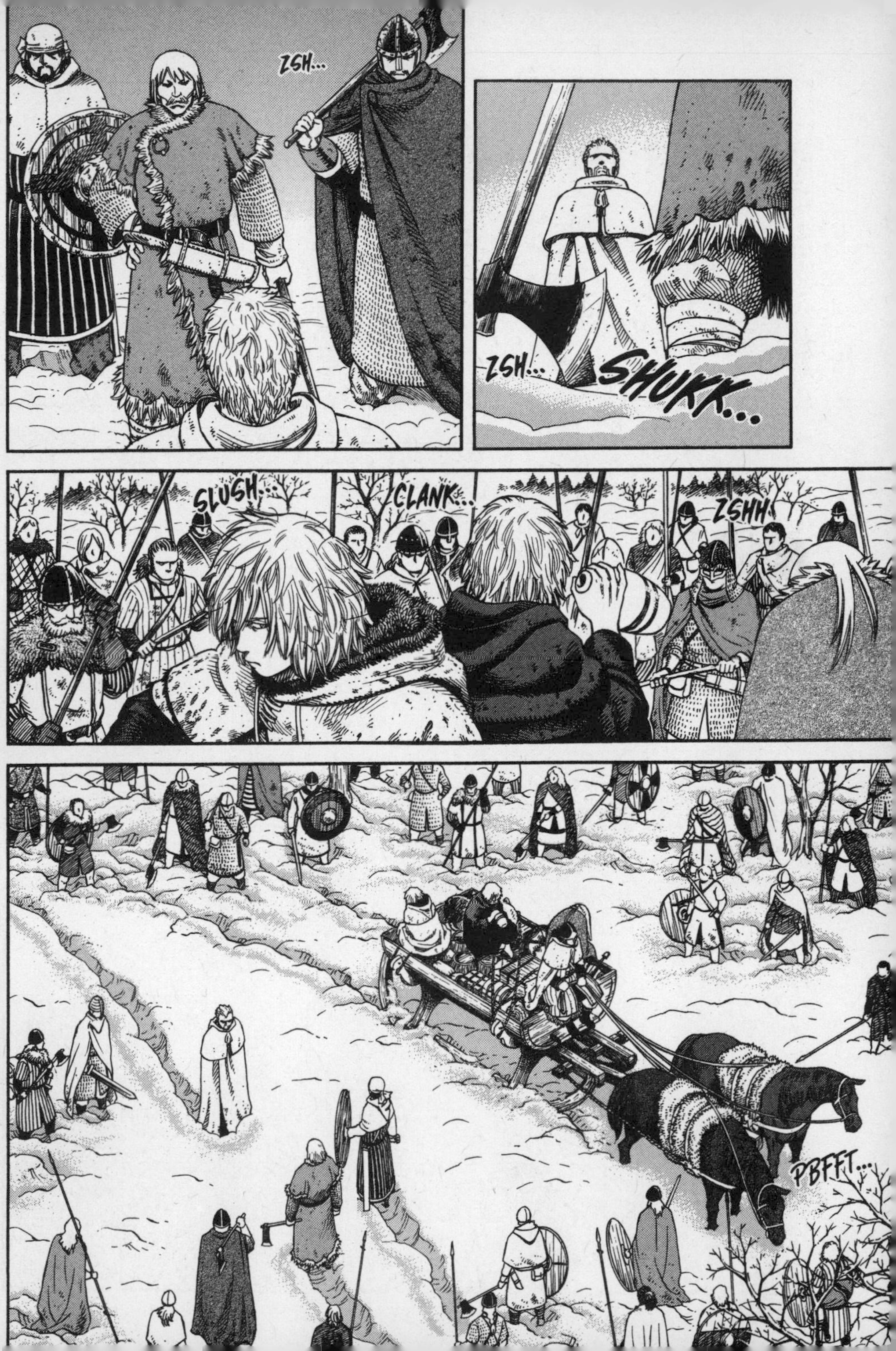
ZSH...
SHUKK...
ZSH...
ZSHH
CLANK...
SLUSH...
PBFFT...

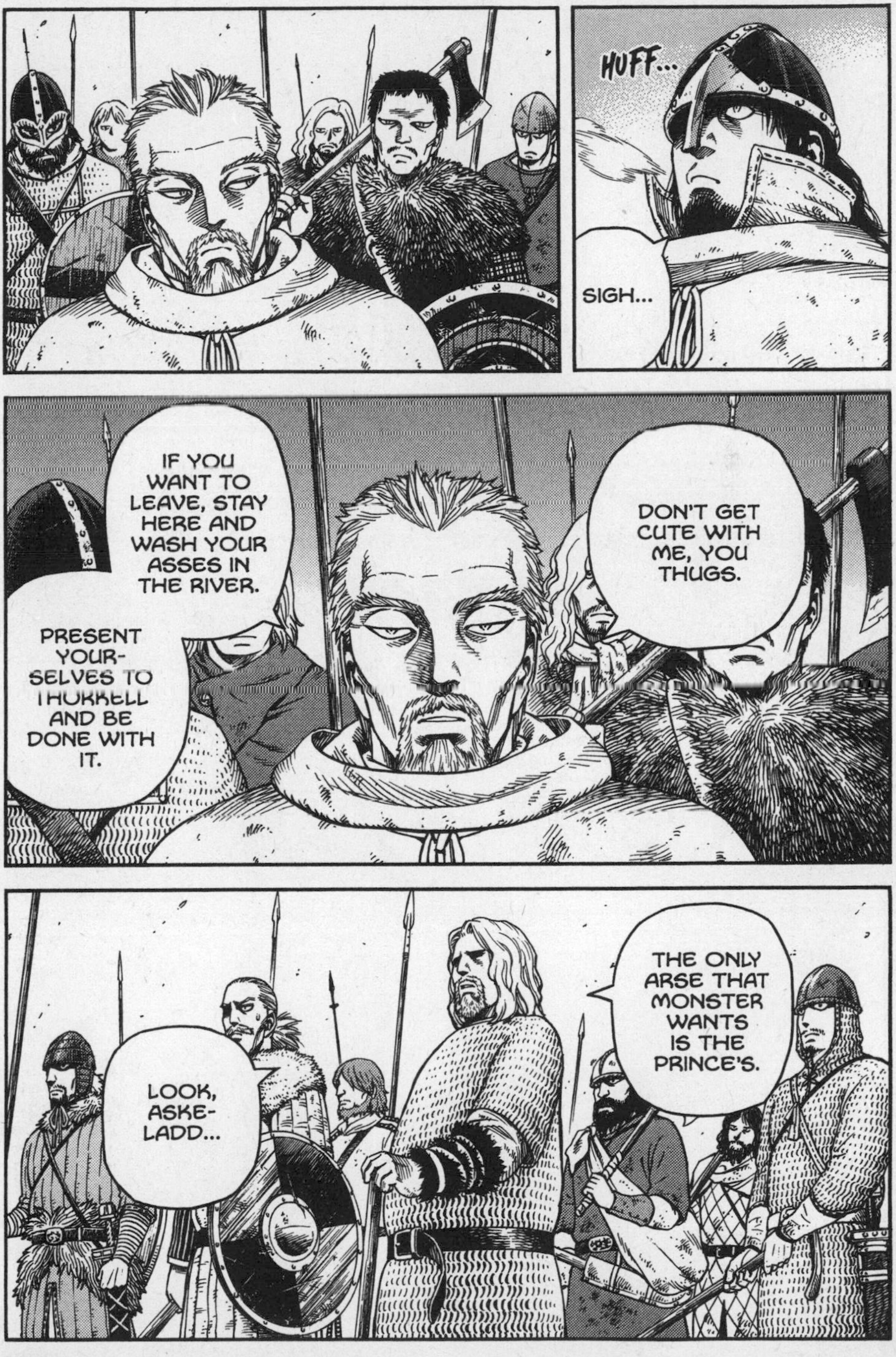
HUFF...
SIGH...
DON'T GET CUTE WITH ME, YOU THUGS.
IF YOU WANT TO LEAVE, STAY HERE AND WASH YOUR ASSES IN THE RIVER.
PRESENT YOURSELVES TO THURKELL AND BE DONE WITH IT.
THE ONLY ARSE THAT MONSTER WANTS IS THE PRINCE'S.
LOOK, ASKELADD...

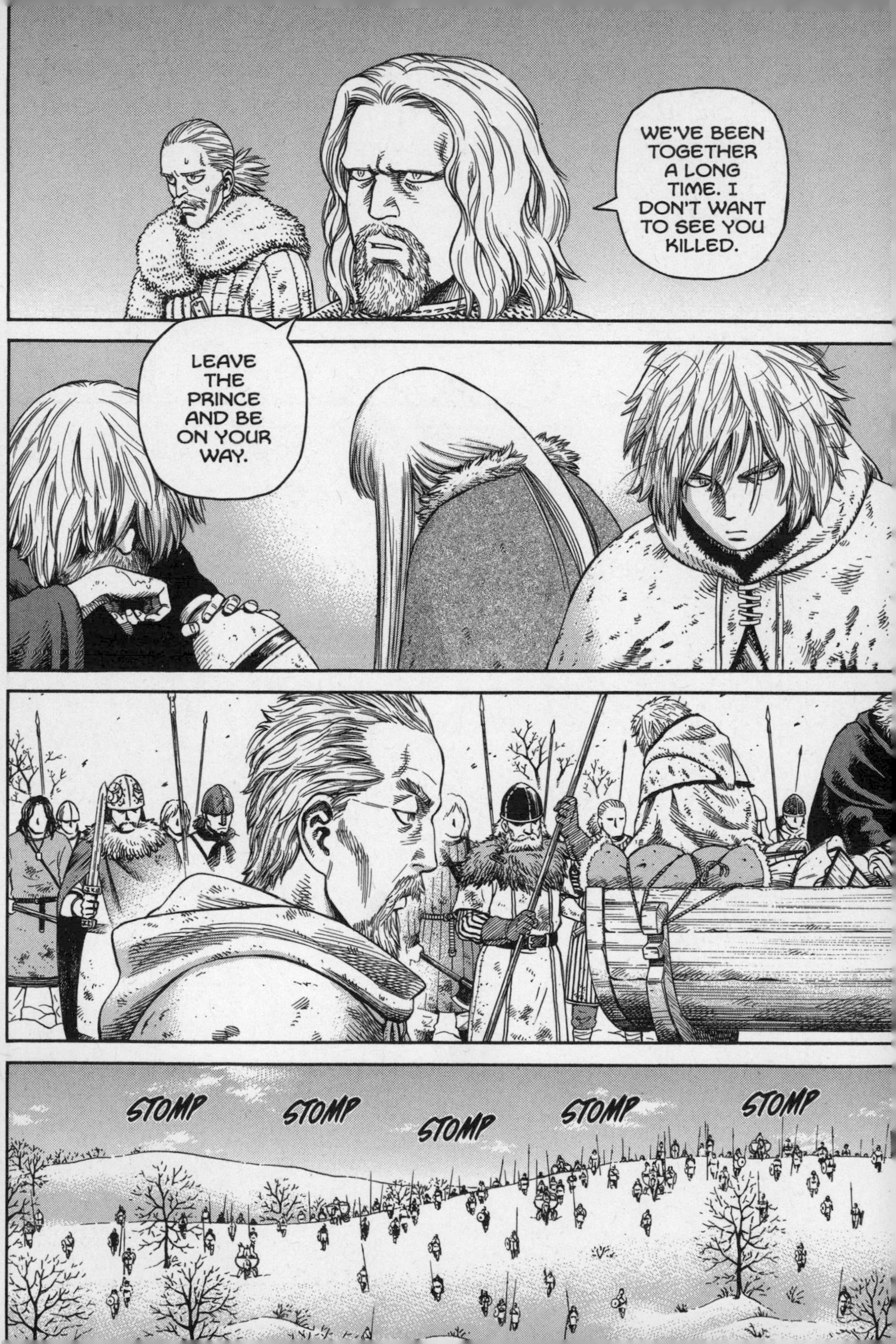
WE'VE BEEN TOGETHER A LONG TIME. I DON'T WANT TO SEE YOU KILLED.
LEAVE THE PRINCE AND BE ON YOUR WAY.
STOMP
STOMP
STOMP
STOMP
STOMP

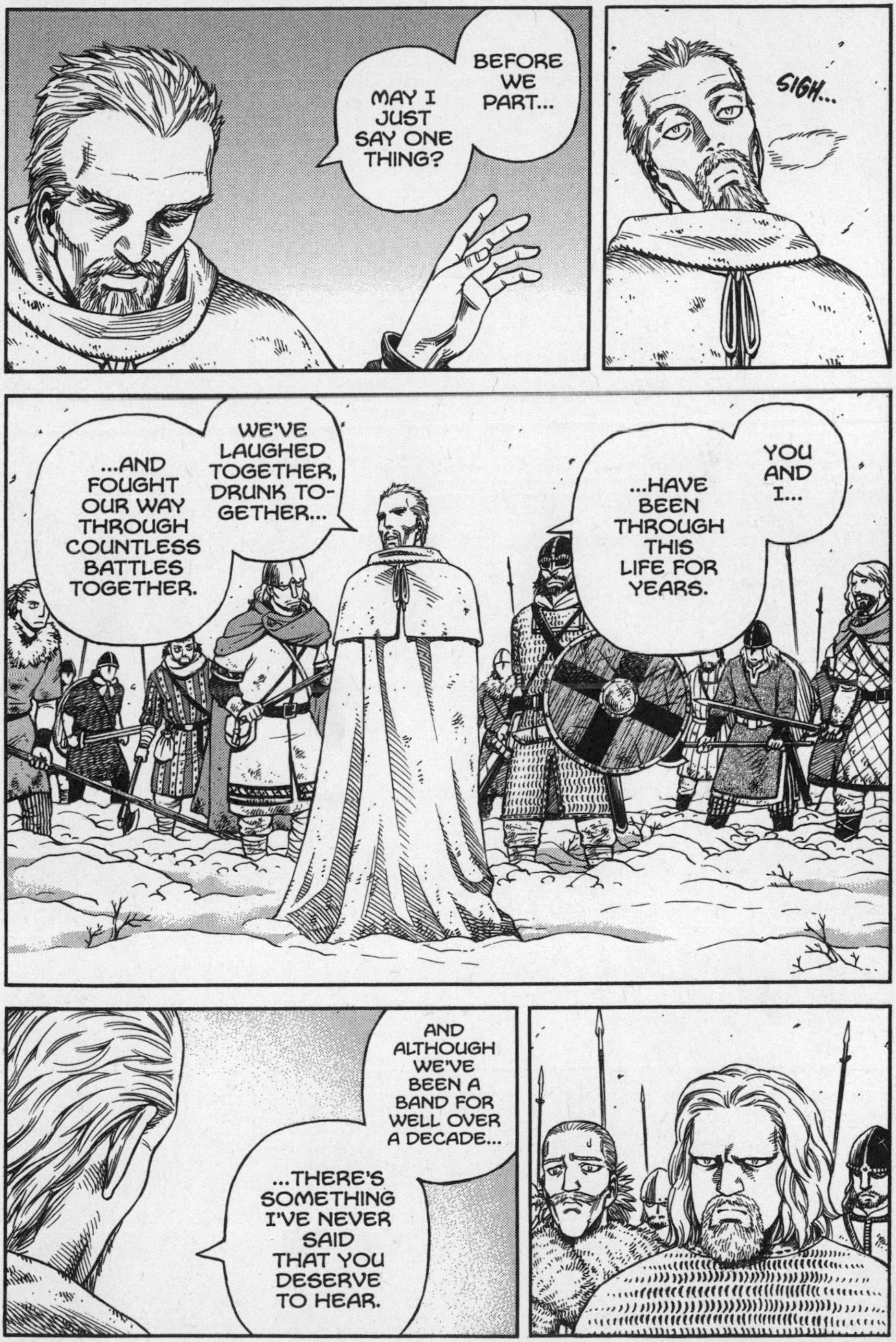
SIGH...
BEFORE WE PART...
MAY I JUST SAY ONE THING?
YOU AND I...
...HAVE BEEN THROUGH THIS LIFE FOR YEARS.
WE'VE LAUGHED TOGETHER, DRUNK TO-GETHER...
...AND FOUGHT OUR WAY THROUGH COUNTLESS BATTLES TOGETHER.
AND ALTHOUGH WE'VE BEEN A BAND FOR WELL OVER A DECADE...
...THERE'S SOMETHING I'VE NEVER SAID THAT YOU DESERVE TO HEAR.

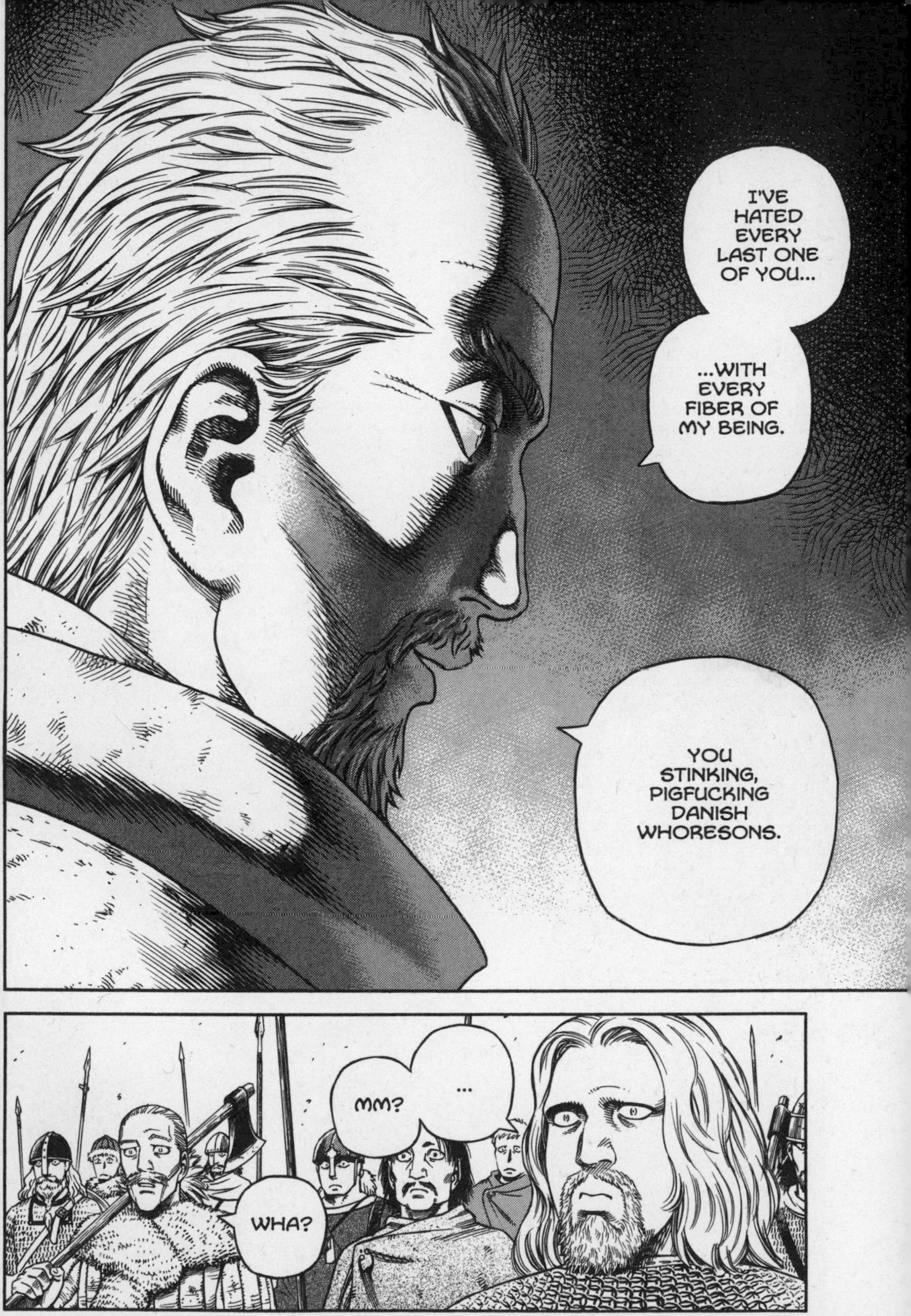
I'VE HATED EVERY LAST ONE OF YOU...
...WITH EVERY FIBER OF MY BEING.
YOU STINKING, PIGFUCKING DANISH WHORESONS.
...
MM?
WHA?

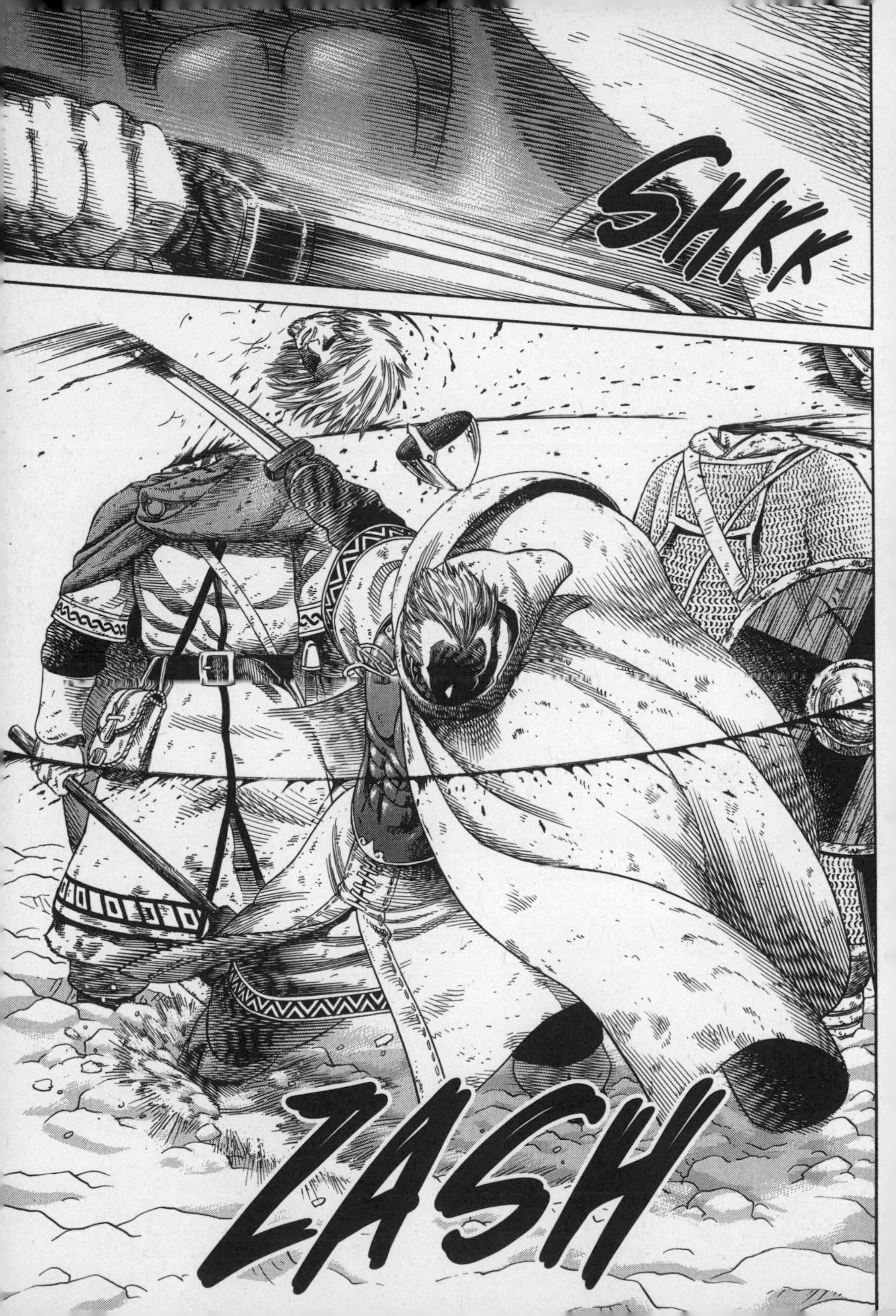
SHKK
ZASH

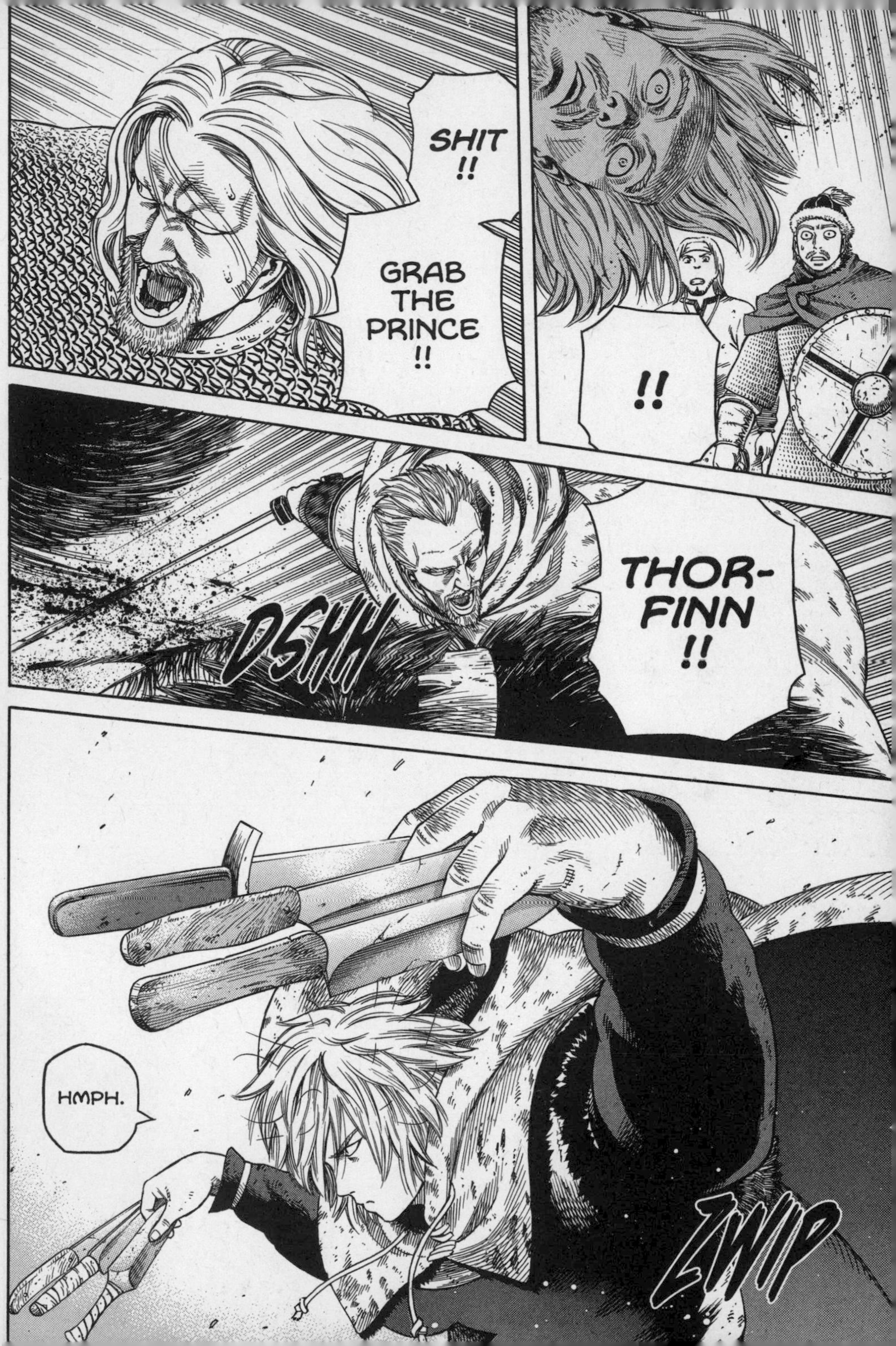
!!
SHIT !!
GRAB THE PRINCE !!
THOR-FINN !!
DSHH
HMPH.
ZWIP

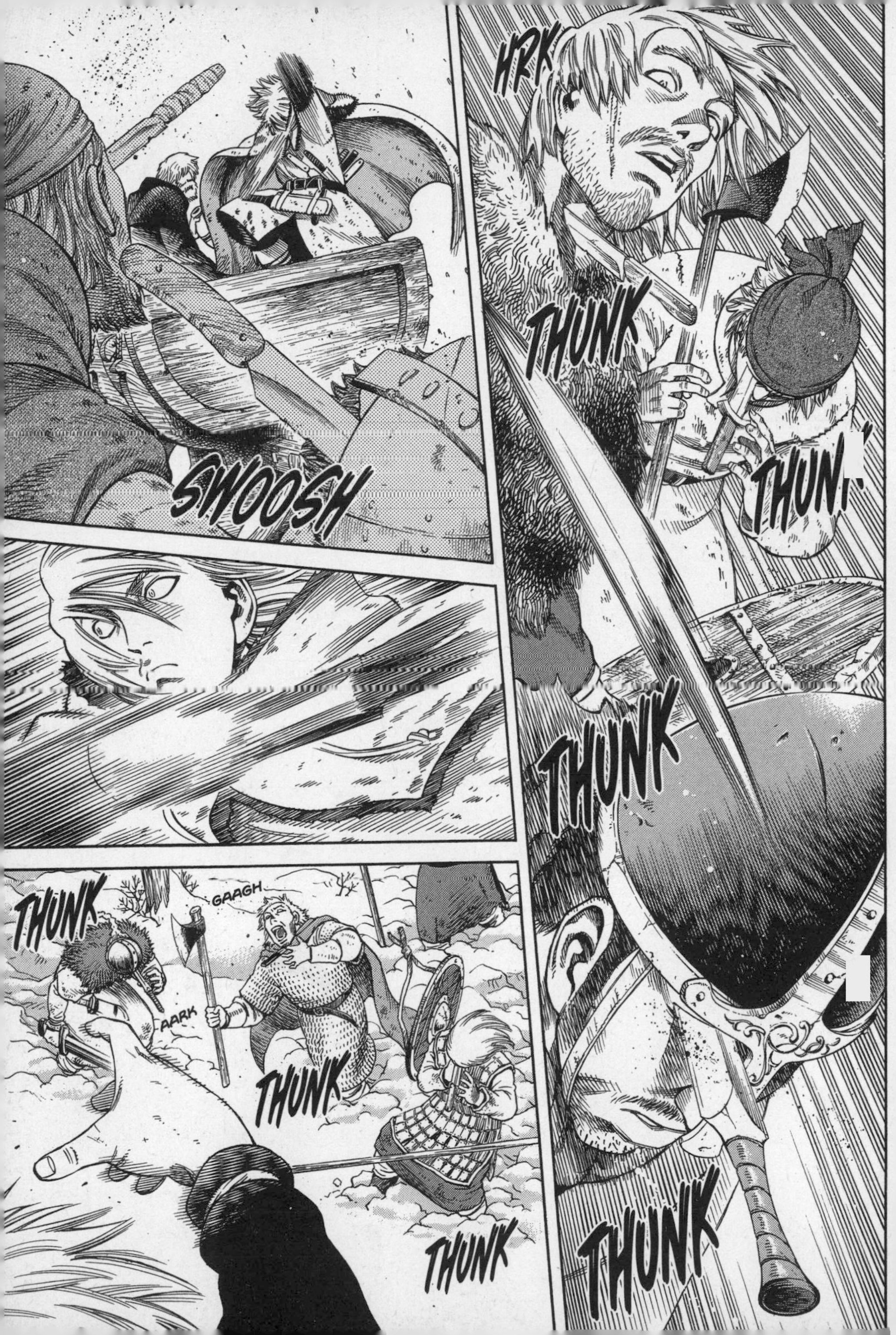
HPK
THUNK
THUN
THUNK
THUNK
SWOOSH
THUNK
GAAGH
AARK
THUNK
THUNK

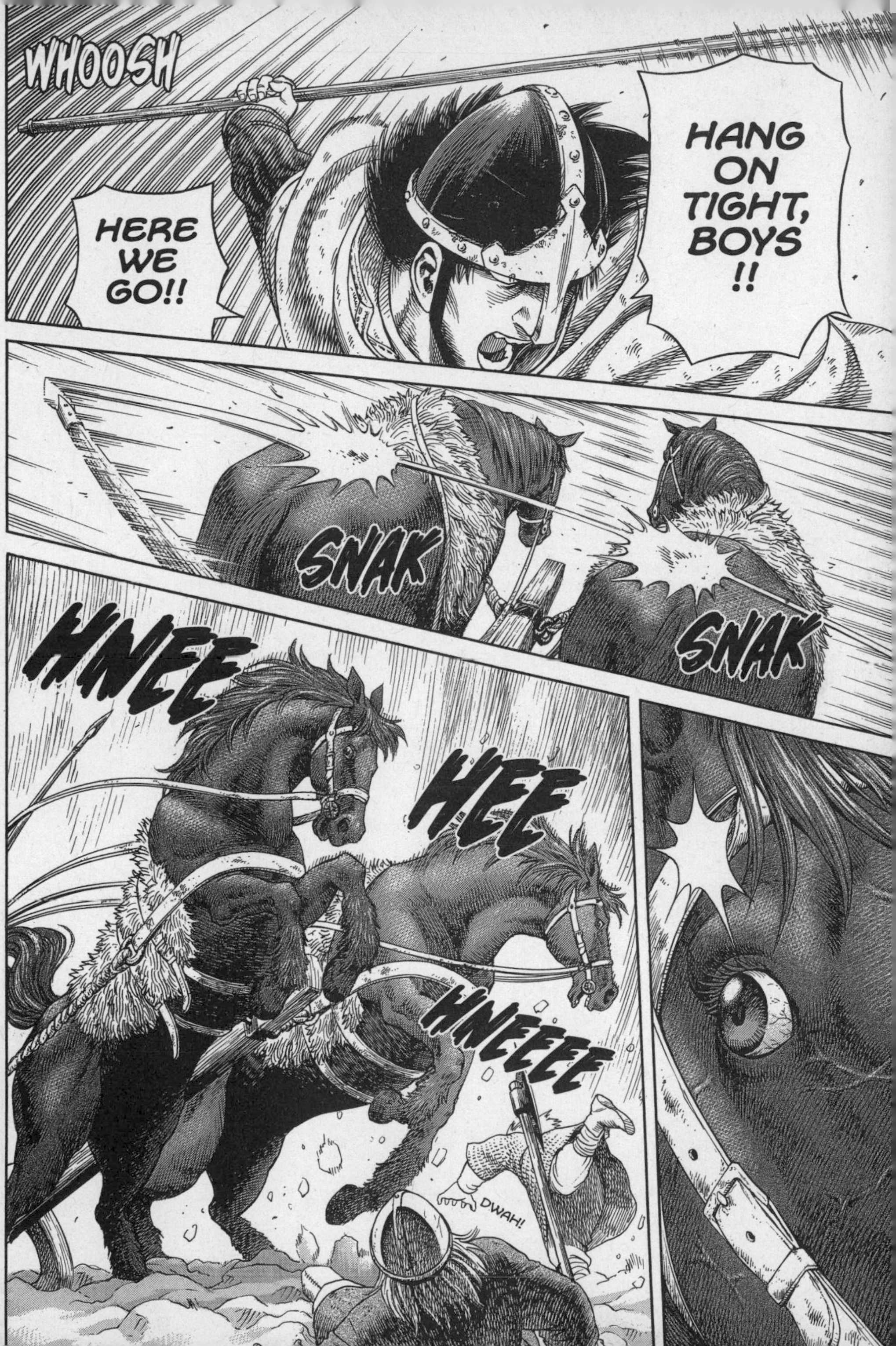

HANG ON TIGHT, BOYS!!
WHOOSH
HERE WE GO!!
SNAK
SNAK
HNEE
HEE
HNEEEEE
DWAH!

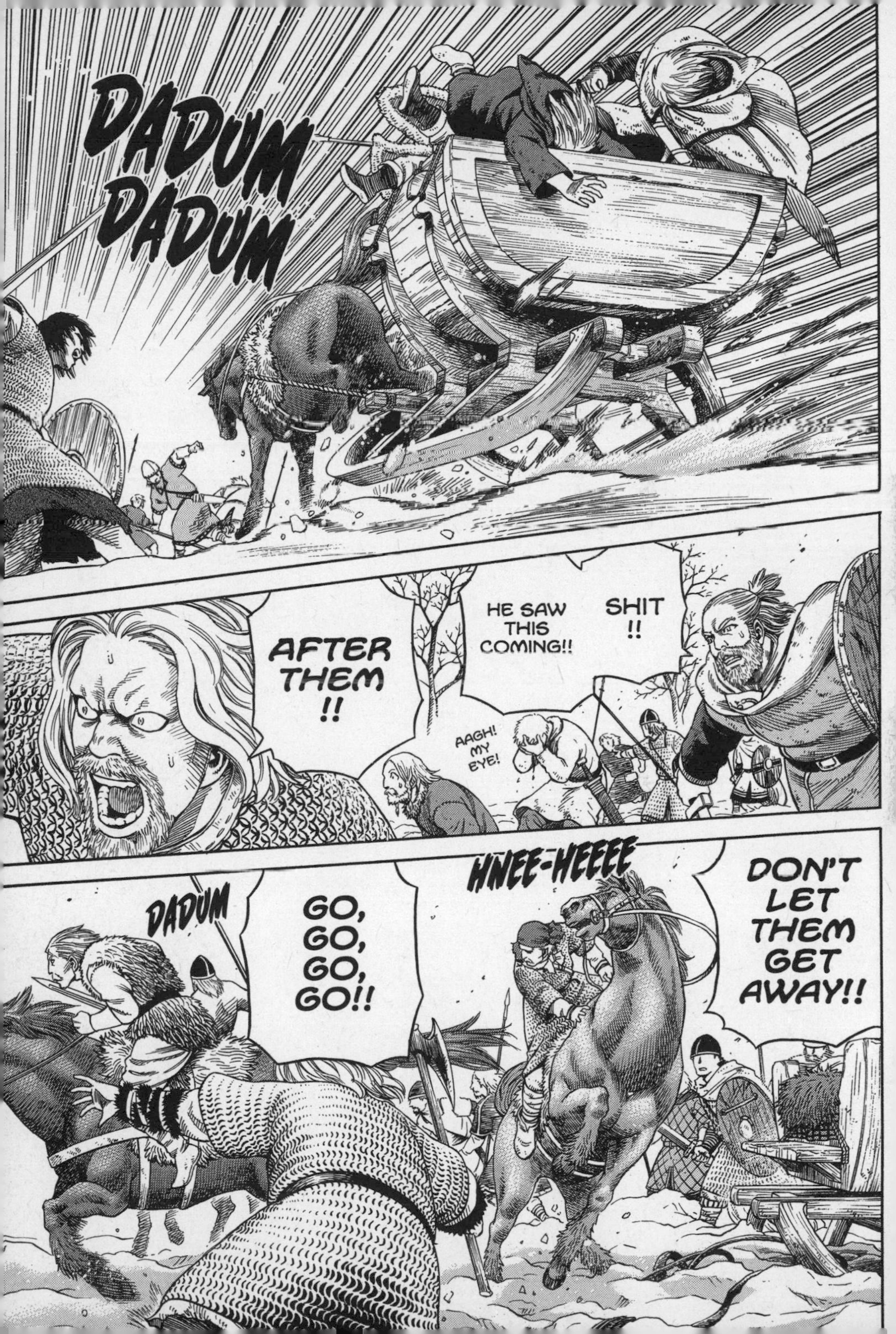
DADUM DADUM
SHIT!!
HE SAW THIS COMING!!
AFTER THEM!!
AAGH! MY EYE!
DON'T LET THEM GET AWAY!!
HNEE-HEEEE
GO, GO, GO, GO!!
DADUM

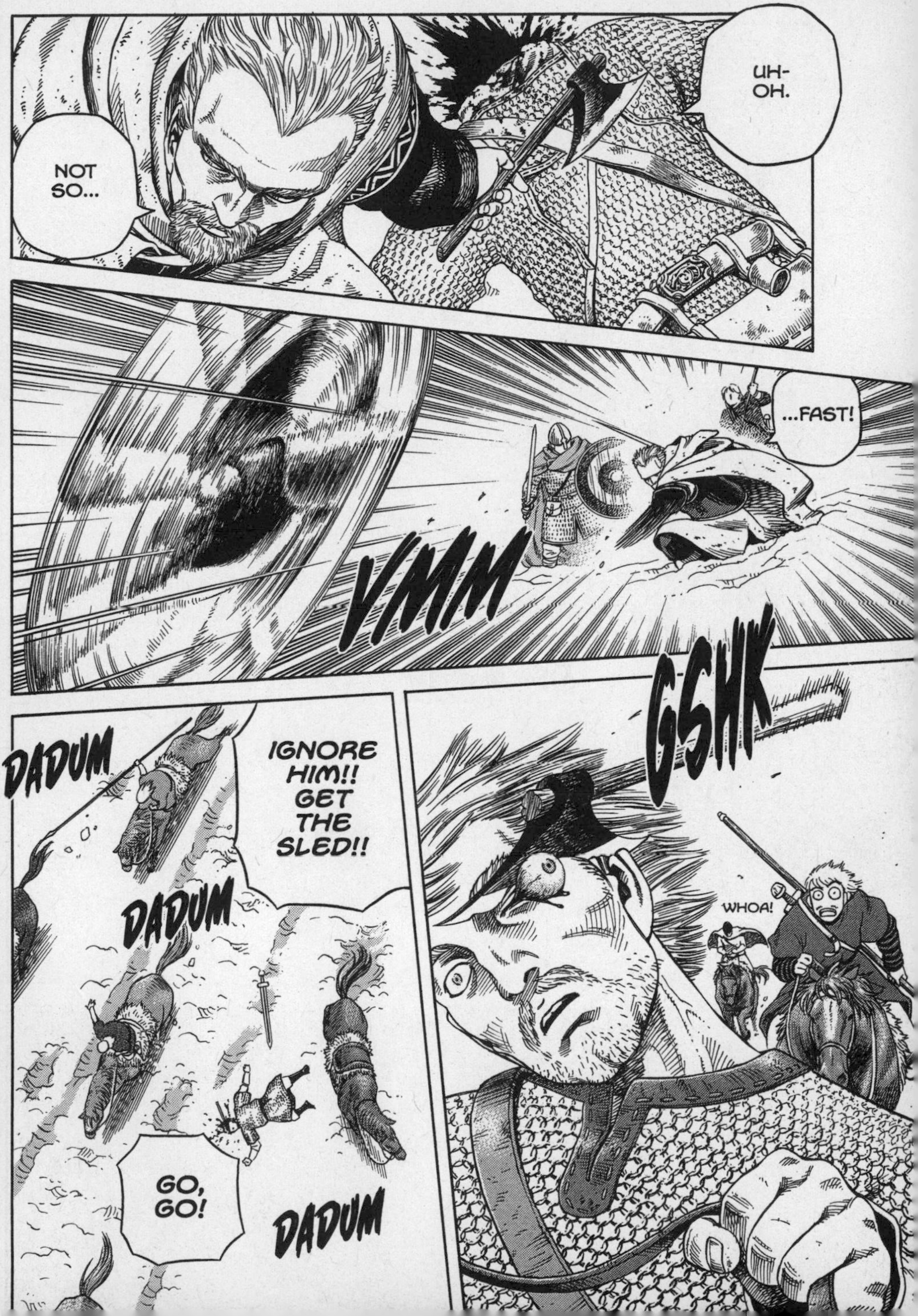
UH-OH.
NOT SO...
...FAST!
VMM
GSHK
WHOA!
IGNORE HIM!! GET THE SLED!!
DADUM
DADUM
GO, GO!
DADUM

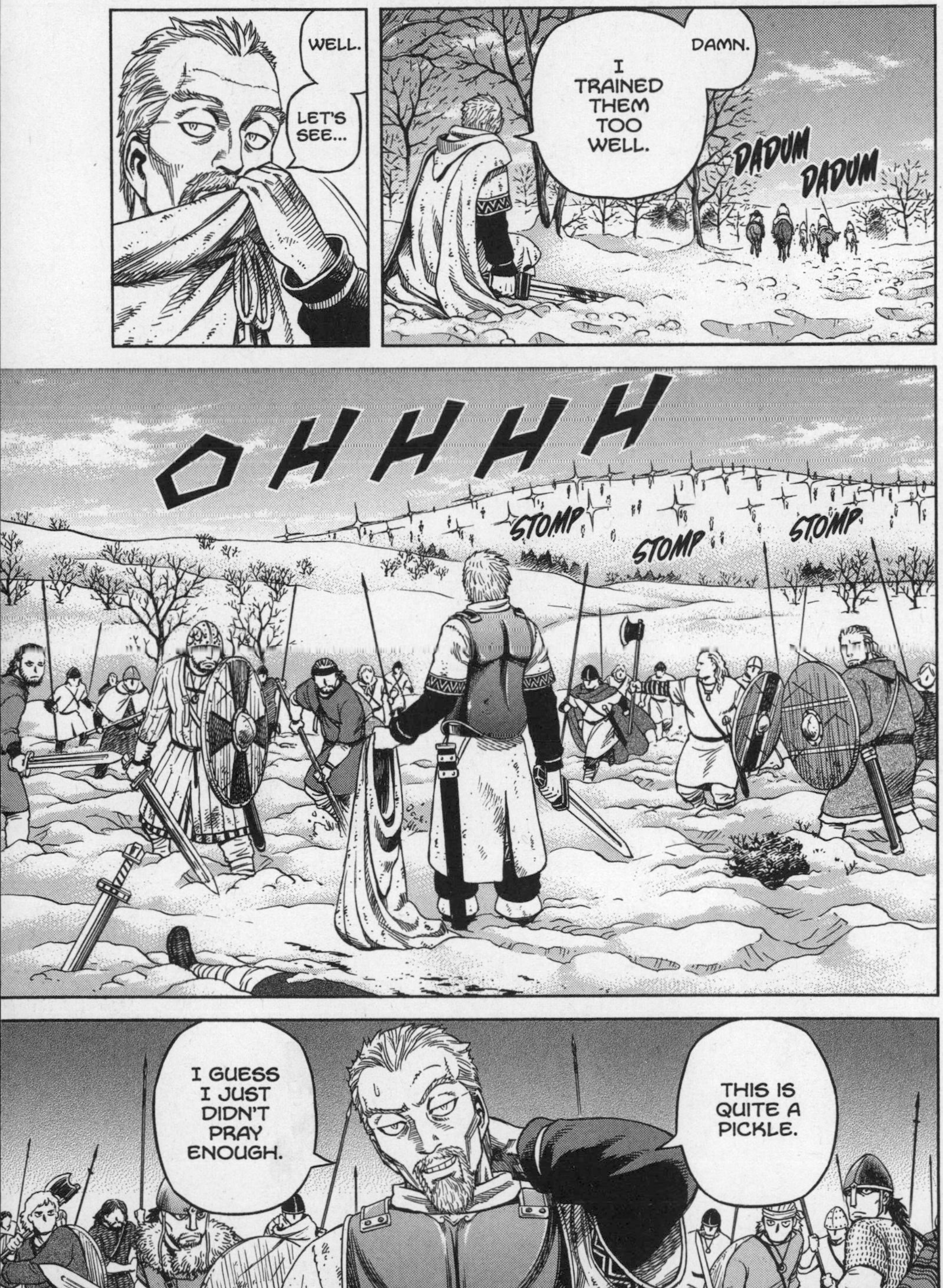
DAMN.
I TRAINED THEM TOO WELL.
DADUM
DADUM
WELL.
LET'S SEE...
OHHHH
STOMP
STOMP
STOMP
THIS IS QUITE A PICKLE.
I GUESS I JUST DIDN'T PRAY ENOUGH.

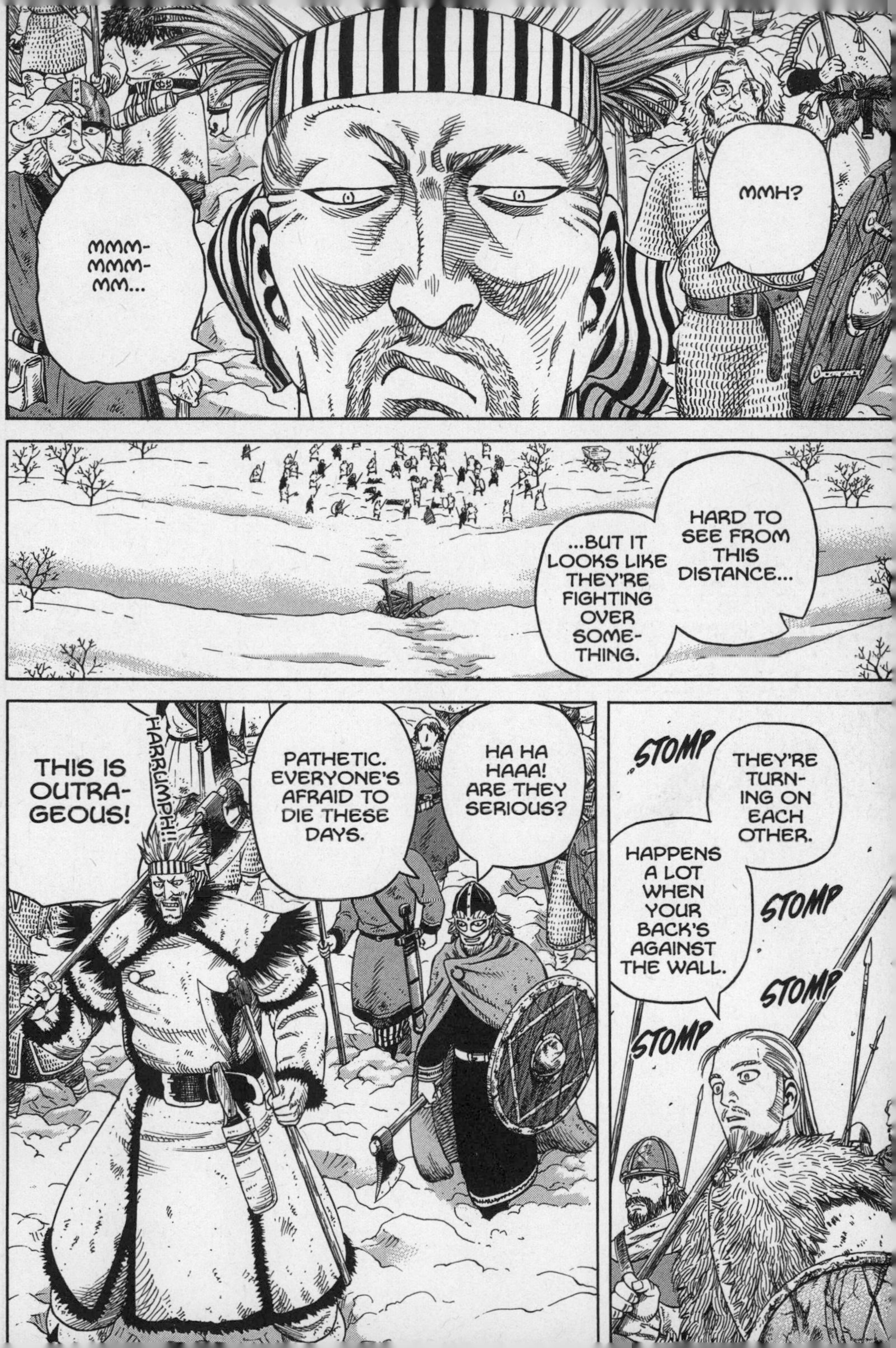
MMH?
MMM-MMM-MM...
HARD TO SEE FROM THIS DISTANCE...
...BUT IT LOOKS LIKE THEY'RE FIGHTING OVER SOME-THING.
STOMP
THEY'RE TURN-ING ON EACH OTHER.
HAPPENS A LOT WHEN YOUR BACK'S AGAINST THE WALL.
STOMP
STOMP
STOMP
HA HA HAAA! ARE THEY SERIOUS?
PATHETIC. EVERYONE'S AFRAID TO DIE THESE DAYS.
HARRUMPH!!
THIS IS OUTRA-GEOUS!

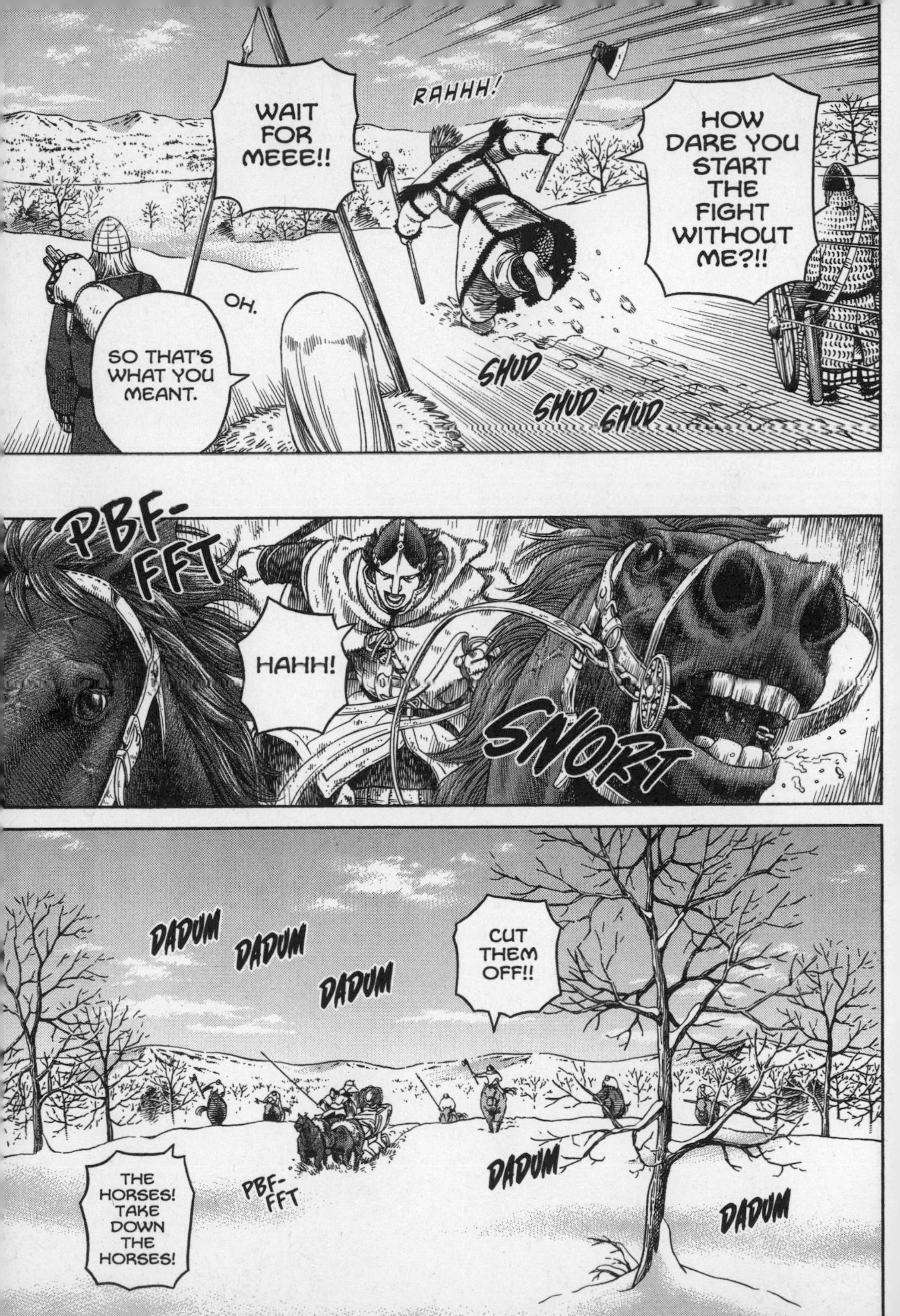
HOW DARE YOU START THE FIGHT WITHOUT ME?!!
RAHHH!
WAIT FOR MEEE!!
OH.
SO THAT'S WHAT YOU MEANT.
SHUD
SHUD
SHUD
SNORT
HAHH!
PBF-FFT
CUT THEM OFF!!
DADUM
DADUM
DADUM
DADUM
DADUM
PBF-FFT
THE HORSES! TAKE DOWN THE HORSES!

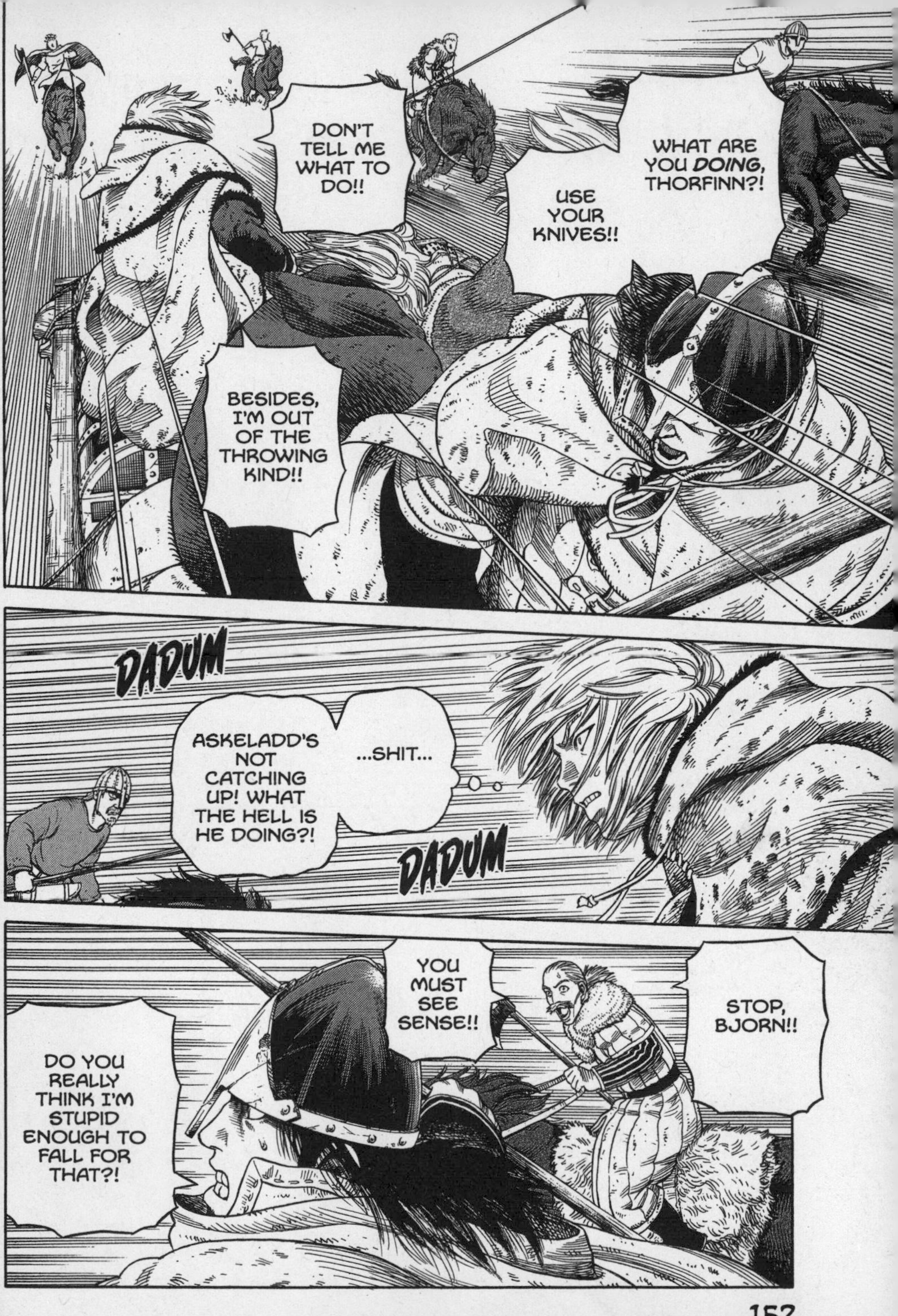
WHAT ARE YOU DOING, THORFINN?!
USE YOUR KNIVES!!
DON'T TELL ME WHAT TO DO!!
BESIDES, I'M OUT OF THE THROWING KIND!!
DADUM
...SHIT...
ASKELADD'S NOT CATCHING UP! WHAT THE HELL IS HE DOING?!
DADUM
STOP, BJORN!!
YOU MUST SEE SENSE!!
DO YOU REALLY THINK I'M STUPID ENOUGH TO FALL FOR THAT?!

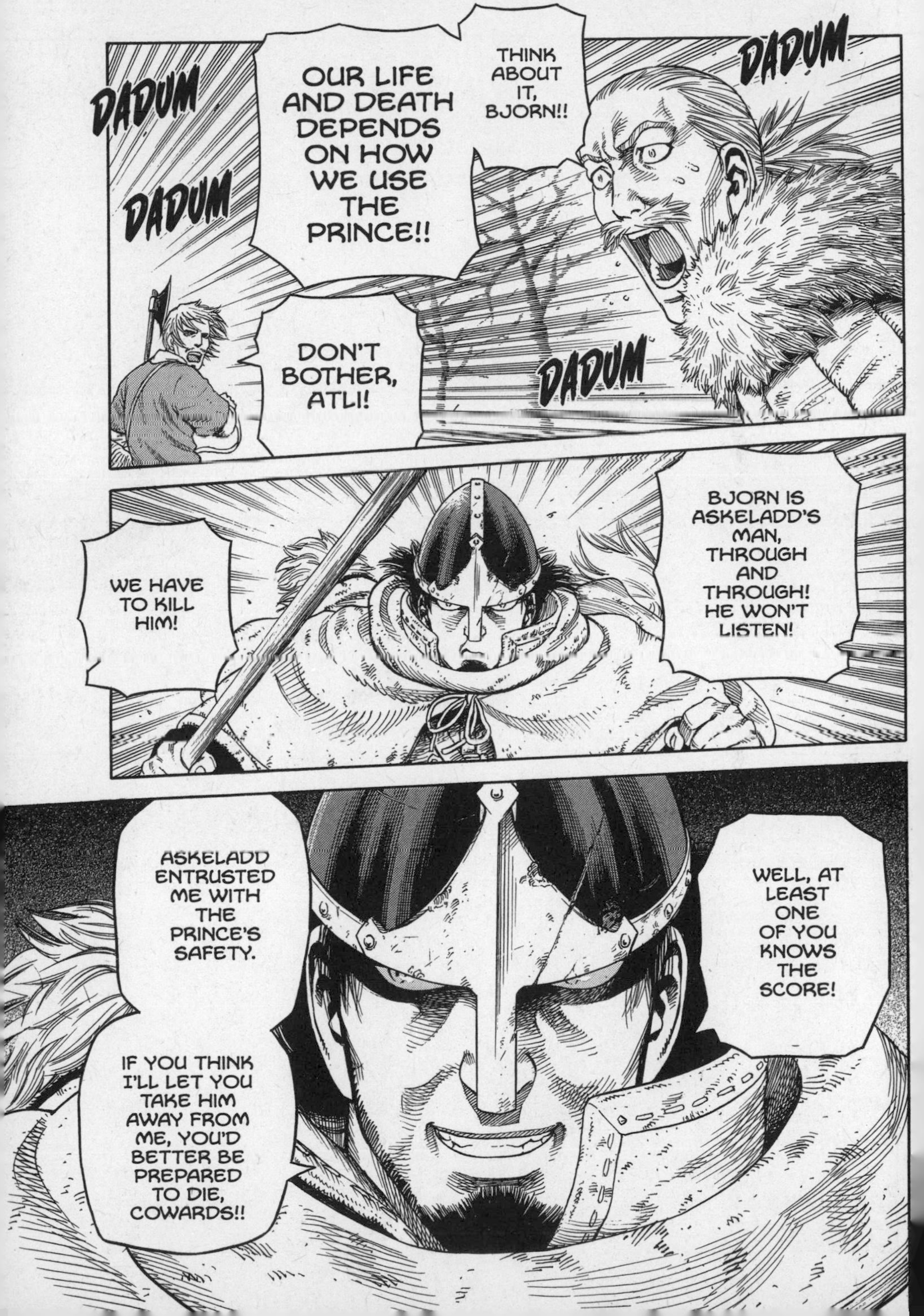
DADUM
THINK ABOUT IT, BJORN!!
OUR LIFE AND DEATH DEPENDS ON HOW WE USE THE PRINCE!!
DADUM
DADUM
DADUM
DON'T BOTHER, ATLI!
BJORN IS ASKELADD'S MAN, THROUGH AND THROUGH! HE WON'T LISTEN!
WE HAVE TO KILL HIM!
WELL, AT LEAST ONE OF YOU KNOWS THE SCORE!
ASKELADD ENTRUSTED ME WITH THE PRINCE'S SAFETY.
IF YOU THINK I'LL LET YOU TAKE HIM AWAY FROM ME, YOU'D BETTER BE PREPARED TO DIE, COWARDS!!

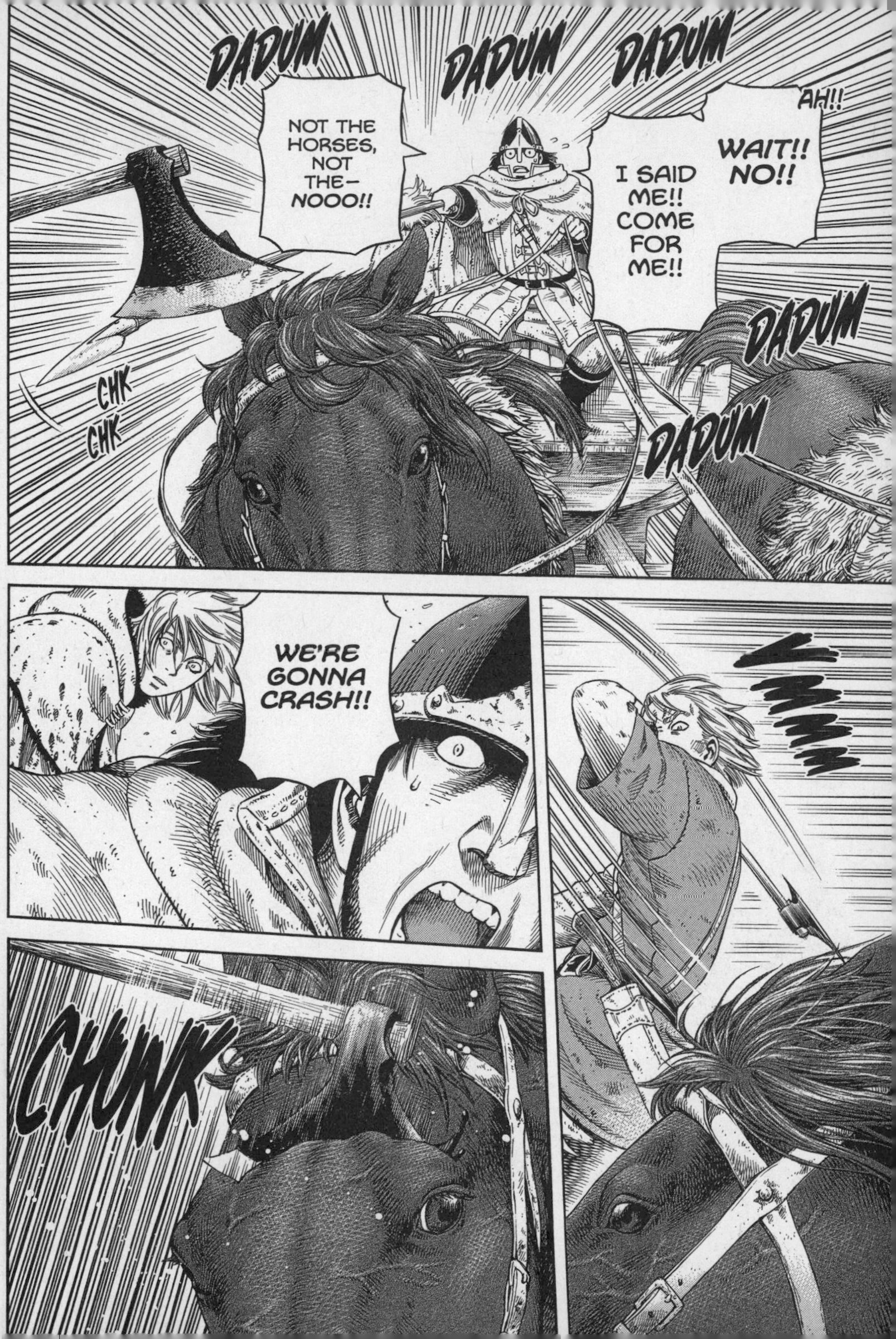
DADUM
AH!!
WAIT!! NO!!
I SAID ME!! COME FOR ME!!
DADUM
NOT THE HORSES, NOT THE— NOOO!!
DADUM
DADUM
DADUM
CHK CHK
WE'RE GONNA CRASH!!
CHUNK

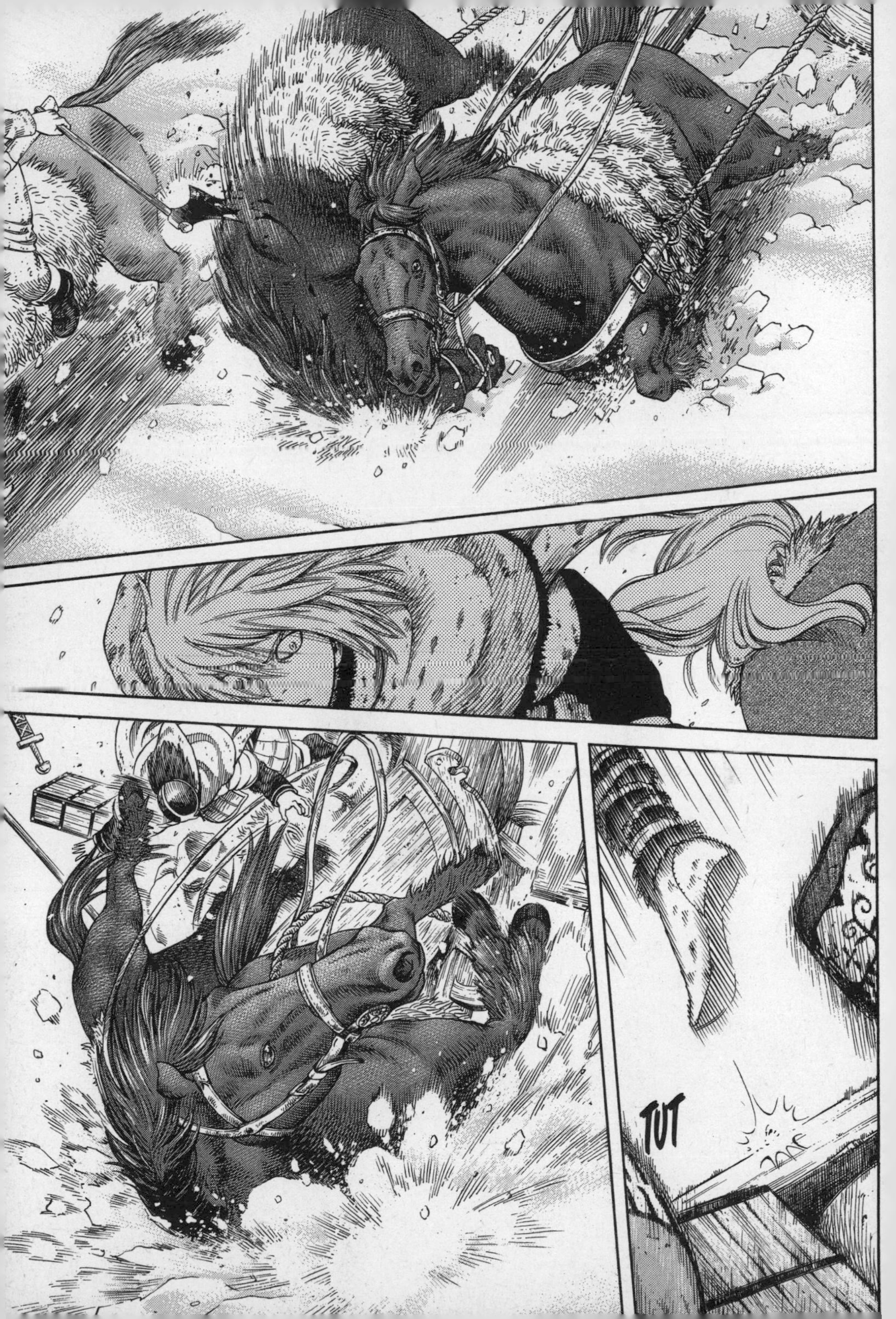
TUT

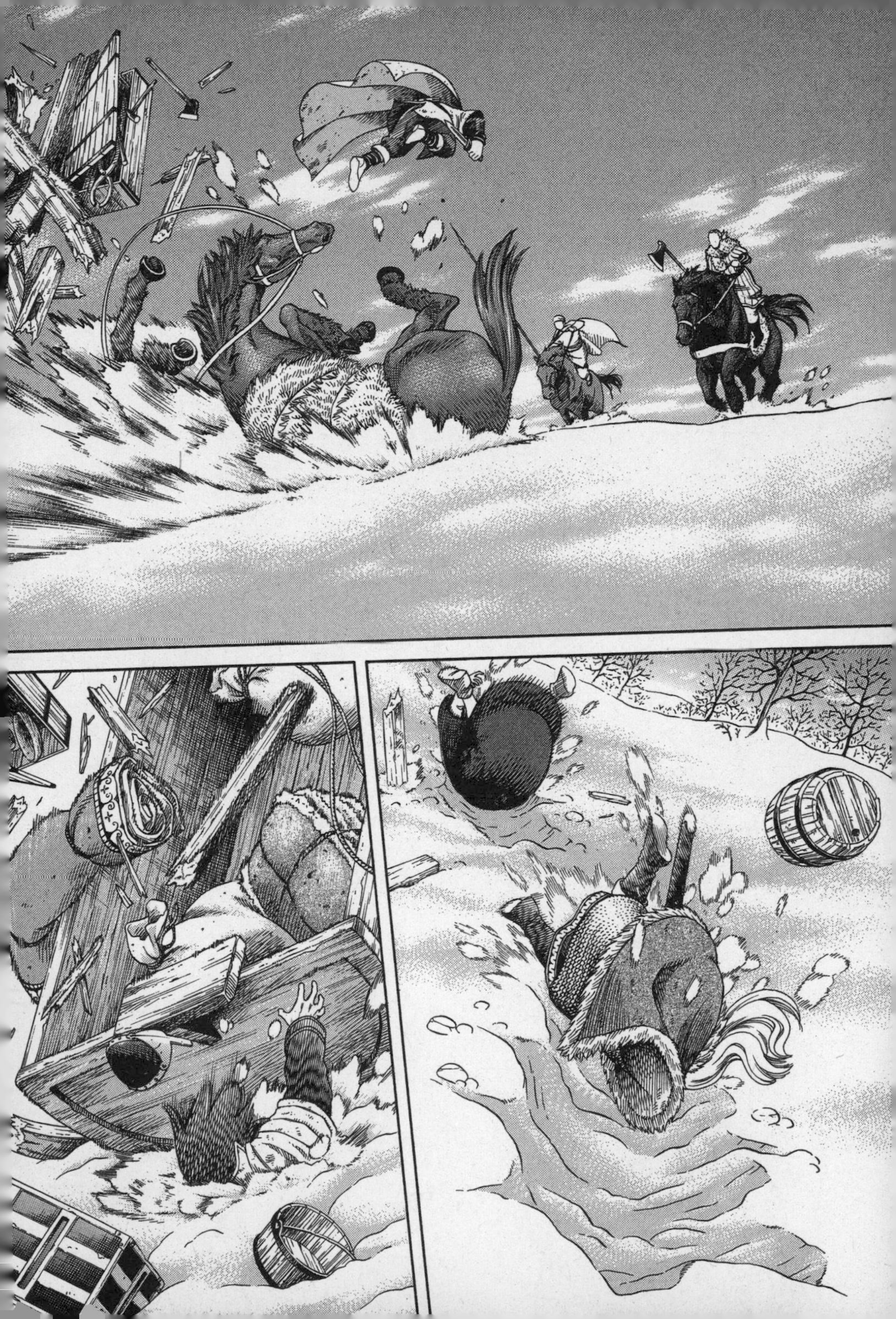

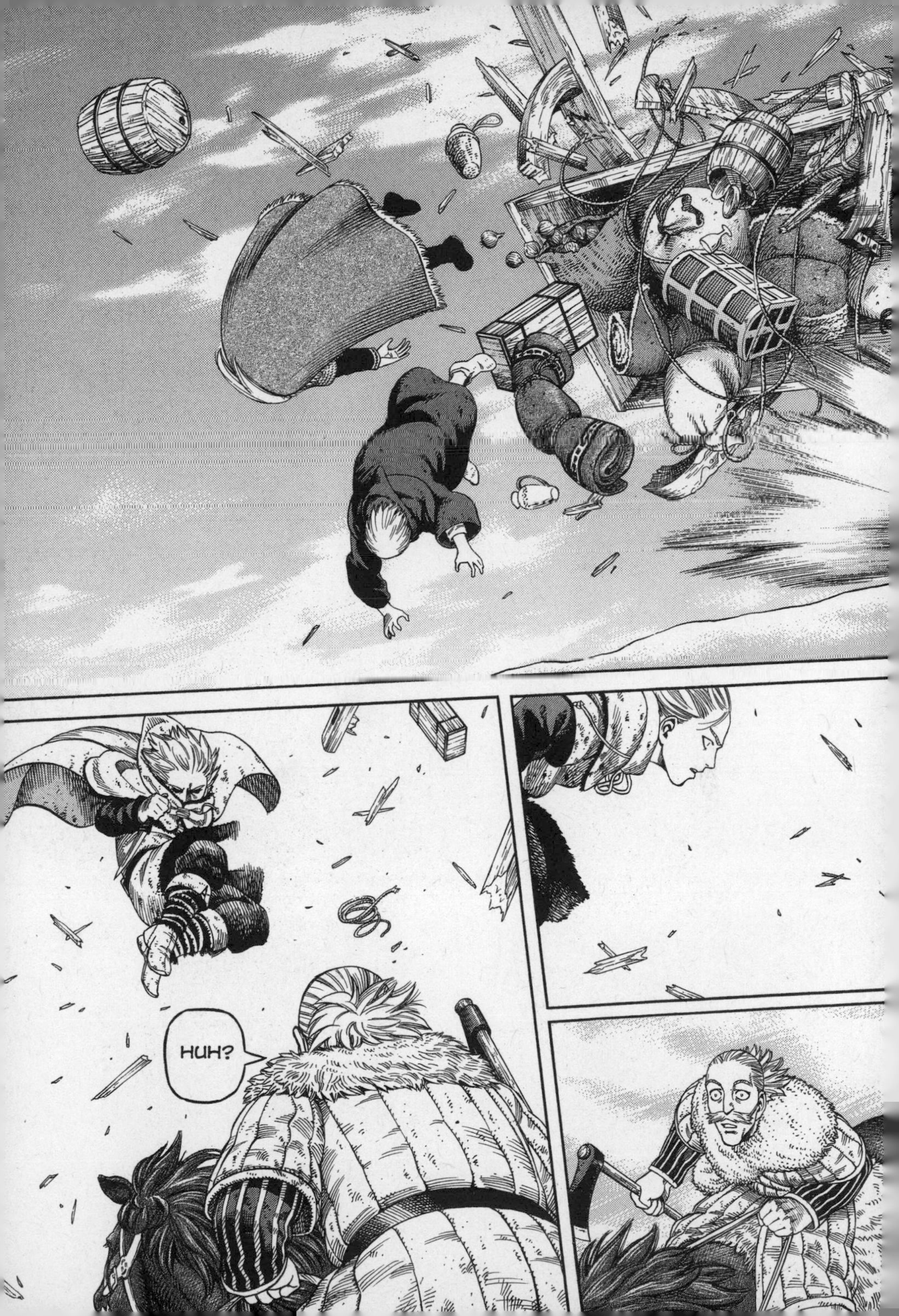
HUH?

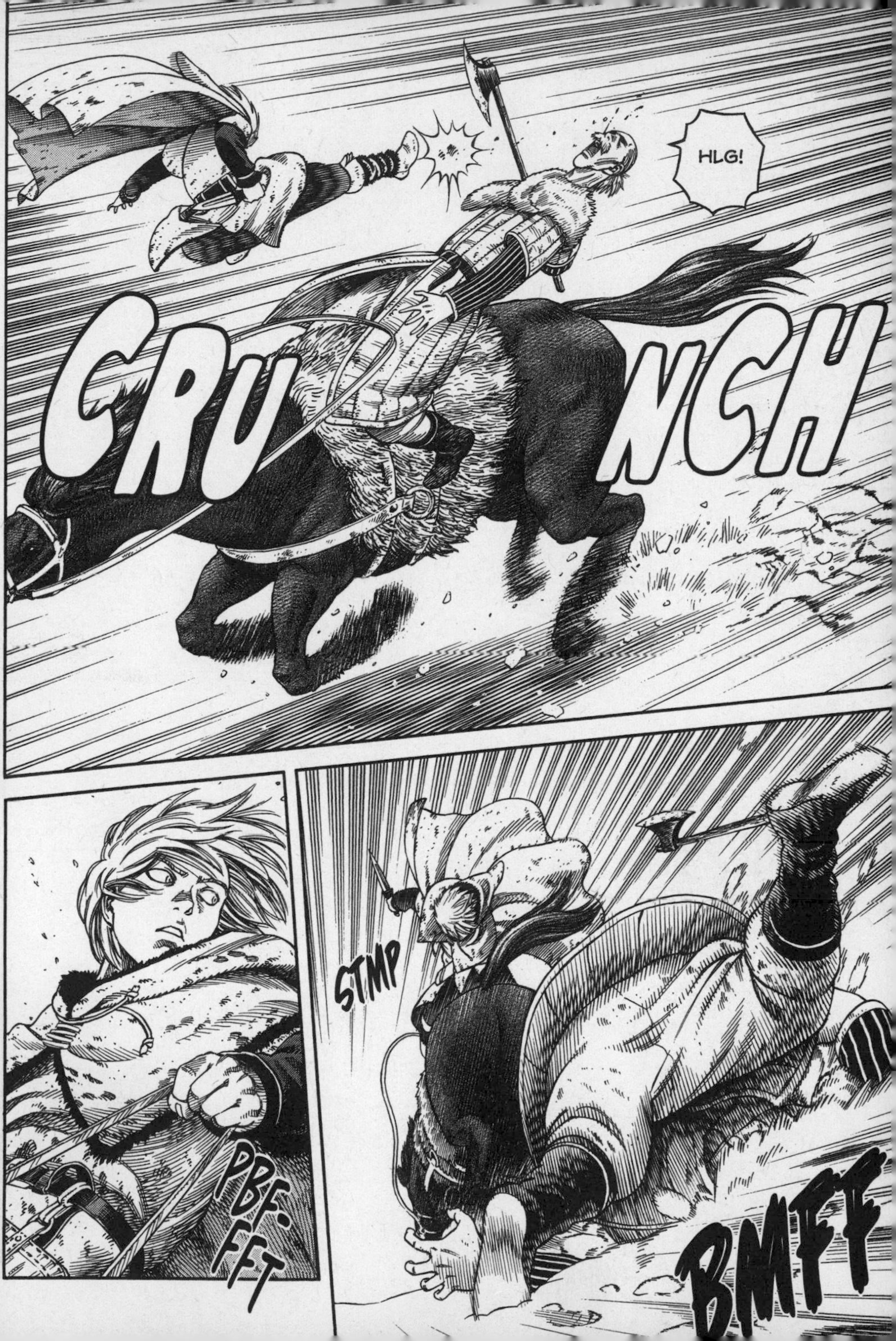
HLG!
CRUNCH
STMP
BMFF
PBF-FFT

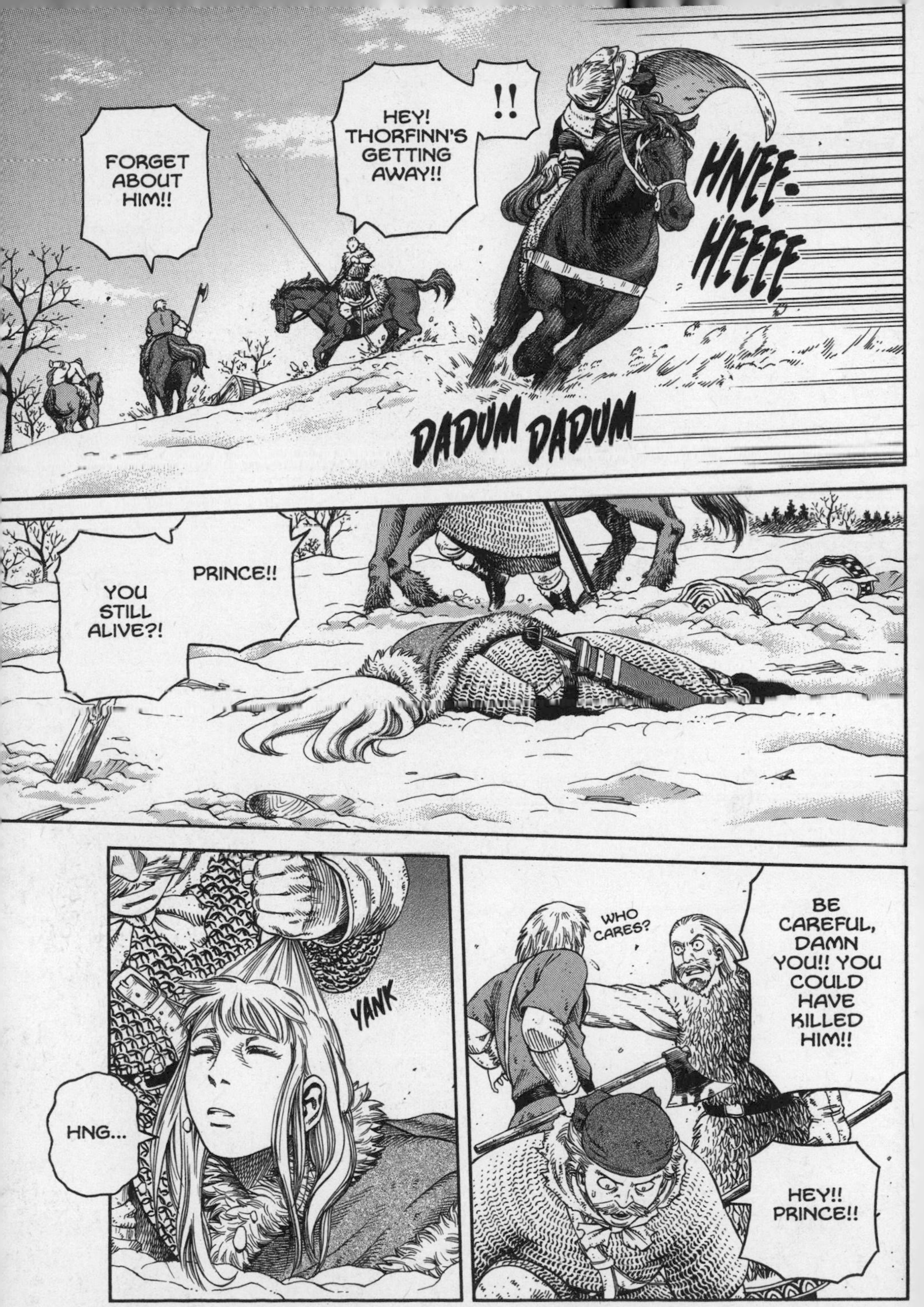
!!
HEY! THORFINN'S GETTING AWAY!!
HNEE-HEEEE
FORGET ABOUT HIM!!
DADUM DADUM
PRINCE!!
YOU STILL ALIVE?!
BE CAREFUL, DAMN YOU!! YOU COULD HAVE KILLED HIM!!
WHO CARES?
HEY!! PRINCE!!
YANK
HNG...

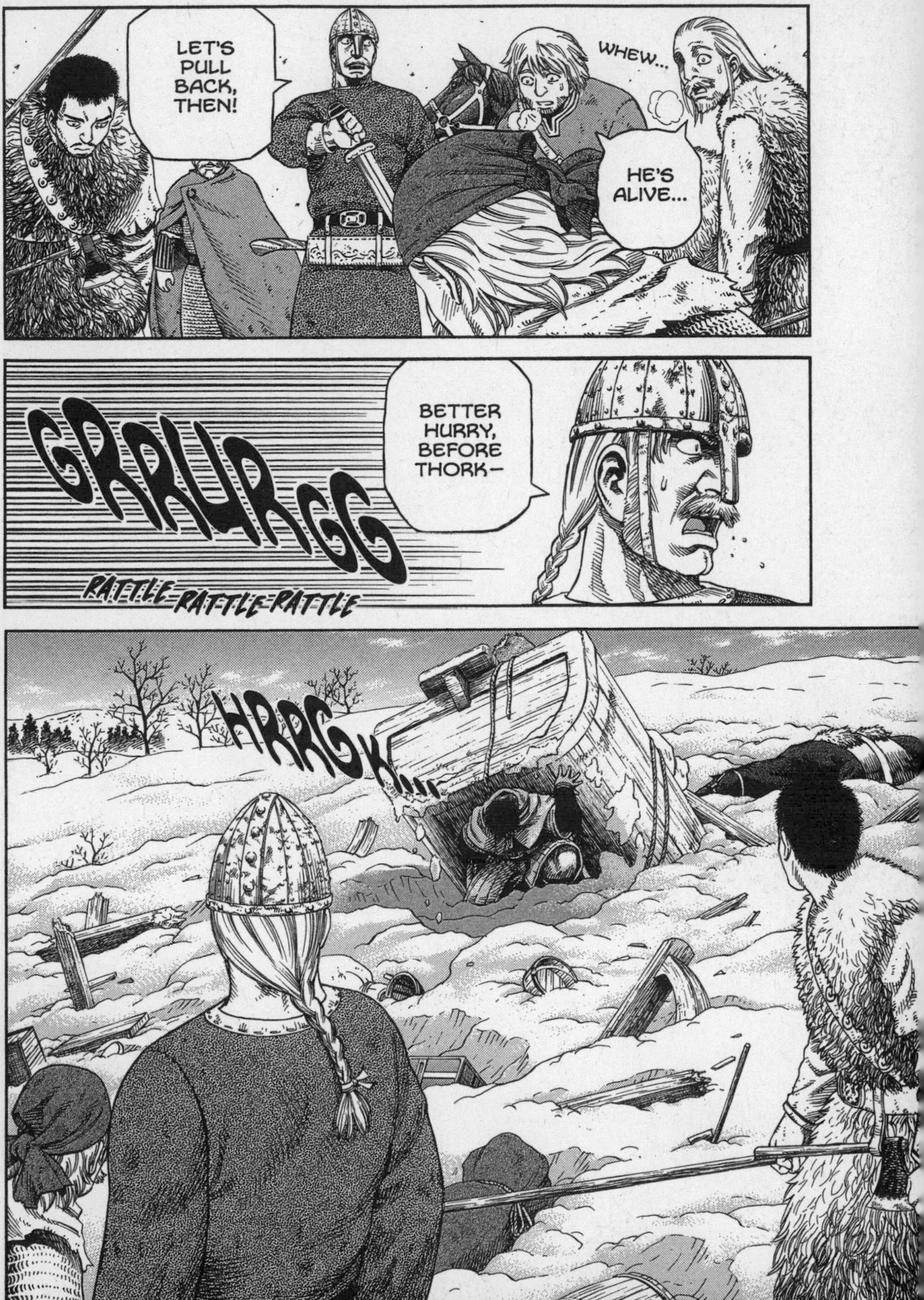
WHEW...
HE'S ALIVE...
LET'S PULL BACK, THEN!
BETTER HURRY, BEFORE THORK–
GRRURGG
RATTLE RATTLE RATTLE
HRRGK...

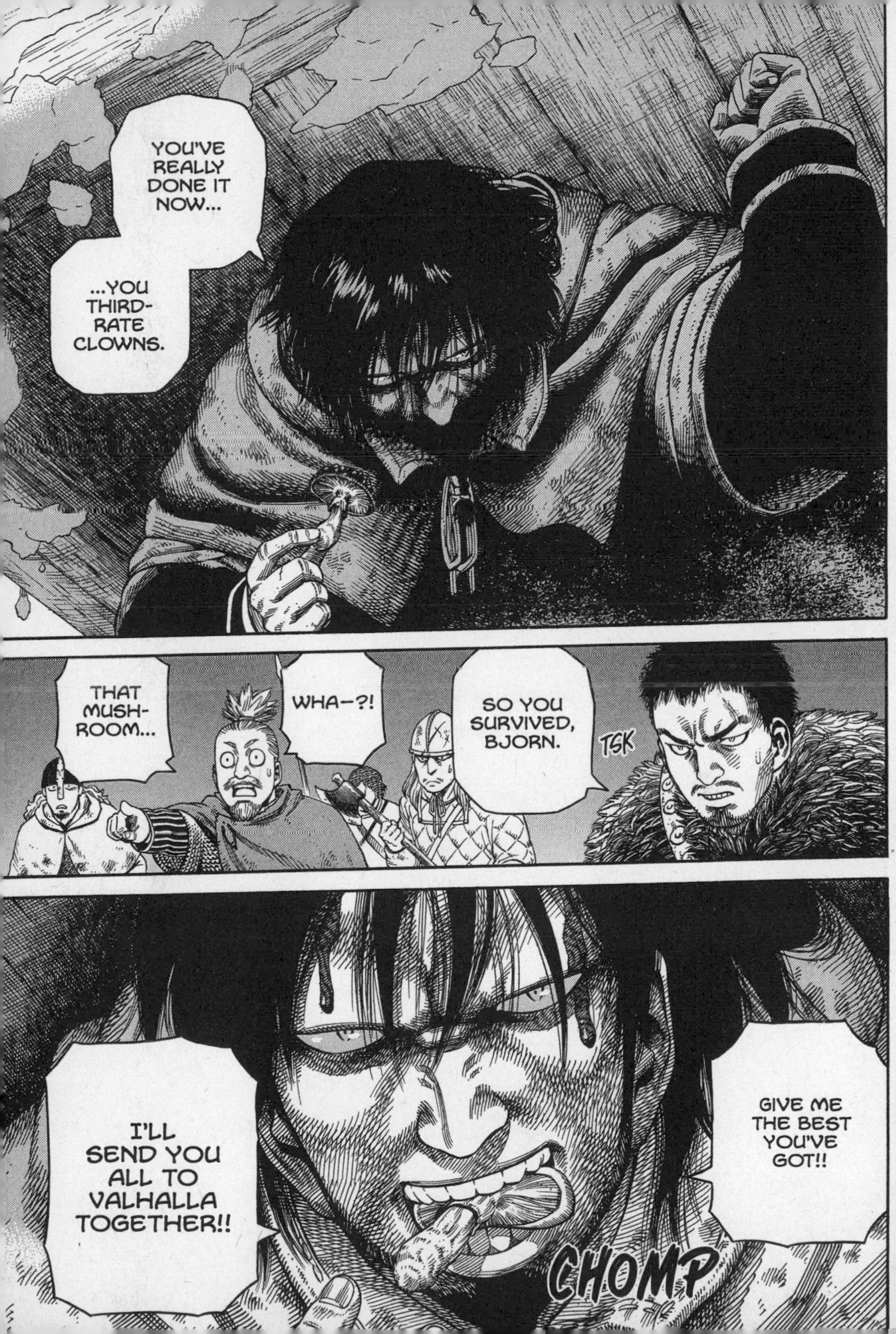
YOU'VE REALLY DONE IT NOW...
...YOU THIRD-RATE CLOWNS.
TSK
SO YOU SURVIVED, BJORN.
WHA-?!
THAT MUSH-ROOM...
GIVE ME THE BEST YOU'VE GOT!!
I'LL SEND YOU ALL TO VALHALLA TOGETHER!!
CHOMP

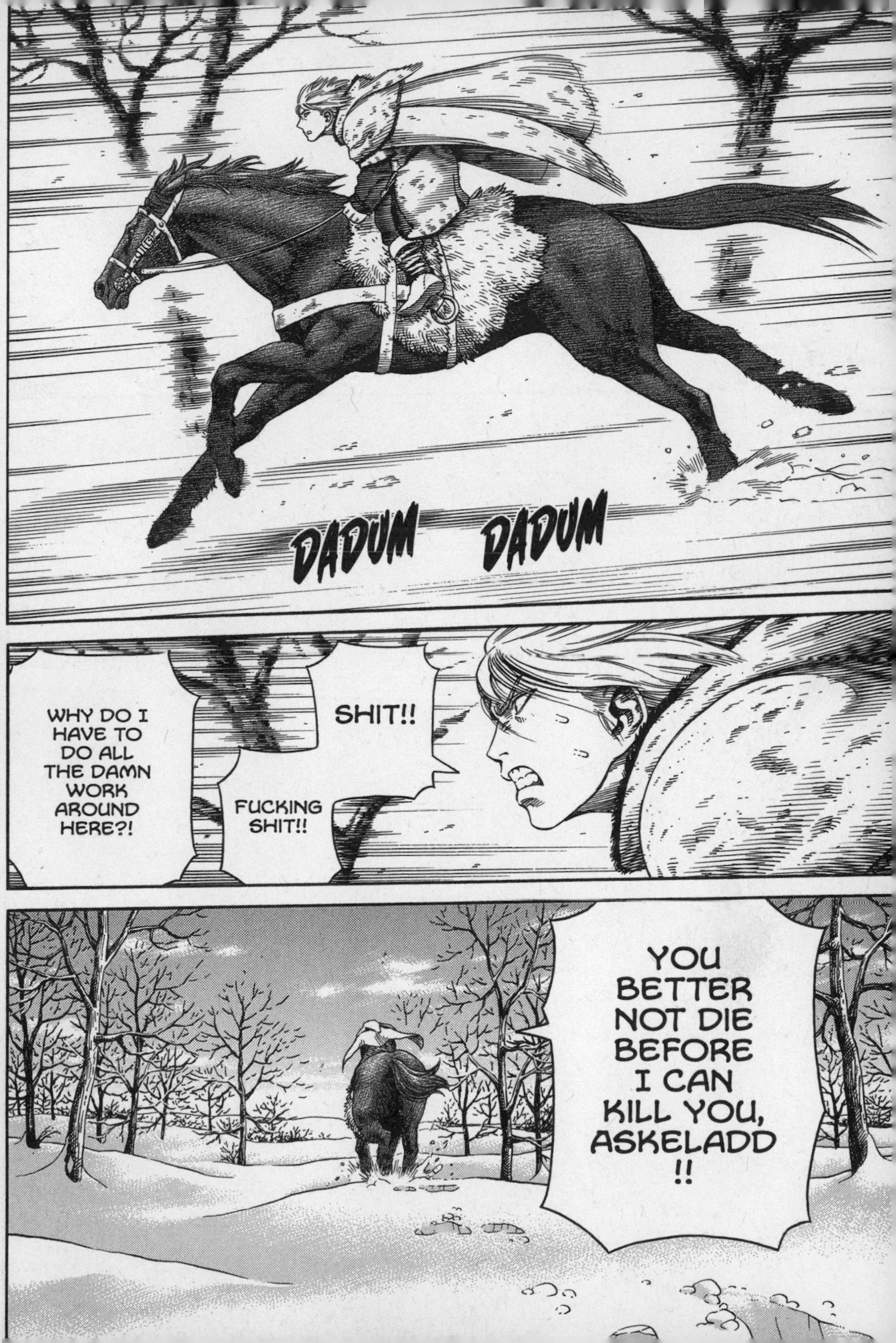
DADUM DADUM
SHIT!!
FUCKING SHIT!!
WHY DO I HAVE TO DO ALL THE DAMN WORK AROUND HERE?!
YOU BETTER NOT DIE BEFORE I CAN KILL YOU, ASKELADD !!

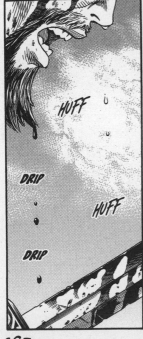

HUFF

DRIP

HUFF

DRIP

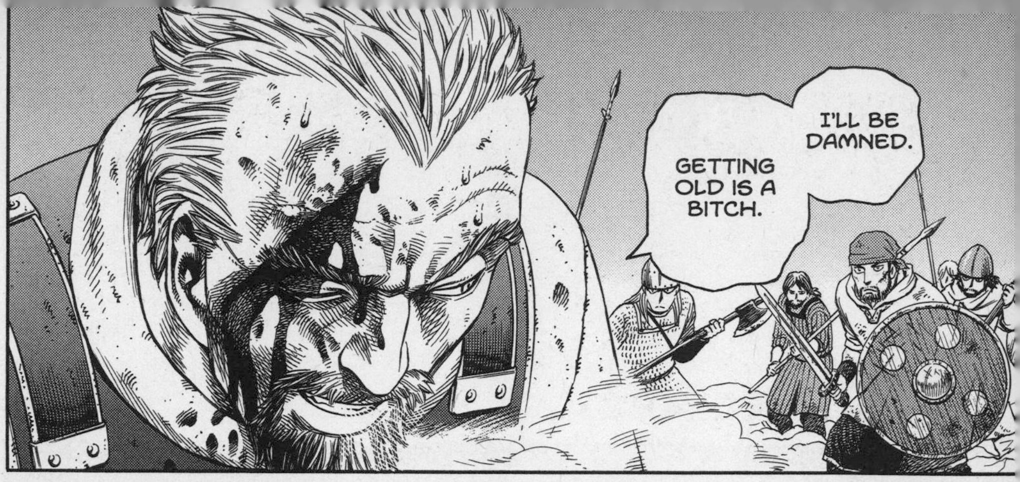
I'LL BE DAMNED.
GETTING OLD IS A BITCH.
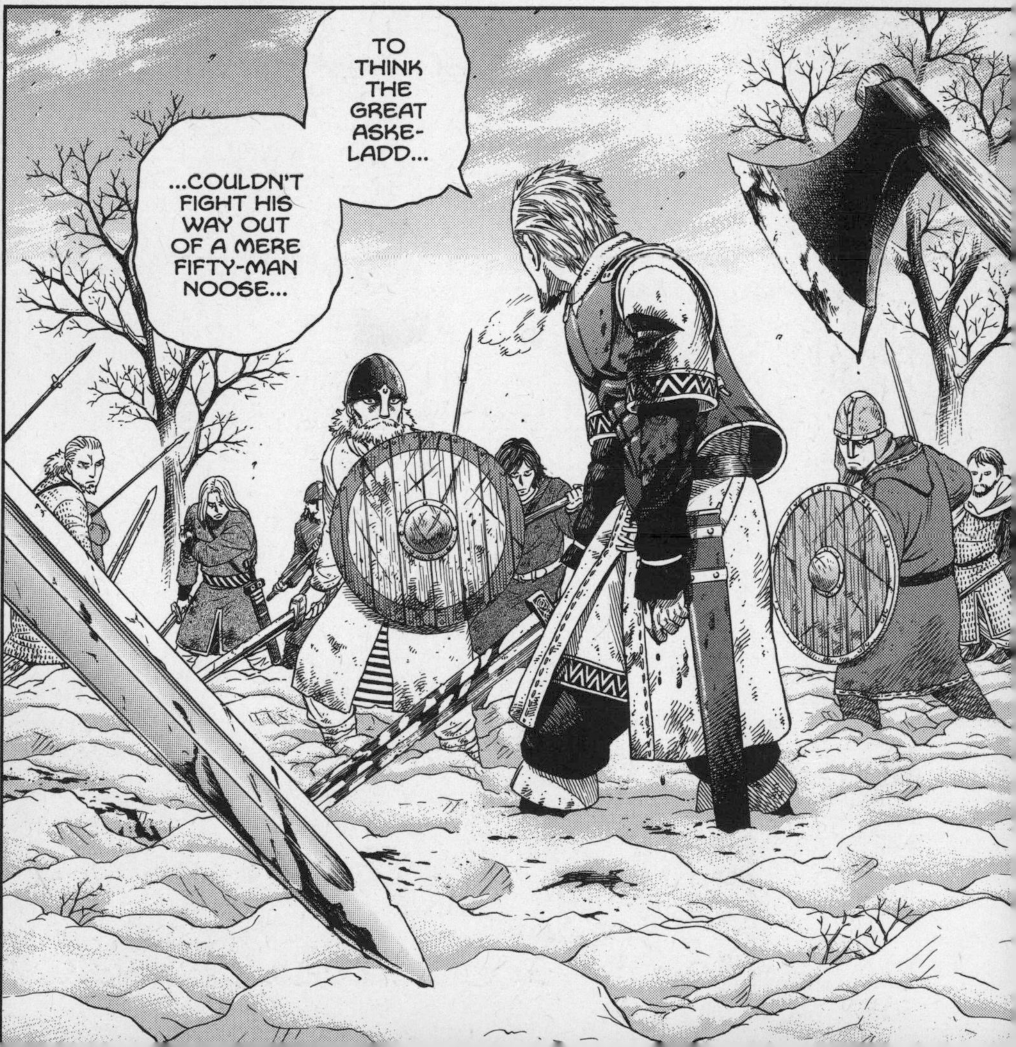
TO THINK THE GREAT ASKE-LADD...
...COULDN'T FIGHT HIS WAY OUT OF A MERE FIFTY-MAN NOOSE...

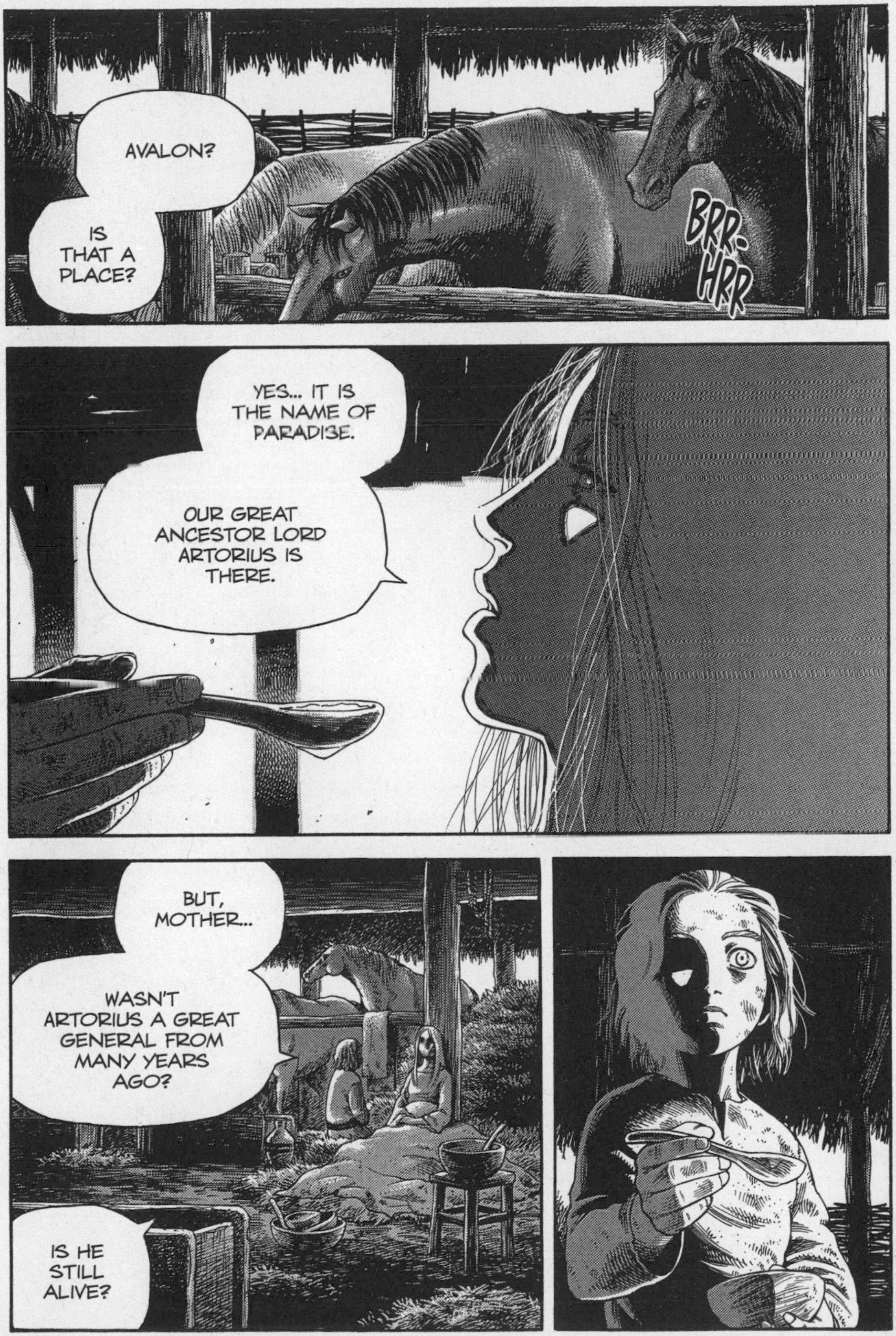
AVALON?
IS THAT A PLACE?
BRR-HRR
YES... IT IS THE NAME OF PARADISE.
OUR GREAT ANCESTOR LORD ARTORIUS IS THERE.
BUT, MOTHER...
WASN'T ARTORIUS A GREAT GENERAL FROM MANY YEARS AGO?
IS HE STILL ALIVE?

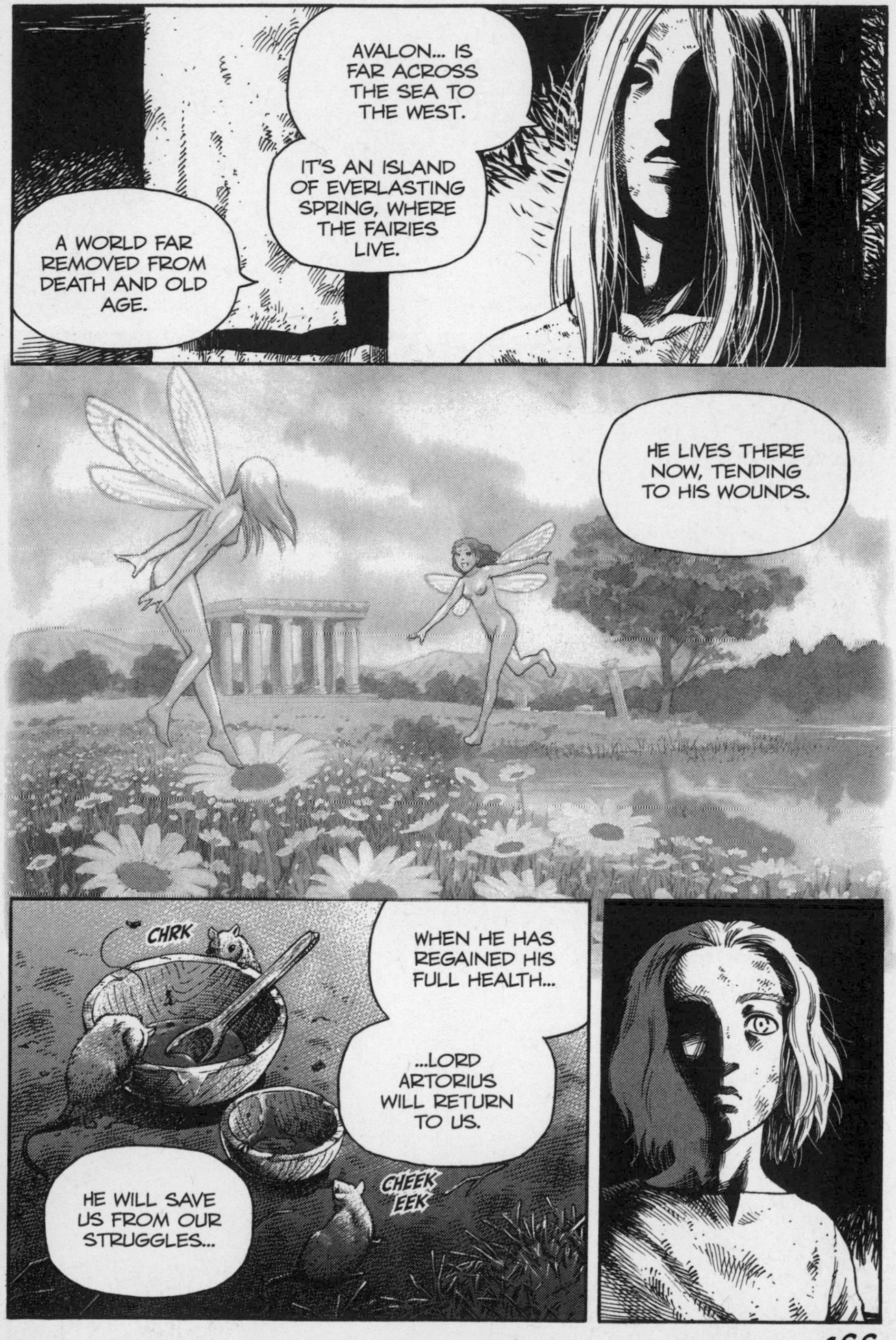
AVALON... IS FAR ACROSS THE SEA TO THE WEST.
IT'S AN ISLAND OF EVERLASTING SPRING, WHERE THE FAIRIES LIVE.
A WORLD FAR REMOVED FROM DEATH AND OLD AGE.
HE LIVES THERE NOW, TENDING TO HIS WOUNDS.
WHEN HE HAS REGAINED HIS FULL HEALTH...
...LORD ARTORIUS WILL RETURN TO US.
CHRK
CHEEK
EEK
HE WILL SAVE US FROM OUR STRUGGLES...

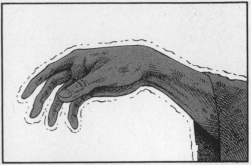

WHEN THAT TIME COMES...

...YOU MUST SERVE HIM, MY SON.

HE IS A WARRIOR, AND A TRUE KING.

BE HIS WISDOM...

BE HIS SWORD...

AND ONE DAY...

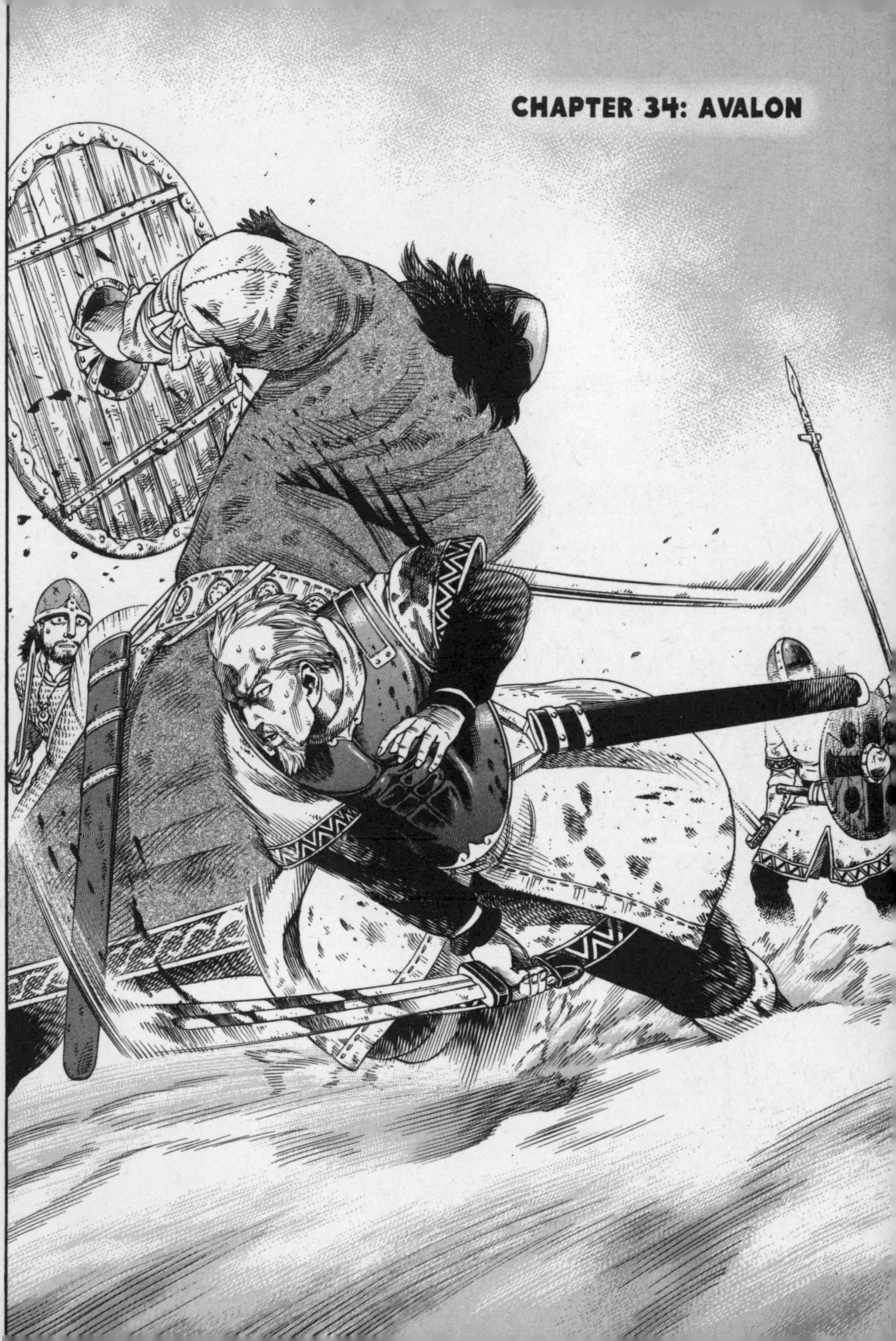
CHAPTER 34: AVALON

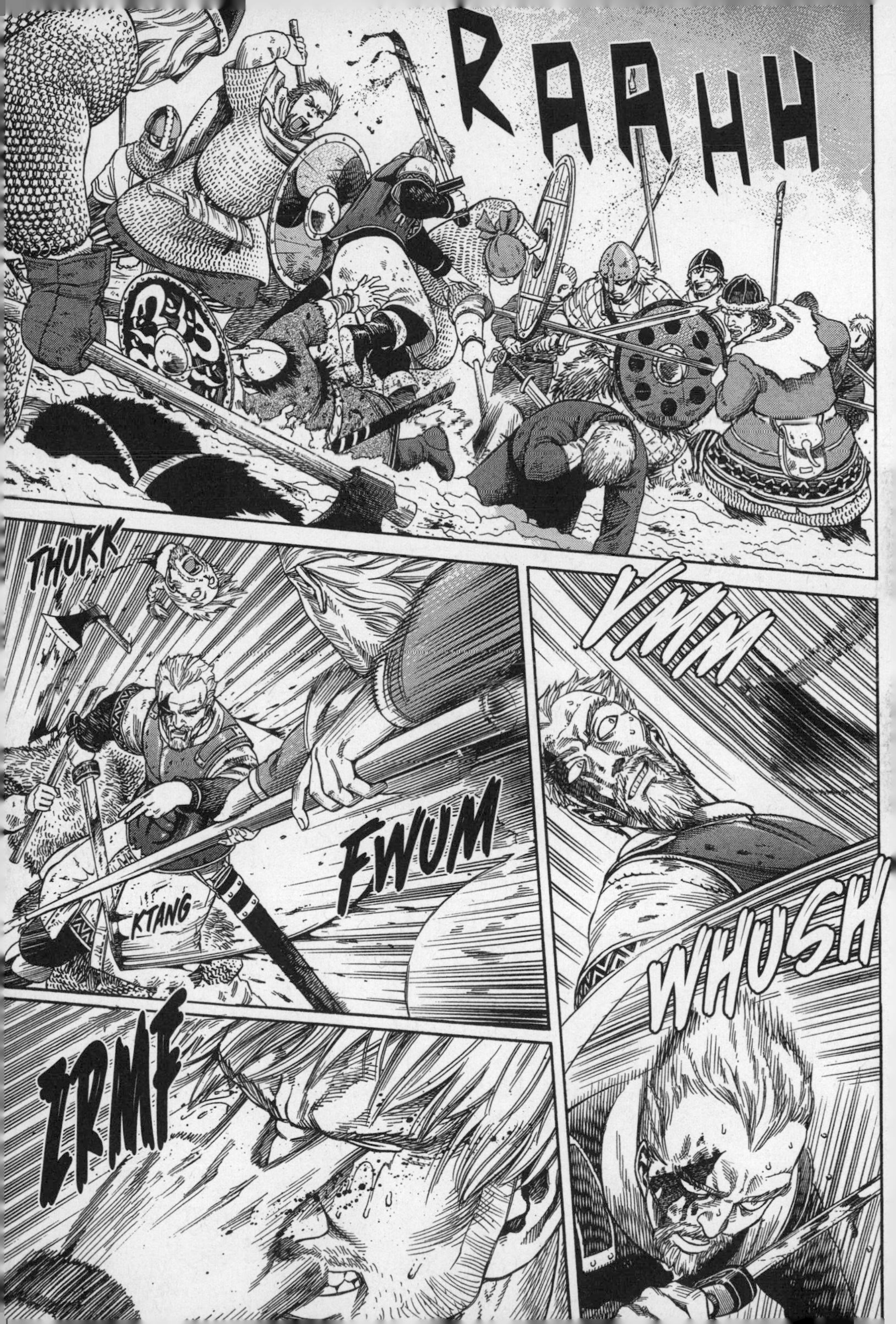
RAAHH
VMM
WHUSH
THUKK
FWUM
KTANG
ZRMF

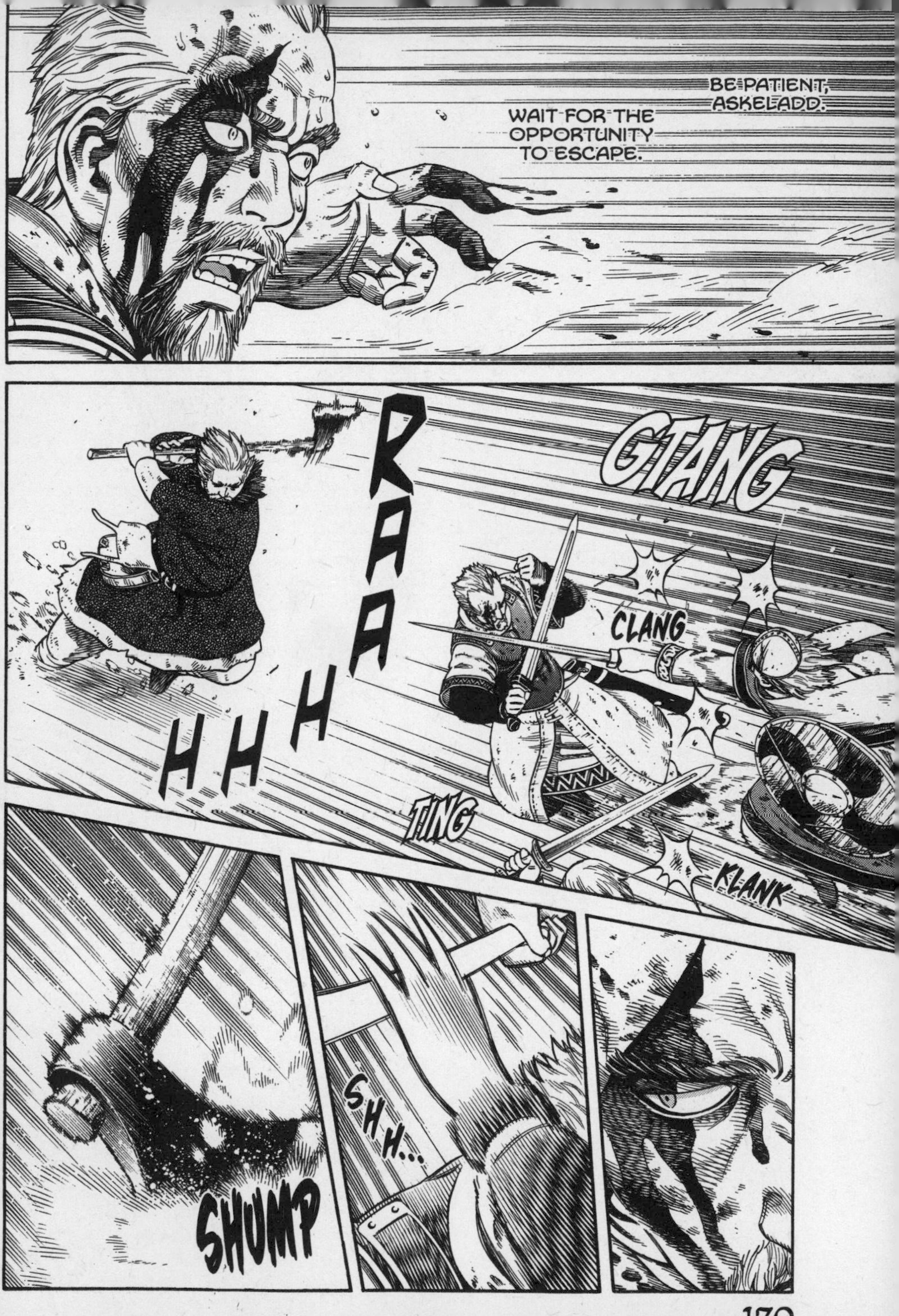
BE PATIENT, ASKELADD.
WAIT FOR THE OPPORTUNITY TO ESCAPE.
GTANG
CLANG
KLANK
TING
RAAAHHH
SHH...
SHUMP

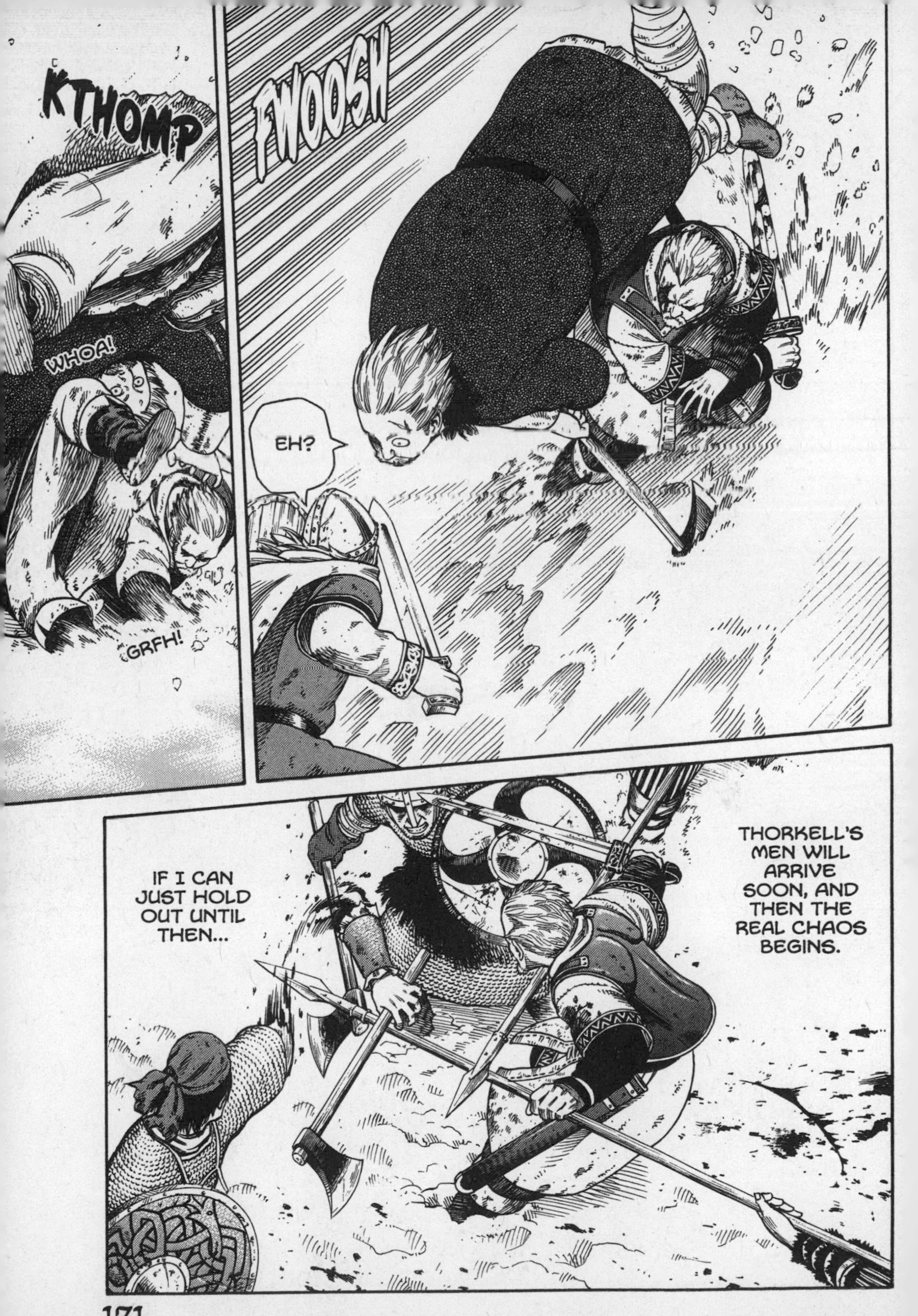
FWOOSH
EH?
KTHOMP
WHOA!
GRFH!
THORKELL'S MEN WILL ARRIVE SOON, AND THEN THE REAL CHAOS BEGINS.
IF I CAN JUST HOLD OUT UNTIL THEN...

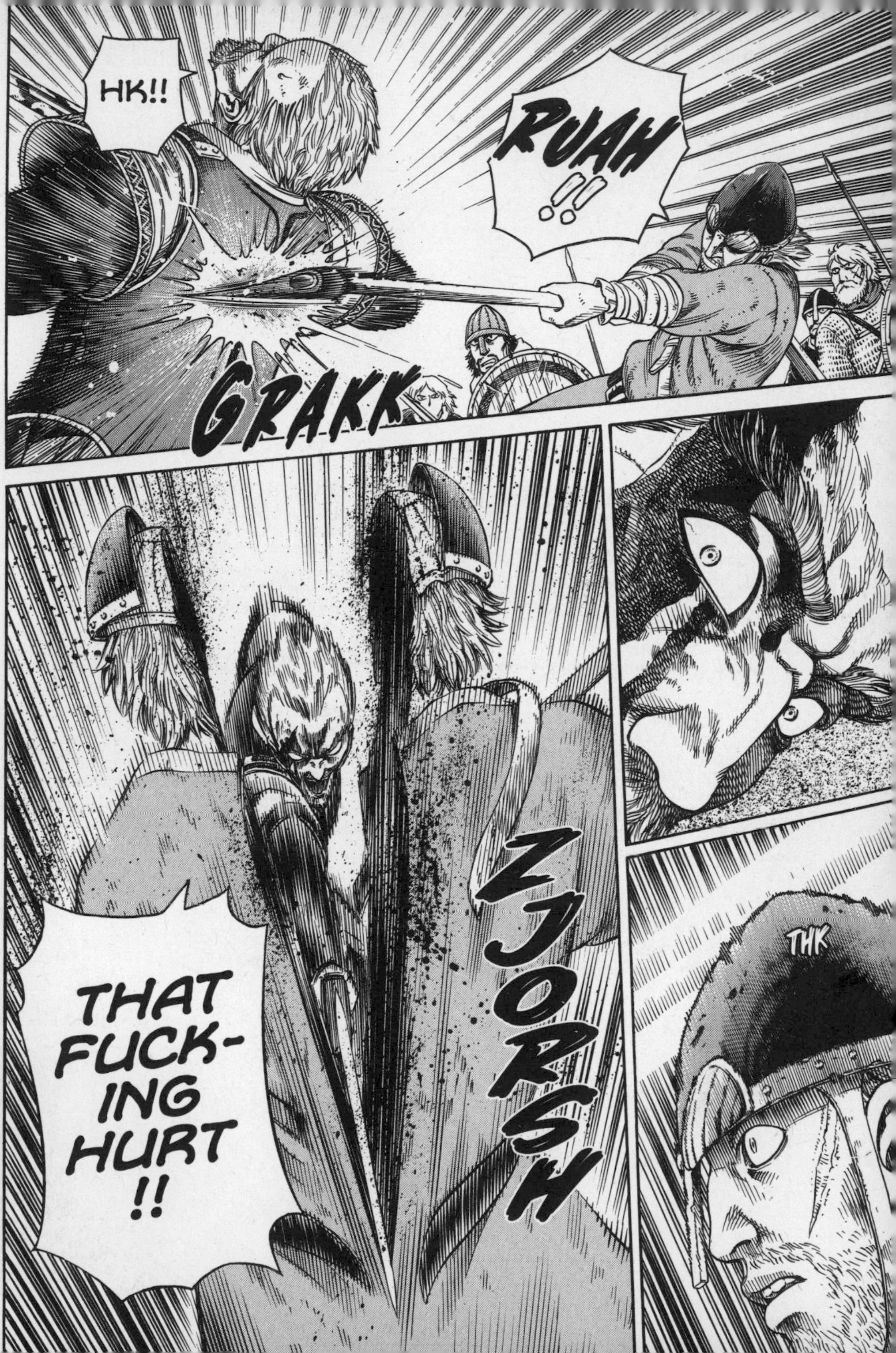
RUAH!!
HK!!
GRAKK
THK
ZJORSH
THAT FUCKING HURT!!

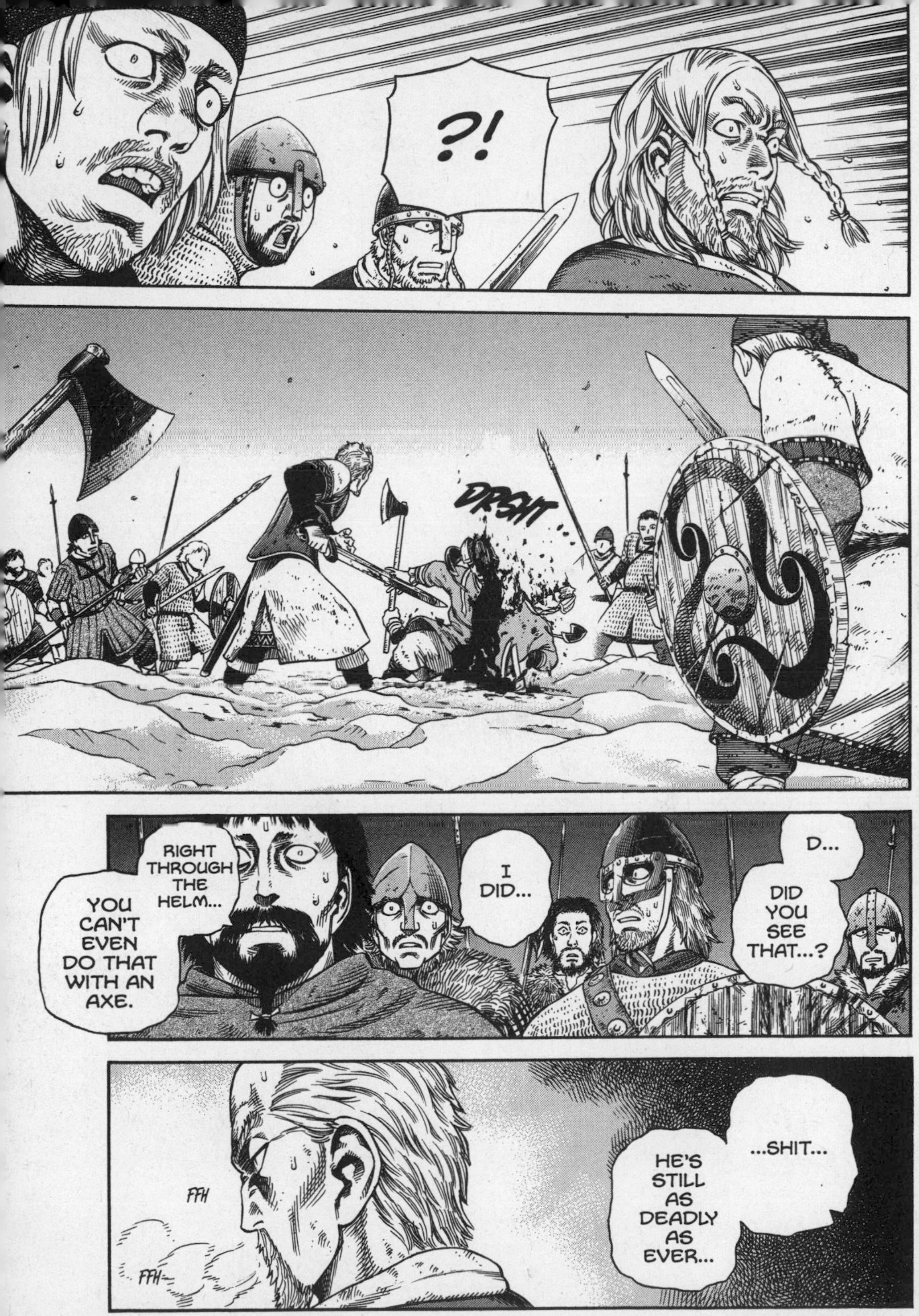
?!
DRSHT
D... DID YOU SEE THAT...?
I DID...
RIGHT THROUGH THE HELM...
YOU CAN'T EVEN DO THAT WITH AN AXE.
...SHIT...
HE'S STILL AS DEADLY AS EVER...
FFH
FFH

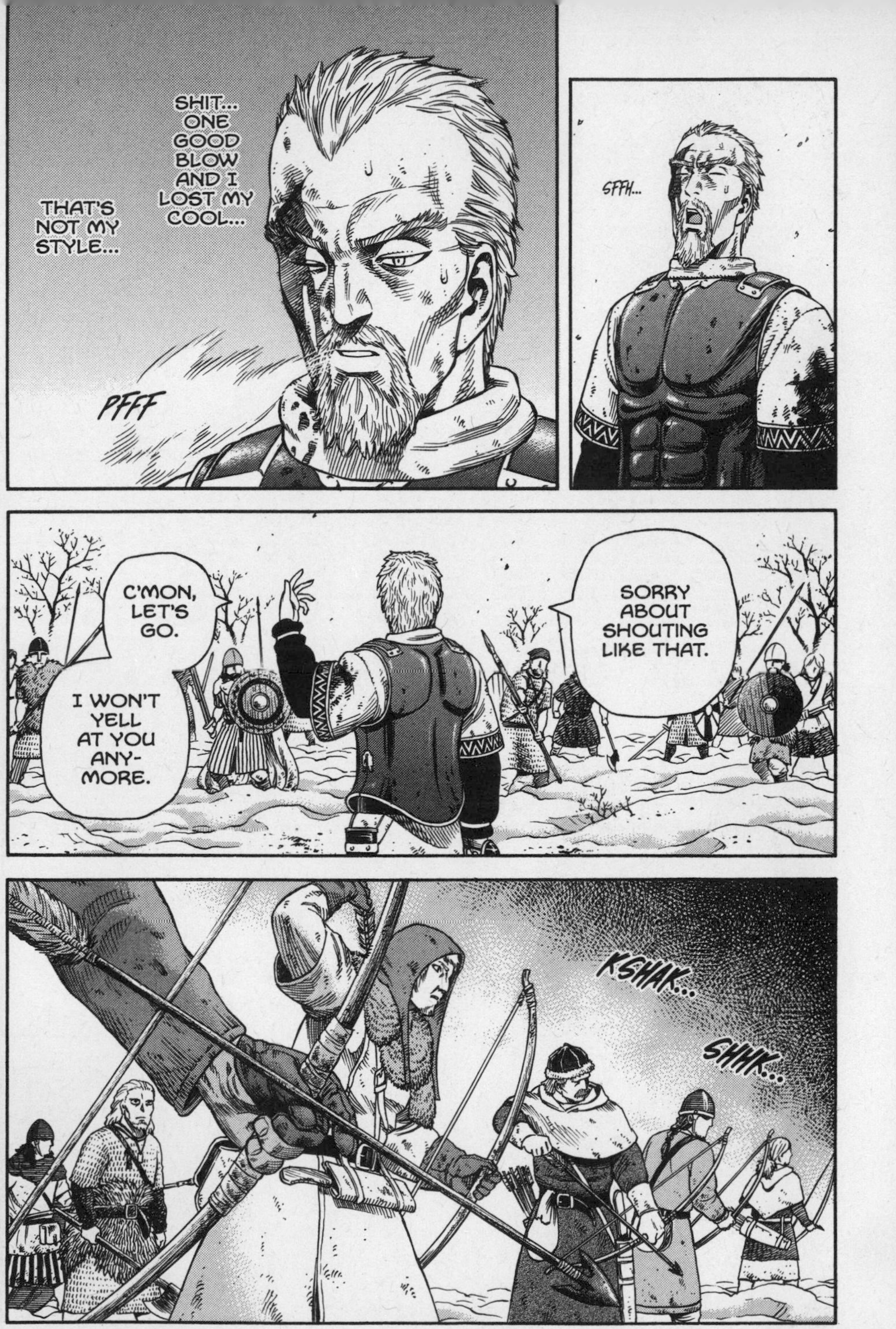
SFFH...
SHIT... ONE GOOD BLOW AND I LOST MY COOL...
THAT'S NOT MY STYLE...
PFFF
SORRY ABOUT SHOUTING LIKE THAT.
C'MON, LET'S GO.
I WON'T YELL AT YOU ANY-MORE.
KSHAK...
SHHK...

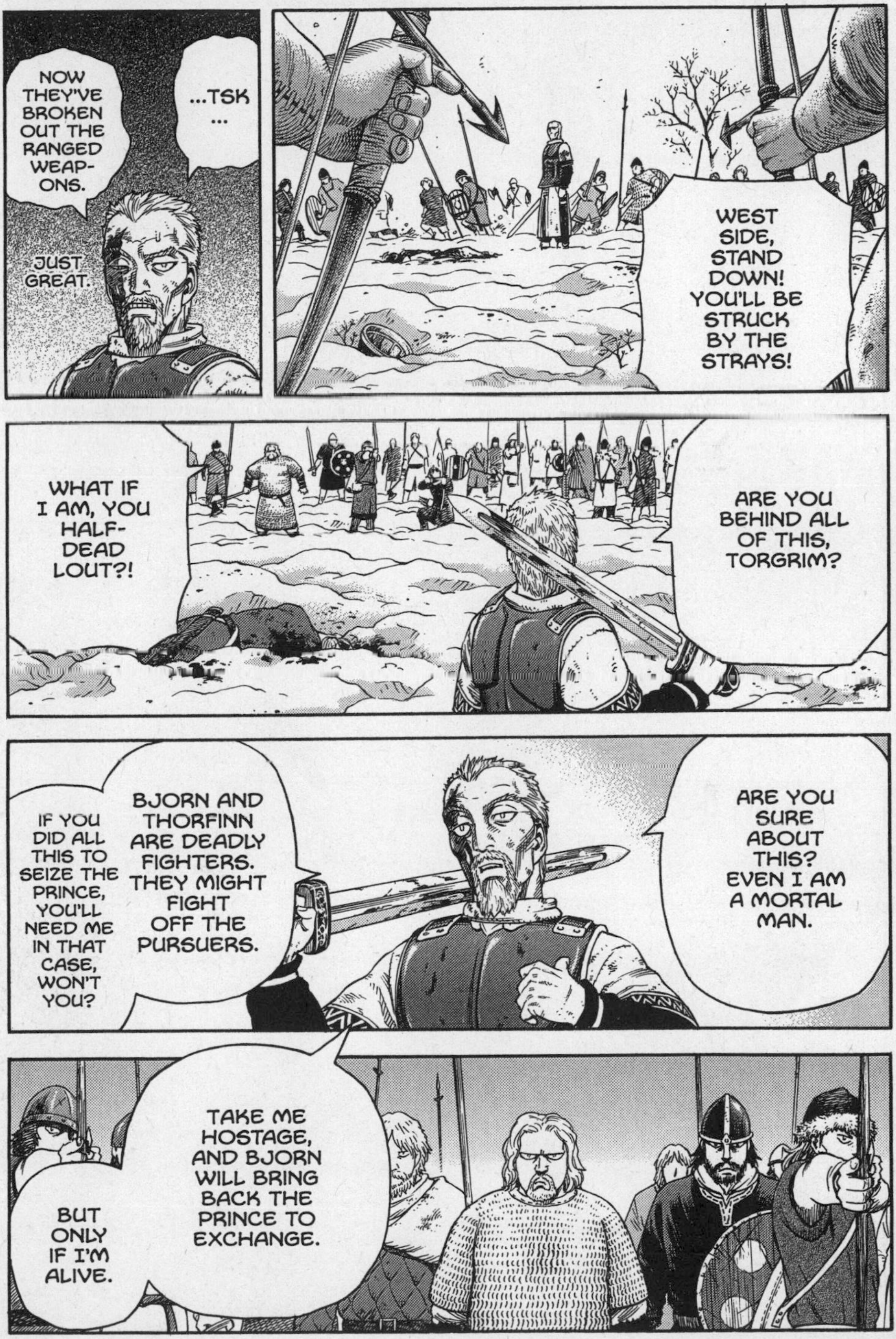
WEST SIDE, STAND DOWN! YOU'LL BE STRUCK BY THE STRAYS!
...TSK ...
NOW THEY'VE BROKEN OUT THE RANGED WEAP-ONS.
JUST GREAT.
ARE YOU BEHIND ALL OF THIS, TORGRIM?
WHAT IF I AM, YOU HALF-DEAD LOUT?!
ARE YOU SURE ABOUT THIS? EVEN I AM A MORTAL MAN.
BJORN AND THORFINN ARE DEADLY FIGHTERS. THEY MIGHT FIGHT OFF THE PURSUERS.
IF YOU DID ALL THIS TO SEIZE THE PRINCE, YOU'LL NEED ME IN THAT CASE, WON'T YOU?
TAKE ME HOSTAGE, AND BJORN WILL BRING BACK THE PRINCE TO EXCHANGE.
BUT ONLY IF I'M ALIVE.

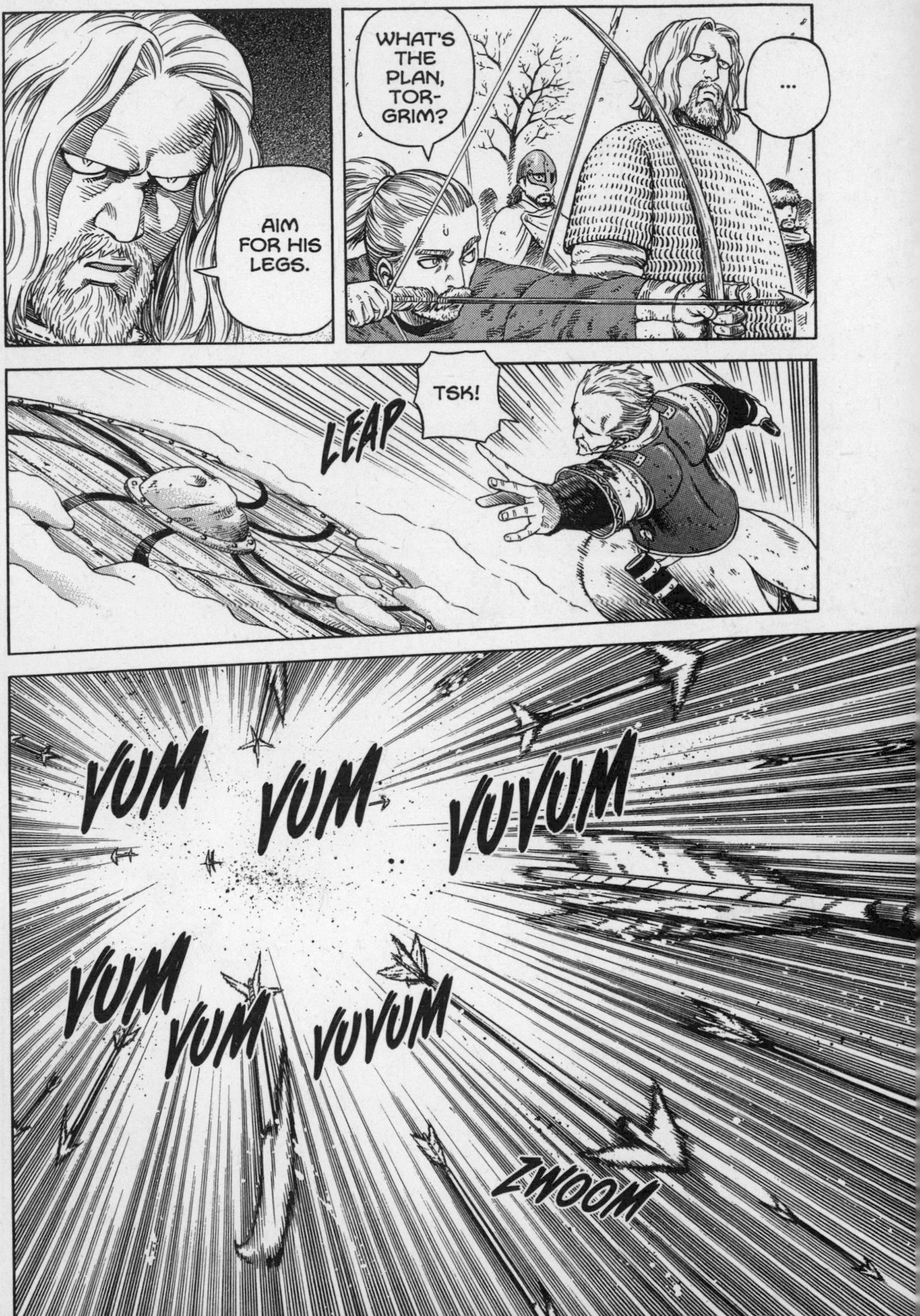
WHAT'S THE PLAN, TOR-GRIM?
...
AIM FOR HIS LEGS.
TSK!
LEAP
VUVUM
VUM
VUM
VUVUM
VUM
VUM
ZWOOM

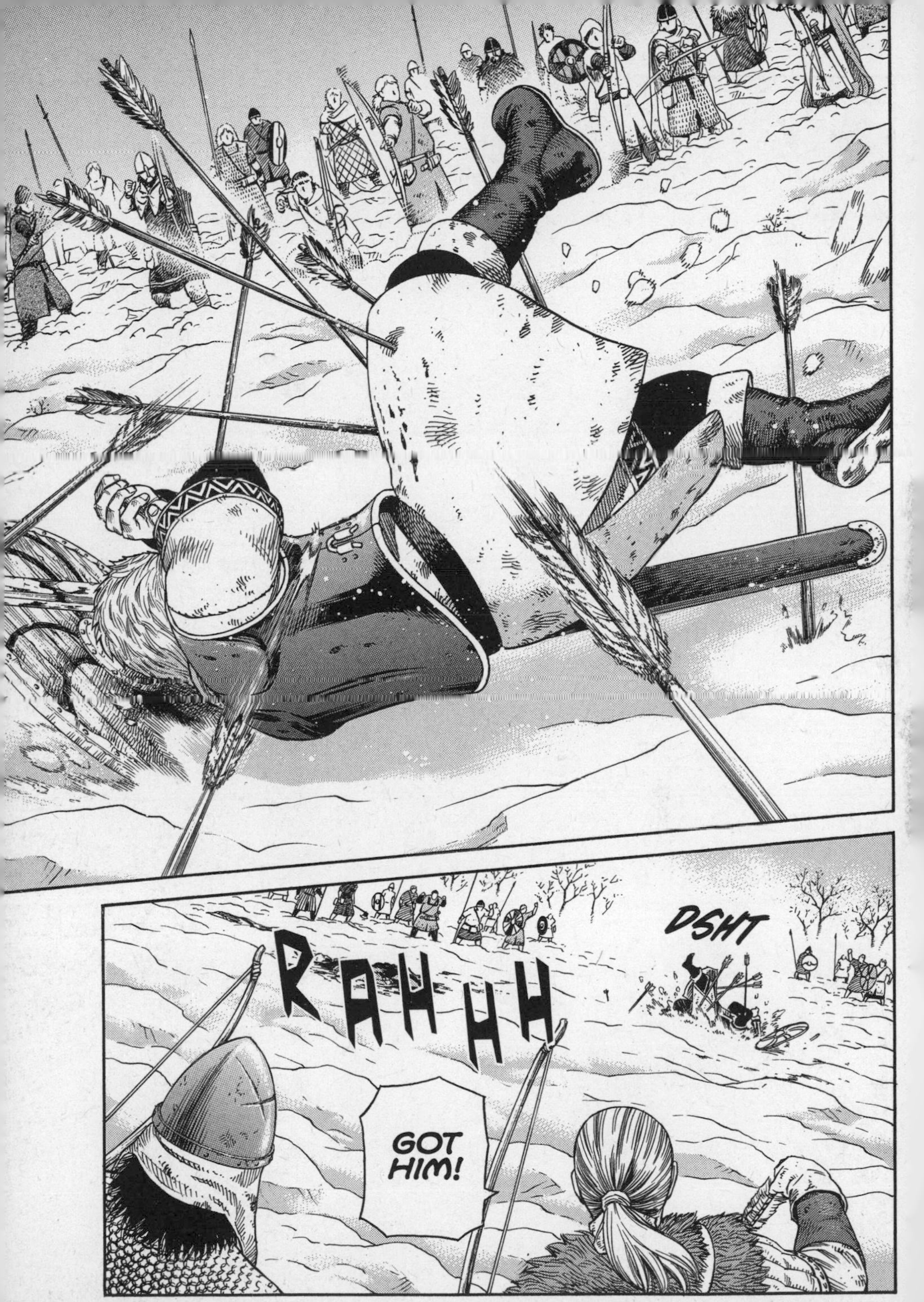
DSHT
RAHHH
GOT HIM!

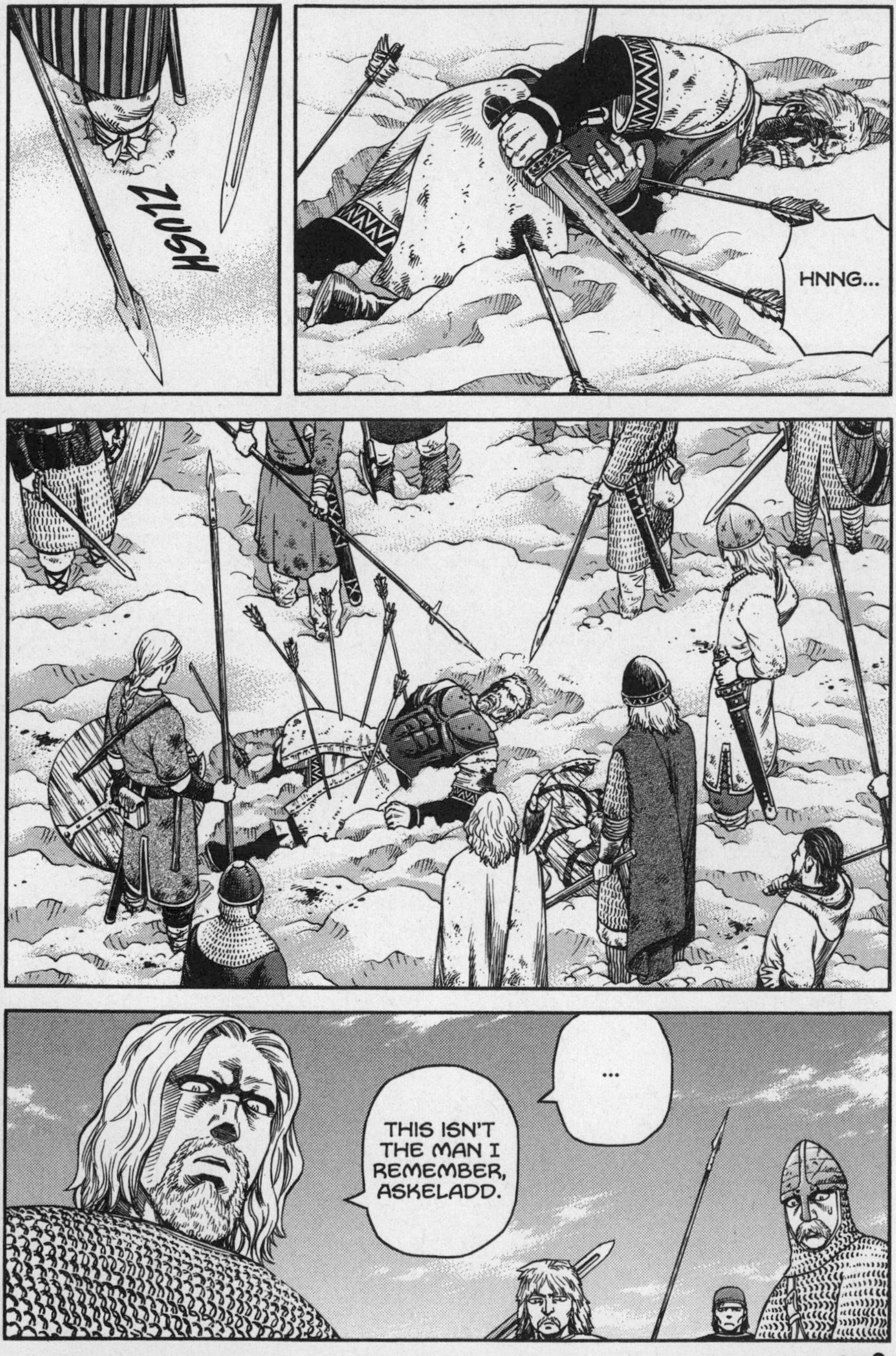
HNNG...
ZLUSH
...
THIS ISN'T THE MAN I REMEMBER, ASKELADD.

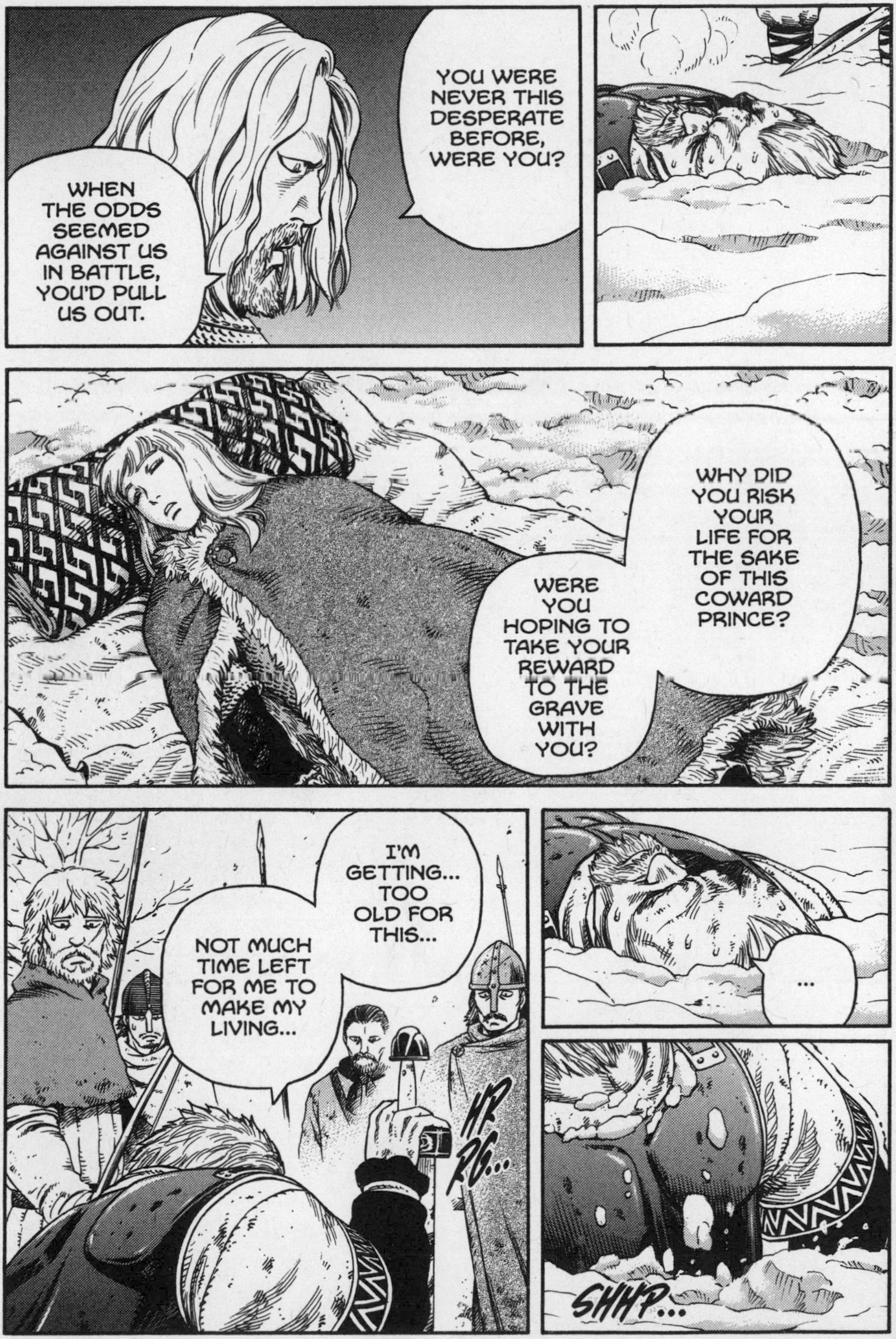

YOU WERE NEVER THIS DESPERATE BEFORE, WERE YOU?
WHEN THE ODDS SEEMED AGAINST US IN BATTLE, YOU'D PULL US OUT.
WHY DID YOU RISK YOUR LIFE FOR THE SAKE OF THIS COWARD PRINCE?
WERE YOU HOPING TO TAKE YOUR REWARD TO THE GRAVE WITH YOU?
...
SHHP...
I'M GETTING... TOO OLD FOR THIS...
NOT MUCH TIME LEFT FOR ME TO MAKE MY LIVING...
HRRG...

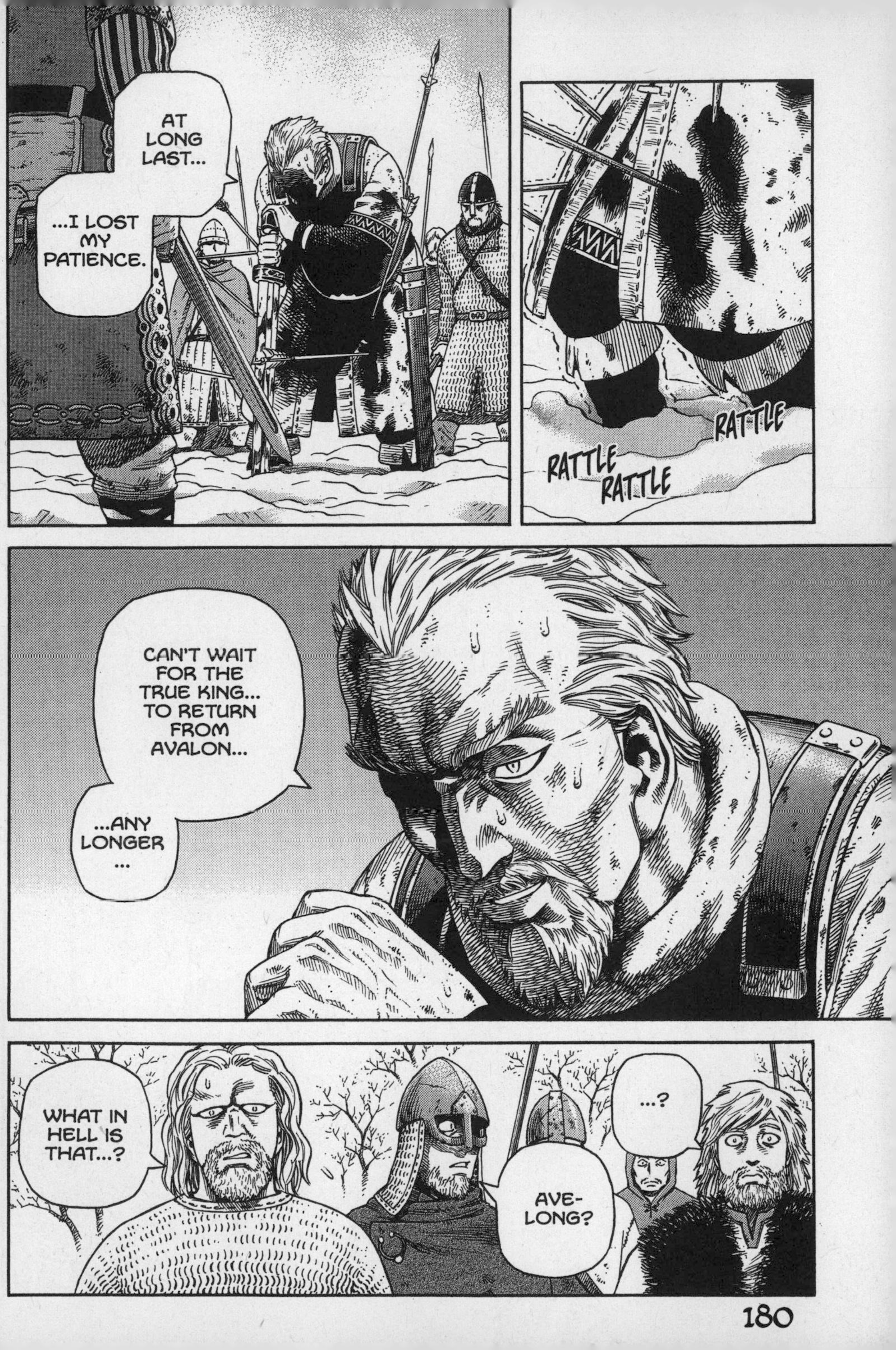
RATTLE
RATTLE
RATTLE
AT LONG LAST...
...I LOST MY PATIENCE.
CAN'T WAIT FOR THE TRUE KING... TO RETURN FROM AVALON...
...ANY LONGER ...
...?
AVE-LONG?
WHAT IN HELL IS THAT...?

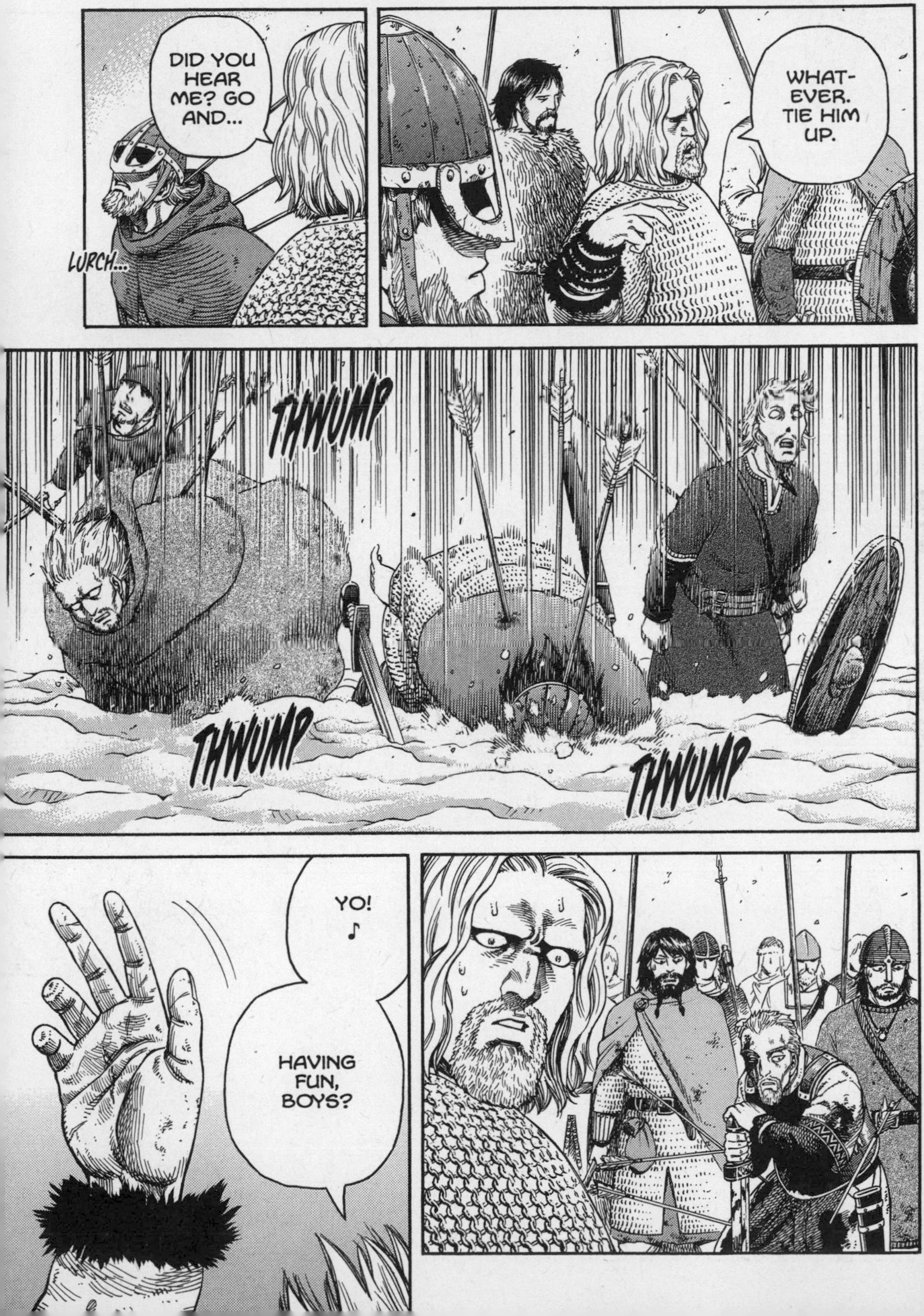
WHAT-EVER. TIE HIM UP.
DID YOU HEAR ME? GO AND...
LURCH...
THWUMP
THWUMP
THWUMP
YO! ♪
HAVING FUN, BOYS?

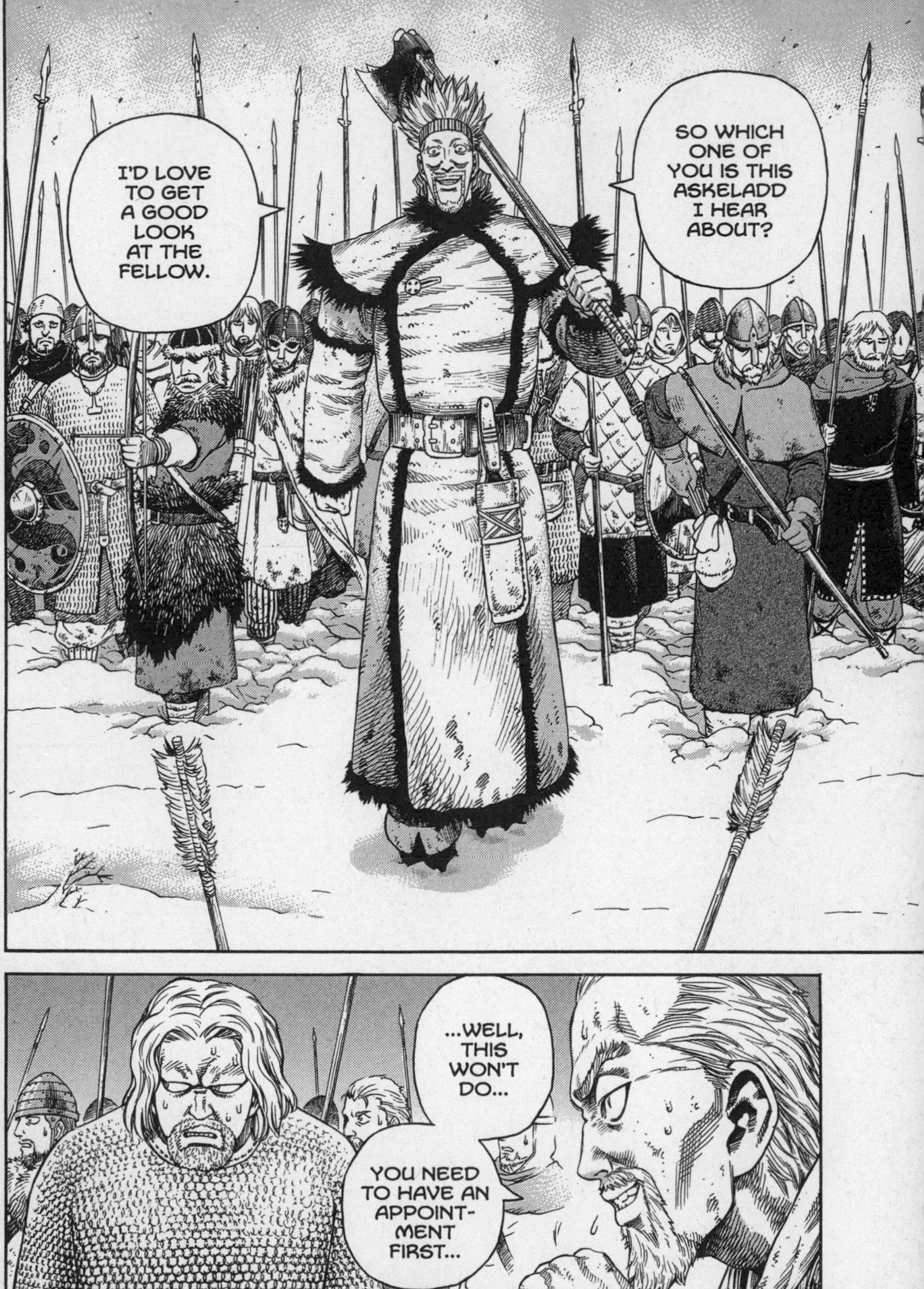
SO WHICH ONE OF YOU IS THIS ASKELADD I HEAR ABOUT?
I'D LOVE TO GET A GOOD LOOK AT THE FELLOW.
...WELL, THIS WON'T DO...
YOU NEED TO HAVE AN APPOINT-MENT FIRST...

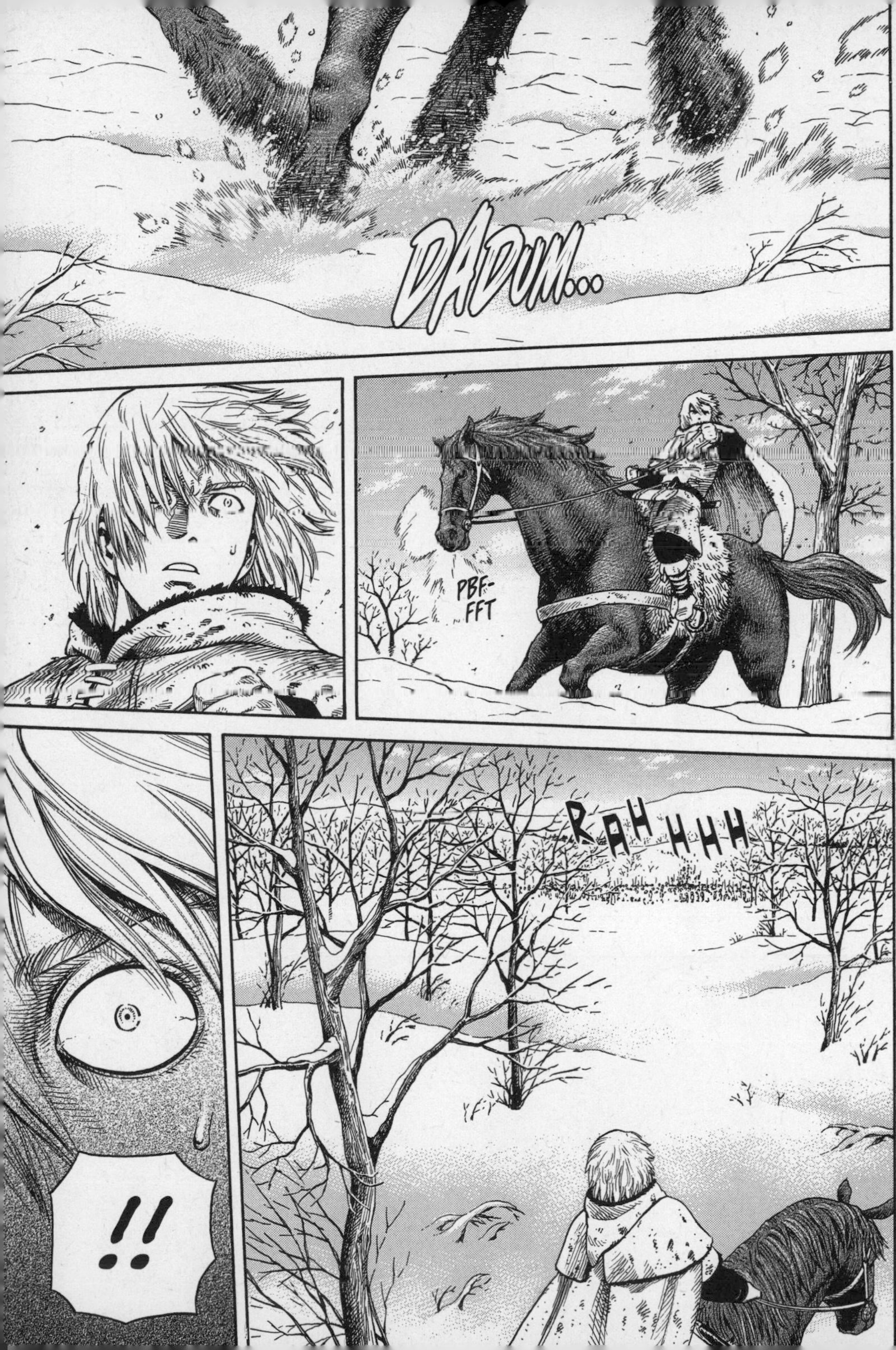
DADUM...
PBF-
FFT
RAHHHH
!!

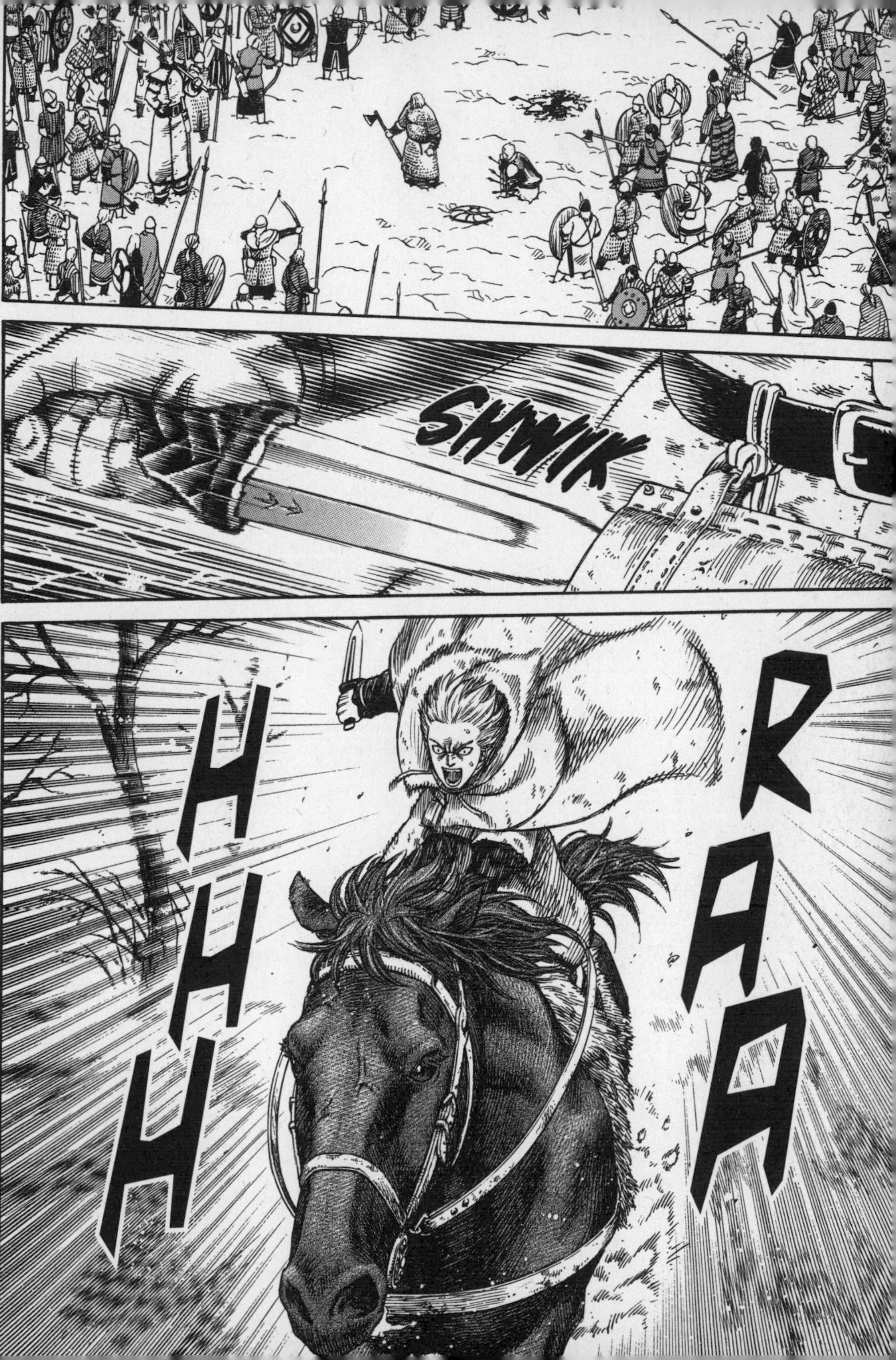
SHWIK
RAAAHHHH

CHAPTER 34 - END

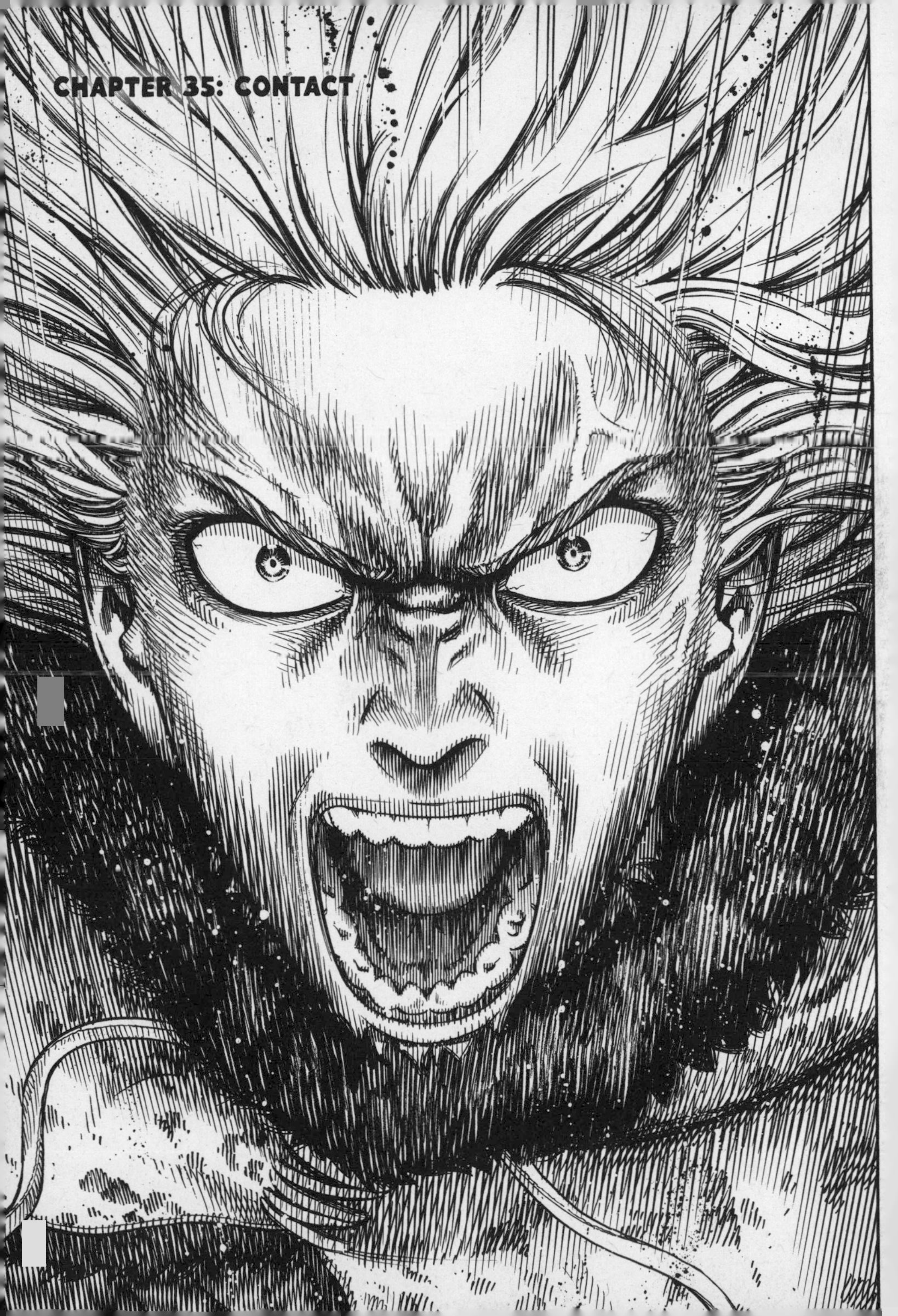
CHAPTER 35: CONTACT

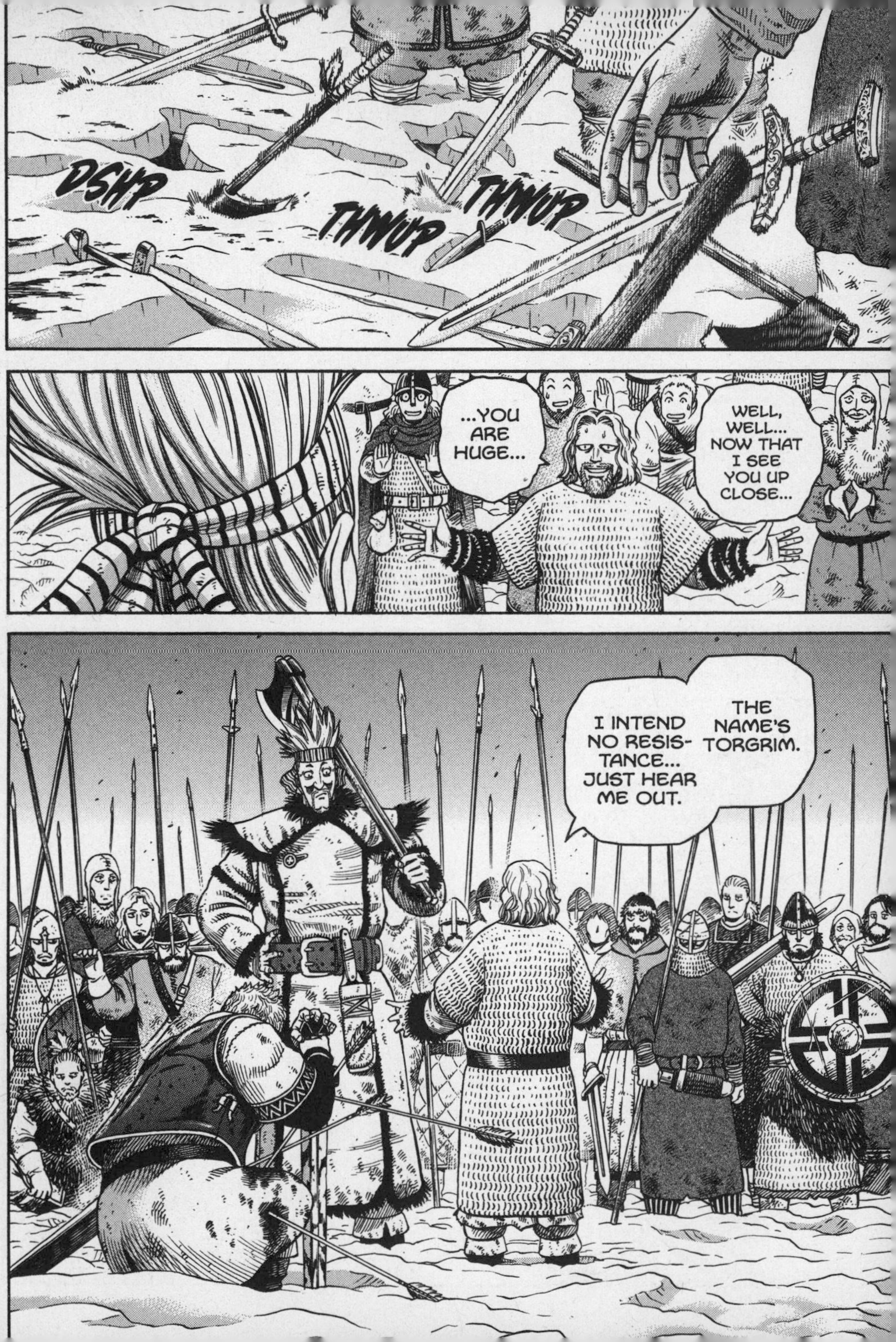
THWUP
THWUP
DSHP
WELL, WELL... NOW THAT I SEE YOU UP CLOSE...
...YOU ARE HUGE...
THE NAME'S TORGRIM.
I INTEND NO RESISTANCE... JUST HEAR ME OUT.

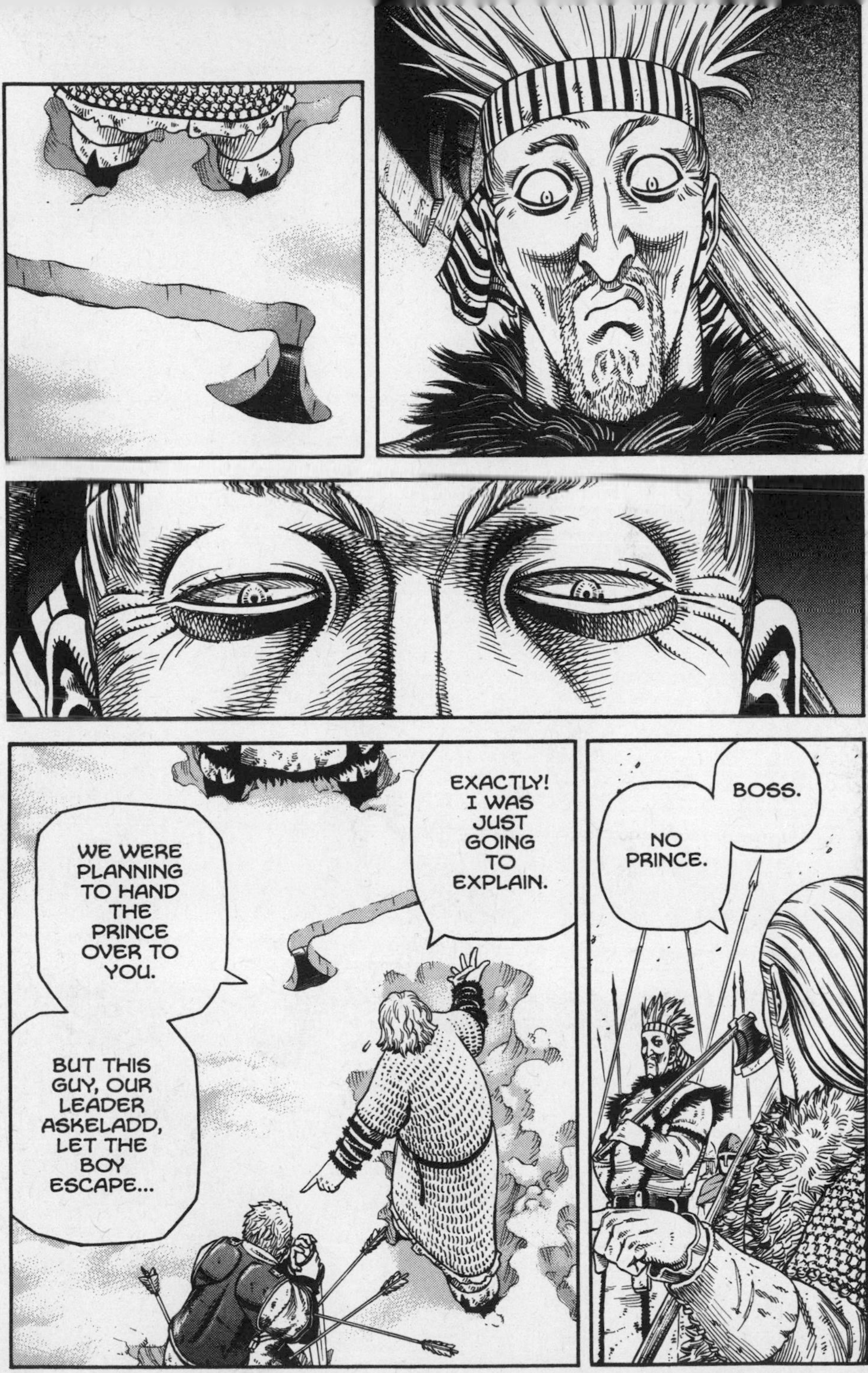
BOSS.
NO PRINCE.
EXACTLY! I WAS JUST GOING TO EXPLAIN.
WE WERE PLANNING TO HAND THE PRINCE OVER TO YOU.
BUT THIS GUY, OUR LEADER ASKELADD, LET THE BOY ESCAPE...

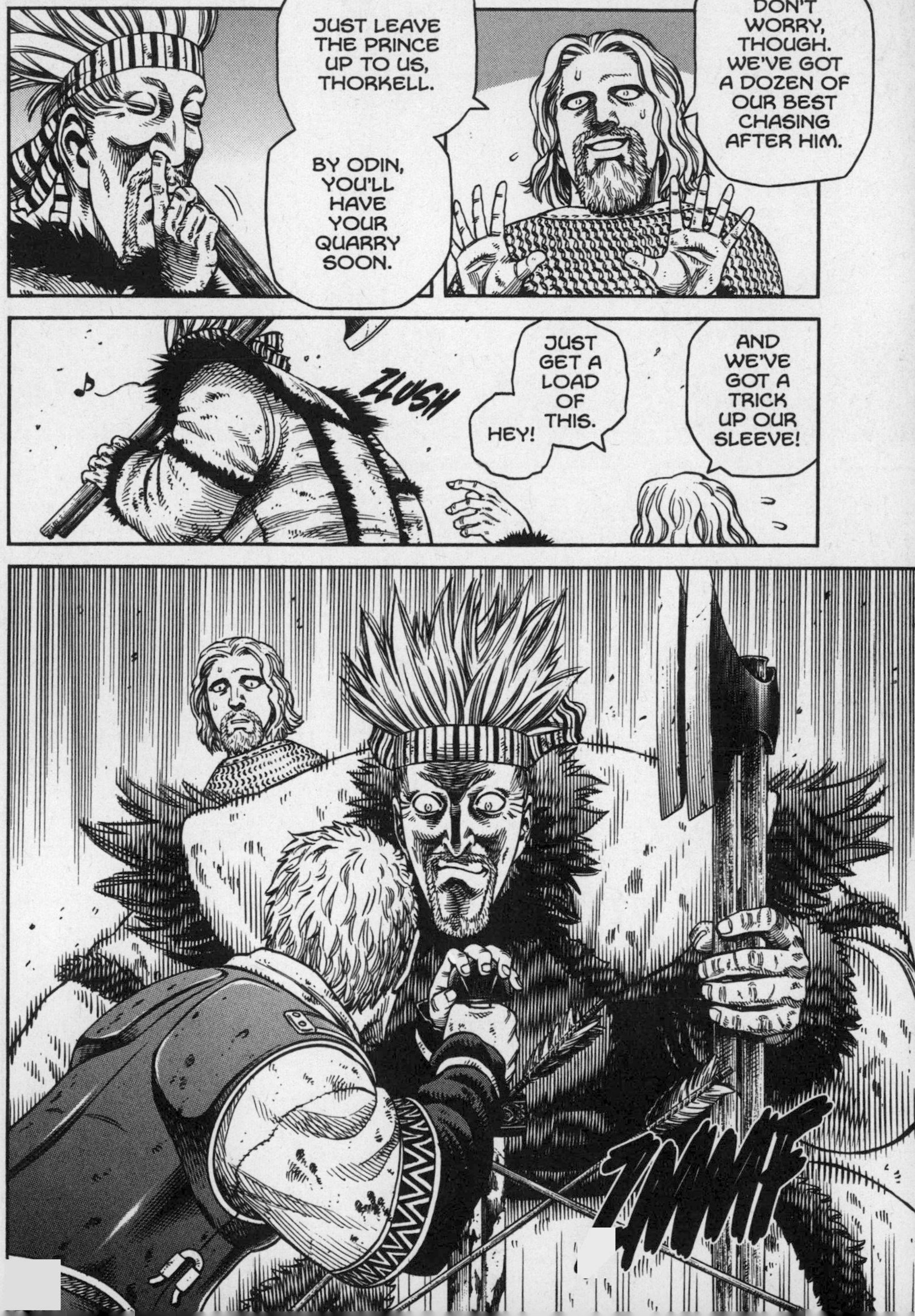
DON'T WORRY, THOUGH. WE'VE GOT A DOZEN OF OUR BEST CHASING AFTER HIM.
JUST LEAVE THE PRINCE UP TO US, THORKELL.
BY ODIN, YOU'LL HAVE YOUR QUARRY SOON.
AND WE'VE GOT A TRICK UP OUR SLEEVE!
JUST GET A LOAD OF THIS.
HEY!
ZLUSH

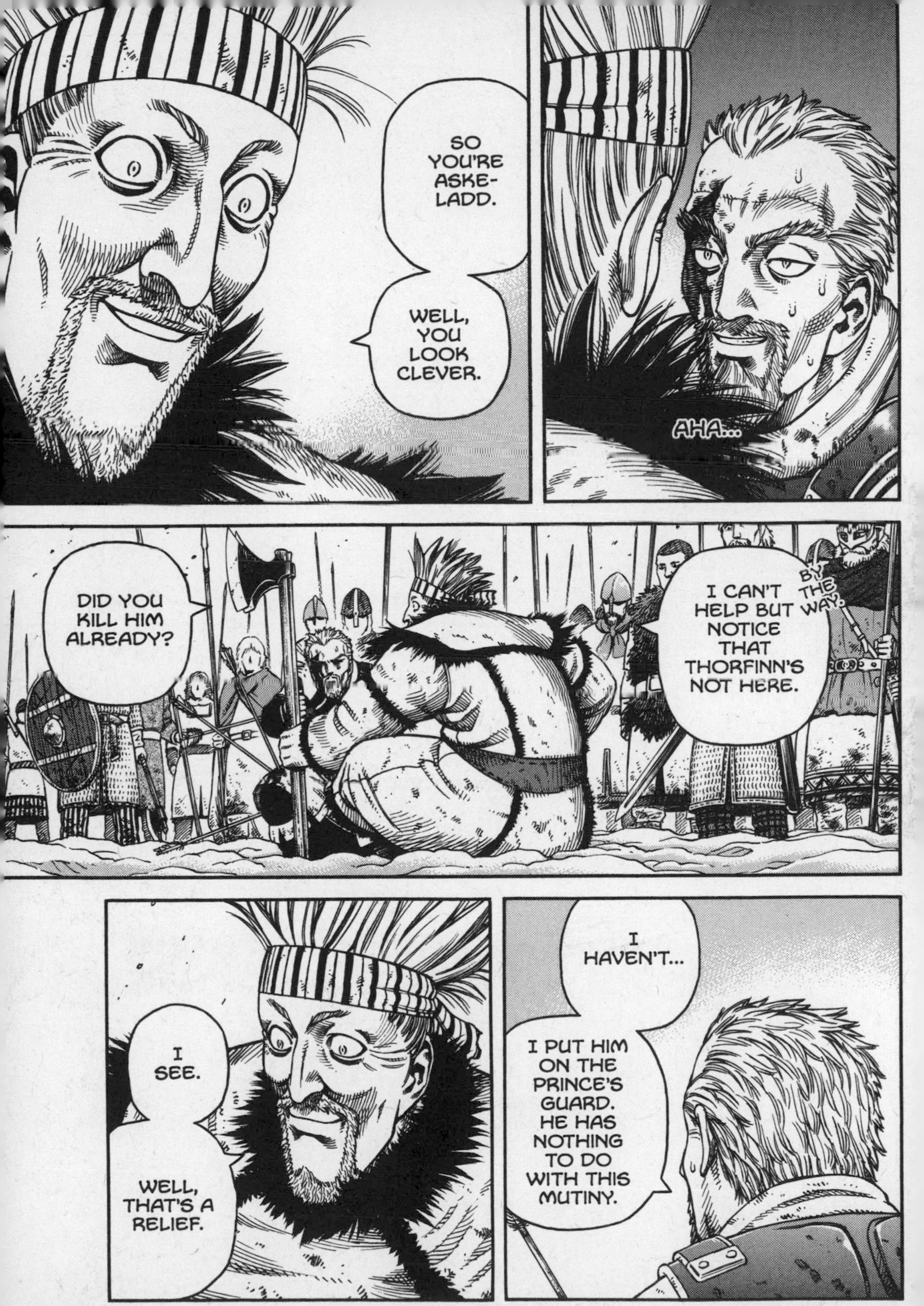
AHA...
SO YOU'RE ASKE-LADD.
WELL, YOU LOOK CLEVER.
BY THE WAY.
I CAN'T HELP BUT NOTICE THAT THORFINN'S NOT HERE.
DID YOU KILL HIM ALREADY?
I HAVEN'T...
I PUT HIM ON THE PRINCE'S GUARD. HE HAS NOTHING TO DO WITH THIS MUTINY.
I SEE.
WELL, THAT'S A RELIEF.

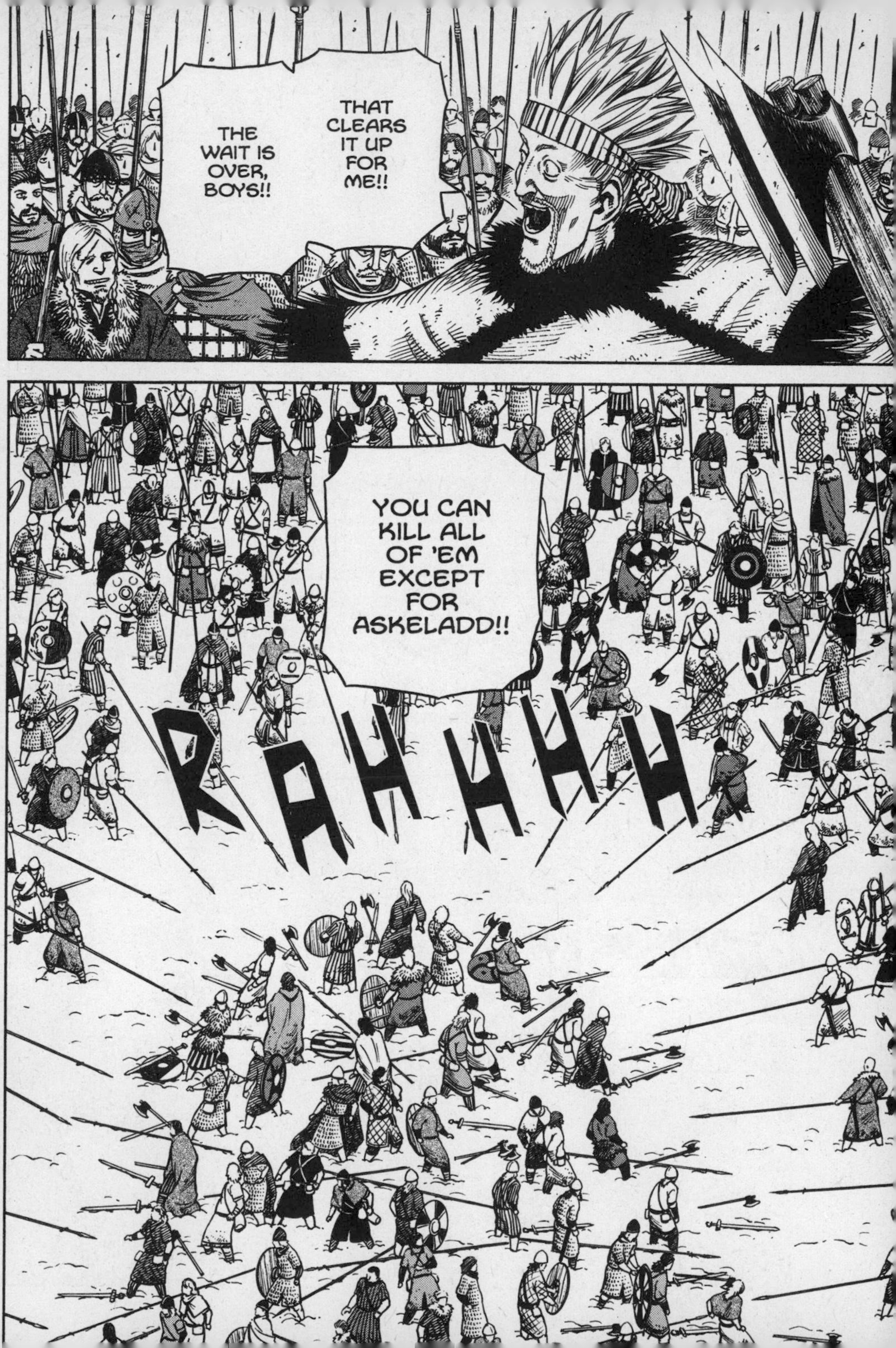
THAT CLEARS IT UP FOR ME!!
THE WAIT IS OVER, BOYS!!
YOU CAN KILL ALL OF 'EM EXCEPT FOR ASKELADD!!
RAHHHH

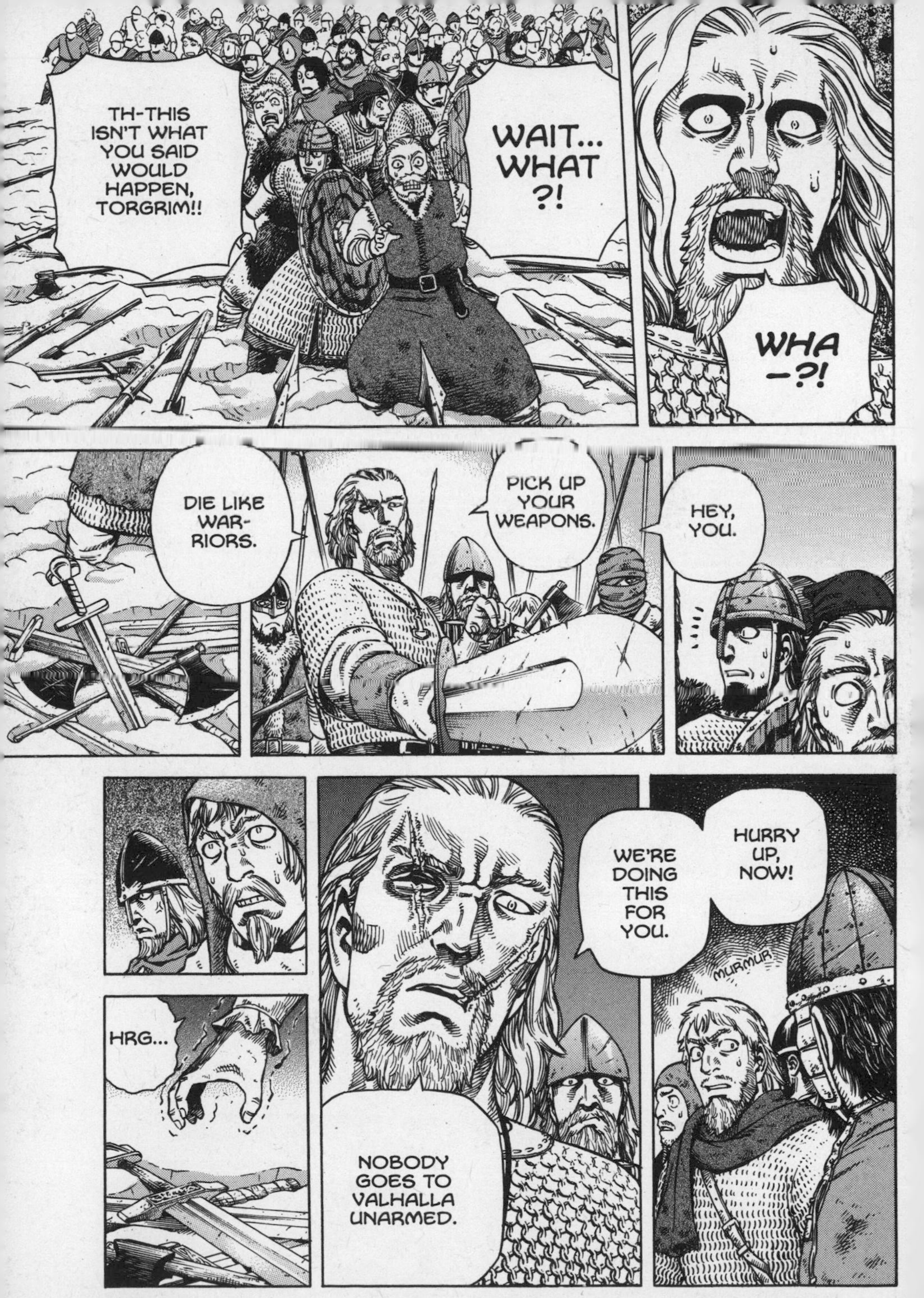
WHA-?!
WAIT... WHAT?!
TH-THIS ISN'T WHAT YOU SAID WOULD HAPPEN, TORGRIM!!
HEY, YOU.
PICK UP YOUR WEAPONS.
DIE LIKE WARRIORS.
HURRY UP, NOW!
WE'RE DOING THIS FOR YOU.
MURMUR
NOBODY GOES TO VALHALLA UNARMED.
HRG...

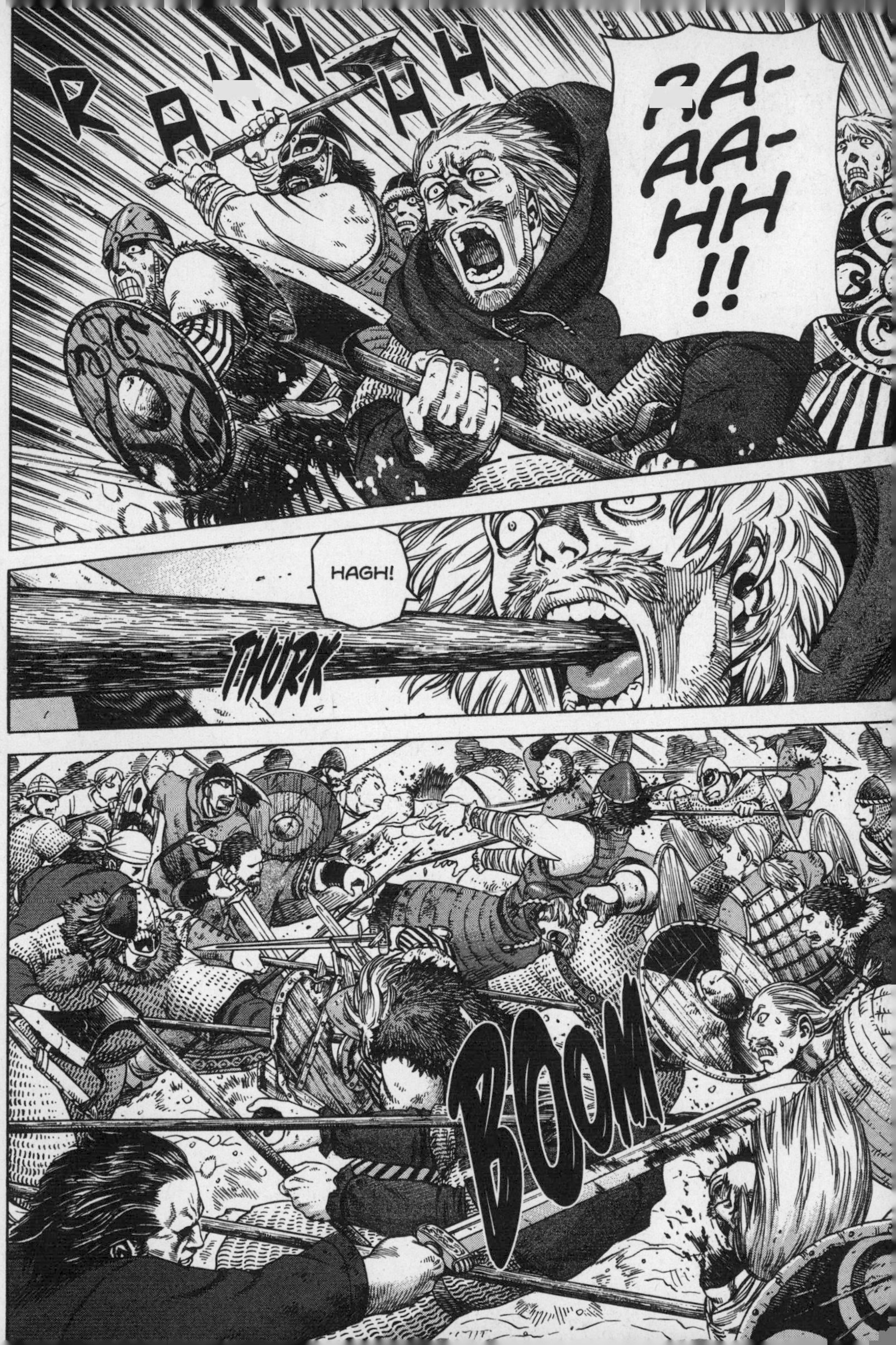
RA-AA-HH!!
RAHHHH
HAGH!
THURK
BOOM

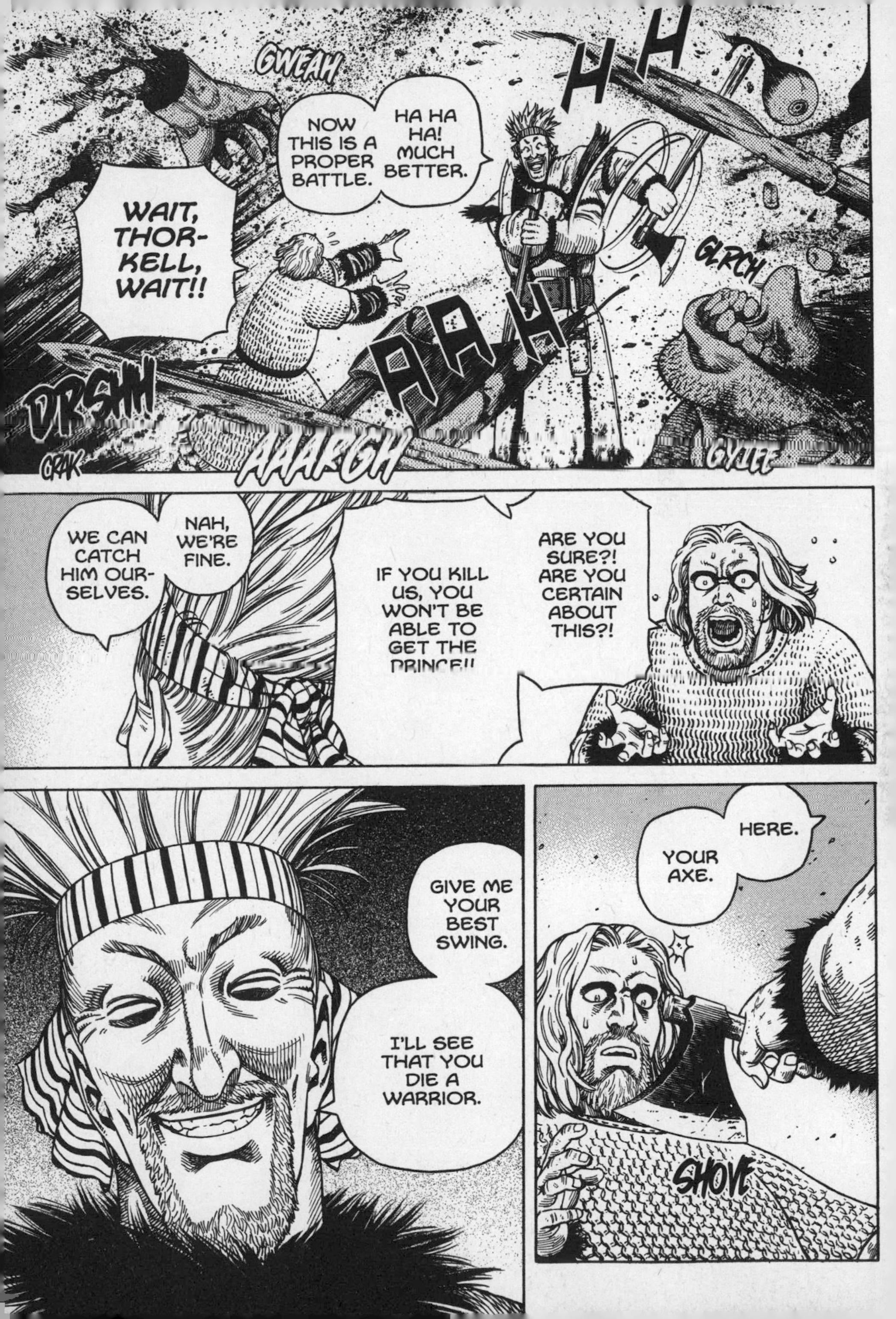

HH
HA HA HA! MUCH BETTER.
NOW THIS IS A PROPER BATTLE.
GWEAH
GLRCH
WAIT, THORKELL, WAIT!!
AAH
GYUFF
AAAARGH
DRSHH
CRAK
ARE YOU SURE?! ARE YOU CERTAIN ABOUT THIS?!
IF YOU KILL US, YOU WON'T BE ABLE TO GET THE PRINCE!!
NAH, WE'RE FINE.
WE CAN CATCH HIM OURSELVES.
HERE.
YOUR AXE.
SHOVE
GIVE ME YOUR BEST SWING.
I'LL SEE THAT YOU DIE A WARRIOR.

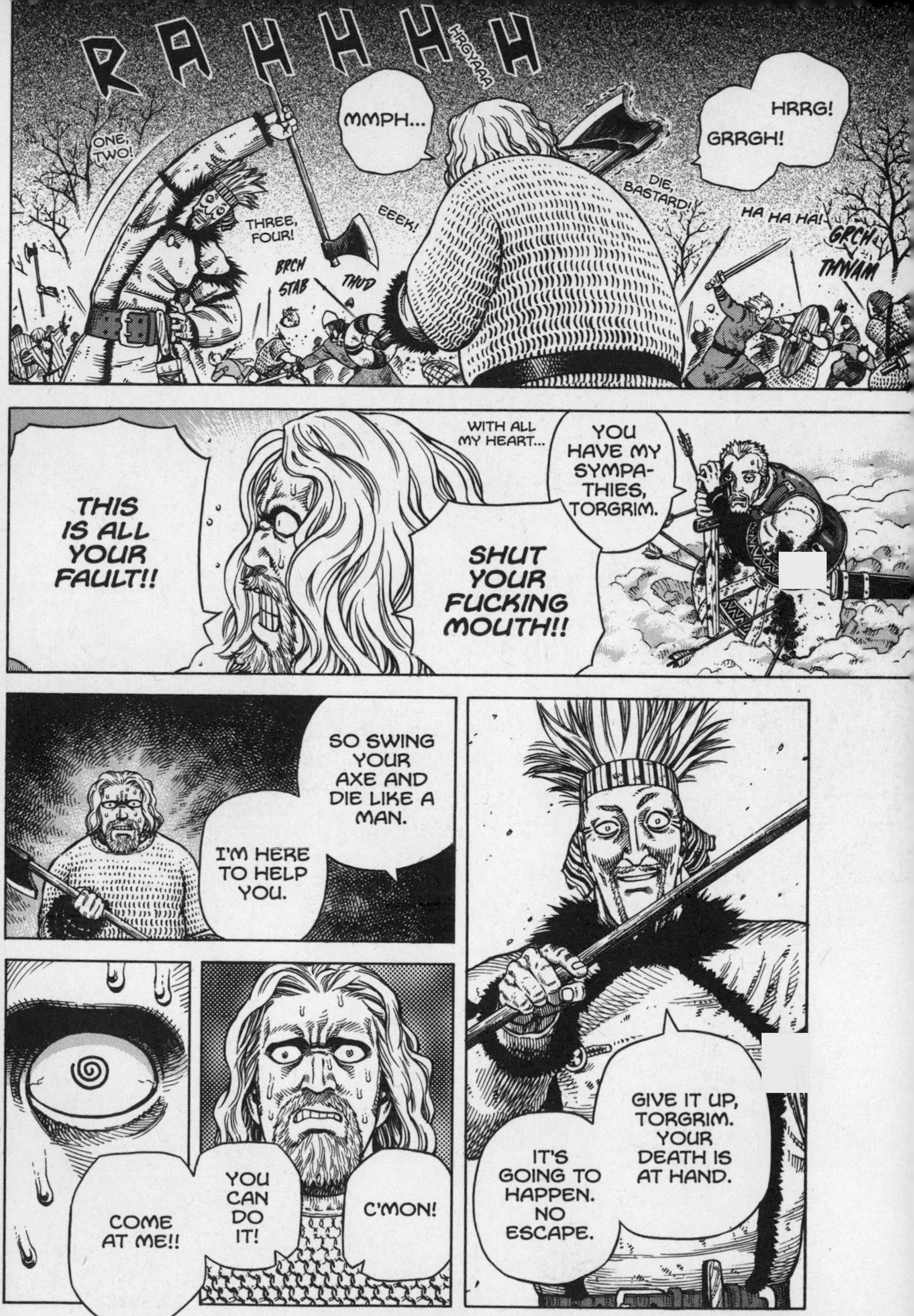
HRRG!
GRRGH!
HRGYAAA
MMPH...
RAHHHH
DIE, BASTARD!
HA HA HA!
GRCH
THWAM
EEEK!
ONE, TWO!
THREE, FOUR!
BRCH
STAB
THUD
YOU HAVE MY SYMPATHIES, TORGRIM.
WITH ALL MY HEART...
SHUT YOUR FUCKING MOUTH!!
THIS IS ALL YOUR FAULT!!
GIVE IT UP, TORGRIM. YOUR DEATH IS AT HAND.
IT'S GOING TO HAPPEN. NO ESCAPE.
SO SWING YOUR AXE AND DIE LIKE A MAN.
I'M HERE TO HELP YOU.
C'MON!
YOU CAN DO IT!
COME AT ME!!

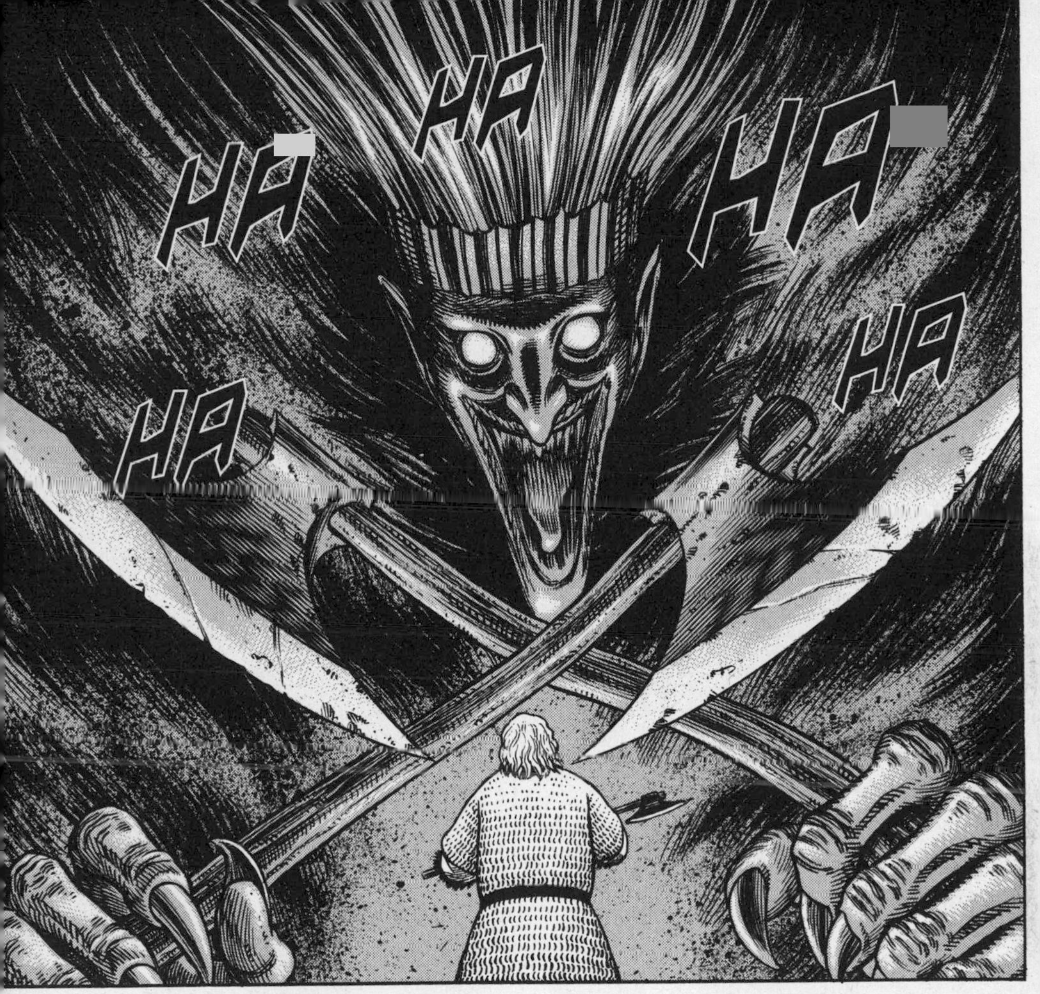
HA
HA
HA
HA
HA

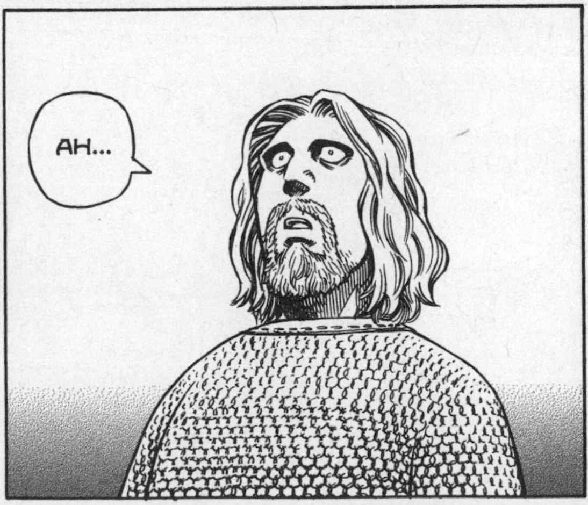
AH...

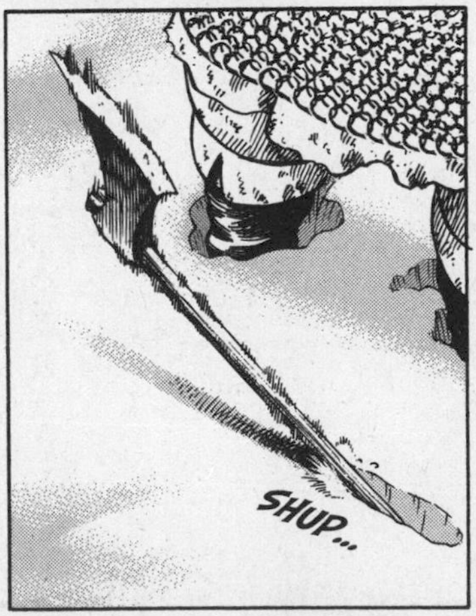
SHUP...

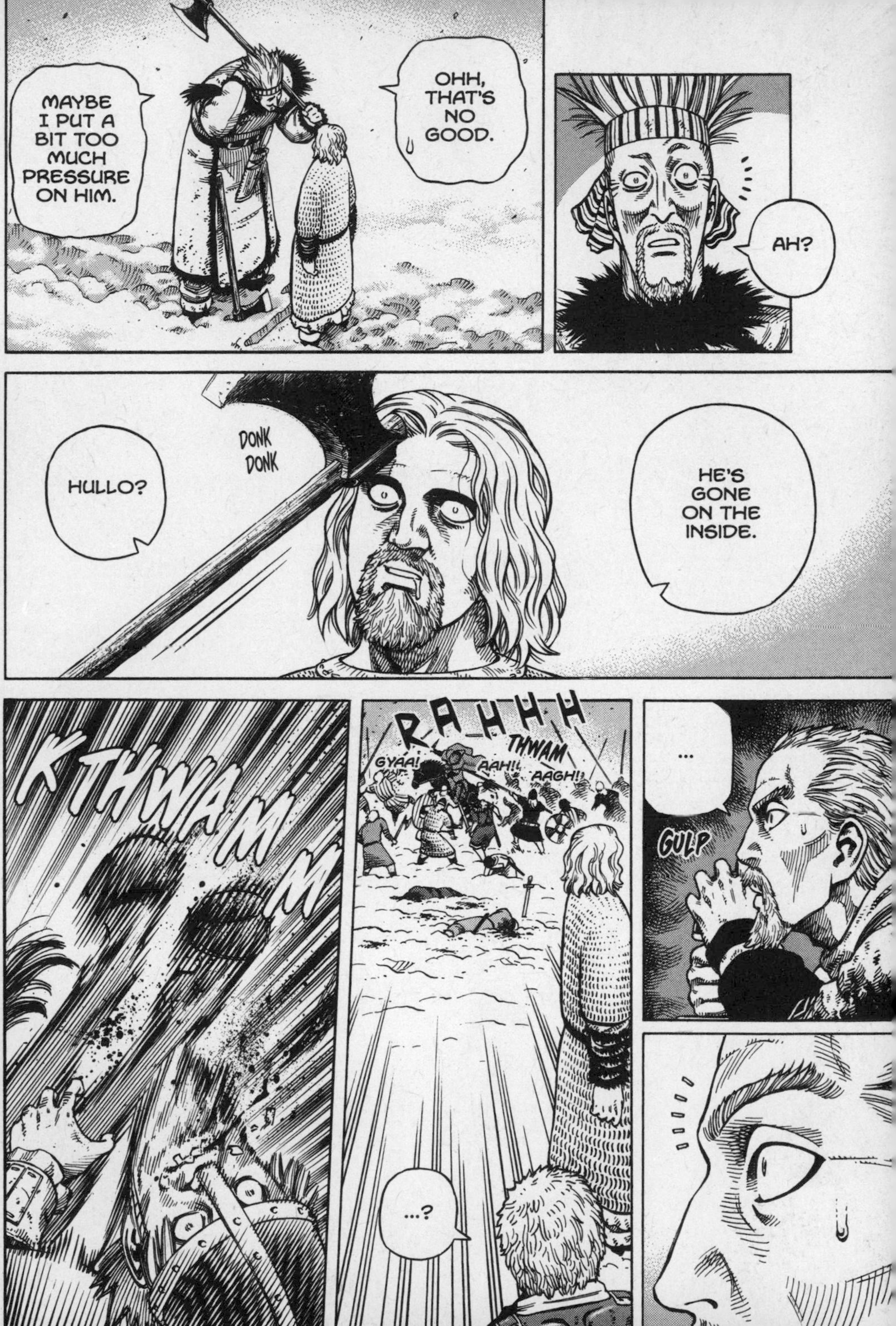
AH?
OHH, THAT'S NO GOOD.
MAYBE I PUT A BIT TOO MUCH PRESSURE ON HIM.
HE'S GONE ON THE INSIDE.
DONK DONK
HULLO?
...
GULP
RAHHH
THWAM
GYAA!
AAH!!
AAGH!!
...?
KTHWAMMM

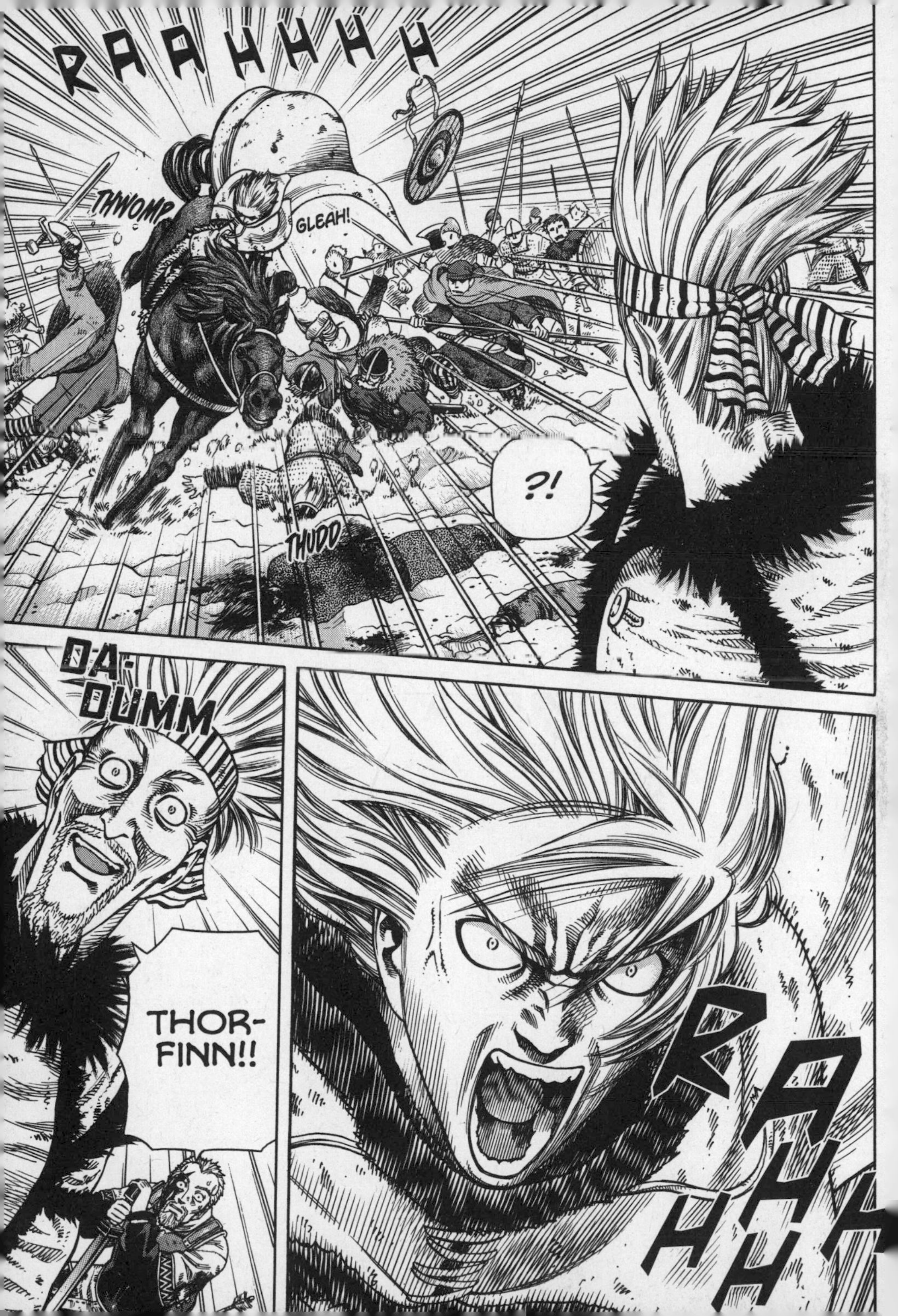
RAAHHHH
THWOMP
GLEAH!
?!
THUDD
RAAHHHH
DA-DUMM
THOR-FINN!!

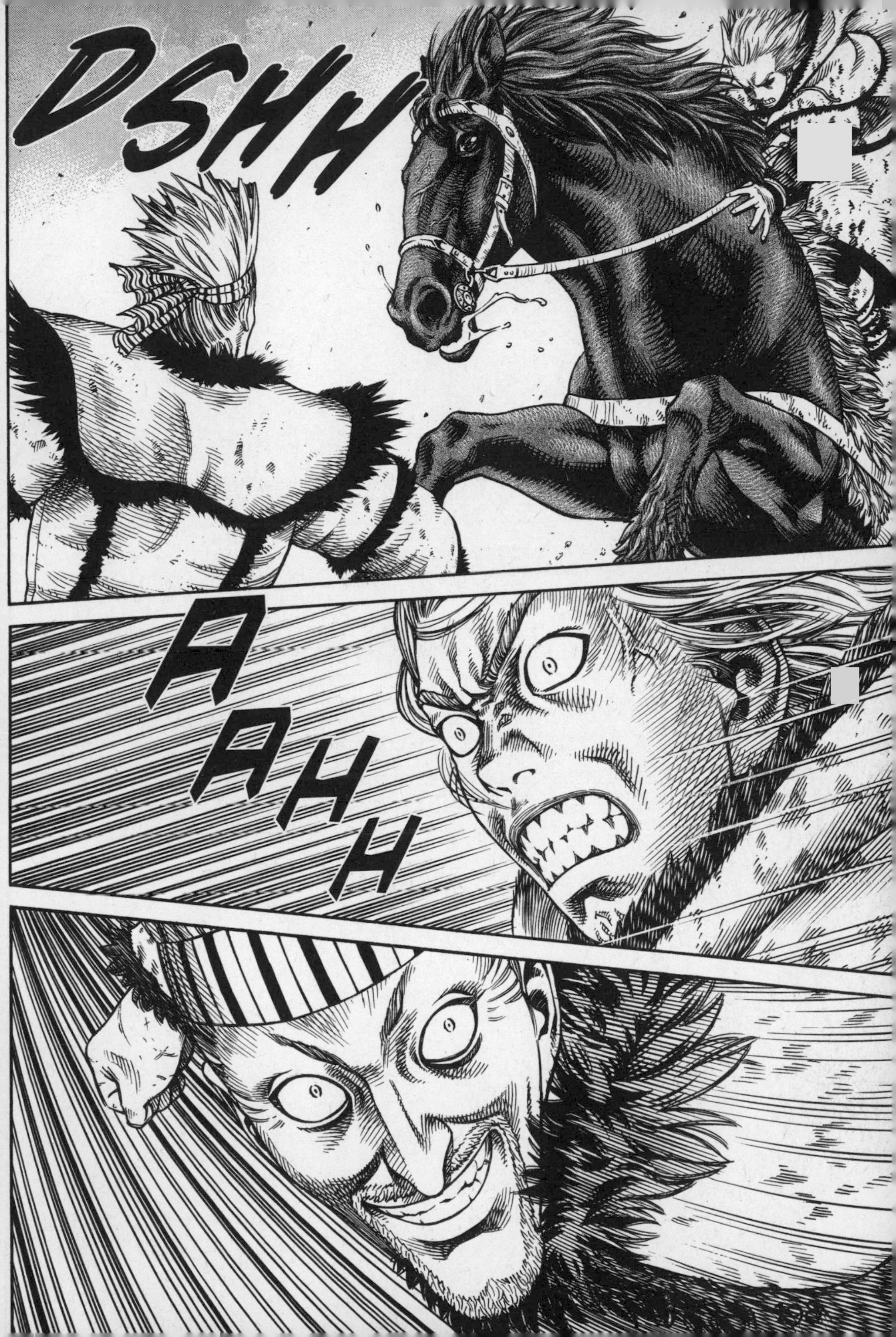
DSHH
AAHH

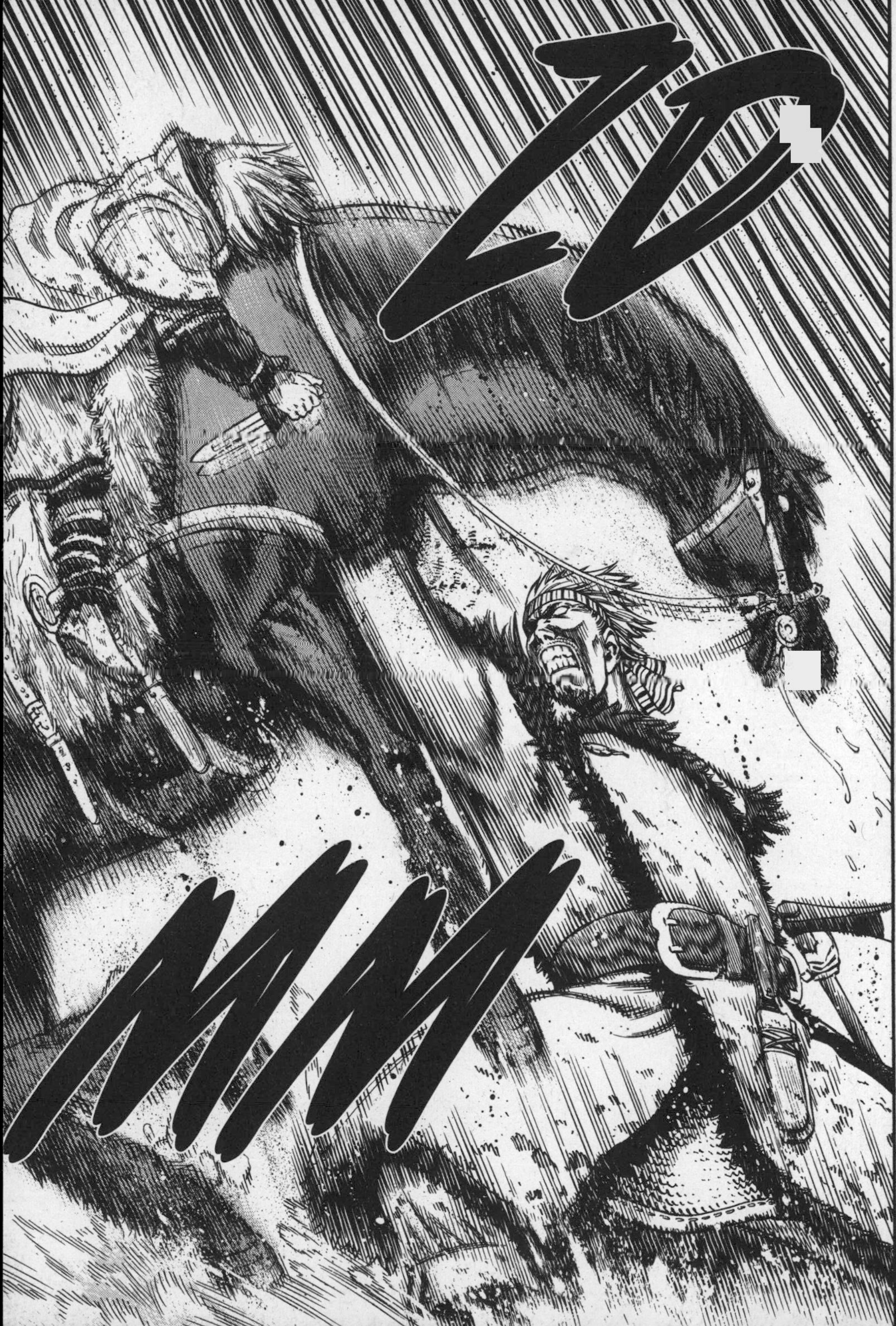

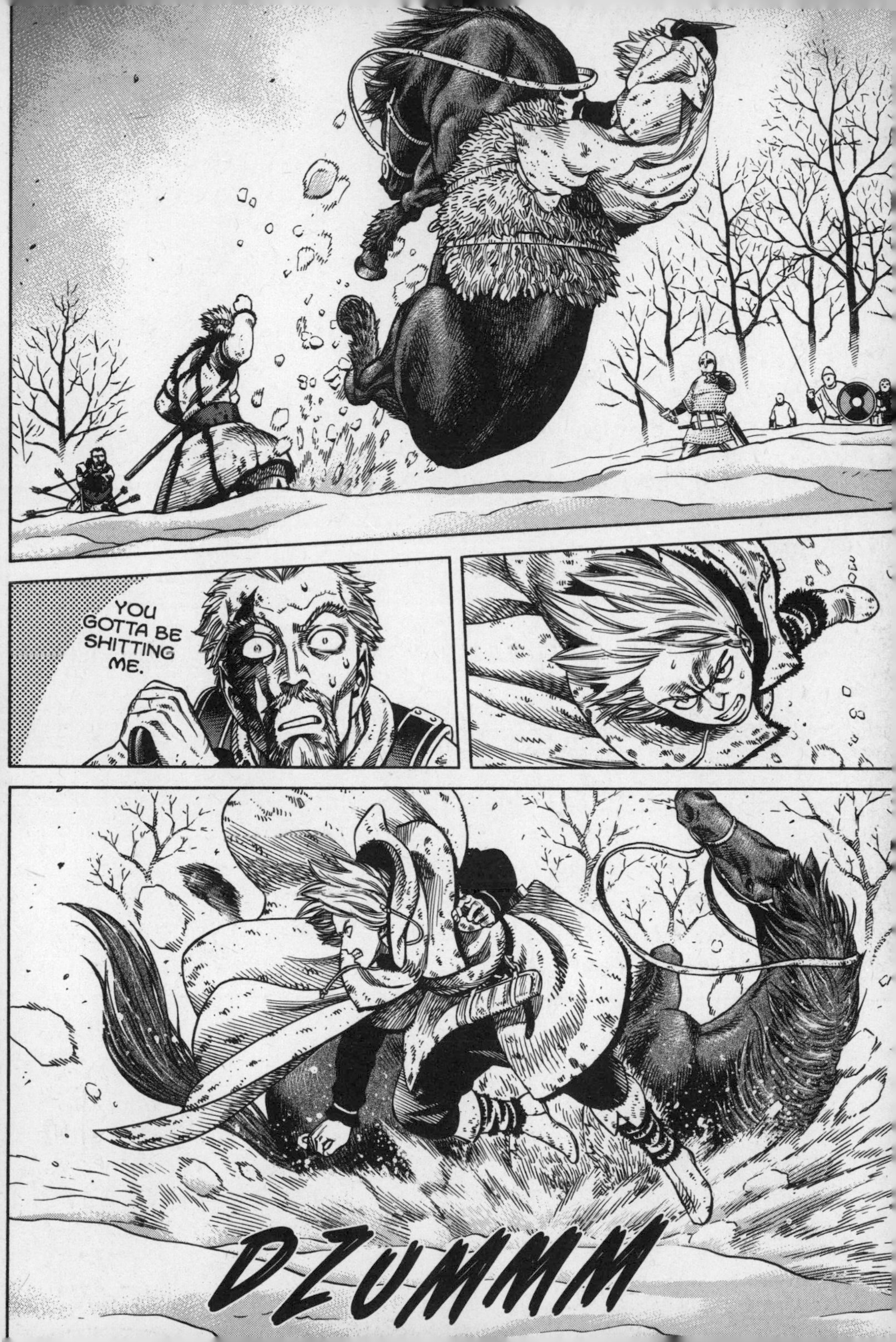
YOU GOTTA BE SHITTING ME.
DZUMMM

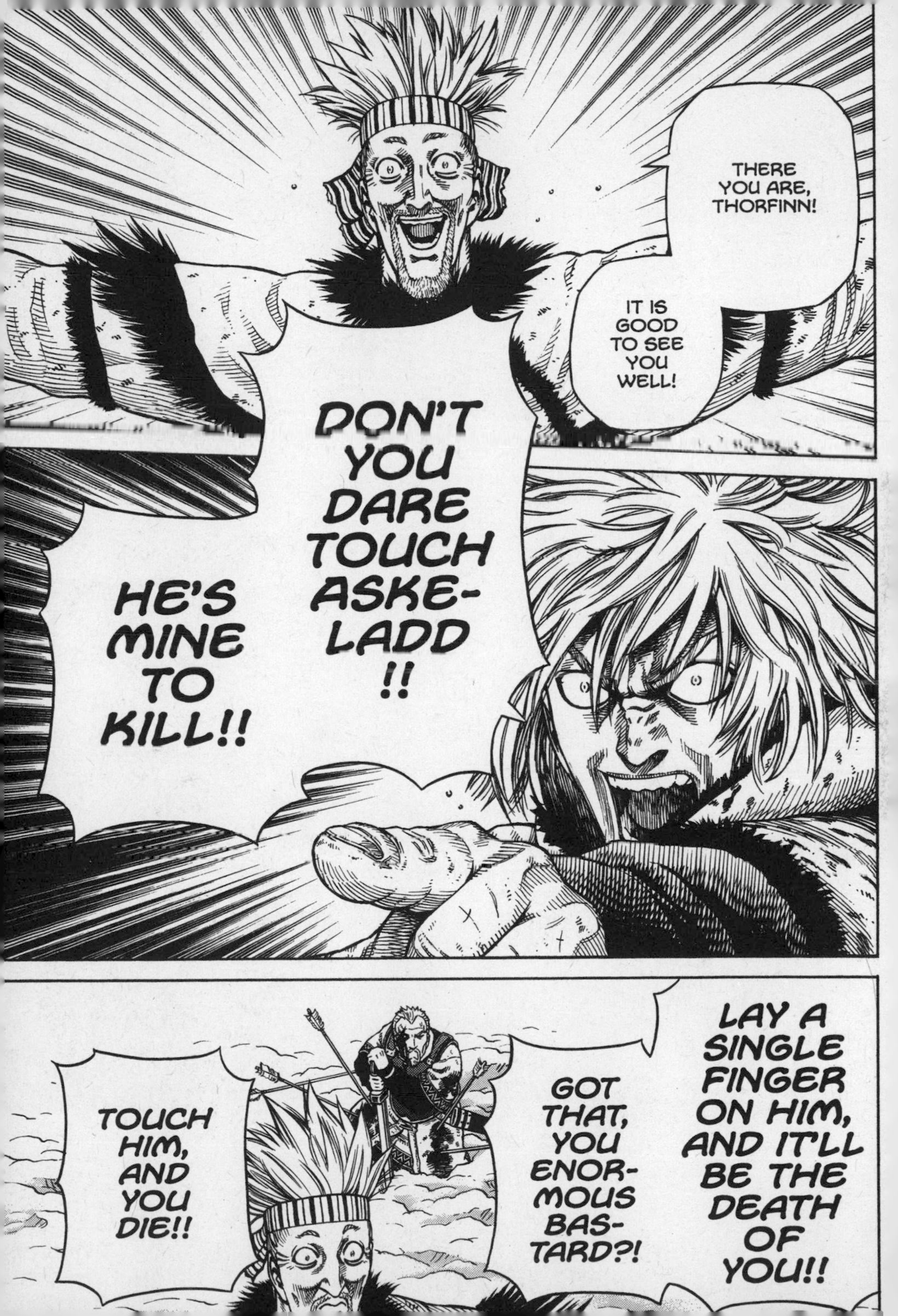
THERE YOU ARE, THORFINN!
IT IS GOOD TO SEE YOU WELL!
DON'T YOU DARE TOUCH ASKELADD!!
HE'S MINE TO KILL!!
LAY A SINGLE FINGER ON HIM, AND IT'LL BE THE DEATH OF YOU!!
GOT THAT, YOU ENORMOUS BASTARD?!
TOUCH HIM, AND YOU DIE!!

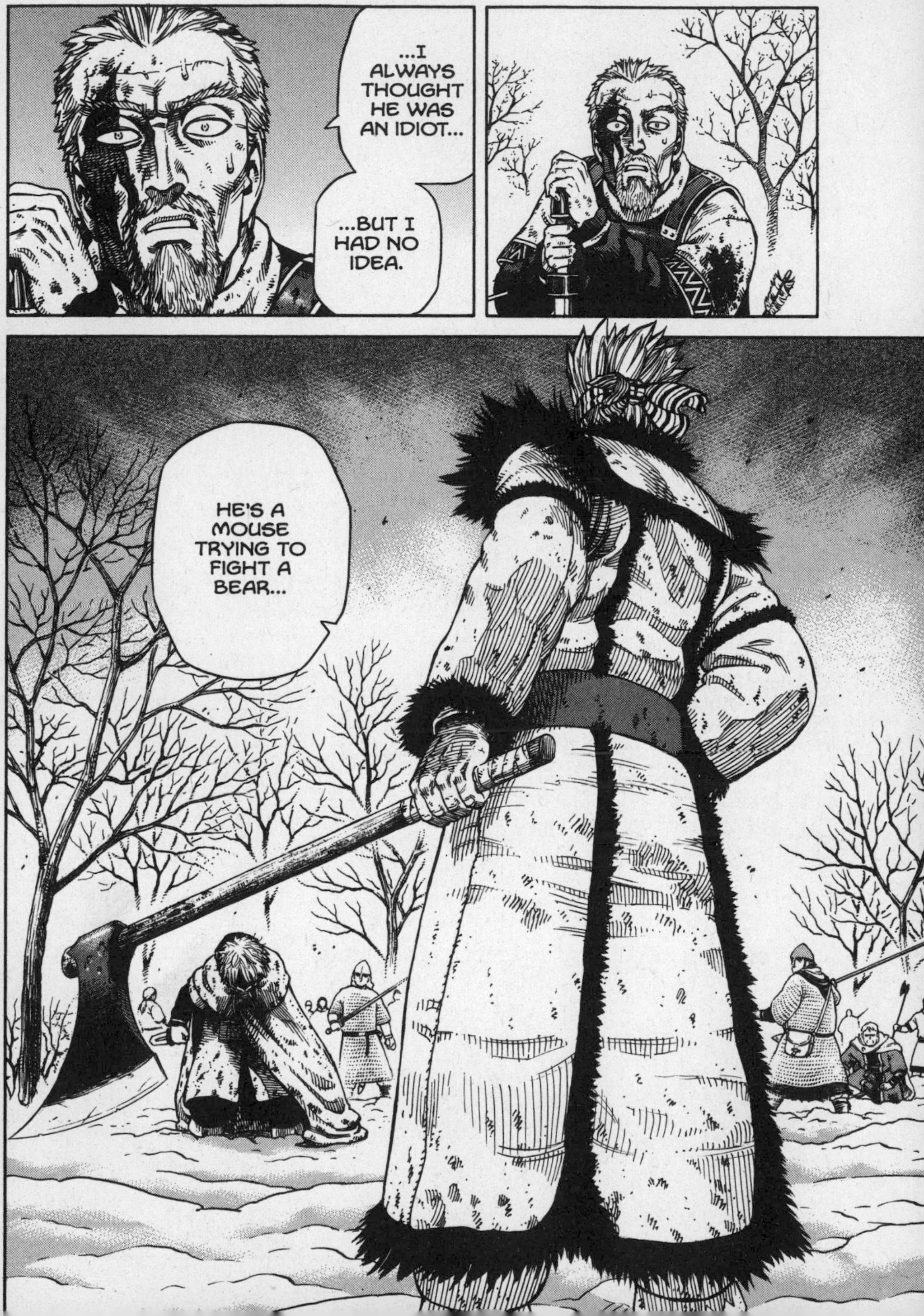
...I ALWAYS THOUGHT HE WAS AN IDIOT...
...BUT I HAD NO IDEA.
HE'S A MOUSE TRYING TO FIGHT A BEAR...

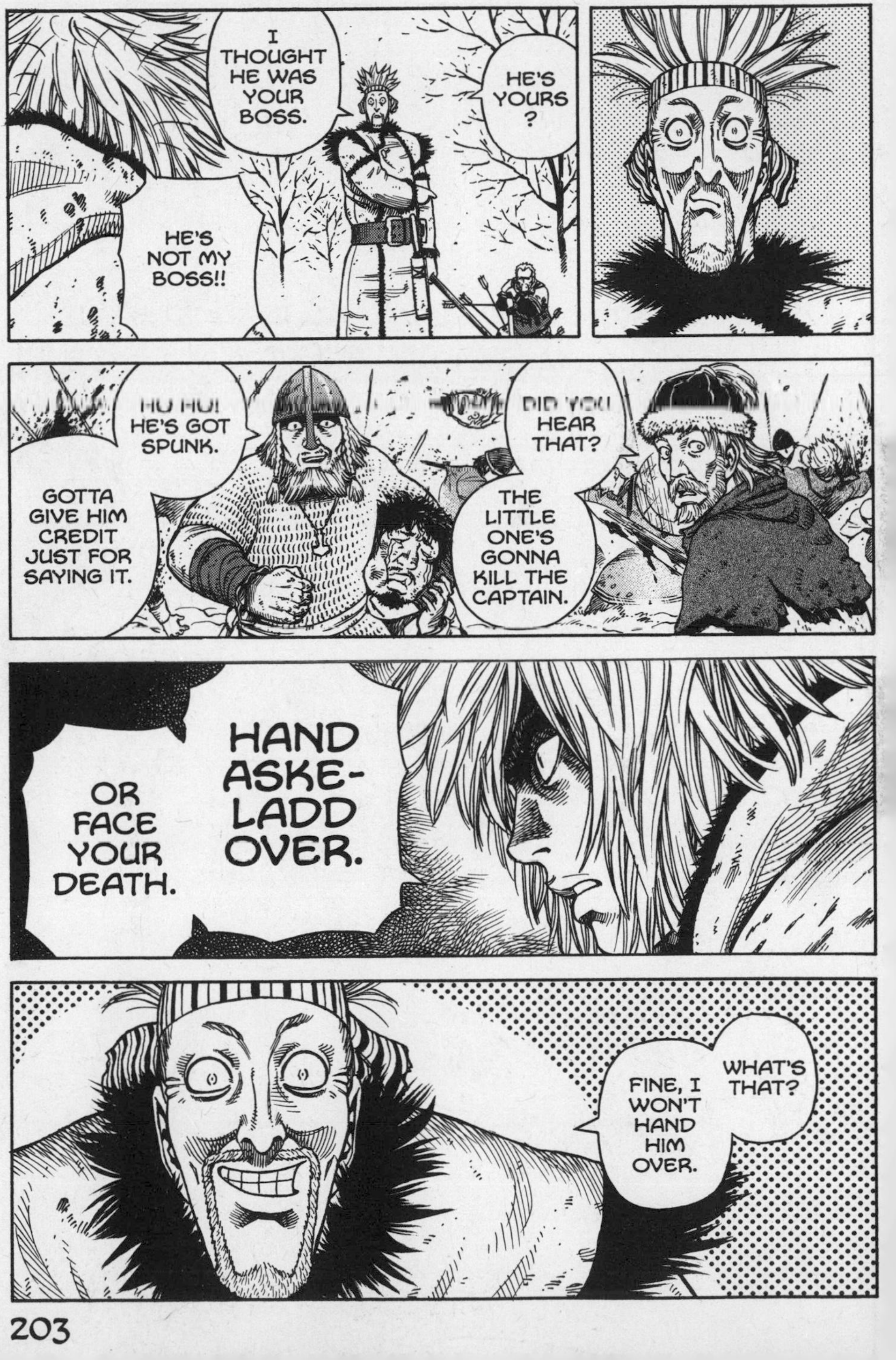
HE'S YOURS ?
I THOUGHT HE WAS YOUR BOSS.
HE'S NOT MY BOSS!!
DID YOU HEAR THAT?
THE LITTLE ONE'S GONNA KILL THE CAPTAIN.
HO HO! HE'S GOT SPUNK.
GOTTA GIVE HIM CREDIT JUST FOR SAYING IT.
HAND ASKE-LADD OVER.
OR FACE YOUR DEATH.
WHAT'S THAT?
FINE, I WON'T HAND HIM OVER.

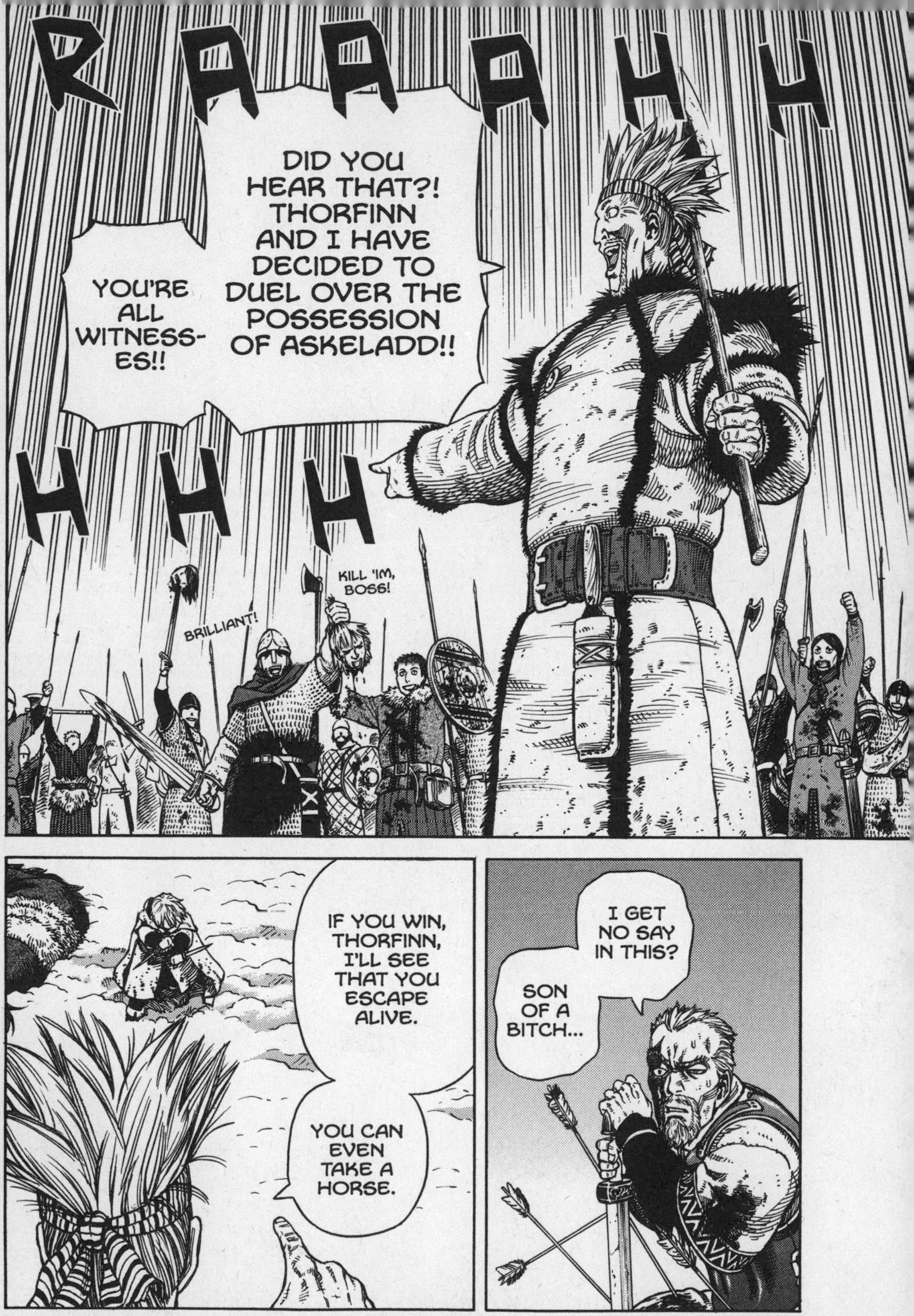
RAAAHH
HHH
DID YOU HEAR THAT?! THORFINN AND I HAVE DECIDED TO DUEL OVER THE POSSESSION OF ASKELADD!!
YOU'RE ALL WITNESS-ES!!
KILL 'IM, BOSS!
BRILLIANT!
I GET NO SAY IN THIS?
SON OF A BITCH...
IF YOU WIN, THORFINN, I'LL SEE THAT YOU ESCAPE ALIVE.
YOU CAN EVEN TAKE A HORSE.

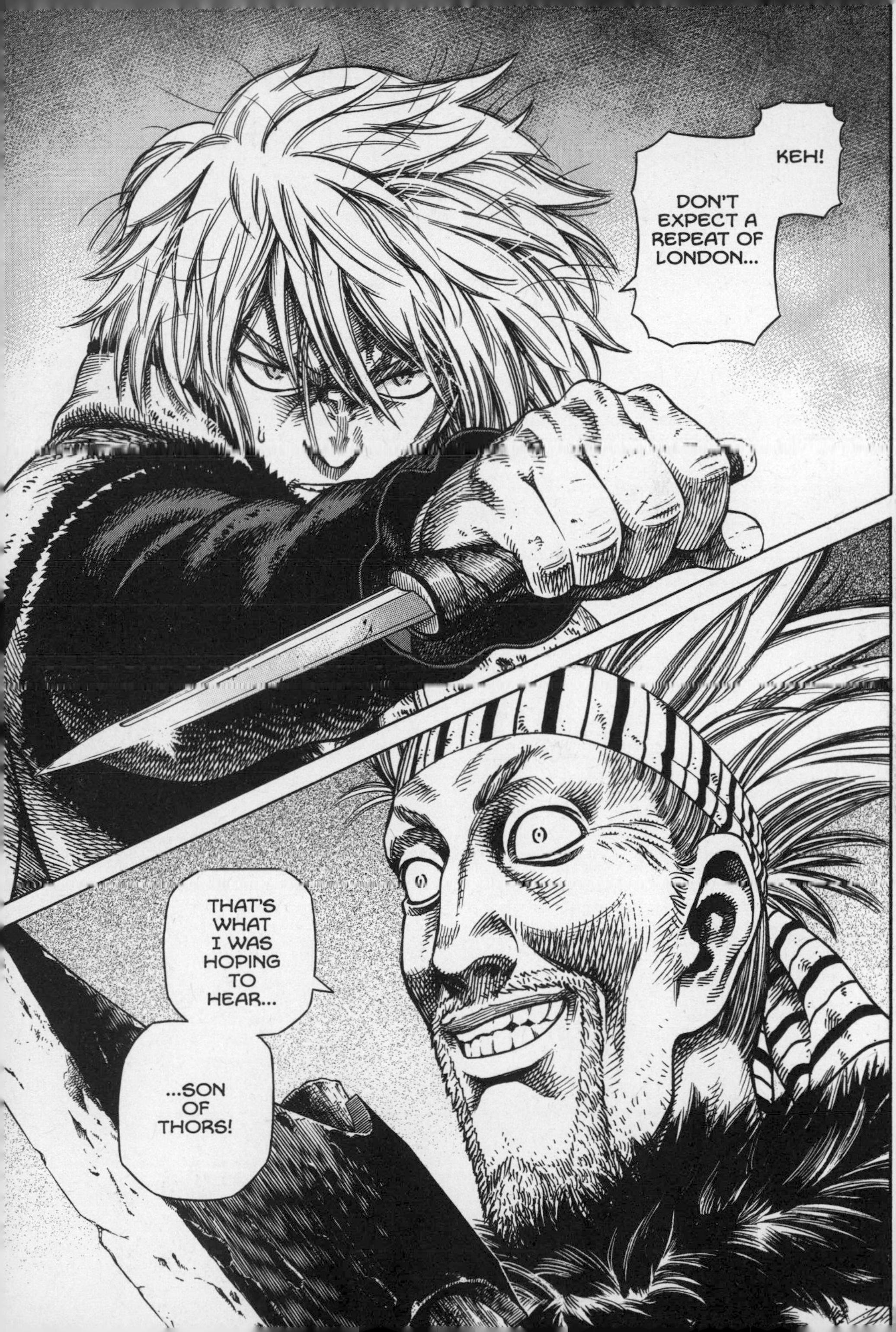
KEH!
DON'T EXPECT A REPEAT OF LONDON...
THAT'S WHAT I WAS HOPING TO HEAR...
...SON OF THORS!

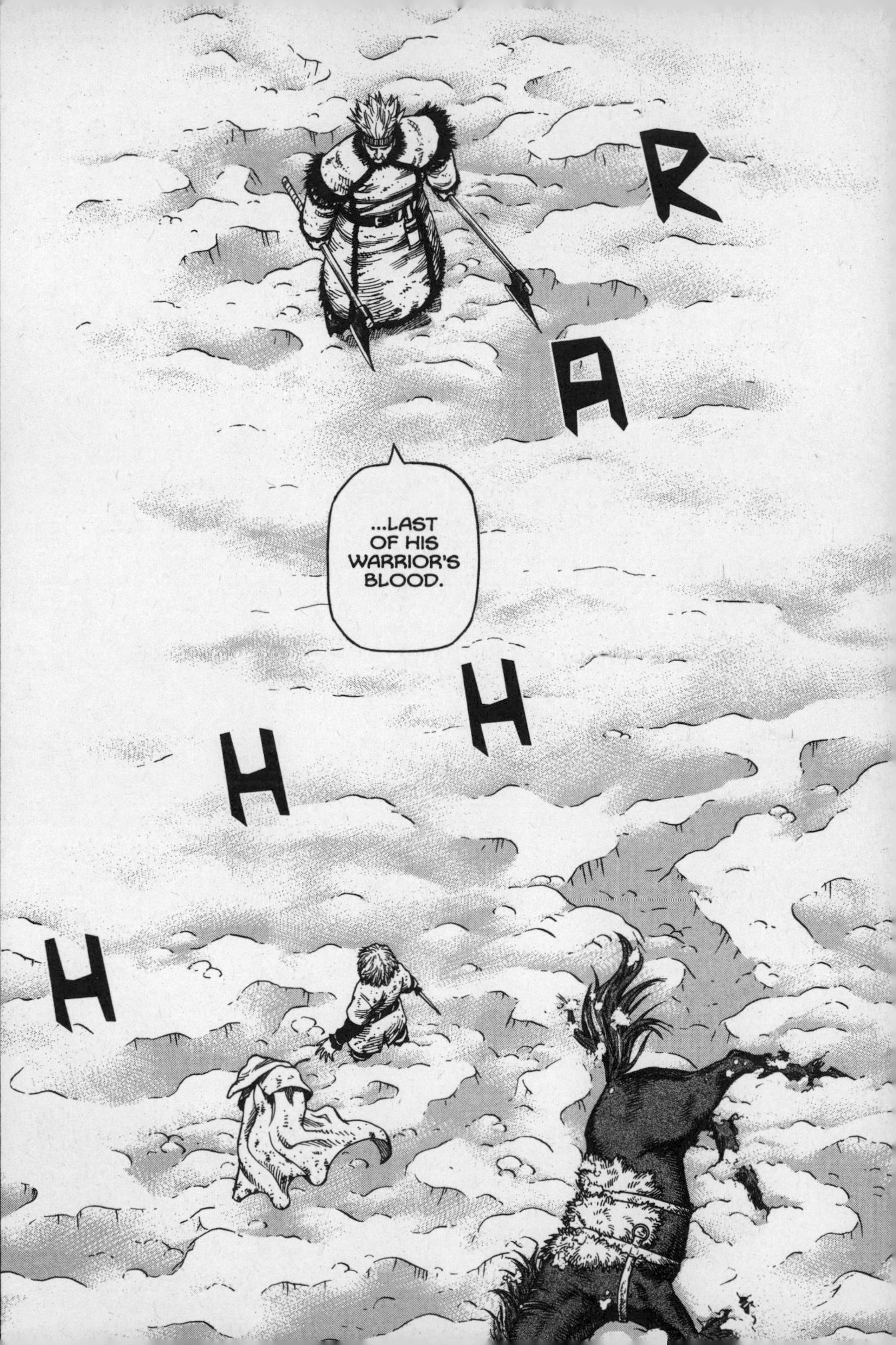
RAHHH
...LAST OF HIS WARRIOR'S BLOOD.

VINLAND SAGA MAP

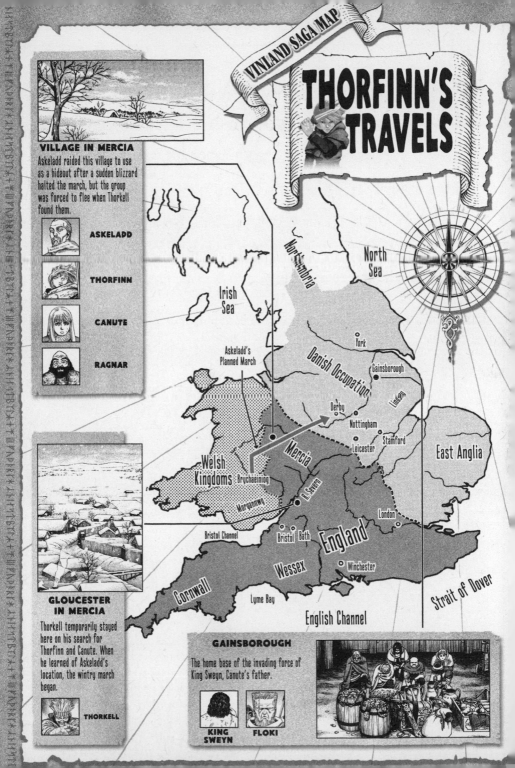

# THORFINN'S TRAVELS

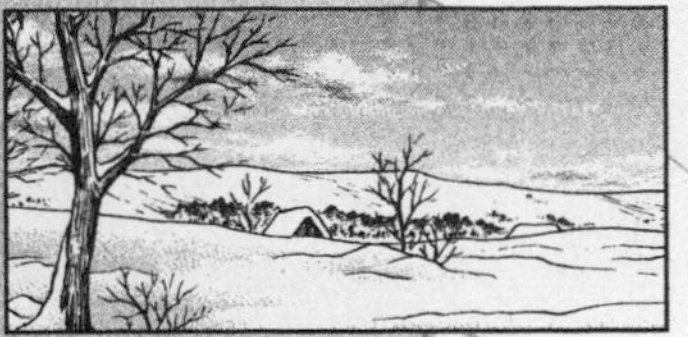

### VILLAGE IN MERCIA

Askeladd raided this village to use as a hideout after a sudden blizzard halted the march, but the group was forced to flee when Thorkell found them.

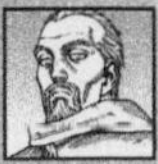
**ASKELADD**

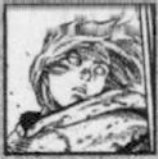
**THORFINN**

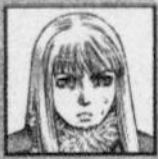
**CANUTE**

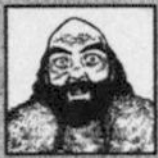
**RAGNAR**

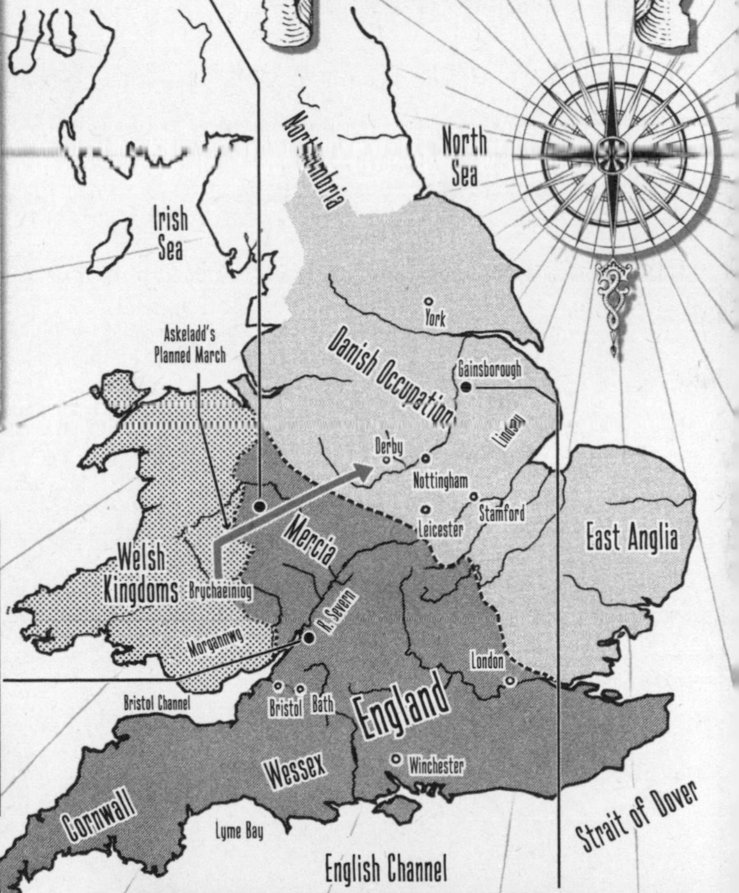

Northumbria
North Sea
Irish Sea
York
Askeladd's Planned March
Danish Occupation
Gainsborough
Lindsey
Derby
Nottingham
Stamford
Leicester
Mercia
East Anglia
Welsh Kingdoms
Brychaeiniog
R. Severn
Morgannwg
London
Bristol Channel
Bristol
Bath
England
Winchester
Wessex
Cornwall
Lyme Bay
English Channel
Strait of Dover


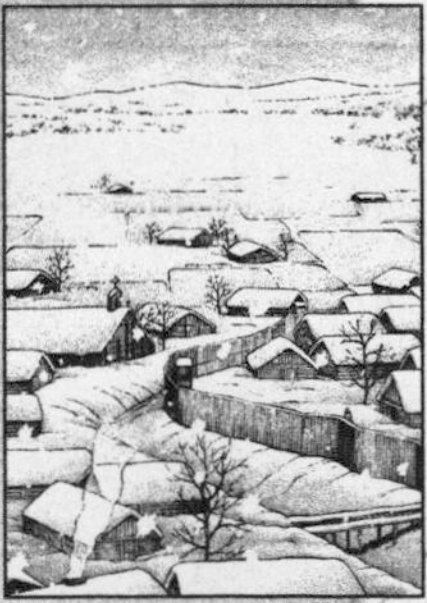

### GLOUCESTER IN MERCIA

Thorkell temporarily stayed here on his search for Thorfinn and Canute. When he learned of Askeladd's location, the wintry march began.

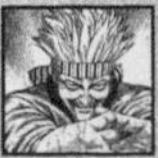
**THORKELL**

### GAINSBOROUGH

The home base of the invading force of King Sweyn, Canute's father.

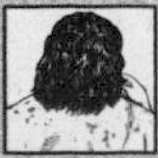
**KING SWEYN**

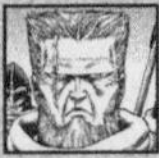
**FLOKI**

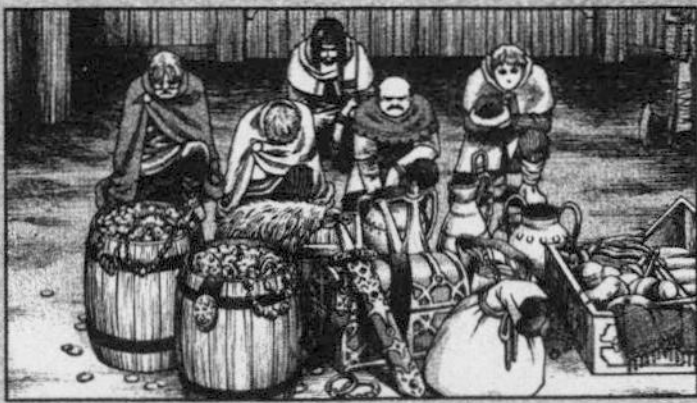

A millennium of history separates me and the Vikings. A thousand years. It's an unfathomably long amount of time. We occasionally stop and ponder the lives of human beings a thousand years ago, but what did the Vikings do? When they took breaks from herding sheep or stood up to stretch their twisted backs after a session at the loom, did they wonder, "How will people live a thousand years in the future?" I hope they did. Could there possibly be a written record of this? How did the Vikings conceptualize life in the 21st century?

**MAKOTO YUKIMURA**

VINLAND SAGA

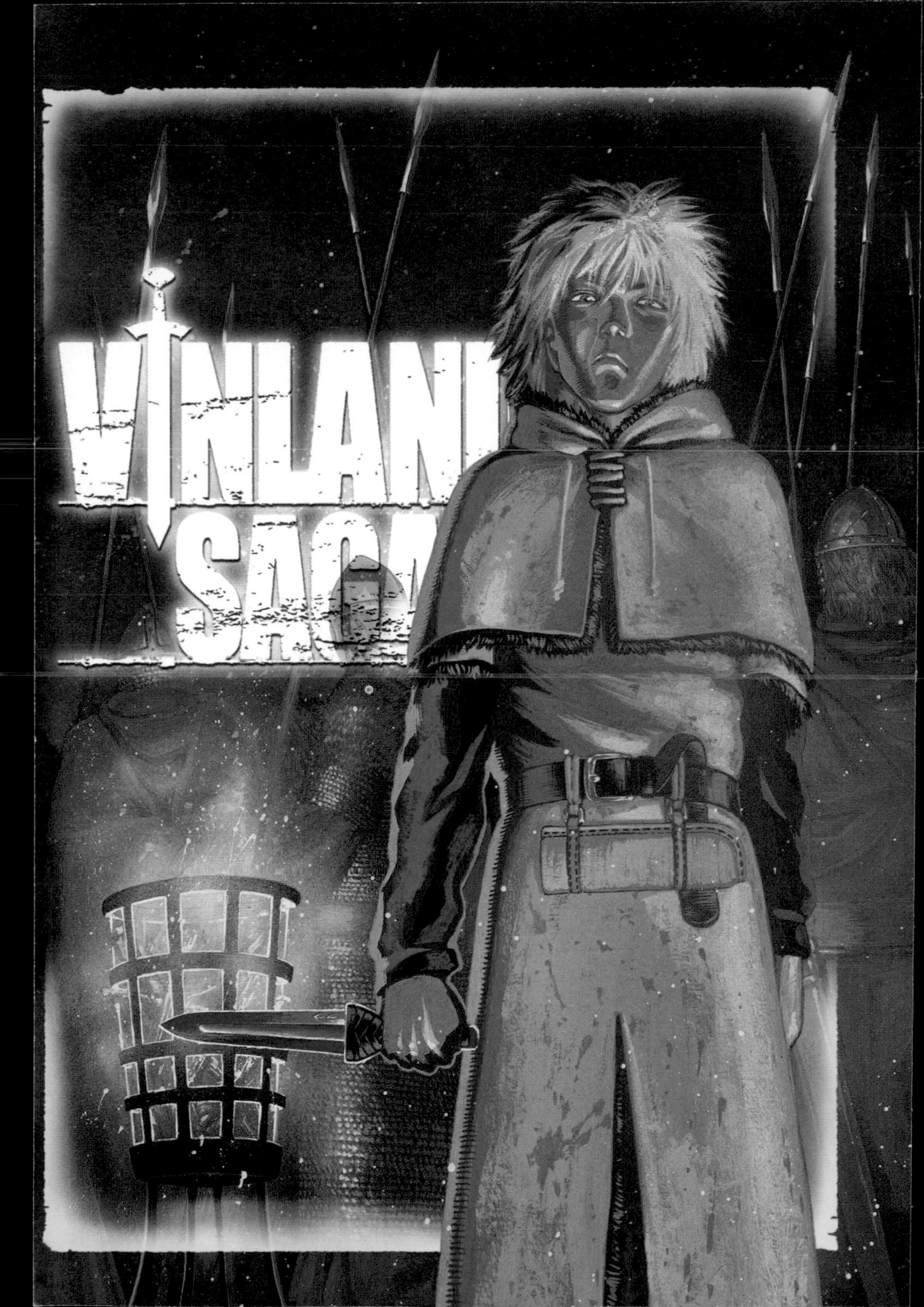
VINLAND
SAGA

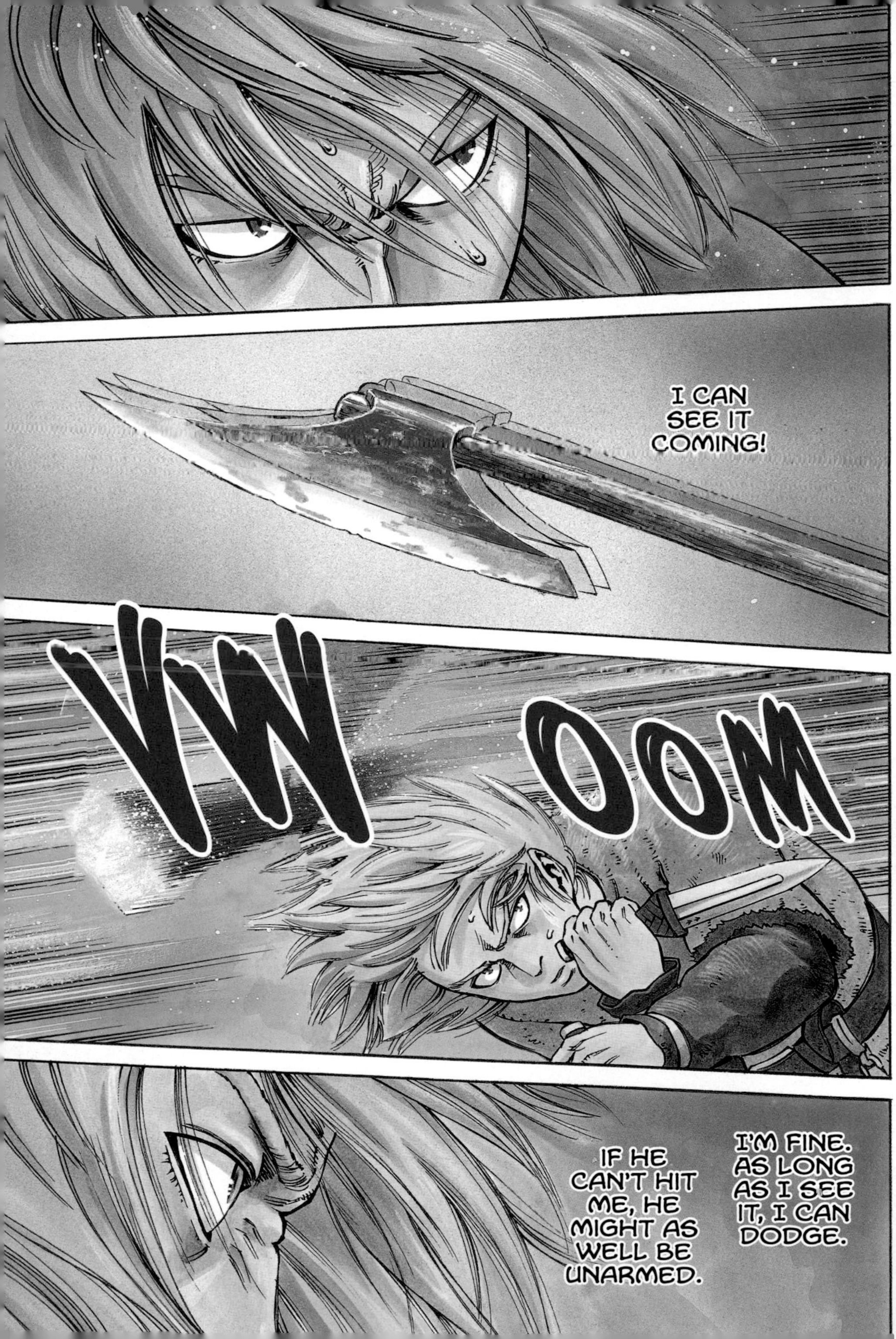
I CAN SEE IT COMING!
VWOOM
I'M FINE. AS LONG AS I SEE IT, I CAN DODGE.
IF HE CAN'T HIT ME, HE MIGHT AS WELL BE UNARMED.

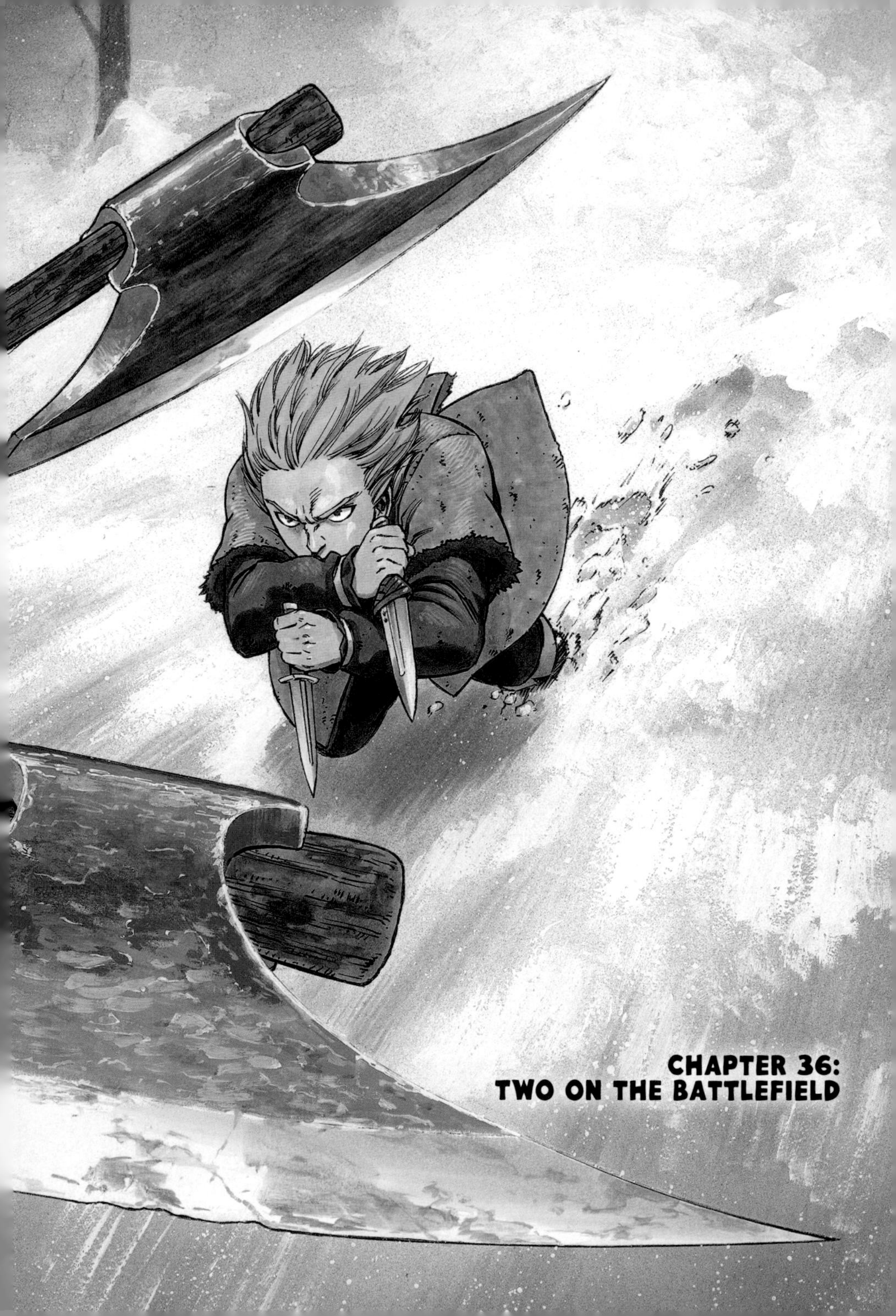
CHAPTER 36:
TWO ON THE BATTLEFIELD

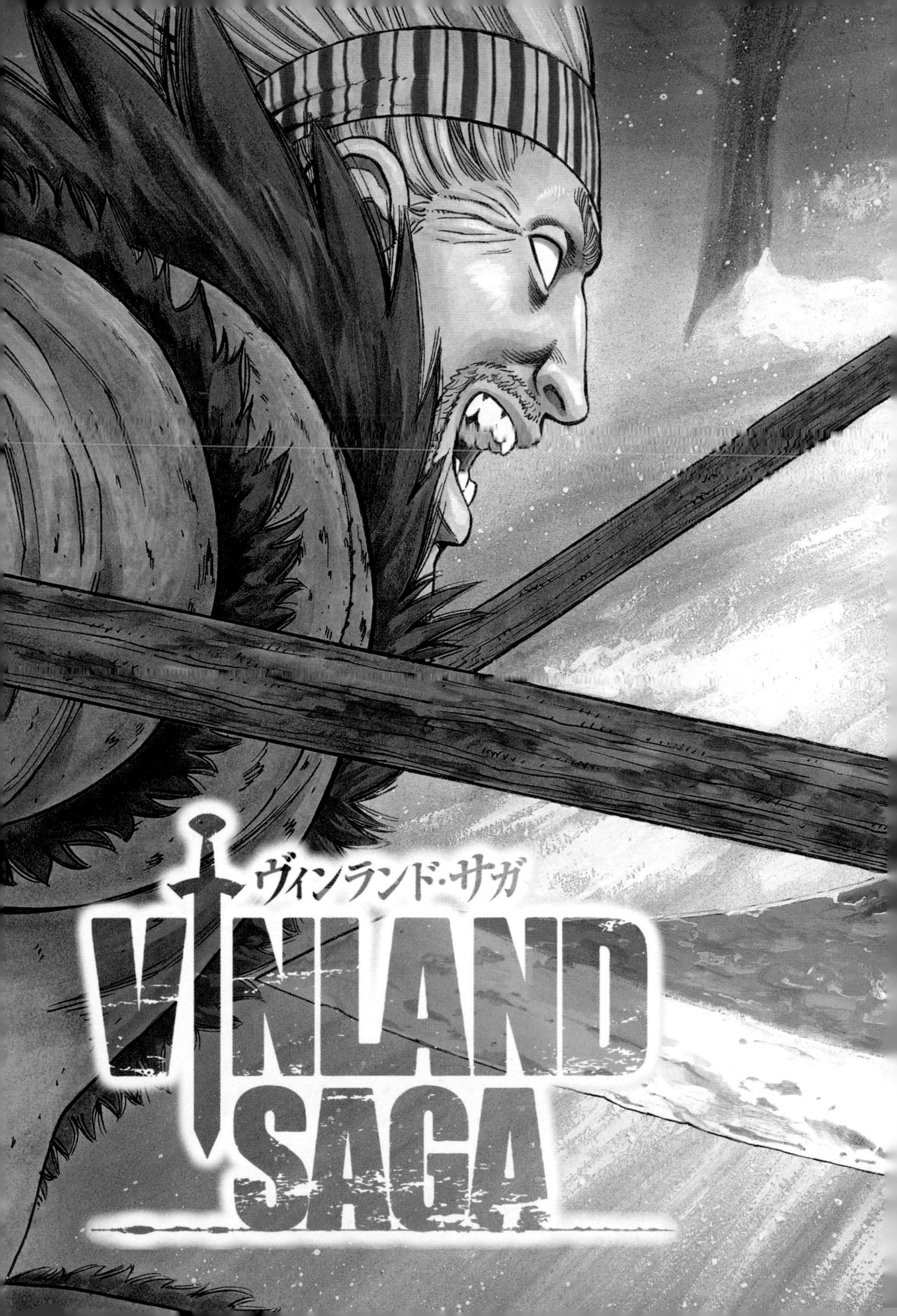
ヴィンランド・サガ
VINLAND
SAGA

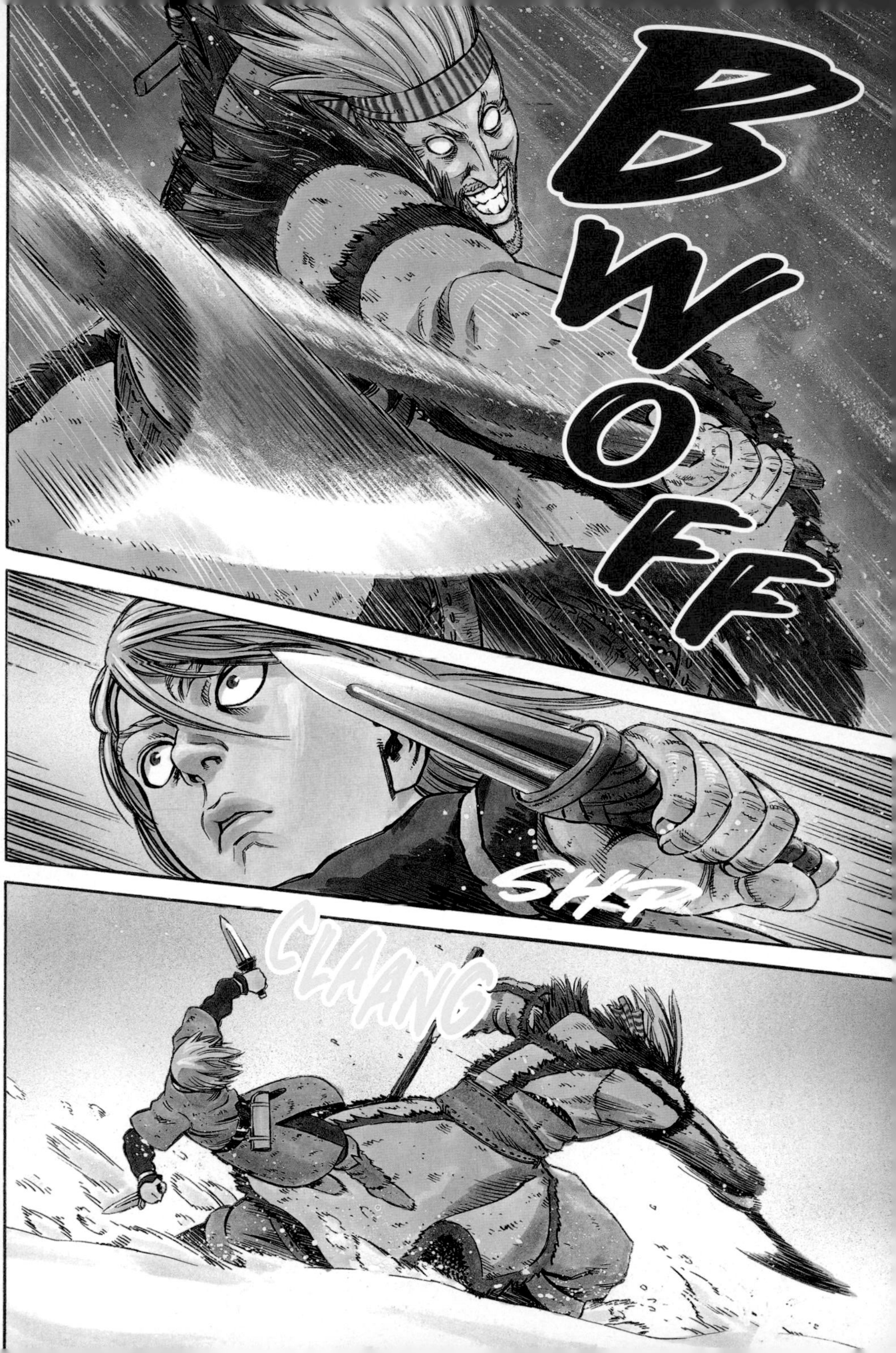
BWOFF
SHP
CLAANG

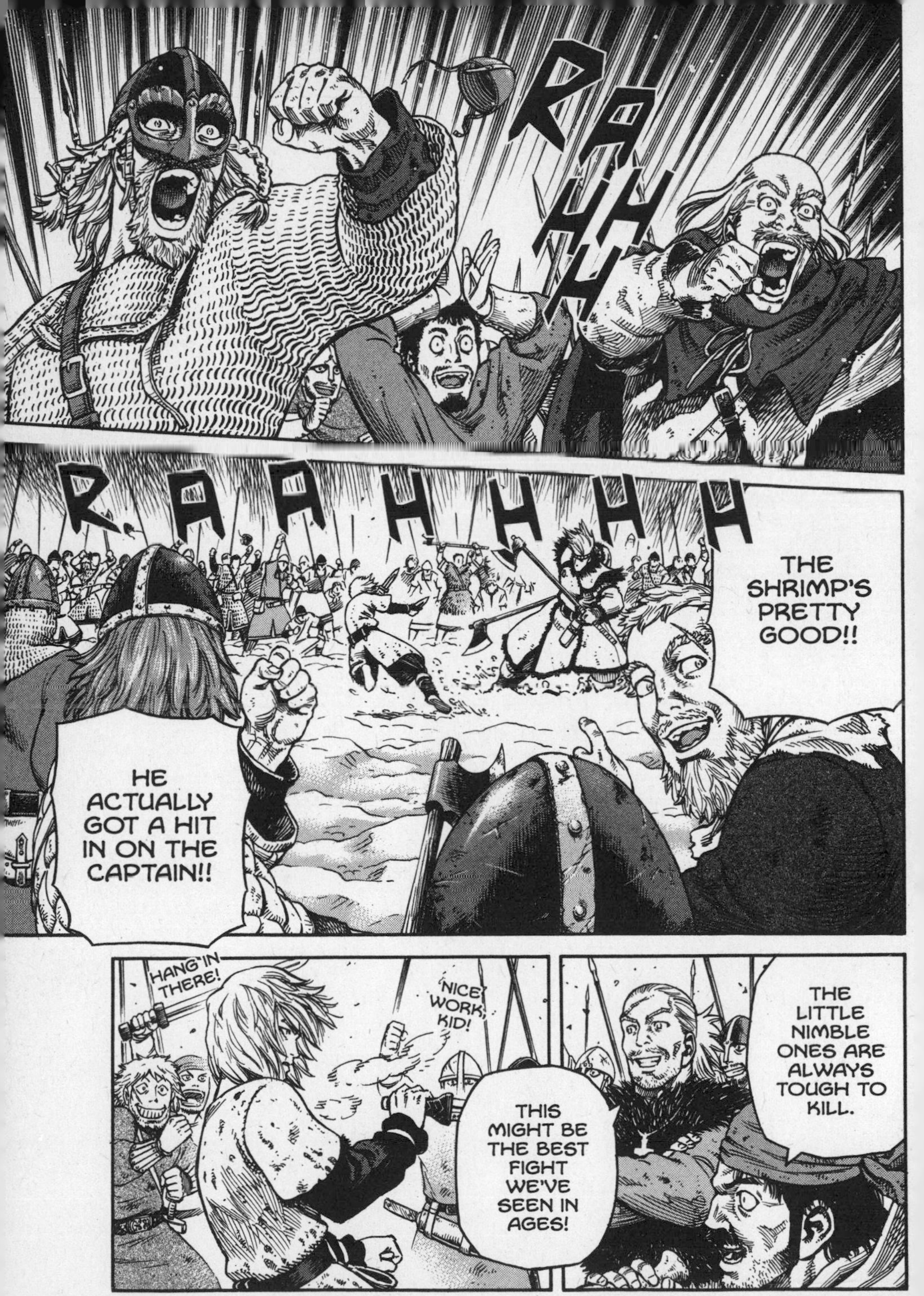
RAHHH
RAAHHHH
THE SHRIMP'S PRETTY GOOD!!
HE ACTUALLY GOT A HIT IN ON THE CAPTAIN!!
THE LITTLE NIMBLE ONES ARE ALWAYS TOUGH TO KILL.
THIS MIGHT BE THE BEST FIGHT WE'VE SEEN IN AGES!
NICE WORK, KID!
HANG IN THERE!

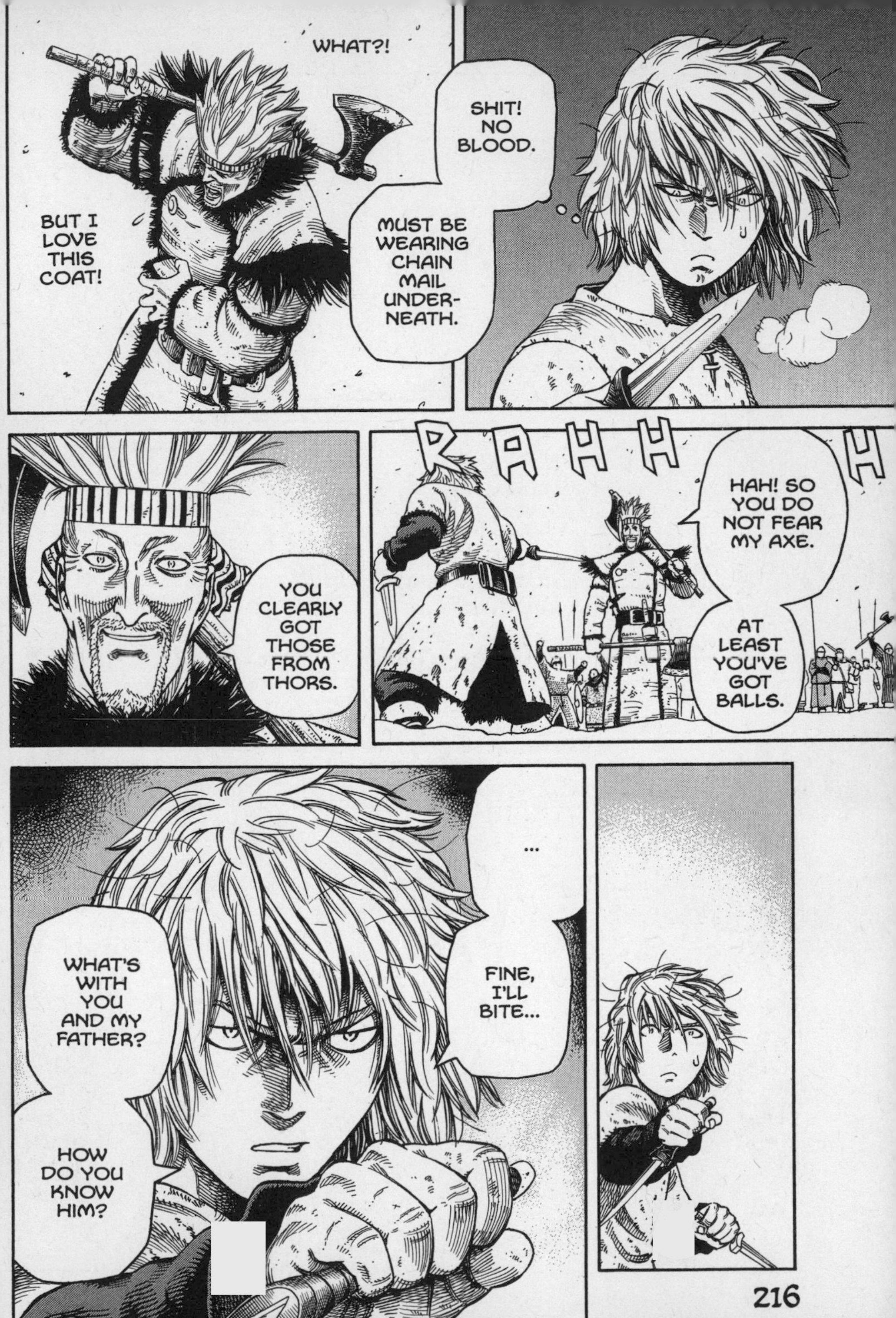
SHIT! NO BLOOD.
MUST BE WEARING CHAIN MAIL UNDER-NEATH.
WHAT?!
BUT I LOVE THIS COAT!
RAHHHH
HAH! SO YOU DO NOT FEAR MY AXE.
AT LEAST YOU'VE GOT BALLS.
YOU CLEARLY GOT THOSE FROM THORS.
...
FINE, I'LL BITE...
WHAT'S WITH YOU AND MY FATHER?
HOW DO YOU KNOW HIM?

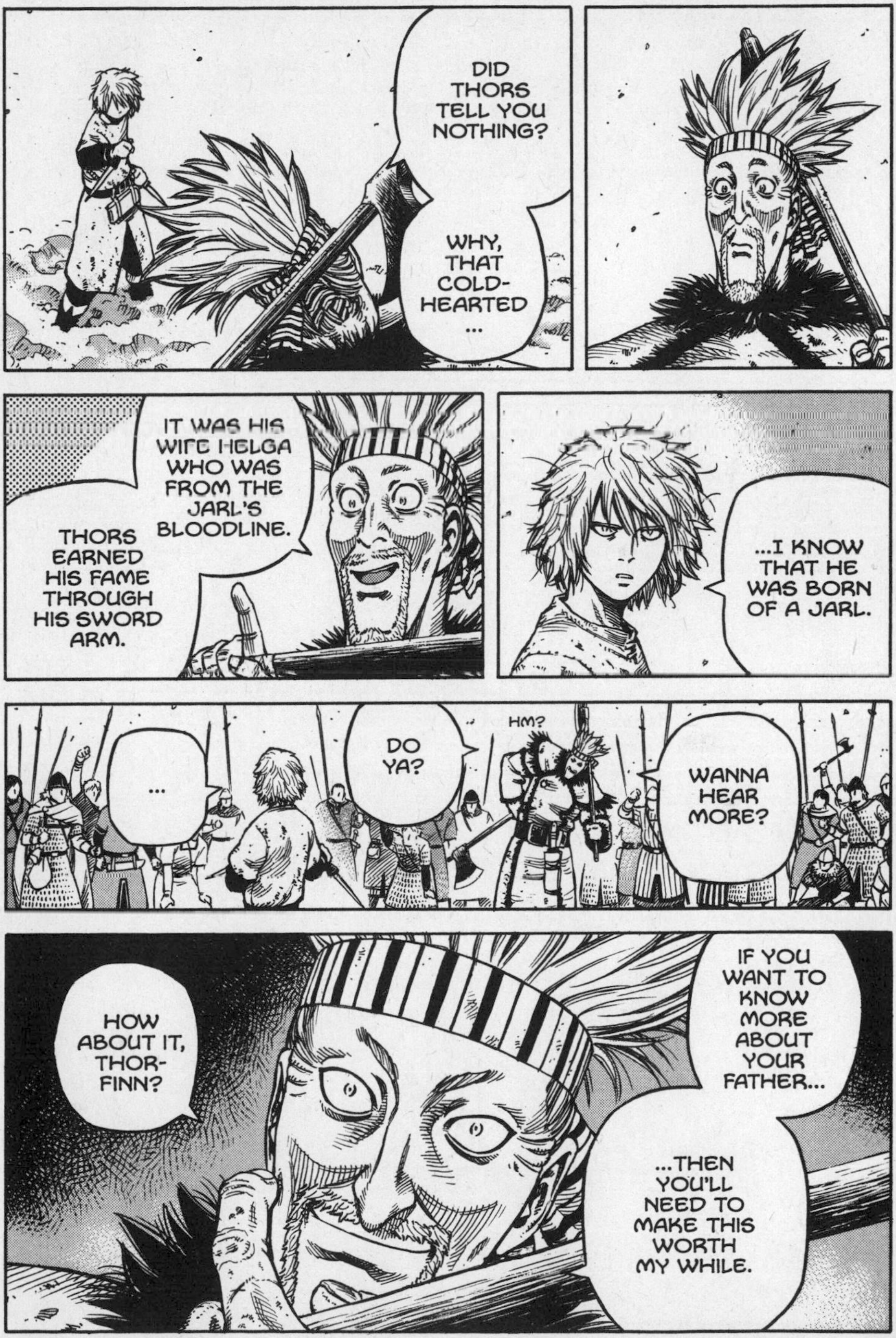
DID THORS TELL YOU NOTHING?
WHY, THAT COLD-HEARTED ...
...I KNOW THAT HE WAS BORN OF A JARL.
IT WAS HIS WIFE HELGA WHO WAS FROM THE JARL'S BLOODLINE.
THORS EARNED HIS FAME THROUGH HIS SWORD ARM.
WANNA HEAR MORE?
HM?
DO YA?
...
IF YOU WANT TO KNOW MORE ABOUT YOUR FATHER...
...THEN YOU'LL NEED TO MAKE THIS WORTH MY WHILE.
HOW ABOUT IT, THORFINN?

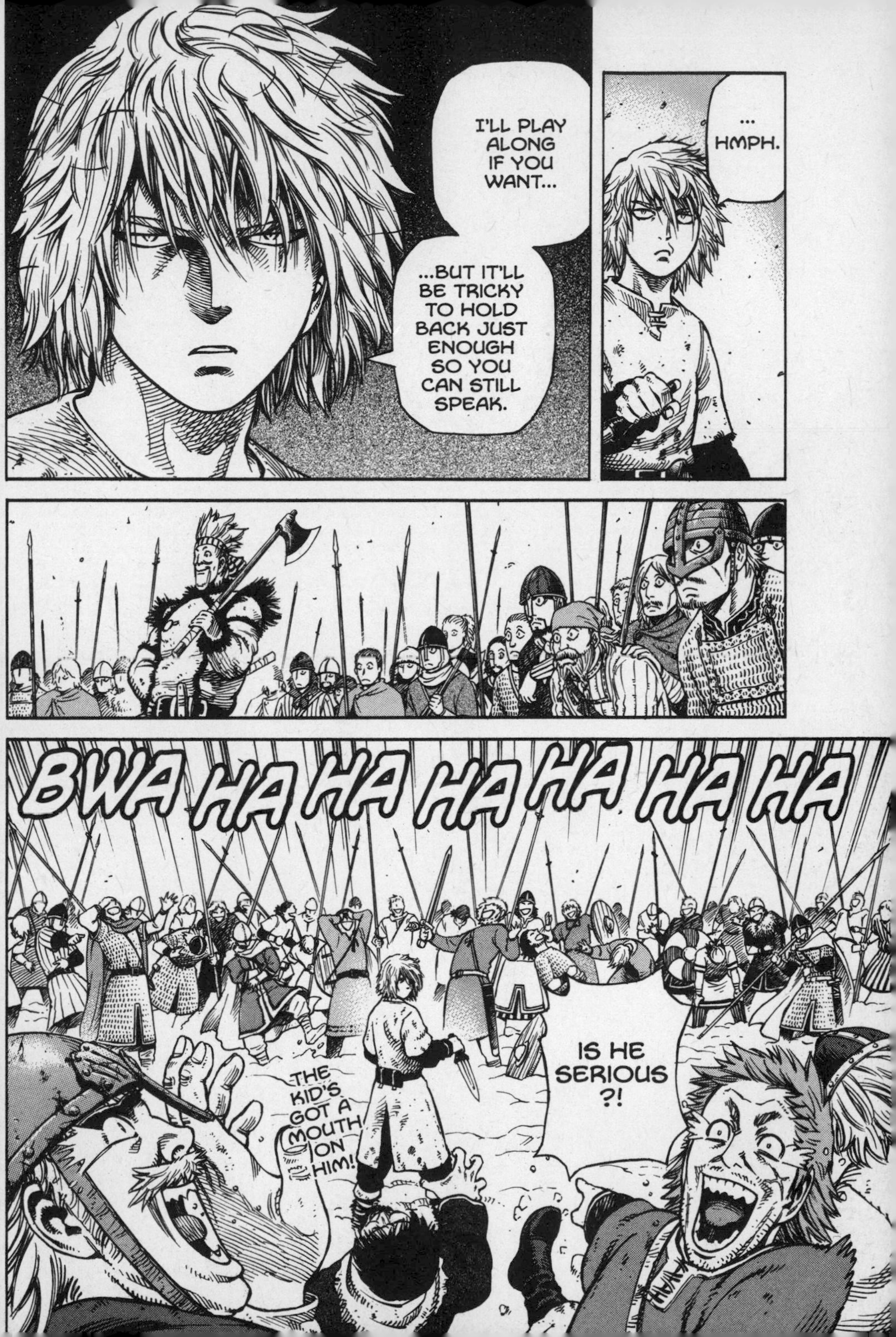
... HMPH.
I'LL PLAY ALONG IF YOU WANT...
...BUT IT'LL BE TRICKY TO HOLD BACK JUST ENOUGH SO YOU CAN STILL SPEAK.
BWA HA HA HA HA HA HA HA
IS HE SERIOUS?!
THE KID'S GOT A MOUTH ON HIM!

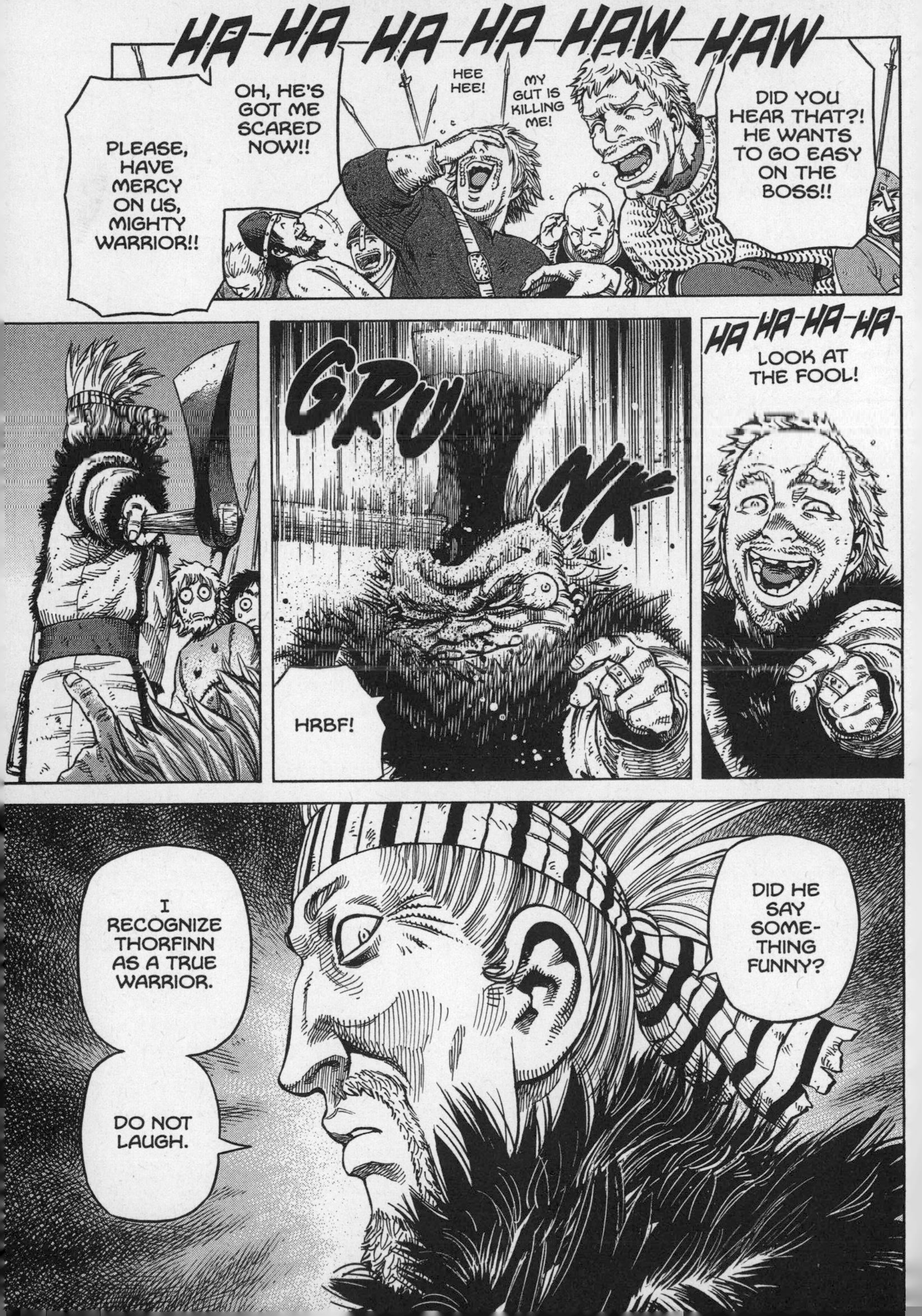
HA-HA-HA-HA-HAW-HAW
DID YOU HEAR THAT?! HE WANTS TO GO EASY ON THE BOSS!!
MY GUT IS KILLING ME!
HEE HEE!
OH, HE'S GOT ME SCARED NOW!!
PLEASE, HAVE MERCY ON US, MIGHTY WARRIOR!!
HA HA-HA-HA
LOOK AT THE FOOL!
GRUNK
HRBF!
DID HE SAY SOMETHING FUNNY?
I RECOGNIZE THORFINN AS A TRUE WARRIOR.
DO NOT LAUGH.

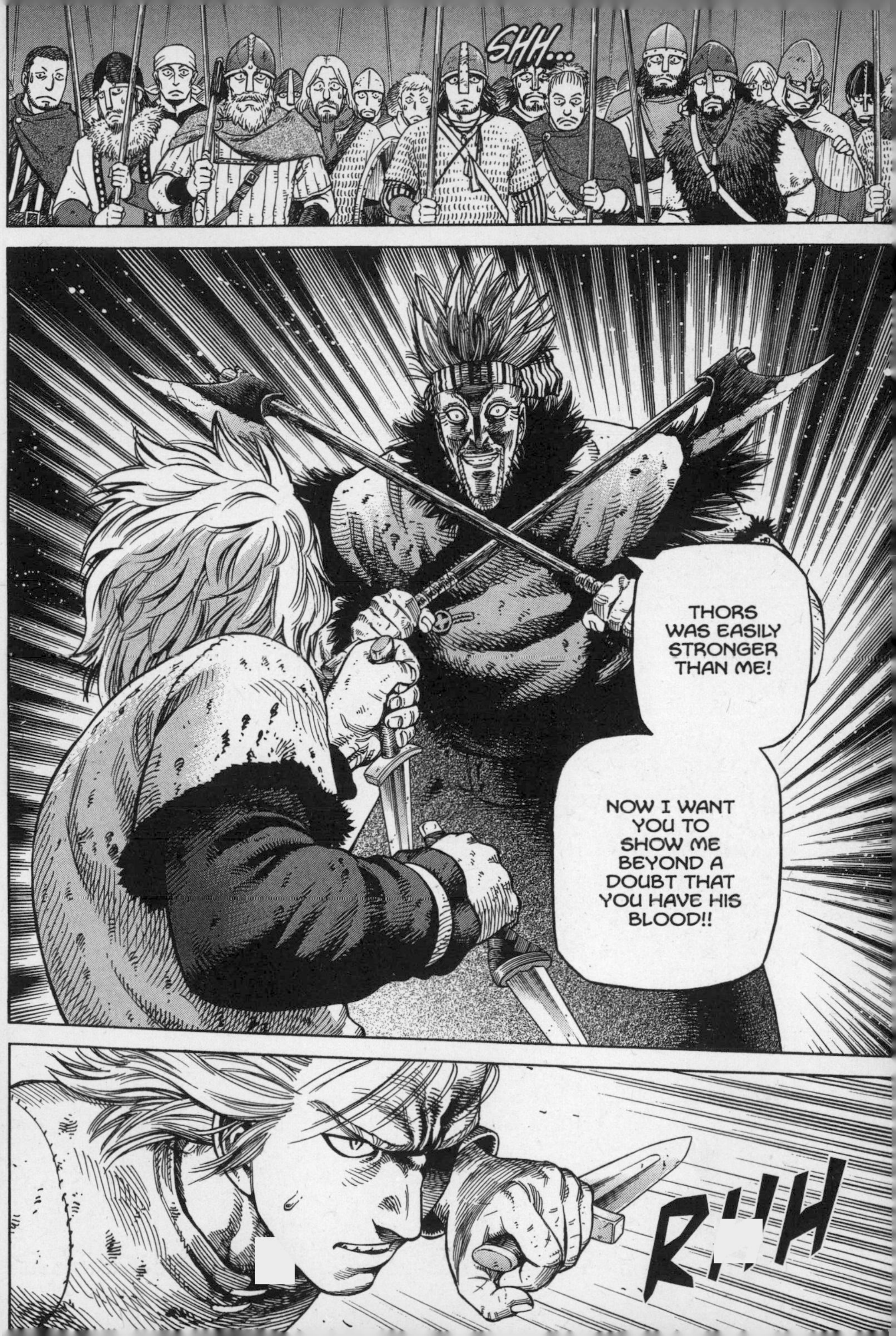SHH...
THORS WAS EASILY STRONGER THAN ME!
NOW I WANT YOU TO SHOW ME BEYOND A DOUBT THAT YOU HAVE HIS BLOOD!!

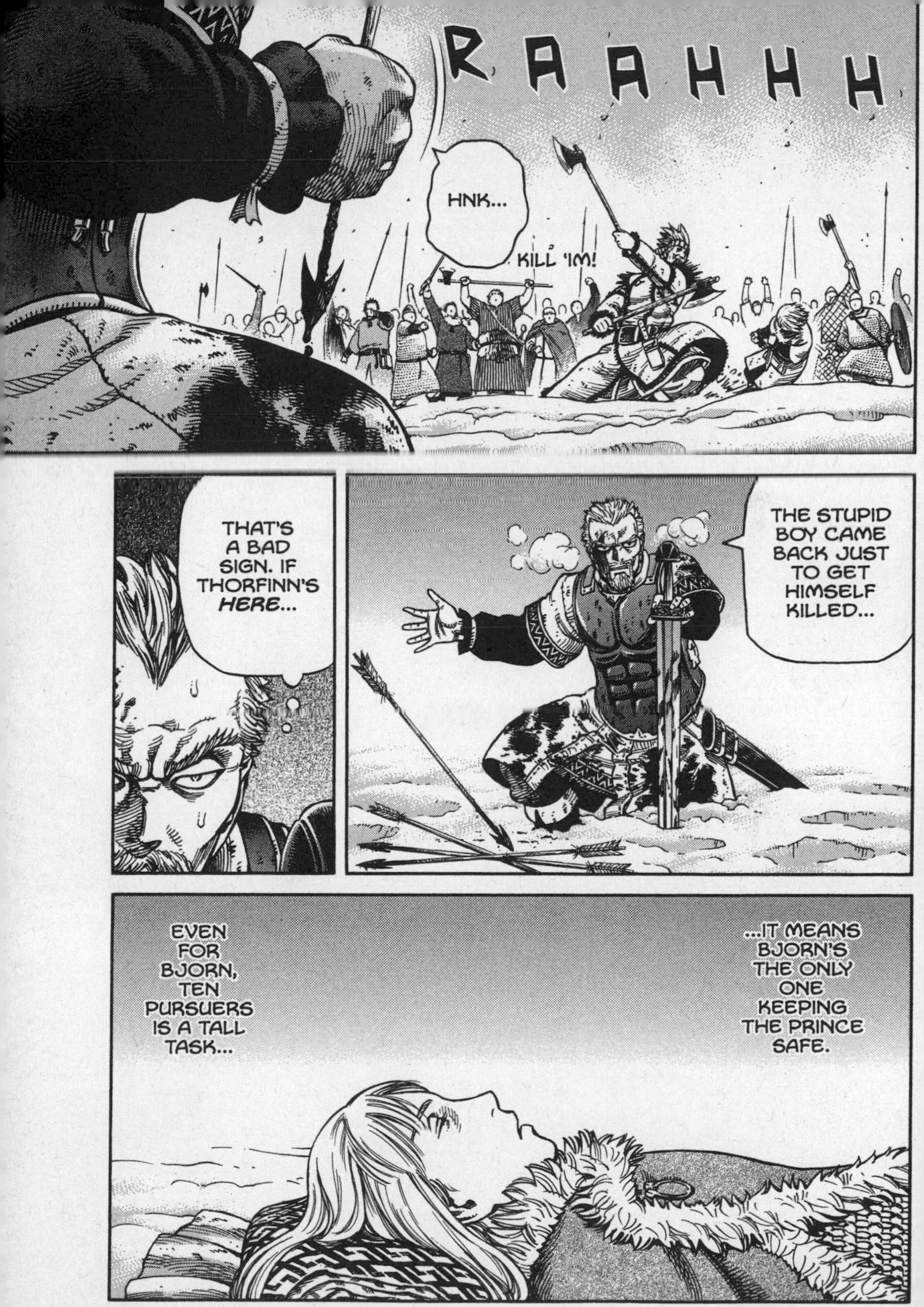
RAAHHH
HNK...
KILL 'IM!
THE STUPID BOY CAME BACK JUST TO GET HIMSELF KILLED...
THAT'S A BAD SIGN. IF THORFINN'S *HERE*...
...IT MEANS BJORN'S THE ONLY ONE KEEPING THE PRINCE SAFE.
EVEN FOR BJORN, TEN PURSUERS IS A TALL TASK...

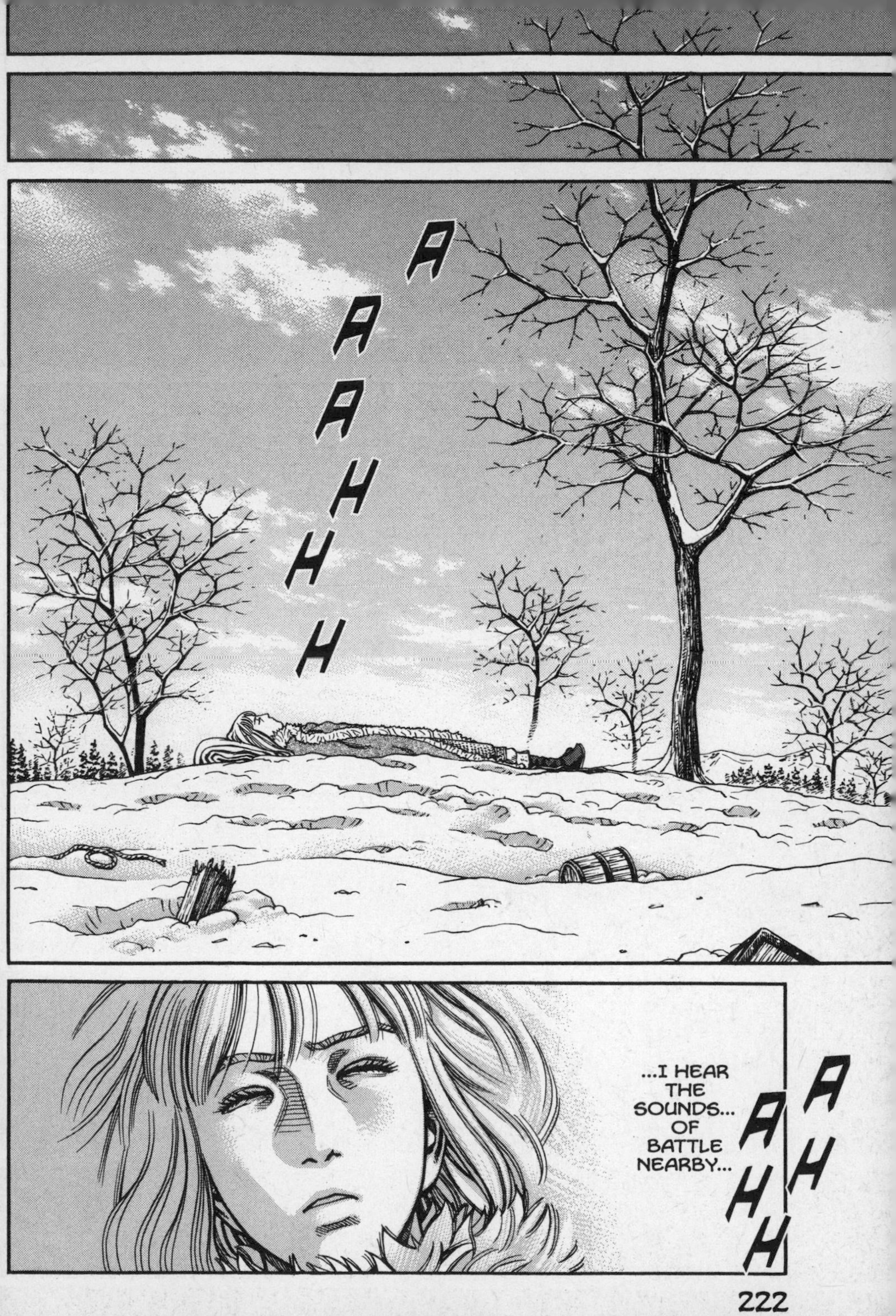
AAAHHH
...I HEAR THE SOUNDS... OF BATTLE NEARBY...
AH
AHH

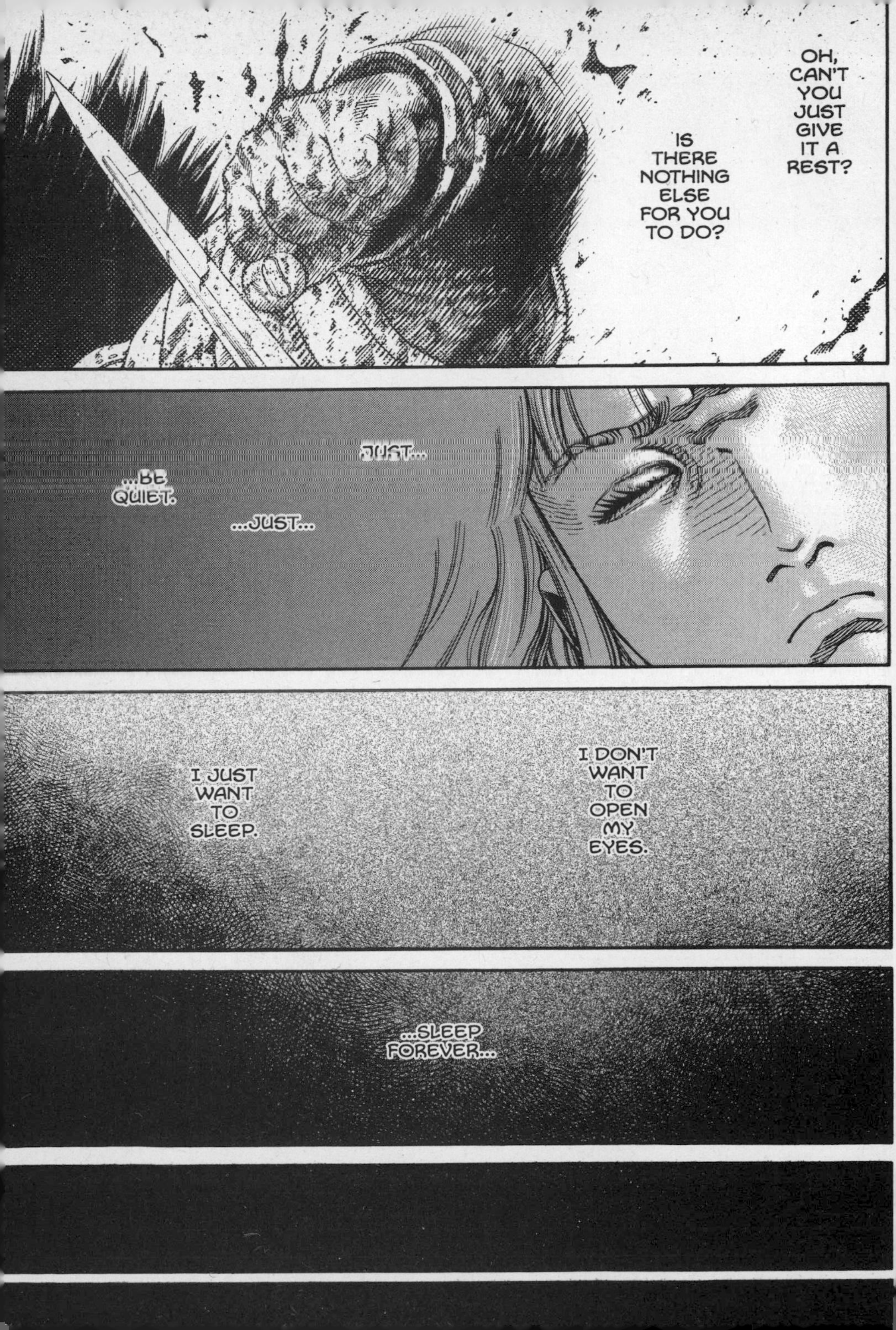
OH, CAN'T YOU JUST GIVE IT A REST?
IS THERE NOTHING ELSE FOR YOU TO DO?
JUST...
...BE QUIET.
...JUST...
I DON'T WANT TO OPEN MY EYES.
I JUST WANT TO SLEEP.
...SLEEP FOREVER...

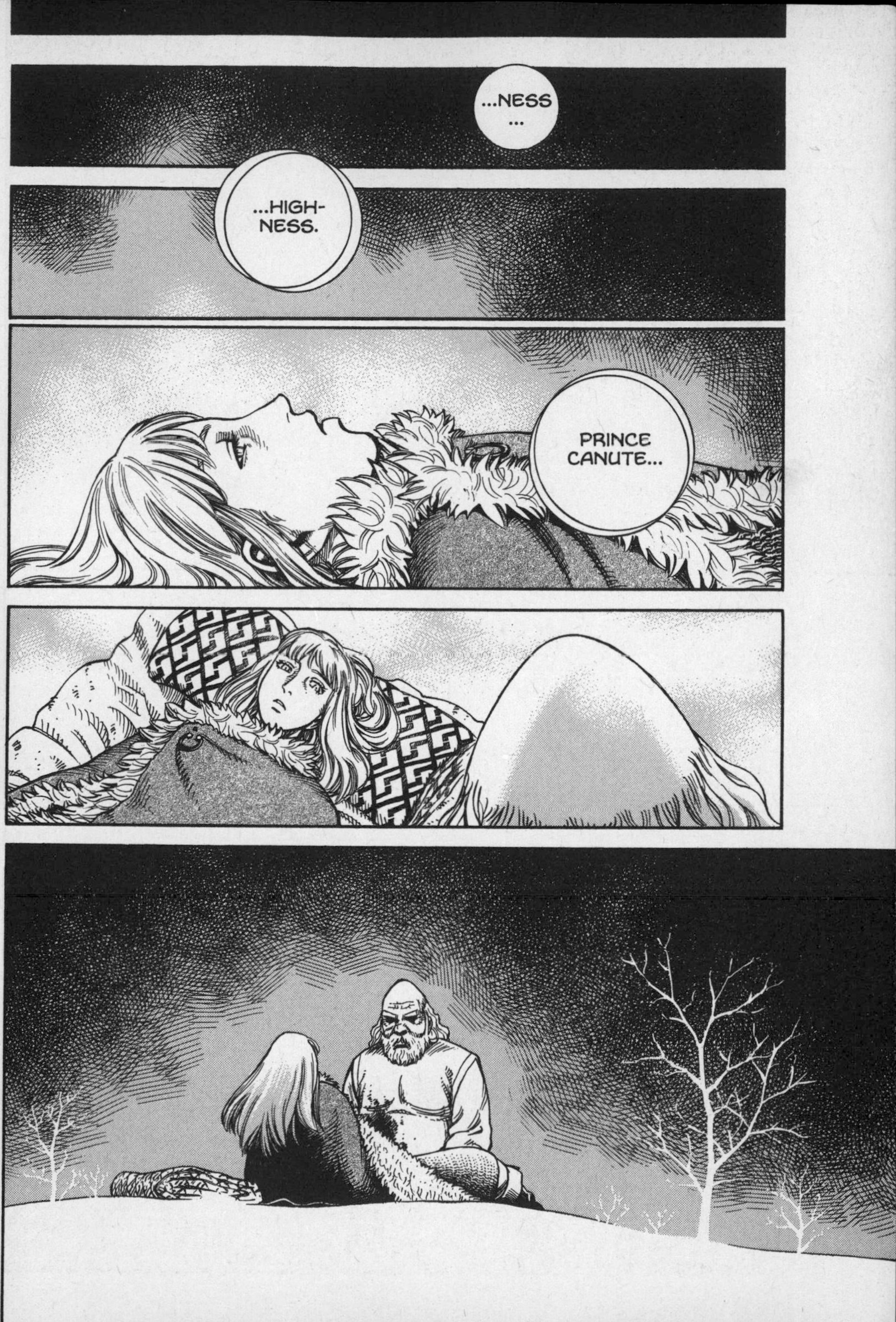
...NESS ...
...HIGH-NESS.
PRINCE CANUTE...

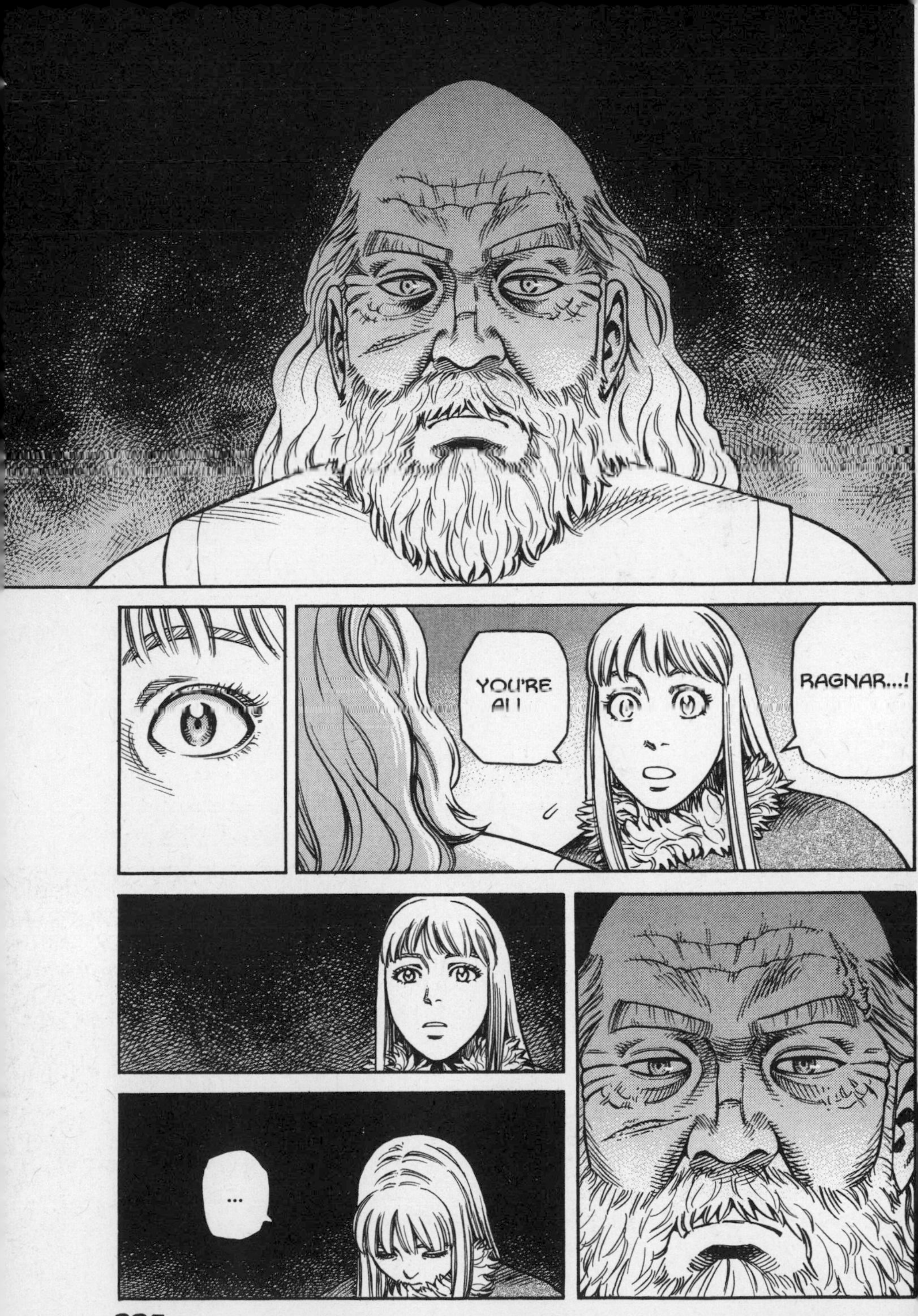
RAGNAR...!
YOU'RE ALI
...

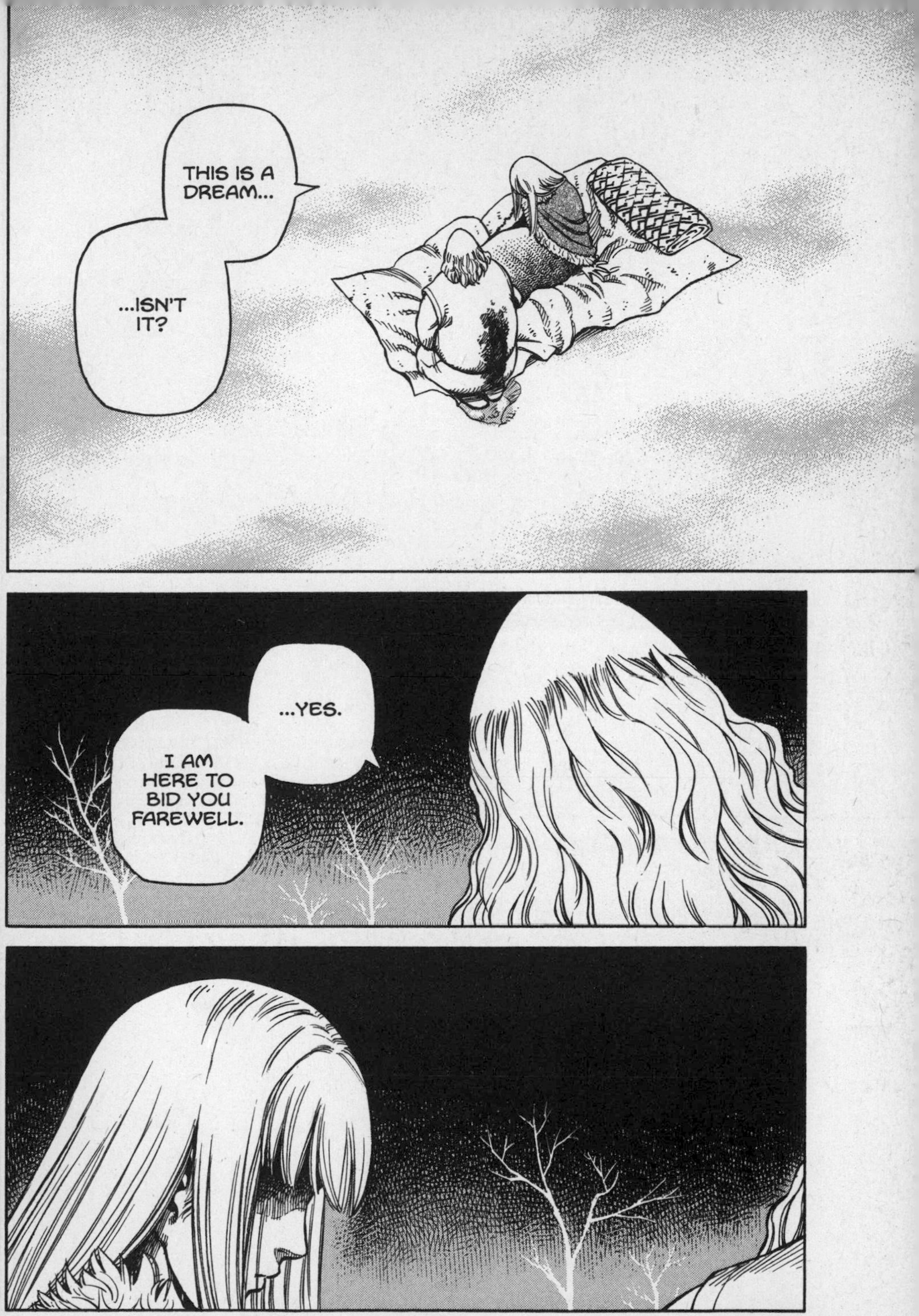
THIS IS A DREAM...
...ISN'T IT?
...YES.
I AM HERE TO BID YOU FAREWELL.

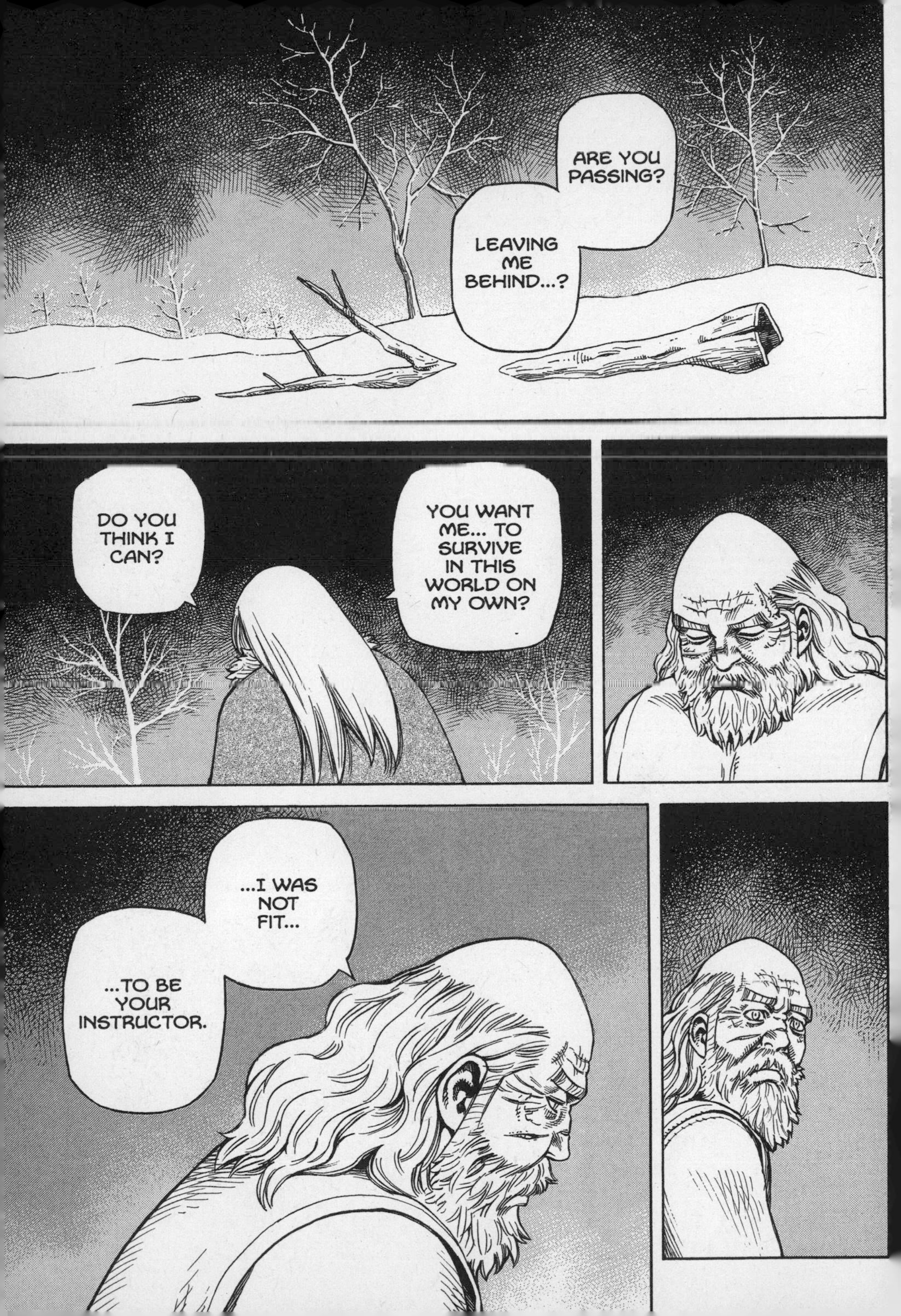
ARE YOU PASSING?
LEAVING ME BEHIND...?
YOU WANT ME... TO SURVIVE IN THIS WORLD ON MY OWN?
DO YOU THINK I CAN?
...I WAS NOT FIT...
...TO BE YOUR INSTRUCTOR.

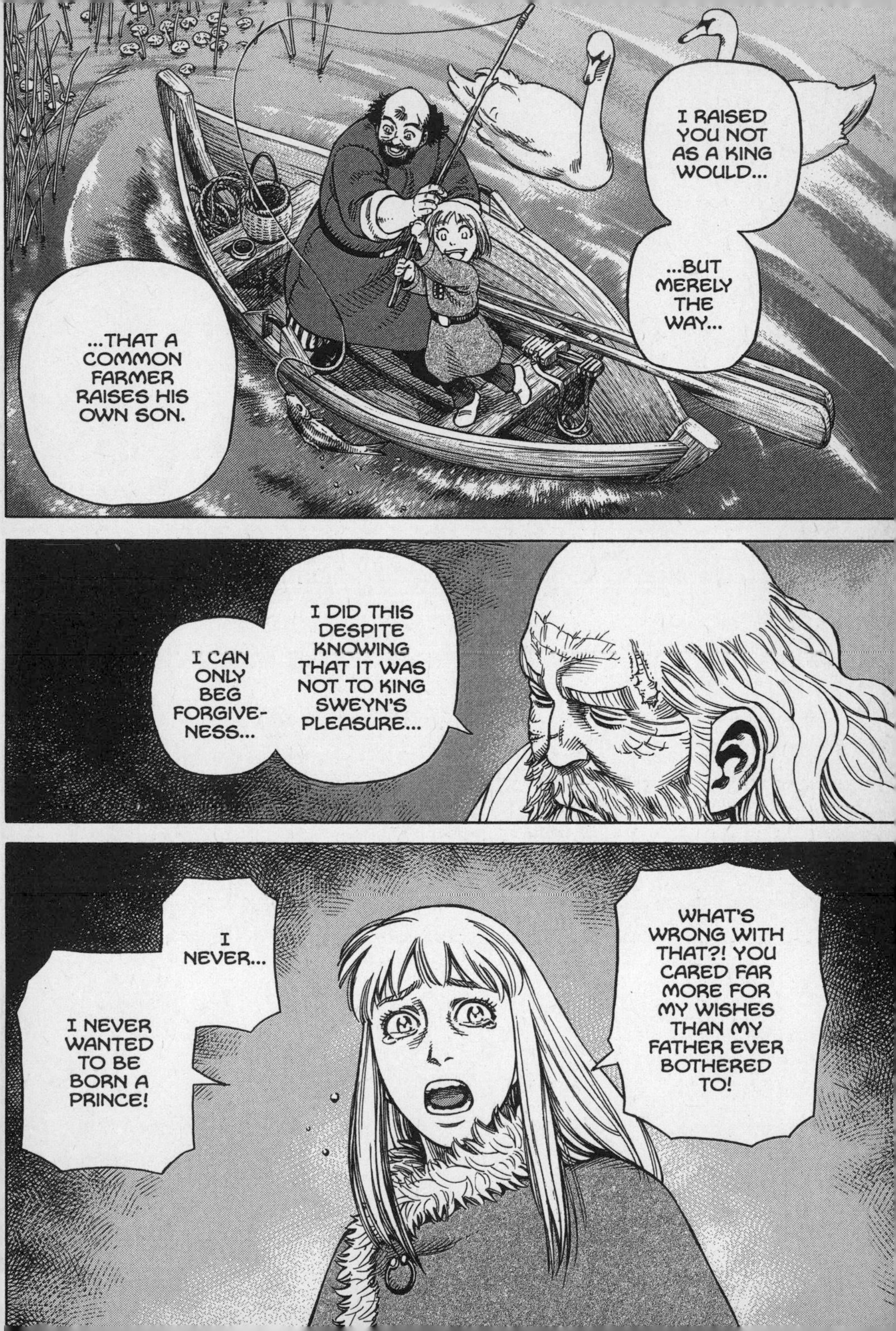
I RAISED YOU NOT AS A KING WOULD...
...BUT MERELY THE WAY...
...THAT A COMMON FARMER RAISES HIS OWN SON.
I DID THIS DESPITE KNOWING THAT IT WAS NOT TO KING SWEYN'S PLEASURE...
I CAN ONLY BEG FORGIVENESS...
WHAT'S WRONG WITH THAT?! YOU CARED FAR MORE FOR MY WISHES THAN MY FATHER EVER BOTHERED TO!
I NEVER...
I NEVER WANTED TO BE BORN A PRINCE!

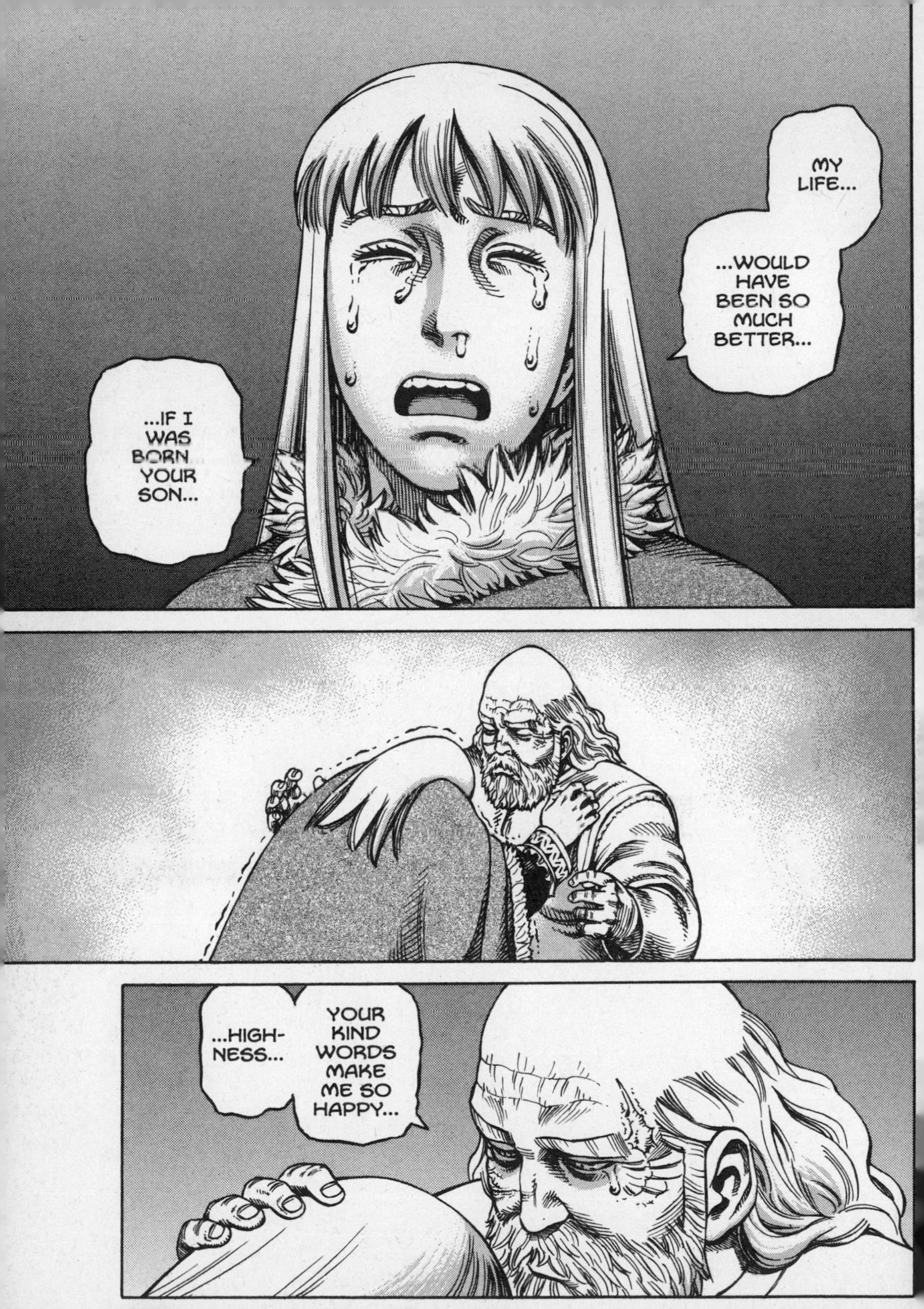
MY LIFE...
...WOULD HAVE BEEN SO MUCH BETTER...
...IF I WAS BORN YOUR SON...
YOUR KIND WORDS MAKE ME SO HAPPY...
...HIGH-NESS...

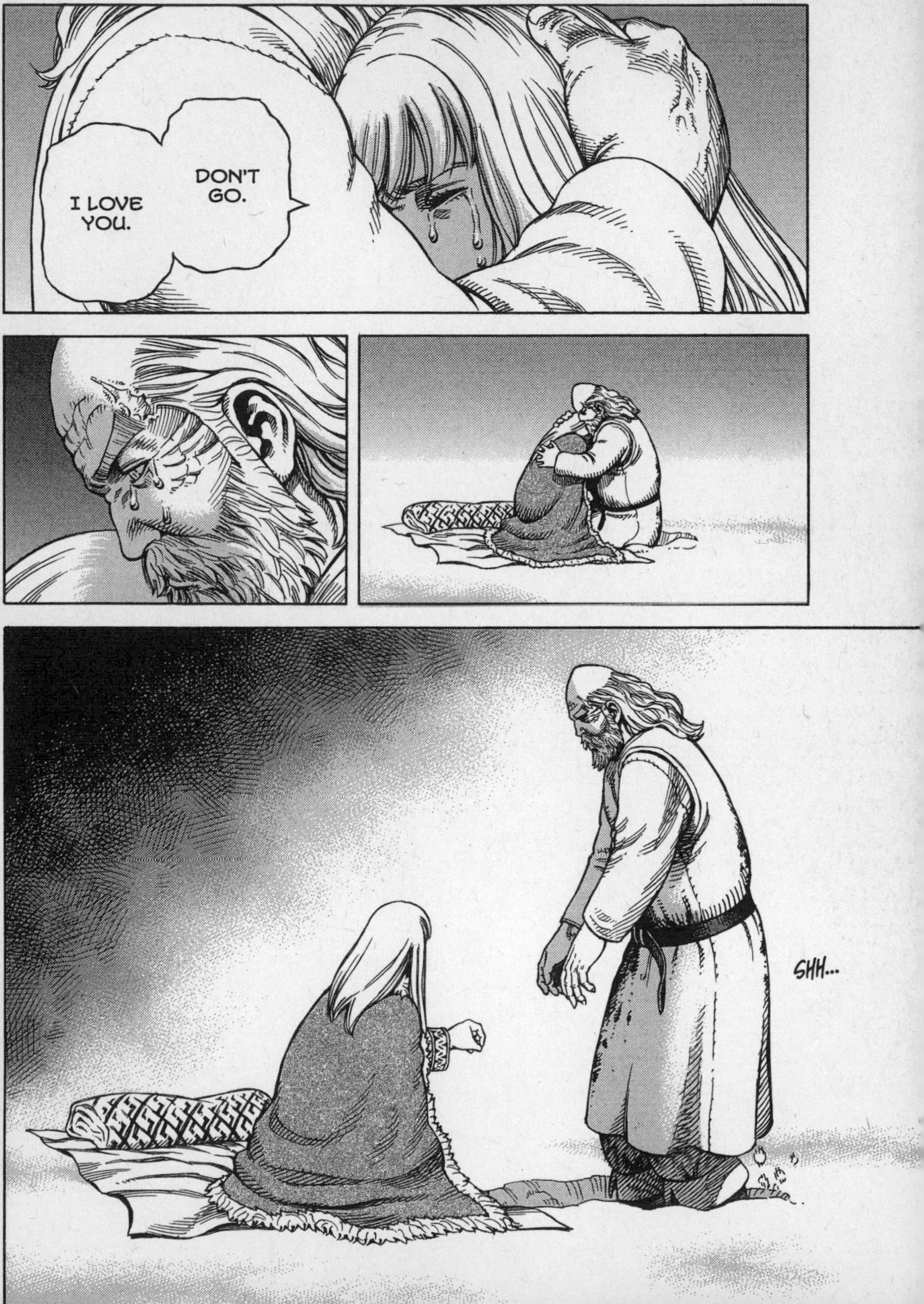
DON'T GO.
I LOVE YOU.
SHH...

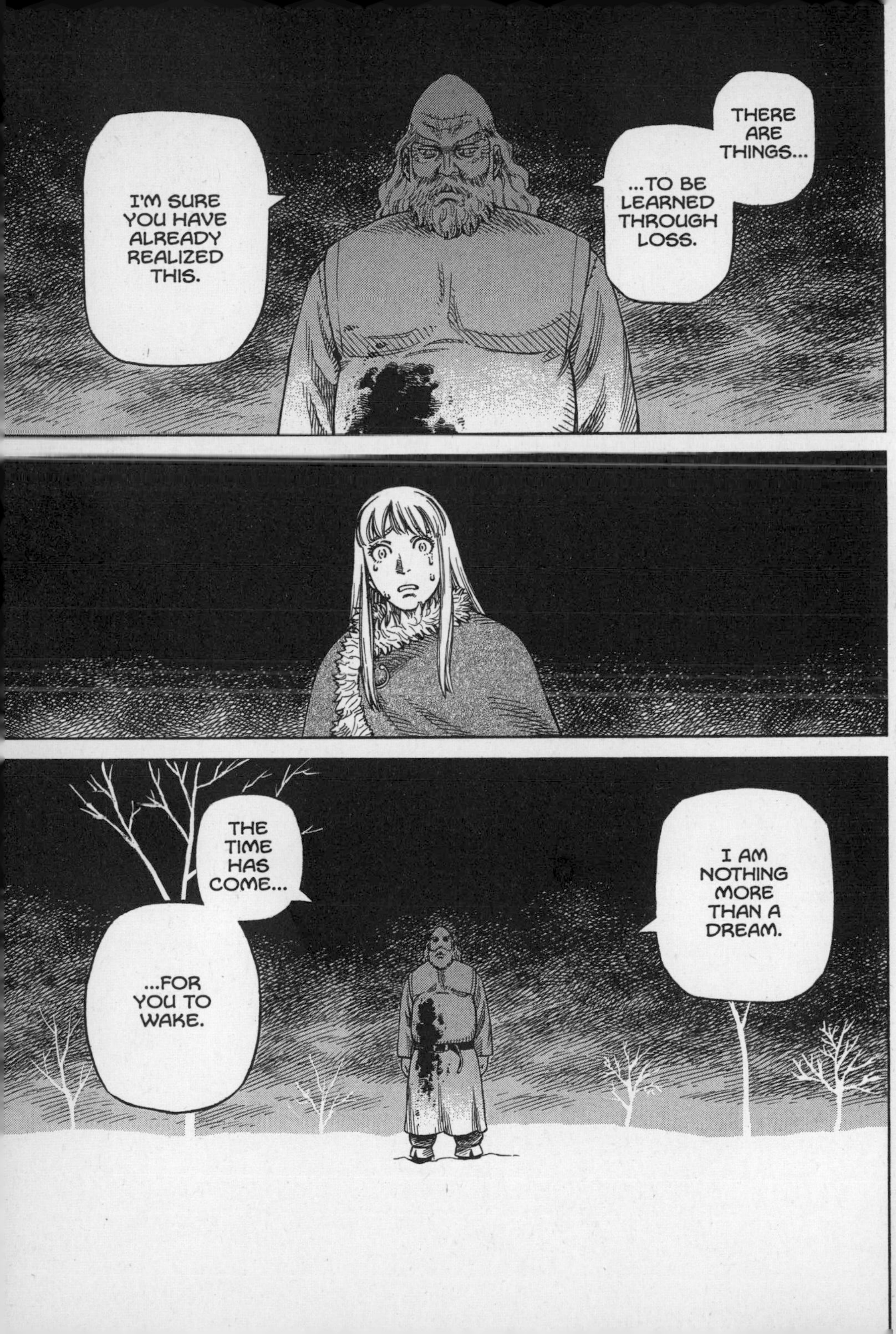
THERE ARE THINGS...
...TO BE LEARNED THROUGH LOSS.
I'M SURE YOU HAVE ALREADY REALIZED THIS.
I AM NOTHING MORE THAN A DREAM.
THE TIME HAS COME...
...FOR YOU TO WAKE.

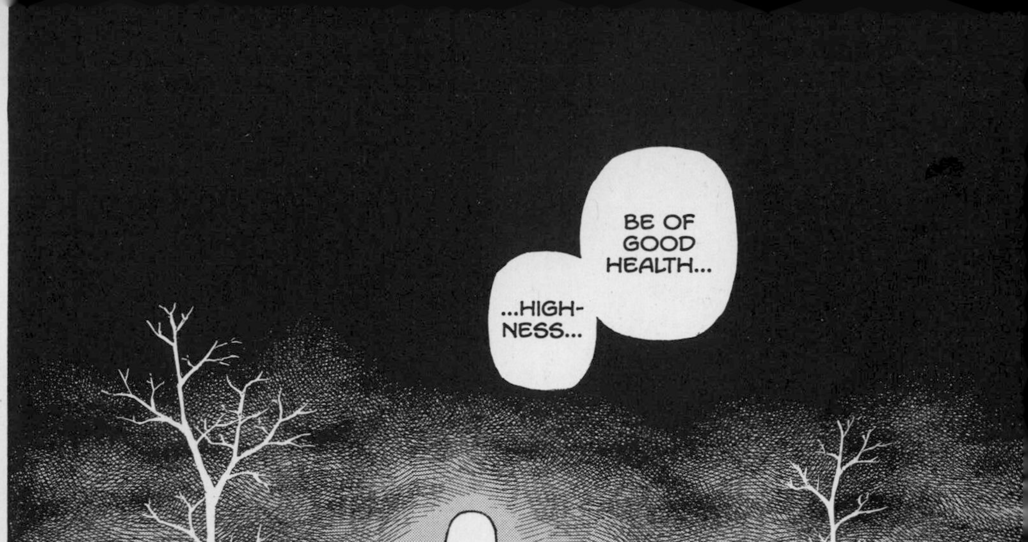
BE OF GOOD HEALTH...
...HIGHNESS...
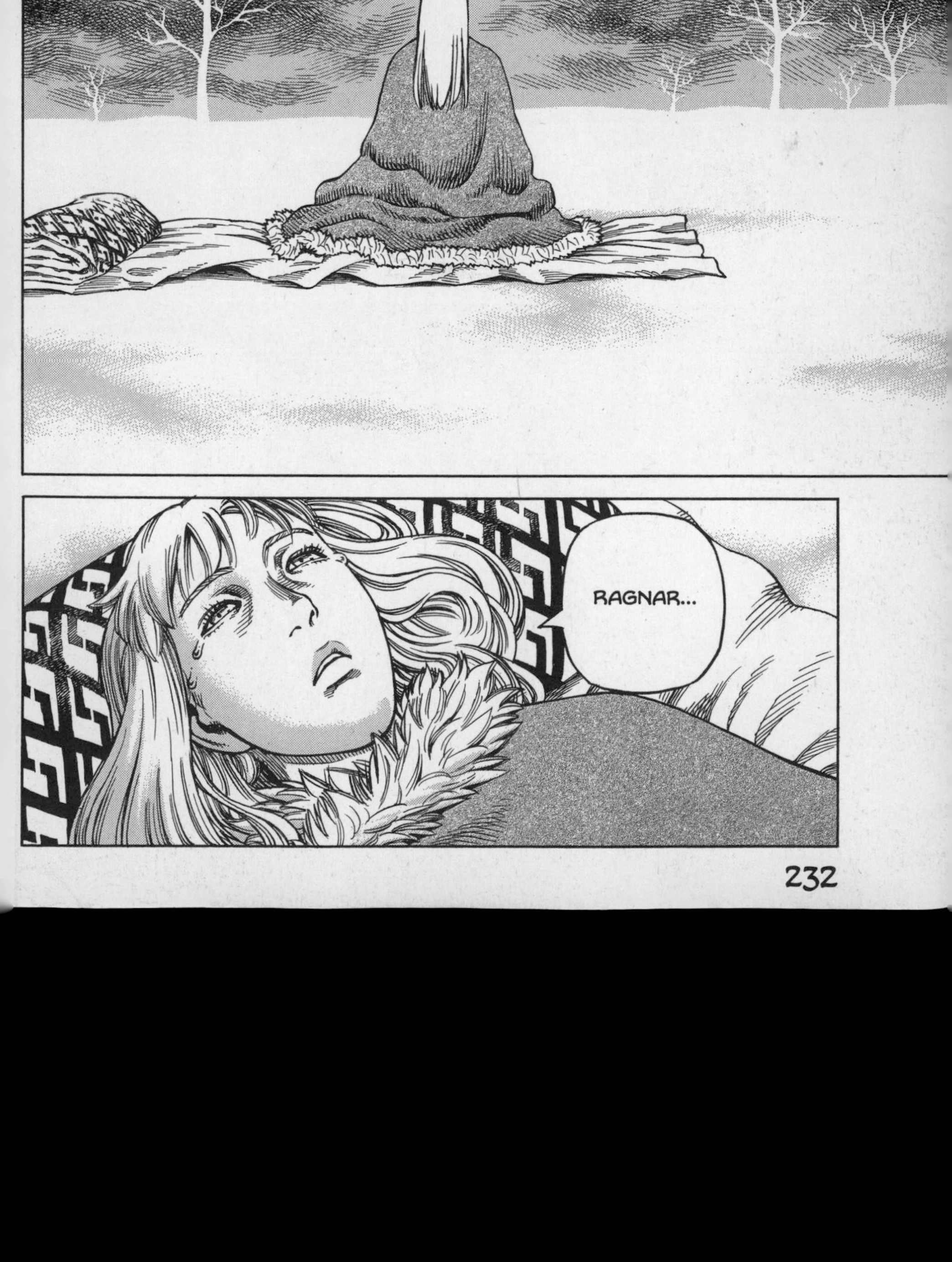
RAGNAR...

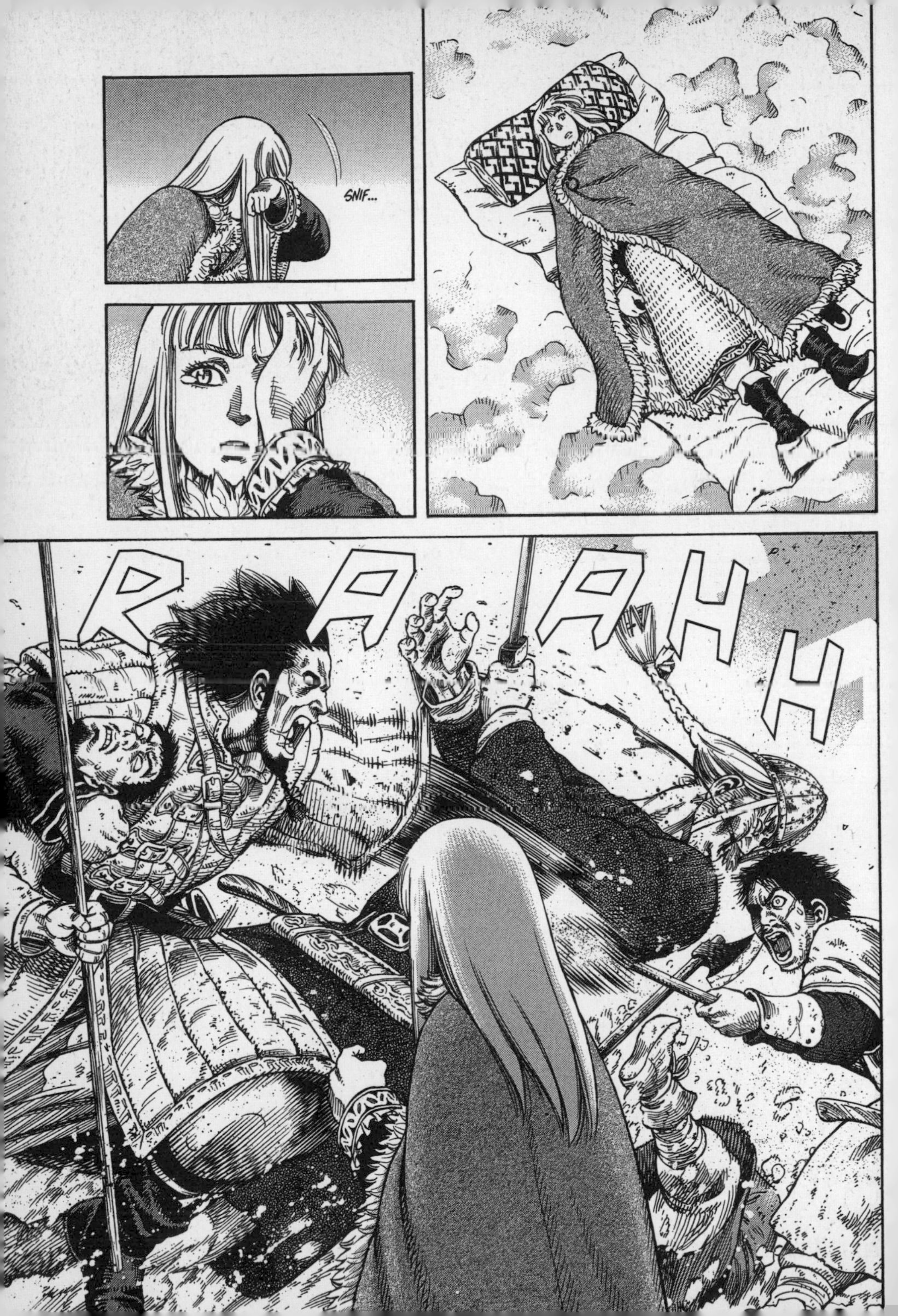
SNIF...
RAAHH

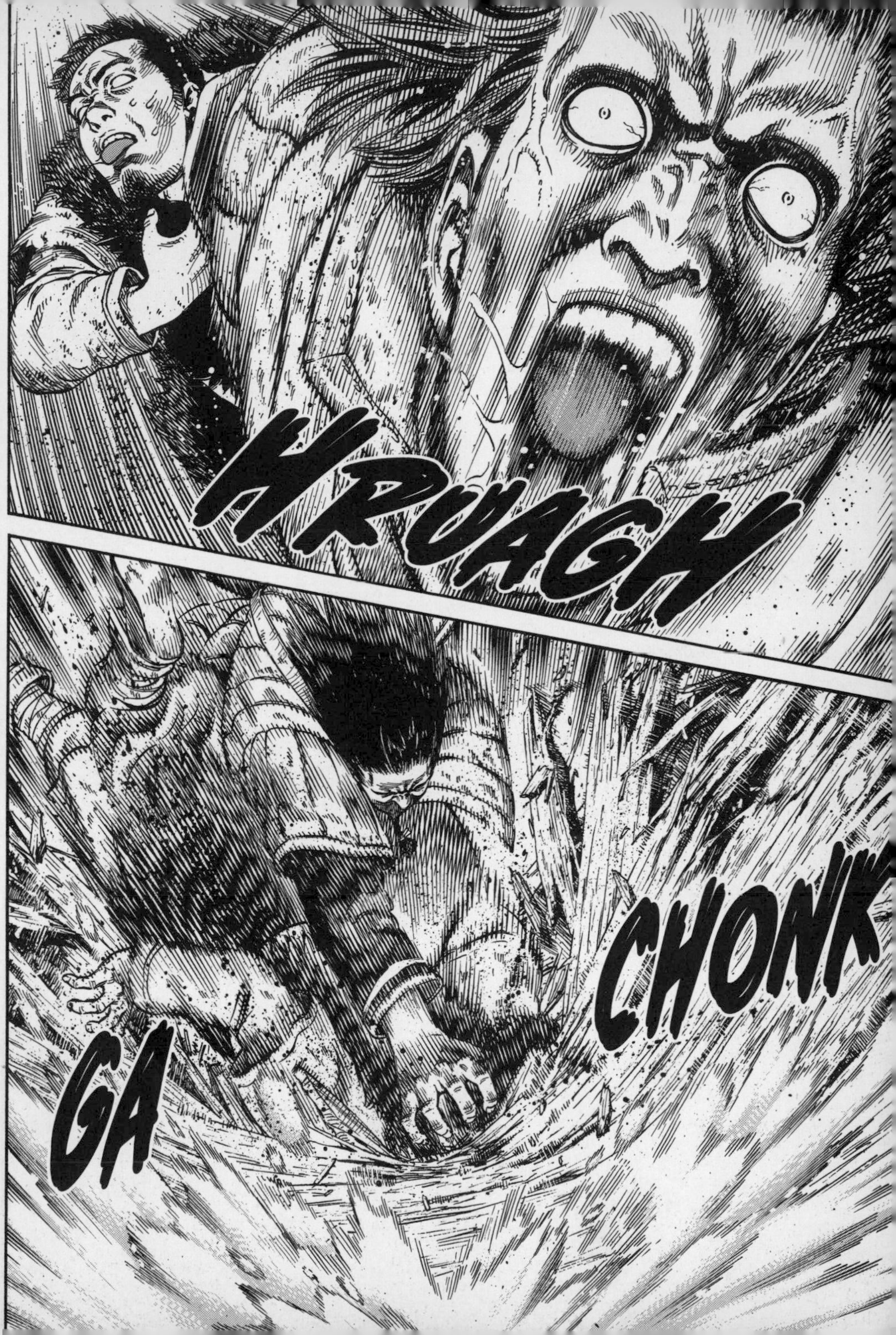
HRUAGH
CHONK
GA

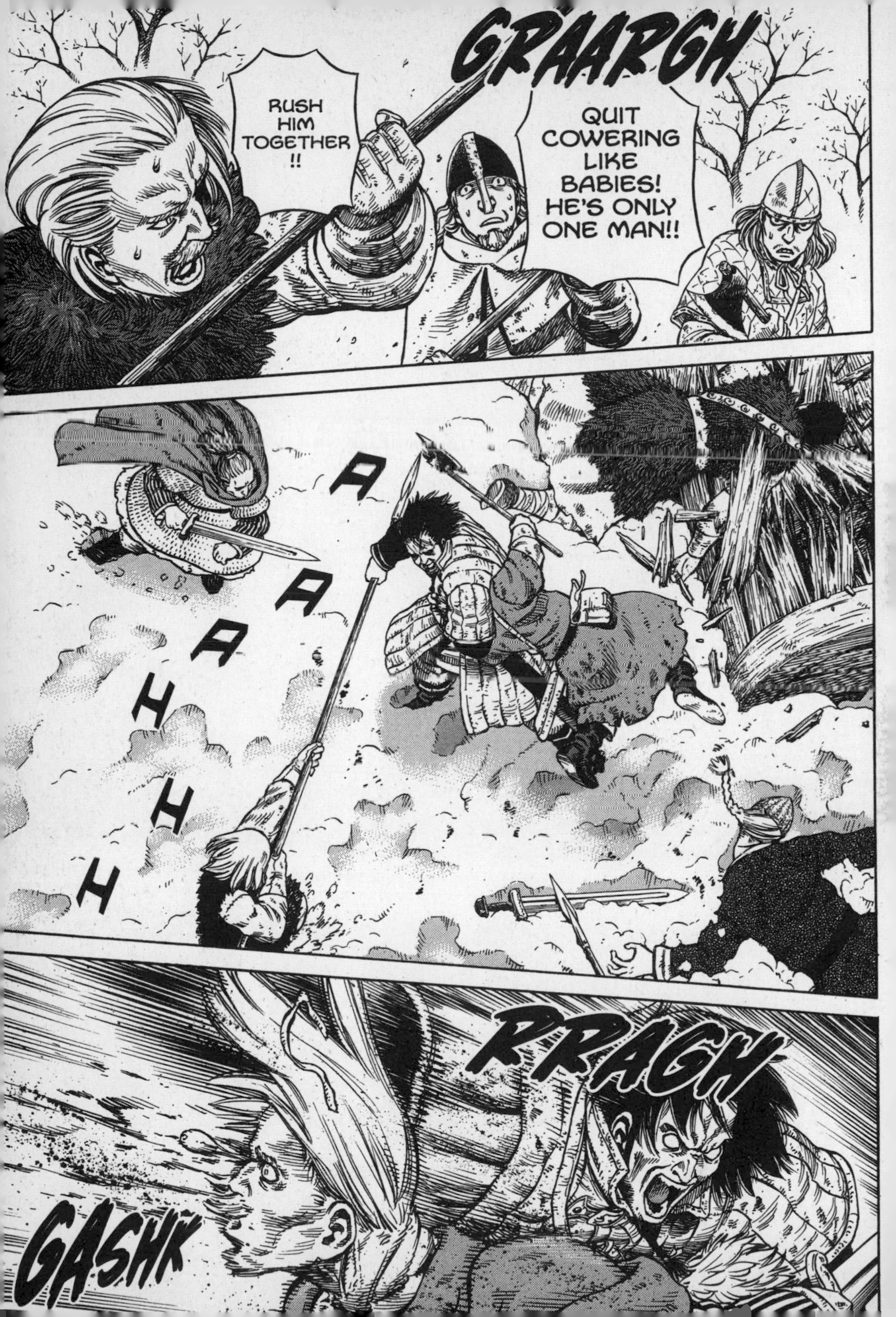
GRAARGH
QUIT COWERING LIKE BABIES! HE'S ONLY ONE MAN!!
RUSH HIM TOGETHER !!
AAAAHHHH
PRAGH
GASHK

SPLT

BSHT

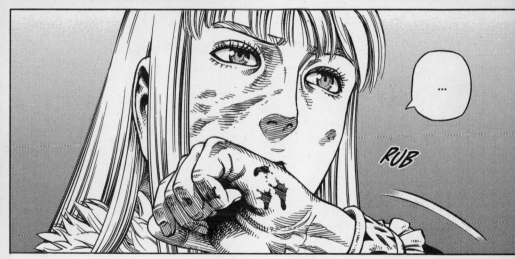

...

RUB

AAA

DO YOU FEEL...

...ANY PAIN?

HH

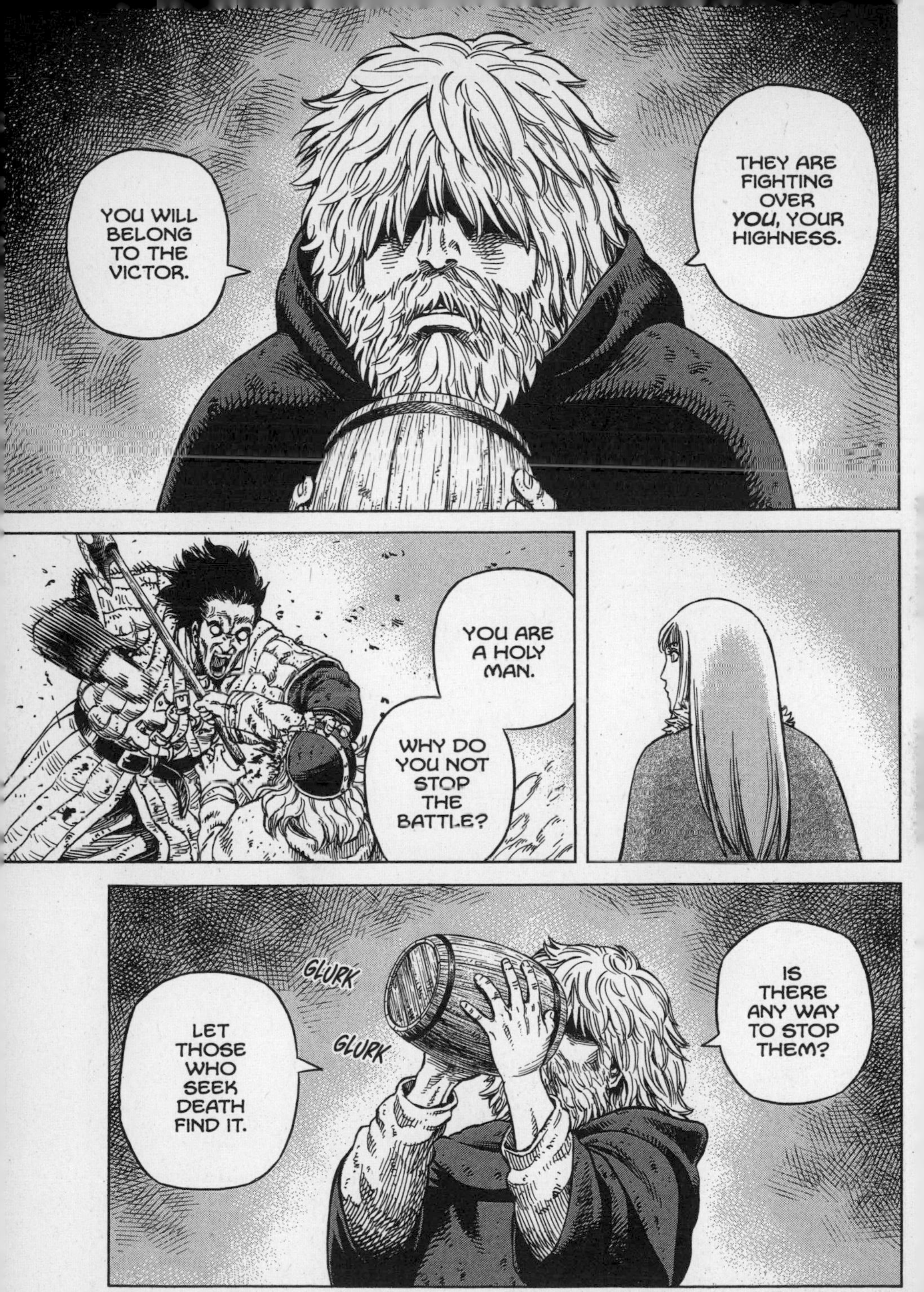
THEY ARE FIGHTING OVER *YOU*, YOUR HIGHNESS.
YOU WILL BELONG TO THE VICTOR.
YOU ARE A HOLY MAN.
WHY DO YOU NOT STOP THE BATTLE?
IS THERE ANY WAY TO STOP THEM?
GLURK
GLURK
LET THOSE WHO SEEK DEATH FIND IT.

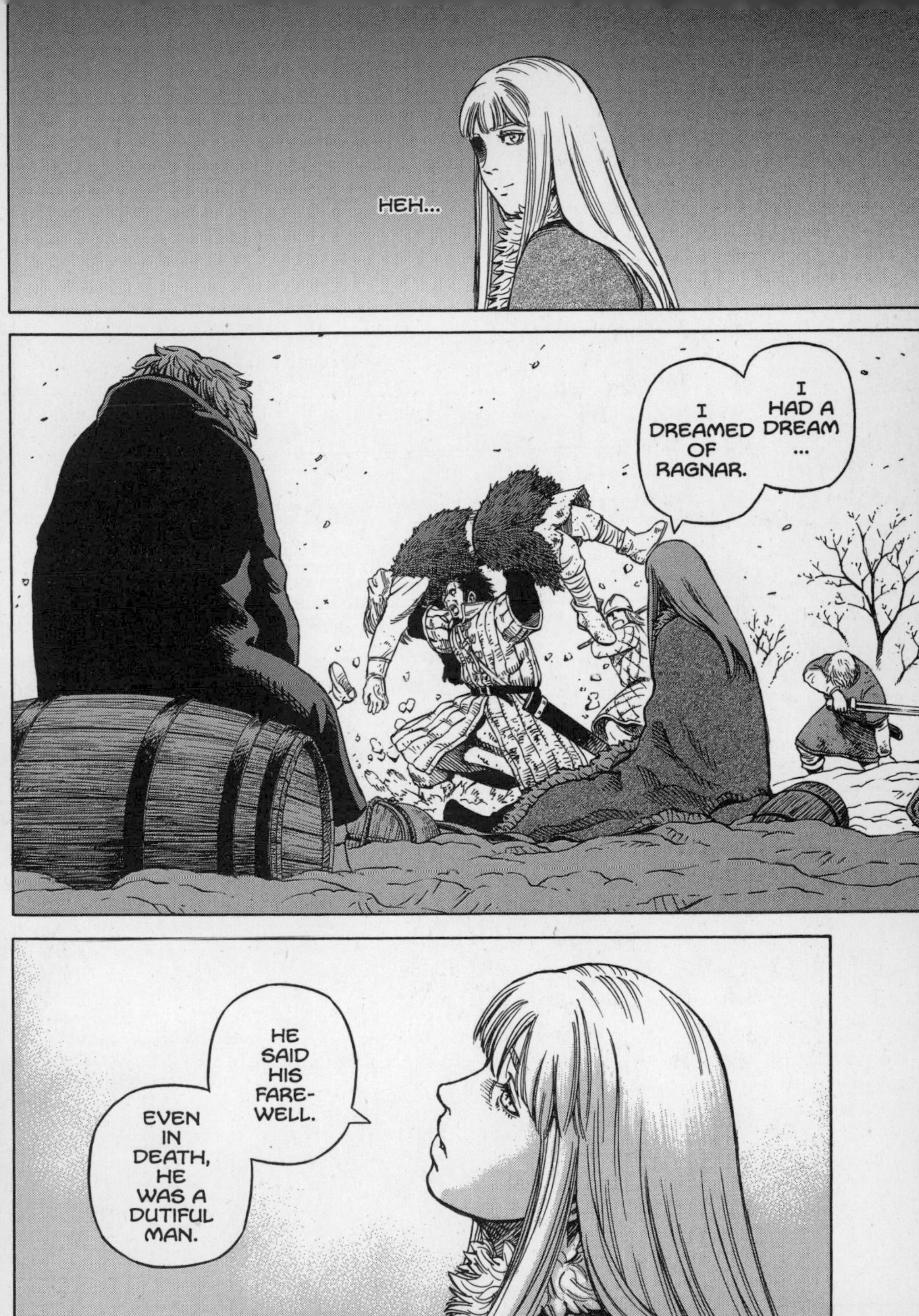
HEH...
I HAD A DREAM ...
I DREAMED OF RAGNAR.
HE SAID HIS FARE-WELL.
EVEN IN DEATH, HE WAS A DUTIFUL MAN.

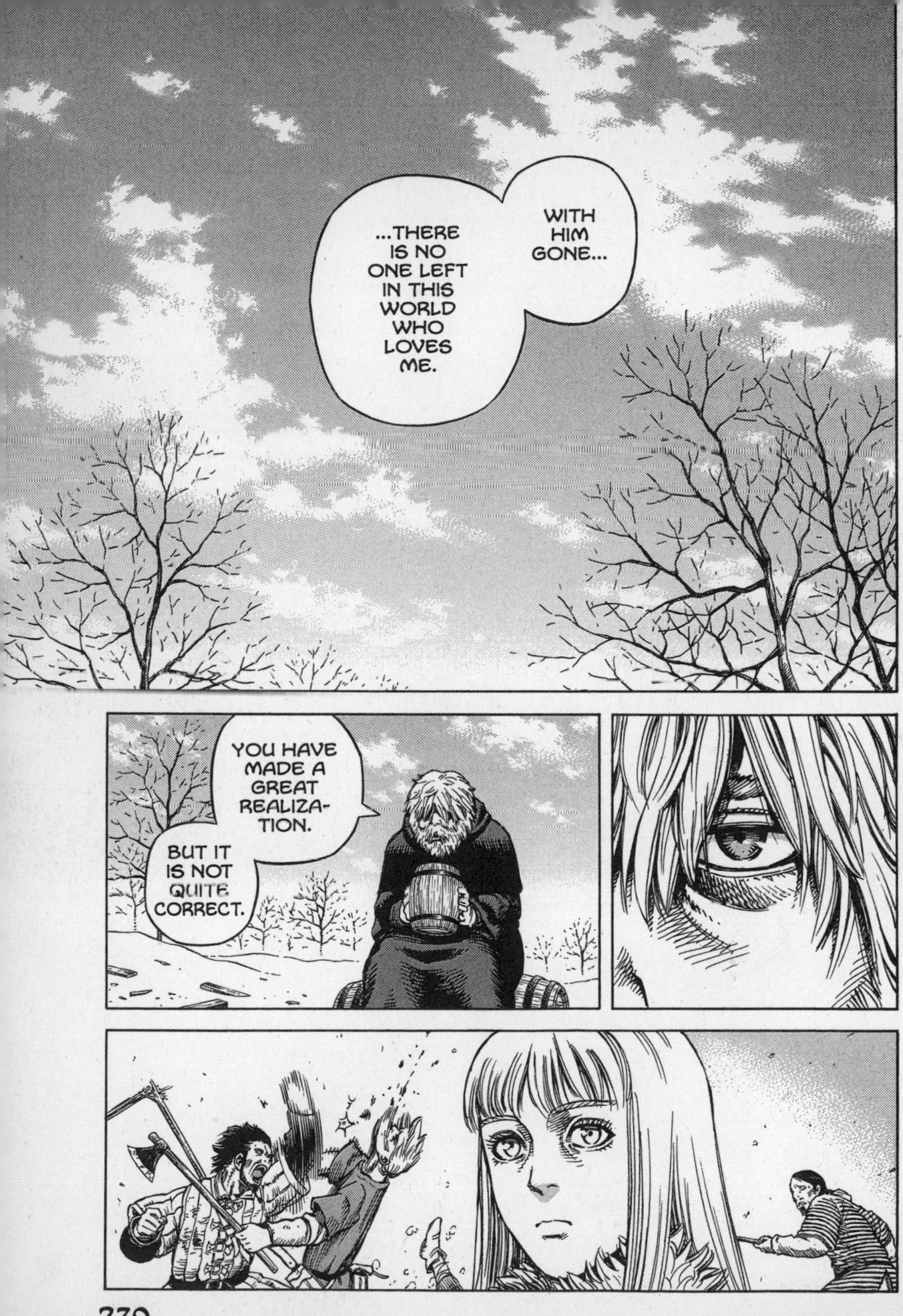
WITH HIM GONE...
...THERE IS NO ONE LEFT IN THIS WORLD WHO LOVES ME.
YOU HAVE MADE A GREAT REALIZA-TION.
BUT IT IS NOT QUITE CORRECT.

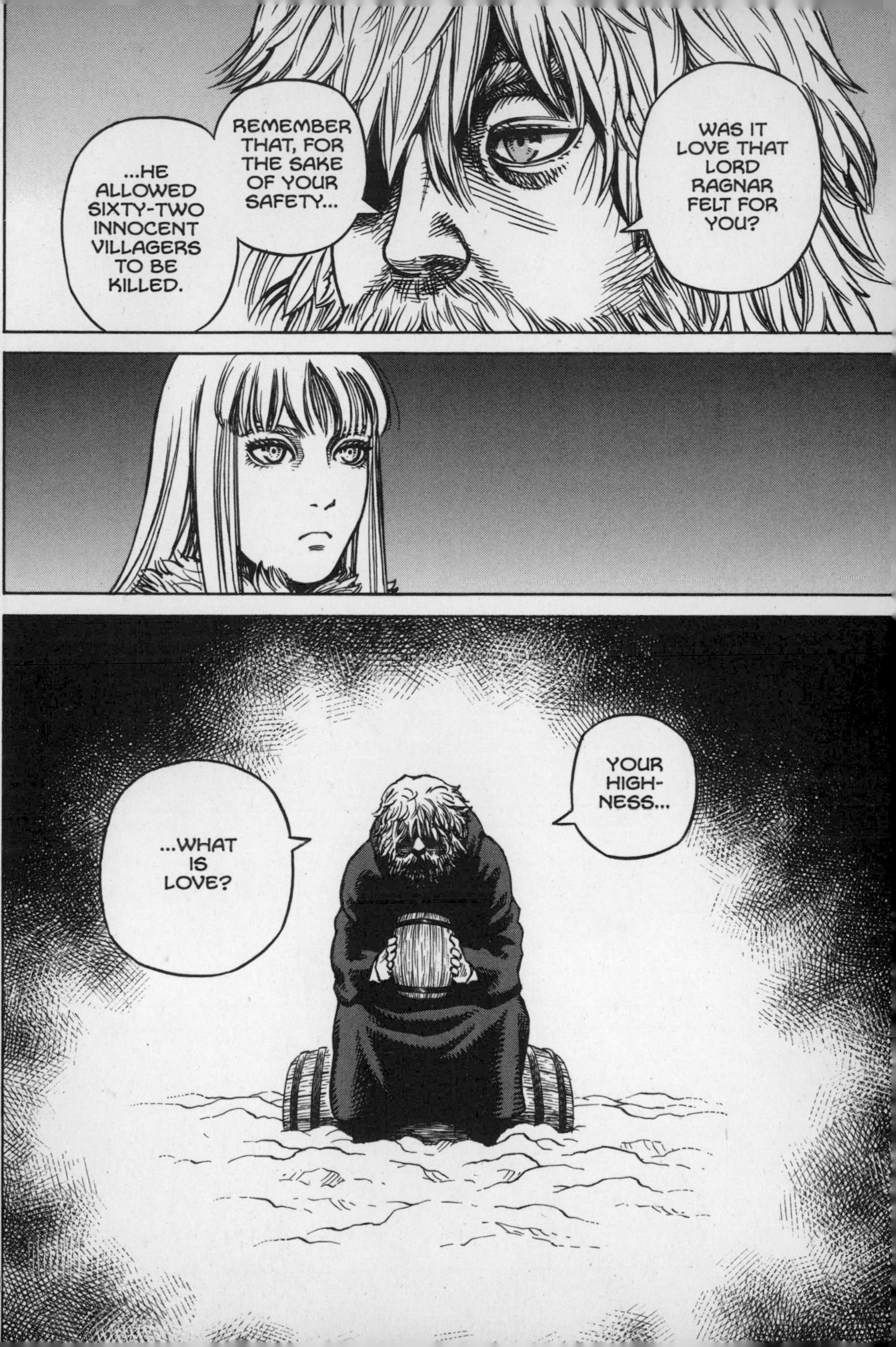
WAS IT LOVE THAT LORD RAGNAR FELT FOR YOU?
REMEMBER THAT, FOR THE SAKE OF YOUR SAFETY...
...HE ALLOWED SIXTY-TWO INNOCENT VILLAGERS TO BE KILLED.
YOUR HIGH-NESS...
...WHAT IS LOVE?

CHAPTER 58 • END

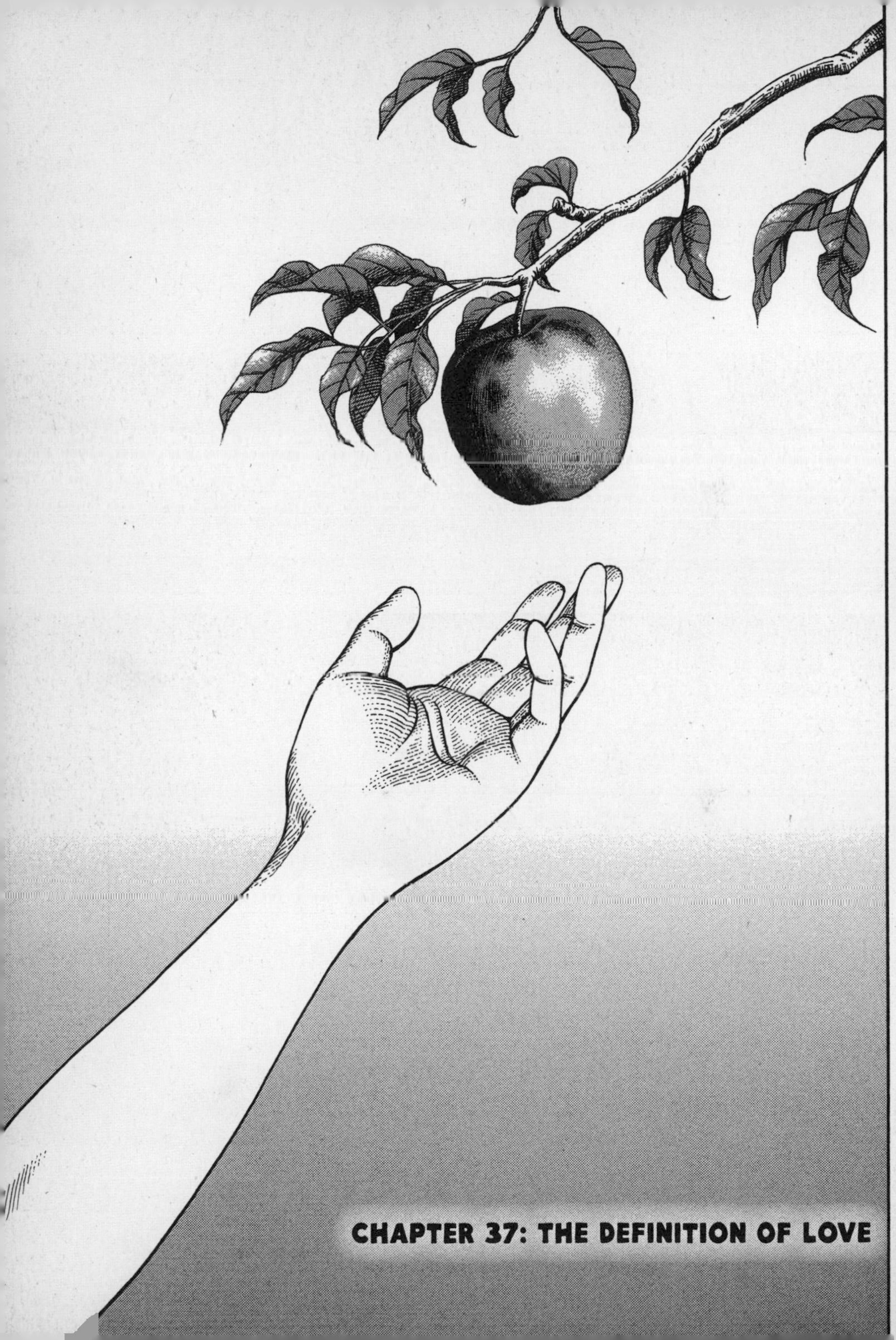

# CHAPTER 37: THE DEFINITION OF LOVE

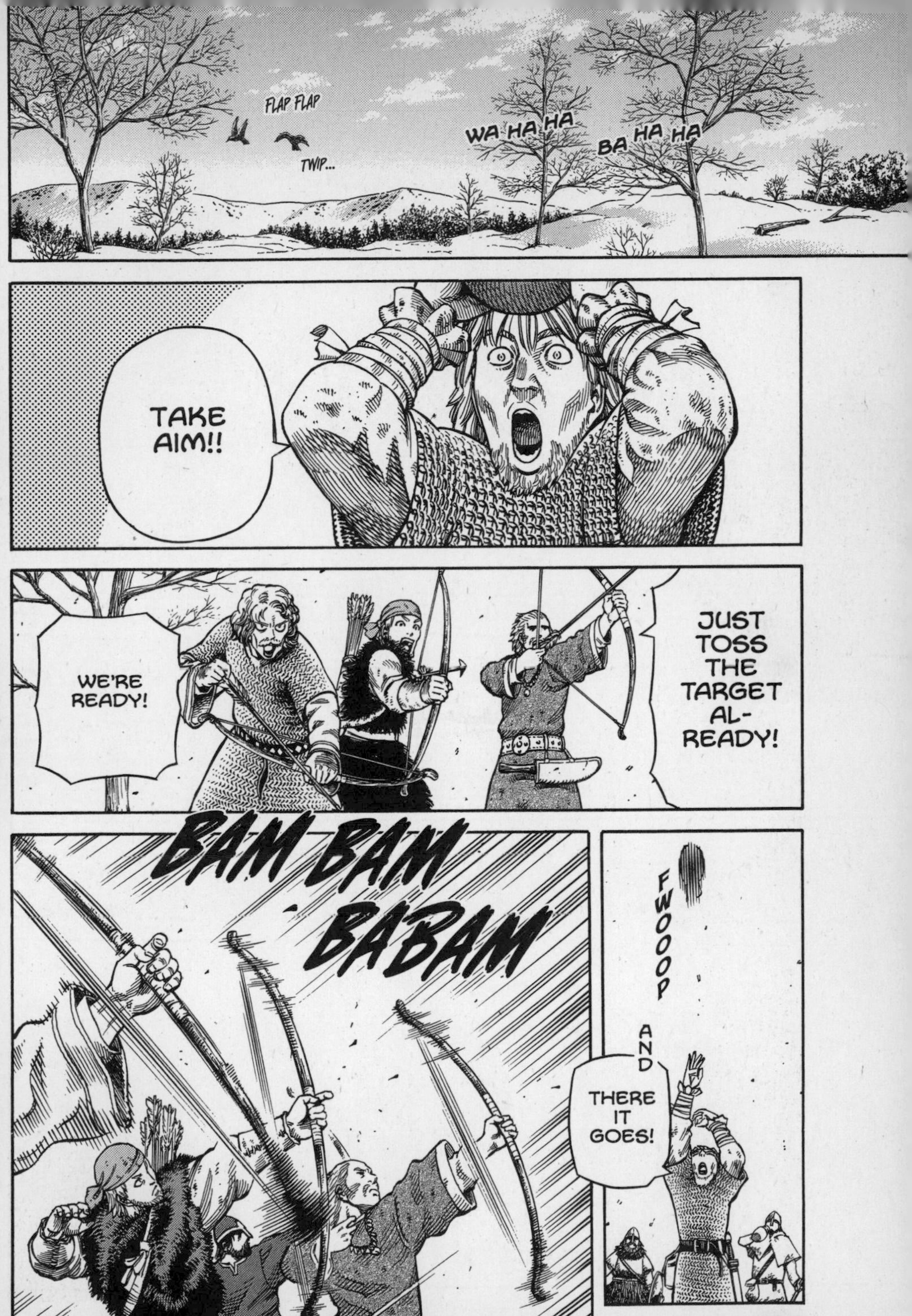
BA HA HA
WA HA HA
FLAP FLAP
TWIP...
TAKE AIM!!
JUST TOSS THE TARGET AL-READY!
WE'RE READY!
FWOOOP
AND THERE IT GOES!
BAM BAM BABAM

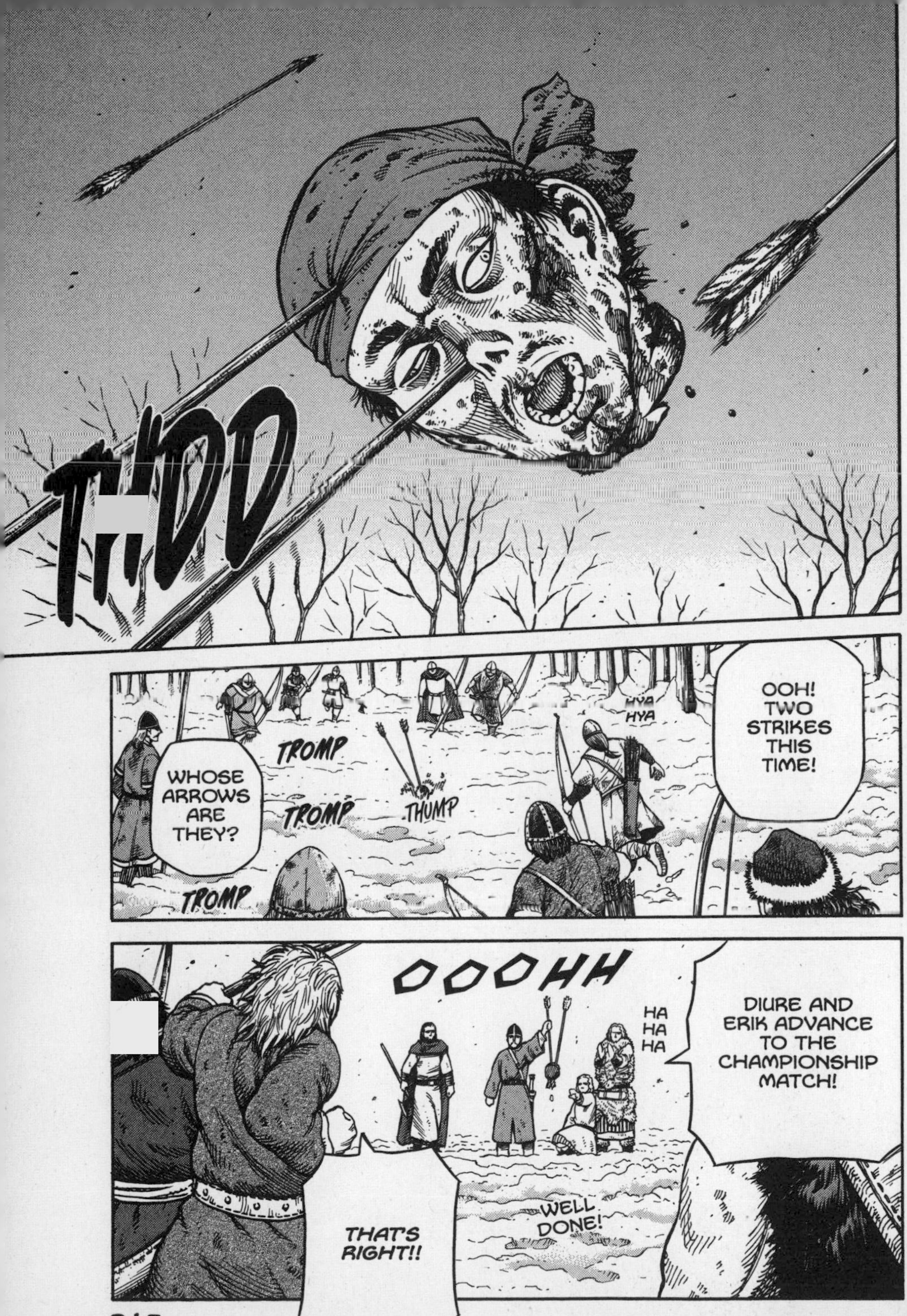
THDD
OOH! TWO STRIKES THIS TIME!
HYA HYA
THUMP
TROMP
TROMP
WHOSE ARROWS ARE THEY?
TROMP
DIURE AND ERIK ADVANCE TO THE CHAMPIONSHIP MATCH!
HA HA HA
OOOHH
WELL DONE!
THAT'S RIGHT!!

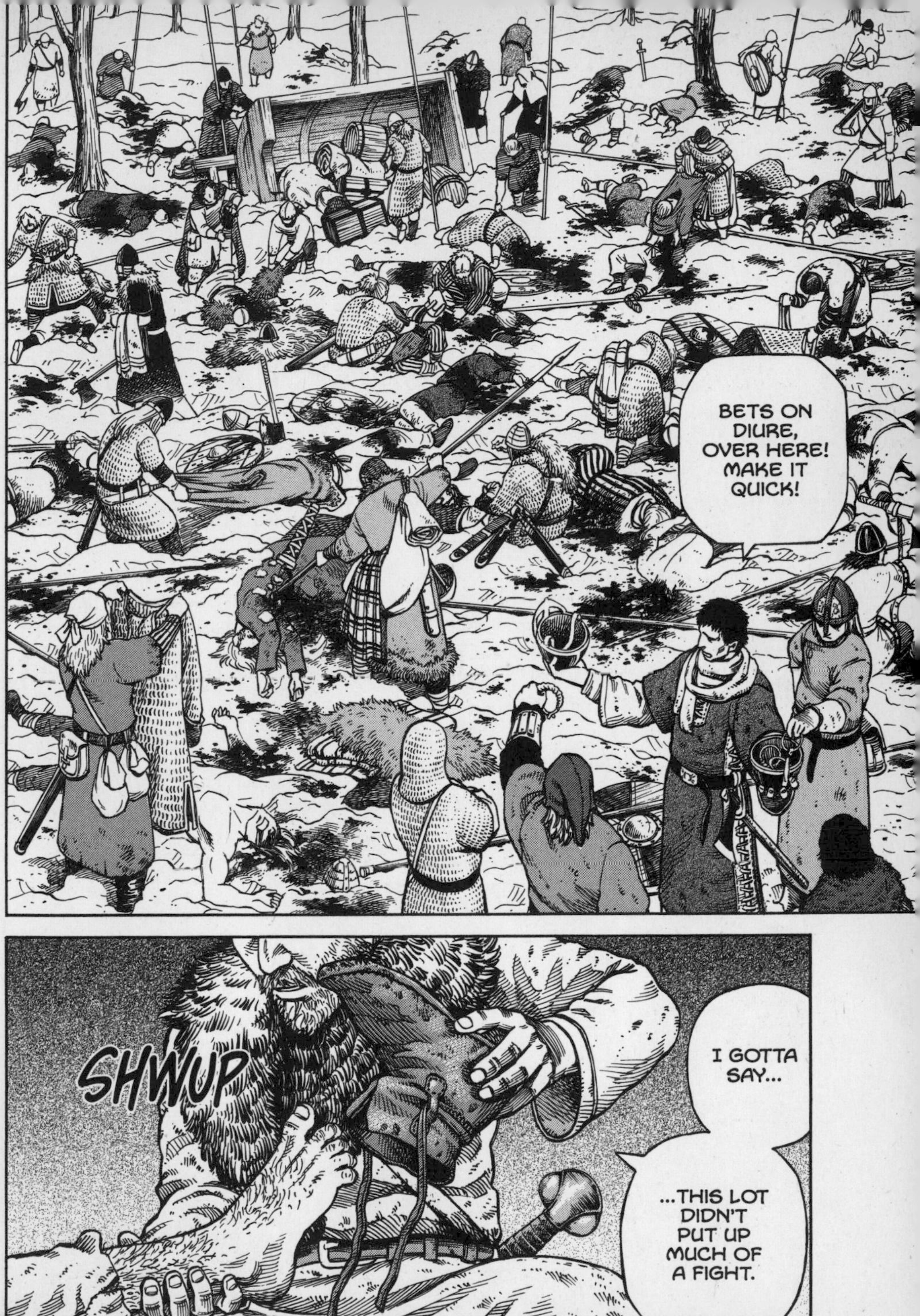
BETS ON DIURE, OVER HERE! MAKE IT QUICK!
SHWUP
I GOTTA SAY...
...THIS LOT DIDN'T PUT UP MUCH OF A FIGHT.

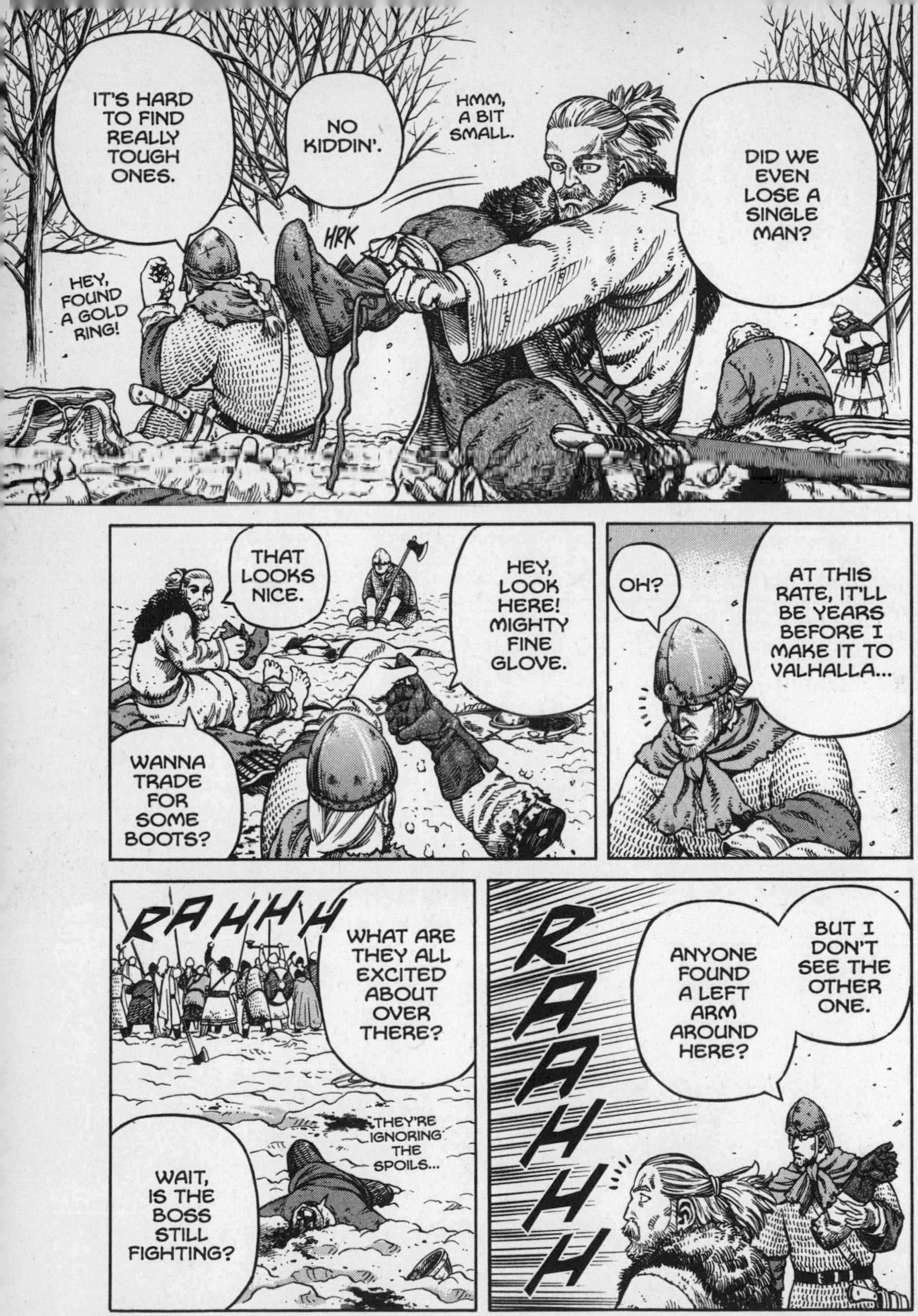
DID WE EVEN LOSE A SINGLE MAN?
HMM, A BIT SMALL.
NO KIDDIN'.
IT'S HARD TO FIND REALLY TOUGH ONES.
HRK
HEY, FOUND A GOLD RING!
AT THIS RATE, IT'LL BE YEARS BEFORE I MAKE IT TO VALHALLA...
OH?
HEY, LOOK HERE! MIGHTY FINE GLOVE.
THAT LOOKS NICE.
WANNA TRADE FOR SOME BOOTS?
BUT I DON'T SEE THE OTHER ONE.
ANYONE FOUND A LEFT ARM AROUND HERE?
RAAAHHHH
WHAT ARE THEY ALL EXCITED ABOUT OVER THERE?
RAHHHH
THEY'RE IGNORING THE SPOILS...
WAIT, IS THE BOSS STILL FIGHTING?

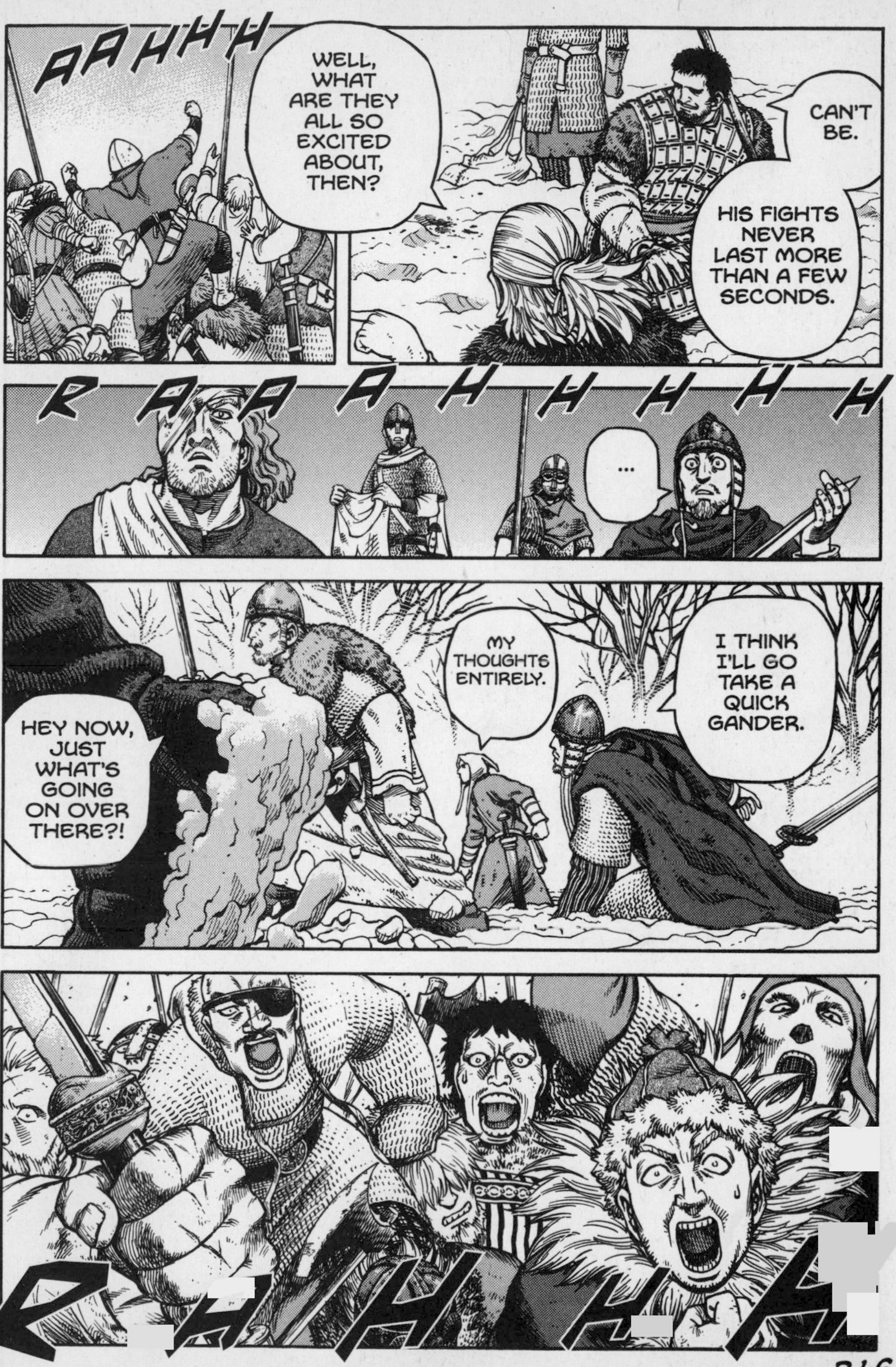
CAN'T BE.
HIS FIGHTS NEVER LAST MORE THAN A FEW SECONDS.
WELL, WHAT ARE THEY ALL SO EXCITED ABOUT, THEN?
AAHHHH
RAAAHHHHH
...
I THINK I'LL GO TAKE A QUICK GANDER.
MY THOUGHTS ENTIRELY.
HEY NOW, JUST WHAT'S GOING ON OVER THERE?!

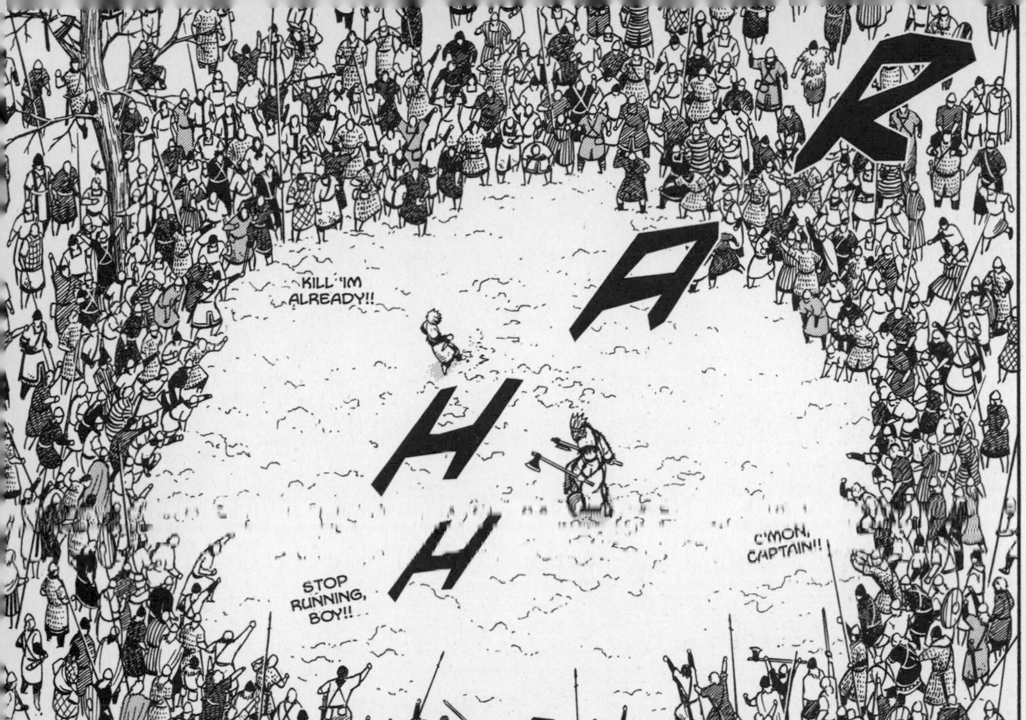
RAAHHHHH
KILL 'IM ALREADY!!
C'MON, CAPTAIN!!
STOP RUNNING, BOY!!
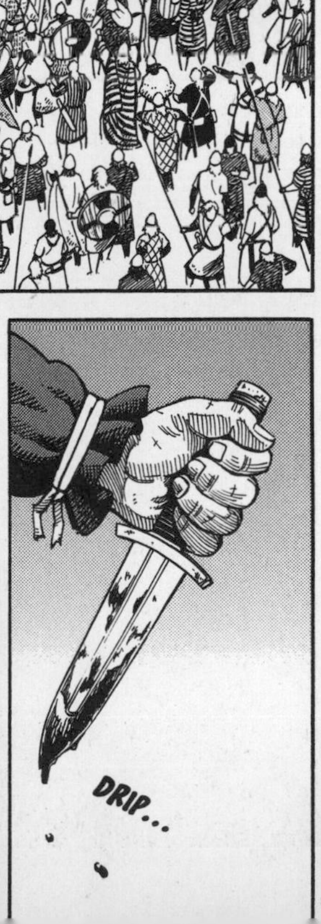
DRIP...
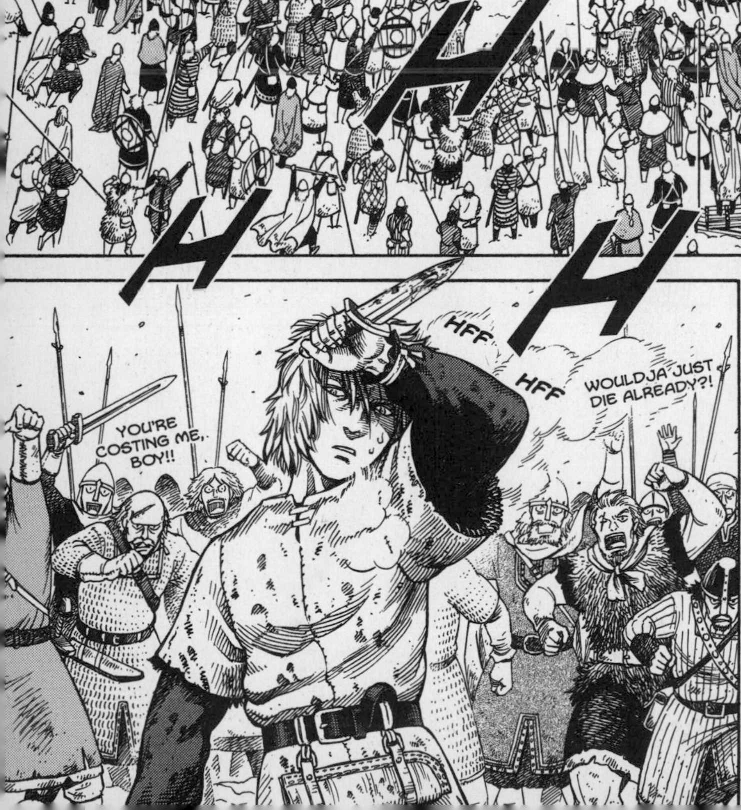
HFF
HFF
WOULDJA JUST DIE ALREADY?!
YOU'RE COSTING ME, BOY!!

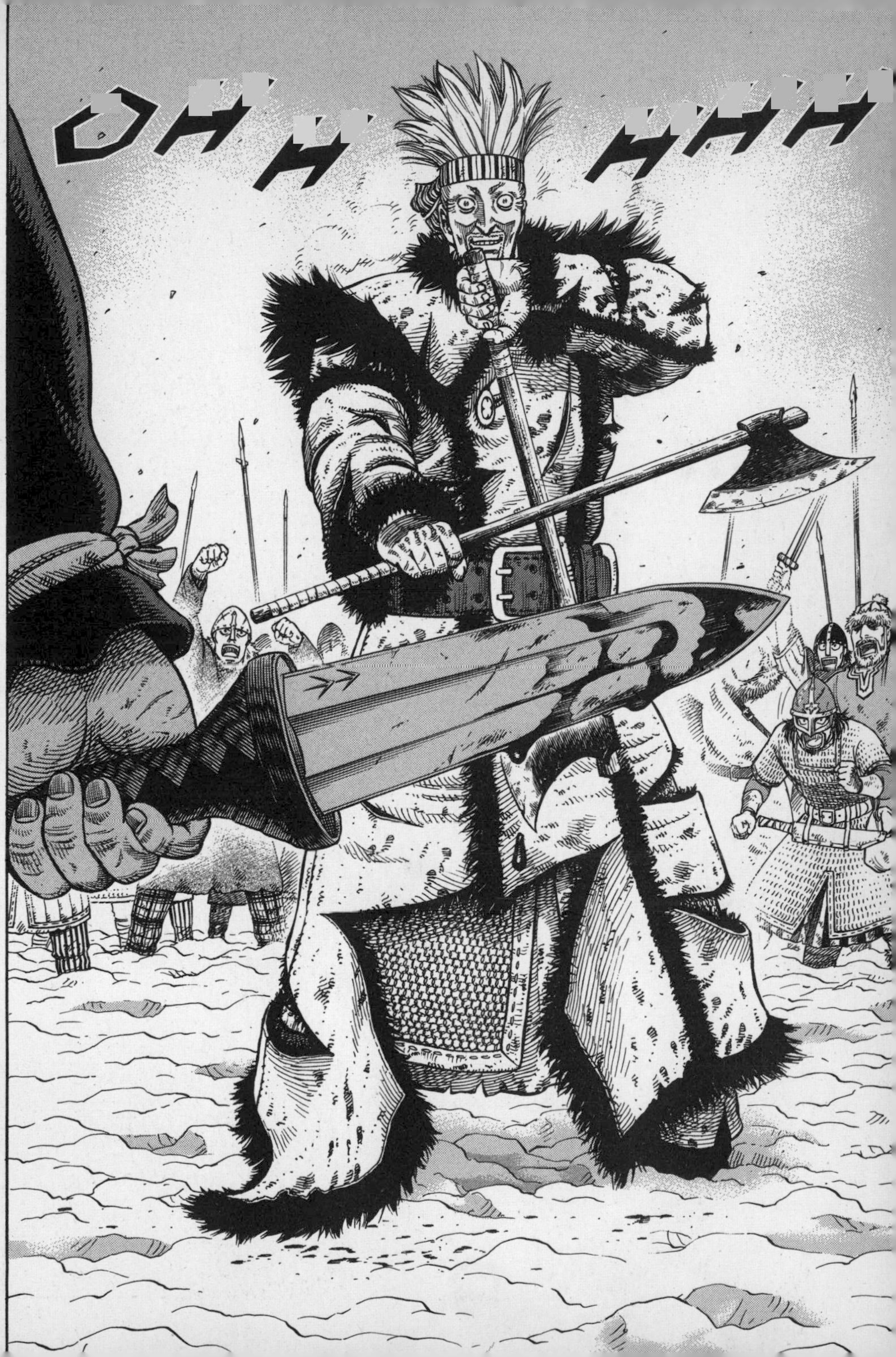
OHH HHHH

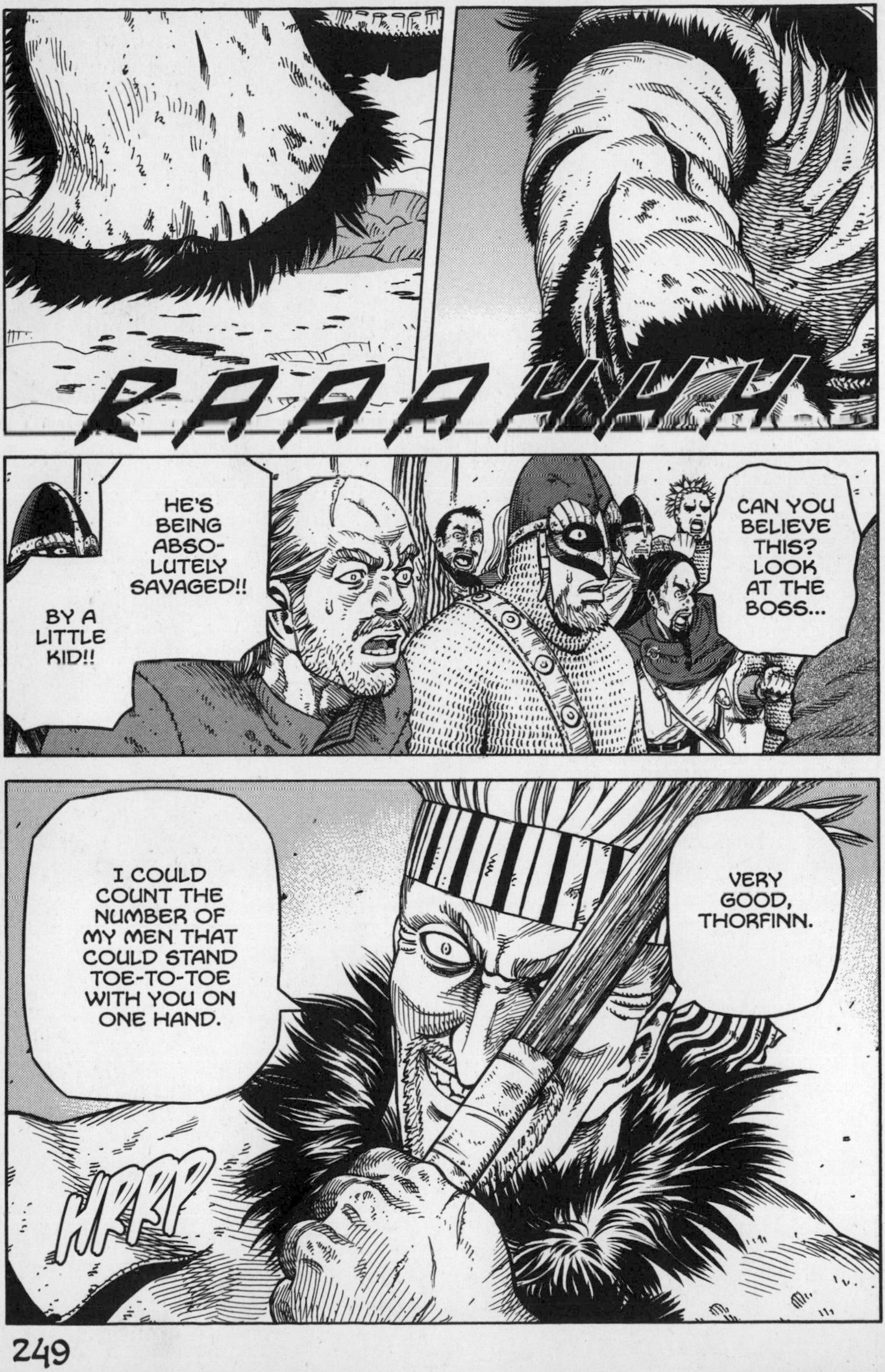
RAAAAHHHH
CAN YOU BELIEVE THIS? LOOK AT THE BOSS...
HE'S BEING ABSO-LUTELY SAVAGED!!
BY A LITTLE KID!!
VERY GOOD, THORFINN.
I COULD COUNT THE NUMBER OF MY MEN THAT COULD STAND TOE-TO-TOE WITH YOU ON ONE HAND.
WHRRP

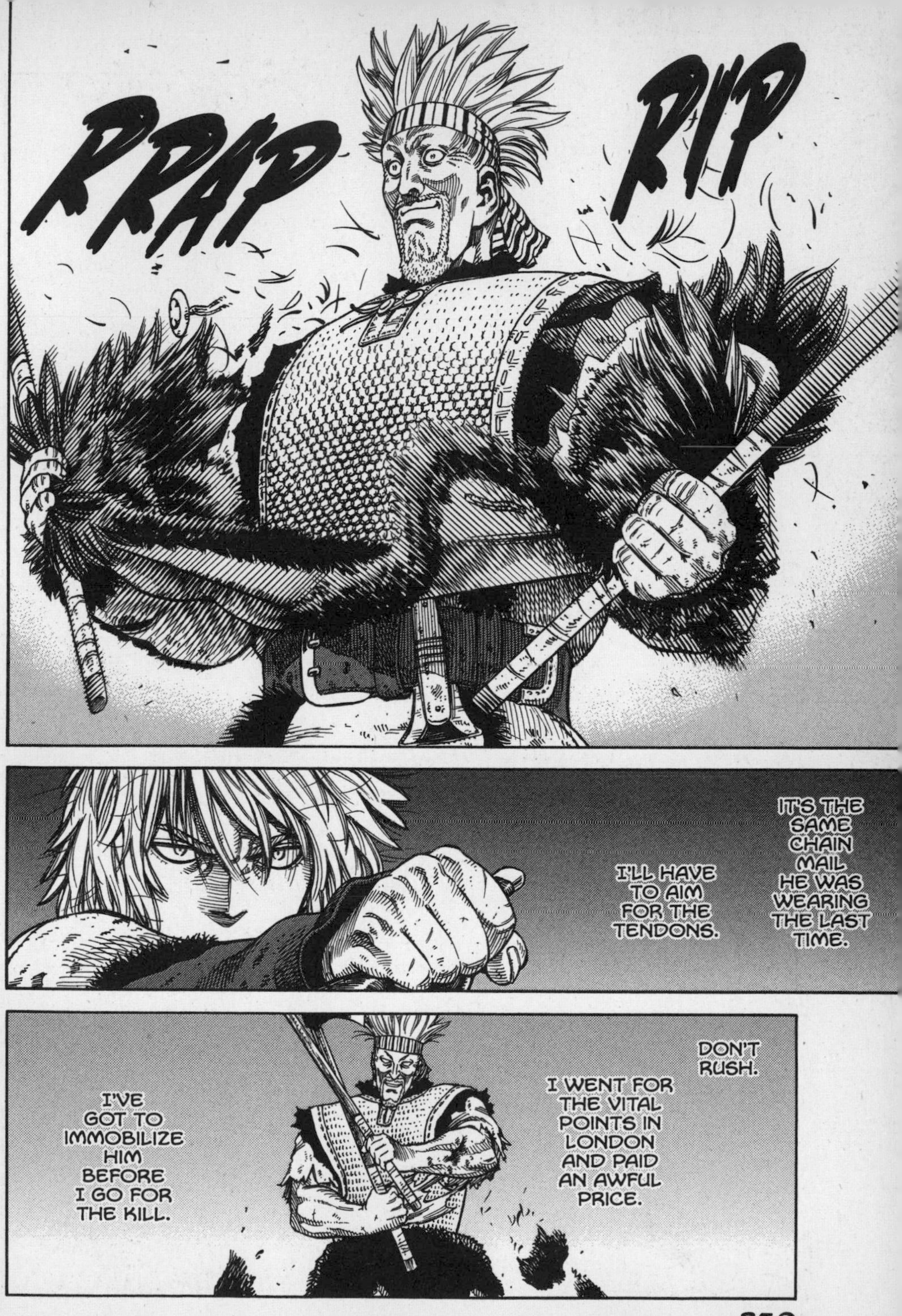
RIP
RRAP
IT'S THE SAME CHAIN MAIL HE WAS WEARING THE LAST TIME.
I'LL HAVE TO AIM FOR THE TENDONS.
DON'T RUSH.
I WENT FOR THE VITAL POINTS IN LONDON AND PAID AN AWFUL PRICE.
I'VE GOT TO IMMOBILIZE HIM BEFORE I GO FOR THE KILL.

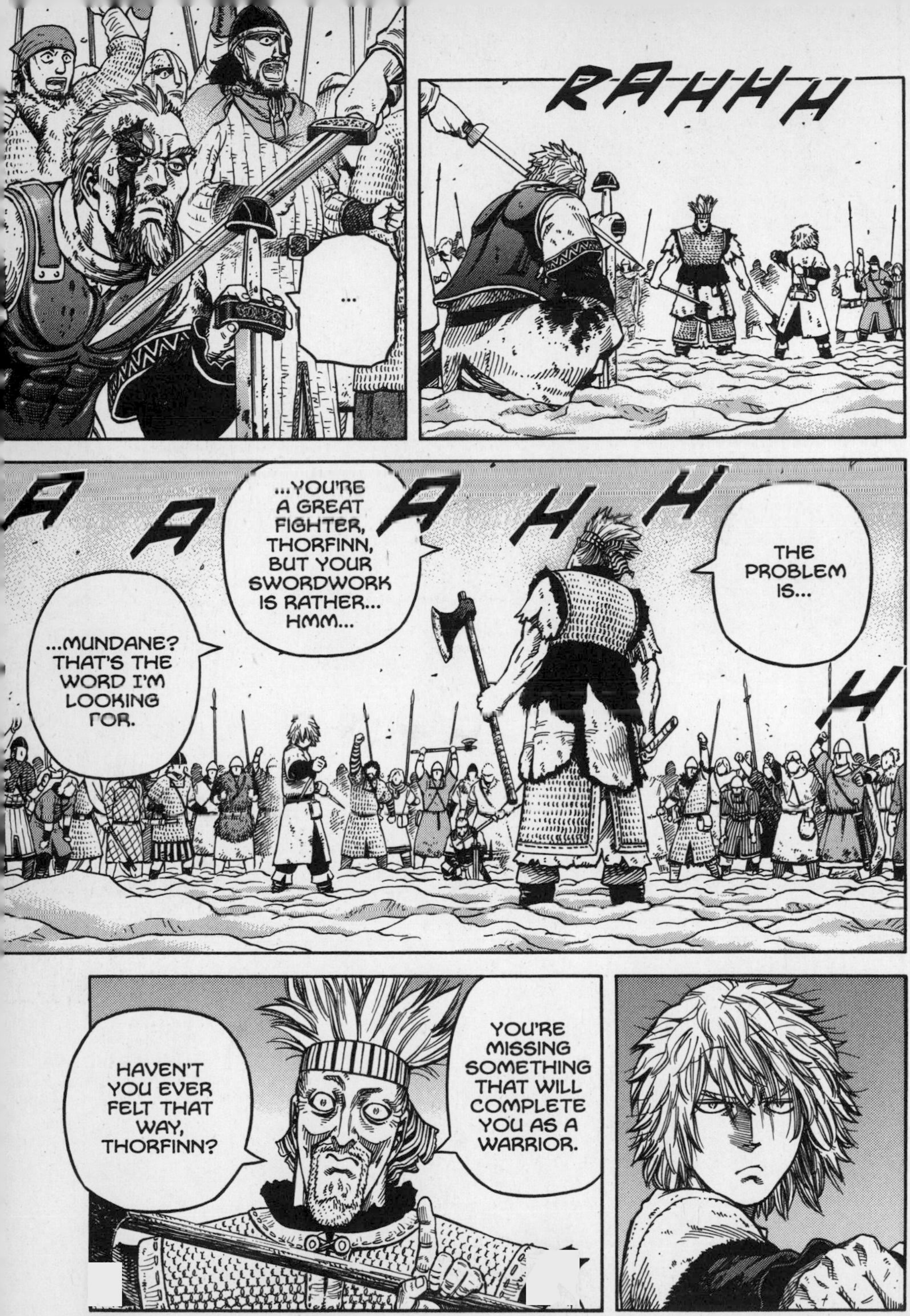
...
RAHHHH
AAAHHH
...YOU'RE A GREAT FIGHTER, THORFINN, BUT YOUR SWORDWORK IS RATHER... HMM...
...MUNDANE? THAT'S THE WORD I'M LOOKING FOR.
THE PROBLEM IS...
YOU'RE MISSING SOMETHING THAT WILL COMPLETE YOU AS A WARRIOR.
HAVEN'T YOU EVER FELT THAT WAY, THORFINN?

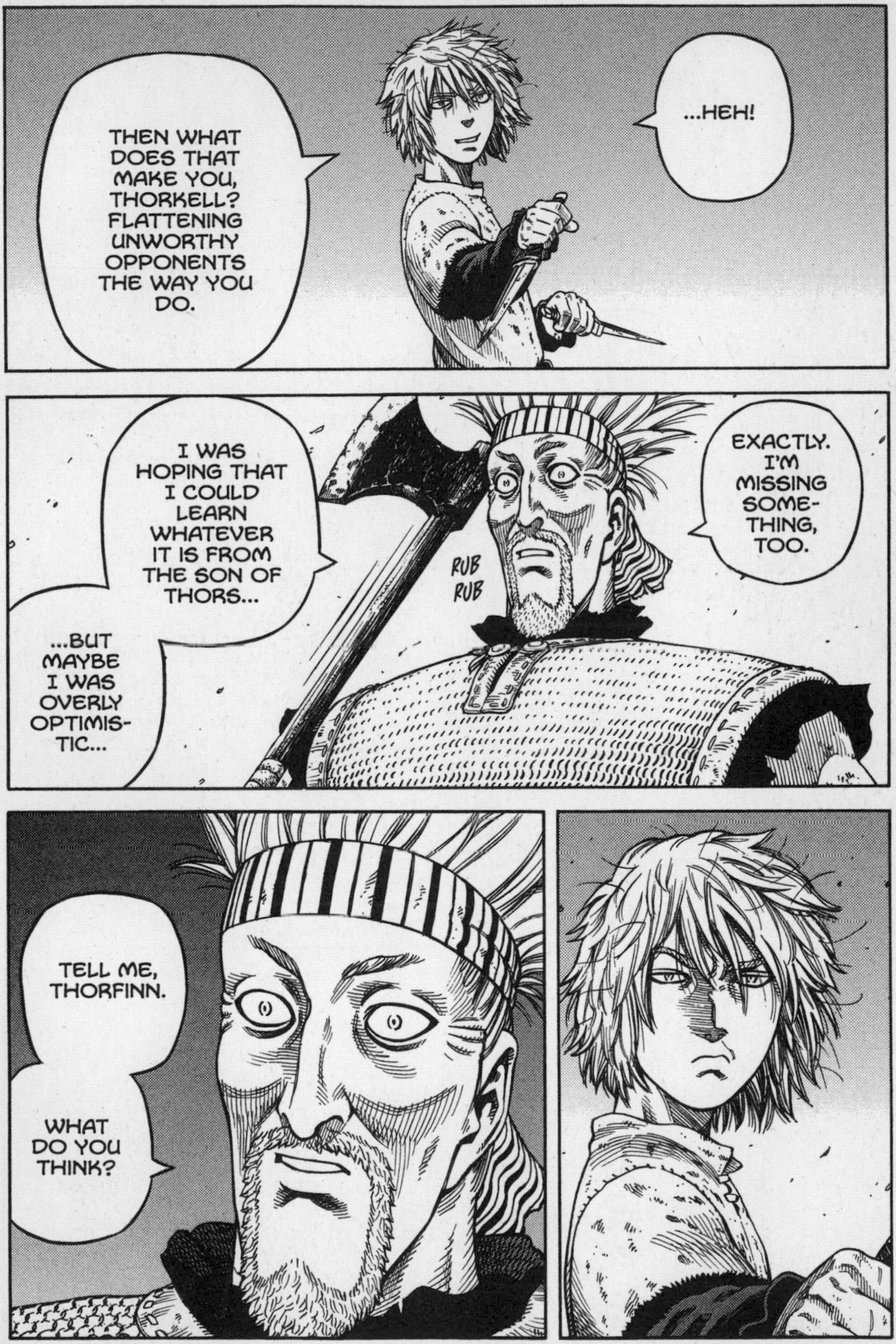
...HEH!
THEN WHAT DOES THAT MAKE YOU, THORKELL? FLATTENING UNWORTHY OPPONENTS THE WAY YOU DO.
EXACTLY. I'M MISSING SOME-THING, TOO.
RUB RUB
I WAS HOPING THAT I COULD LEARN WHATEVER IT IS FROM THE SON OF THORS...
...BUT MAYBE I WAS OVERLY OPTIMIS-TIC...
TELL ME, THORFINN.
WHAT DO YOU THINK?

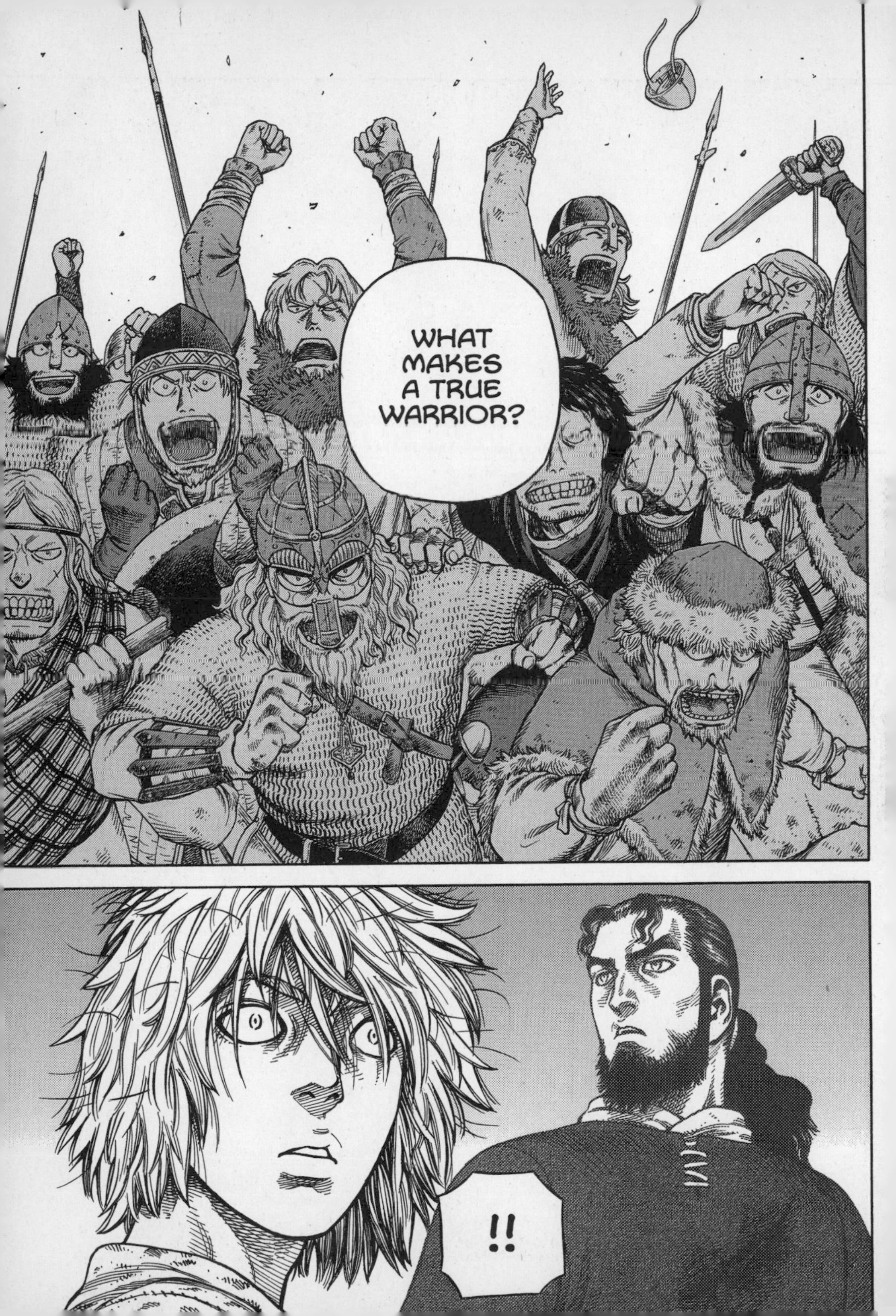
WHAT MAKES A TRUE WARRIOR?
!!

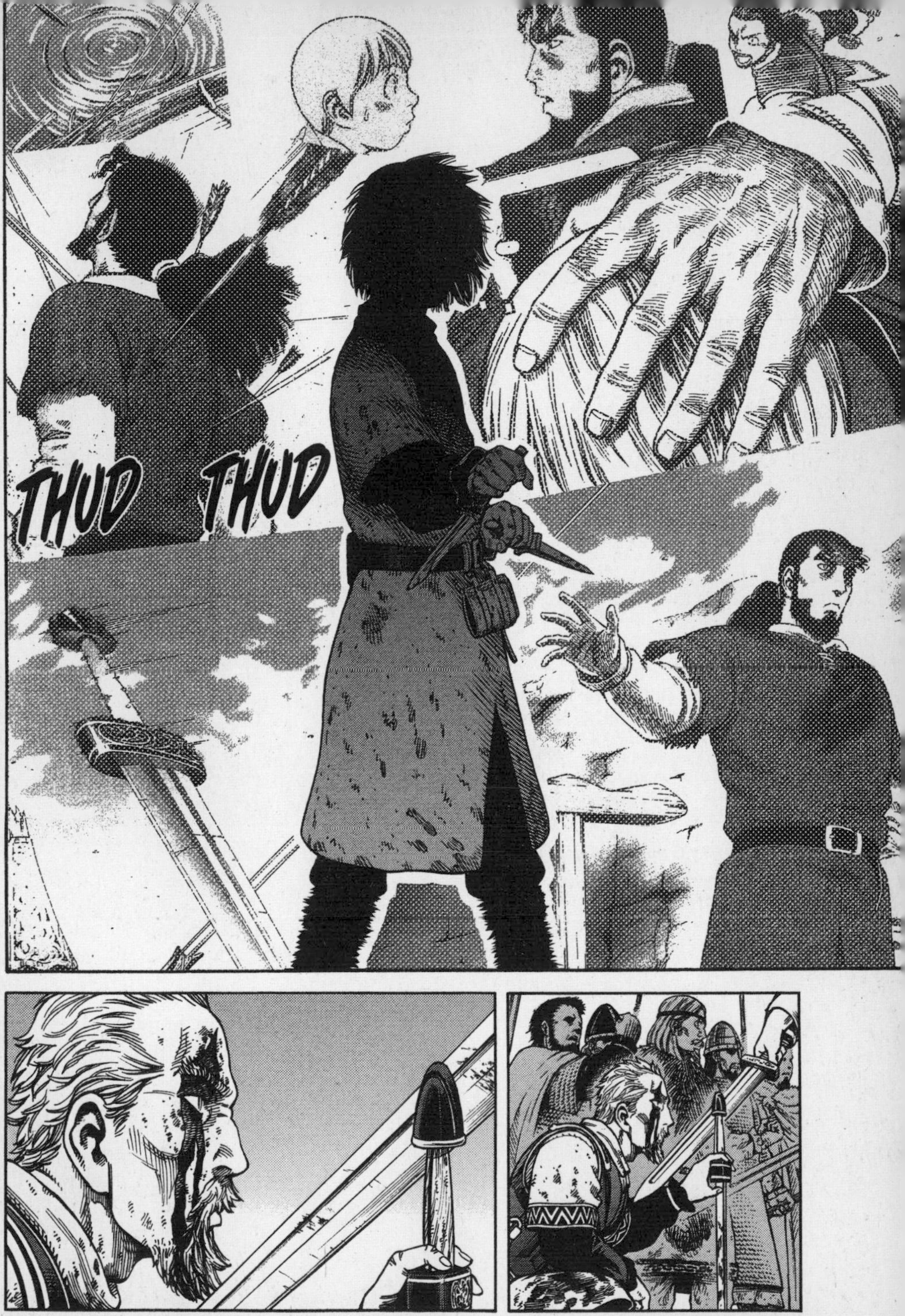
THUD
THUD

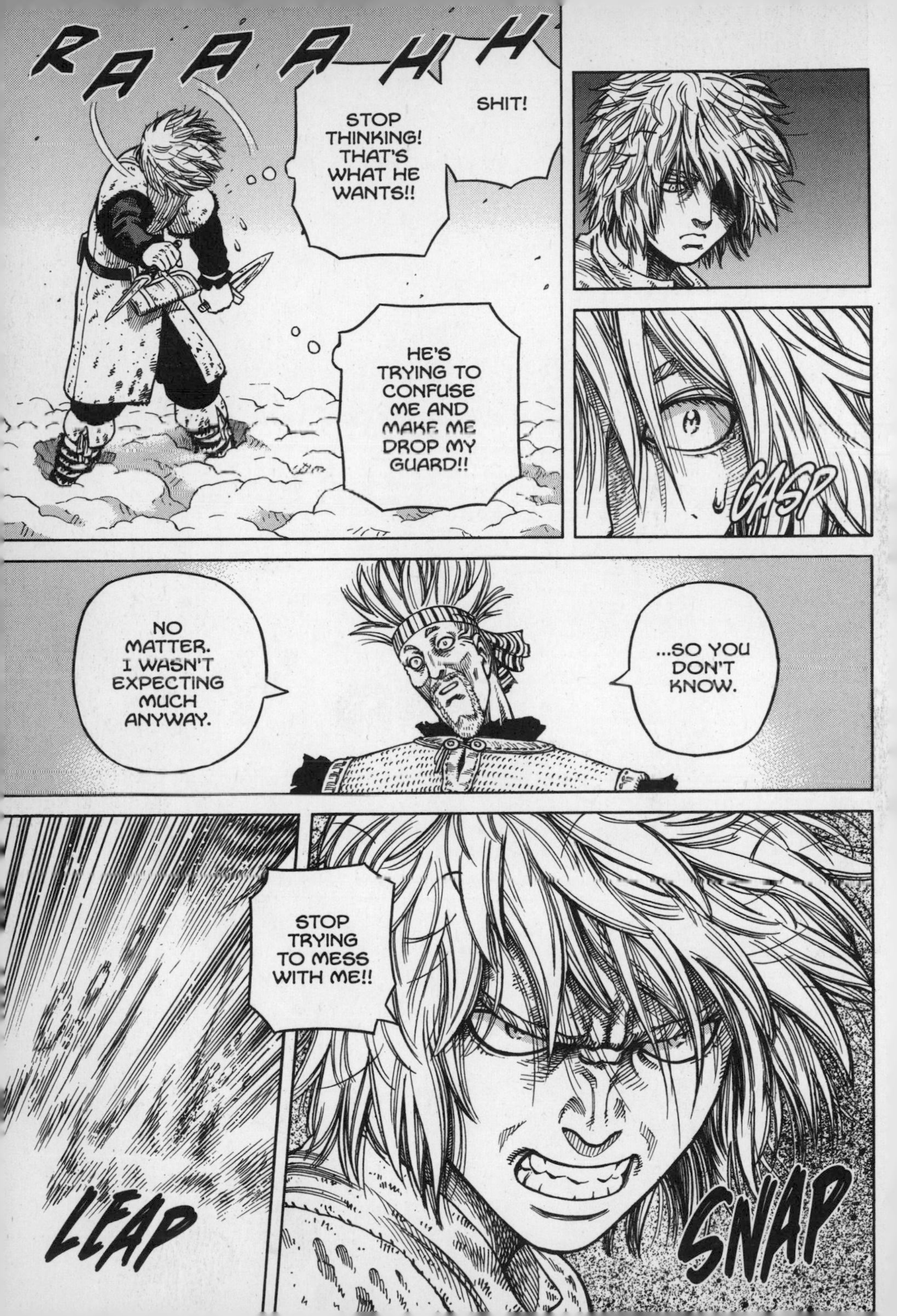
GASP
RAAAAHH
SHIT!
STOP THINKING! THAT'S WHAT HE WANTS!!
HE'S TRYING TO CONFUSE ME AND MAKE ME DROP MY GUARD!!
...SO YOU DON'T KNOW.
NO MATTER. I WASN'T EXPECTING MUCH ANYWAY.
STOP TRYING TO MESS WITH ME!!
SNAP
LEAP

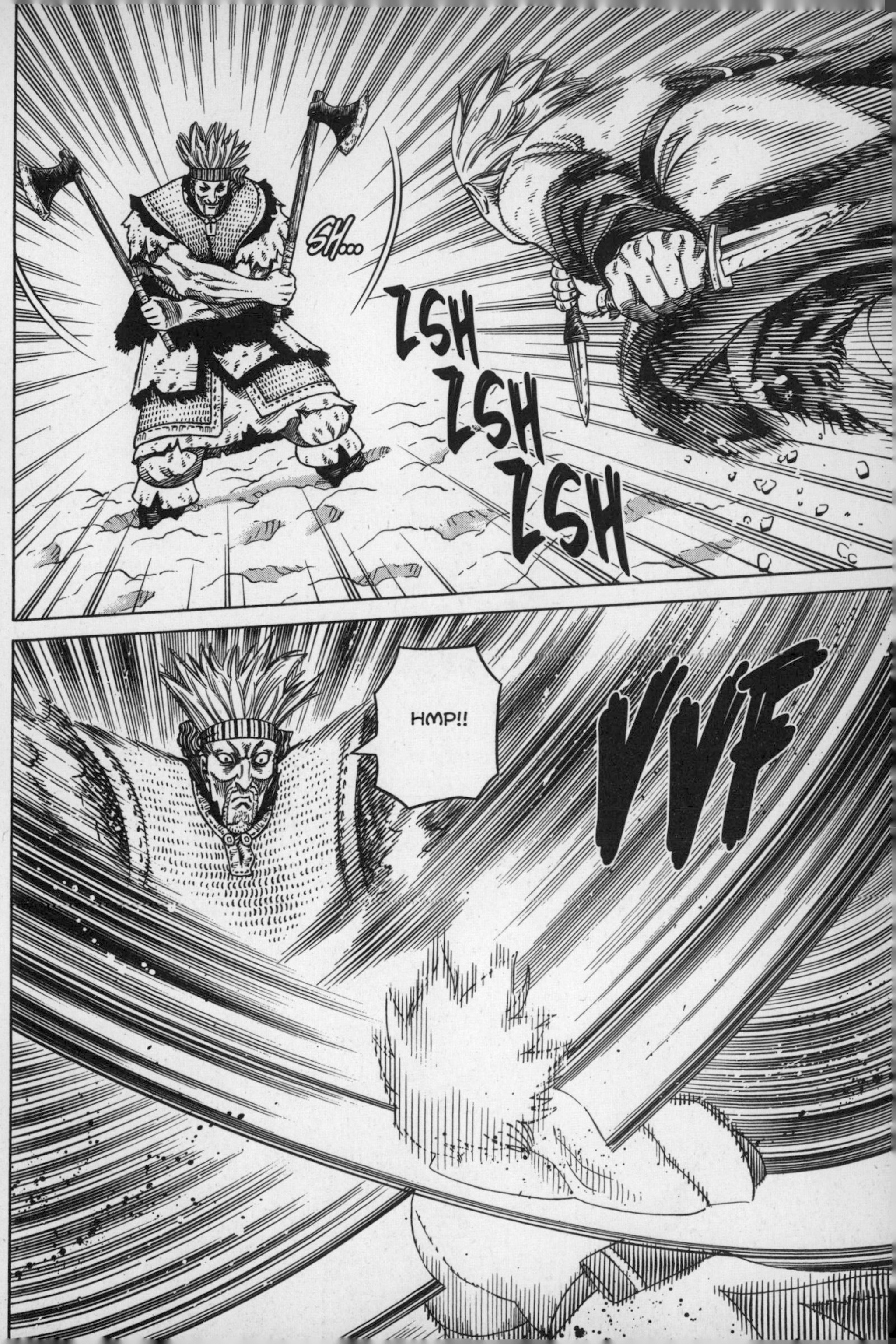
ZSH ZSH ZSH
SH...
VVF
HMP!!

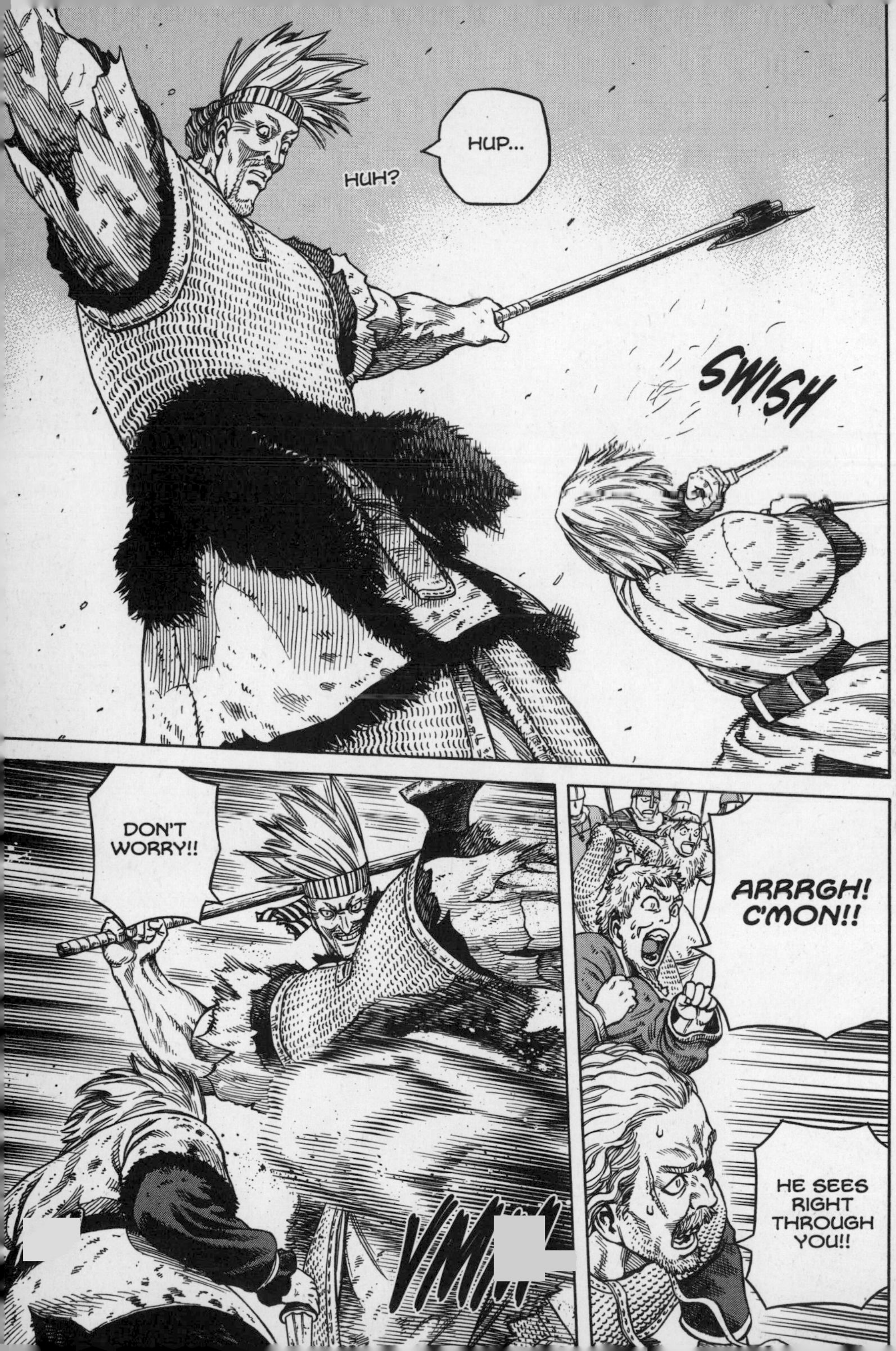
HUP...
HUH?
SWISH
ARRRGH! C'MON!!
HE SEES RIGHT THROUGH YOU!!
DON'T WORRY!!

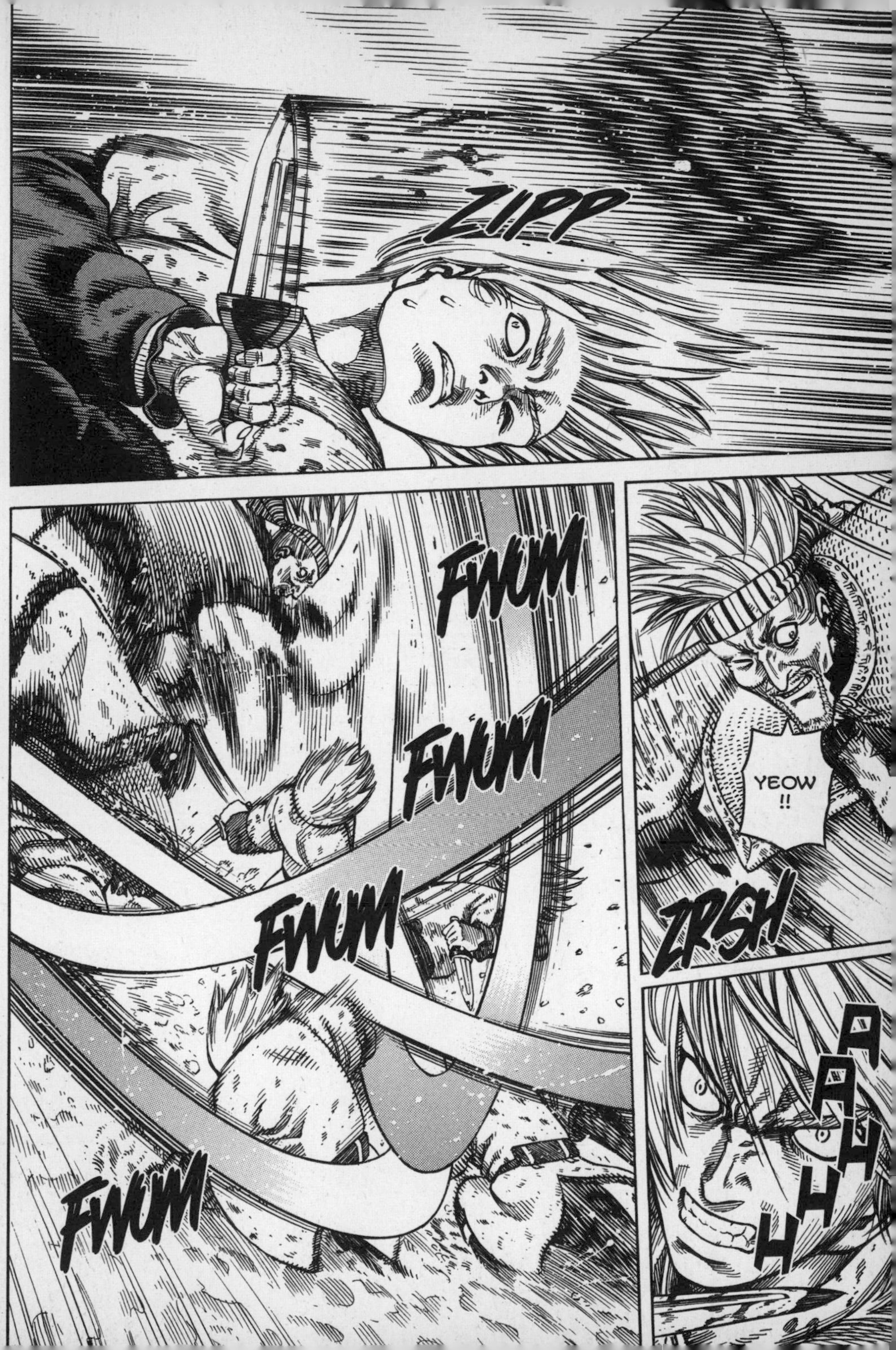
ZIPP
YEOW !!
ZRSH
AAHHH
FWUM
FWUM
FWUM
FWUM

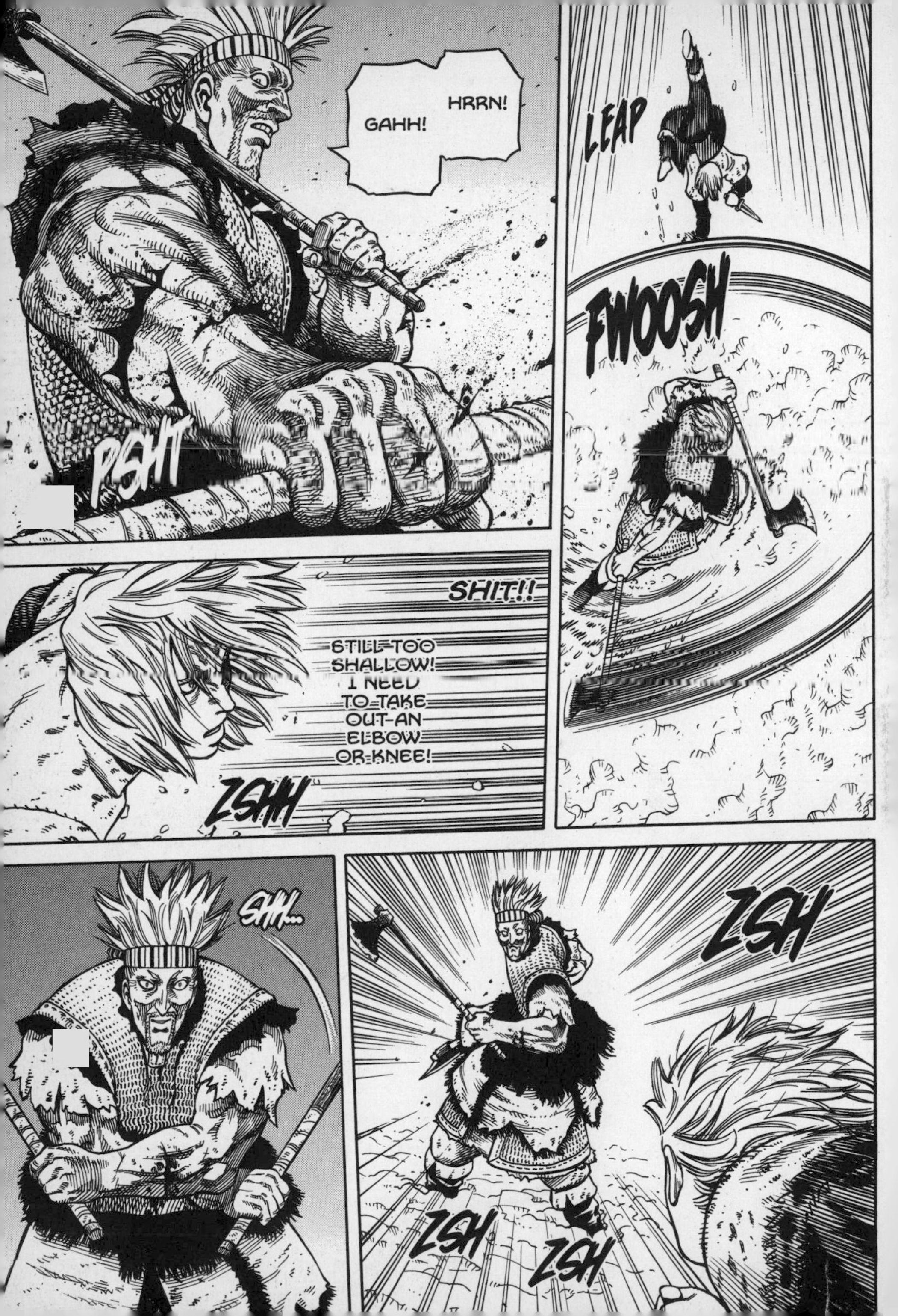
LEAP
FWOOSH
HRRN! GAHH!
PSHT
SHIT!!
STILL TOO SHALLOW! I NEED TO TAKE OUT AN ELBOW OR KNEE!
ZSHH
ZSH
ZSH
ZSH
SHH...

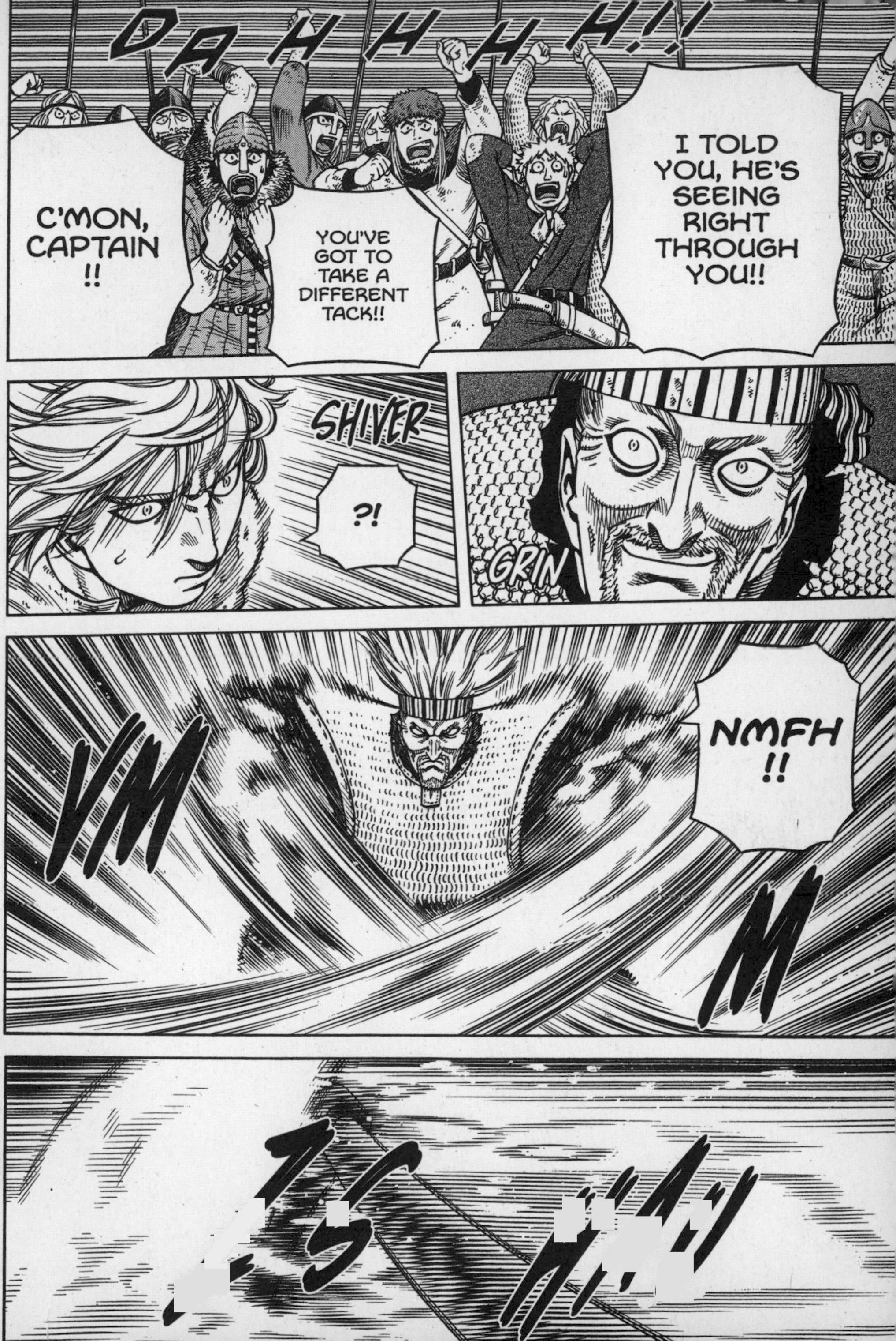
OAHHHHH!!
I TOLD YOU, HE'S SEEING RIGHT THROUGH YOU!!
YOU'VE GOT TO TAKE A DIFFERENT TACK!!
C'MON, CAPTAIN!!
GRIN
SHIVER
?!
NMFH!!
VMM

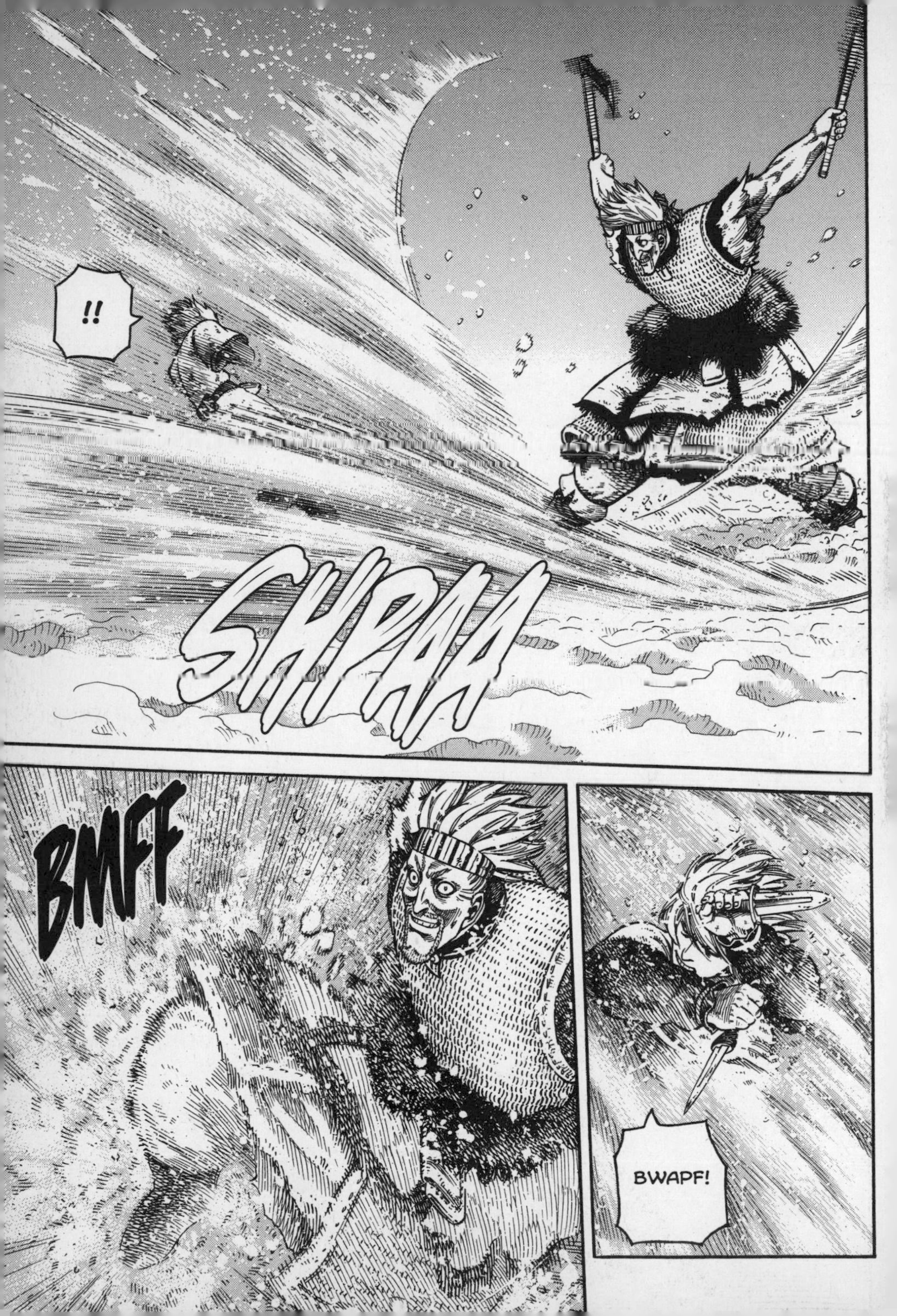
!!
SHPAA
BWAPF!
BMFF

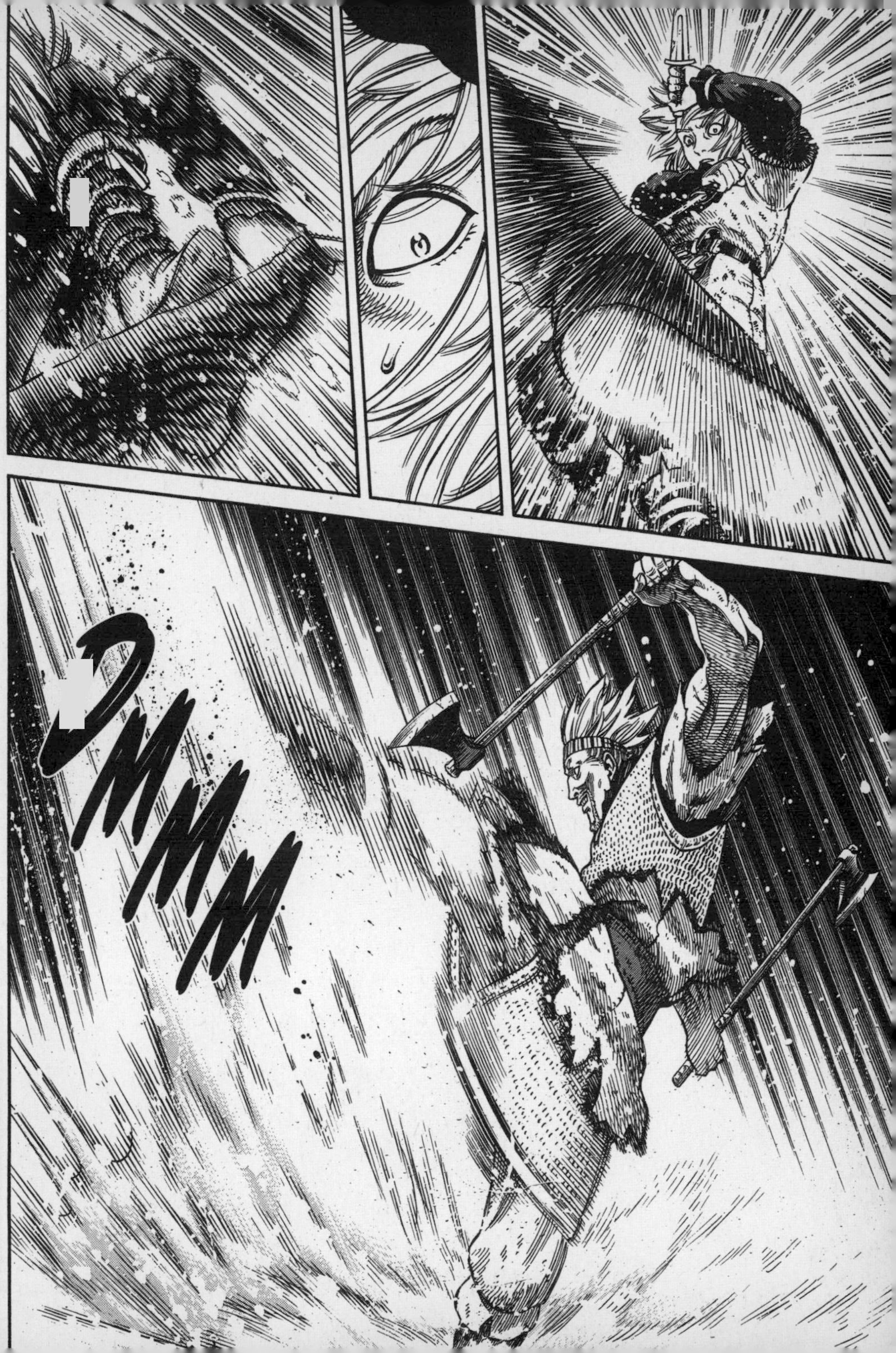

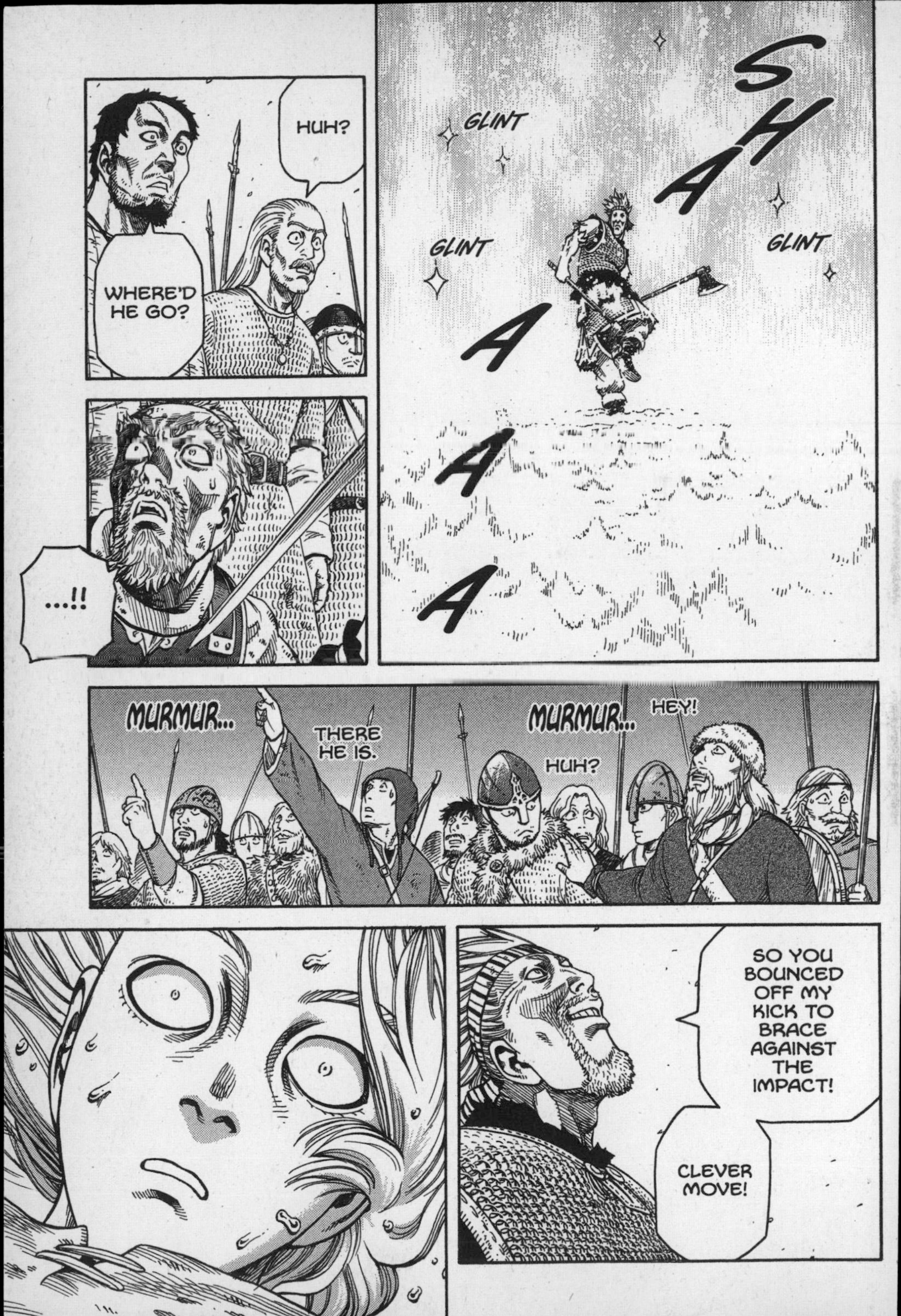
SHAAAAA
GLINT
GLINT
GLINT
HUH?
WHERE'D HE GO?
...!!
HEY!
MURMUR...
HUH?
THERE HE IS.
MURMUR...
SO YOU BOUNCED OFF MY KICK TO BRACE AGAINST THE IMPACT!
CLEVER MOVE!

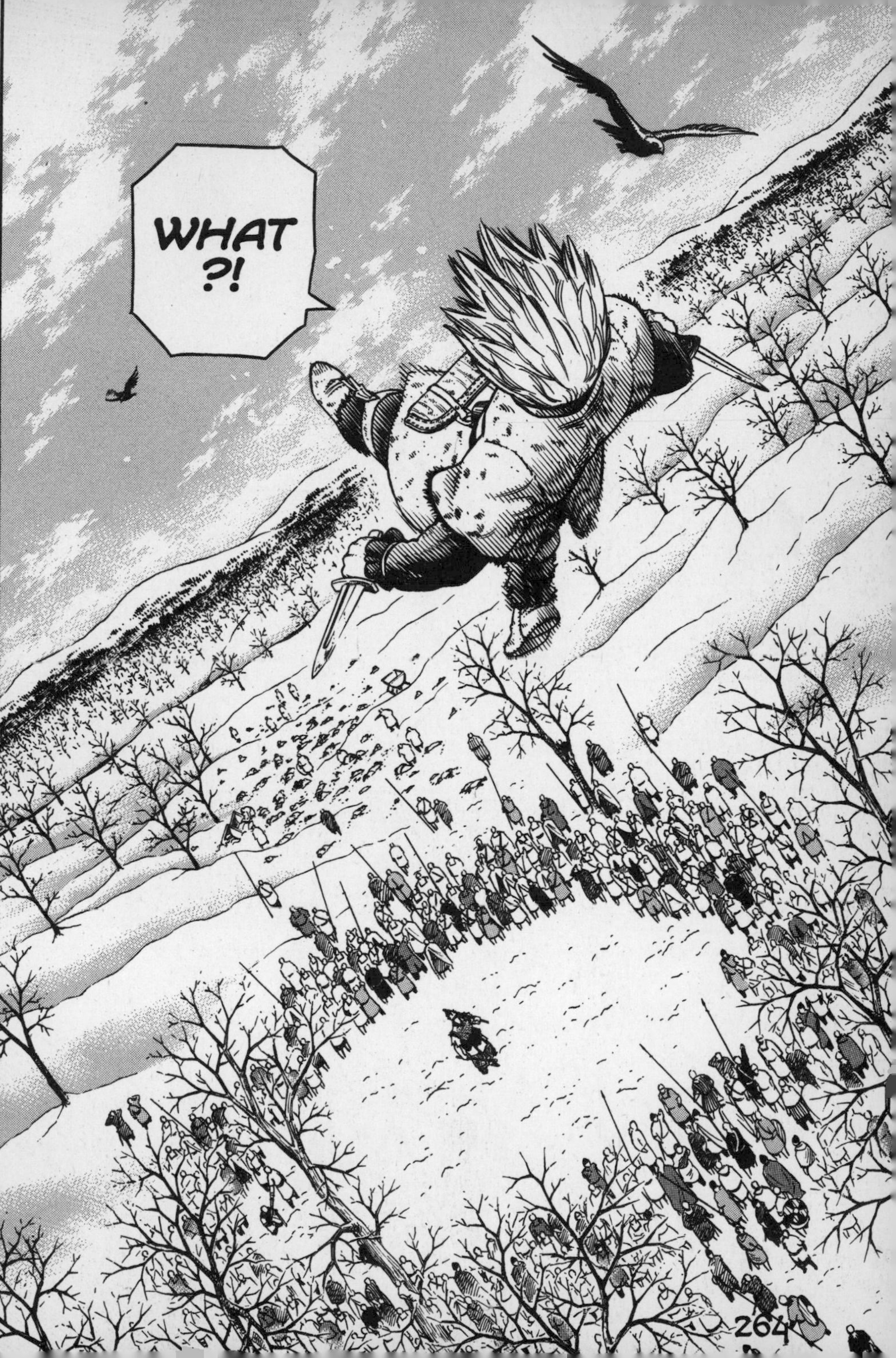
WHAT ?!

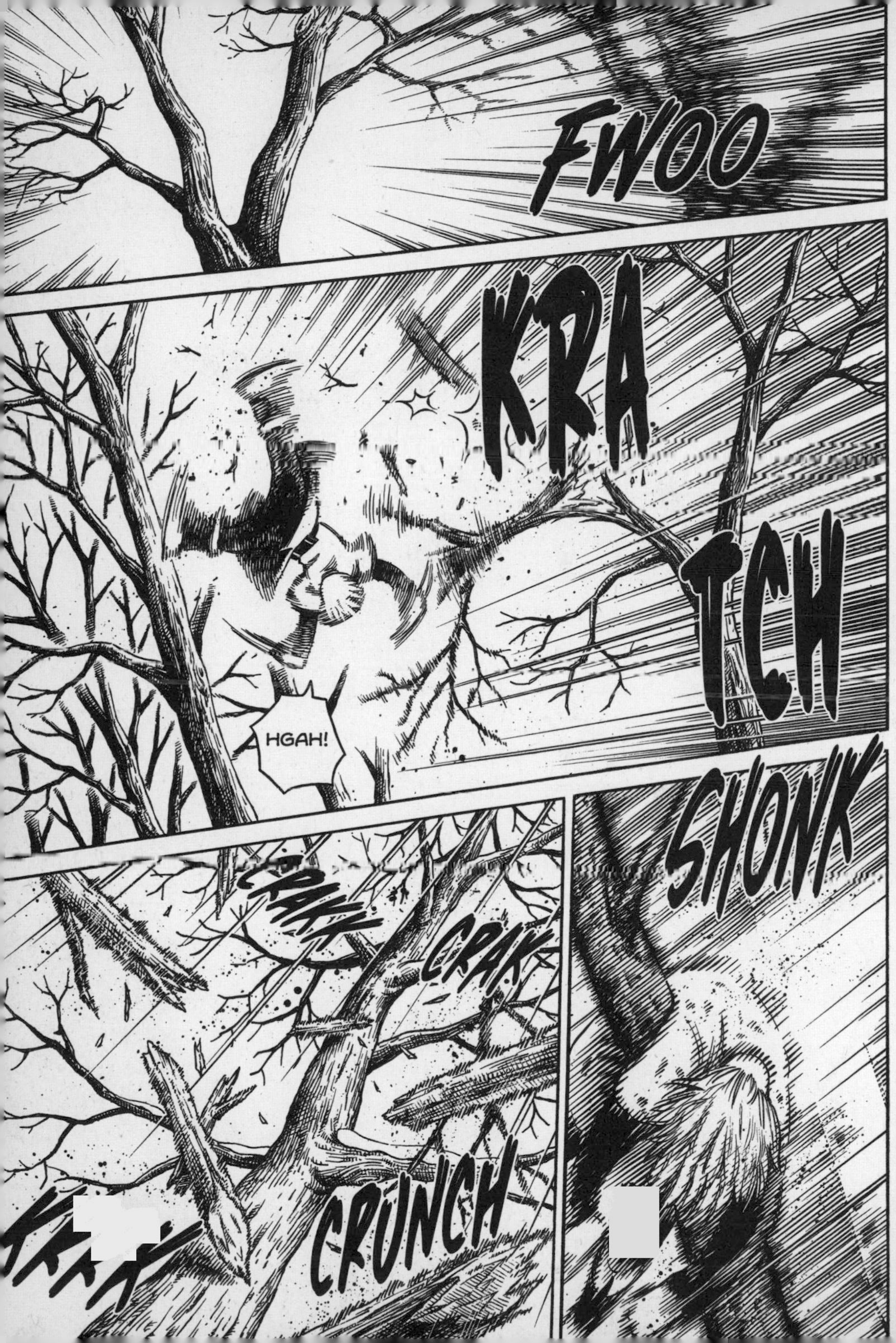
FWOO
KRA
TCH
HGAH!
SHONK
CRAKK
CRAK
CRUNCH

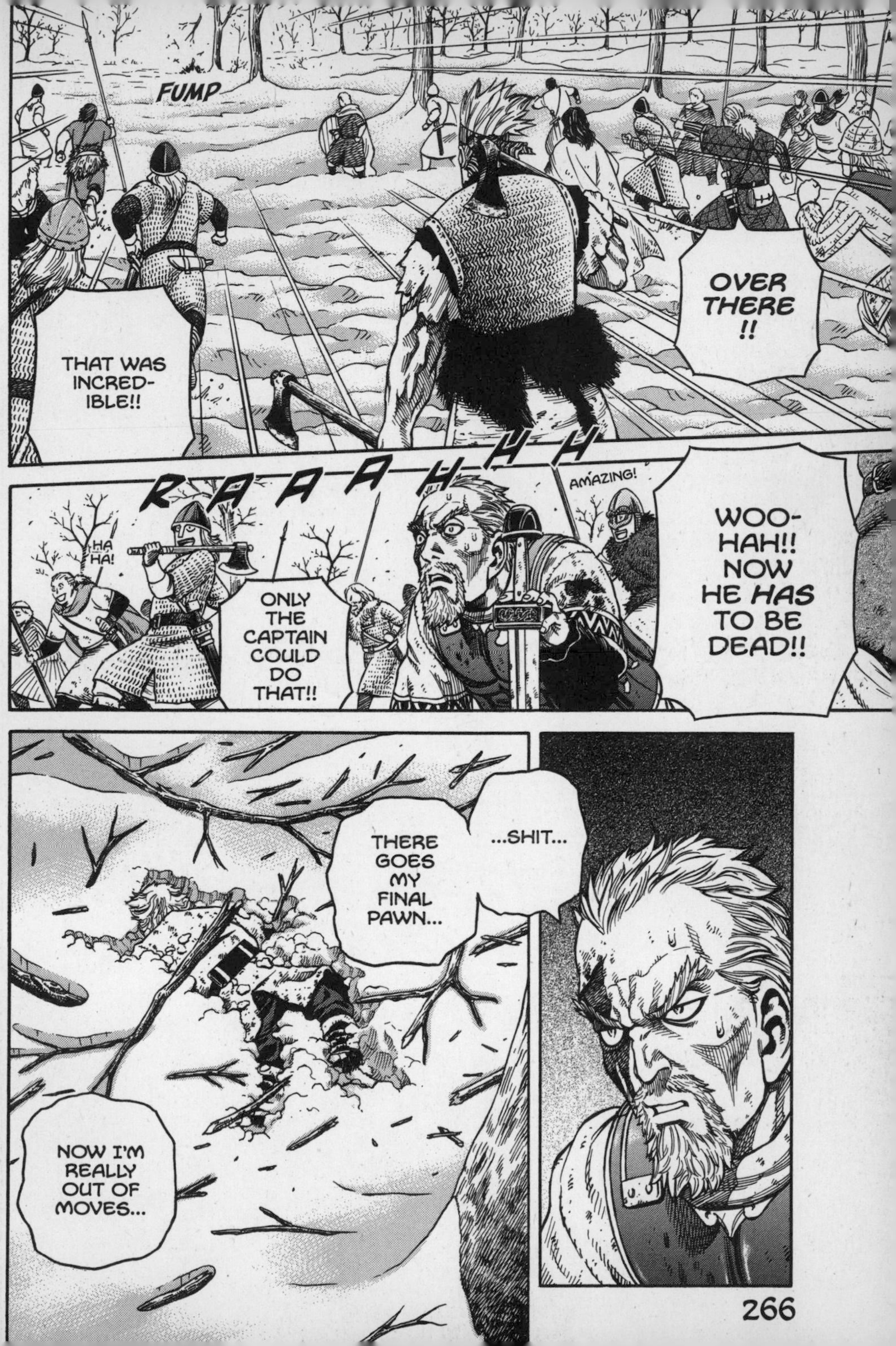
OVER THERE!!
FUMP
THAT WAS INCREDIBLE!!
RAAAAHHHH
WOO-HAH!! NOW HE HAS TO BE DEAD!!
AMAZING!
ONLY THE CAPTAIN COULD DO THAT!!
HA HA!
...SHIT...
THERE GOES MY FINAL PAWN...
NOW I'M REALLY OUT OF MOVES...

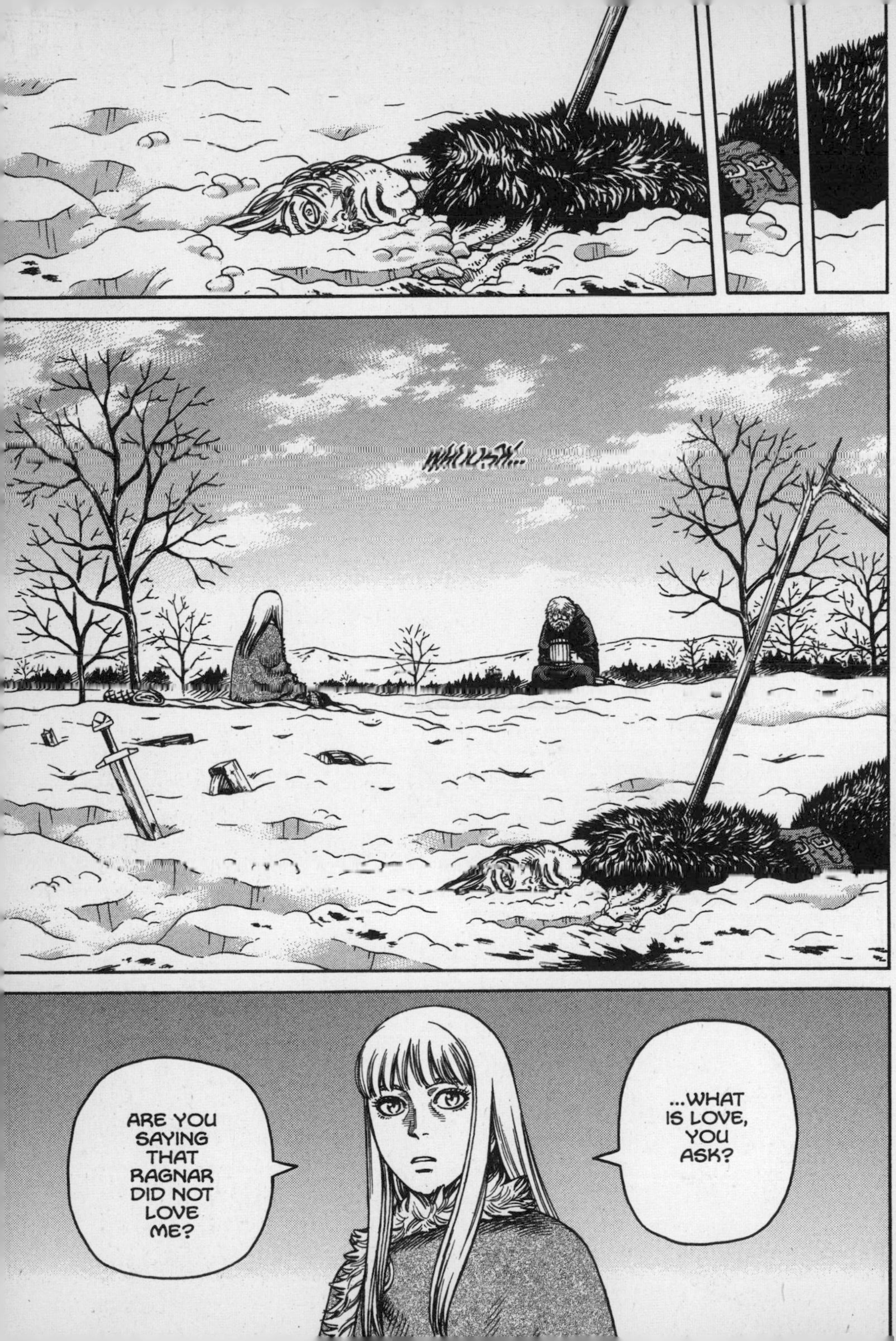
WHUUSH...
...WHAT IS LOVE, YOU ASK?
ARE YOU SAYING THAT RAGNAR DID NOT LOVE ME?

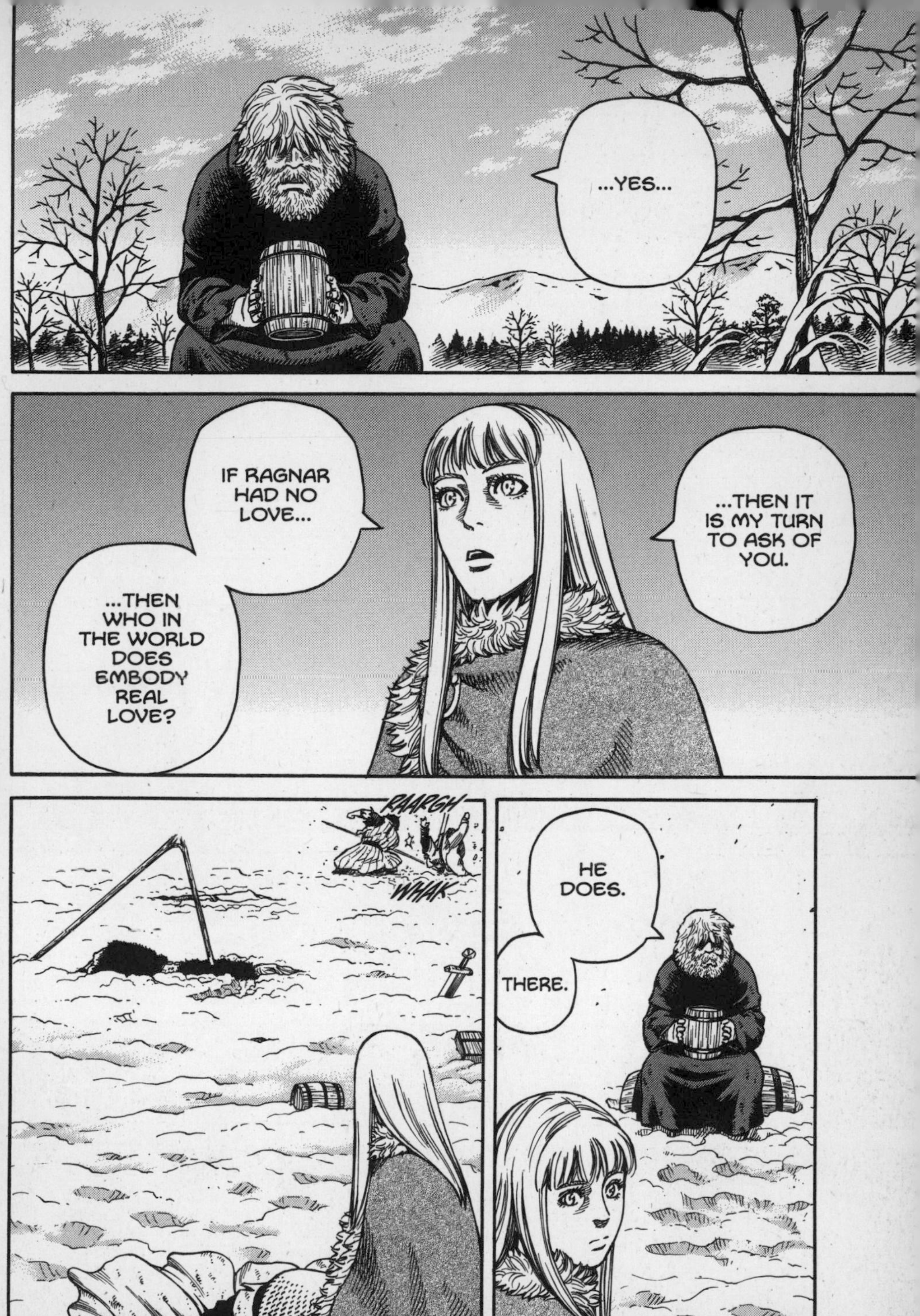
...YES...
...THEN IT IS MY TURN TO ASK OF YOU.
IF RAGNAR HAD NO LOVE...
...THEN WHO IN THE WORLD DOES EMBODY REAL LOVE?
HE DOES.
THERE.
RAARGH
WHAK

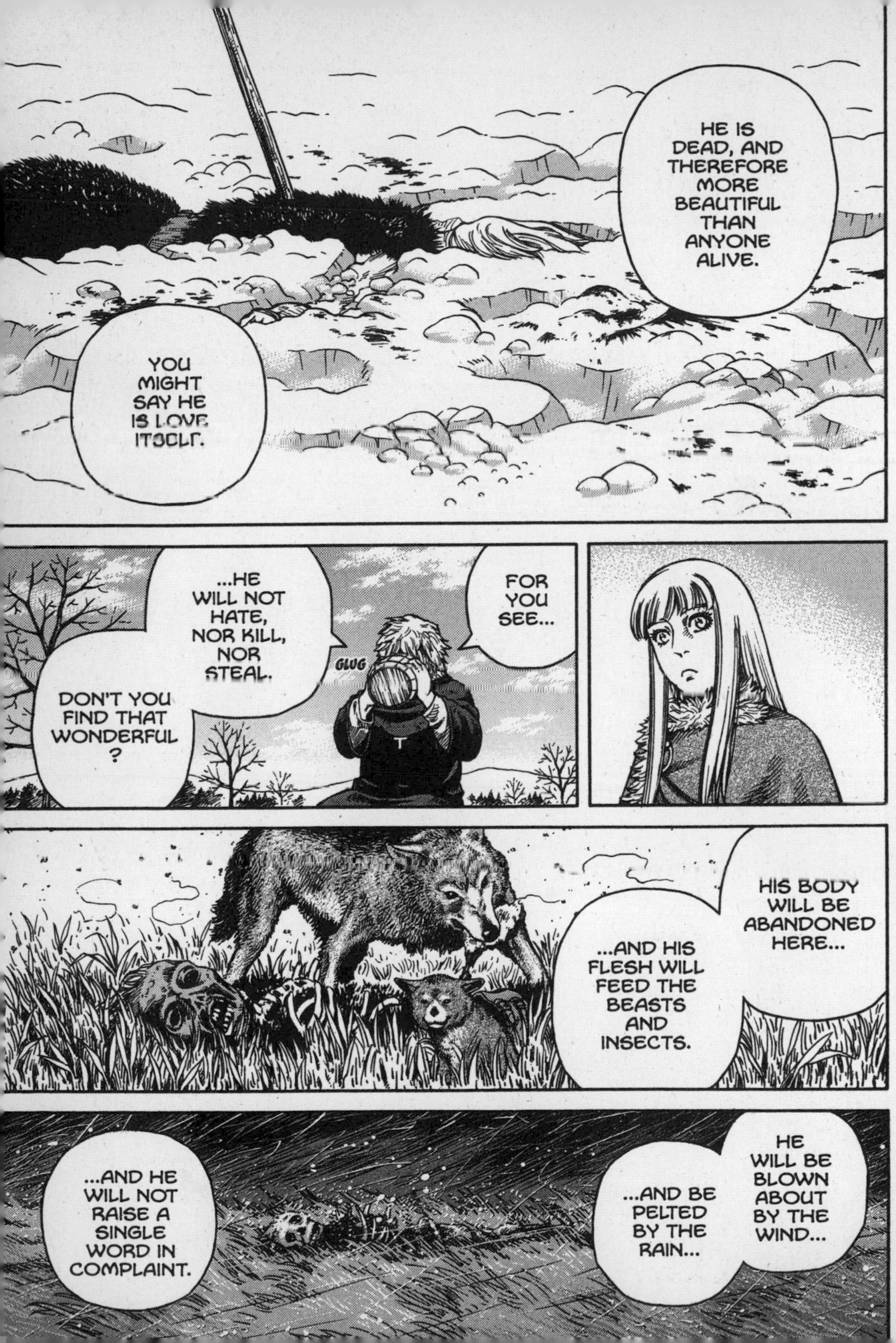
HE IS DEAD, AND THEREFORE MORE BEAUTIFUL THAN ANYONE ALIVE.
YOU MIGHT SAY HE IS LOVE ITSELF.
FOR YOU SEE...
...HE WILL NOT HATE, NOR KILL, NOR STEAL.
GLUG
DON'T YOU FIND THAT WONDERFUL?
HIS BODY WILL BE ABANDONED HERE...
...AND HIS FLESH WILL FEED THE BEASTS AND INSECTS.
HE WILL BE BLOWN ABOUT BY THE WIND...
...AND BE PELTED BY THE RAIN...
...AND HE WILL NOT RAISE A SINGLE WORD IN COMPLAINT.

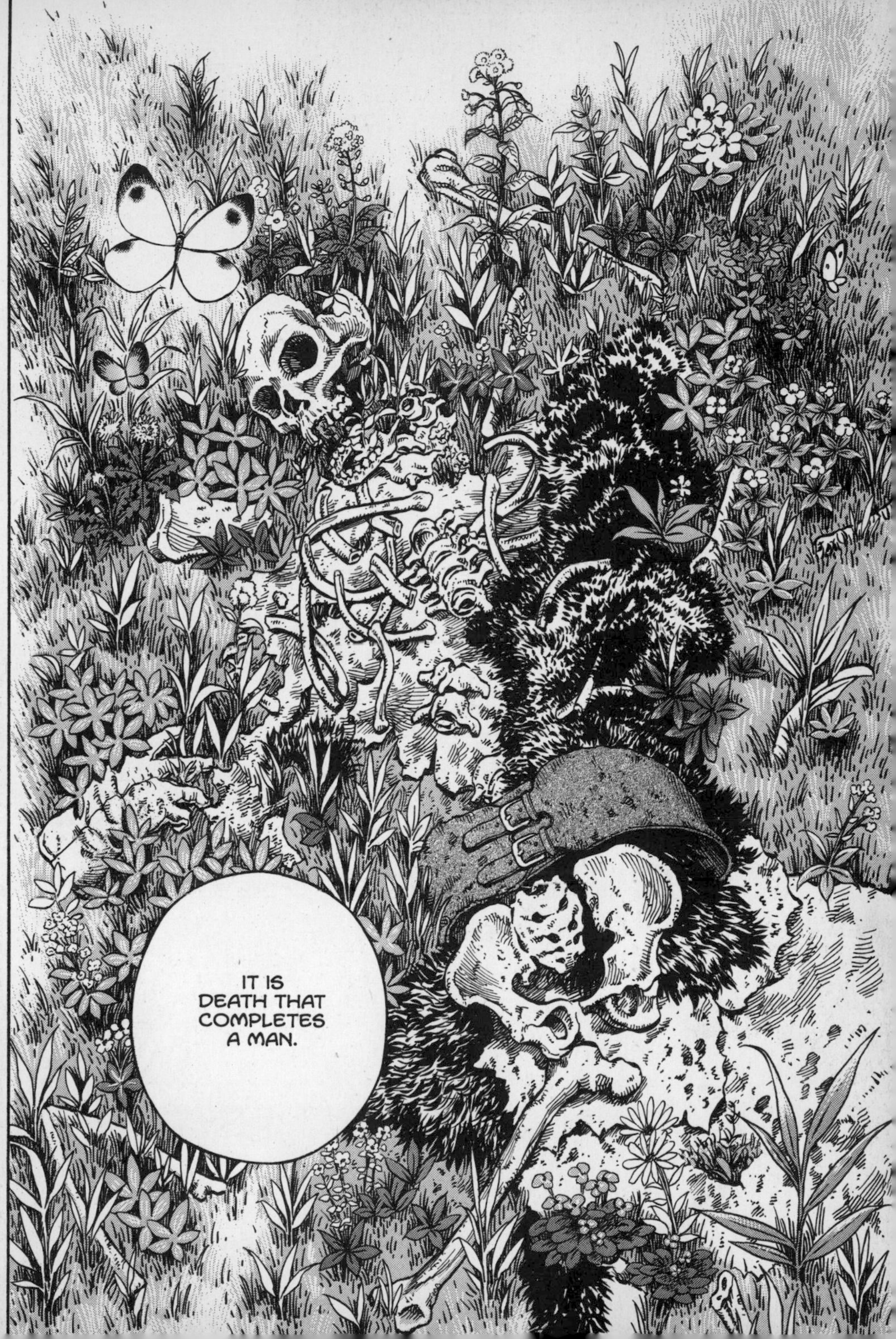
IT IS DEATH THAT COMPLETES A MAN.

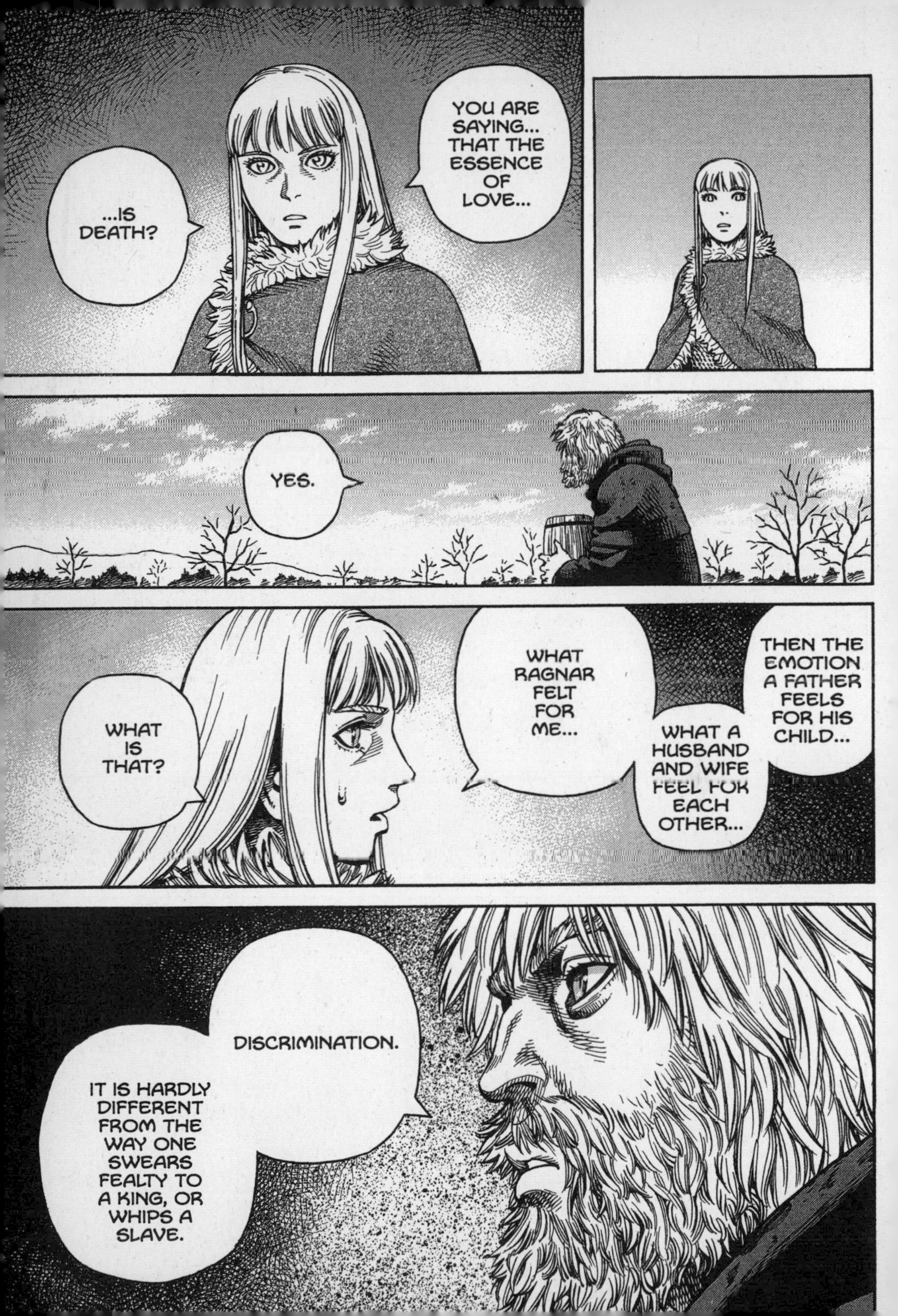
YOU ARE SAYING... THAT THE ESSENCE OF LOVE...
...IS DEATH?
YES.
THEN THE EMOTION A FATHER FEELS FOR HIS CHILD...
WHAT A HUSBAND AND WIFE FEEL FOR EACH OTHER...
WHAT RAGNAR FELT FOR ME...
WHAT IS THAT?
DISCRIMINATION.
IT IS HARDLY DIFFERENT FROM THE WAY ONE SWEARS FEALTY TO A KING, OR WHIPS A SLAVE.

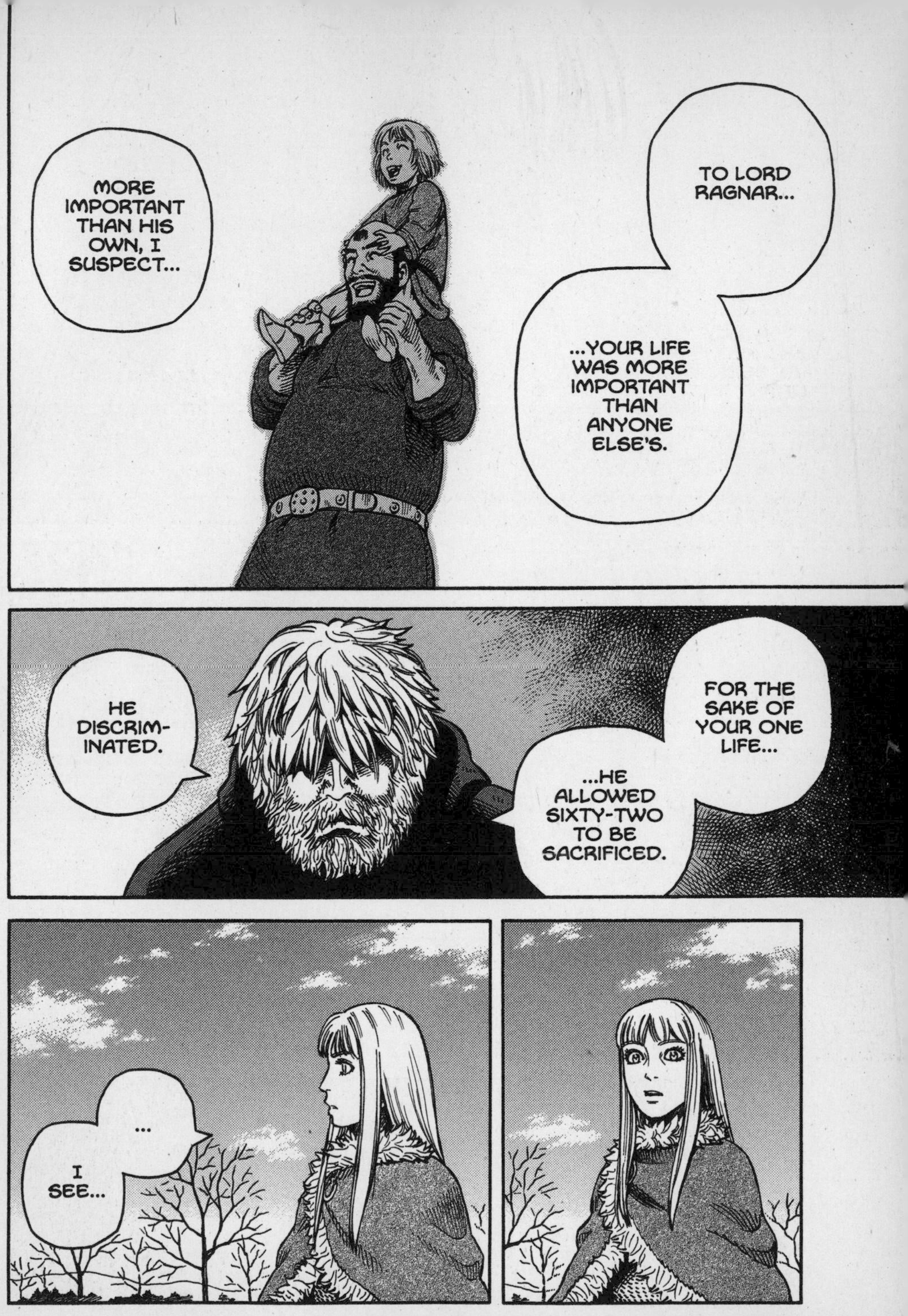
TO LORD RAGNAR...
...YOUR LIFE WAS MORE IMPORTANT THAN ANYONE ELSE'S.
MORE IMPORTANT THAN HIS OWN, I SUSPECT...
FOR THE SAKE OF YOUR ONE LIFE...
...HE ALLOWED SIXTY-TWO TO BE SACRIFICED.
HE DISCRIMINATED.
...
I SEE...

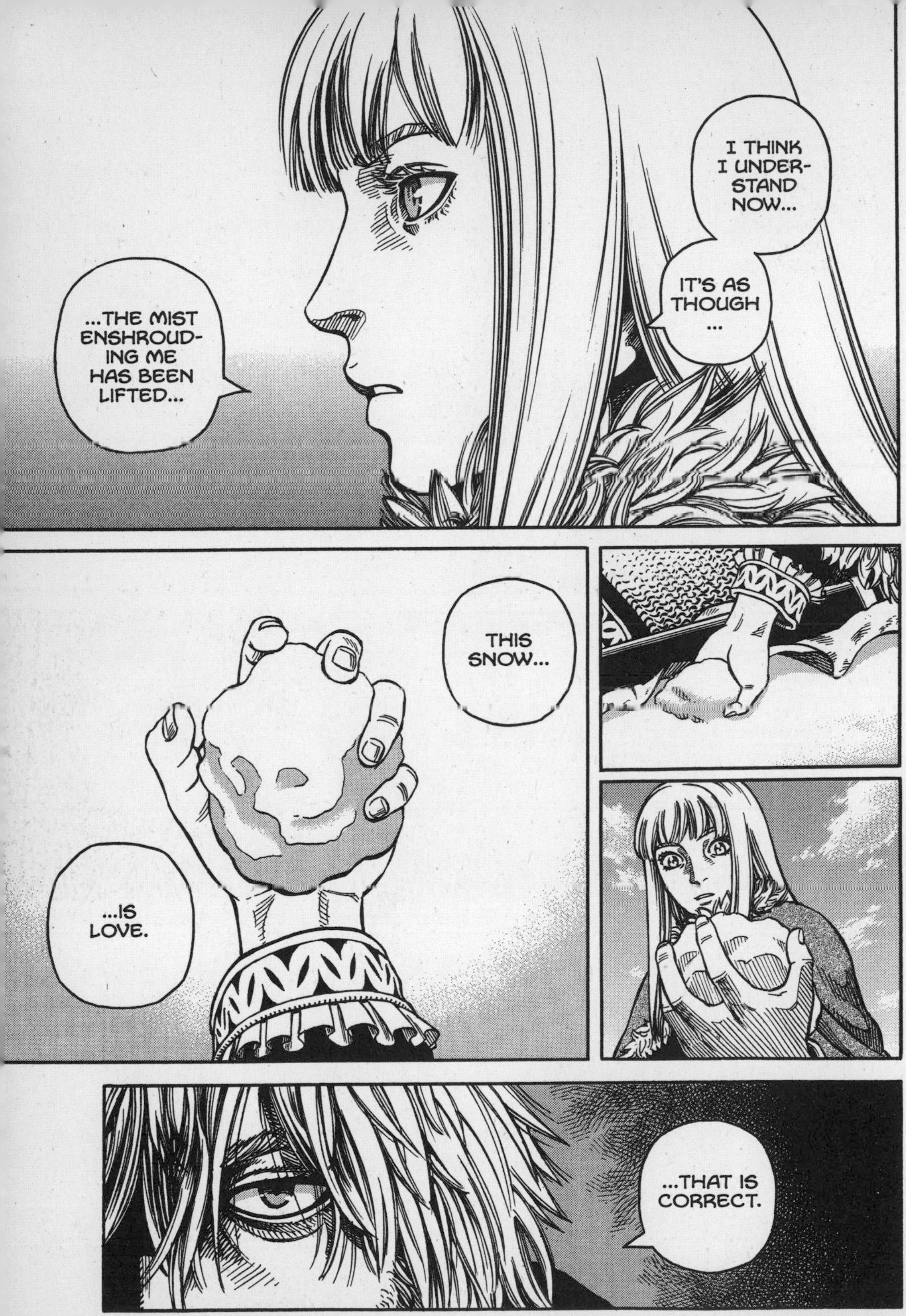

I THINK I UNDER-STAND NOW...
IT'S AS THOUGH ...
...THE MIST ENSHROUD-ING ME HAS BEEN LIFTED...
THIS SNOW...
...IS LOVE.
...THAT IS CORRECT.

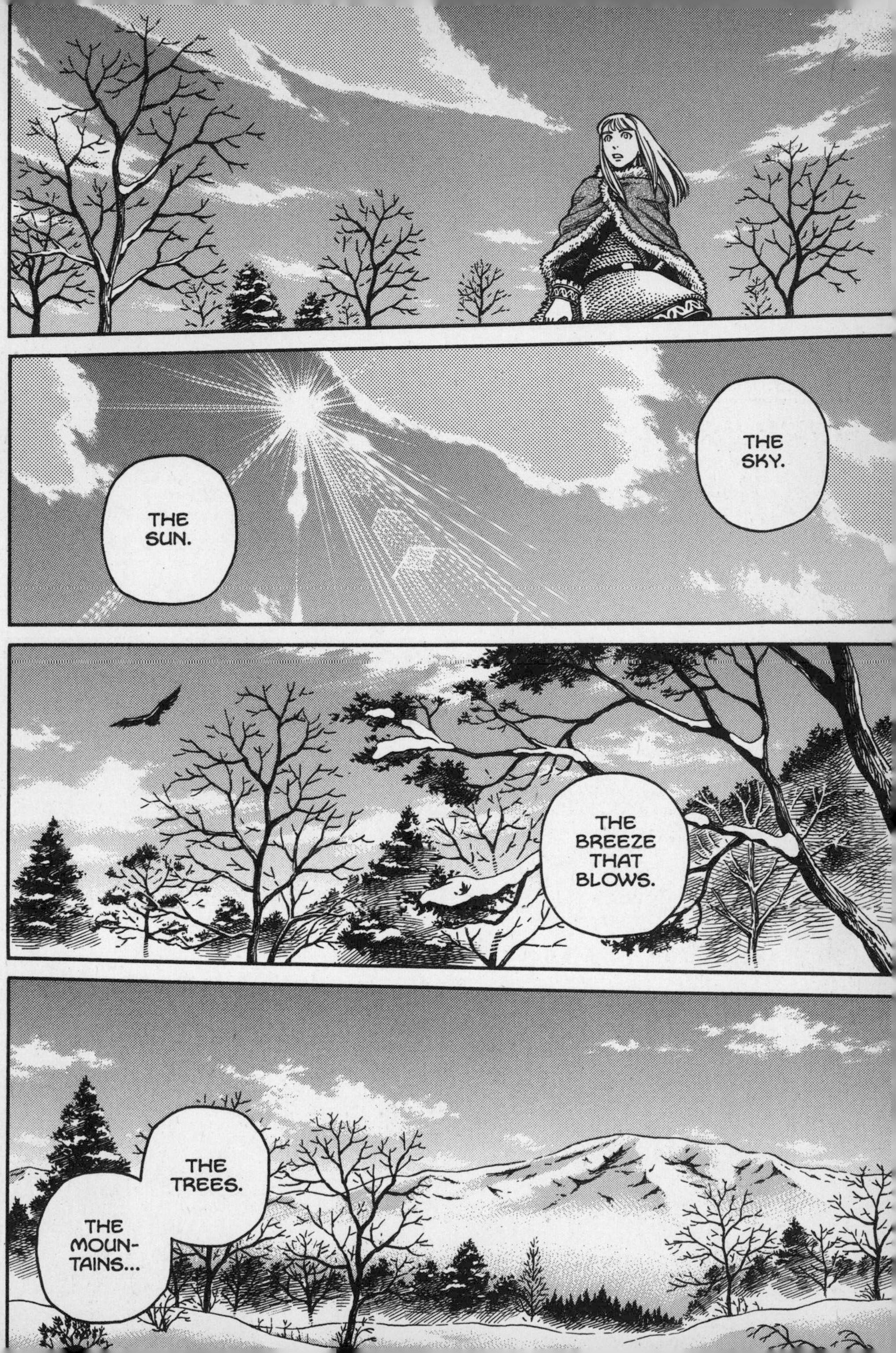
THE SKY.
THE SUN.
THE BREEZE THAT BLOWS.
THE TREES.
THE MOUN-TAINS...

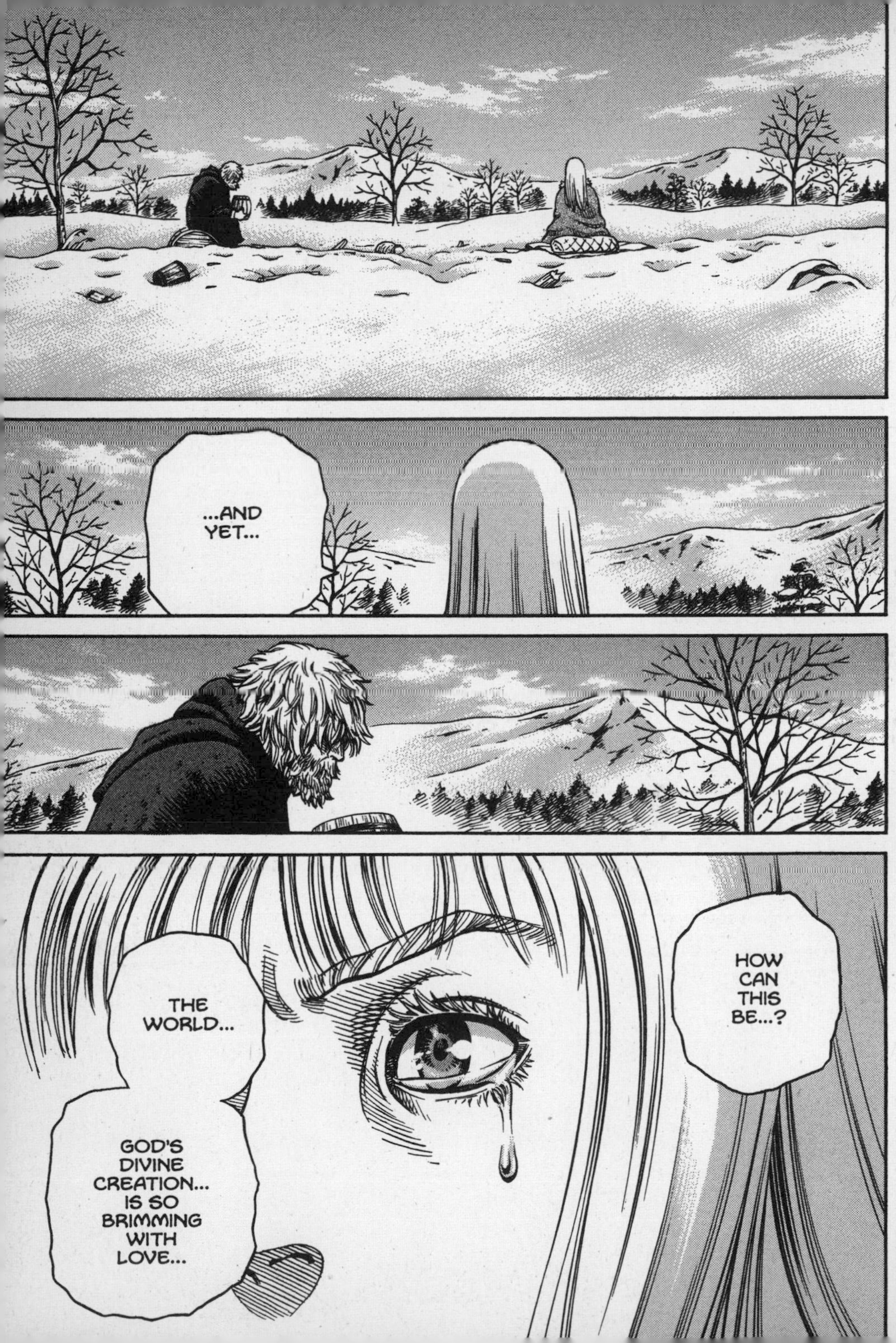
...AND YET...
HOW CAN THIS BE...?
THE WORLD...
GOD'S DIVINE CREATION... IS SO BRIMMING WITH LOVE...

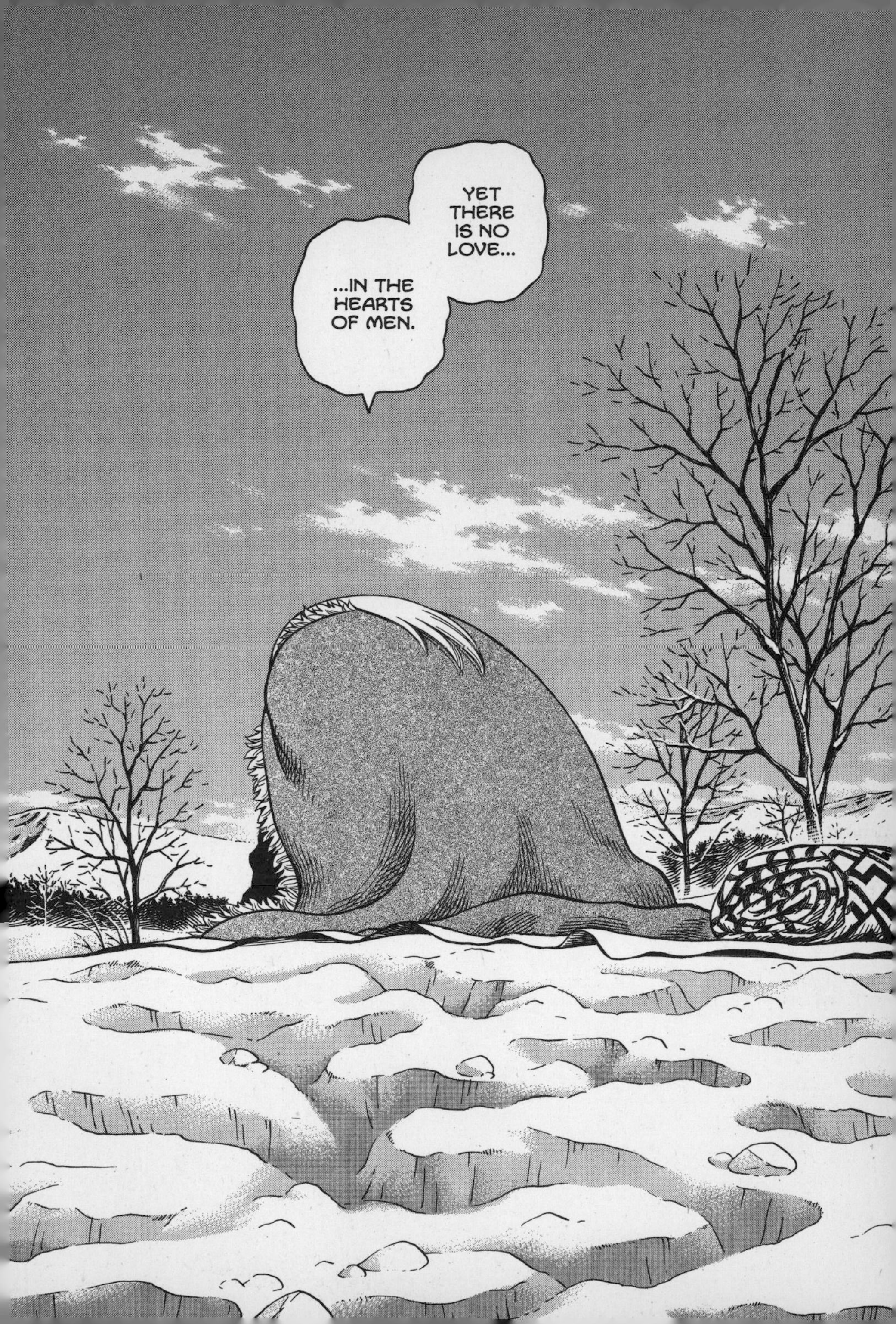
YET THERE IS NO LOVE...
...IN THE HEARTS OF MEN.

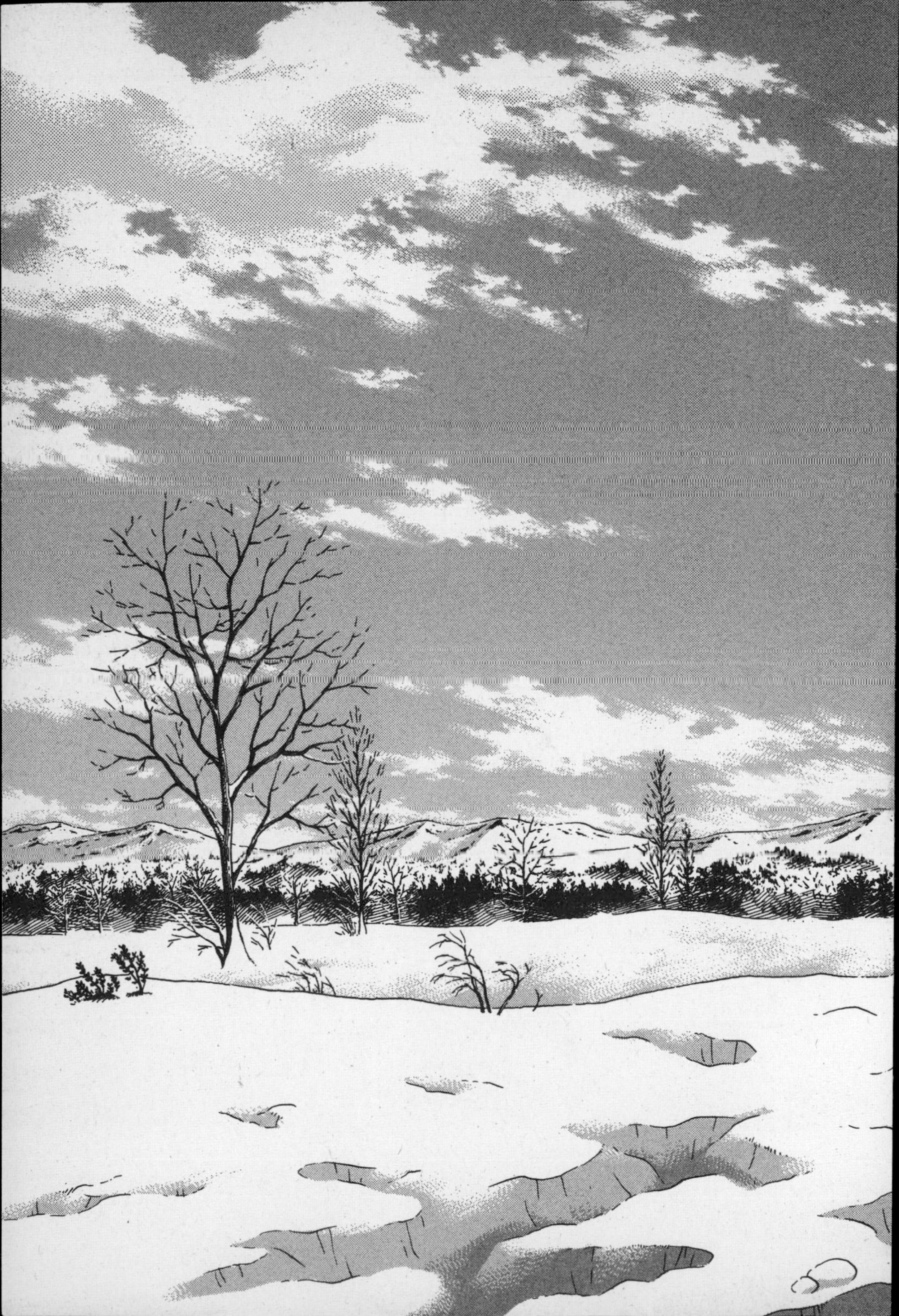

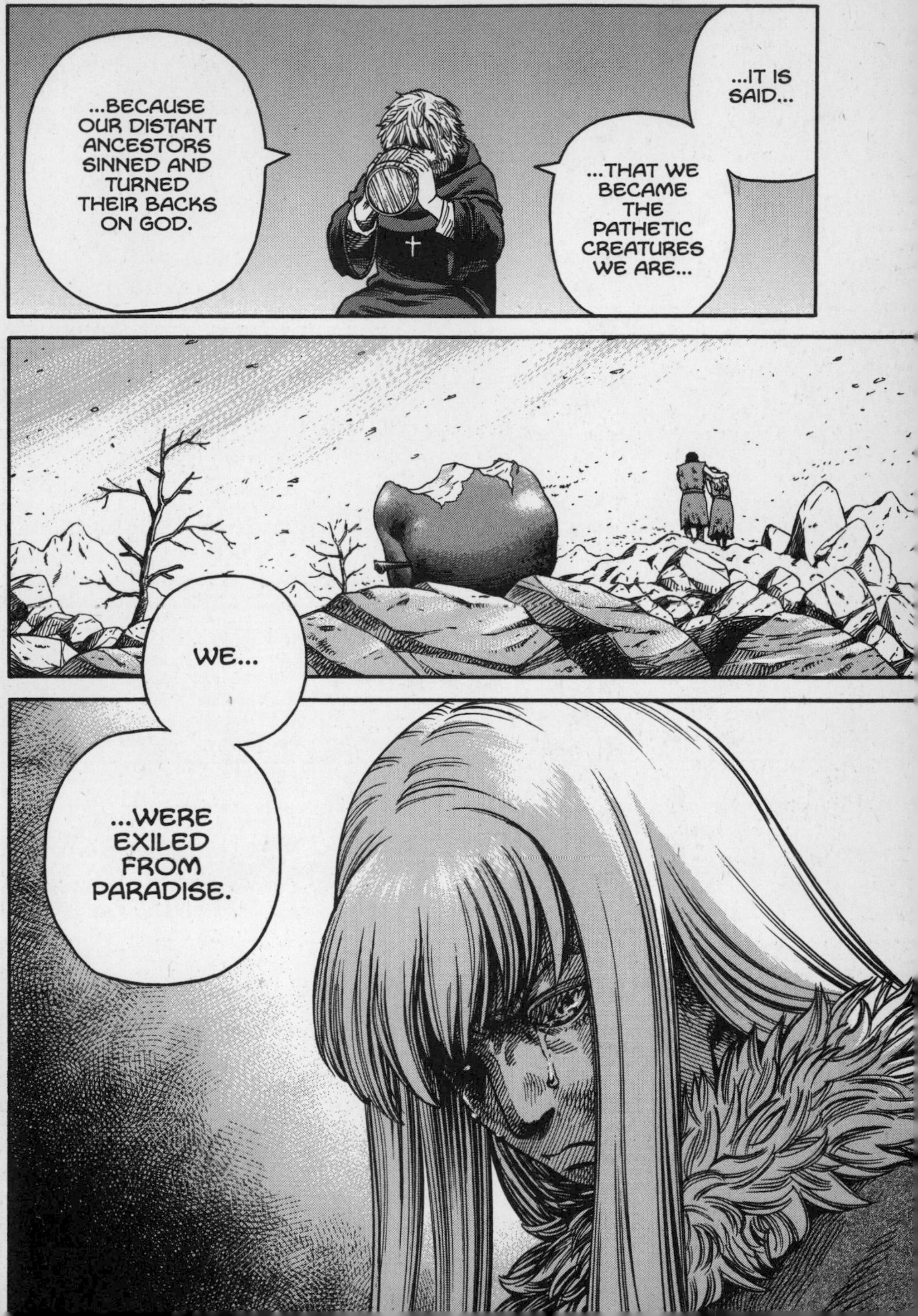
...IT IS SAID...
...THAT WE BECAME THE PATHETIC CREATURES WE ARE...
...BECAUSE OUR DISTANT ANCESTORS SINNED AND TURNED THEIR BACKS ON GOD.
WE...
...WERE EXILED FROM PARADISE.

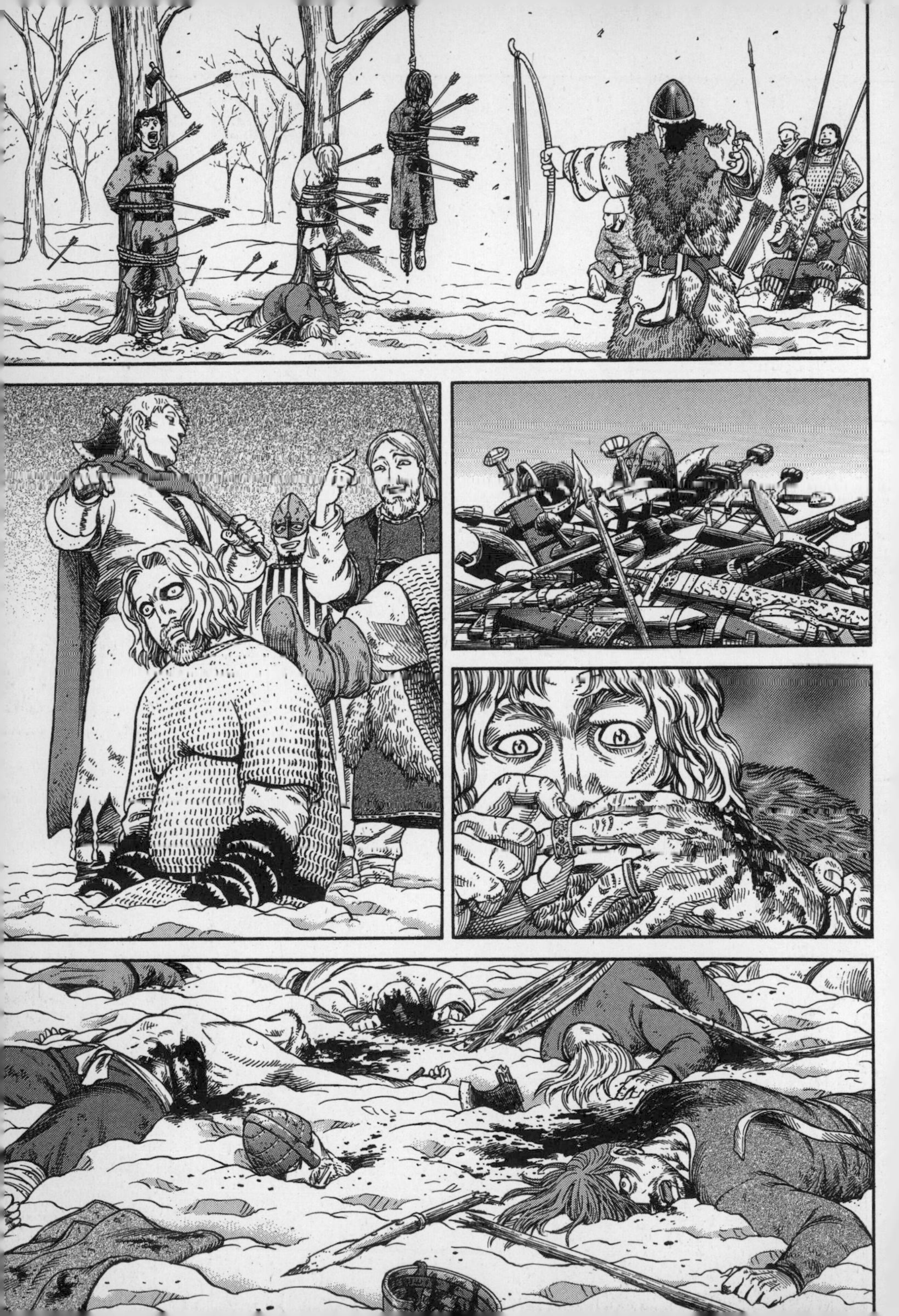

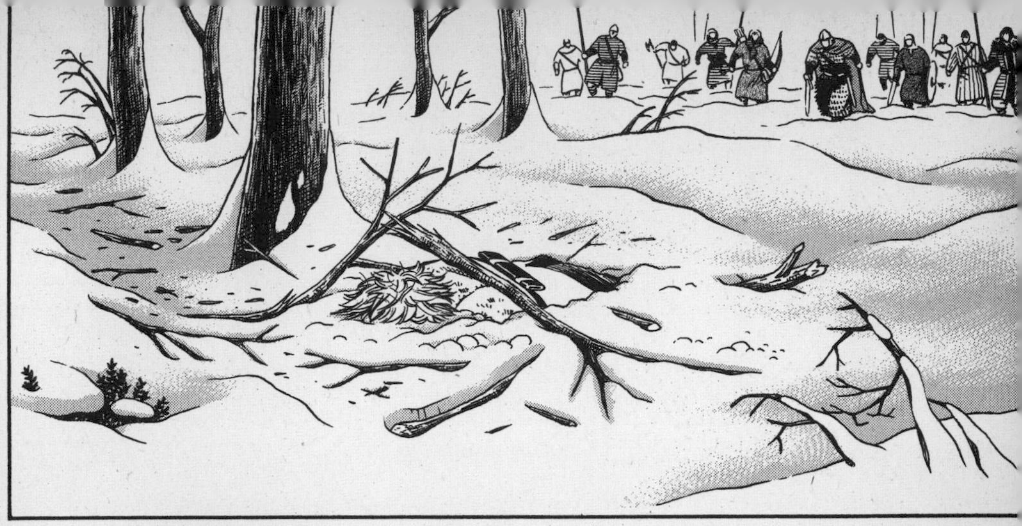

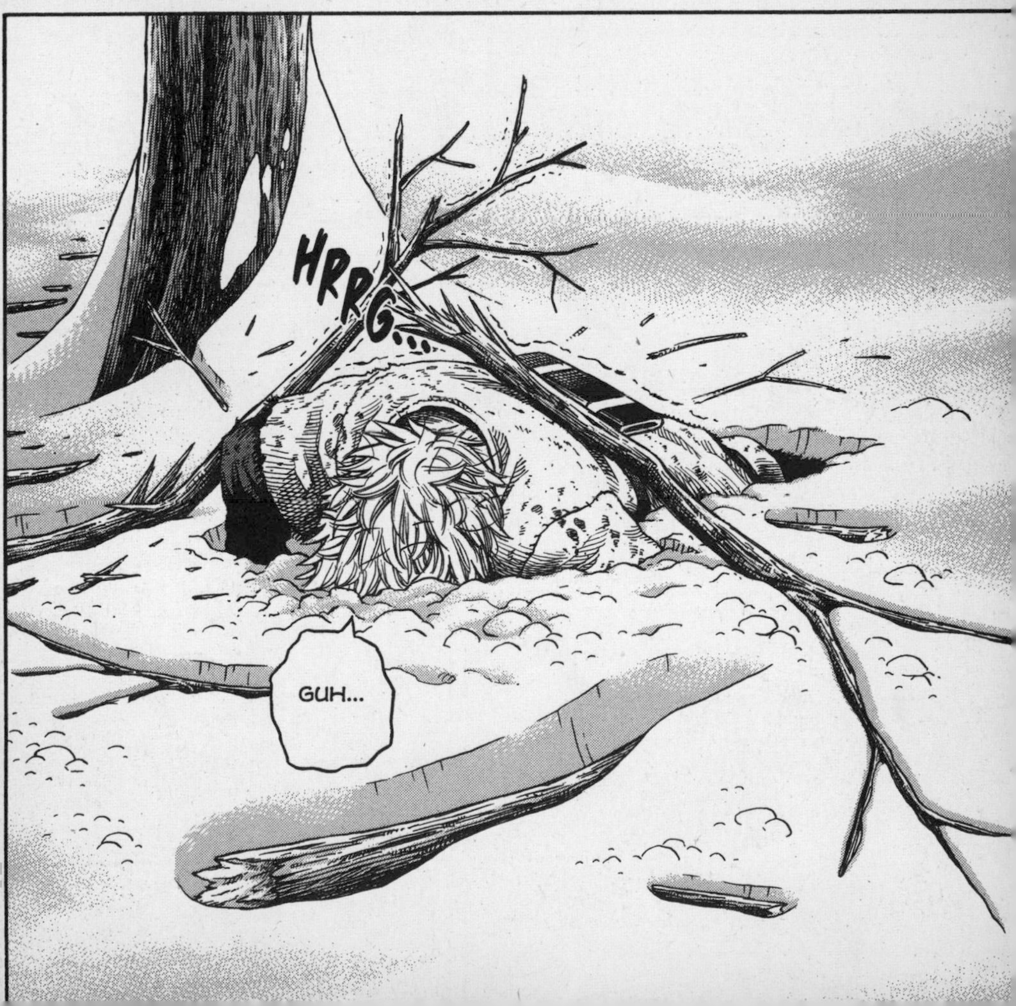
HRRG...
GUH...

CHAPTER 37 • END

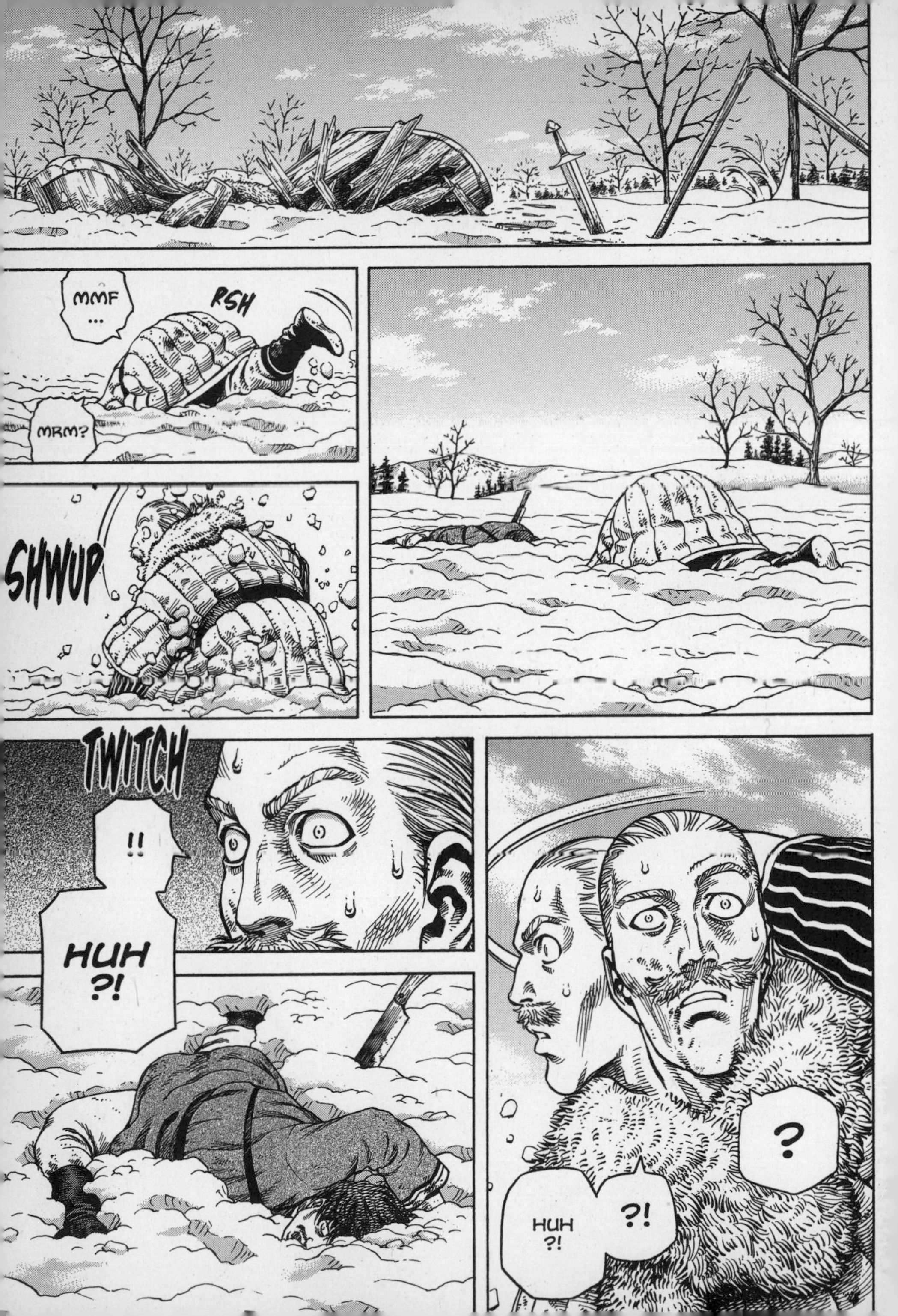
MMF ...
RSH
MRM?
SHWUP
?
?!
HUH ?!
TWITCH
!!
HUH ?!

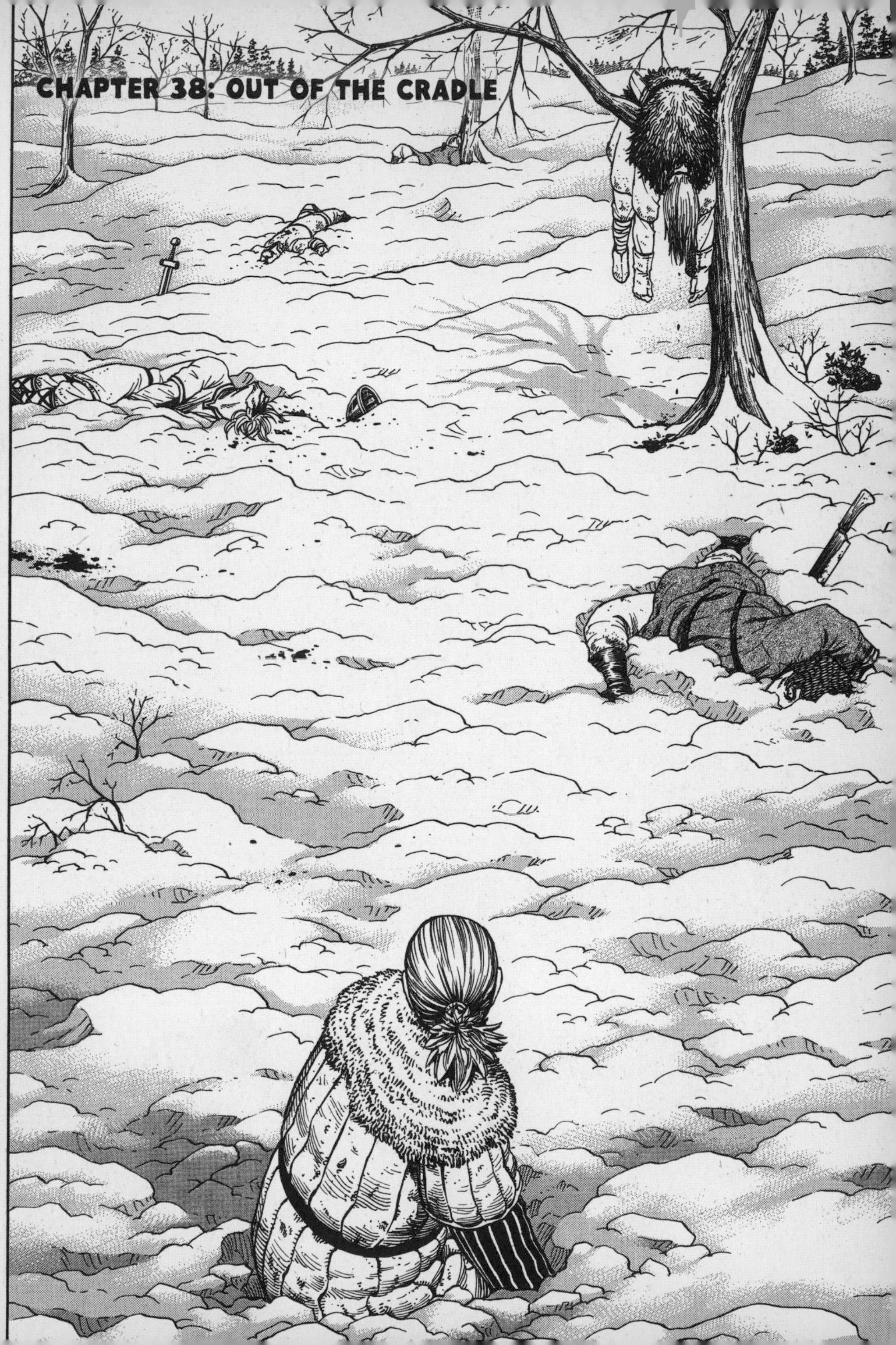
CHAPTER 38: OUT OF THE CRADLE

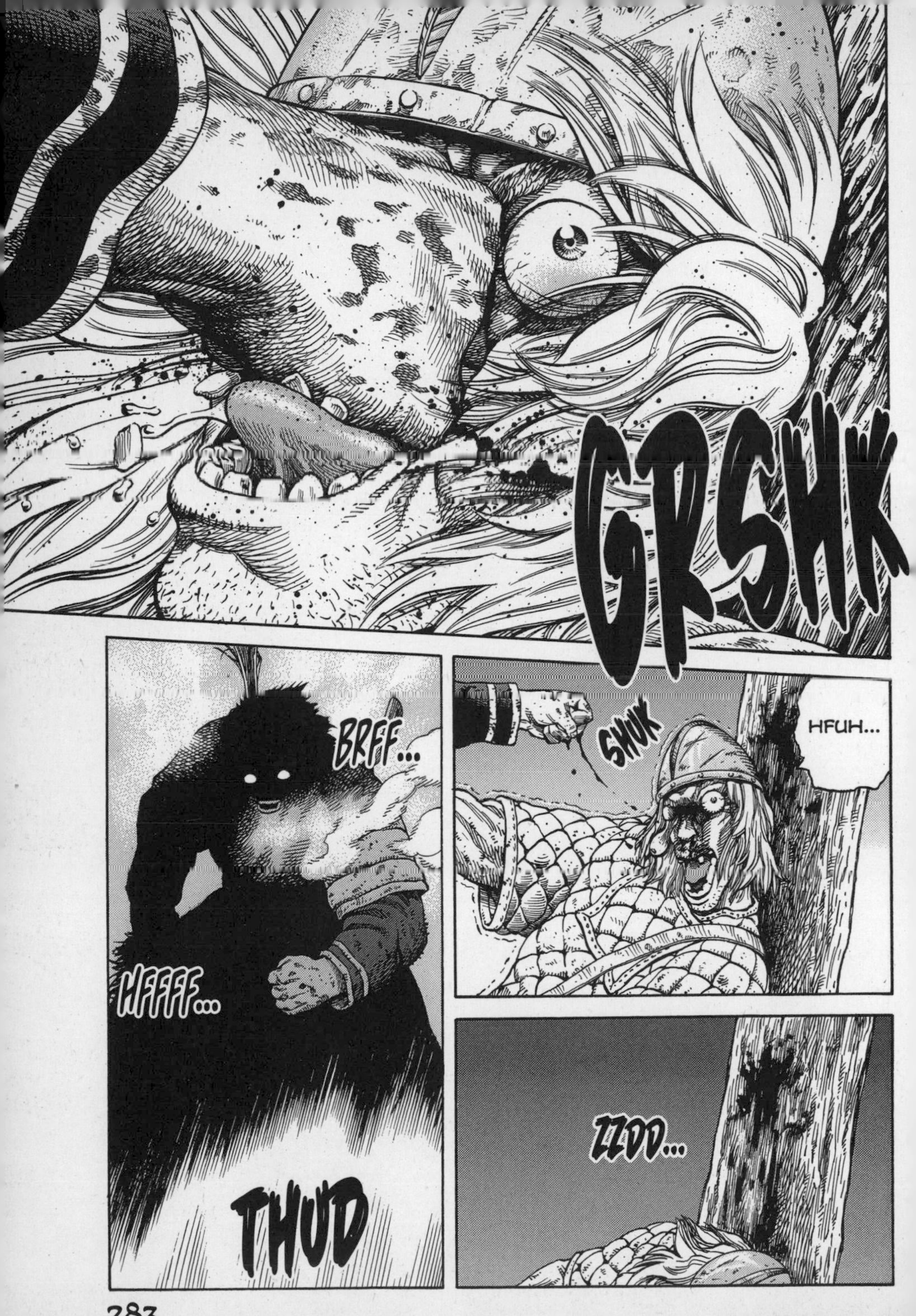
GRSHK
SHUK
HFUH...
ZZDD...
BRFF...
HFFFF...
THUD

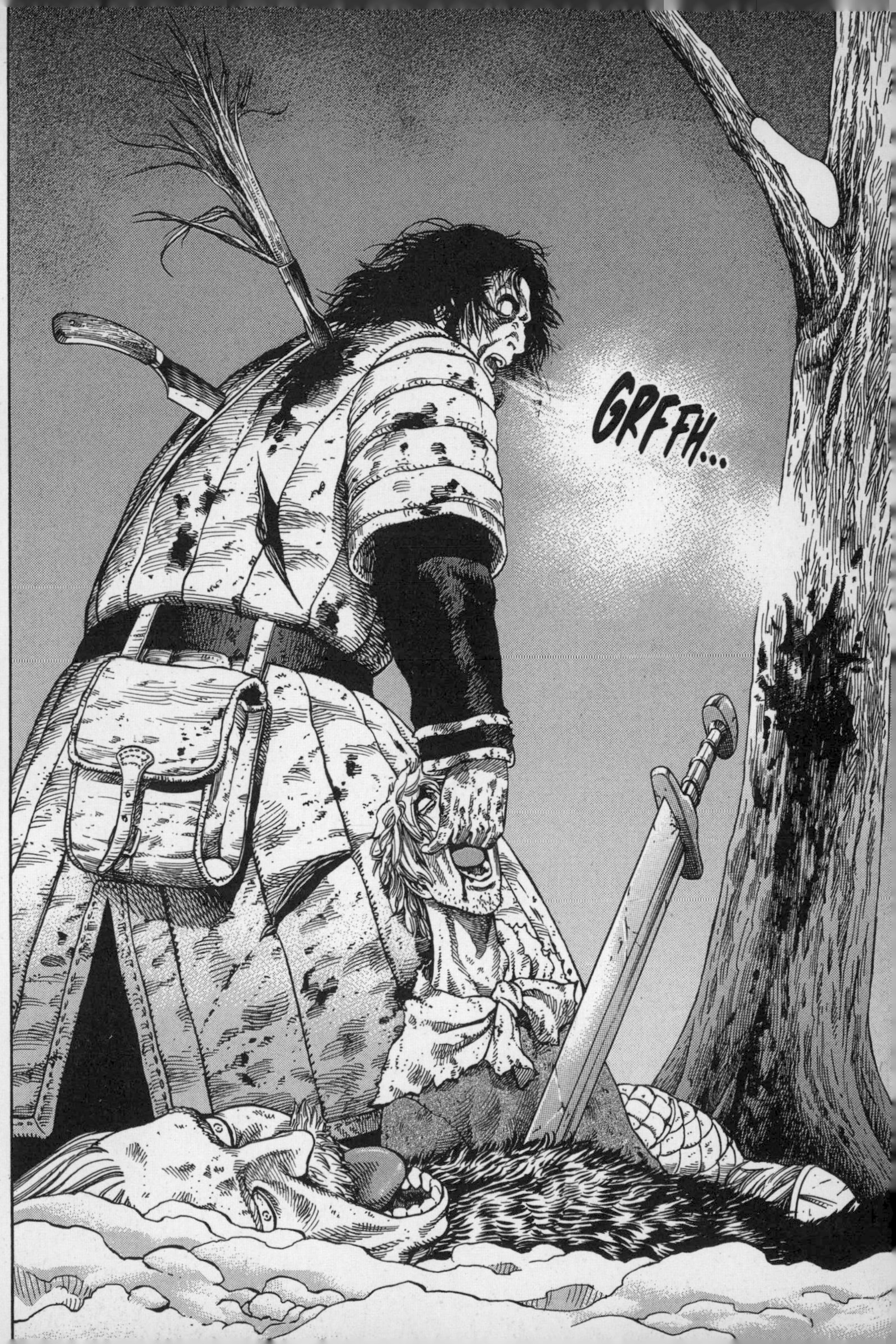
GRFFH...

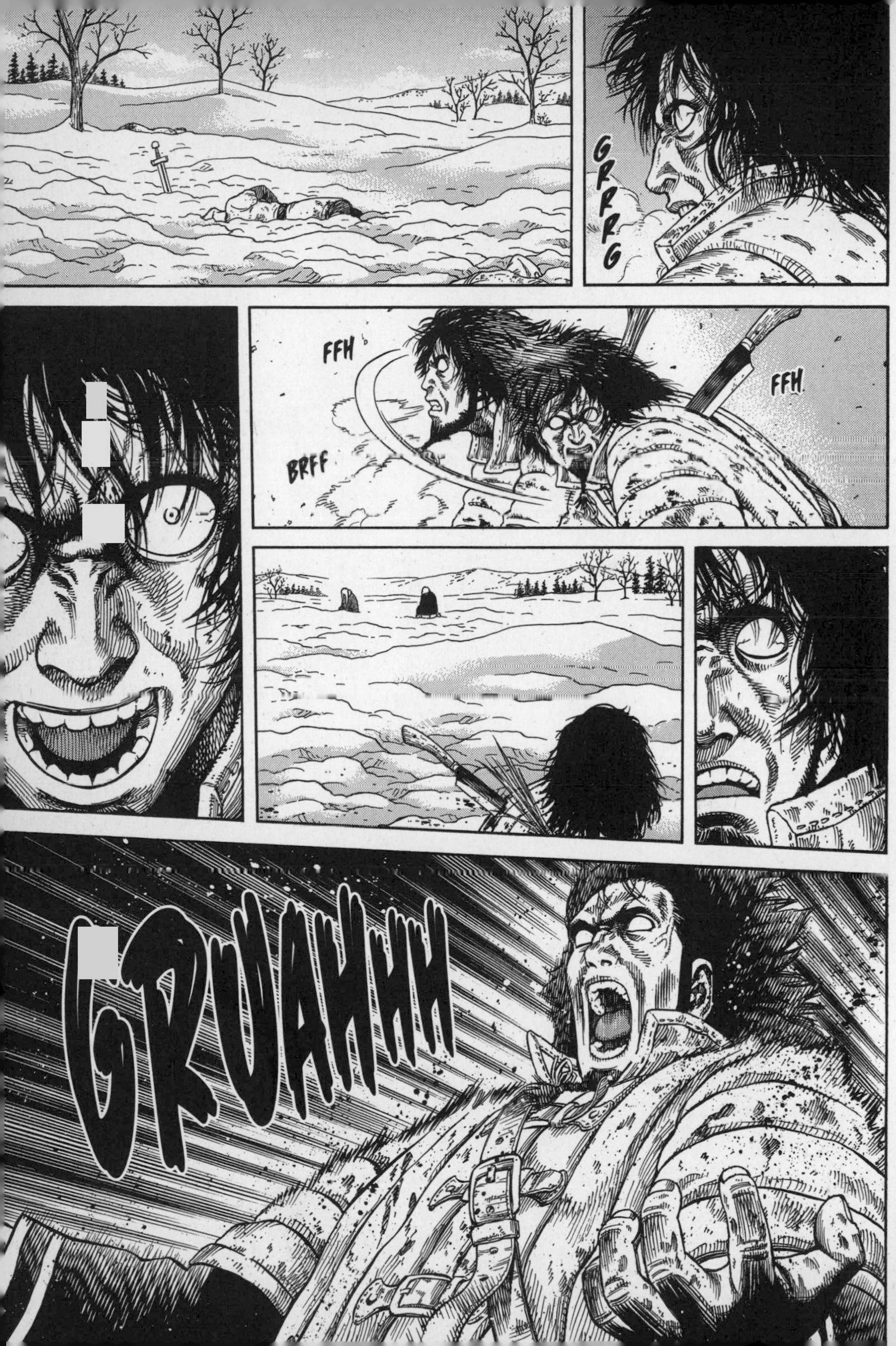
GRRRG
FFH
FFH
BRFF
GRUAHHH

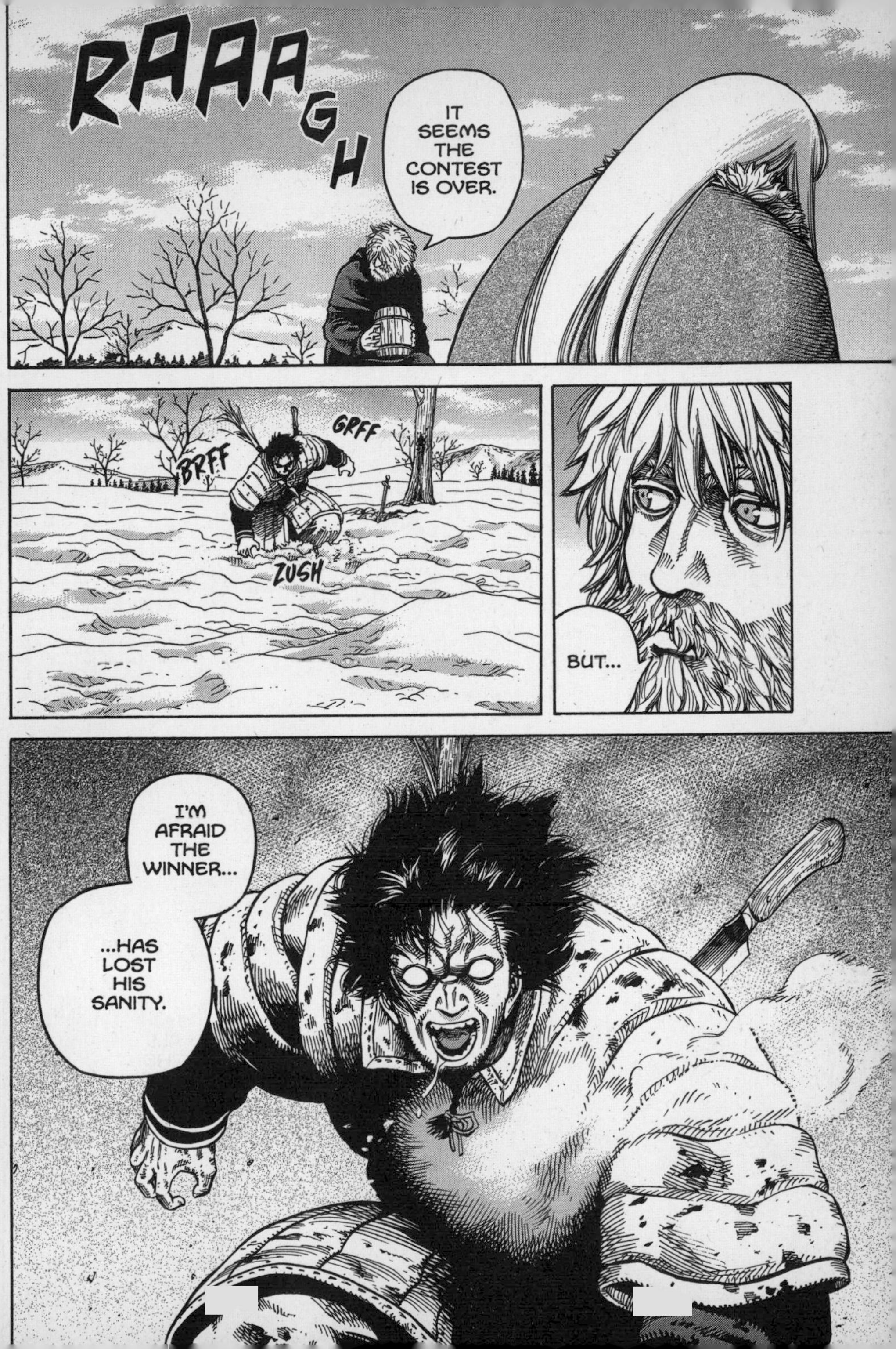
RAAAGH
IT SEEMS THE CONTEST IS OVER.
BUT...
GRFF
BRFF
ZUSH
I'M AFRAID THE WINNER...
...HAS LOST HIS SANITY.

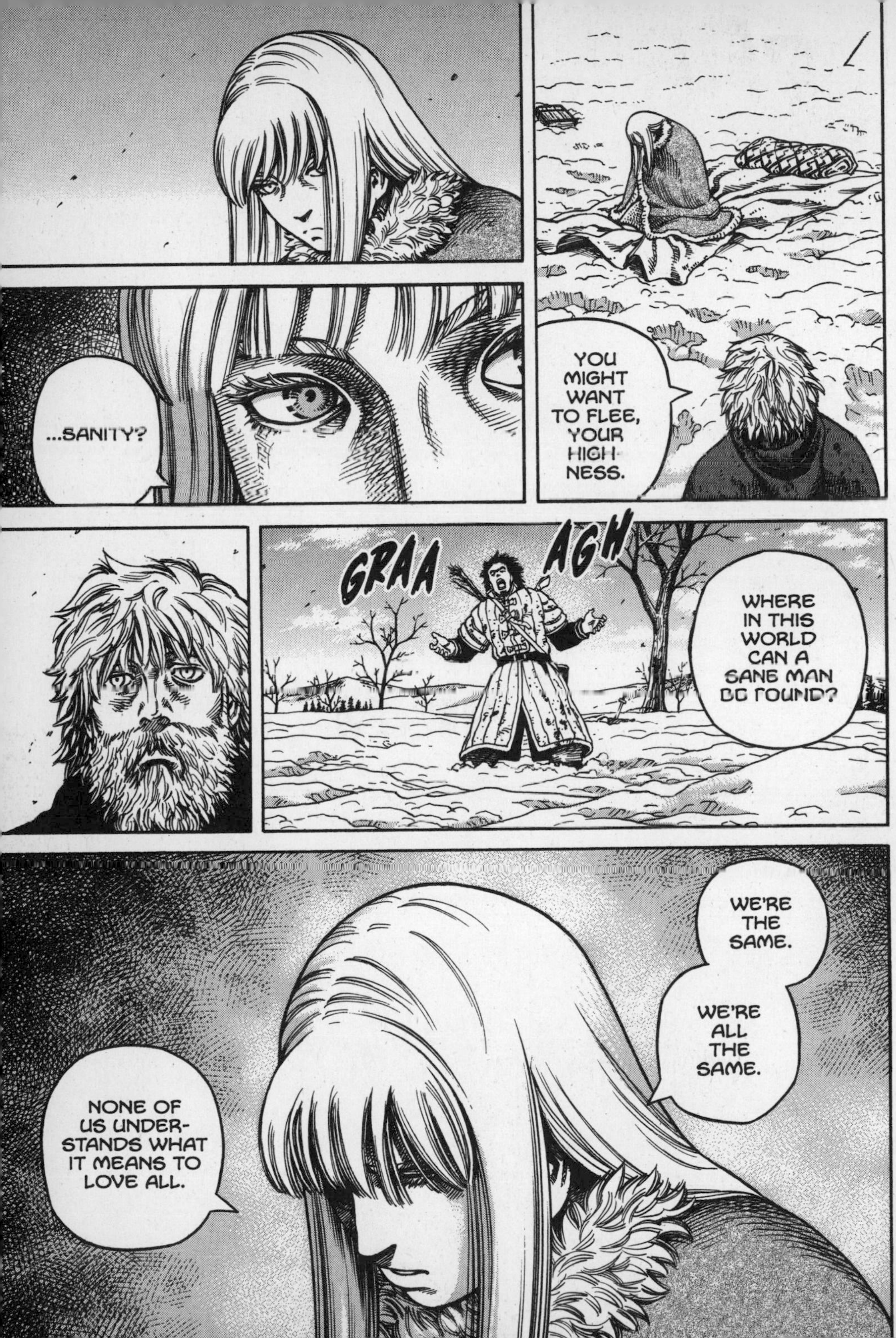
YOU MIGHT WANT TO FLEE, YOUR HIGHNESS.
...SANITY?
GRAA AGH
WHERE IN THIS WORLD CAN A SANE MAN BE FOUND?
WE'RE THE SAME.
WE'RE ALL THE SAME.
NONE OF US UNDER-STANDS WHAT IT MEANS TO LOVE ALL.

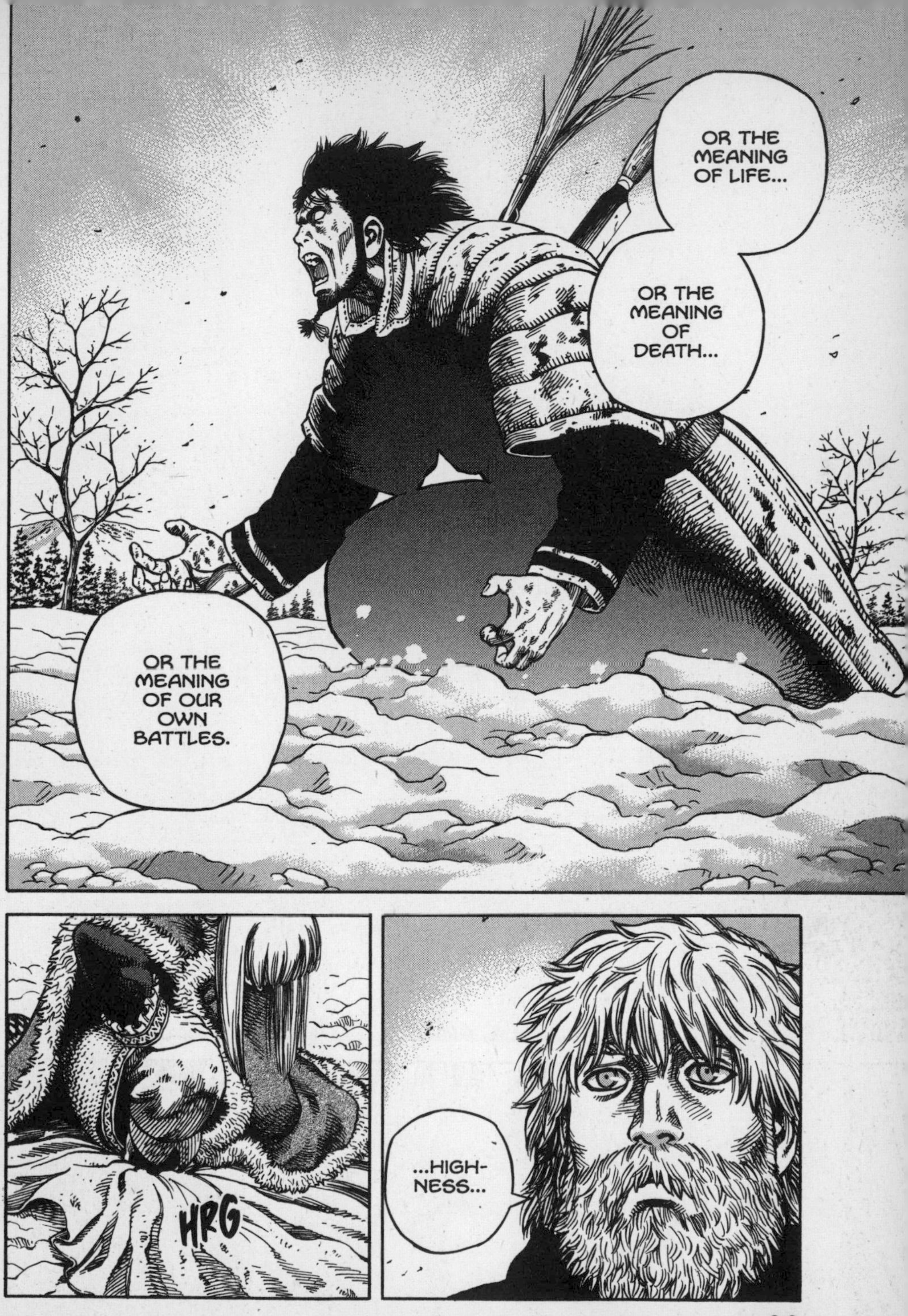
OR THE MEANING OF LIFE...
OR THE MEANING OF DEATH...
OR THE MEANING OF OUR OWN BATTLES.
...HIGH-NESS...
HRG

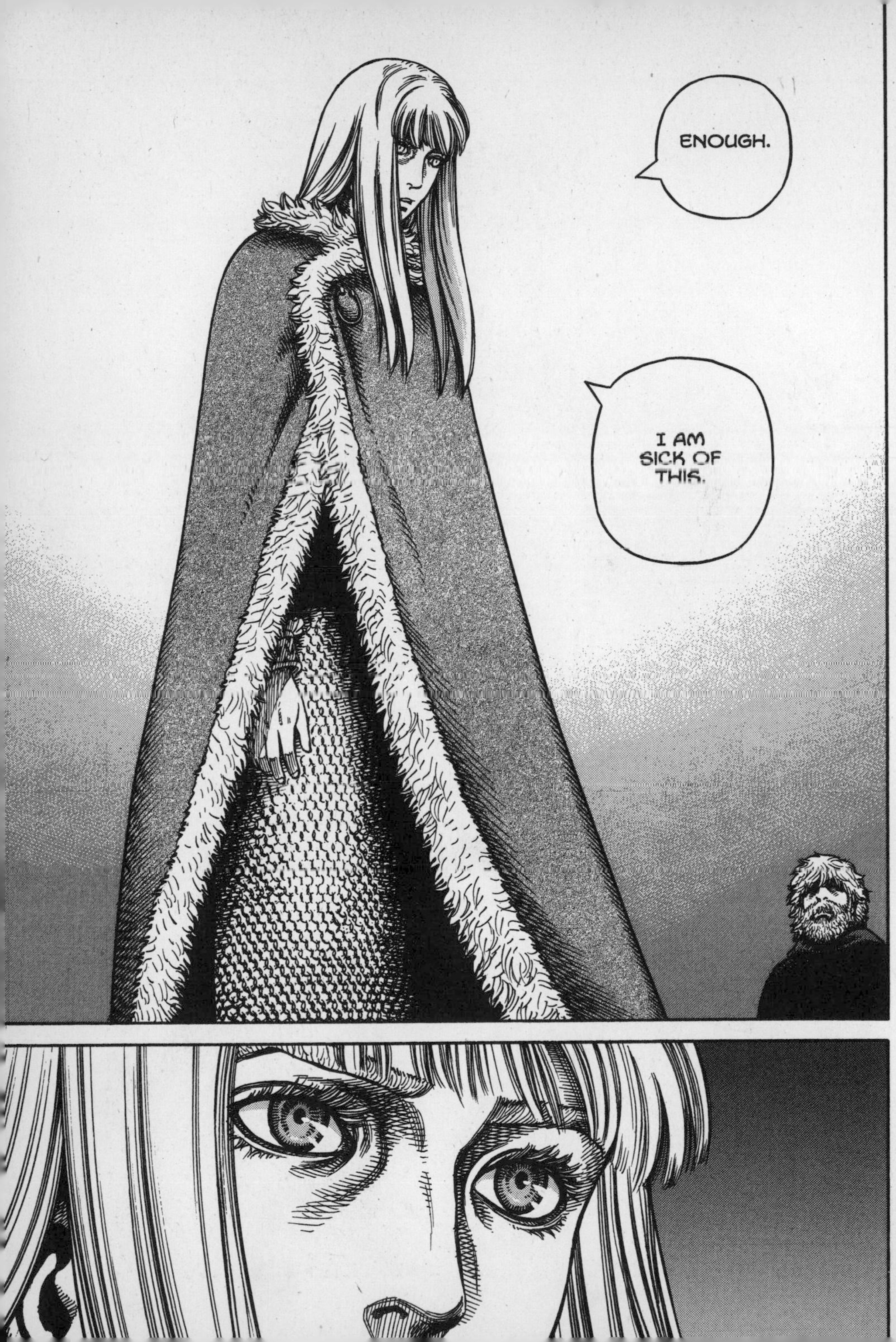
ENOUGH.
I AM SICK OF THIS.

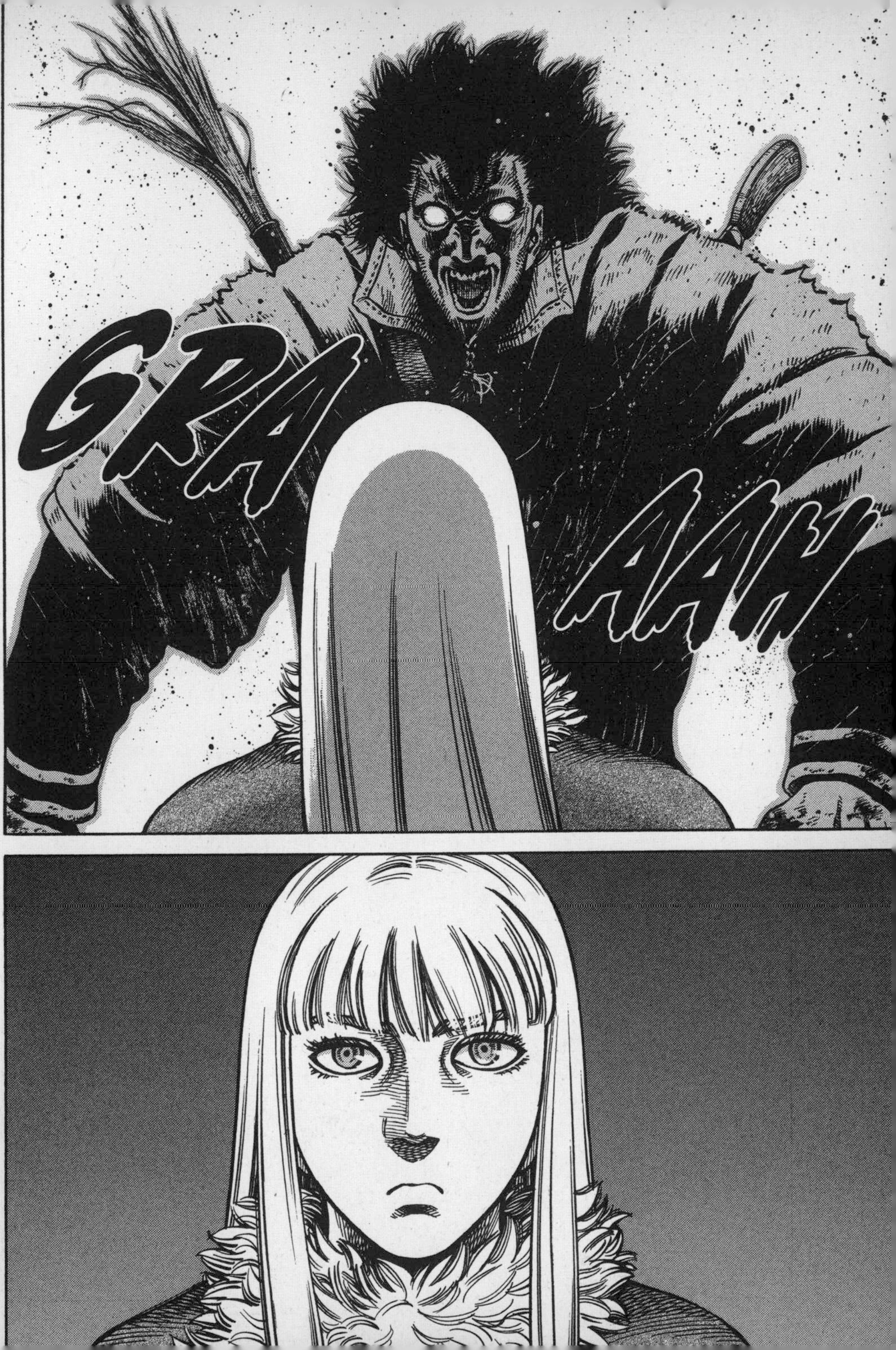
GRA
AAH

CHAPTER 38 • END

# CHAPTER 39: THE KING AWAKENS

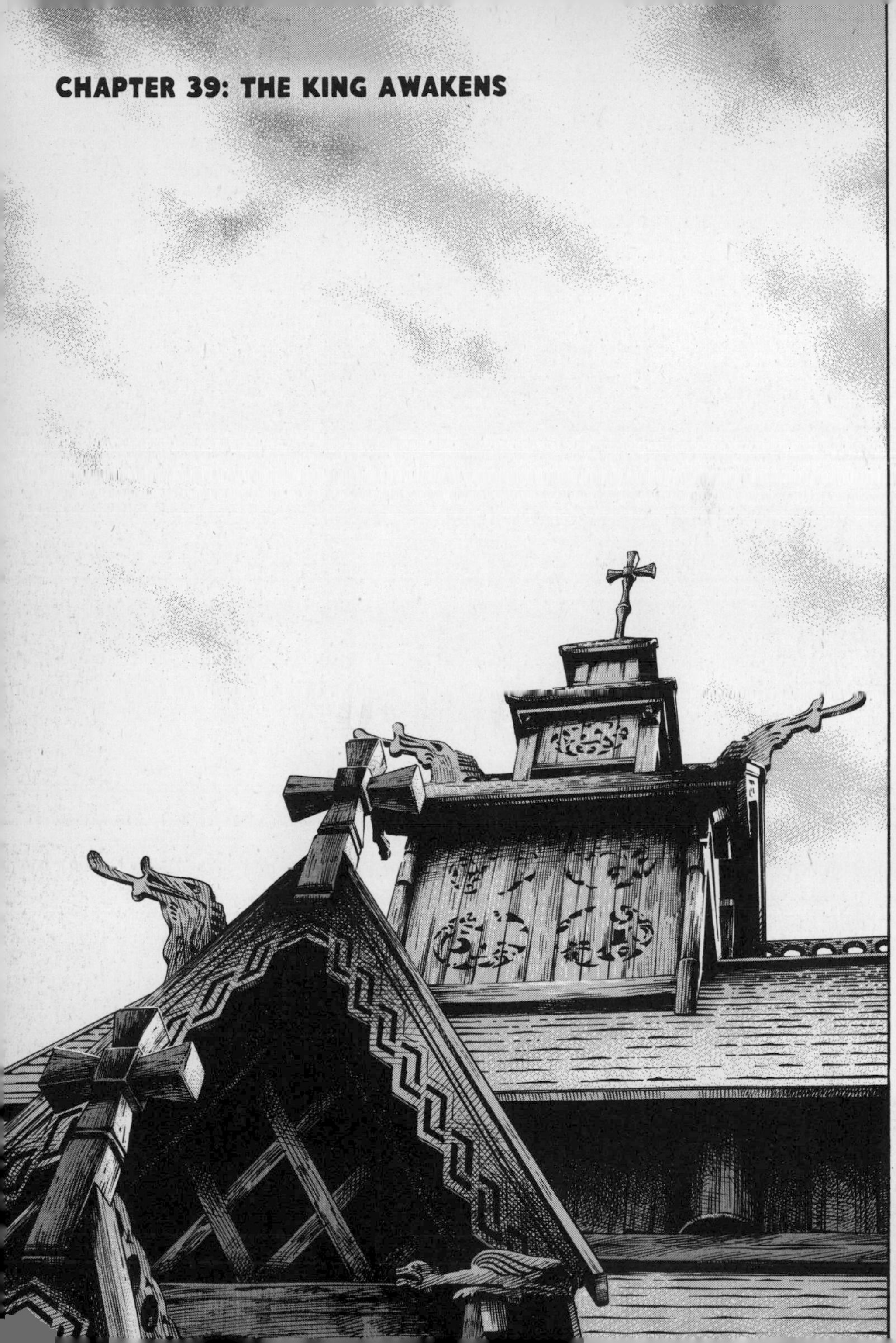

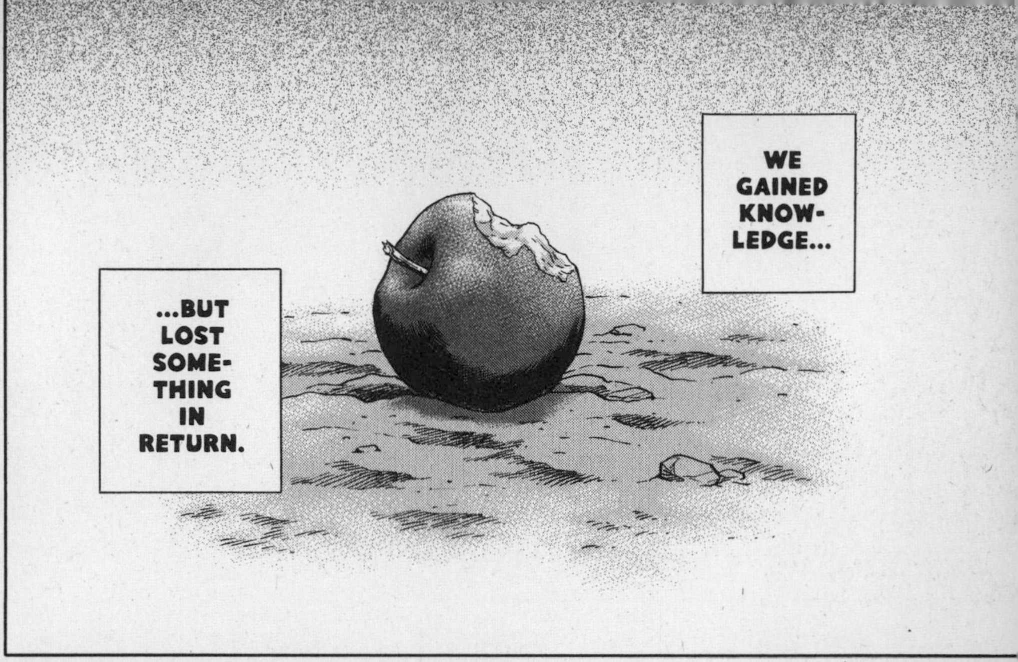
WE GAINED KNOW-LEDGE...
...BUT LOST SOME-THING IN RETURN.
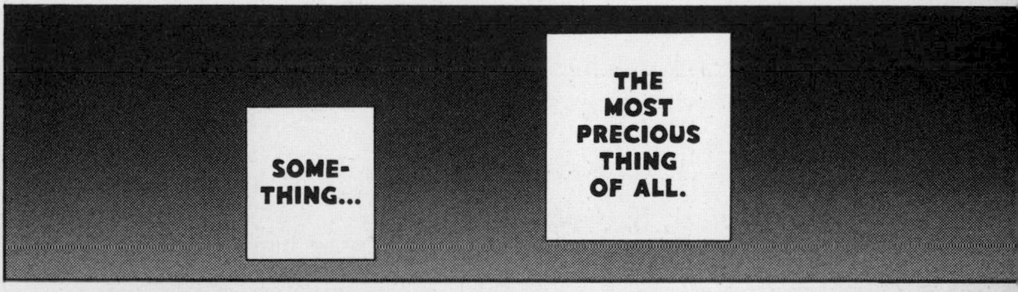
THE MOST PRECIOUS THING OF ALL.
SOME-THING...
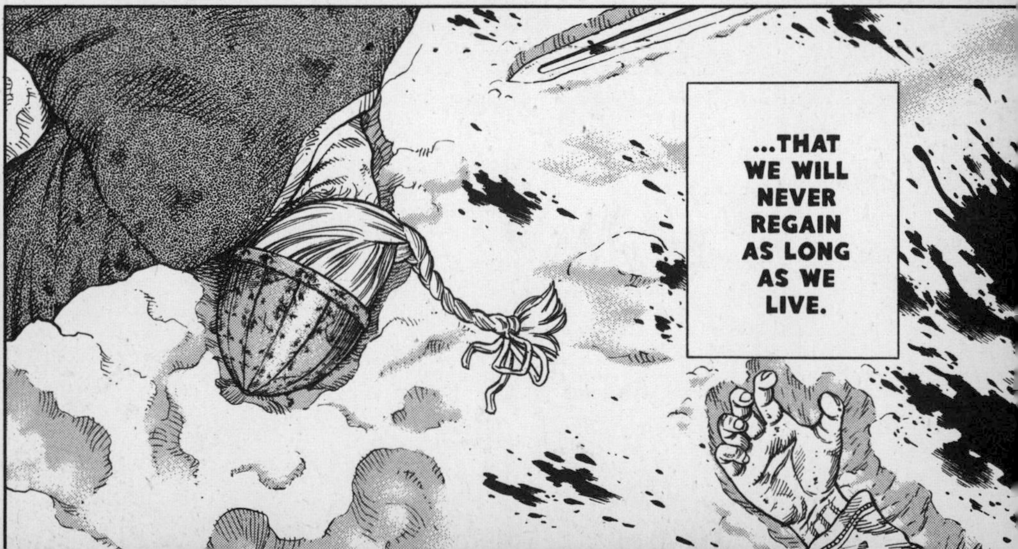
...THAT WE WILL NEVER REGAIN AS LONG AS WE LIVE.

GRRRGG...

...

AND YET...

WE WILL NEVER HAVE IT BACK.

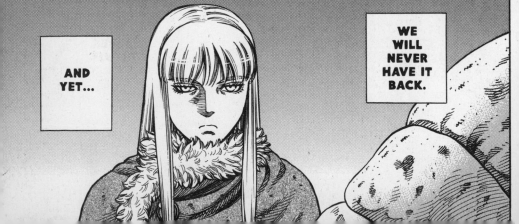

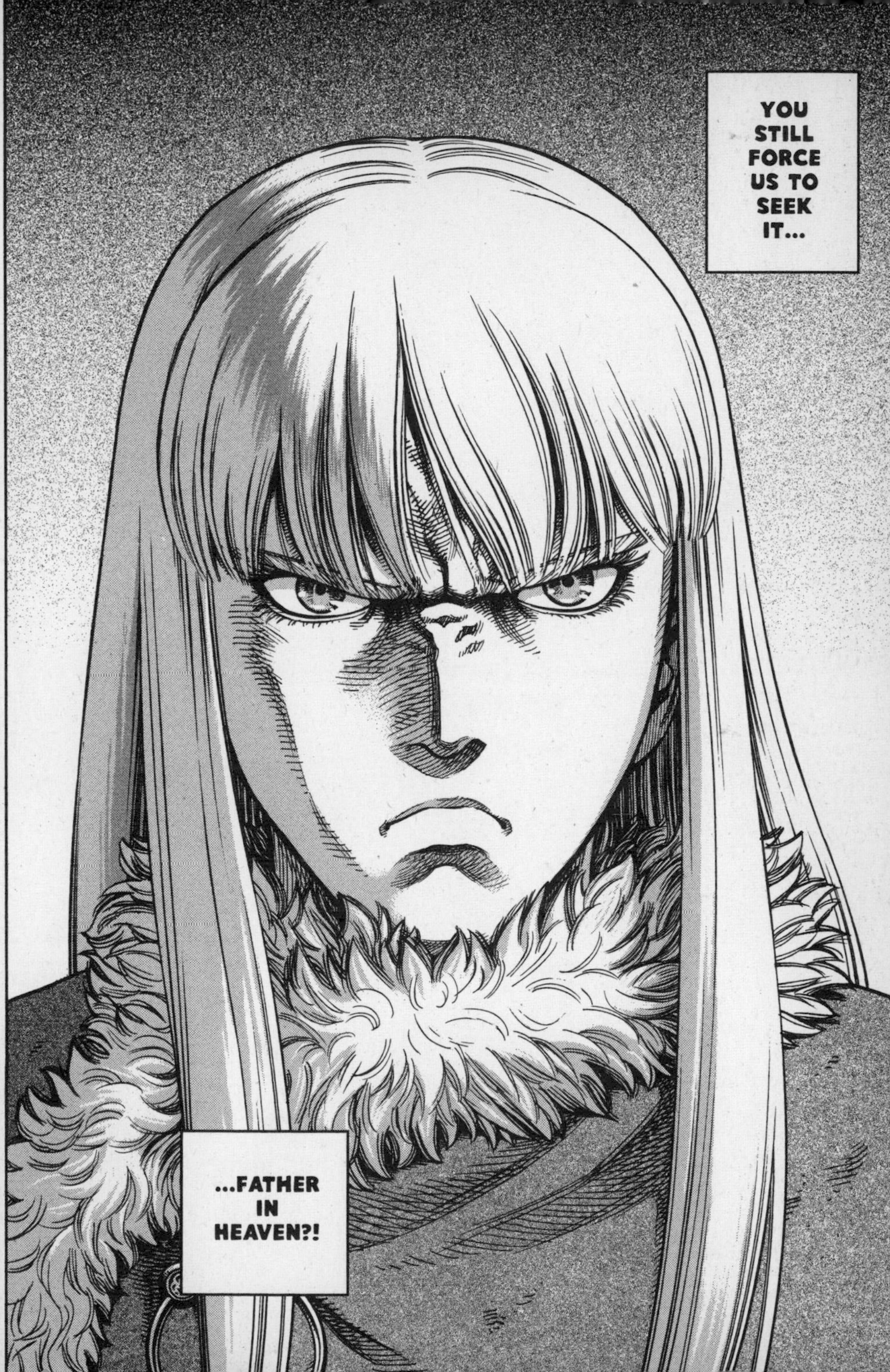
YOU STILL FORCE US TO SEEK IT...
...FATHER IN HEAVEN?!

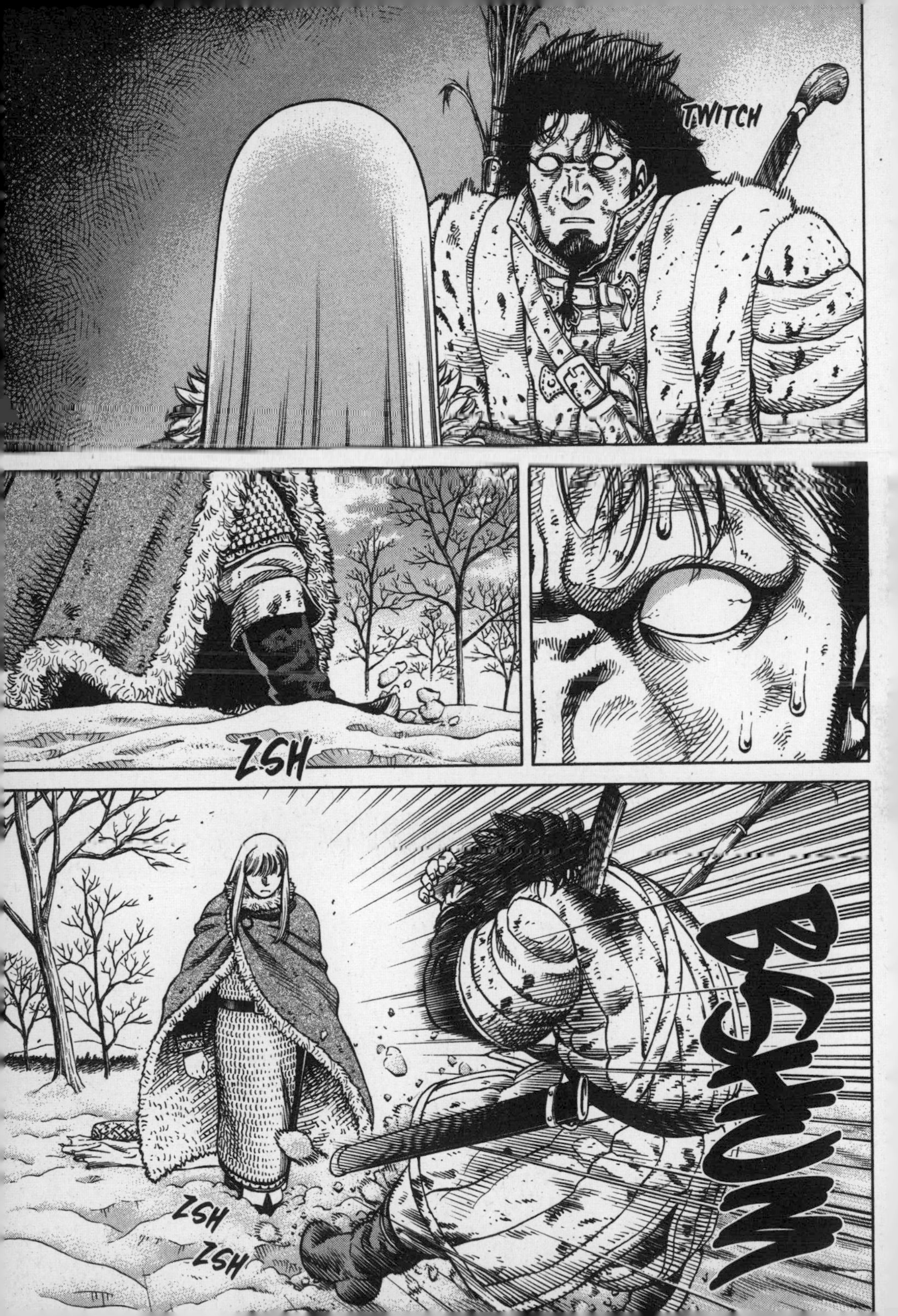
TWITCH
ZSH
BASHUM
ZSH
ZSH

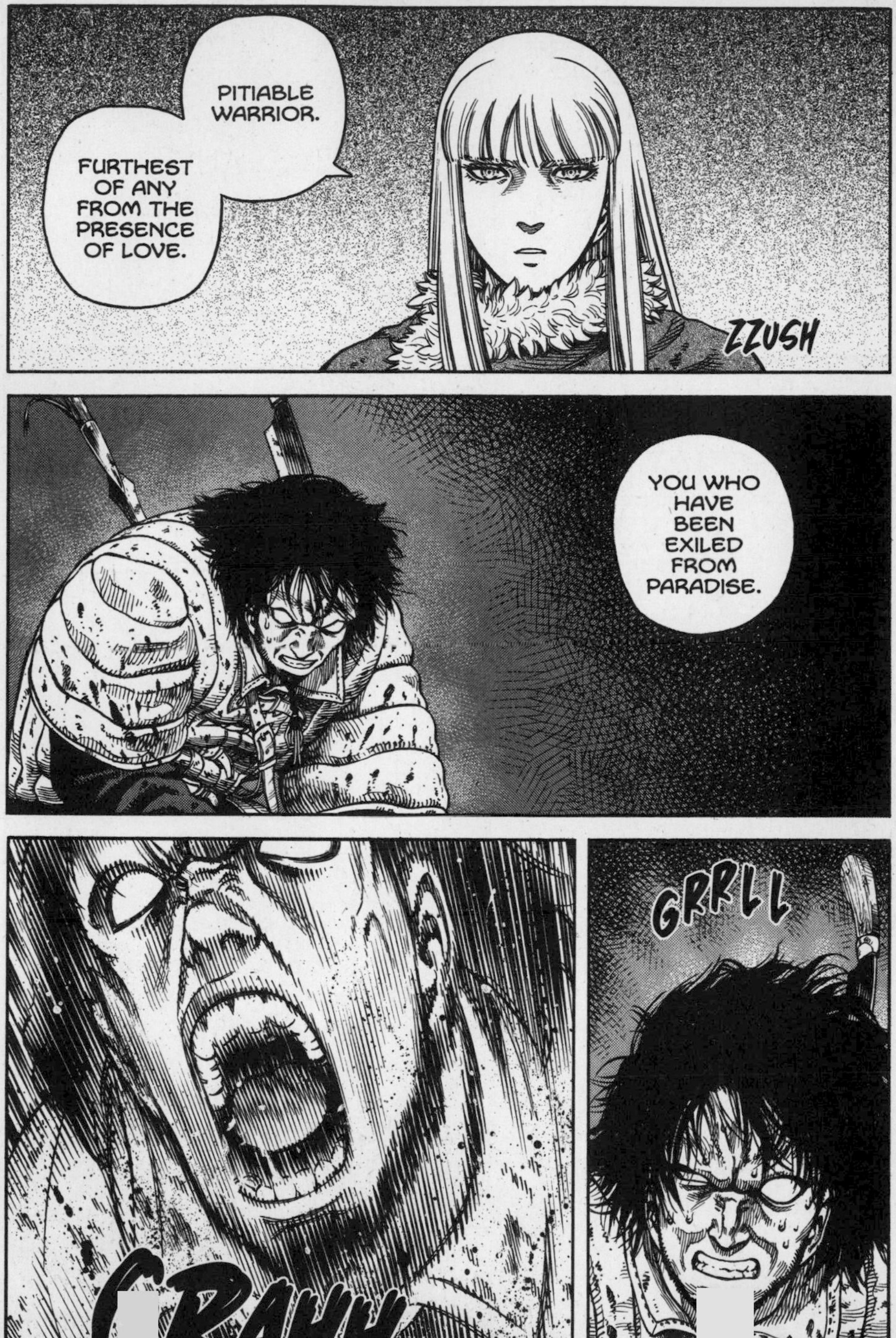
PITIABLE WARRIOR.
FURTHEST OF ANY FROM THE PRESENCE OF LOVE.
ZZUSH
YOU WHO HAVE BEEN EXILED FROM PARADISE.
GRRLL
CRAHH

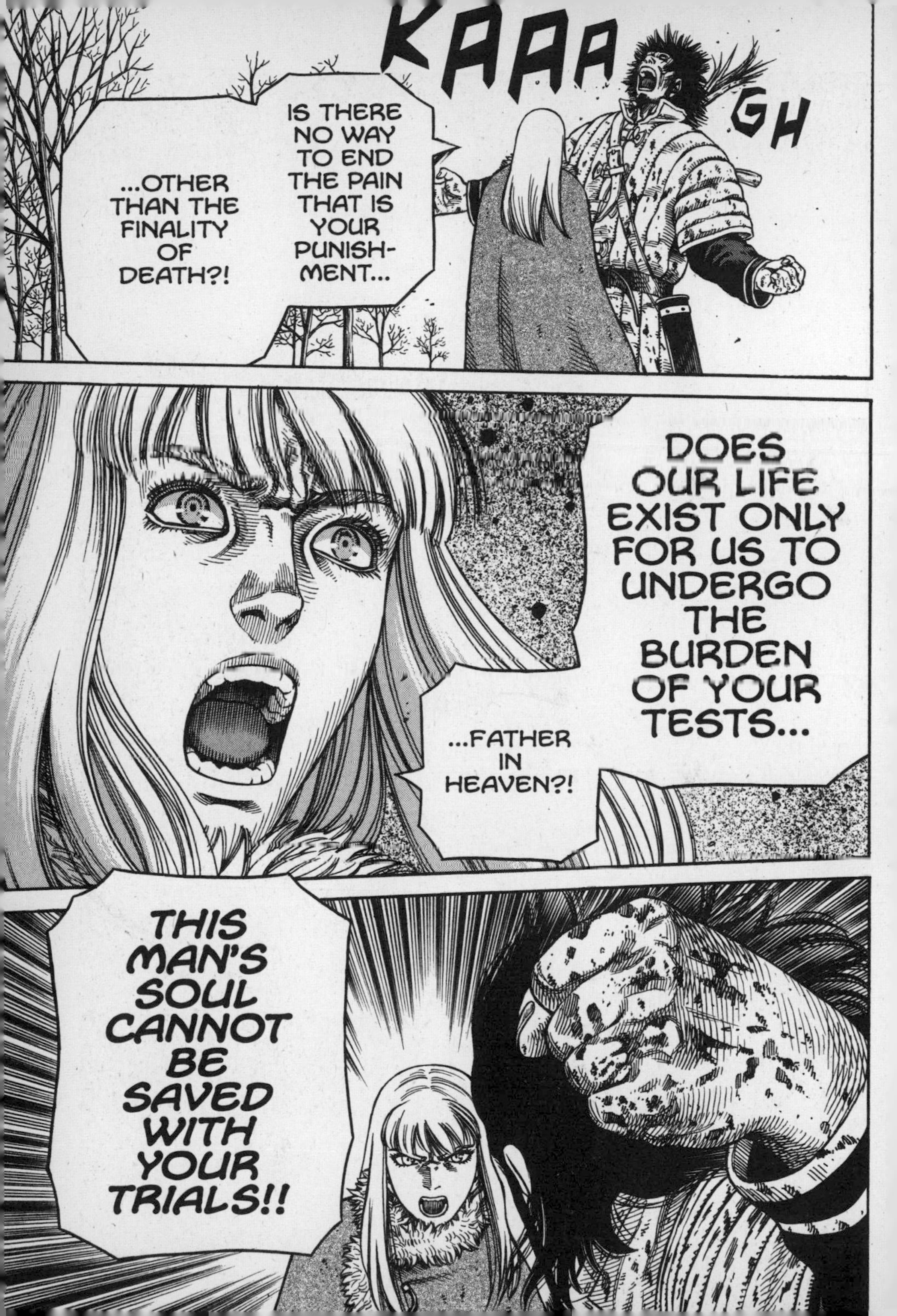
KAAAGH
IS THERE NO WAY TO END THE PAIN THAT IS YOUR PUNISHMENT...
...OTHER THAN THE FINALITY OF DEATH?!
DOES OUR LIFE EXIST ONLY FOR US TO UNDERGO THE BURDEN OF YOUR TESTS...
...FATHER IN HEAVEN?!
THIS MAN'S SOUL CANNOT BE SAVED WITH YOUR TRIALS!!

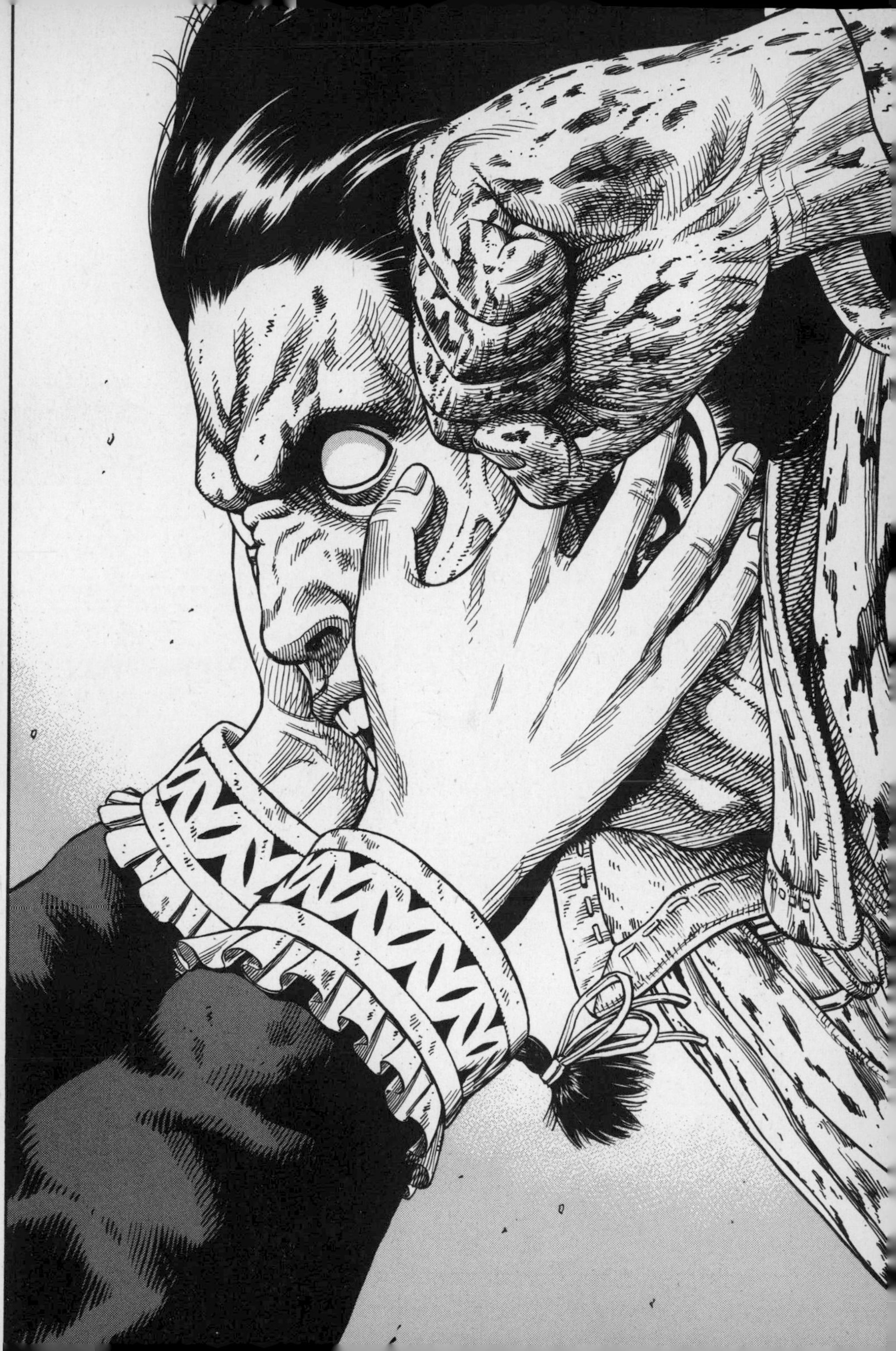

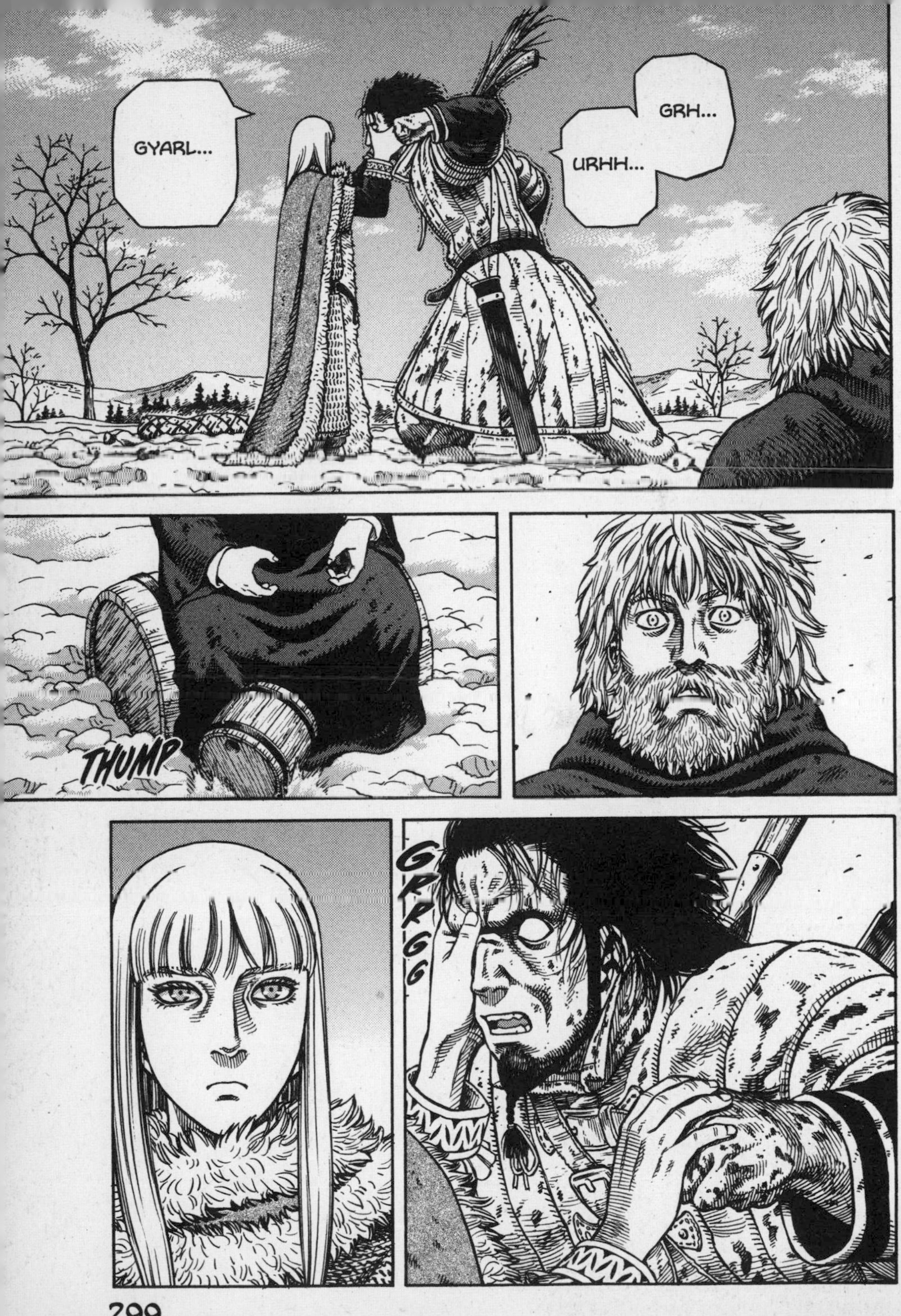
GRH...
URHH...
GYARL...
THUMP
GRRGG

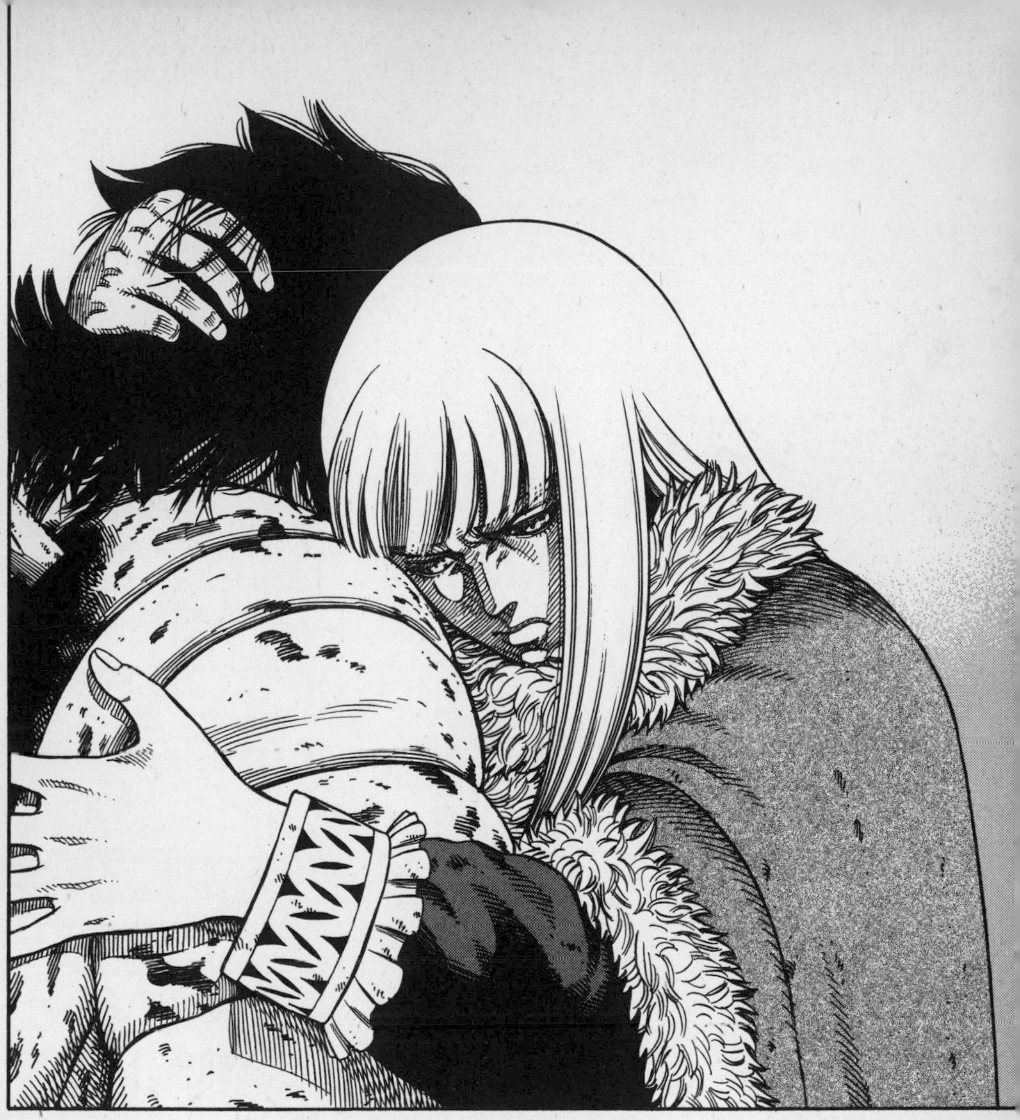
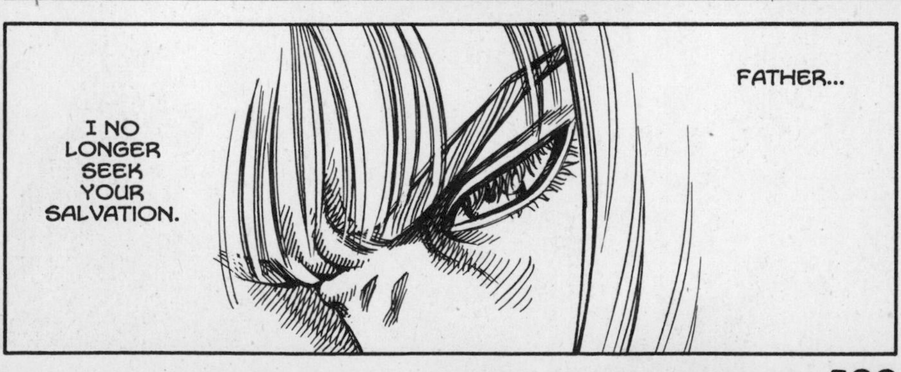
FATHER...
I NO LONGER SEEK YOUR SALVATION.

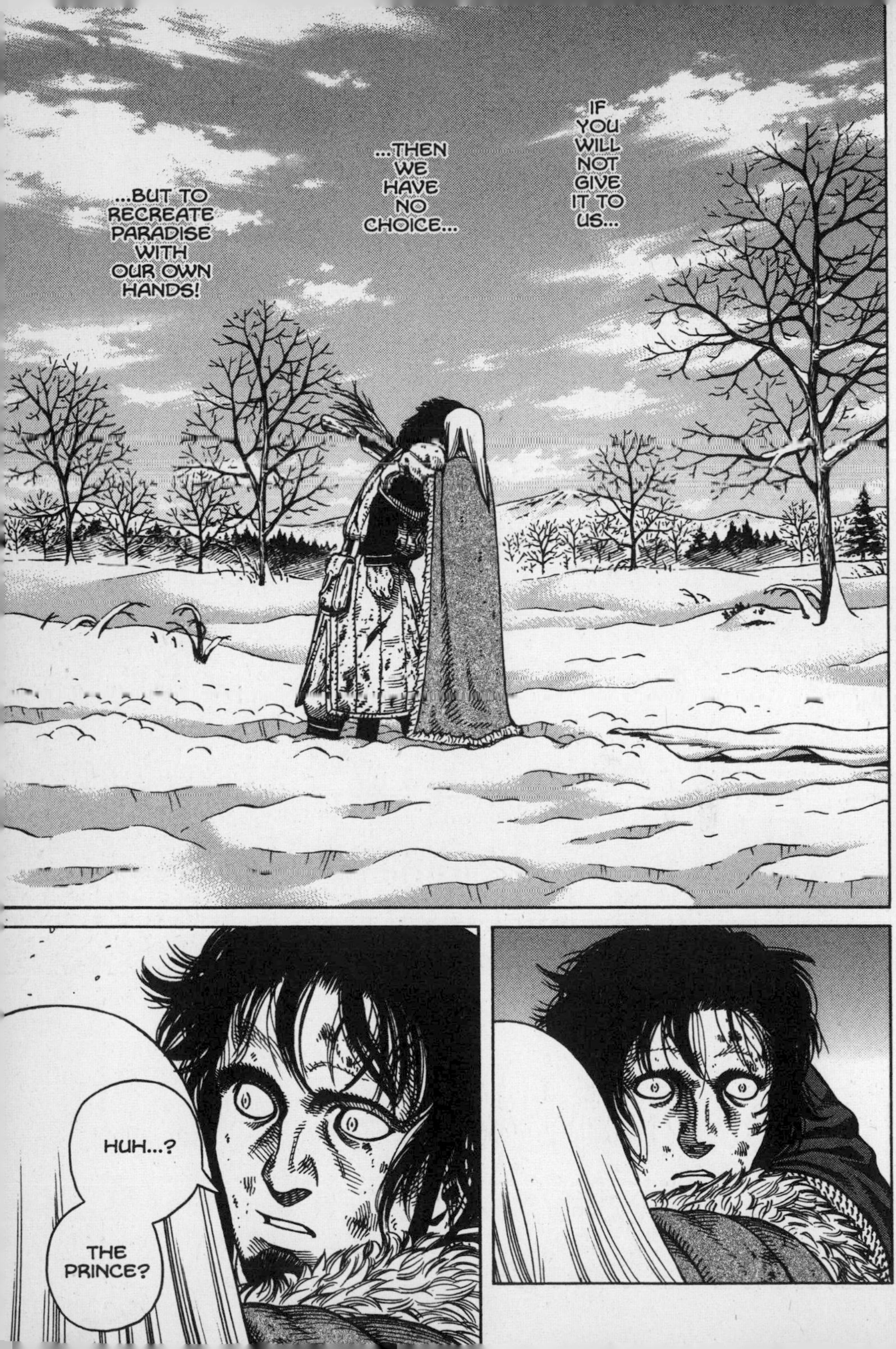
IF YOU WILL NOT GIVE IT TO US...
...THEN WE HAVE NO CHOICE...
...BUT TO RECREATE PARADISE WITH OUR OWN HANDS!
HUH...?
THE PRINCE?

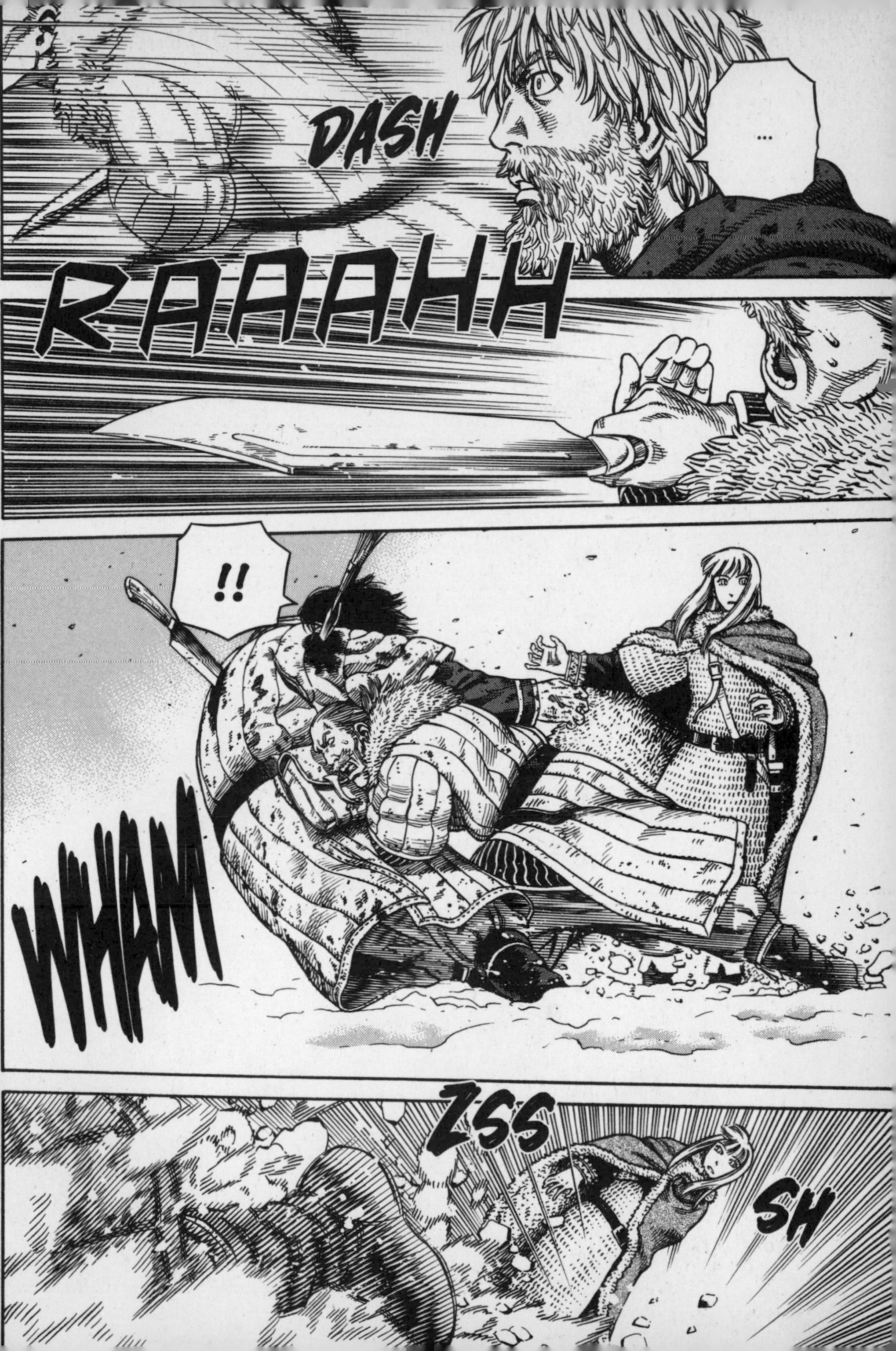
...
DASH
RAAAAHH
!!
WHAM
ZSS
SH

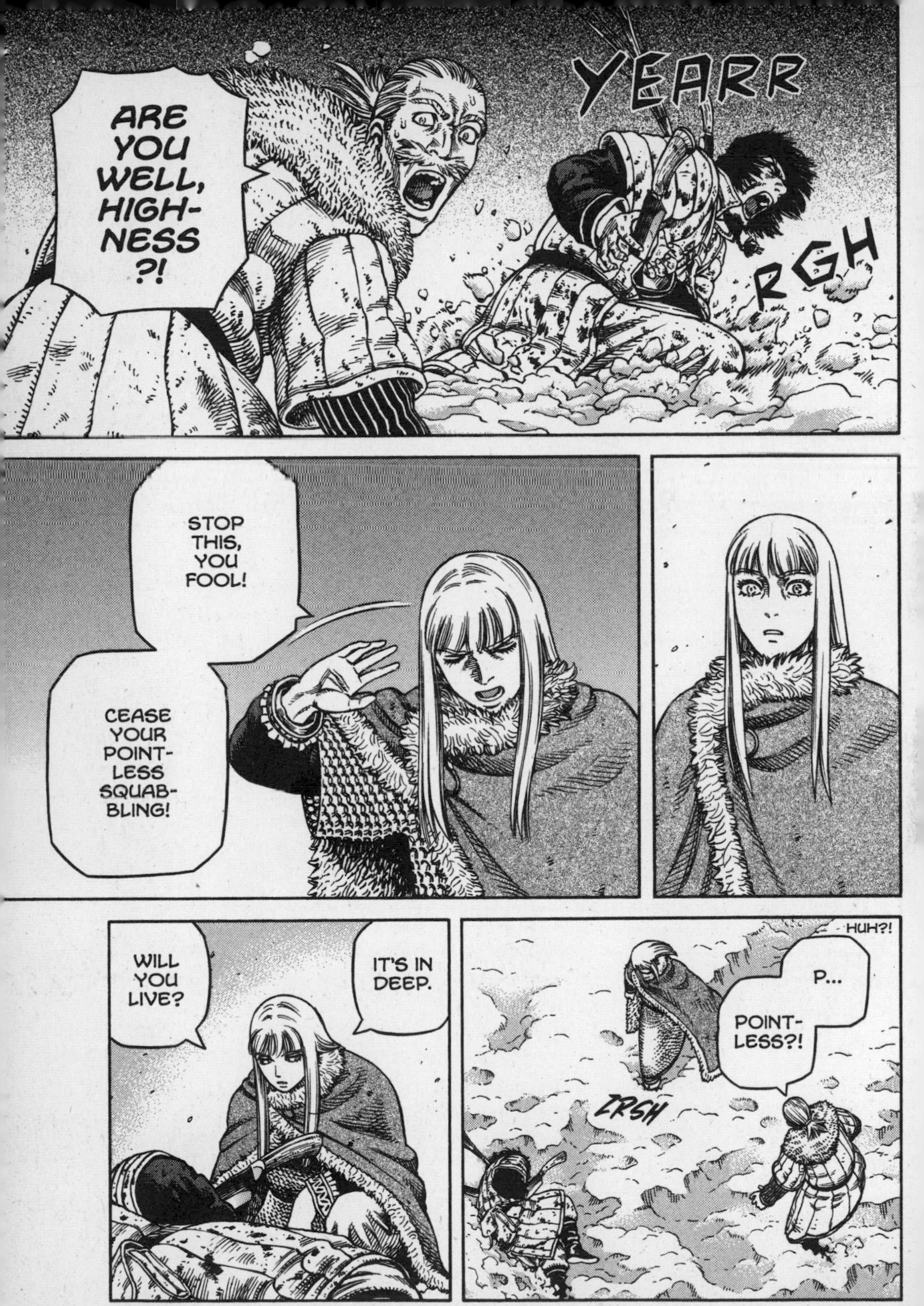
YEARR
RGH
ARE YOU WELL, HIGHNESS?!
STOP THIS, YOU FOOL!
CEASE YOUR POINTLESS SQUABBLING!
HUH?!
P... POINTLESS?!
ZRSH
IT'S IN DEEP.
WILL YOU LIVE?

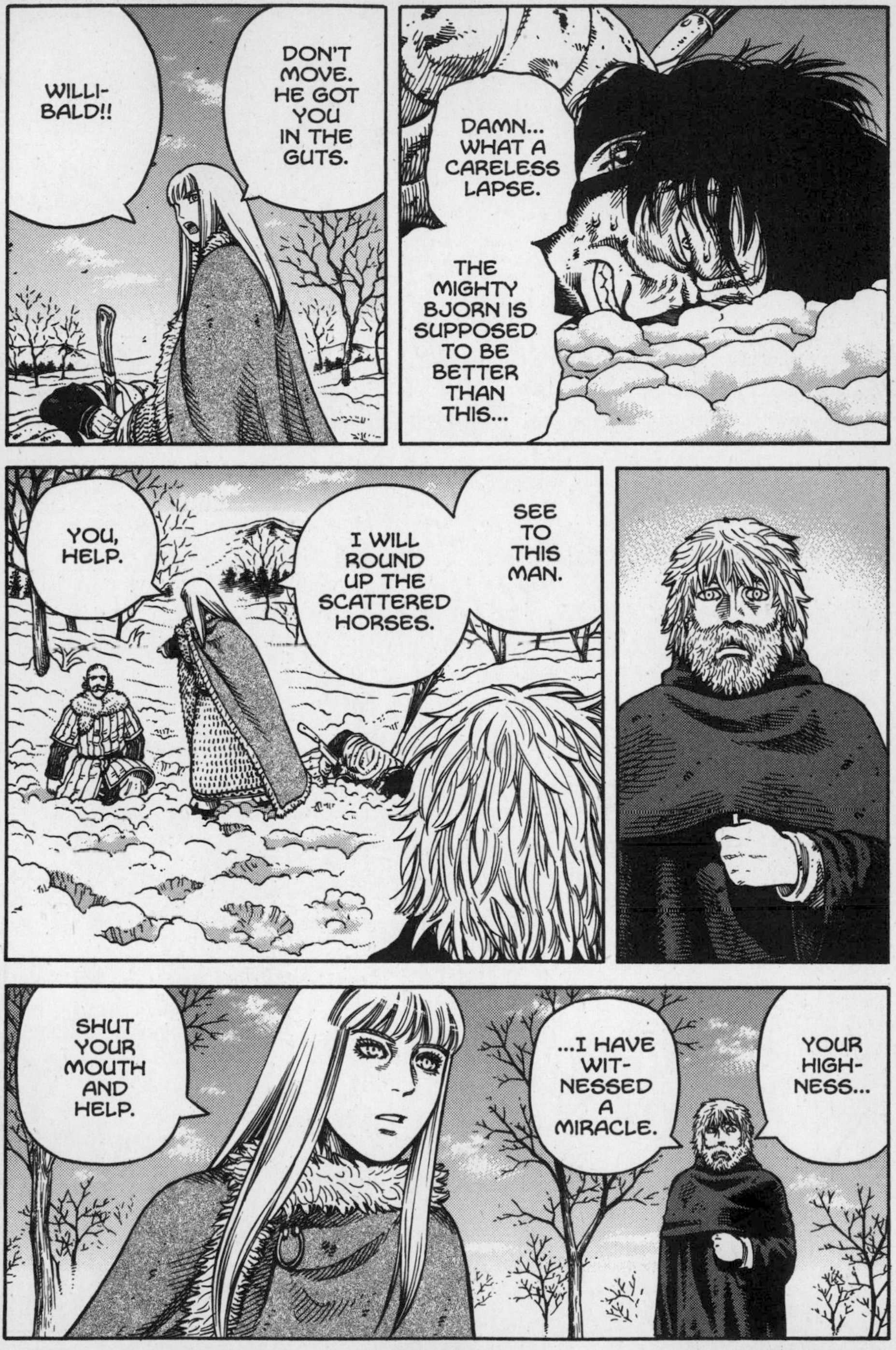
DAMN... WHAT A CARELESS LAPSE.
THE MIGHTY BJORN IS SUPPOSED TO BE BETTER THAN THIS...
DON'T MOVE. HE GOT YOU IN THE GUTS.
WILLI-BALD!!
SEE TO THIS MAN.
I WILL ROUND UP THE SCATTERED HORSES.
YOU, HELP.
YOUR HIGH-NESS...
...I HAVE WIT-NESSED A MIRACLE.
SHUT YOUR MOUTH AND HELP.

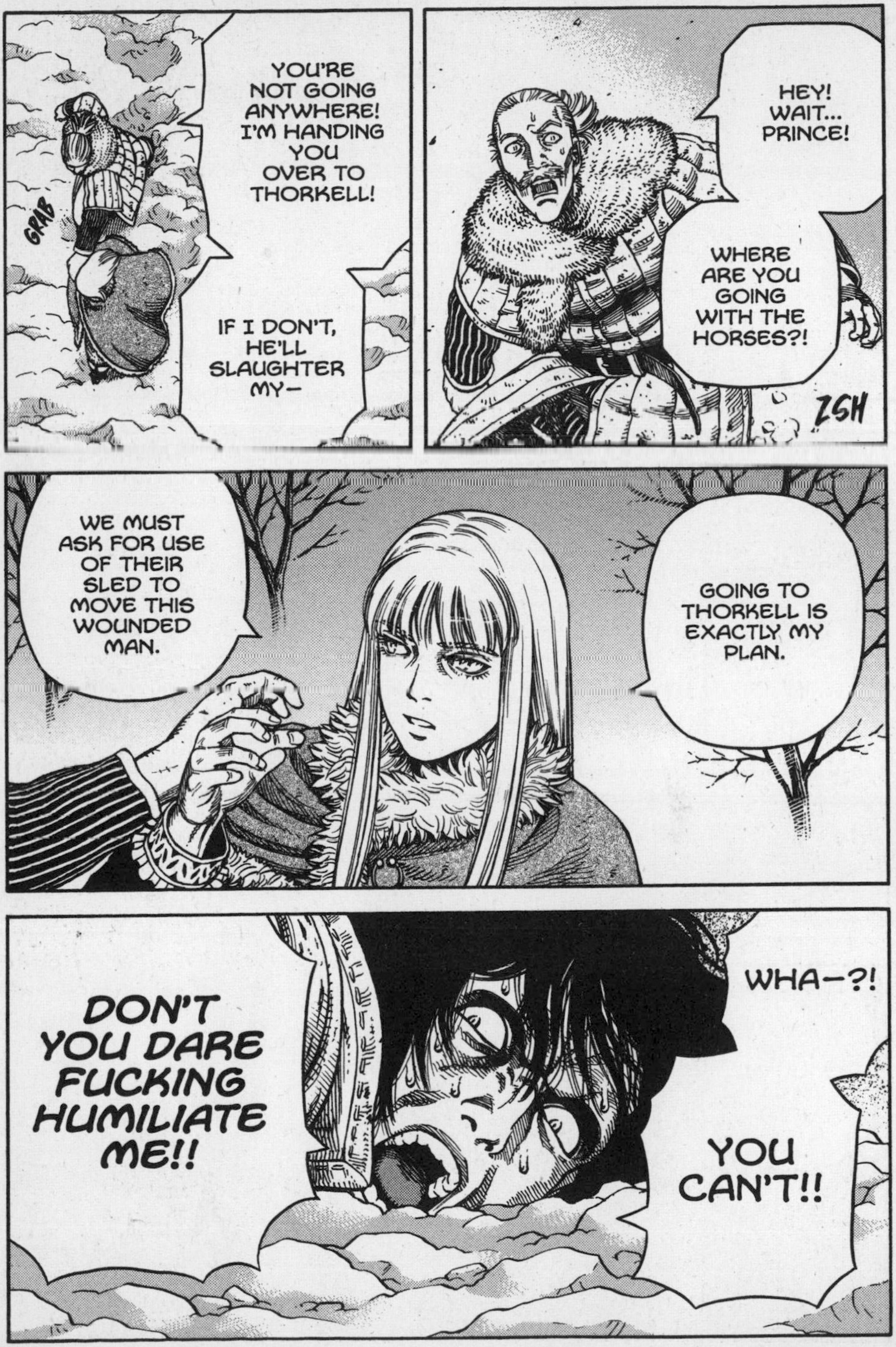
HEY! WAIT... PRINCE!
WHERE ARE YOU GOING WITH THE HORSES?!
ZSH
GRAB
YOU'RE NOT GOING ANYWHERE! I'M HANDING YOU OVER TO THORKELL!
IF I DON'T, HE'LL SLAUGHTER MY—
GOING TO THORKELL IS EXACTLY MY PLAN.
WE MUST ASK FOR USE OF THEIR SLED TO MOVE THIS WOUNDED MAN.
WHA—?!
YOU CAN'T!!
DON'T YOU DARE FUCKING HUMILIATE ME!!

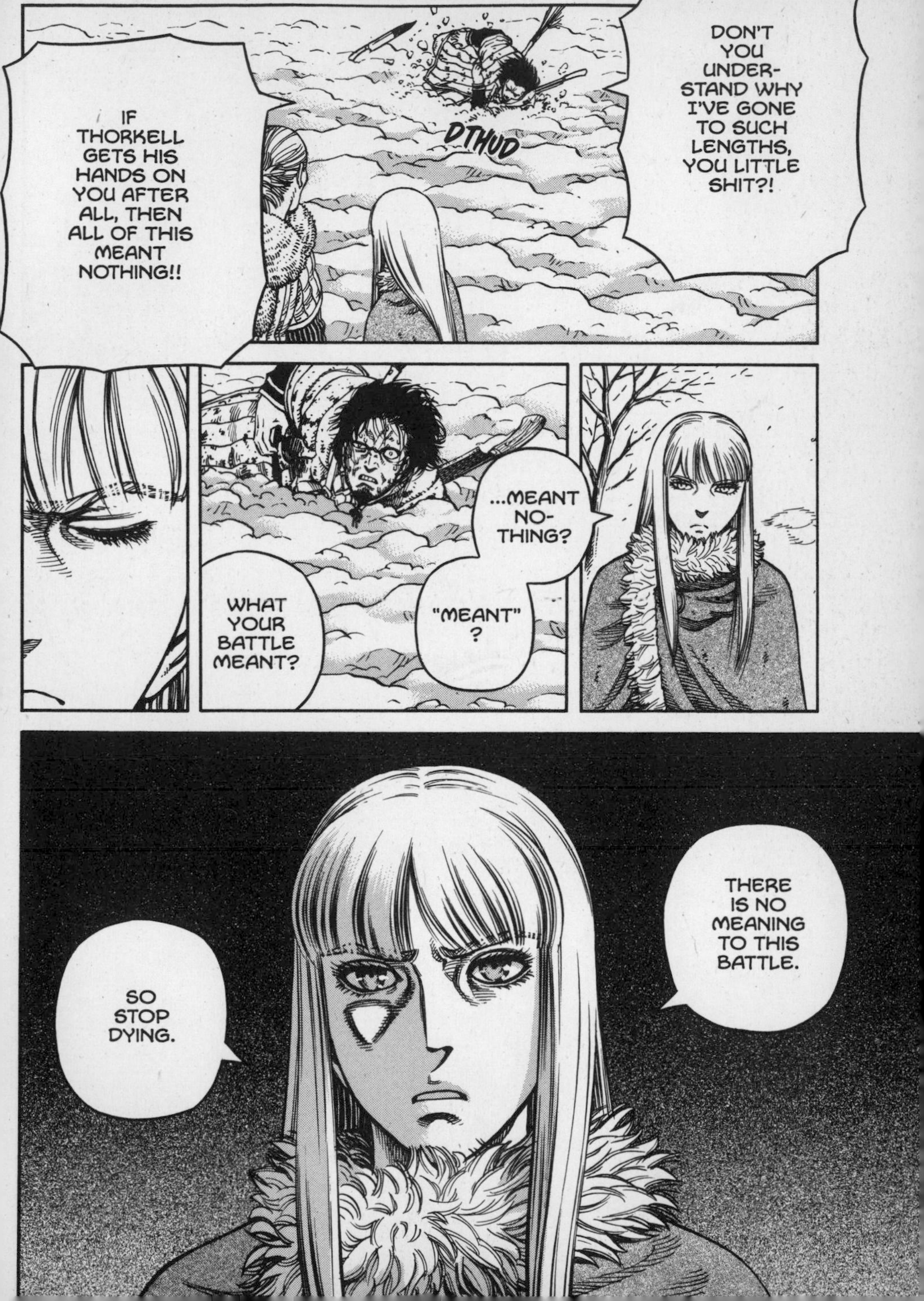
DON'T YOU UNDER-STAND WHY I'VE GONE TO SUCH LENGTHS, YOU LITTLE SHIT?!
IF THORKELL GETS HIS HANDS ON YOU AFTER ALL, THEN ALL OF THIS MEANT NOTHING!!
DTHUD
...MEANT NO-THING?
"MEANT" ?
WHAT YOUR BATTLE MEANT?
THERE IS NO MEANING TO THIS BATTLE.
SO STOP DYING.

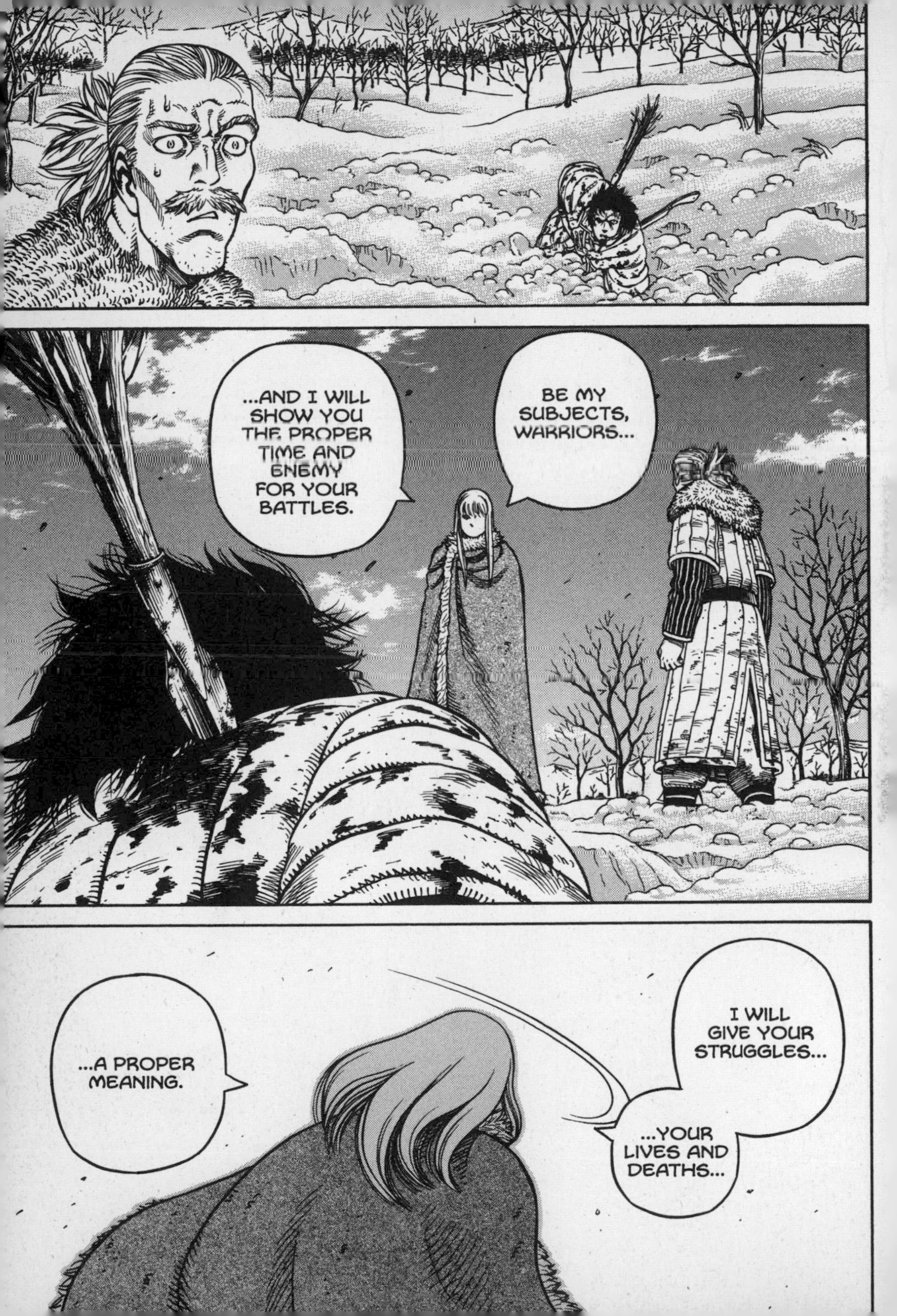
BE MY SUBJECTS, WARRIORS...
...AND I WILL SHOW YOU THE PROPER TIME AND ENEMY FOR YOUR BATTLES.
I WILL GIVE YOUR STRUGGLES...
...YOUR LIVES AND DEATHS...
...A PROPER MEANING.

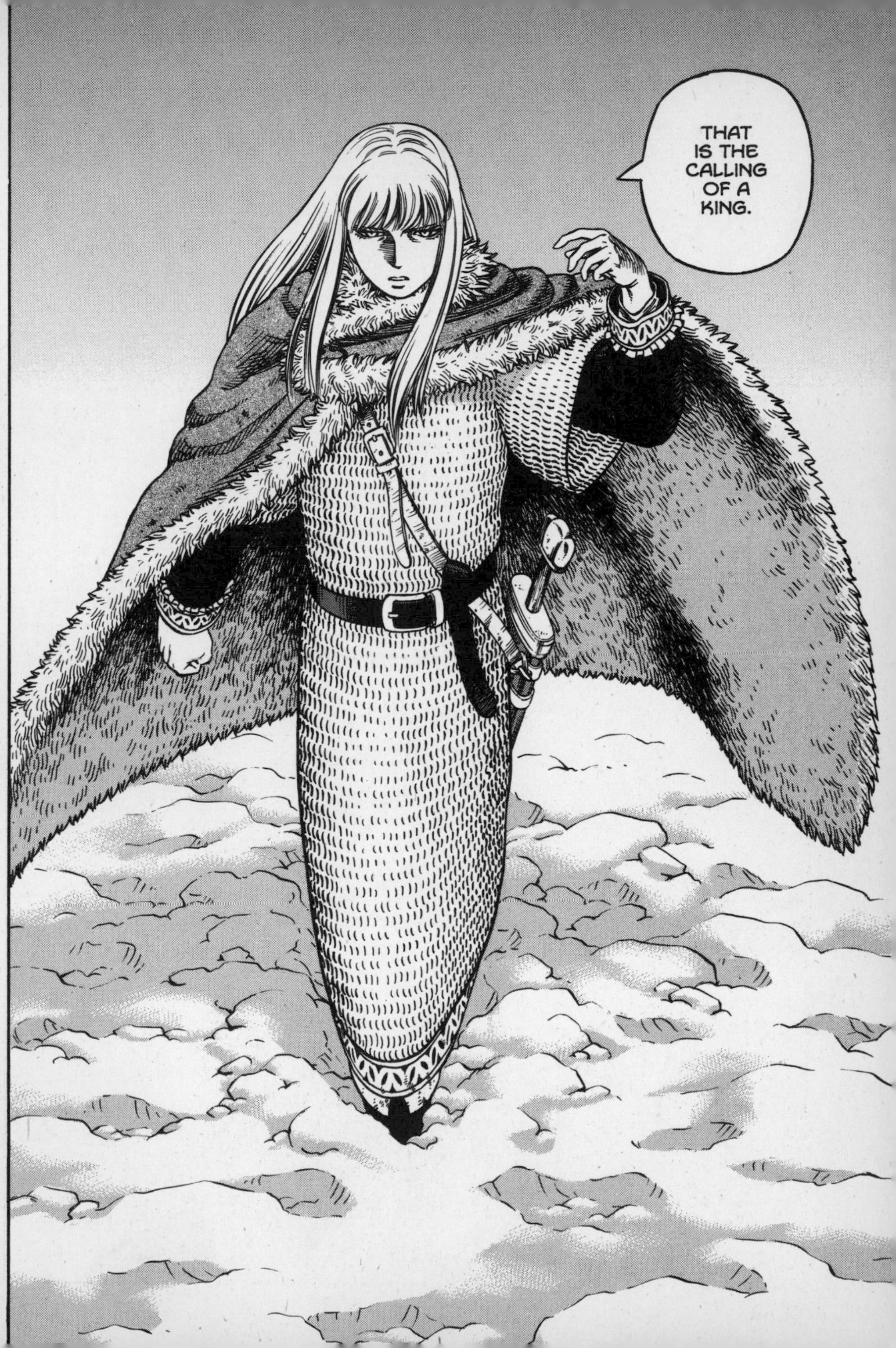
THAT IS THE CALLING OF A KING.

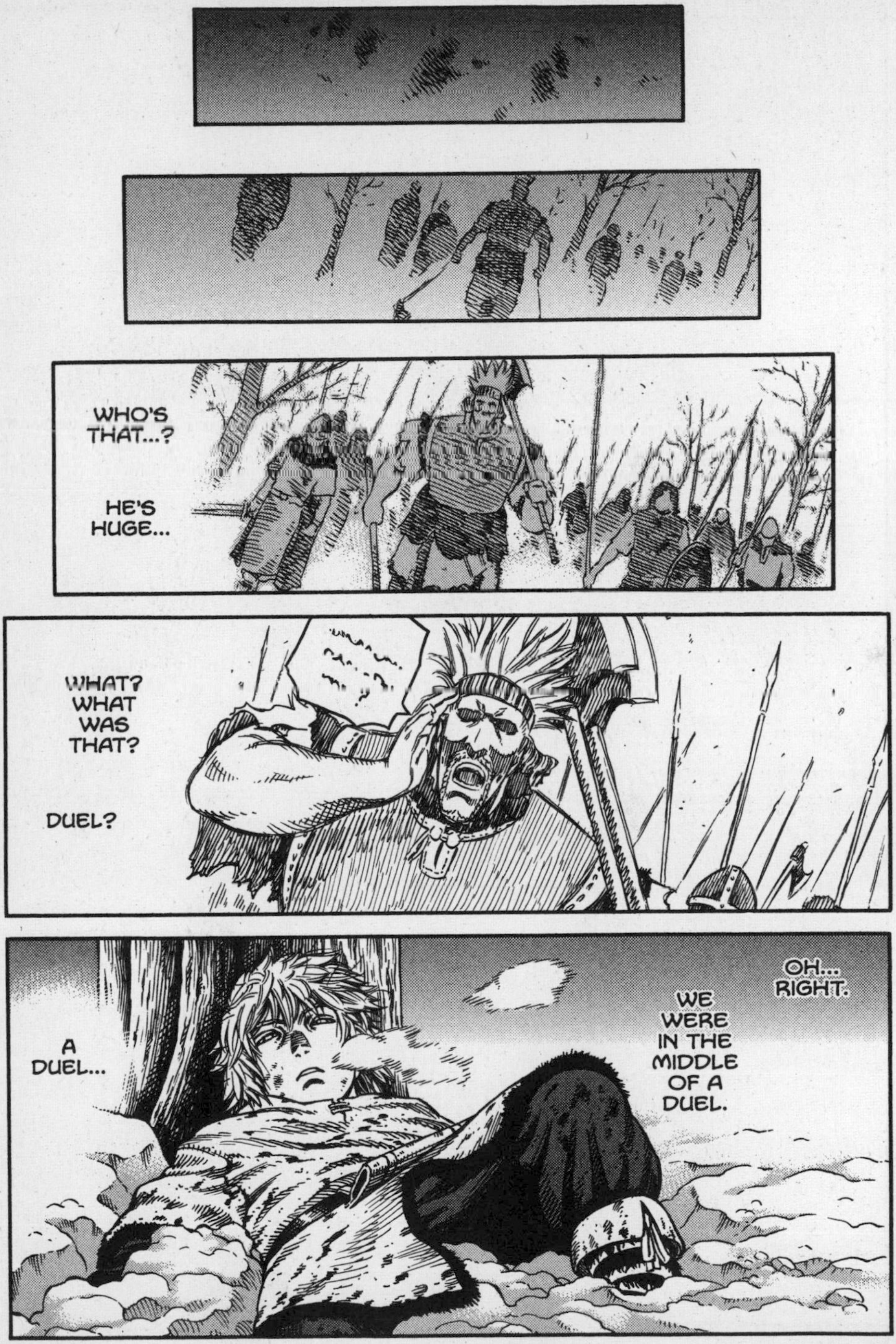
WHO'S THAT...?
HE'S HUGE...
WHAT? WHAT WAS THAT?
DUEL?
OH... RIGHT.
WE WERE IN THE MIDDLE OF A DUEL.
A DUEL...

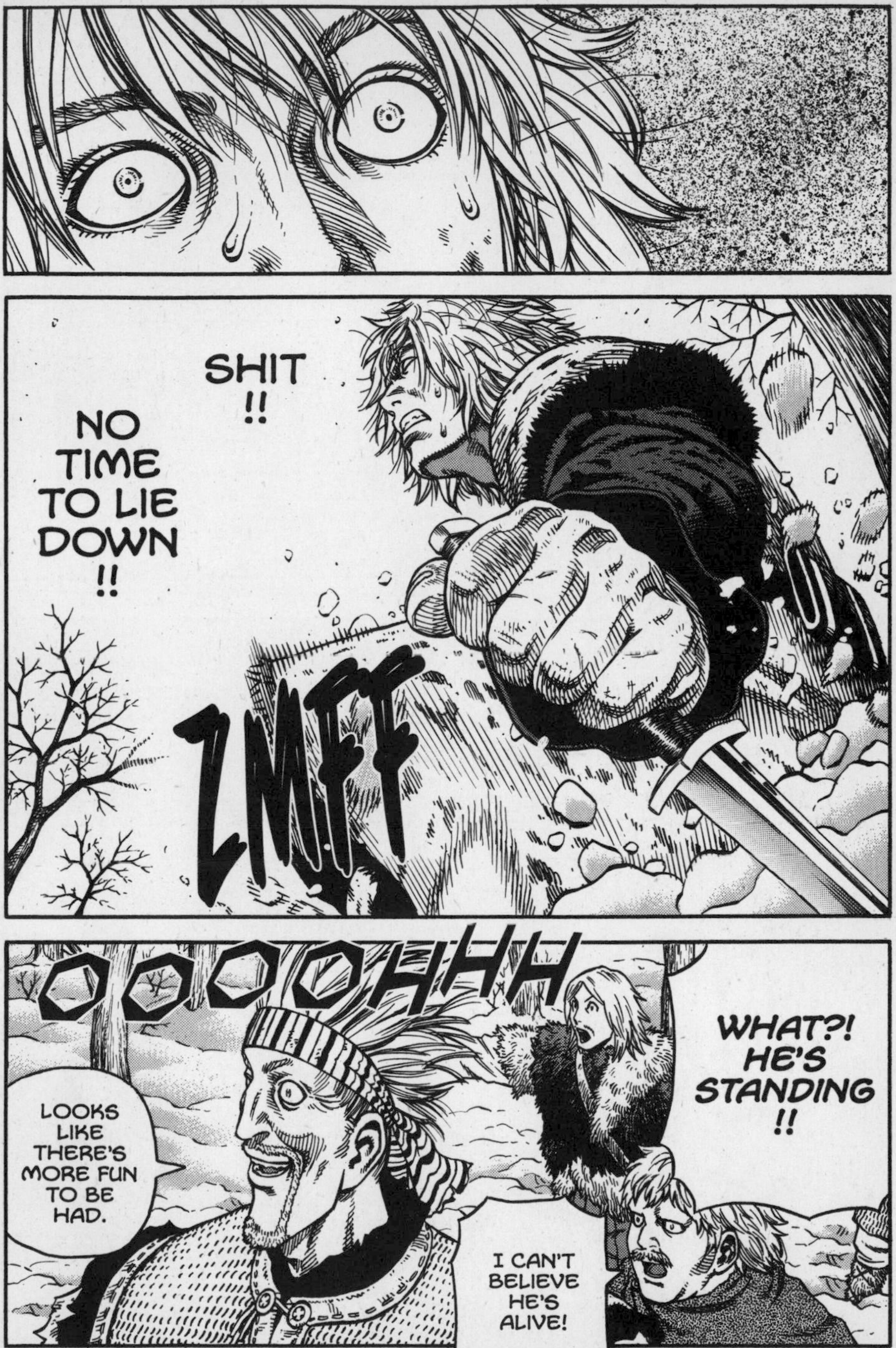
SHIT!!
NO TIME TO LIE DOWN!!
ZMFF
OOOOHHH
WHAT?! HE'S STANDING!!
I CAN'T BELIEVE HE'S ALIVE!
LOOKS LIKE THERE'S MORE FUN TO BE HAD.

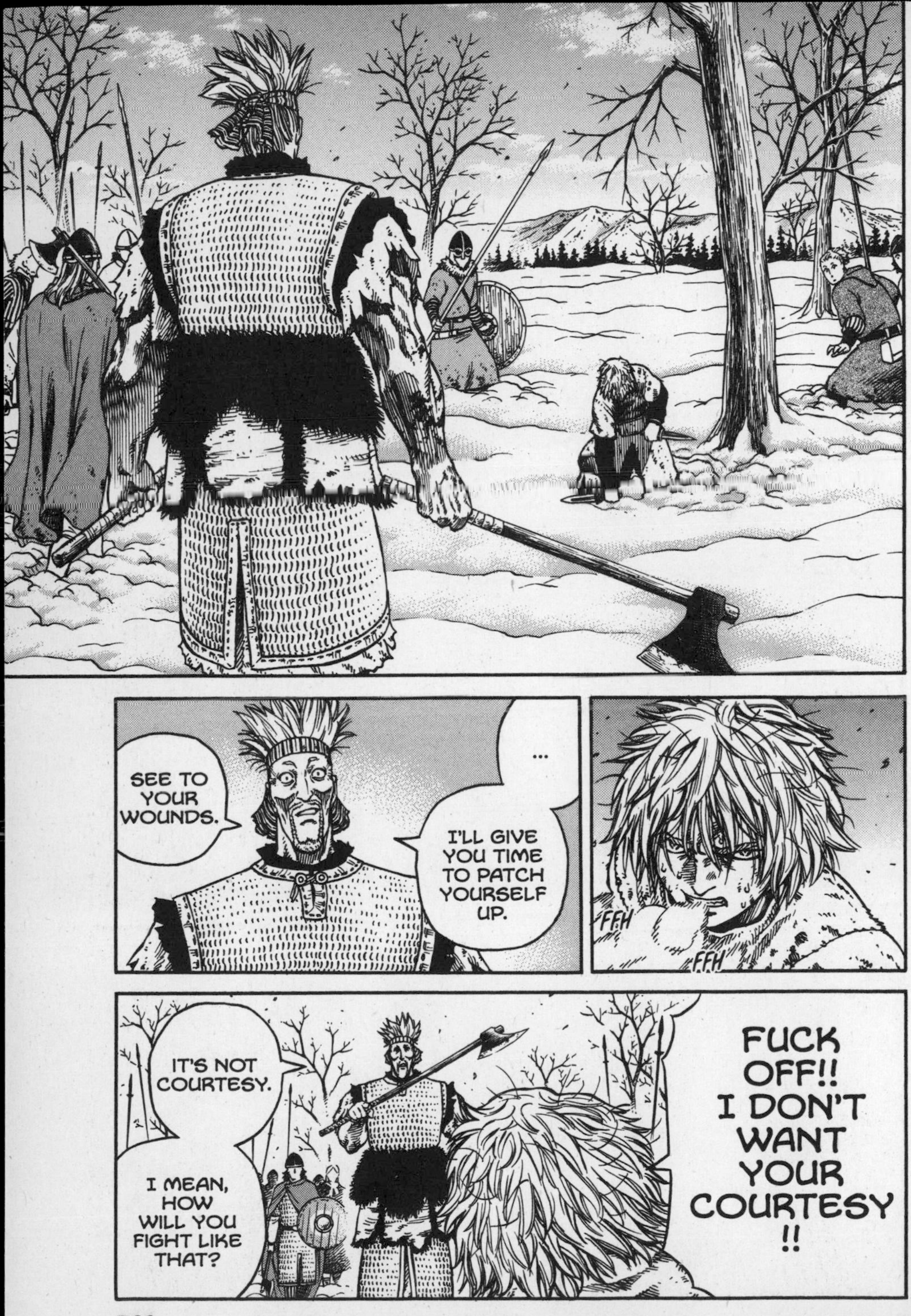
FFH
FFH
...
I'LL GIVE YOU TIME TO PATCH YOURSELF UP.
SEE TO YOUR WOUNDS.
FUCK OFF!! I DON'T WANT YOUR COURTESY!!
IT'S NOT COURTESY.
I MEAN, HOW WILL YOU FIGHT LIKE THAT?

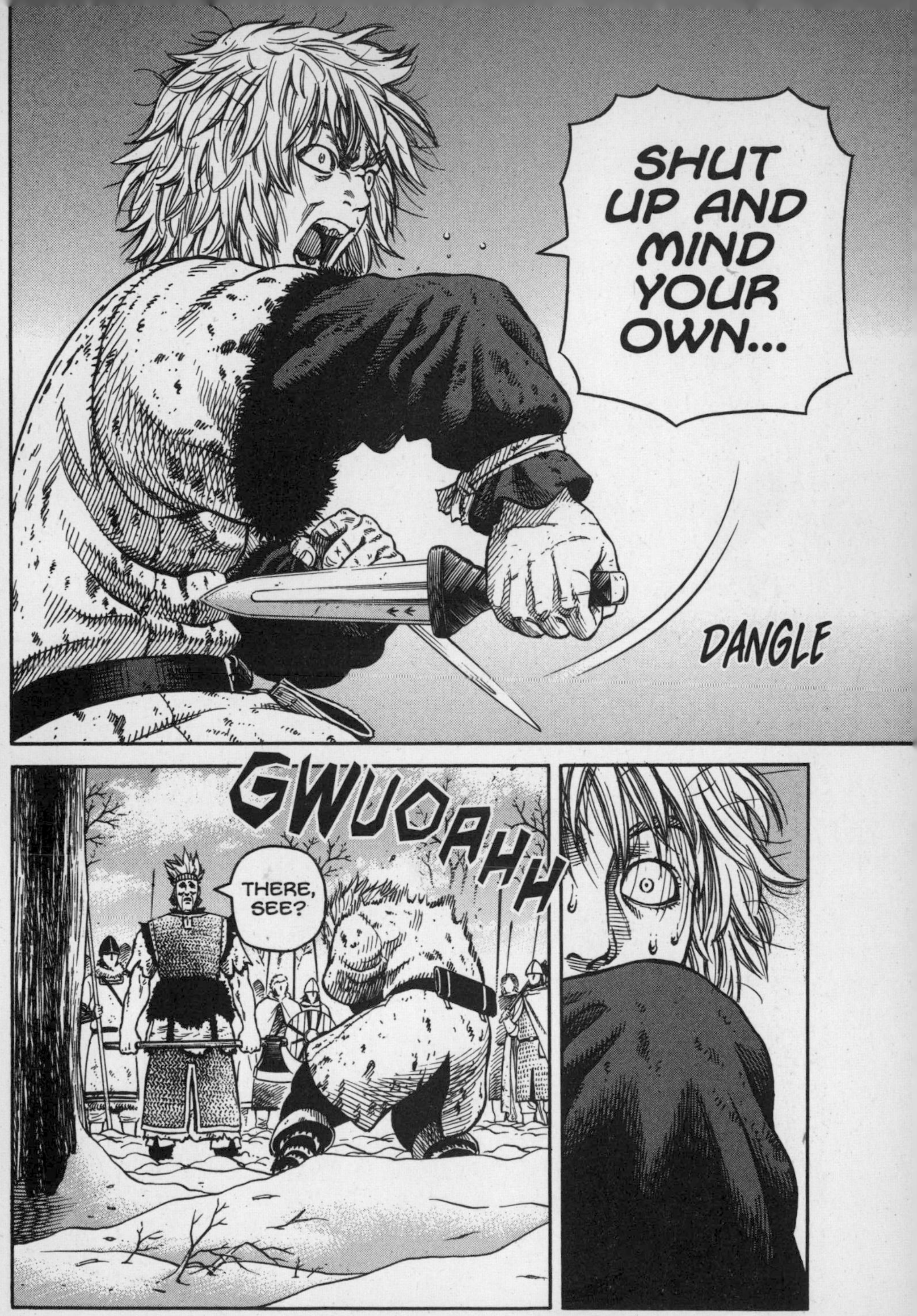
SHUT UP AND MIND YOUR OWN...
DANGLE
GWUOAHH
THERE, SEE?

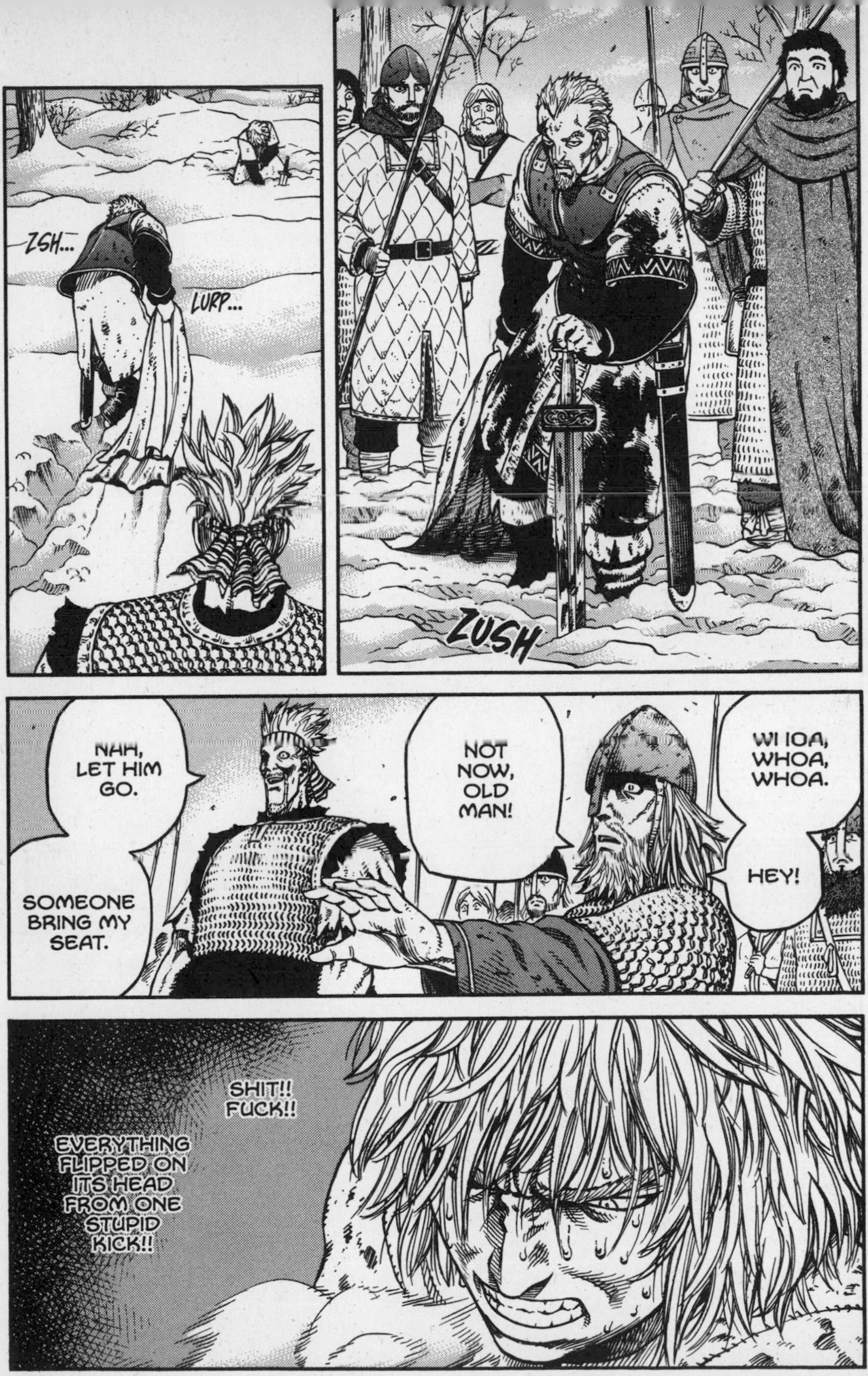
ZUSH
ZSH...
LURP...
WHOA, WHOA, WHOA.
HEY!
NOT NOW, OLD MAN!
NAH, LET HIM GO.
SOMEONE BRING MY SEAT.
SHIT!! FUCK!!
EVERYTHING FLIPPED ON ITS HEAD FROM ONE STUPID KICK!!

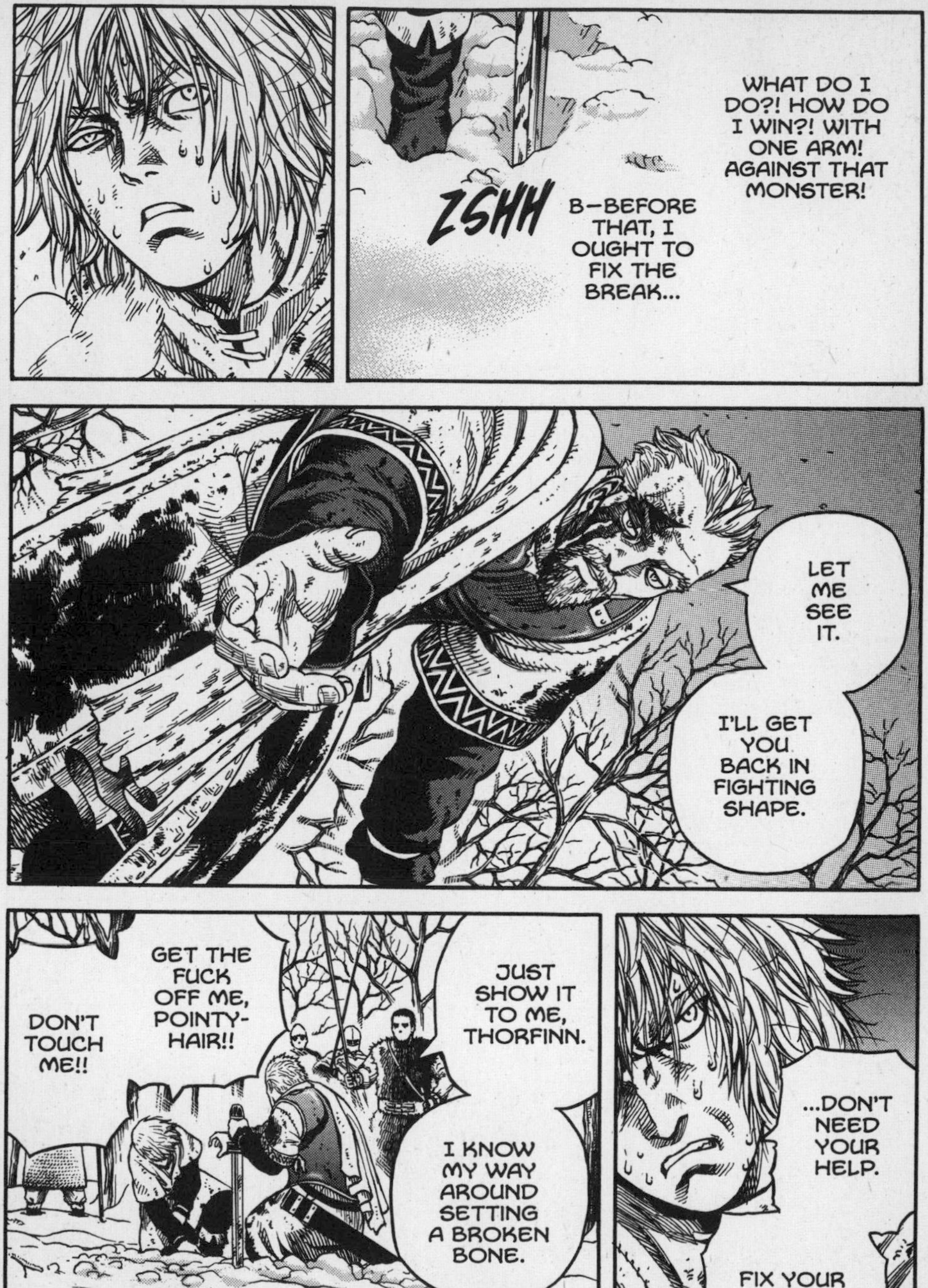
WHAT DO I DO?! HOW DO I WIN?! WITH ONE ARM! AGAINST THAT MONSTER!
B—BEFORE THAT, I OUGHT TO FIX THE BREAK...
ZSHH
LET ME SEE IT.
I'LL GET YOU BACK IN FIGHTING SHAPE.
...DON'T NEED YOUR HELP.
FIX YOUR OWN WOUNDS.
JUST SHOW IT TO ME, THORFINN.
I KNOW MY WAY AROUND SETTING A BROKEN BONE.
GET THE FUCK OFF ME, POINTY-HAIR!!
DON'T TOUCH ME!!

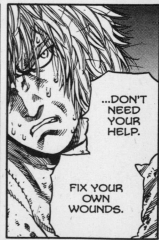

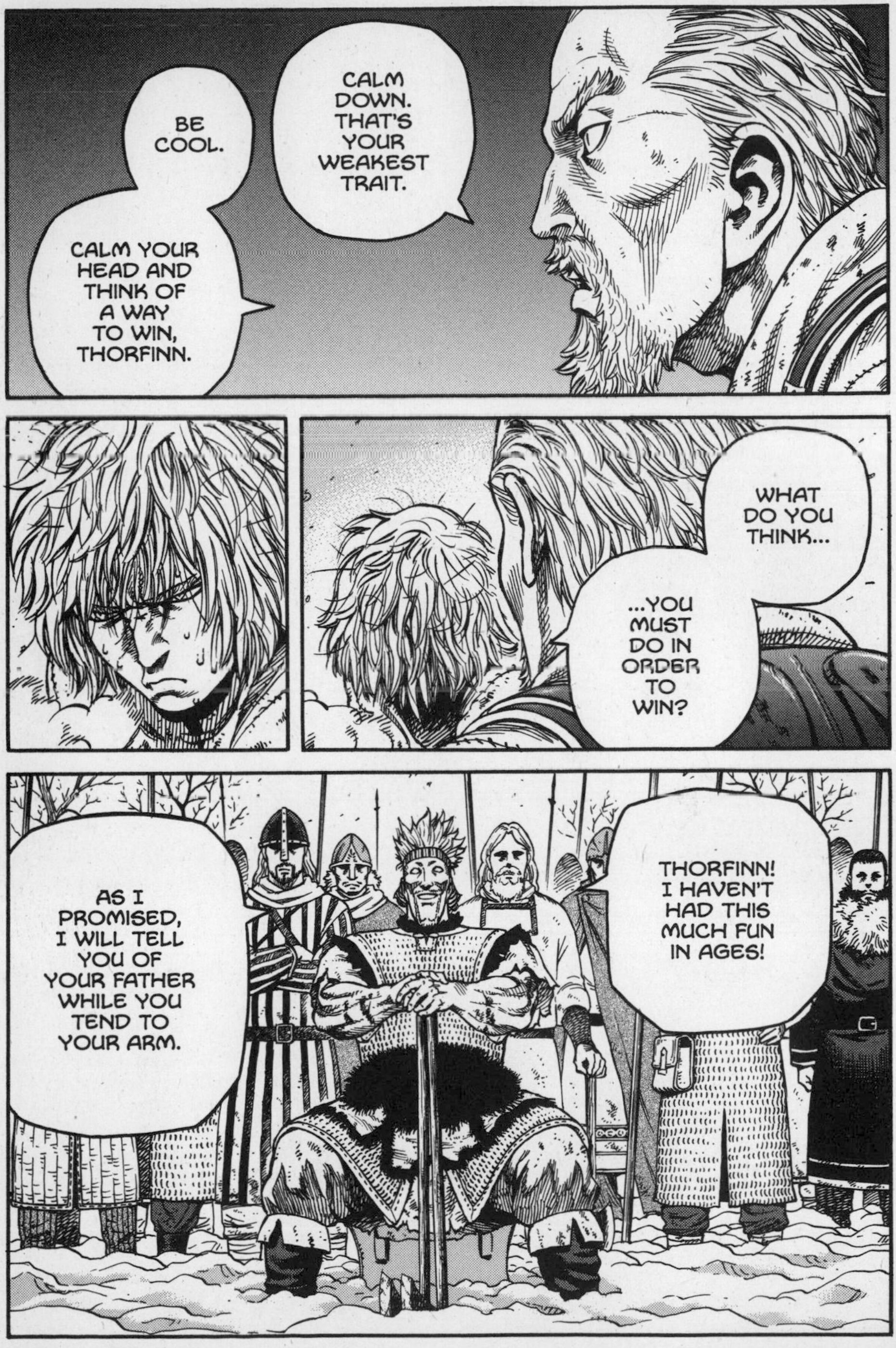
CALM DOWN. THAT'S YOUR WEAKEST TRAIT.
BE COOL.
CALM YOUR HEAD AND THINK OF A WAY TO WIN, THORFINN.
WHAT DO YOU THINK...
...YOU MUST DO IN ORDER TO WIN?
THORFINN! I HAVEN'T HAD THIS MUCH FUN IN AGES!
AS I PROMISED, I WILL TELL YOU OF YOUR FATHER WHILE YOU TEND TO YOUR ARM.

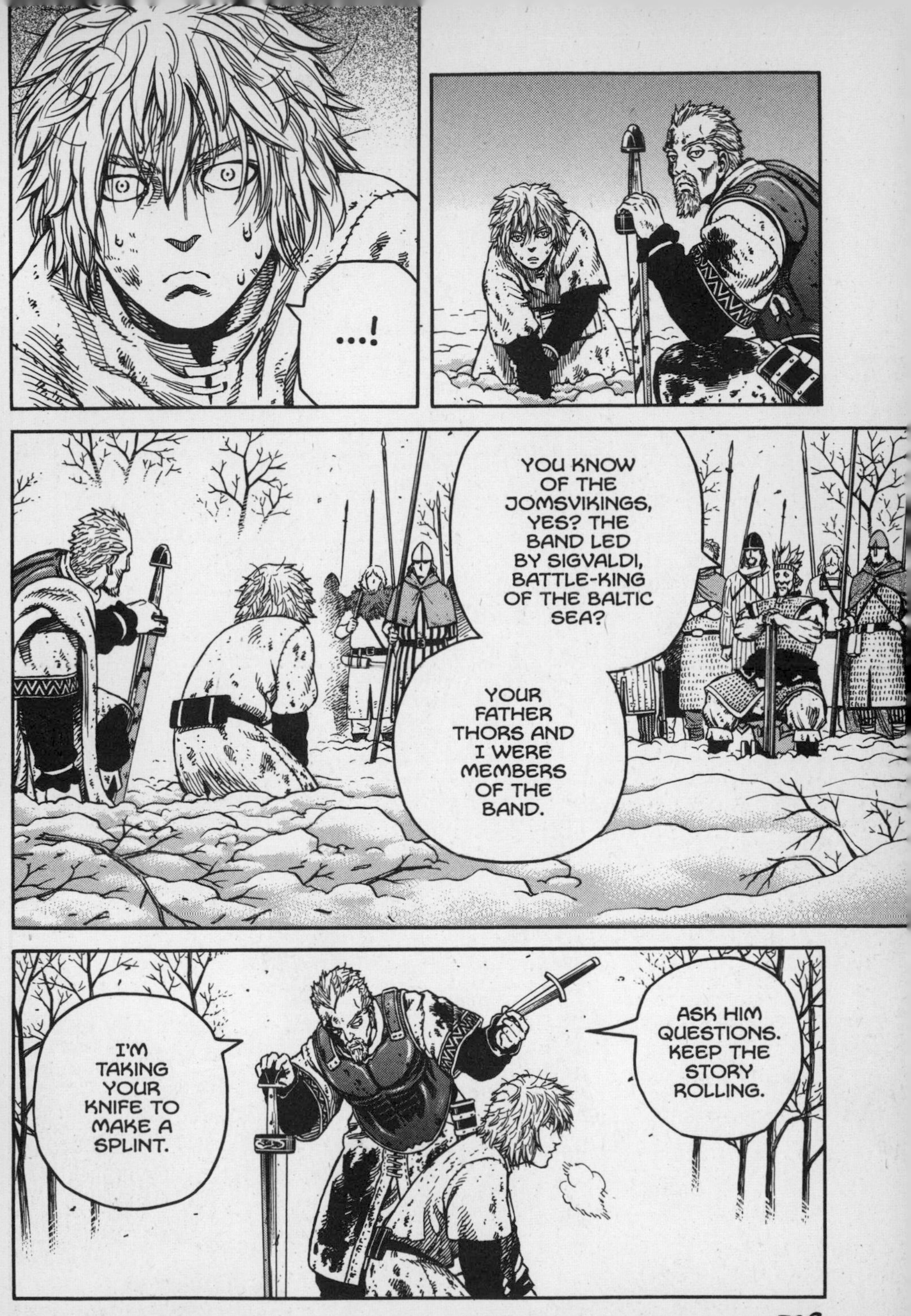
...!
YOU KNOW OF THE JOMSVIKINGS, YES? THE BAND LED BY SIGVALDI, BATTLE-KING OF THE BALTIC SEA?
YOUR FATHER THORS AND I WERE MEMBERS OF THE BAND.
ASK HIM QUESTIONS. KEEP THE STORY ROLLING.
I'M TAKING YOUR KNIFE TO MAKE A SPLINT.

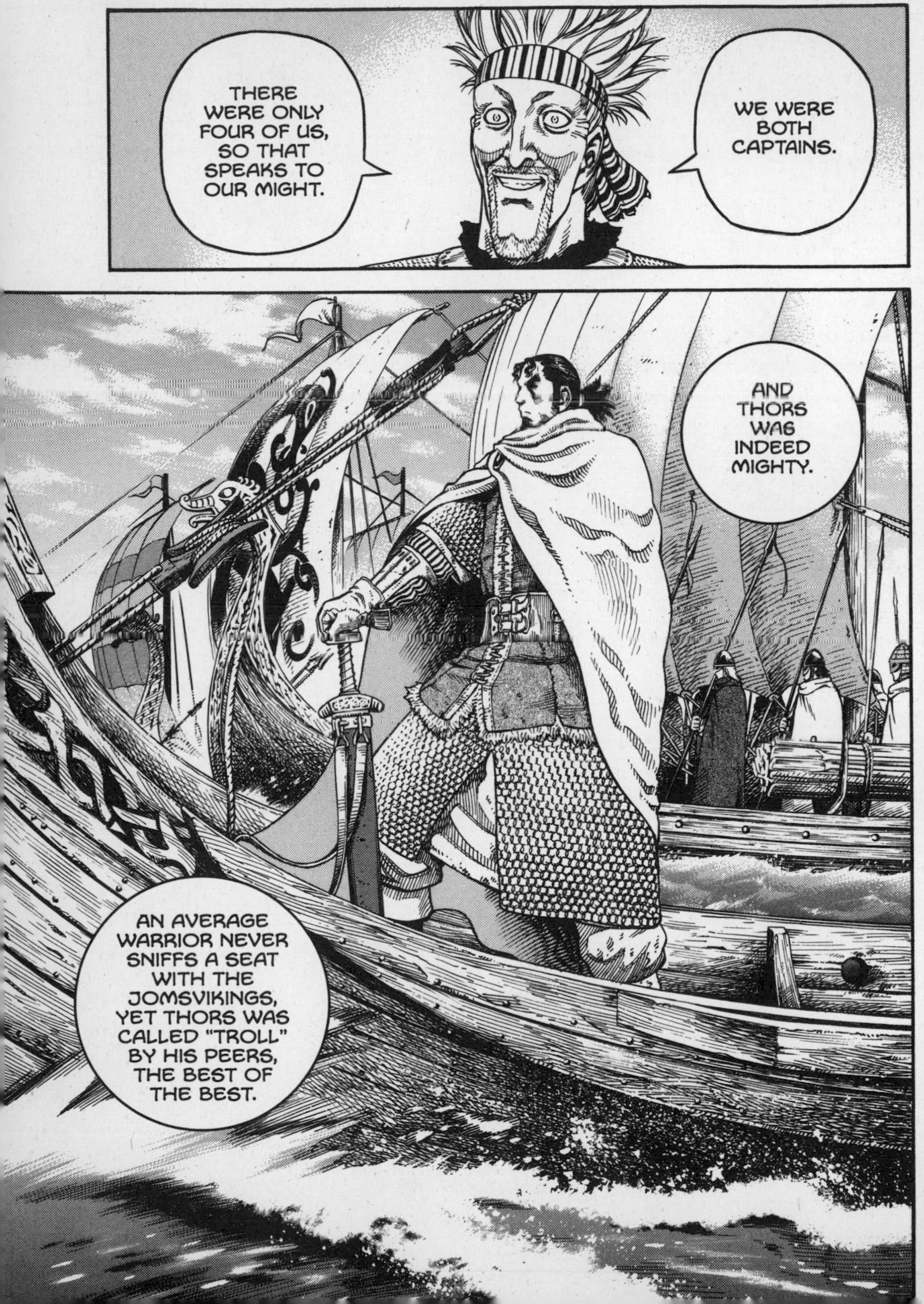
WE WERE BOTH CAPTAINS.
THERE WERE ONLY FOUR OF US, SO THAT SPEAKS TO OUR MIGHT.
AND THORS WAS INDEED MIGHTY.
AN AVERAGE WARRIOR NEVER SNIFFS A SEAT WITH THE JOMSVIKINGS, YET THORS WAS CALLED "TROLL" BY HIS PEERS, THE BEST OF THE BEST.

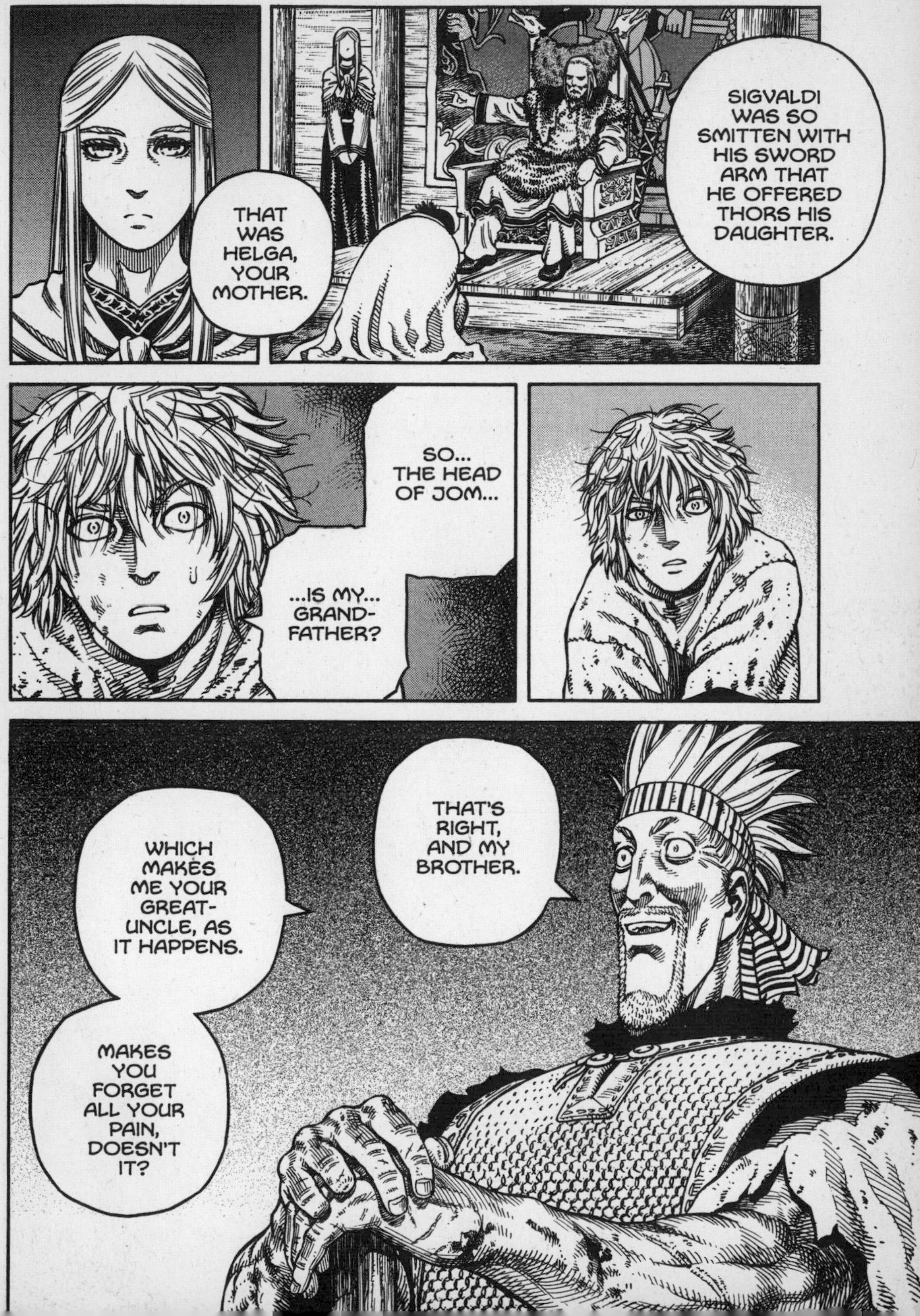
SIGVALDI WAS SO SMITTEN WITH HIS SWORD ARM THAT HE OFFERED THORS HIS DAUGHTER.
THAT WAS HELGA, YOUR MOTHER.
SO... THE HEAD OF JOM...
...IS MY... GRAND-FATHER?
THAT'S RIGHT, AND MY BROTHER.
WHICH MAKES ME YOUR GREAT-UNCLE, AS IT HAPPENS.
MAKES YOU FORGET ALL YOUR PAIN, DOESN'T IT?

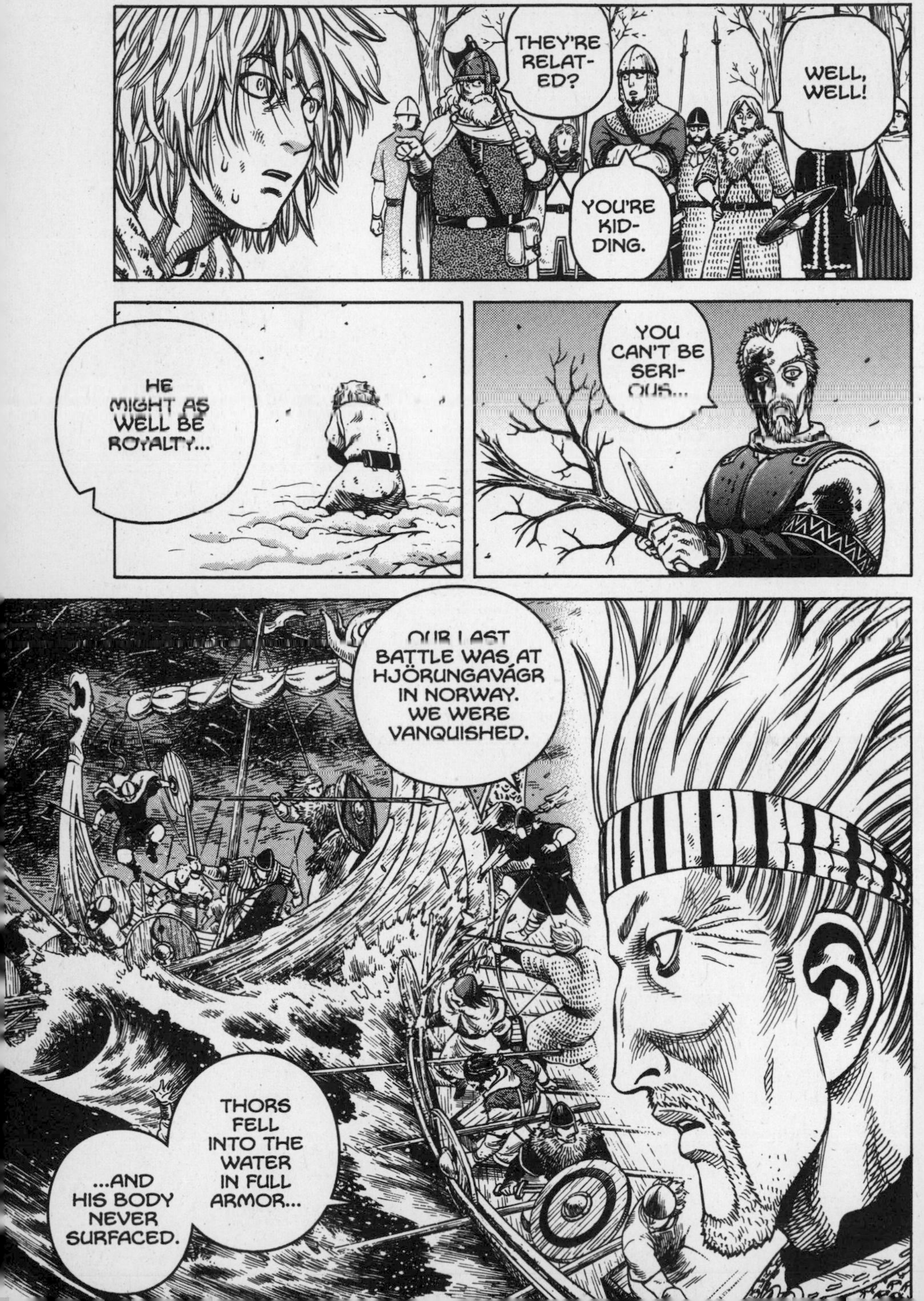
WELL, WELL!
THEY'RE RELATED?
YOU'RE KIDDING.
YOU CAN'T BE SERIOUS...
HE MIGHT AS WELL BE ROYALTY...
OUR LAST BATTLE WAS AT HJÖRUNGAVÁGR IN NORWAY. WE WERE VANQUISHED.
THORS FELL INTO THE WATER IN FULL ARMOR...
...AND HIS BODY NEVER SURFACED.

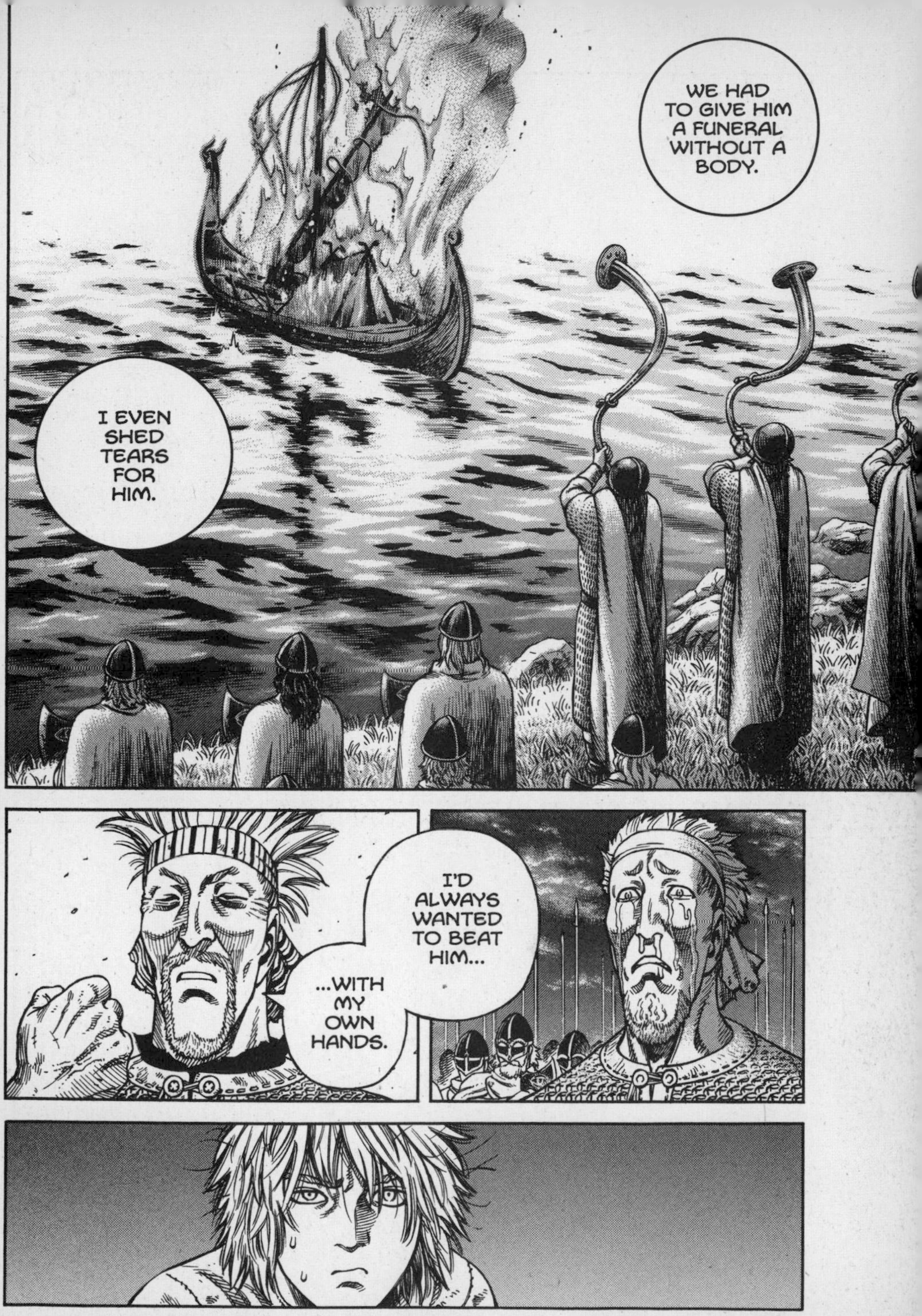
WE HAD TO GIVE HIM A FUNERAL WITHOUT A BODY.
I EVEN SHED TEARS FOR HIM.
I'D ALWAYS WANTED TO BEAT HIM...
...WITH MY OWN HANDS.

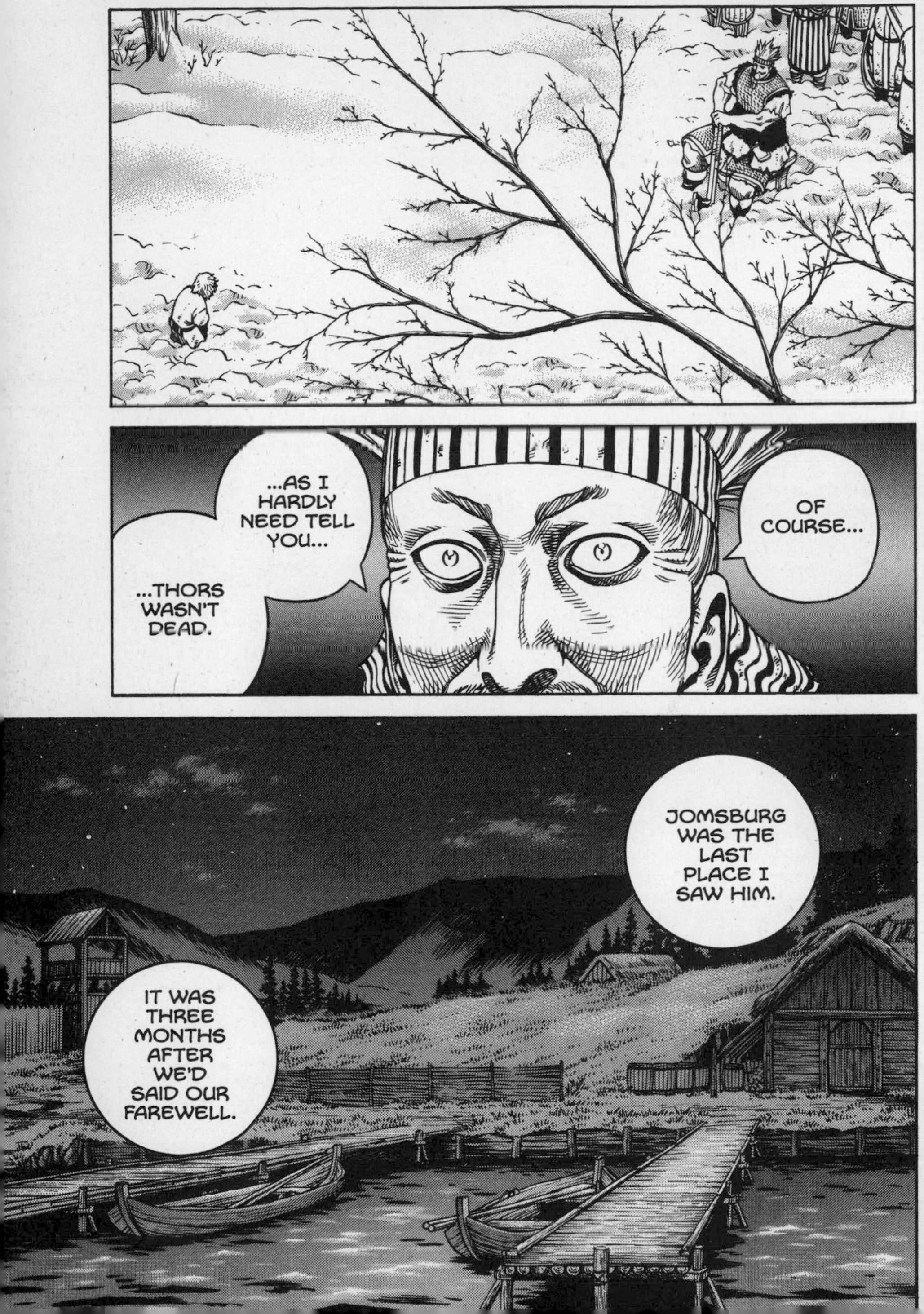
OF COURSE...
...AS I HARDLY NEED TELL YOU...
...THORS WASN'T DEAD.
JOMSBURG WAS THE LAST PLACE I SAW HIM.
IT WAS THREE MONTHS AFTER WE'D SAID OUR FAREWELL.

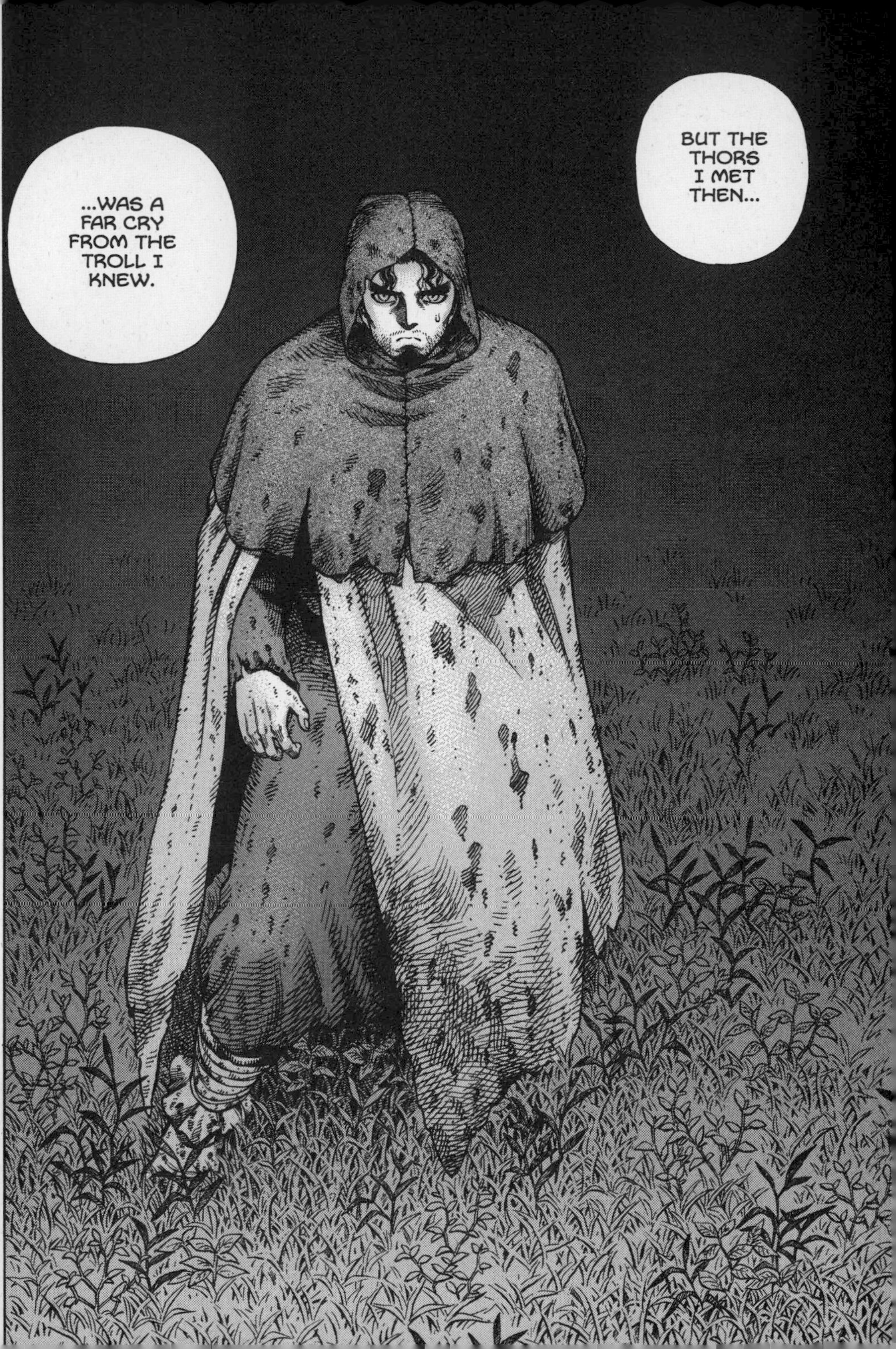
BUT THE THORS I MET THEN...
...WAS A FAR CRY FROM THE TROLL I KNEW.

CHAPTER 39 - END

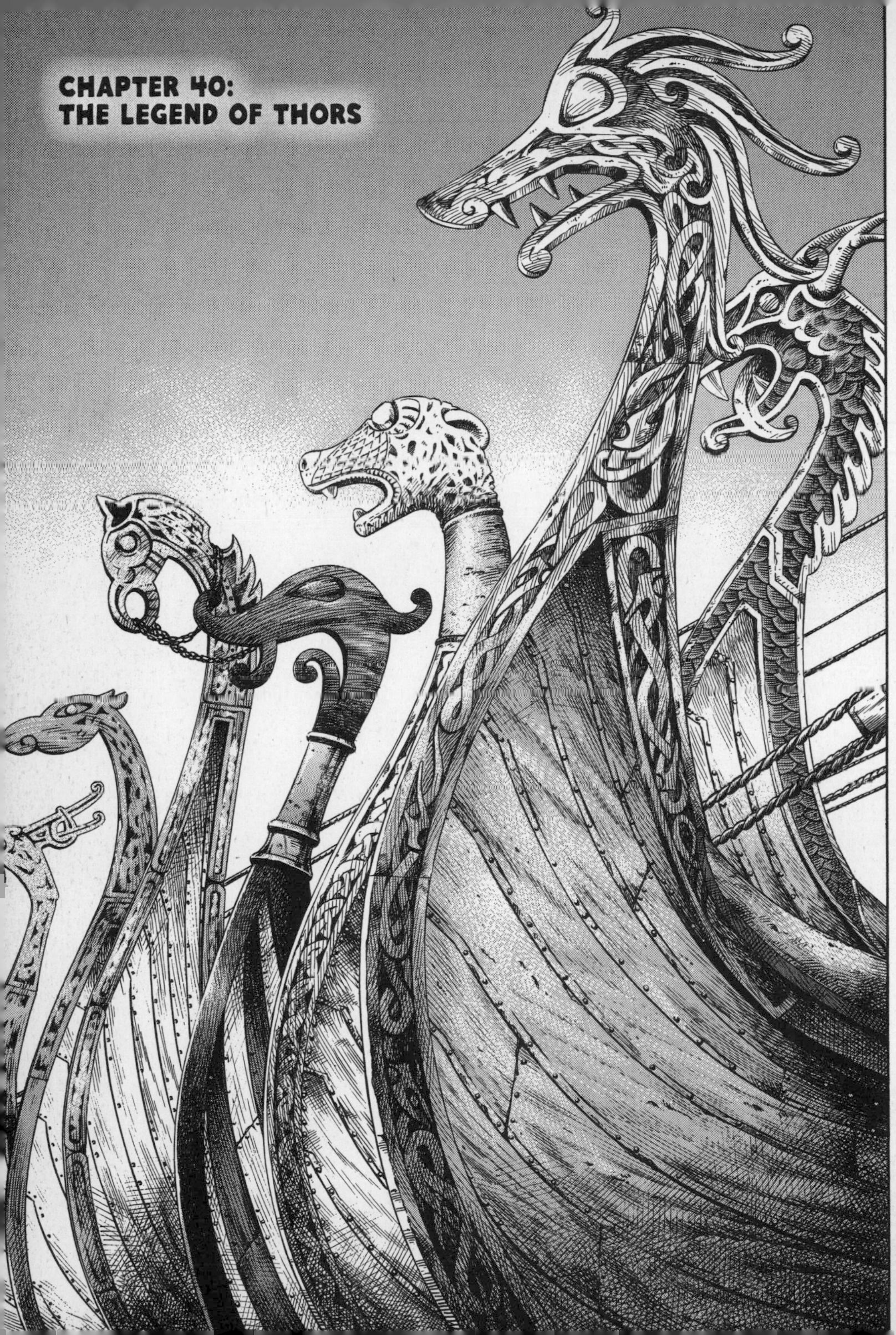
CHAPTER 40:
THE LEGEND OF THORS

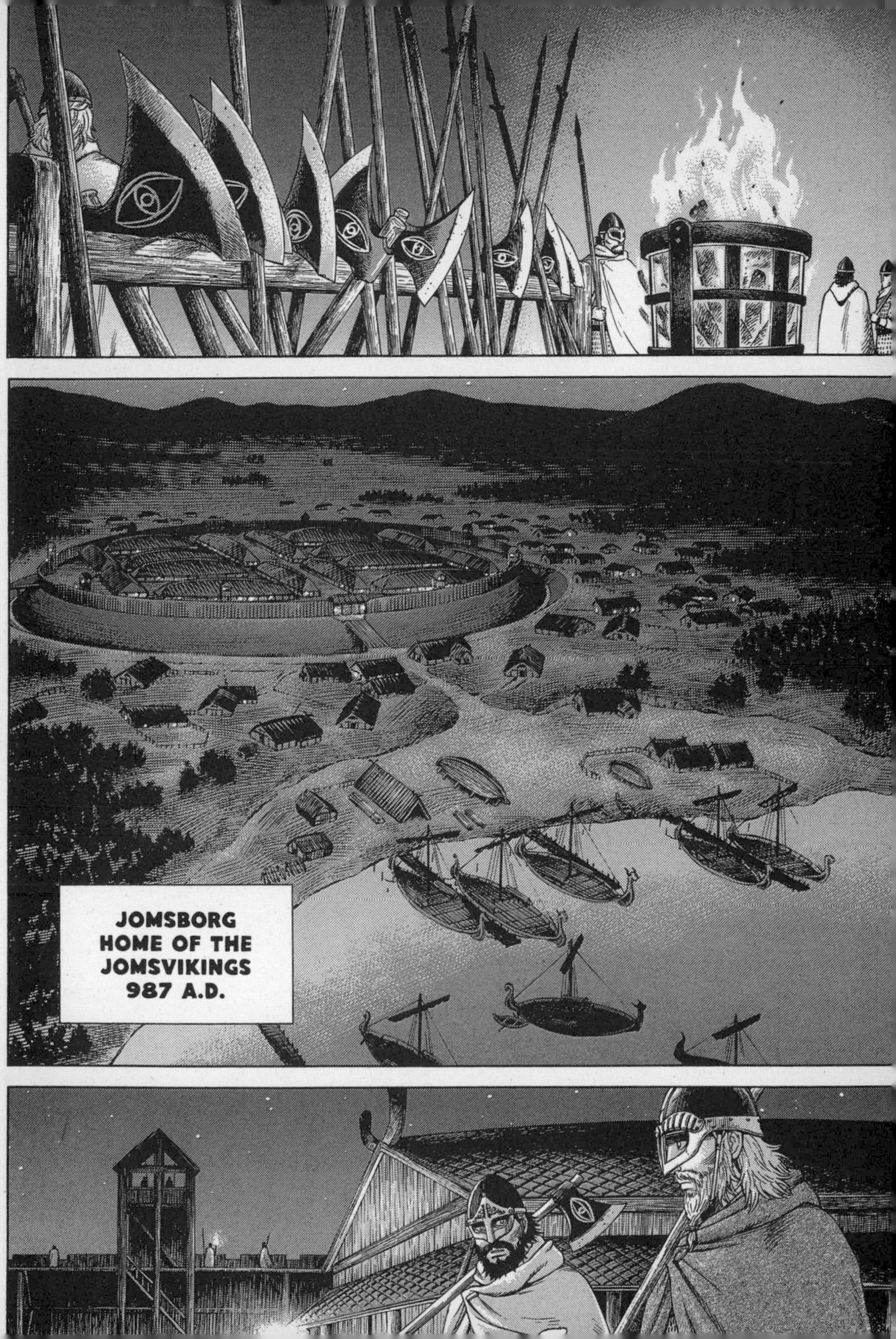
JOMSBORG
HOME OF THE
JOMSVIKINGS
987 A.D.

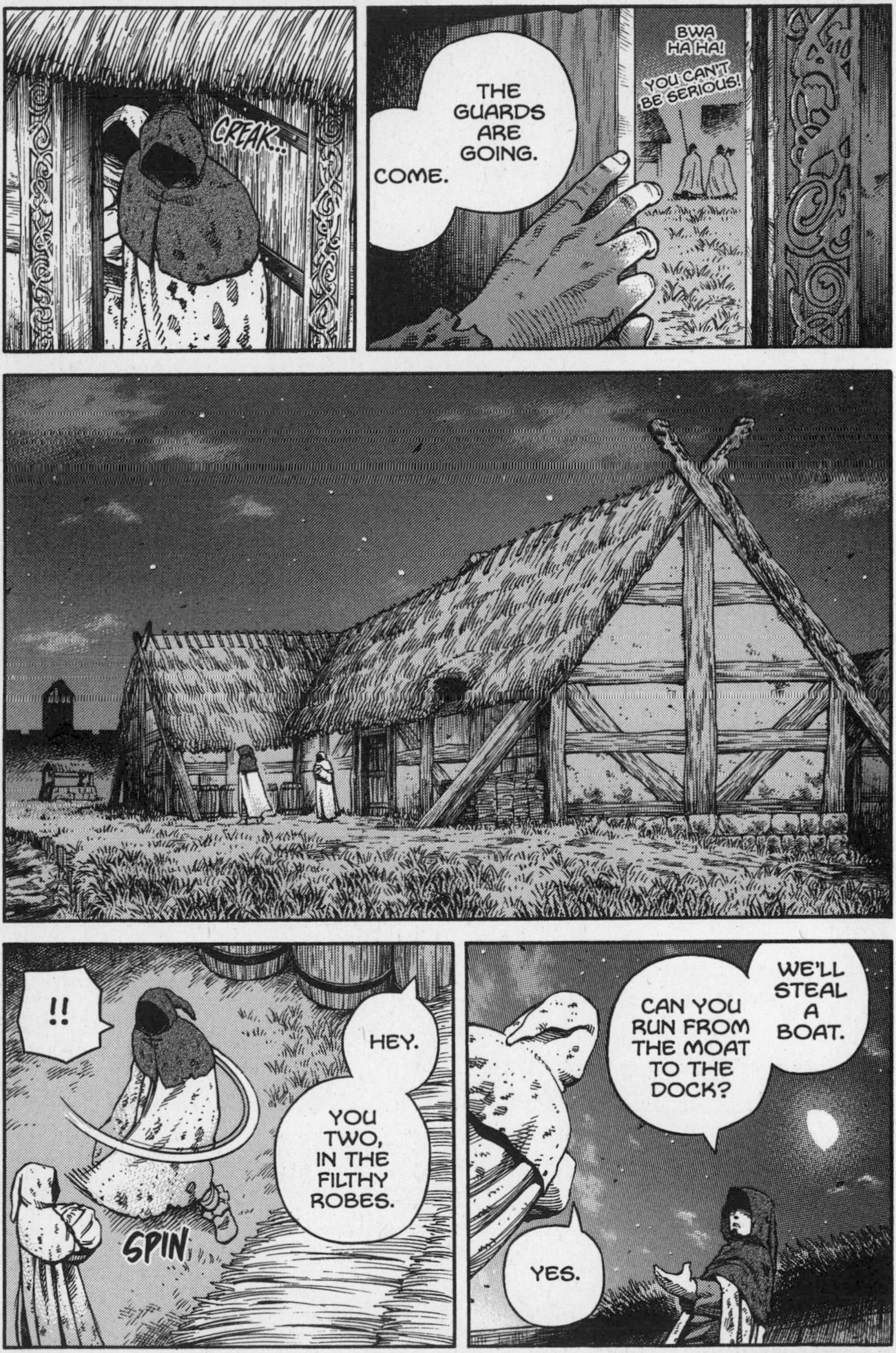
BWA HA HA! YOU CAN'T BE SERIOUS!
THE GUARDS ARE GOING.
COME.
CREAK...
WE'LL STEAL A BOAT.
CAN YOU RUN FROM THE MOAT TO THE DOCK?
YES.
HEY.
!!
YOU TWO, IN THE FILTHY ROBES.
SPIN

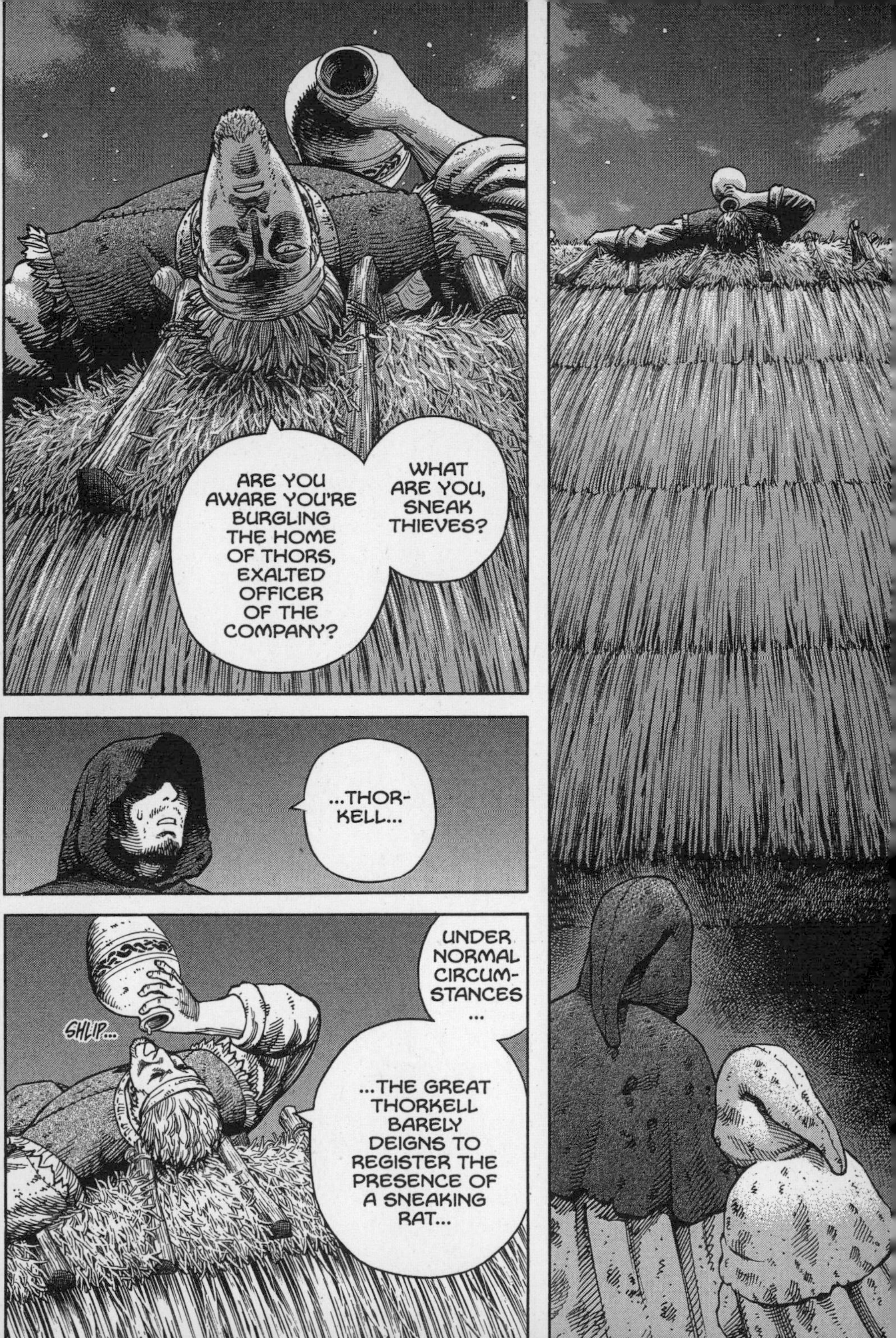
WHAT ARE YOU, SNEAK THIEVES?
ARE YOU AWARE YOU'RE BURGLING THE HOME OF THORS, EXALTED OFFICER OF THE COMPANY?
...THOR-KELL...
UNDER NORMAL CIRCUM-STANCES...
SHLIP...
...THE GREAT THORKELL BARELY DEIGNS TO REGISTER THE PRESENCE OF A SNEAKING RAT...

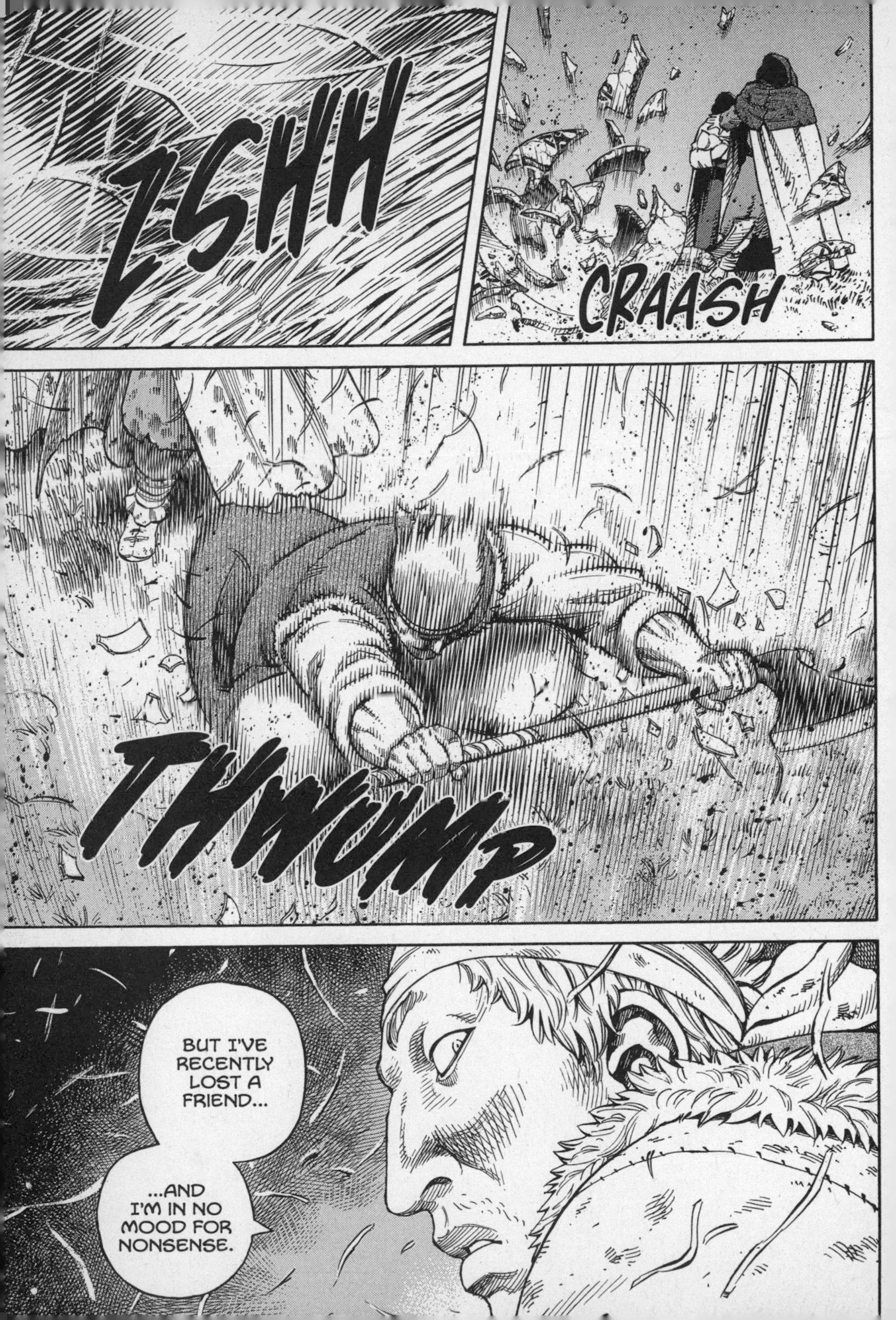
CRAASH
ZSHH
THWUMP
BUT I'VE RECENTLY LOST A FRIEND...
...AND I'M IN NO MOOD FOR NONSENSE.

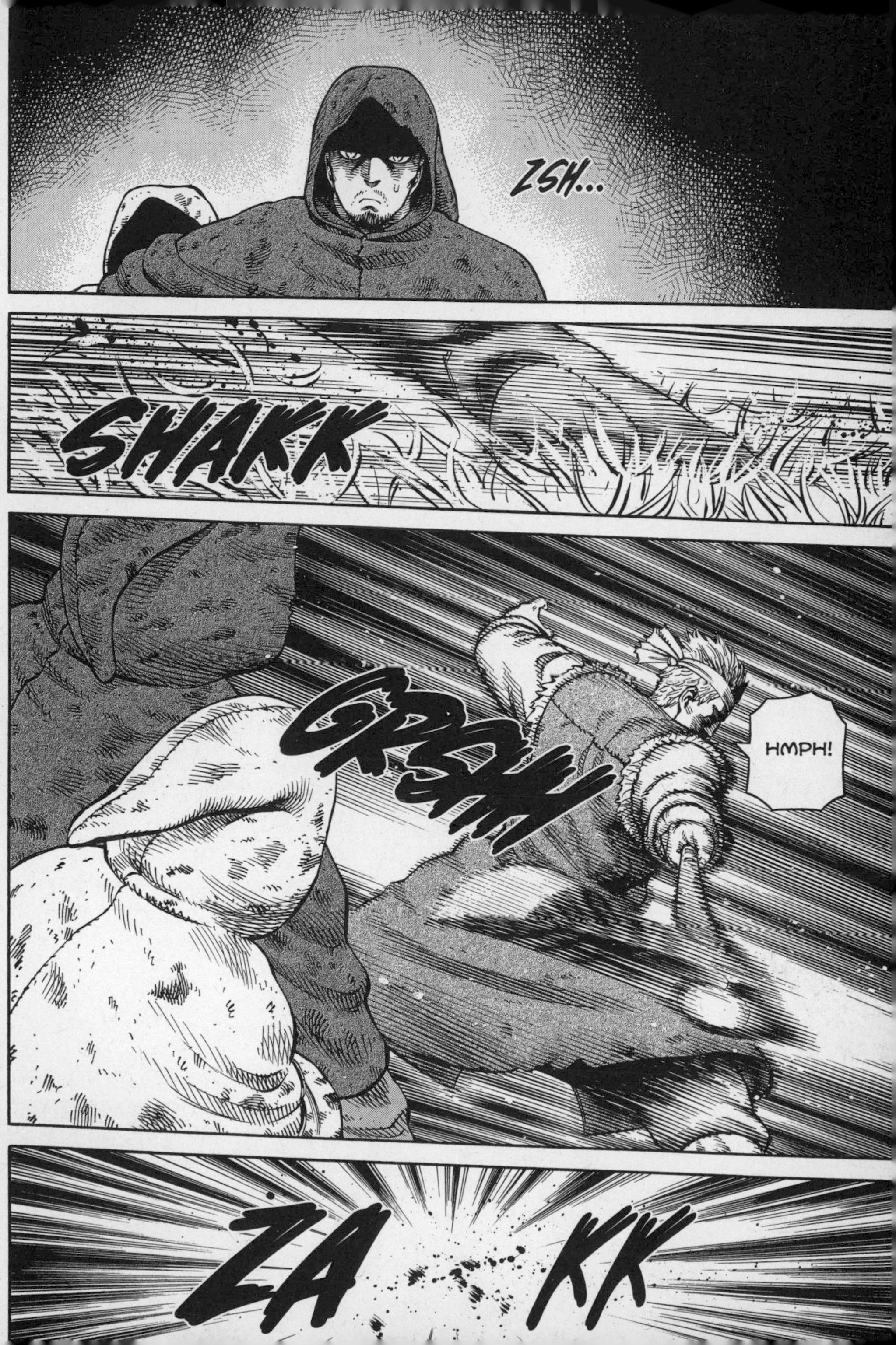
ZSH...
SHAKK
HMPH!
GRSH
ZA KK

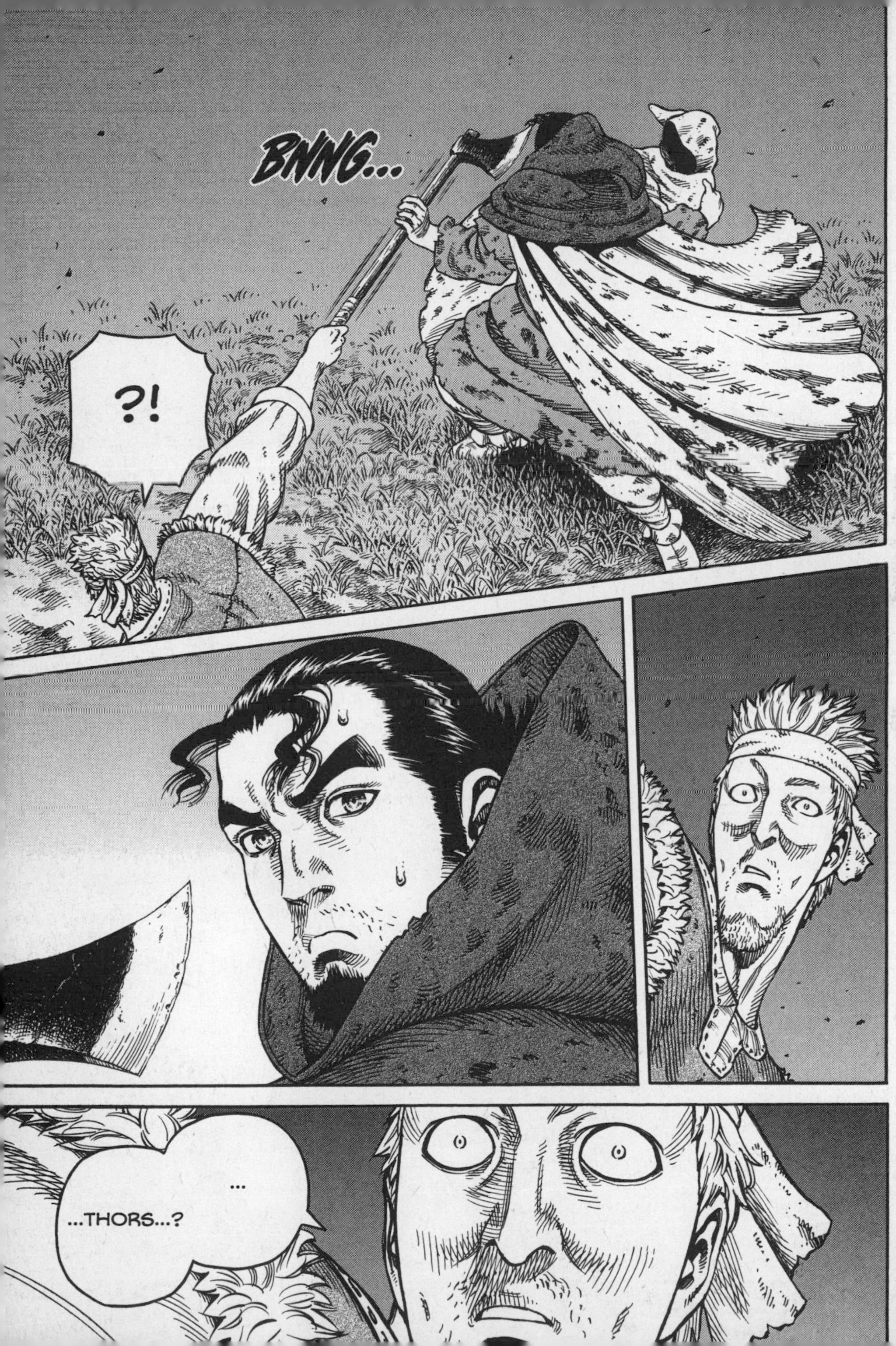
BNNG...
?!
...
...THORS...?

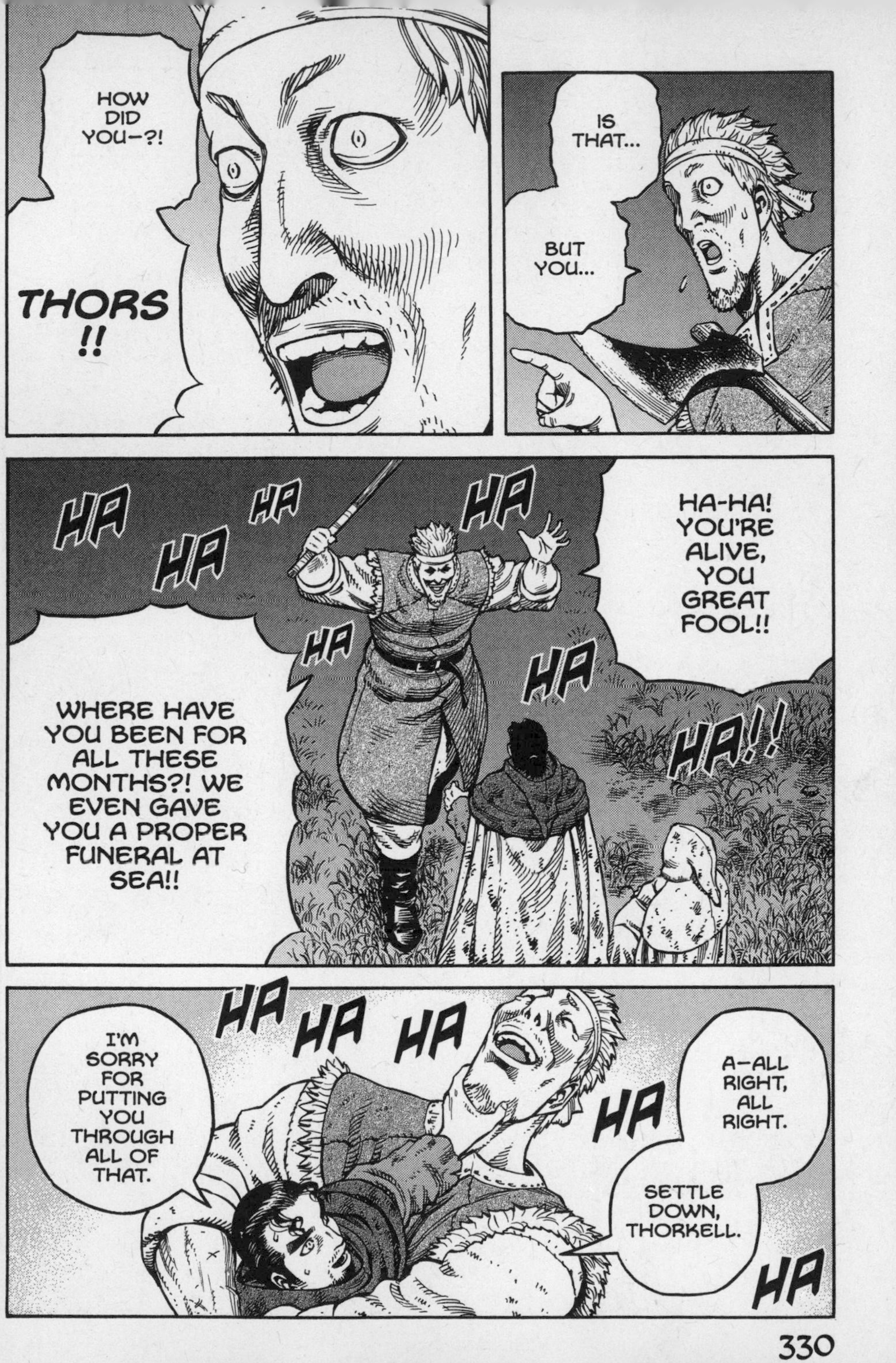
IS THAT...
BUT YOU...
HOW DID YOU-?!
THORS !!
HA-HA! YOU'RE ALIVE, YOU GREAT FOOL!!
HA
HA
HA
HA
HA
HA
HA!!
WHERE HAVE YOU BEEN FOR ALL THESE MONTHS?! WE EVEN GAVE YOU A PROPER FUNERAL AT SEA!!
A-ALL RIGHT, ALL RIGHT.
SETTLE DOWN, THORKELL.
HA
HA
HA
HA
HA
I'M SORRY FOR PUTTING YOU THROUGH ALL OF THAT.

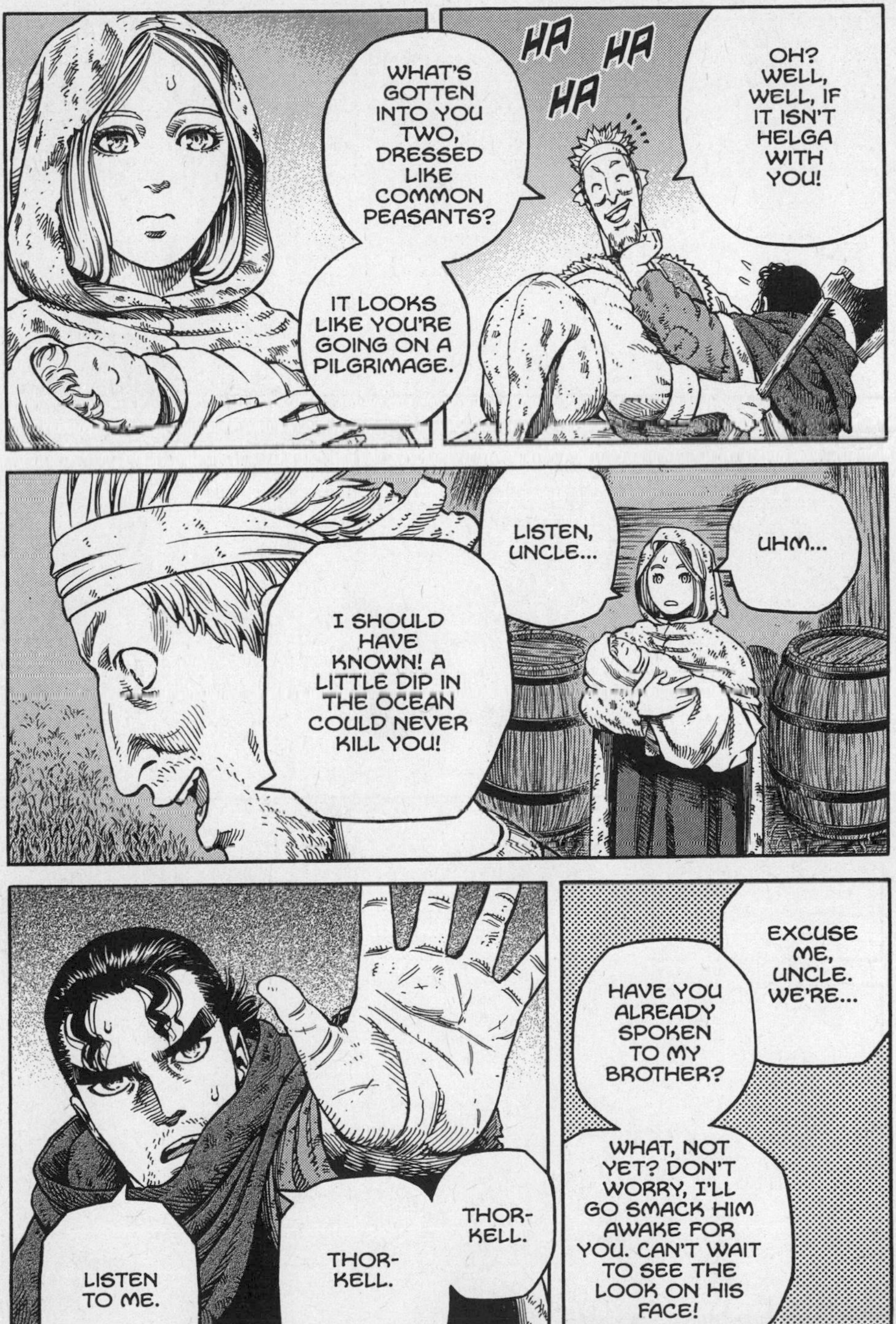
OH? WELL, WELL, IF IT ISN'T HELGA WITH YOU!
HA HA HA
WHAT'S GOTTEN INTO YOU TWO, DRESSED LIKE COMMON PEASANTS?
IT LOOKS LIKE YOU'RE GOING ON A PILGRIMAGE.
UHM...
LISTEN, UNCLE...
I SHOULD HAVE KNOWN! A LITTLE DIP IN THE OCEAN COULD NEVER KILL YOU!
EXCUSE ME, UNCLE. WE'RE...
HAVE YOU ALREADY SPOKEN TO MY BROTHER?
WHAT, NOT YET? DON'T WORRY, I'LL GO SMACK HIM AWAKE FOR YOU. CAN'T WAIT TO SEE THE LOOK ON HIS FACE!
THOR-KELL.
THOR-KELL.
LISTEN TO ME.

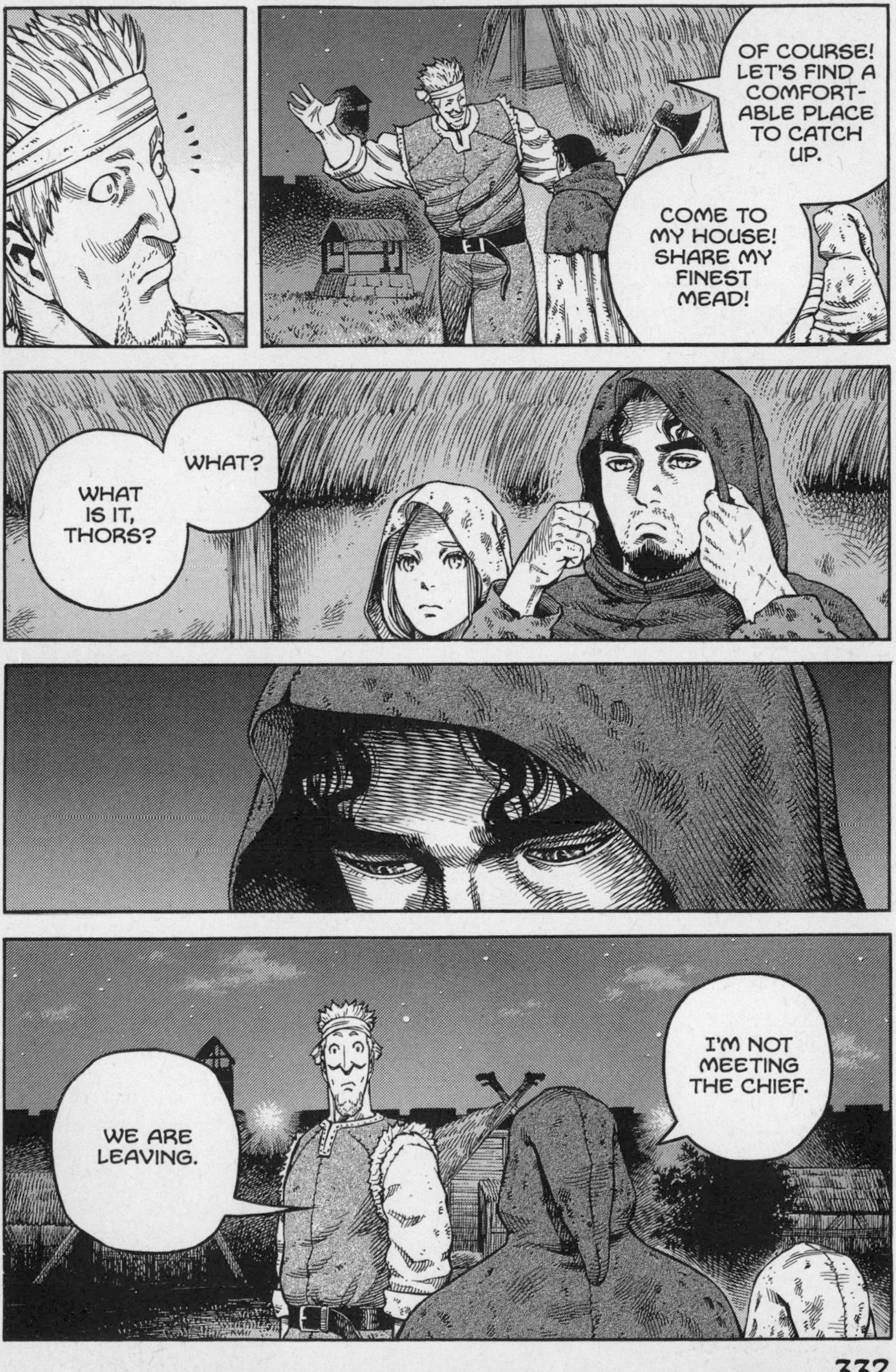
OF COURSE! LET'S FIND A COMFORT-ABLE PLACE TO CATCH UP.
COME TO MY HOUSE! SHARE MY FINEST MEAD!
WHAT?
WHAT IS IT, THORS?
I'M NOT MEETING THE CHIEF.
WE ARE LEAVING.

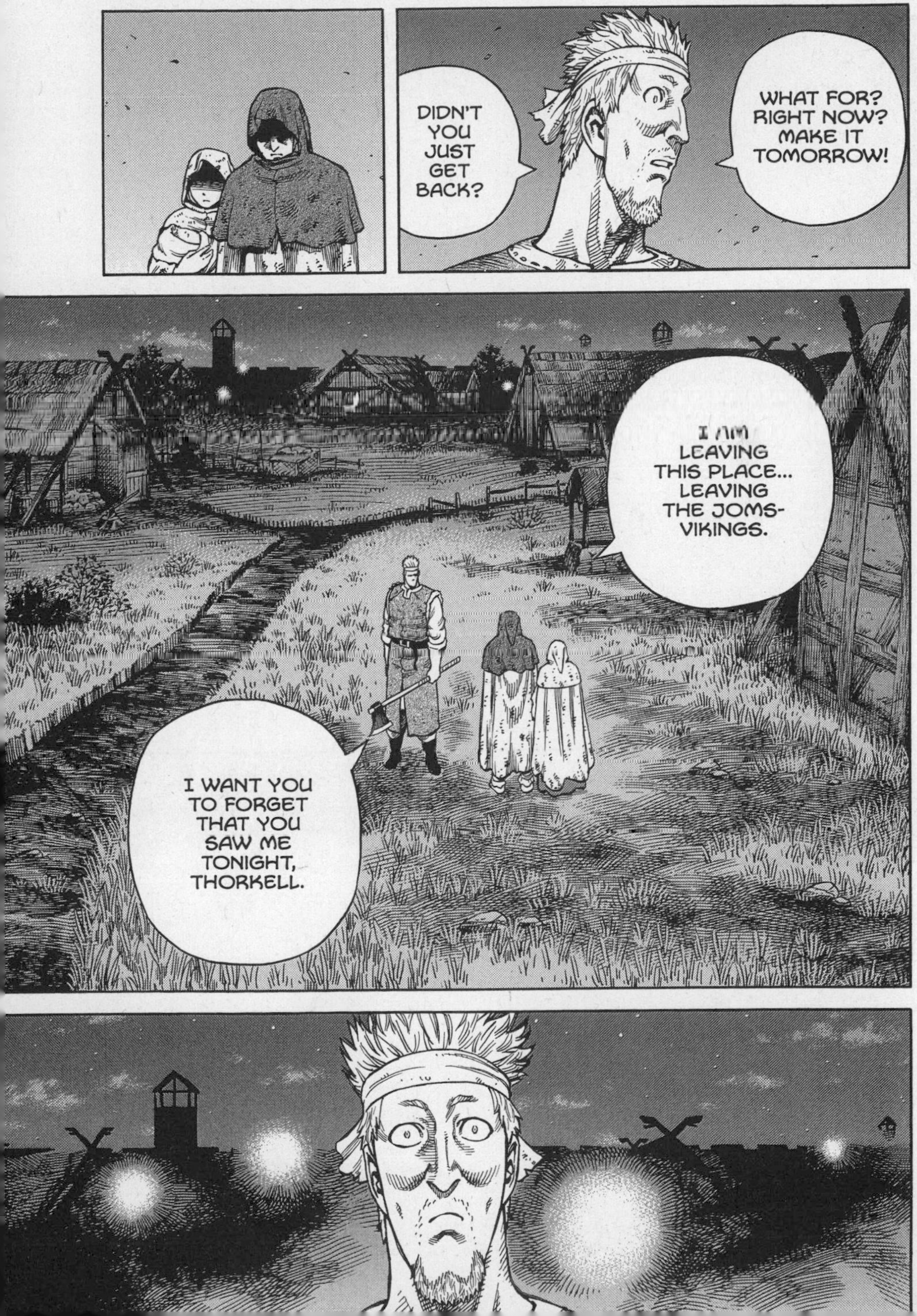
WHAT FOR? RIGHT NOW? MAKE IT TOMORROW!
DIDN'T YOU JUST GET BACK?
I AM LEAVING THIS PLACE... LEAVING THE JOMS-VIKINGS.
I WANT YOU TO FORGET THAT YOU SAW ME TONIGHT, THORKELL.

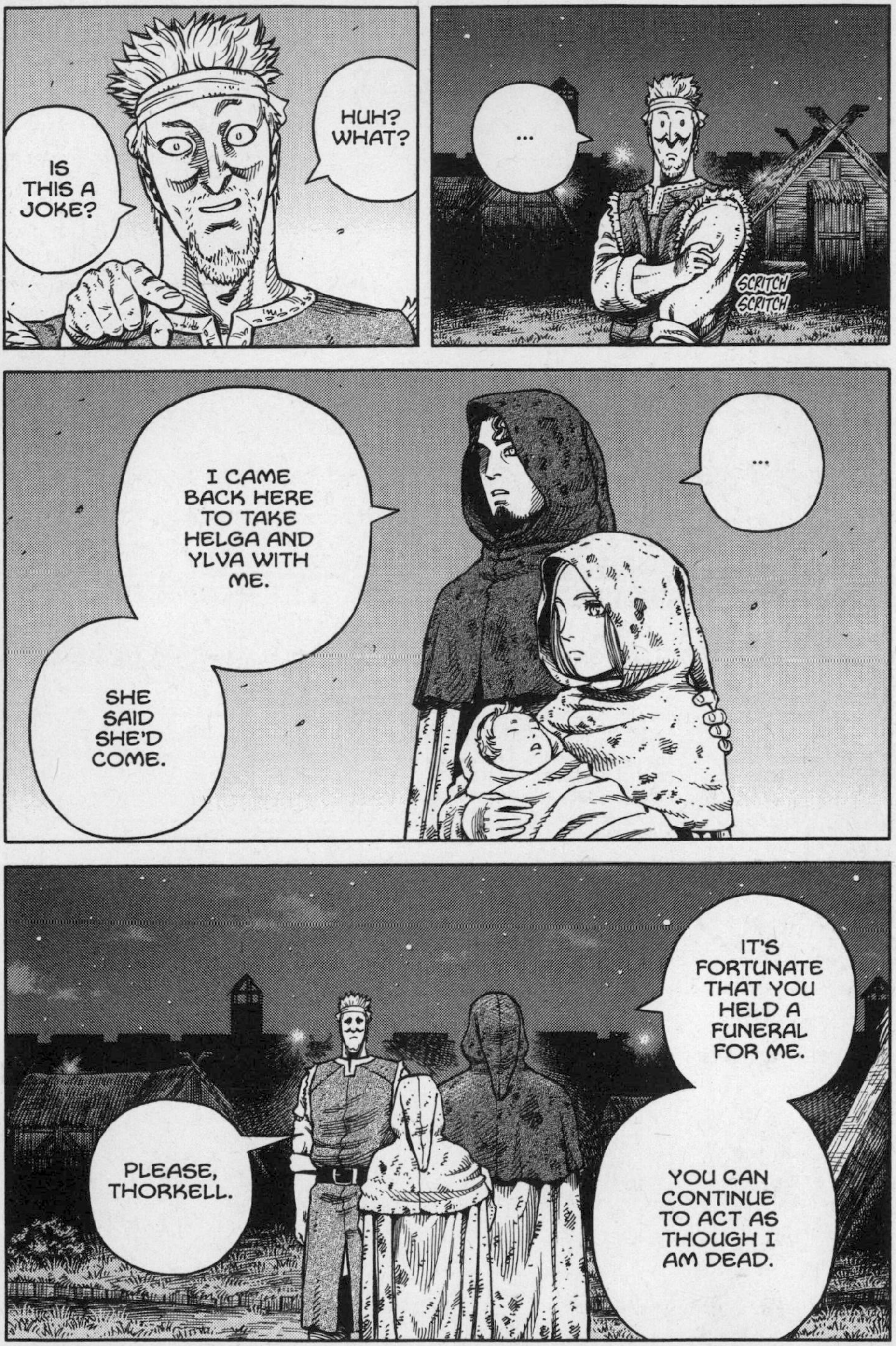
...
SCRITCH SCRITCH
HUH? WHAT?
IS THIS A JOKE?
...
I CAME BACK HERE TO TAKE HELGA AND YLVA WITH ME.
SHE SAID SHE'D COME.
IT'S FORTUNATE THAT YOU HELD A FUNERAL FOR ME.
YOU CAN CONTINUE TO ACT AS THOUGH I AM DEAD.
PLEASE, THORKELL.

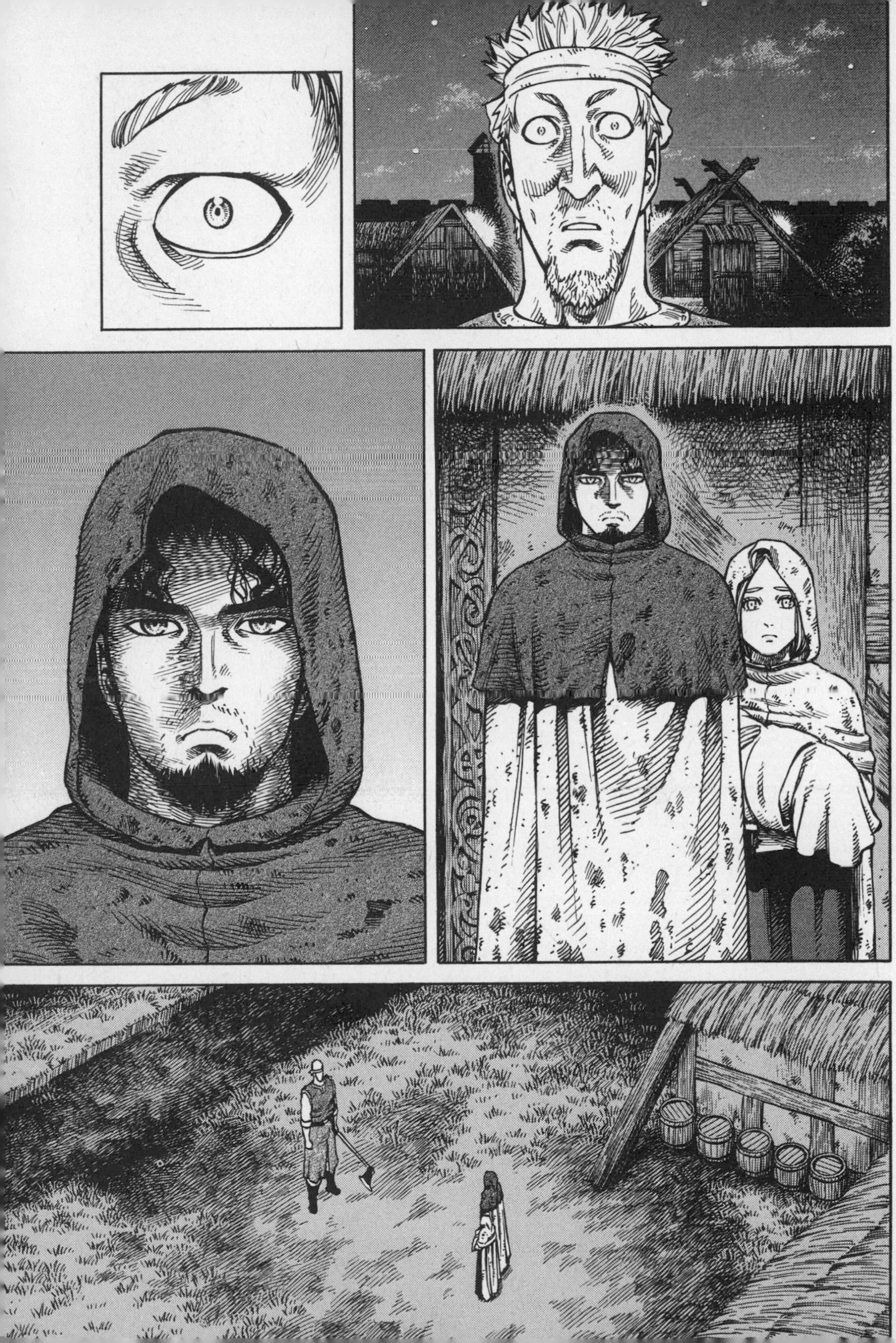

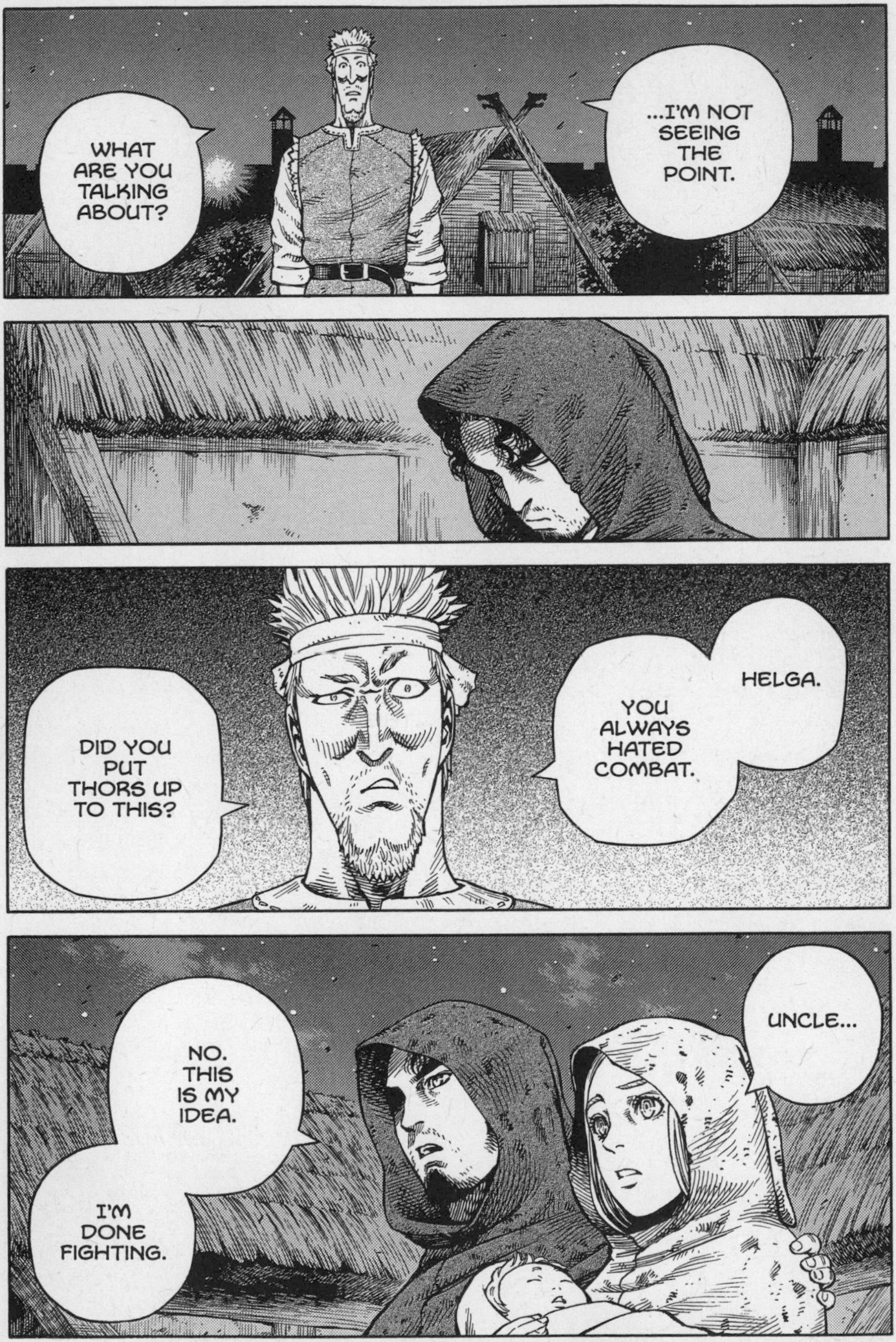
...I'M NOT SEEING THE POINT.
WHAT ARE YOU TALKING ABOUT?
HELGA.
YOU ALWAYS HATED COMBAT.
DID YOU PUT THORS UP TO THIS?
UNCLE...
NO. THIS IS MY IDEA.
I'M DONE FIGHTING.

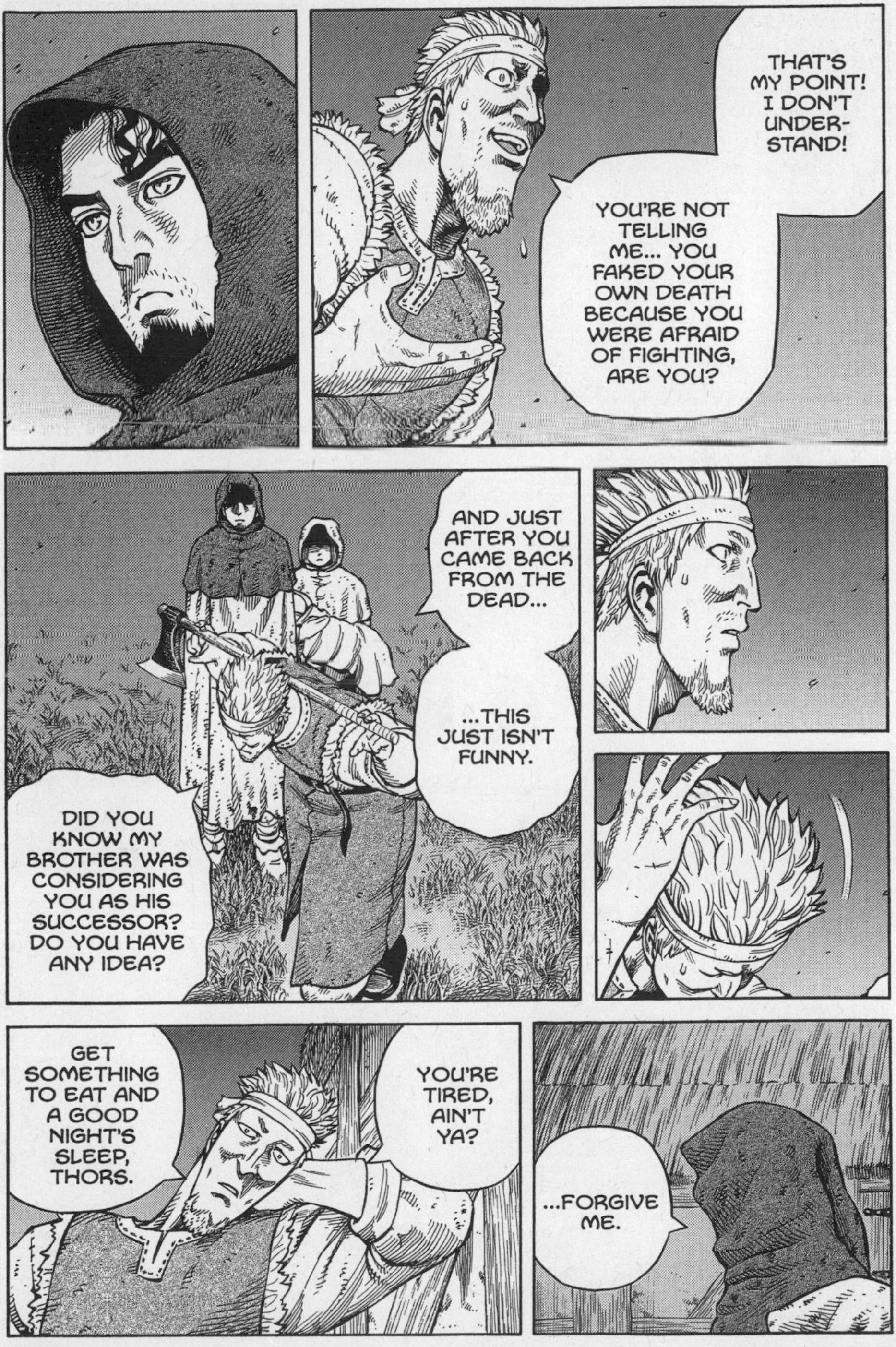
THAT'S MY POINT! I DON'T UNDER-STAND!
YOU'RE NOT TELLING ME... YOU FAKED YOUR OWN DEATH BECAUSE YOU WERE AFRAID OF FIGHTING, ARE YOU?
AND JUST AFTER YOU CAME BACK FROM THE DEAD...
...THIS JUST ISN'T FUNNY.
DID YOU KNOW MY BROTHER WAS CONSIDERING YOU AS HIS SUCCESSOR? DO YOU HAVE ANY IDEA?
...FORGIVE ME.
YOU'RE TIRED, AIN'T YA?
GET SOMETHING TO EAT AND A GOOD NIGHT'S SLEEP, THORS.

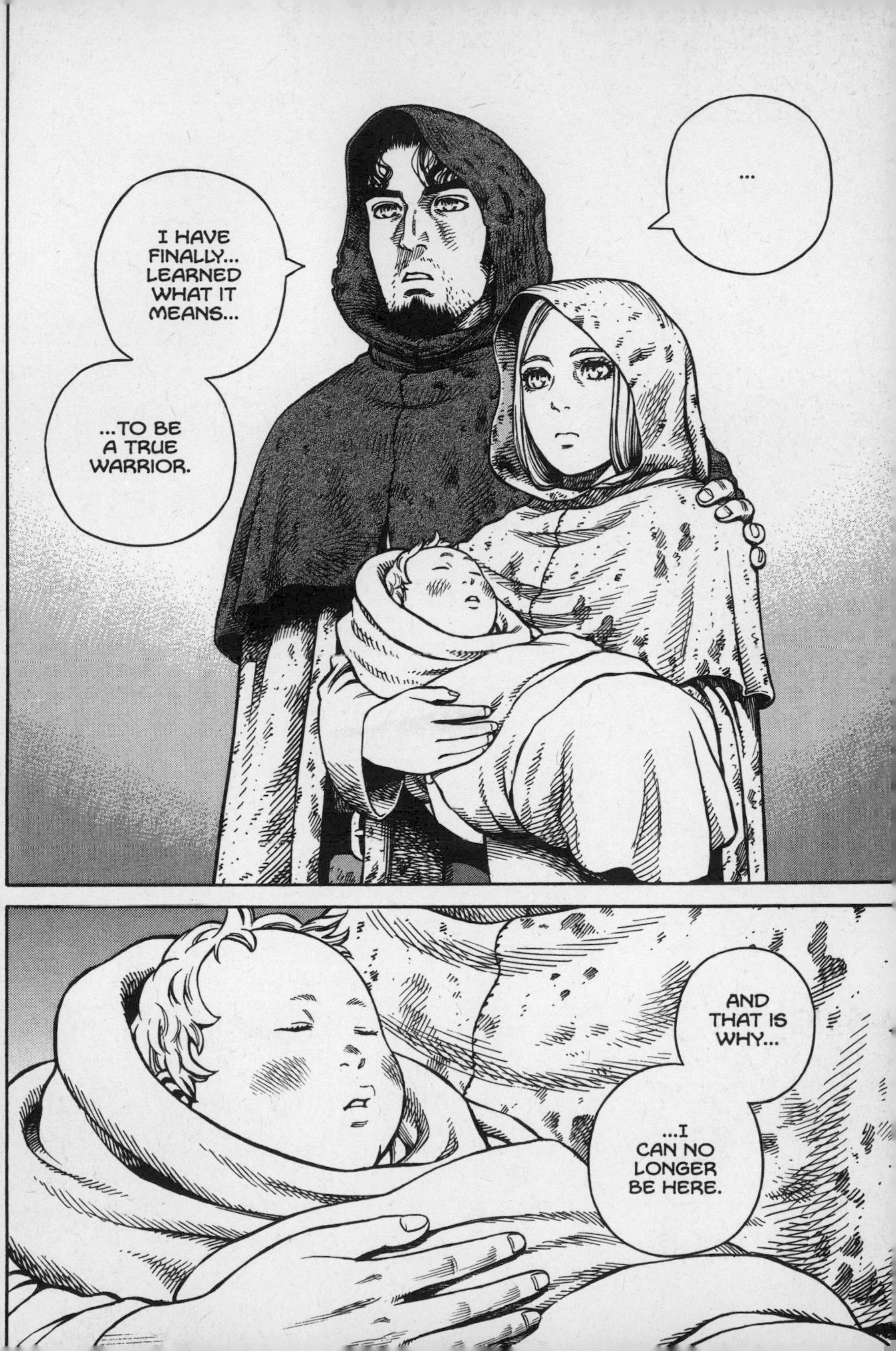
...
I HAVE FINALLY... LEARNED WHAT IT MEANS...
...TO BE A TRUE WARRIOR.
AND THAT IS WHY...
...I CAN NO LONGER BE HERE.

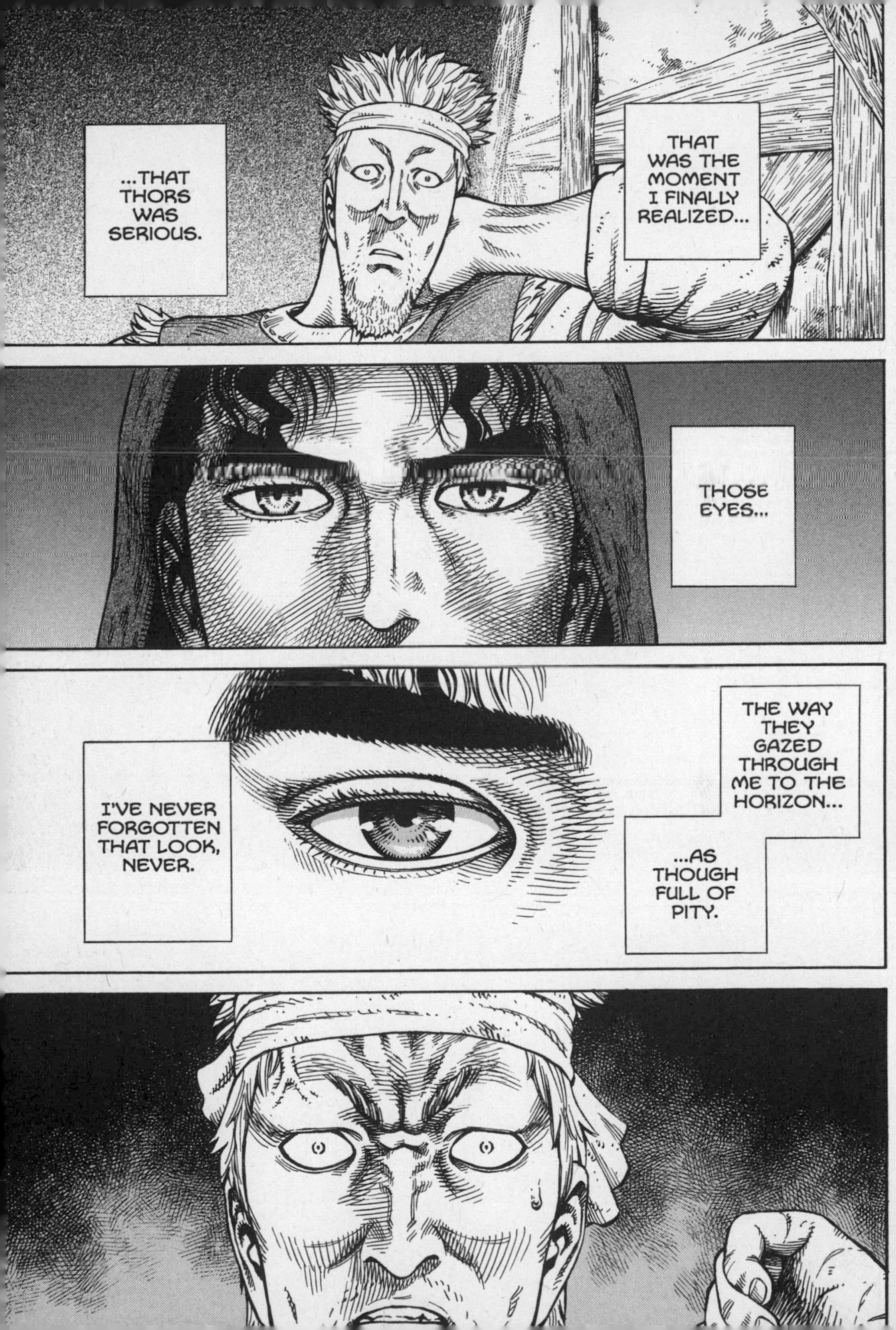
THAT WAS THE MOMENT I FINALLY REALIZED...
...THAT THORS WAS SERIOUS.
THOSE EYES...
THE WAY THEY GAZED THROUGH ME TO THE HORIZON...
...AS THOUGH FULL OF PITY.
I'VE NEVER FORGOTTEN THAT LOOK, NEVER.

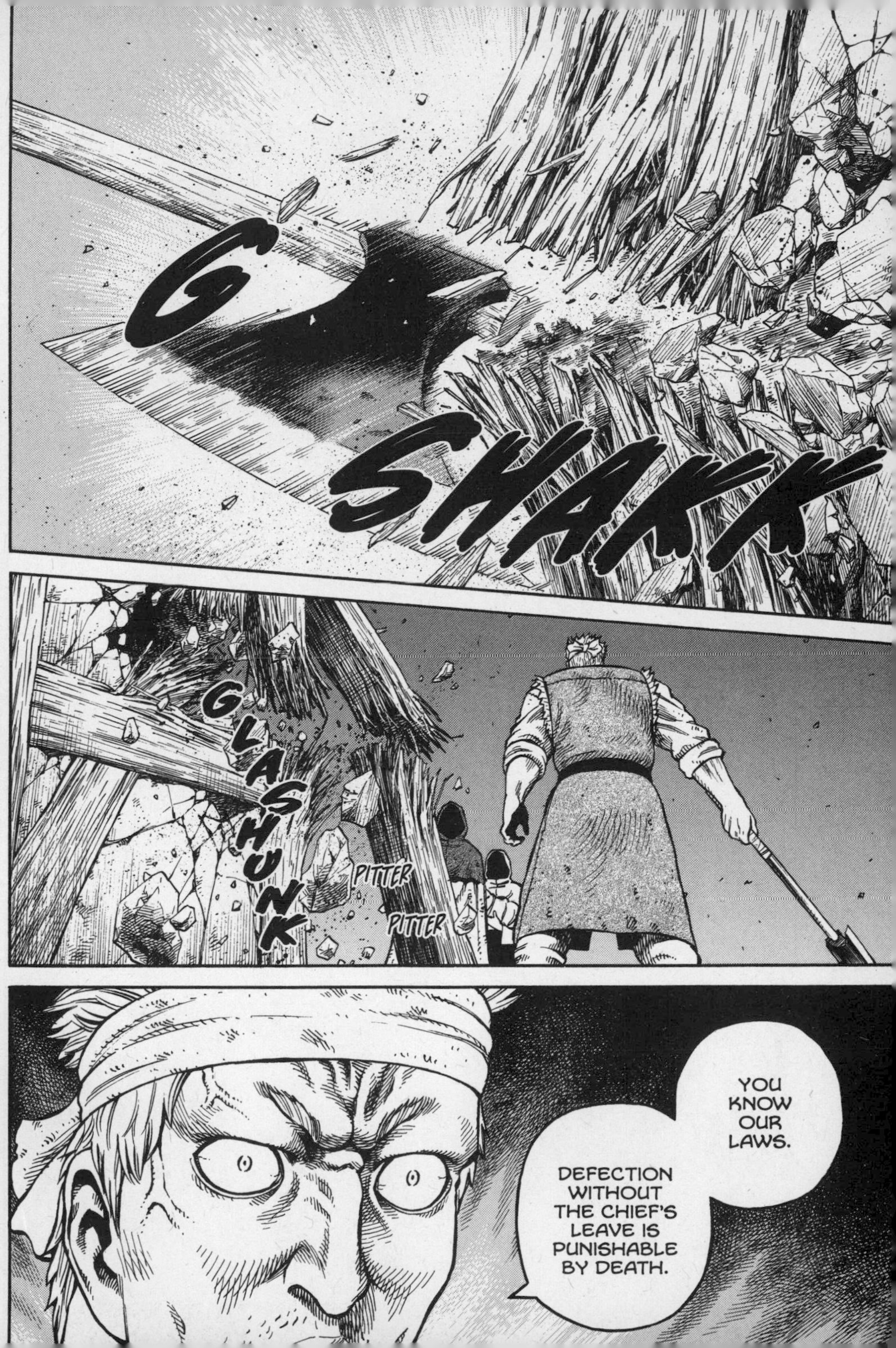

GSHAKK
GLASHUNK
PITTER
PITTER
YOU KNOW OUR LAWS.
DEFECTION WITHOUT THE CHIEF'S LEAVE IS PUNISHABLE BY DEATH.

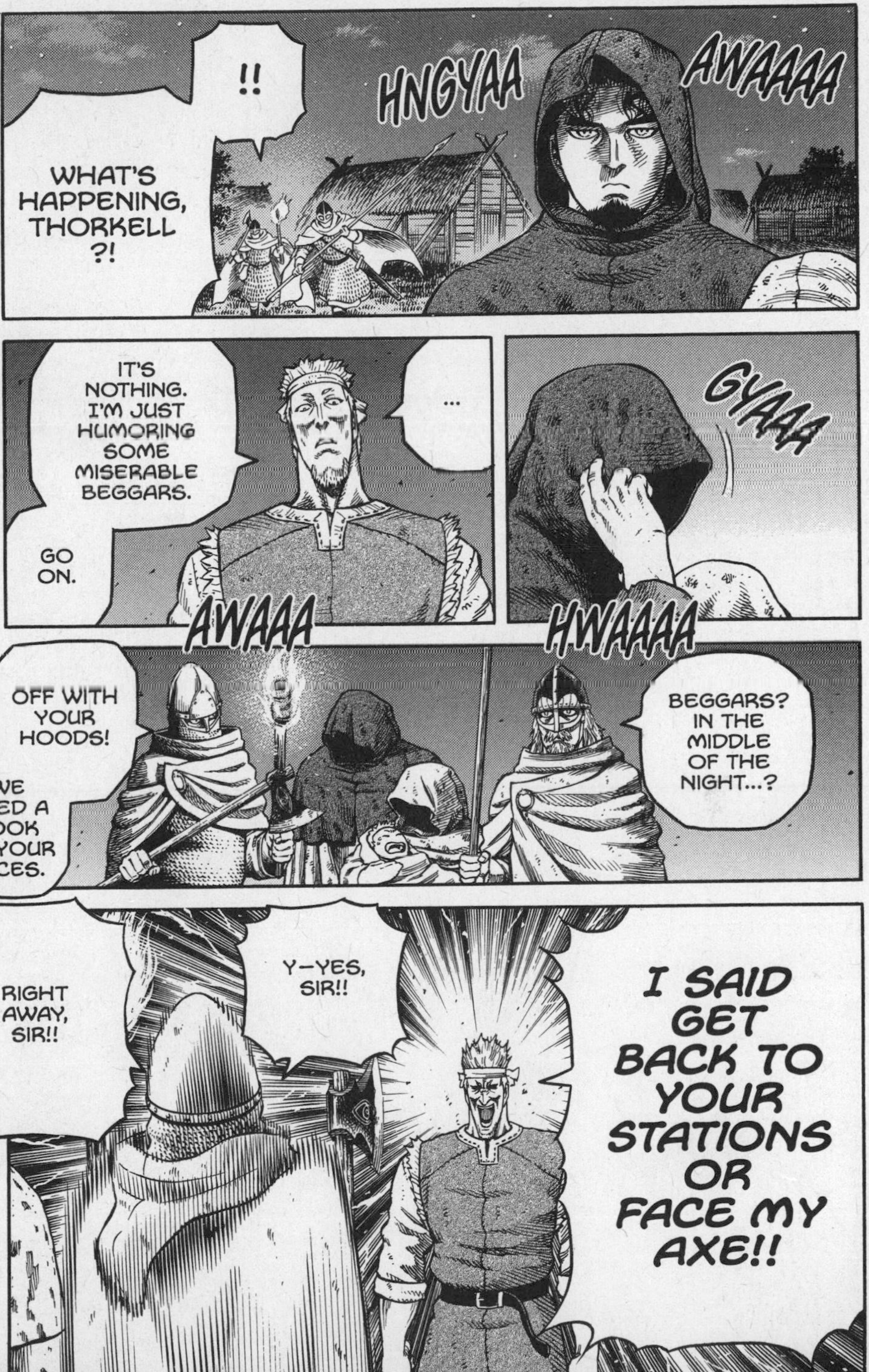
HNGYAA AWAAAAA
!!
WHAT'S HAPPENING, THORKELL ?!
GYAAAA
...
IT'S NOTHING. I'M JUST HUMORING SOME MISERABLE BEGGARS.
GO ON.
AWAAA HWAAAAA
BEGGARS? IN THE MIDDLE OF THE NIGHT...?
OFF WITH YOUR HOODS!
WE NEED A LOOK AT YOUR FACES.
I SAID GET BACK TO YOUR STATIONS OR FACE MY AXE!!
Y-YES, SIR!!
RIGHT AWAY, SIR!!

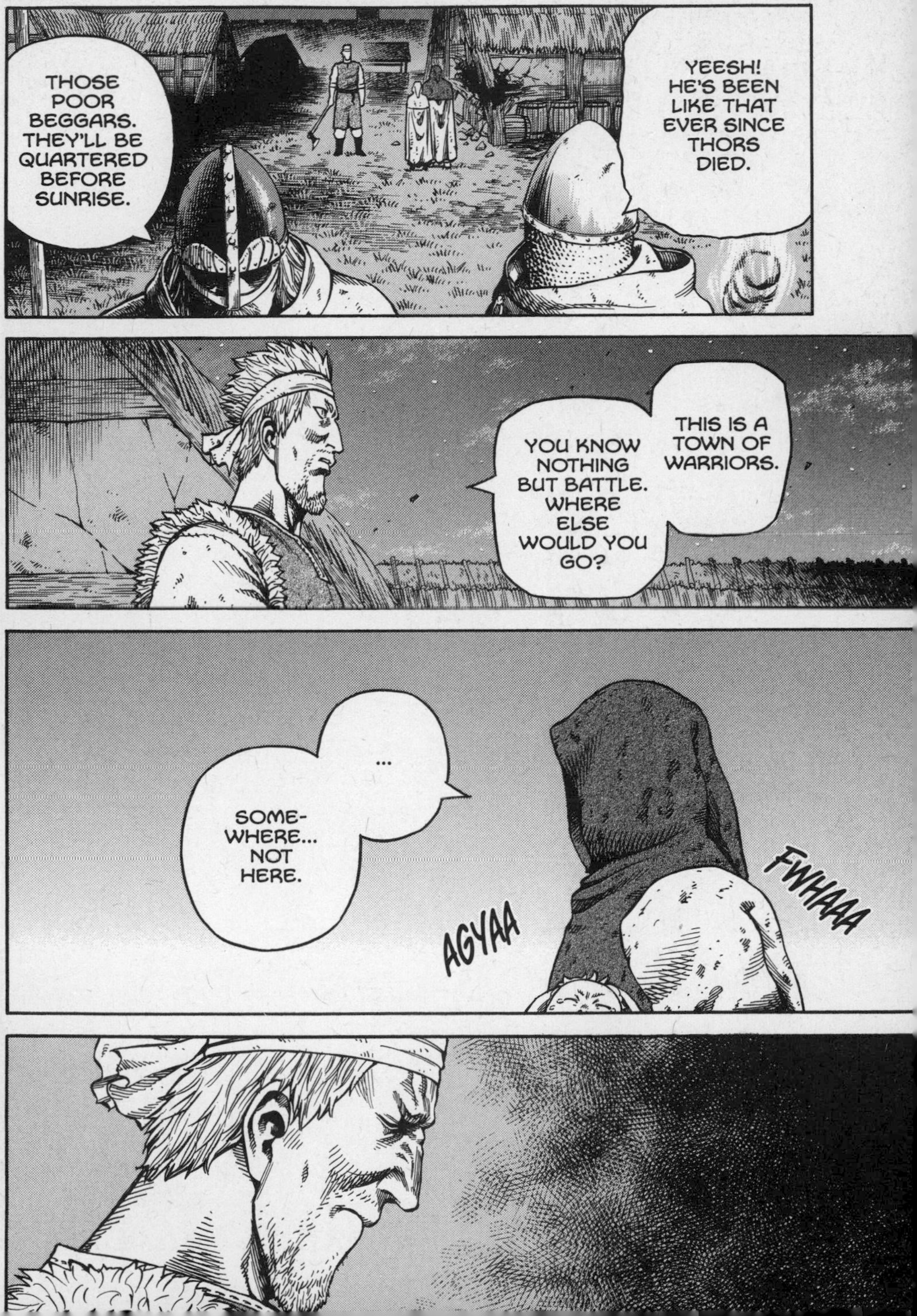
YEESH! HE'S BEEN LIKE THAT EVER SINCE THORS DIED.
THOSE POOR BEGGARS. THEY'LL BE QUARTERED BEFORE SUNRISE.
THIS IS A TOWN OF WARRIORS.
YOU KNOW NOTHING BUT BATTLE. WHERE ELSE WOULD YOU GO?
...
SOME-WHERE... NOT HERE.
FWHAAA
AGYAA

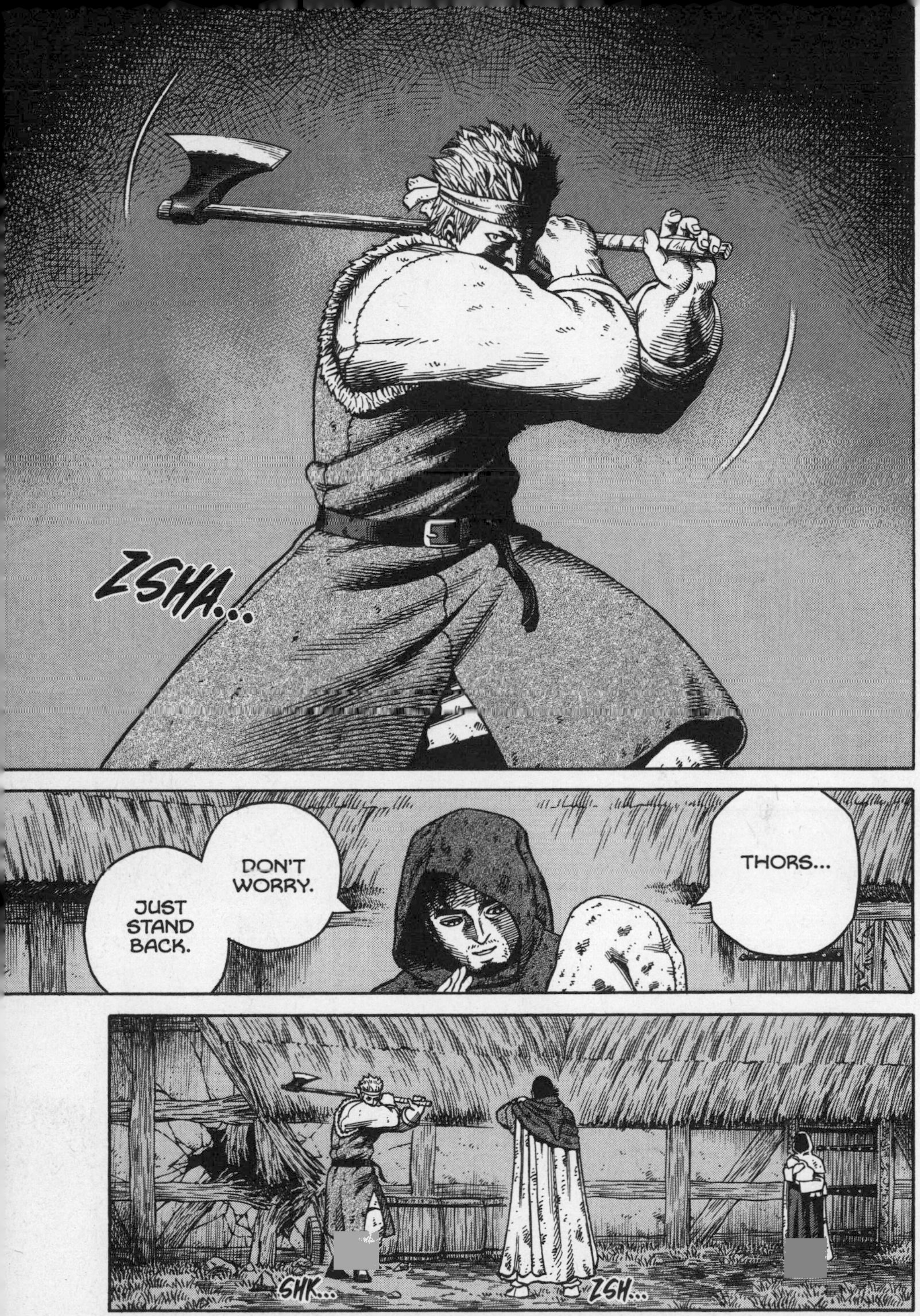
ZSHA...
THORS...
DON'T WORRY.
JUST STAND BACK.
ZSH...
SHK...

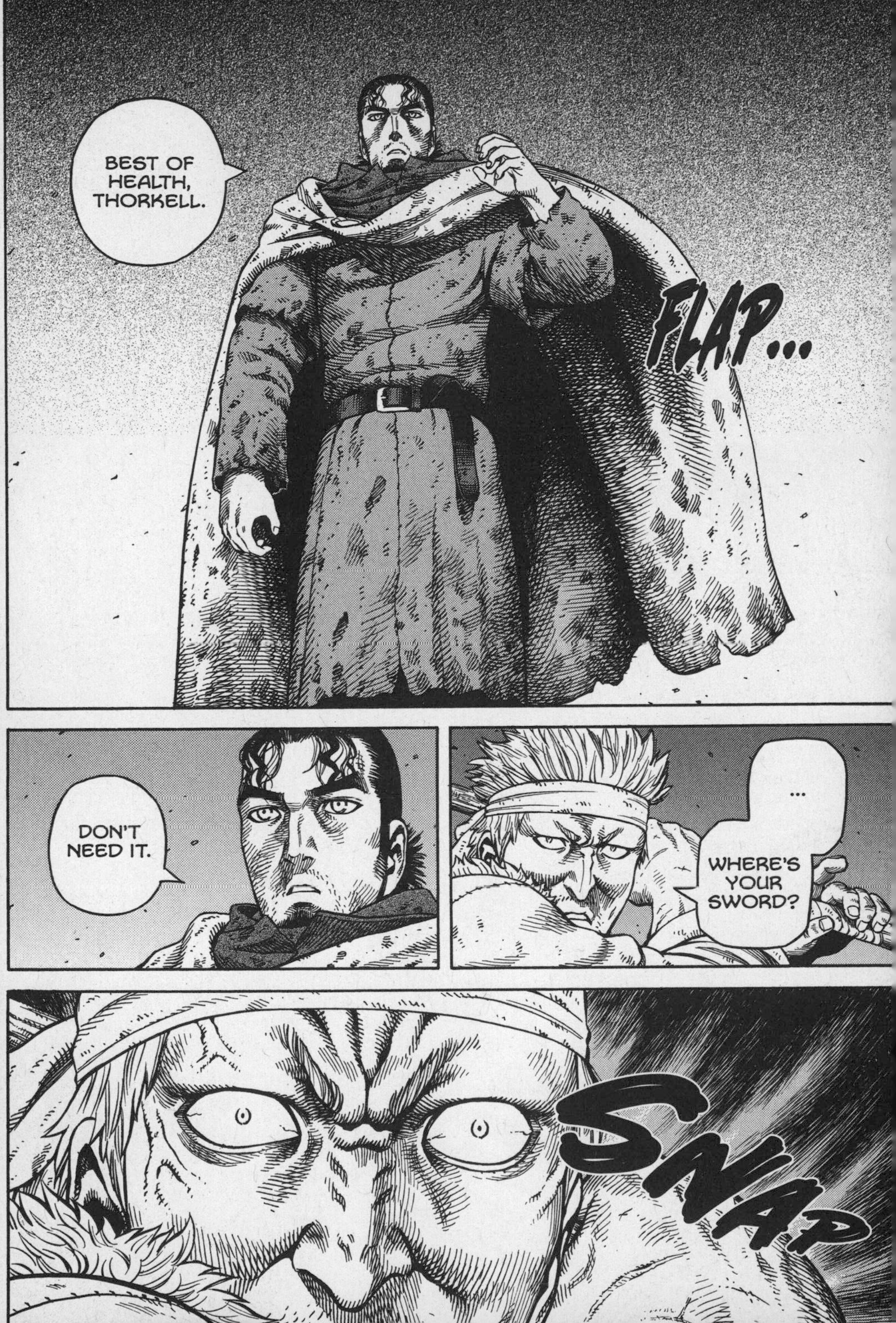
BEST OF HEALTH, THORKELL.
FLAP...
...
WHERE'S YOUR SWORD?
DON'T NEED IT.
SNAP

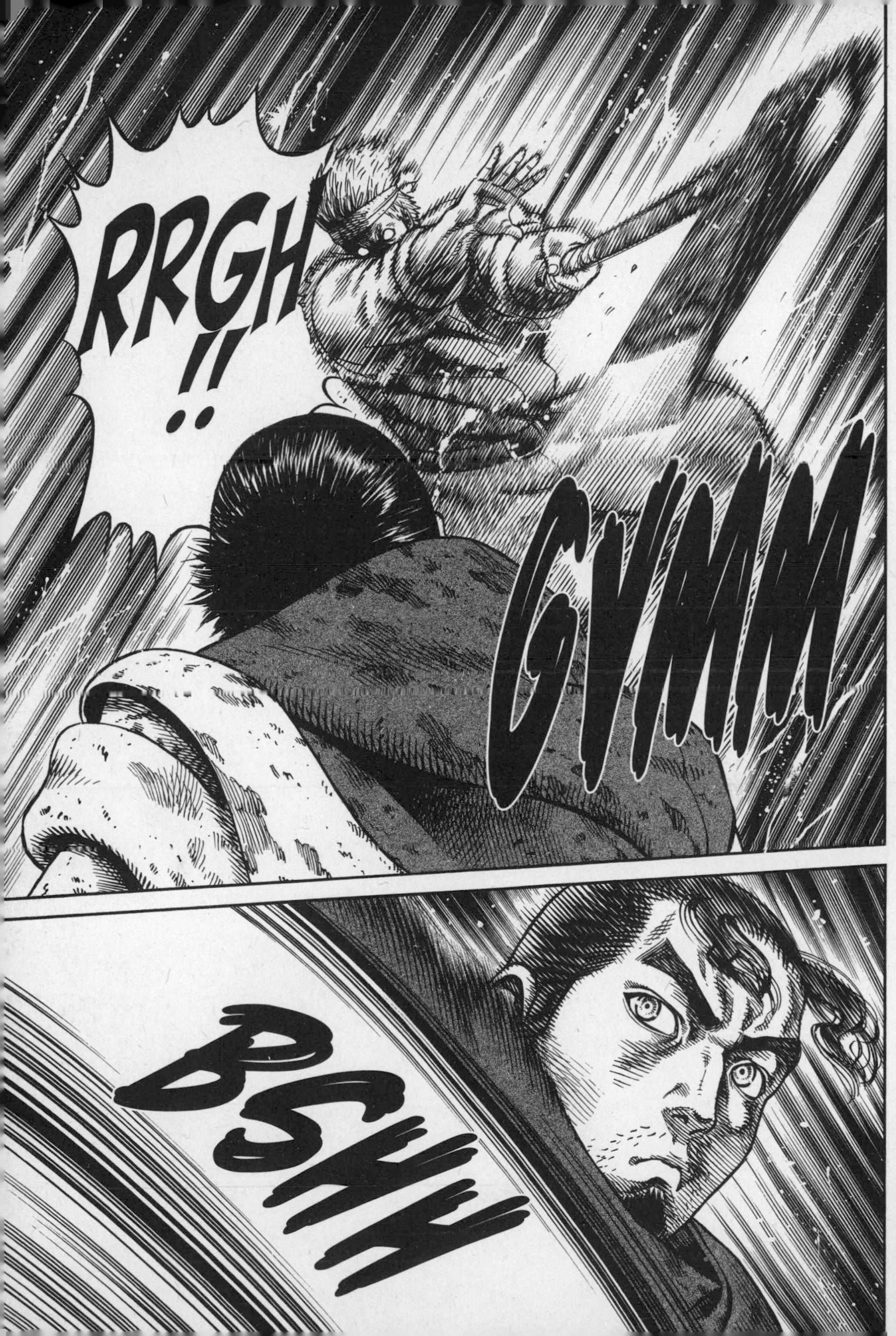
RRGH!!
GYMMM
BSHH

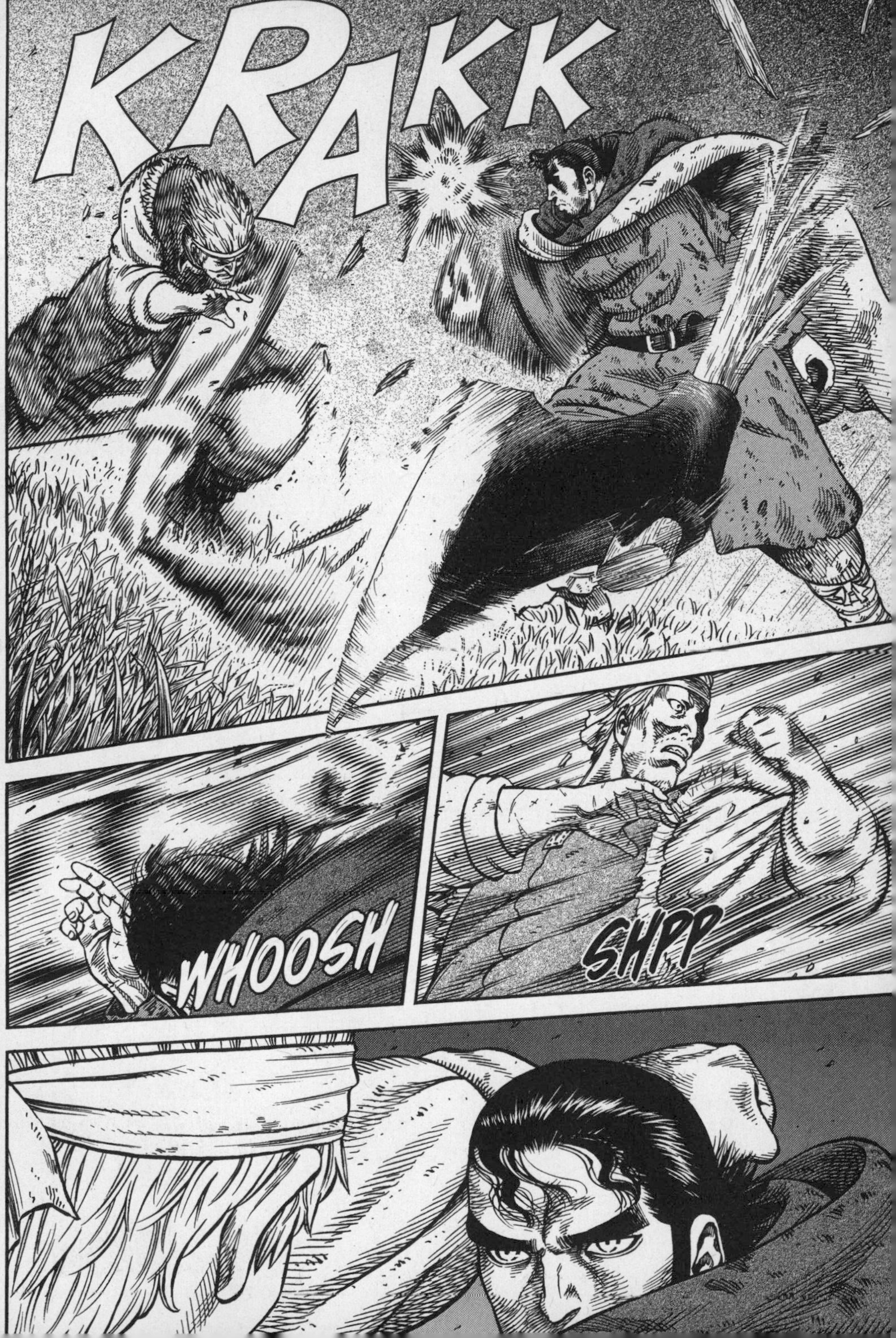
KRAKK
SHPP
WHOOSH

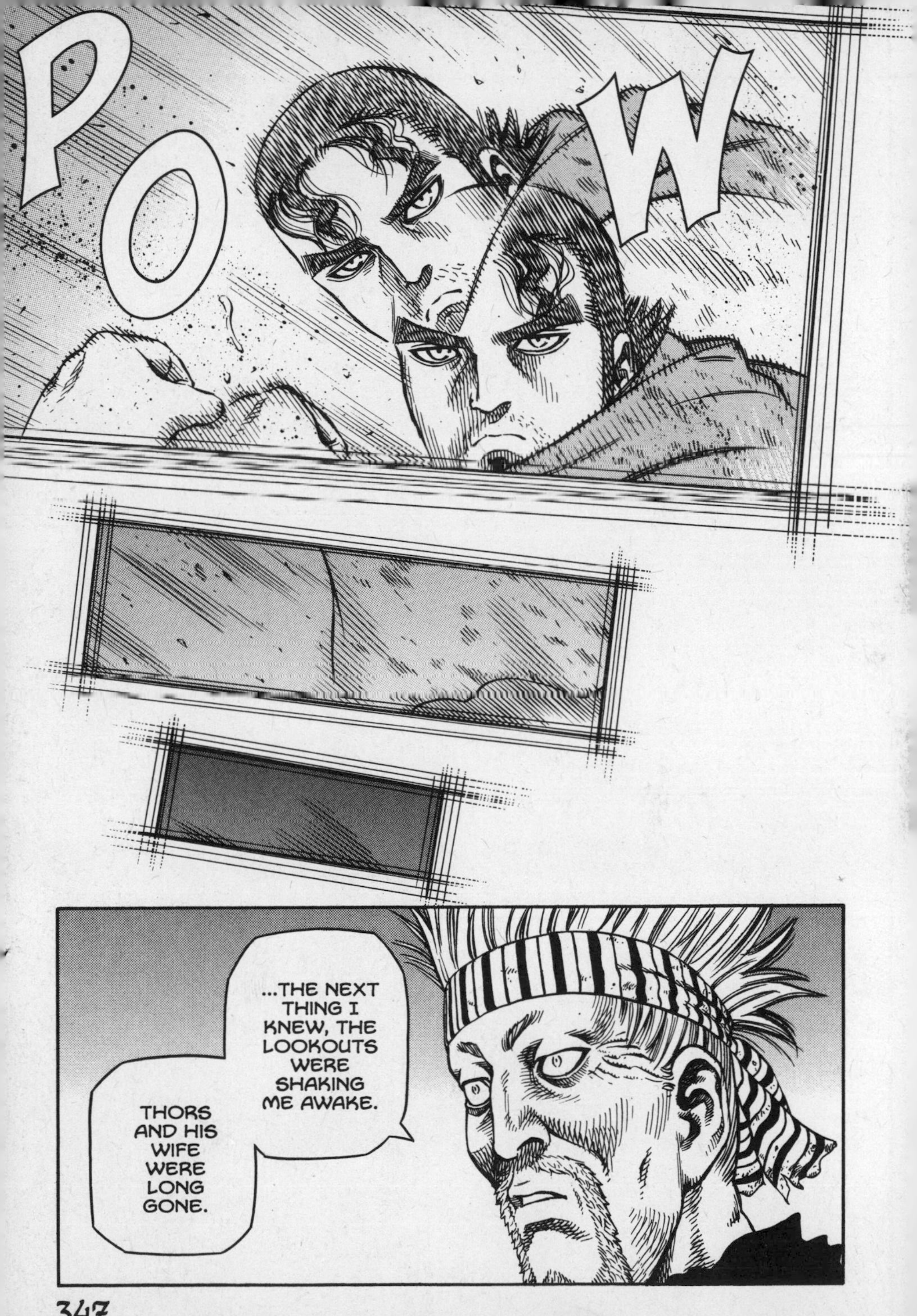
POW
...THE NEXT THING I KNEW, THE LOOKOUTS WERE SHAKING ME AWAKE.
THORS AND HIS WIFE WERE LONG GONE.

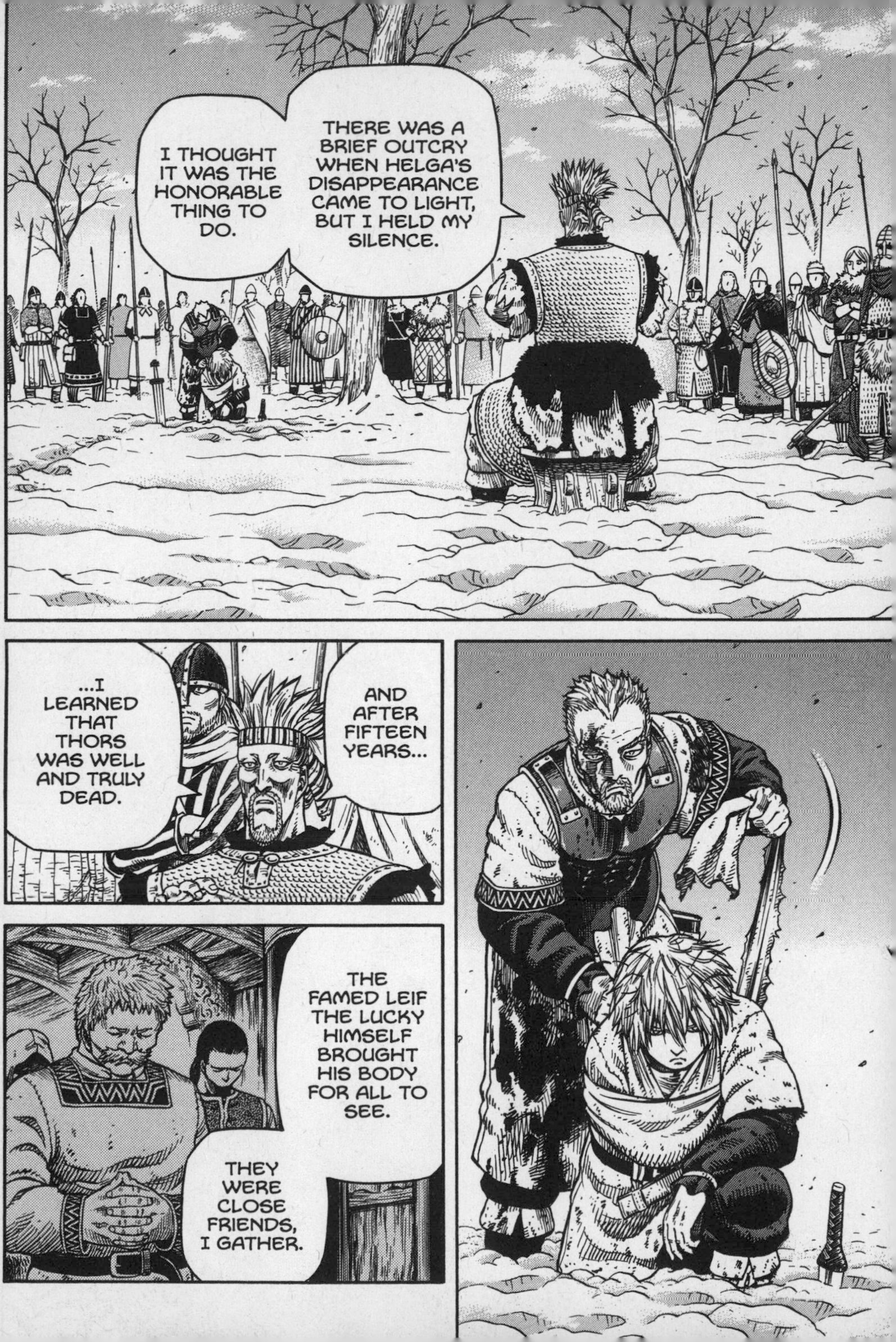
THERE WAS A BRIEF OUTCRY WHEN HELGA'S DISAPPEARANCE CAME TO LIGHT, BUT I HELD MY SILENCE.
I THOUGHT IT WAS THE HONORABLE THING TO DO.
AND AFTER FIFTEEN YEARS...
...I LEARNED THAT THORS WAS WELL AND TRULY DEAD.
THE FAMED LEIF THE LUCKY HIMSELF BROUGHT HIS BODY FOR ALL TO SEE.
THEY WERE CLOSE FRIENDS, I GATHER.

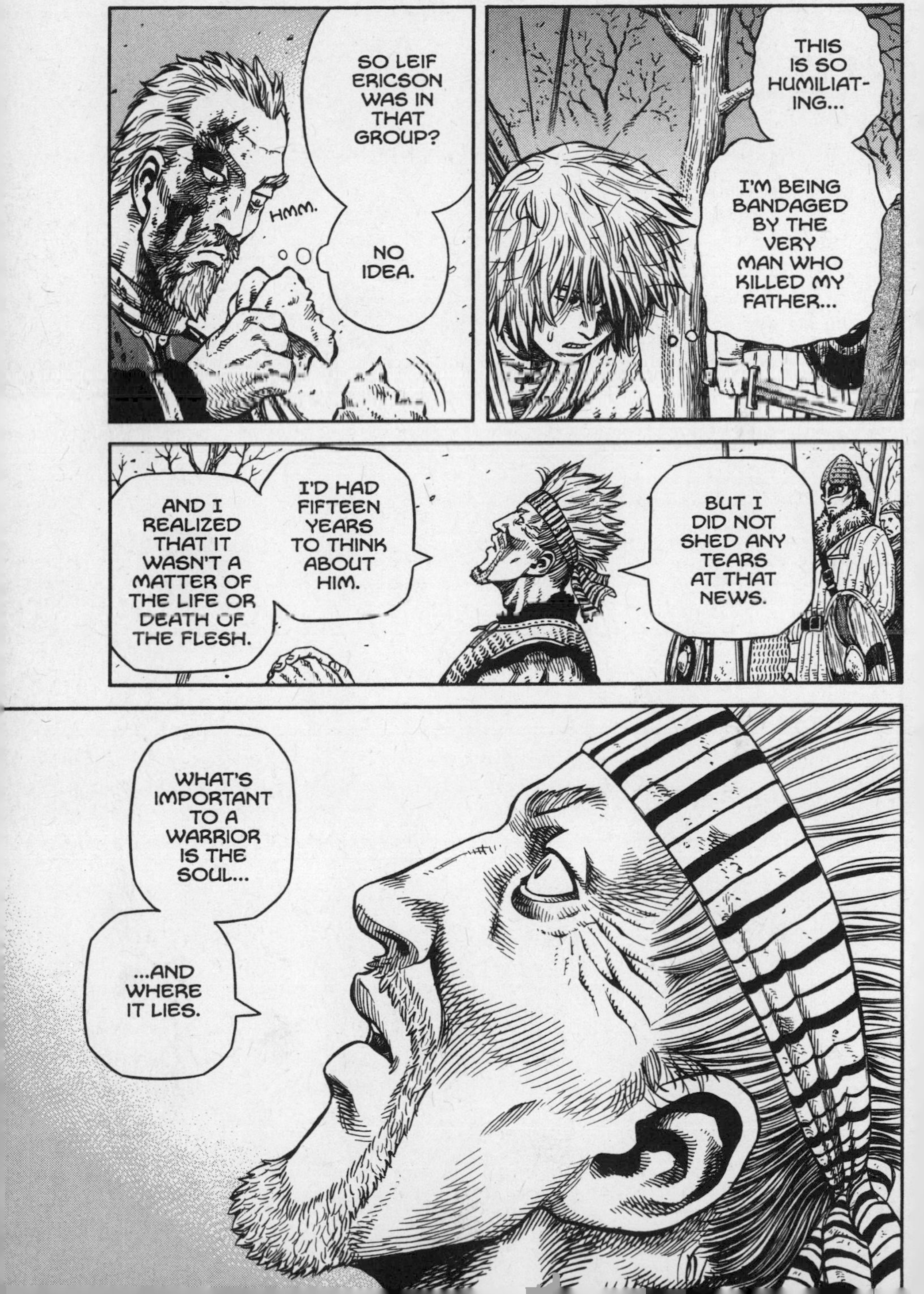
THIS IS SO HUMILIAT-ING...
I'M BEING BANDAGED BY THE VERY MAN WHO KILLED MY FATHER...
SO LEIF ERICSON WAS IN THAT GROUP?
HMM.
NO IDEA.
BUT I DID NOT SHED ANY TEARS AT THAT NEWS.
I'D HAD FIFTEEN YEARS TO THINK ABOUT HIM.
AND I REALIZED THAT IT WASN'T A MATTER OF THE LIFE OR DEATH OF THE FLESH.
WHAT'S IMPORTANT TO A WARRIOR IS THE SOUL...
...AND WHERE IT LIES.

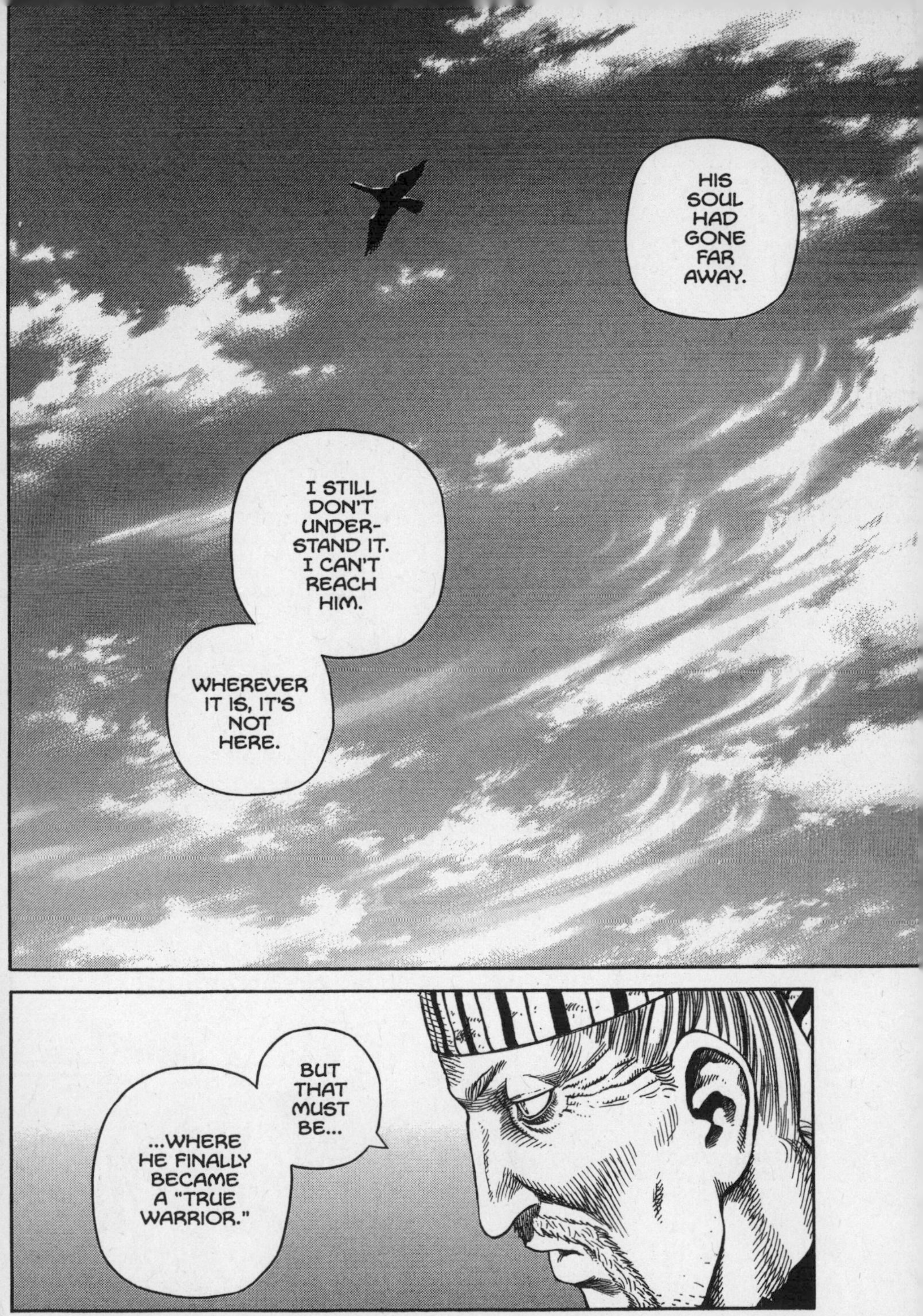
HIS SOUL HAD GONE FAR AWAY.
I STILL DON'T UNDER-STAND IT. I CAN'T REACH HIM.
WHEREVER IT IS, IT'S NOT HERE.
BUT THAT MUST BE...
...WHERE HE FINALLY BECAME A "TRUE WARRIOR."

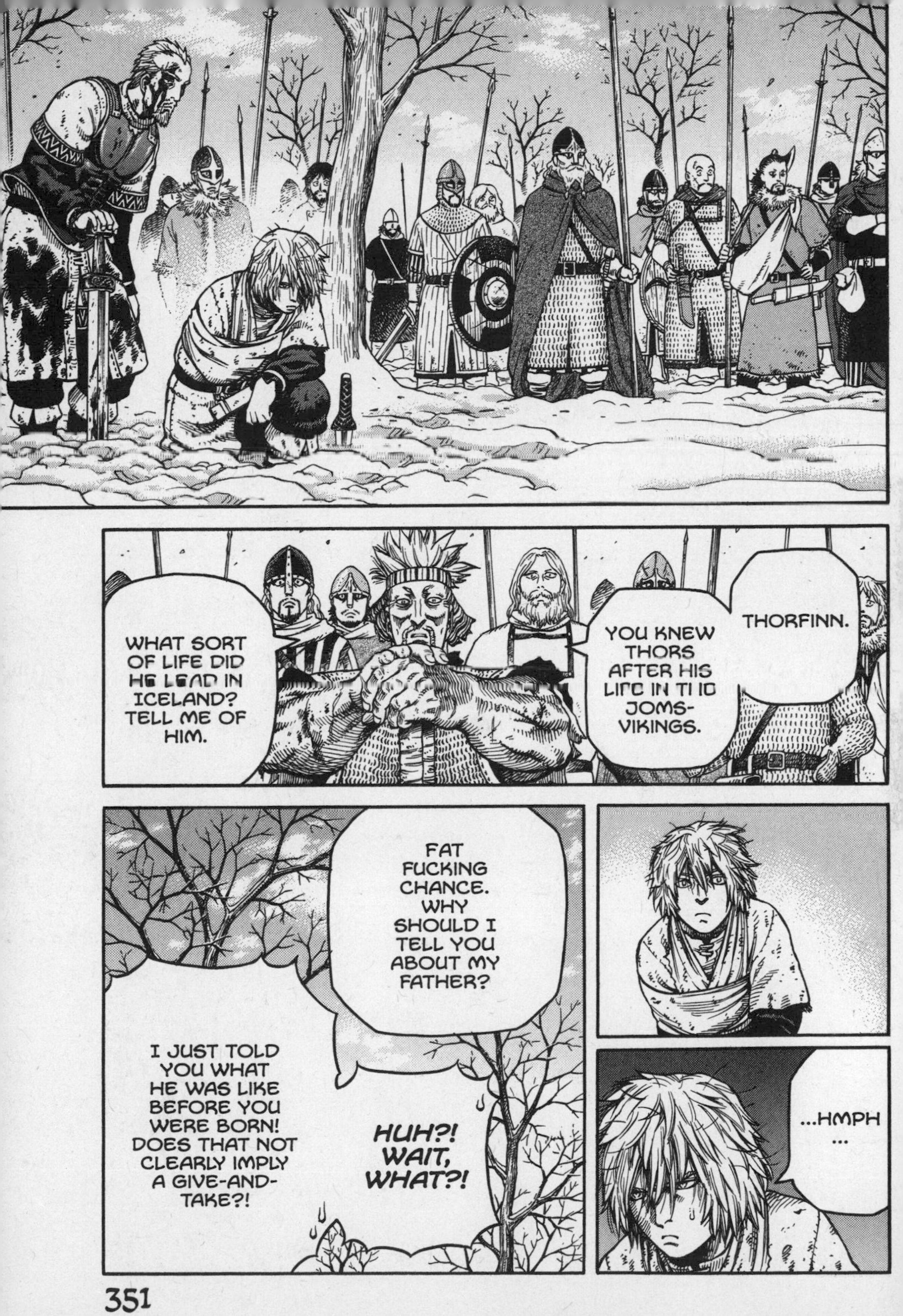
THORFINN.
YOU KNEW THORS AFTER HIS LIFE IN THE JOMS-VIKINGS.
WHAT SORT OF LIFE DID HE LEAD IN ICELAND? TELL ME OF HIM.
...HMPH ...
FAT FUCKING CHANCE. WHY SHOULD I TELL YOU ABOUT MY FATHER?
HUH?! WAIT, WHAT?!
I JUST TOLD YOU WHAT HE WAS LIKE BEFORE YOU WERE BORN! DOES THAT NOT CLEARLY IMPLY A GIVE-AND-TAKE?!

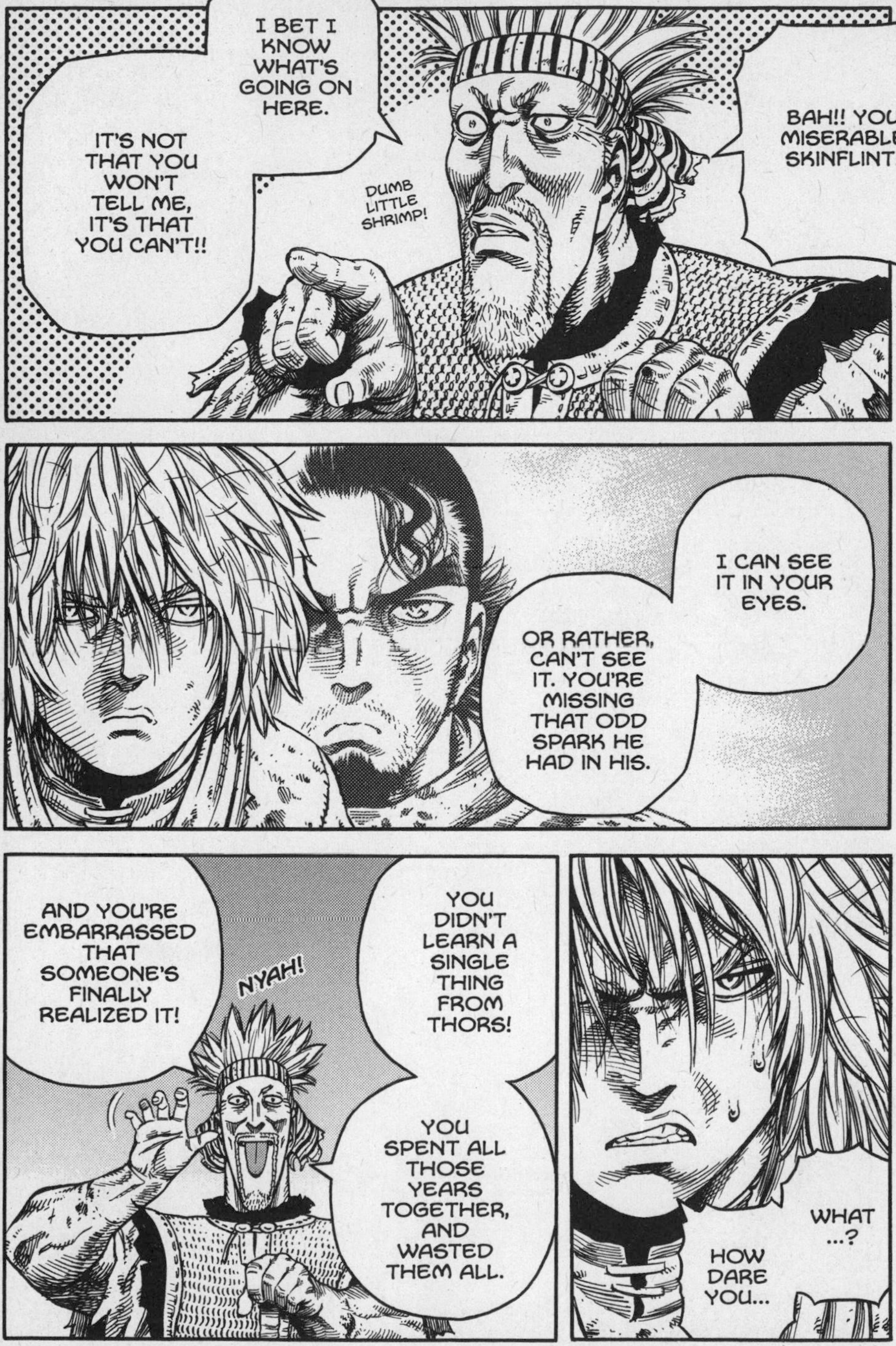
BAH!! YOU MISERABLE SKINFLINT!
I BET I KNOW WHAT'S GOING ON HERE.
IT'S NOT THAT YOU WON'T TELL ME, IT'S THAT YOU CAN'T!!
DUMB LITTLE SHRIMP!
I CAN SEE IT IN YOUR EYES.
OR RATHER, CAN'T SEE IT. YOU'RE MISSING THAT ODD SPARK HE HAD IN HIS.
WHAT ...?
HOW DARE YOU...
YOU DIDN'T LEARN A SINGLE THING FROM THORS!
AND YOU'RE EMBARRASSED THAT SOMEONE'S FINALLY REALIZED IT!
NYAH!
YOU SPENT ALL THOSE YEARS TOGETHER, AND WASTED THEM ALL.

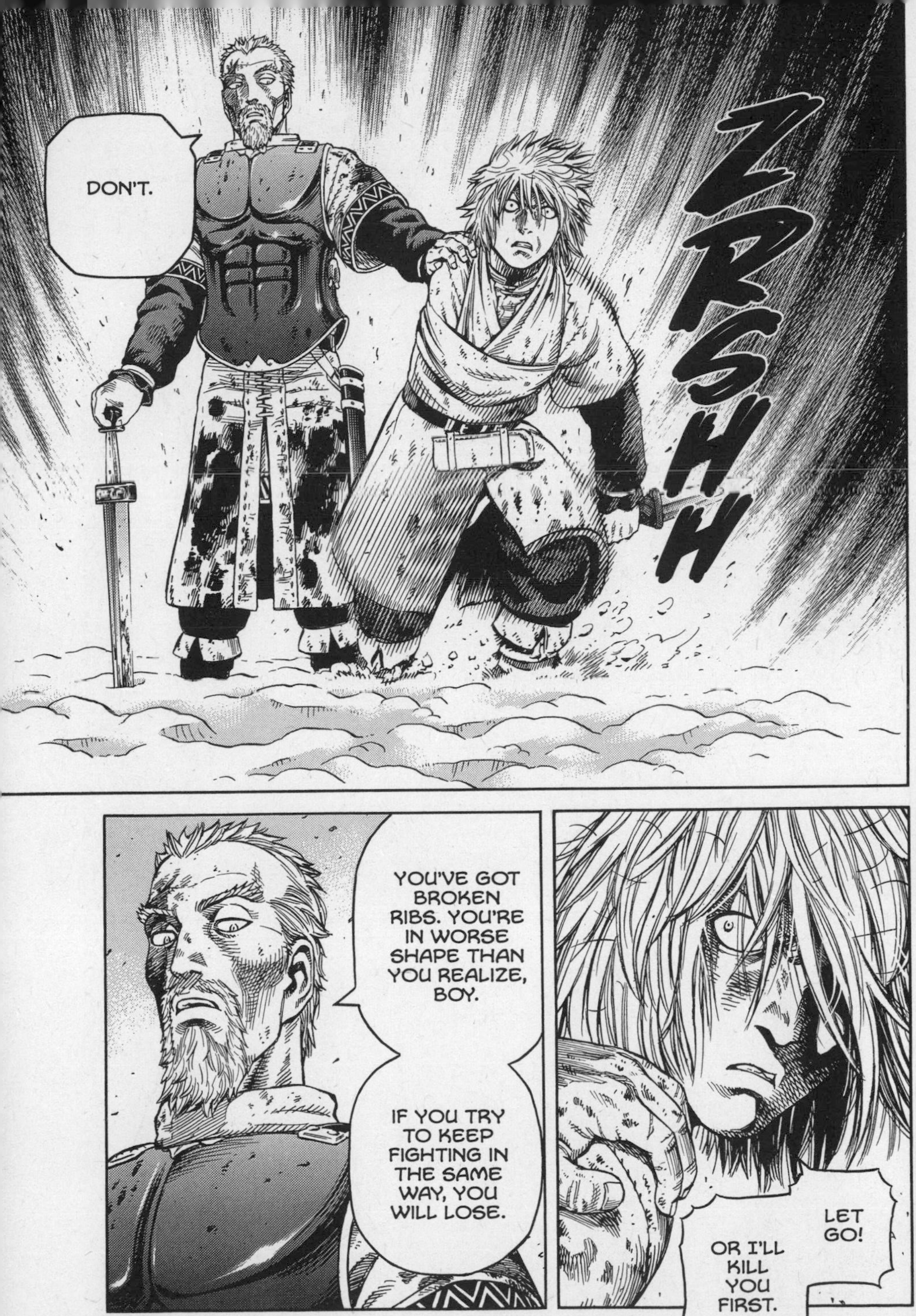
ZRSHHH
DON'T.
LET GO!
OR I'LL KILL YOU FIRST.
YOU'VE GOT BROKEN RIBS. YOU'RE IN WORSE SHAPE THAN YOU REALIZE, BOY.
IF YOU TRY TO KEEP FIGHTING IN THE SAME WAY, YOU WILL LOSE.

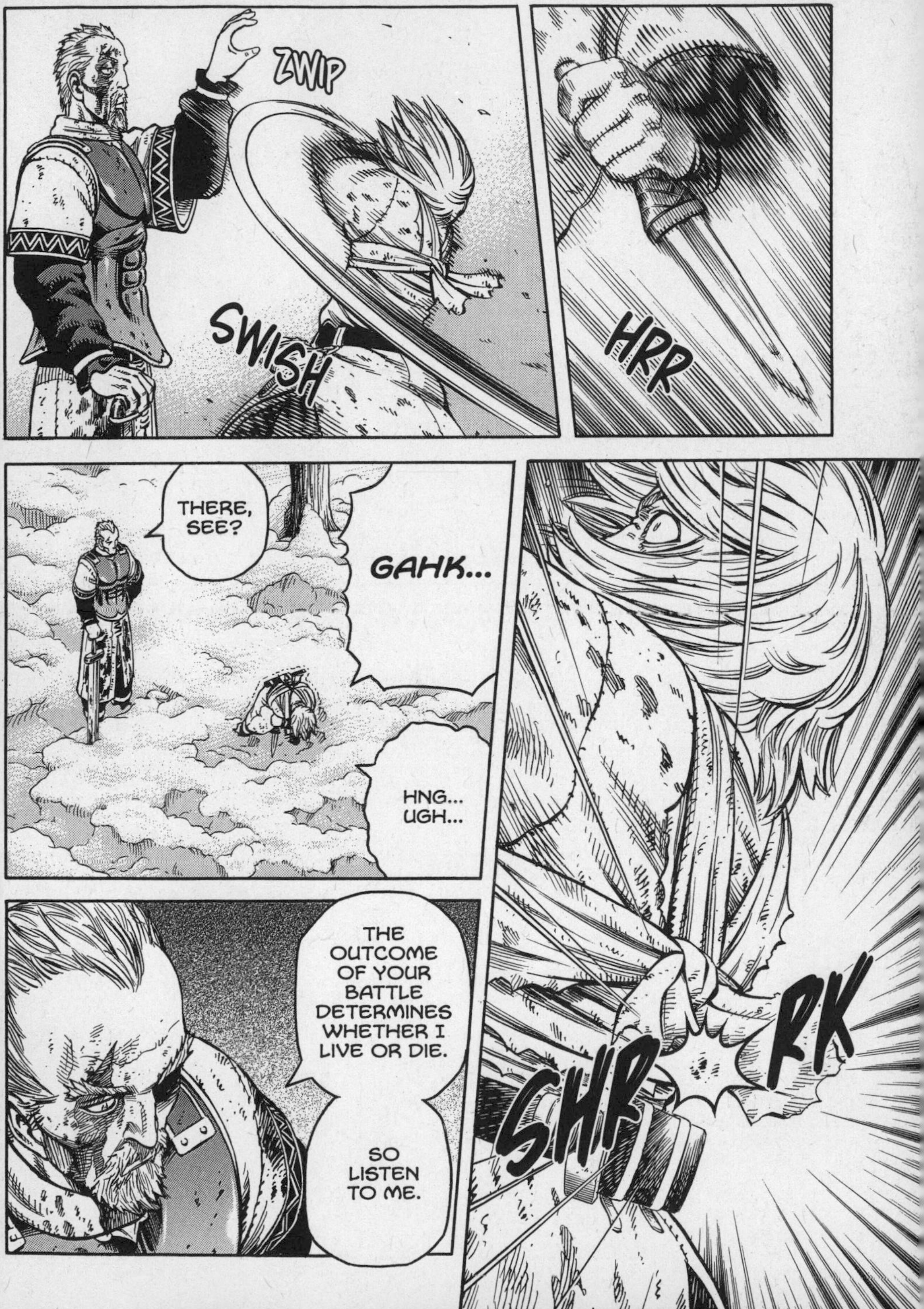
HRR
ZWIP
SWISH
SHR
RK
THERE, SEE?
GAHK...
HNG... UGH...
THE OUTCOME OF YOUR BATTLE DETERMINES WHETHER I LIVE OR DIE.
SO LISTEN TO ME.

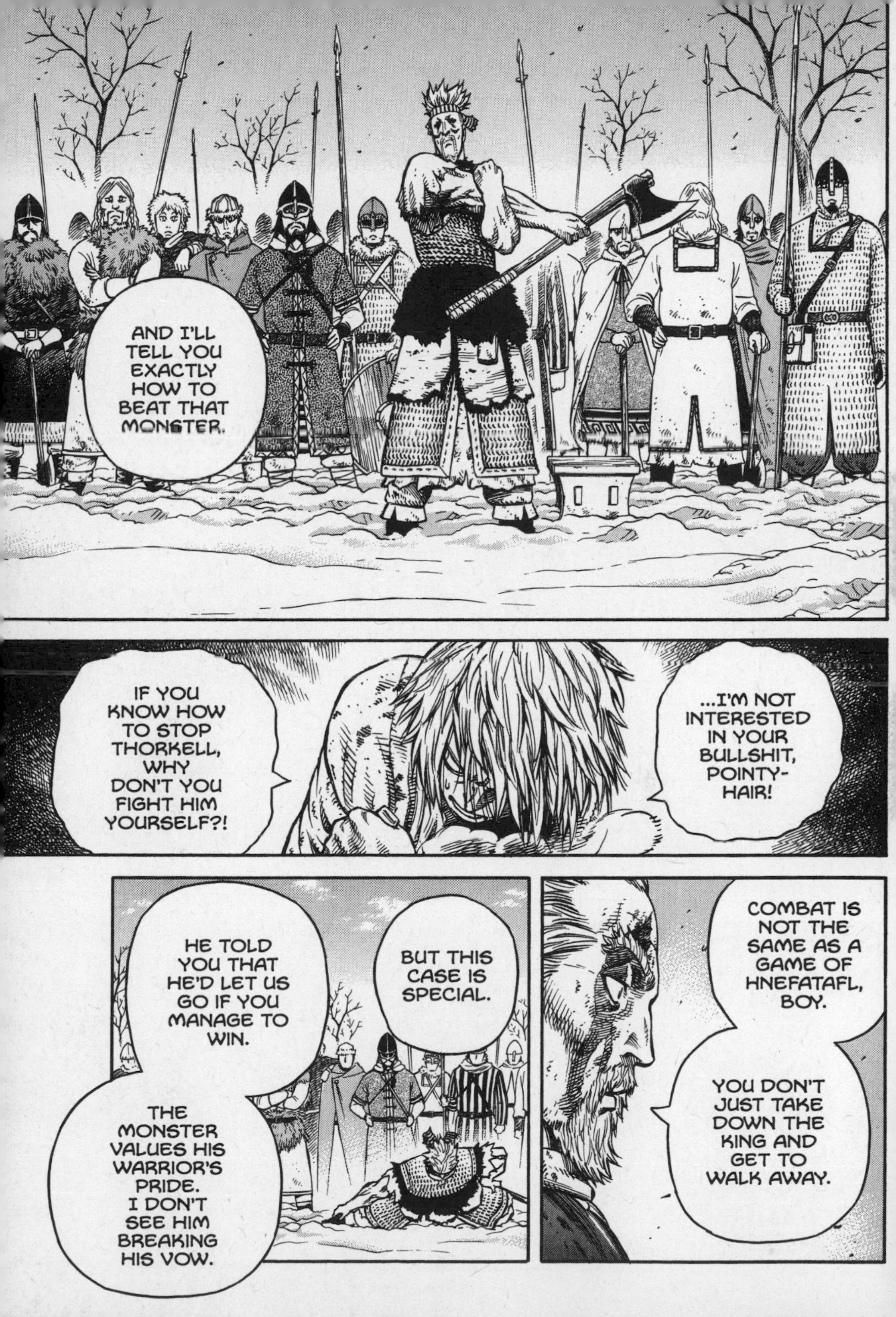
AND I'LL TELL YOU EXACTLY HOW TO BEAT THAT MONSTER.
...I'M NOT INTERESTED IN YOUR BULLSHIT, POINTY-HAIR!
IF YOU KNOW HOW TO STOP THORKELL, WHY DON'T YOU FIGHT HIM YOURSELF?!
COMBAT IS NOT THE SAME AS A GAME OF HNEFATAFL, BOY.
YOU DON'T JUST TAKE DOWN THE KING AND GET TO WALK AWAY.
BUT THIS CASE IS SPECIAL.
HE TOLD YOU THAT HE'D LET US GO IF YOU MANAGE TO WIN.
THE MONSTER VALUES HIS WARRIOR'S PRIDE. I DON'T SEE HIM BREAKING HIS VOW.

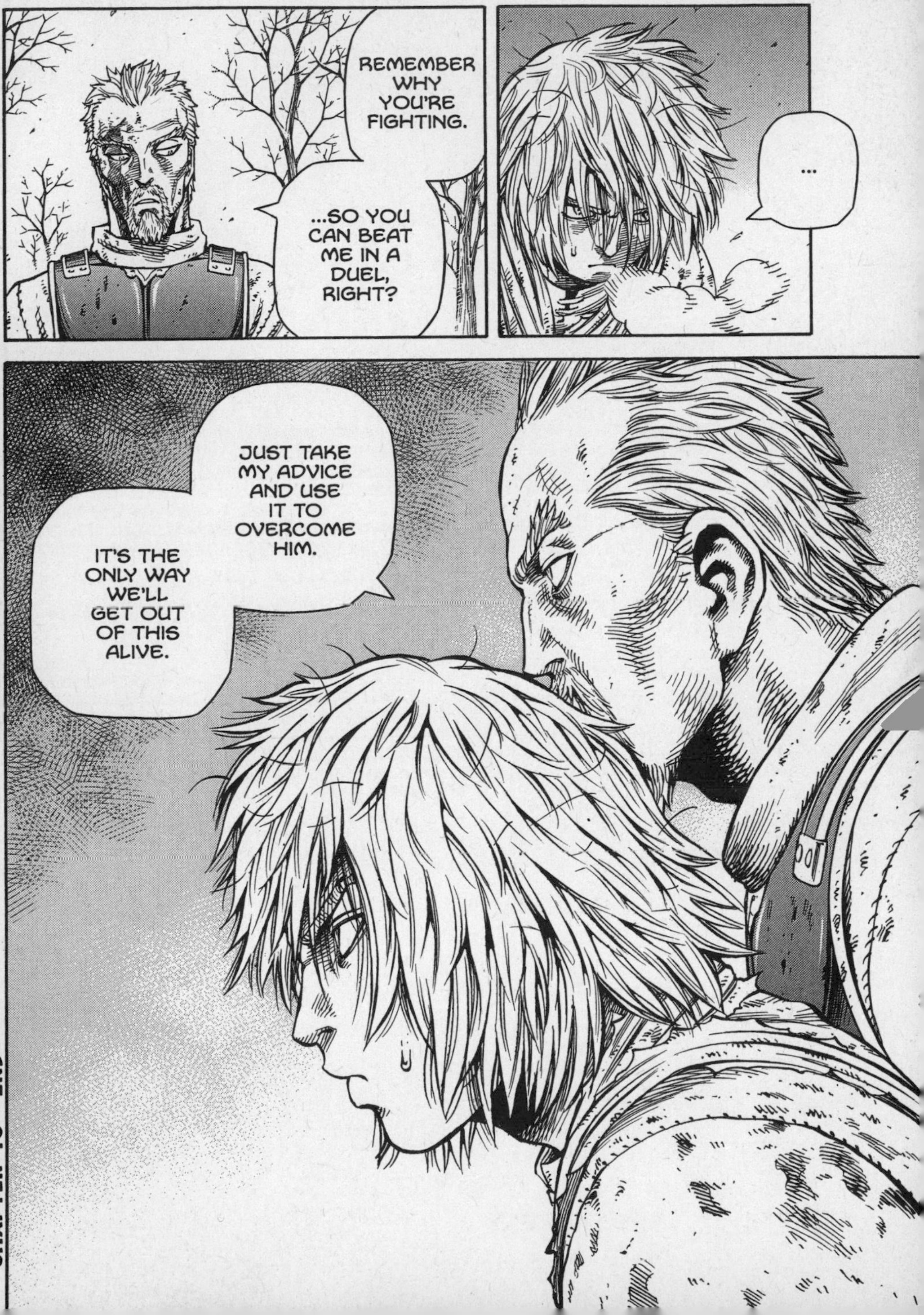
...
REMEMBER WHY YOU'RE FIGHTING.
...SO YOU CAN BEAT ME IN A DUEL, RIGHT?
JUST TAKE MY ADVICE AND USE IT TO OVERCOME HIM.
IT'S THE ONLY WAY WE'LL GET OUT OF THIS ALIVE.

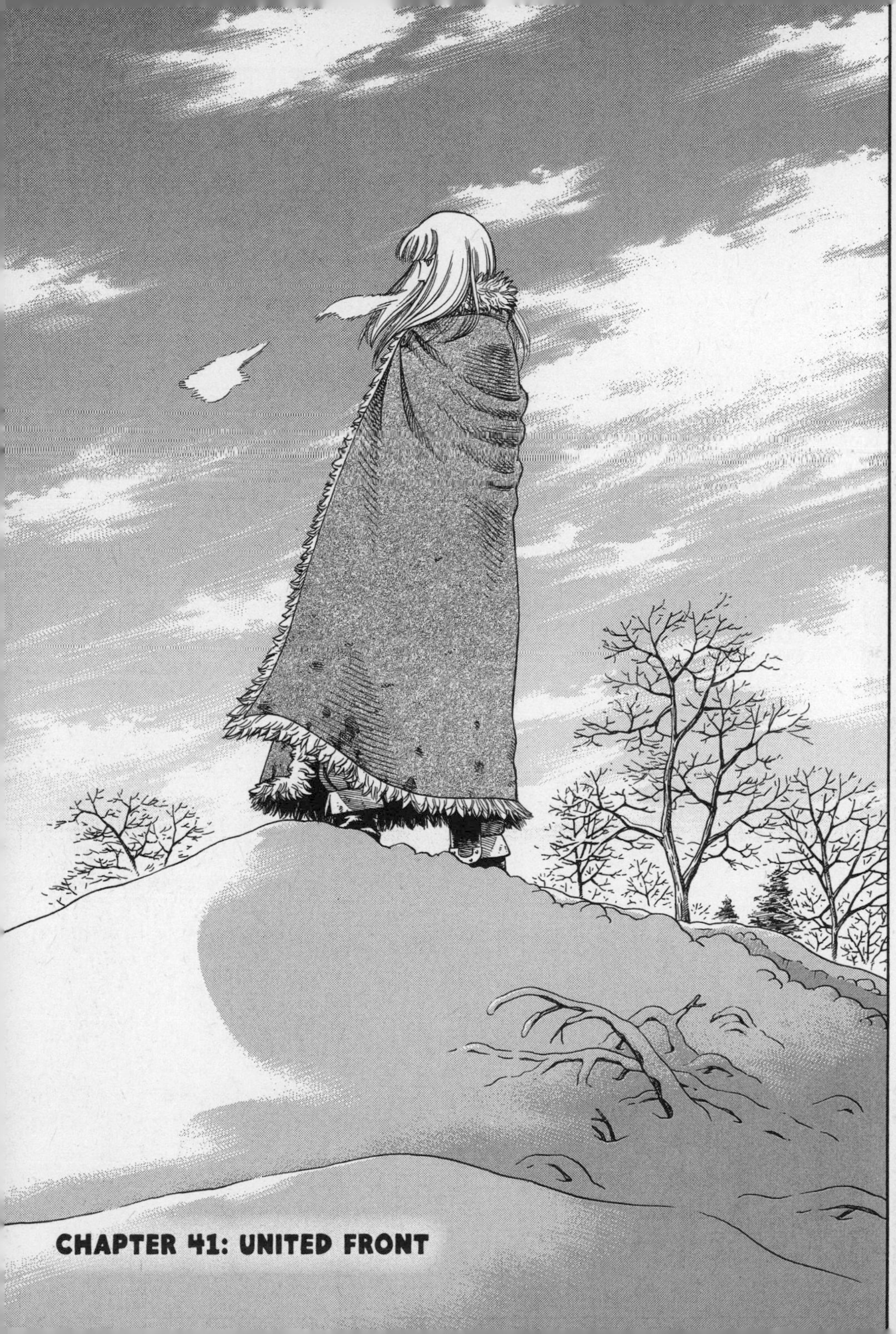

CHAPTER 41: UNITED FRONT

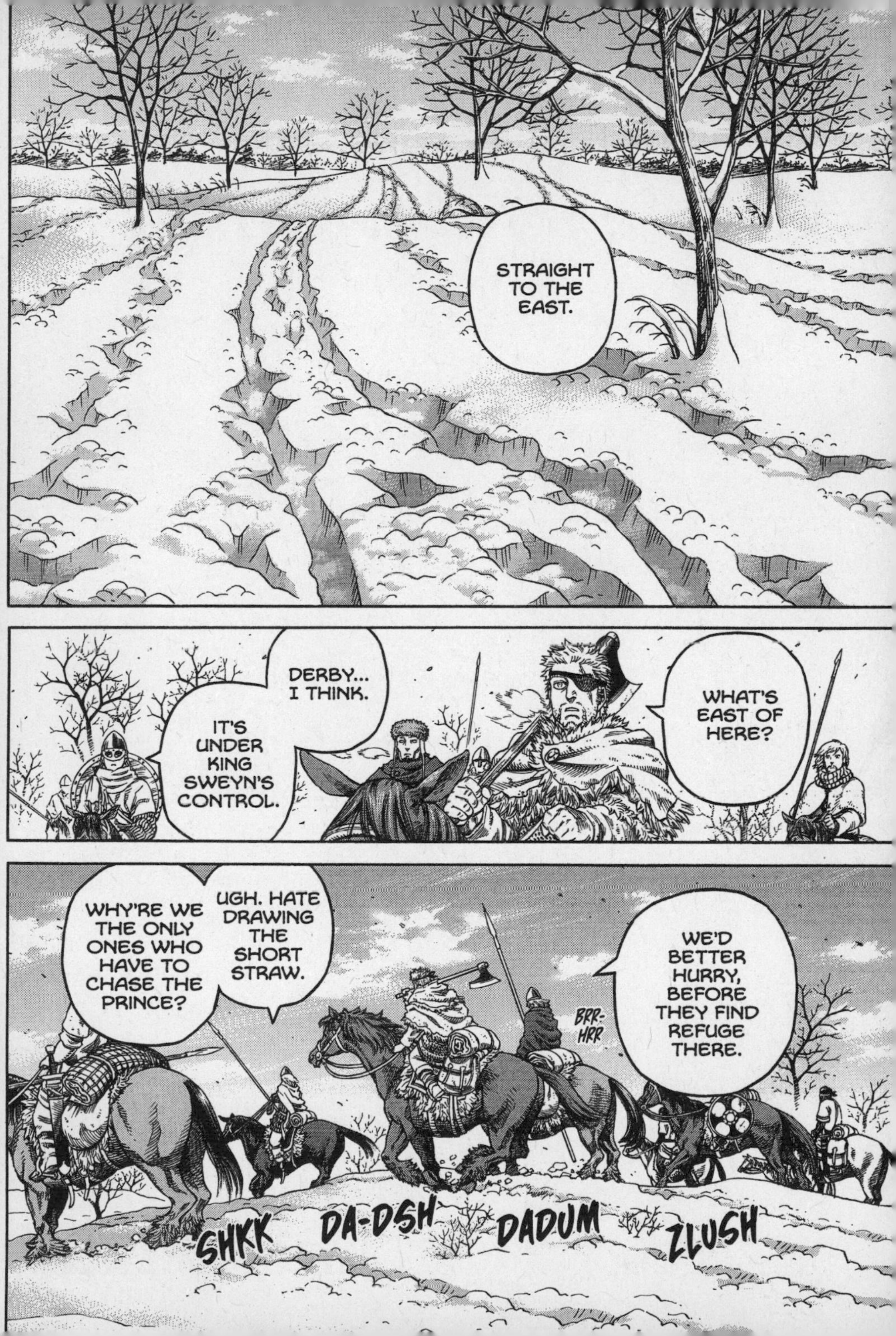
STRAIGHT TO THE EAST.
WHAT'S EAST OF HERE?
DERBY... I THINK.
IT'S UNDER KING SWEYN'S CONTROL.
WE'D BETTER HURRY, BEFORE THEY FIND REFUGE THERE.
BRR-HRR
UGH. HATE DRAWING THE SHORT STRAW.
WHY'RE WE THE ONLY ONES WHO HAVE TO CHASE THE PRINCE?
ZLUSH
DADUM
DA-DSH
SHKK

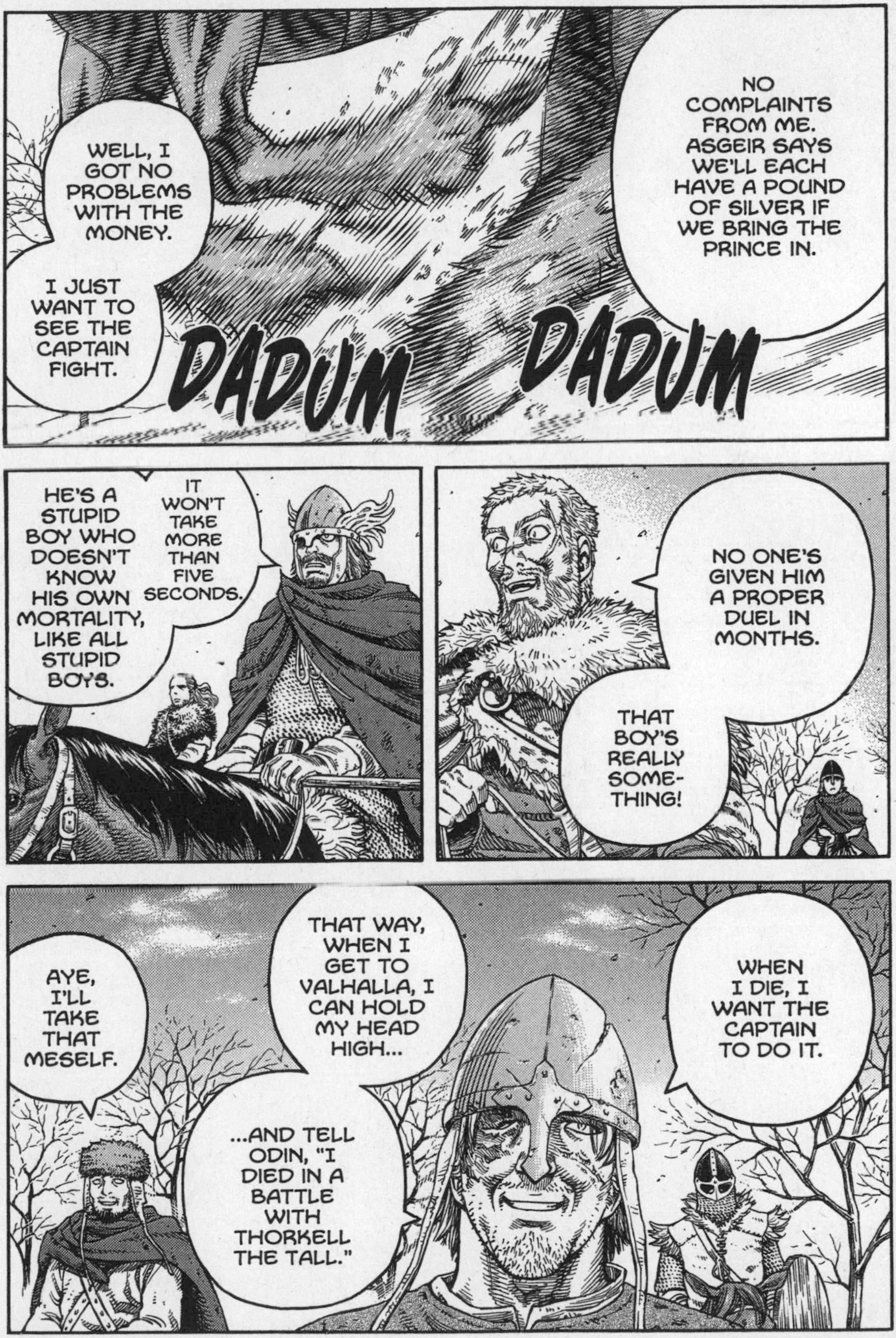
NO COMPLAINTS FROM ME. ASGEIR SAYS WE'LL EACH HAVE A POUND OF SILVER IF WE BRING THE PRINCE IN.
DADUM
DADUM
WELL, I GOT NO PROBLEMS WITH THE MONEY.
I JUST WANT TO SEE THE CAPTAIN FIGHT.
NO ONE'S GIVEN HIM A PROPER DUEL IN MONTHS.
THAT BOY'S REALLY SOME-THING!
IT WON'T TAKE MORE THAN FIVE SECONDS.
HE'S A STUPID BOY WHO DOESN'T KNOW HIS OWN MORTALITY, LIKE ALL STUPID BOYS.
WHEN I DIE, I WANT THE CAPTAIN TO DO IT.
THAT WAY, WHEN I GET TO VALHALLA, I CAN HOLD MY HEAD HIGH...
...AND TELL ODIN, "I DIED IN A BATTLE WITH THORKELL THE TALL."
AYE, I'LL TAKE THAT MESELF.

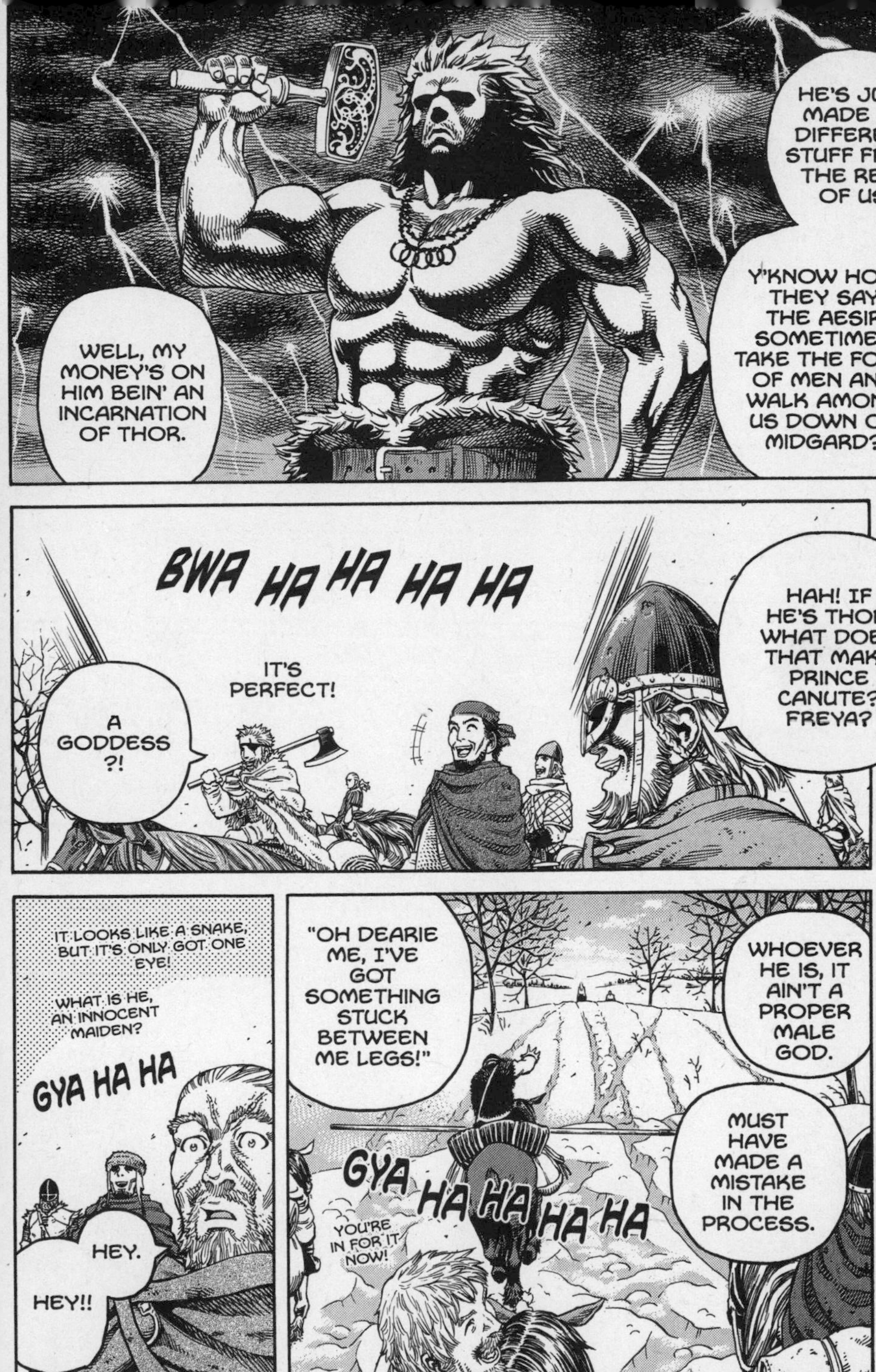
HE'S JUST MADE OF DIFFERENT STUFF FROM THE REST OF US.
Y'KNOW HOW THEY SAY THE AESIR SOMETIMES TAKE THE FORM OF MEN AND WALK AMONG US DOWN ON MIDGARD?
WELL, MY MONEY'S ON HIM BEIN' AN INCARNATION OF THOR.
HAH! IF HE'S THOR, WHAT DOES THAT MAKE PRINCE CANUTE? FREYA?
BWA HA HA HA HA
IT'S PERFECT!
A GODDESS ?!
WHOEVER HE IS, IT AIN'T A PROPER MALE GOD.
"OH DEARIE ME, I'VE GOT SOMETHING STUCK BETWEEN ME LEGS!"
MUST HAVE MADE A MISTAKE IN THE PROCESS.
GYA HA HA HA HA
YOU'RE IN FOR IT NOW!
IT LOOKS LIKE A SNAKE, BUT IT'S ONLY GOT ONE EYE!
WHAT IS HE, AN INNOCENT MAIDEN?
GYA HA HA
HEY.
HEY!!

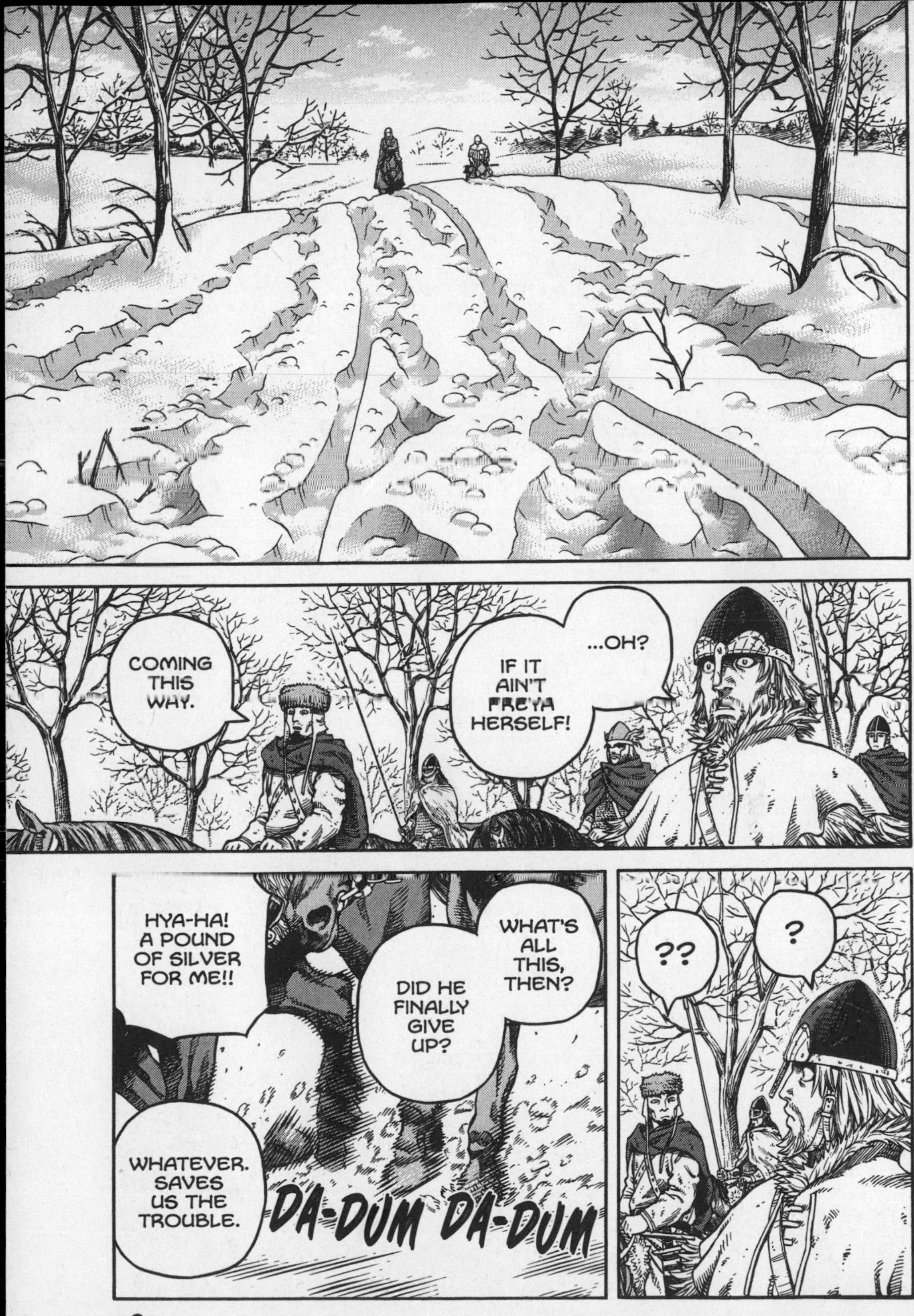
...OH?
IF IT AIN'T FREYA HERSELF!
COMING THIS WAY.
?
??
WHAT'S ALL THIS, THEN?
DID HE FINALLY GIVE UP?
HYA-HA! A POUND OF SILVER FOR ME!!
WHATEVER. SAVES US THE TROUBLE.
DA-DUM DA-DUM

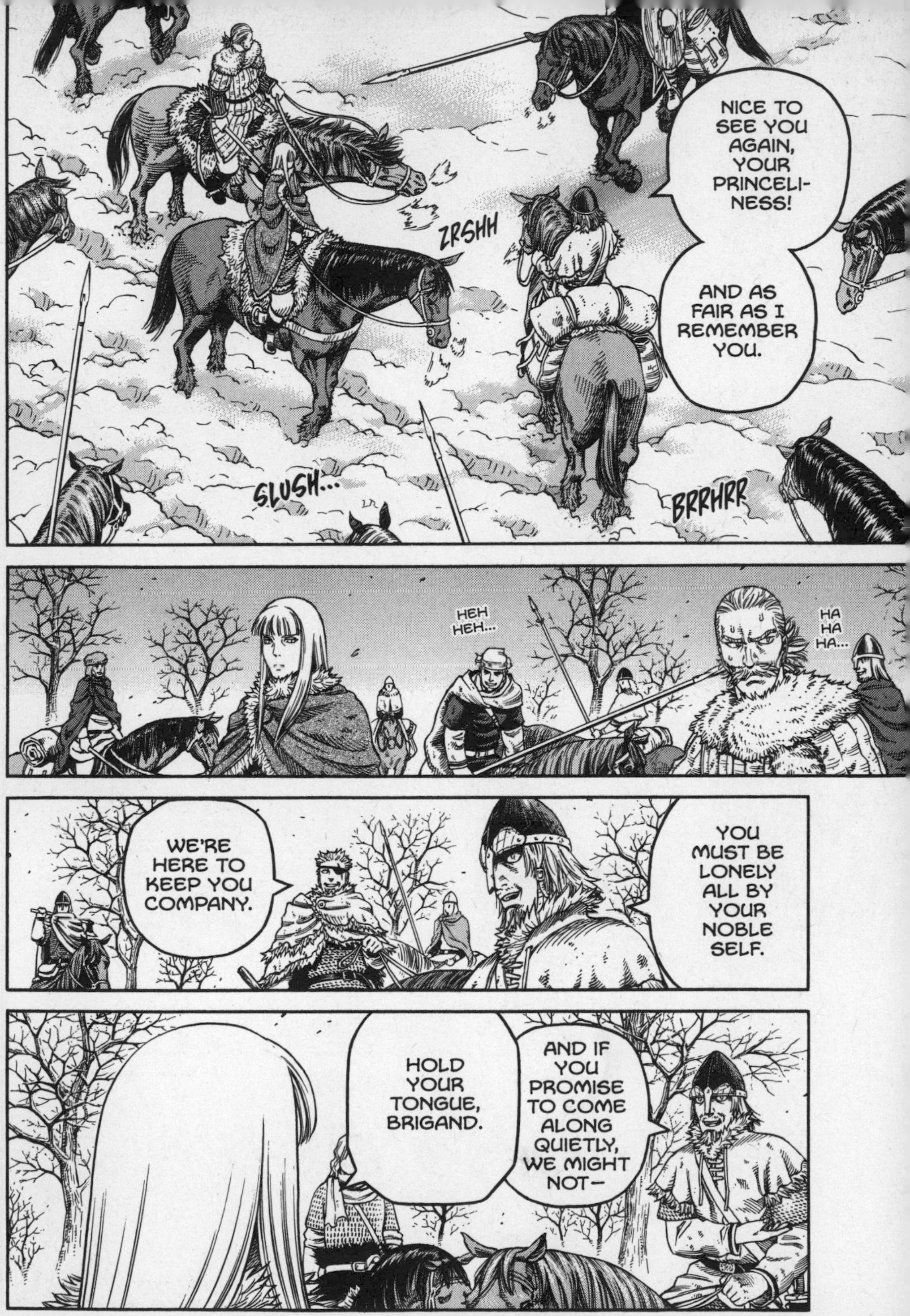
NICE TO SEE YOU AGAIN, YOUR PRINCELINESS!
AND AS FAIR AS I REMEMBER YOU.
ZRSHH
BRRHRR
SLUSH...
HA HA HA...
HEH HEH...
YOU MUST BE LONELY ALL BY YOUR NOBLE SELF.
WE'RE HERE TO KEEP YOU COMPANY.
AND IF YOU PROMISE TO COME ALONG QUIETLY, WE MIGHT NOT—
HOLD YOUR TONGUE, BRIGAND.

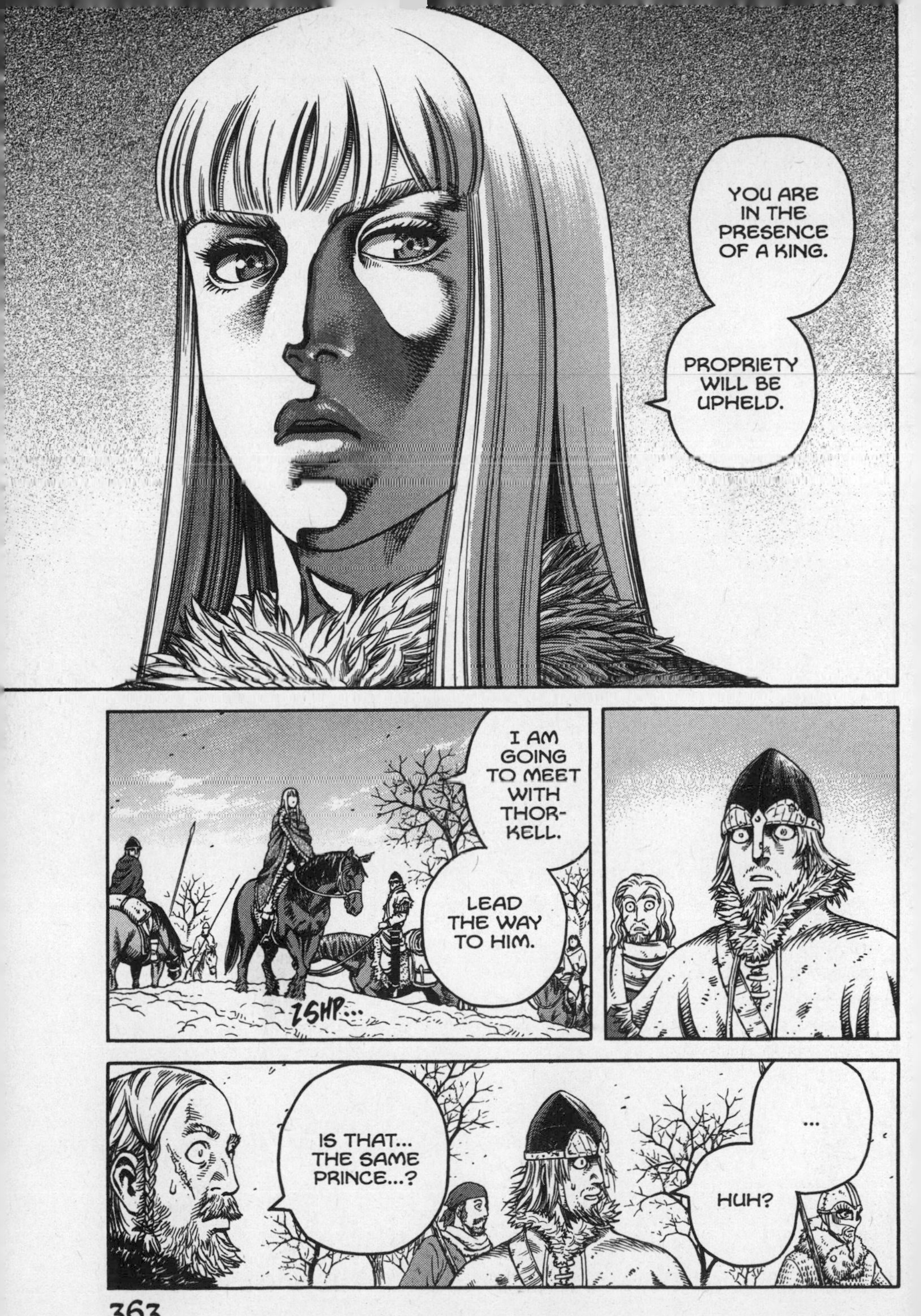
YOU ARE IN THE PRESENCE OF A KING.
PROPRIETY WILL BE UPHELD.
I AM GOING TO MEET WITH THOR-KELL.
LEAD THE WAY TO HIM.
ZSHP...
...
HUH?
IS THAT... THE SAME PRINCE...?

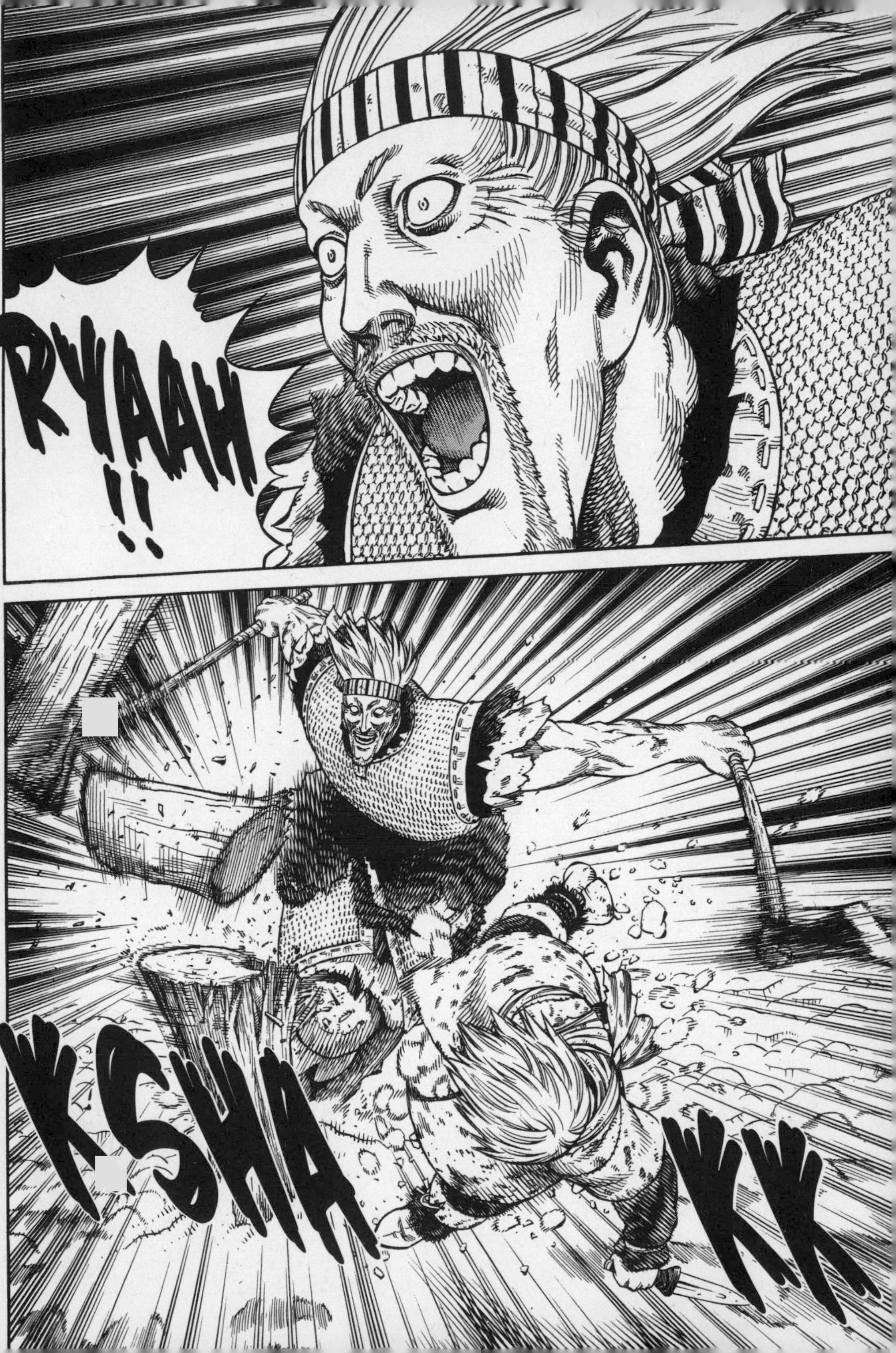
RYAAH!!!
KSHA KKK

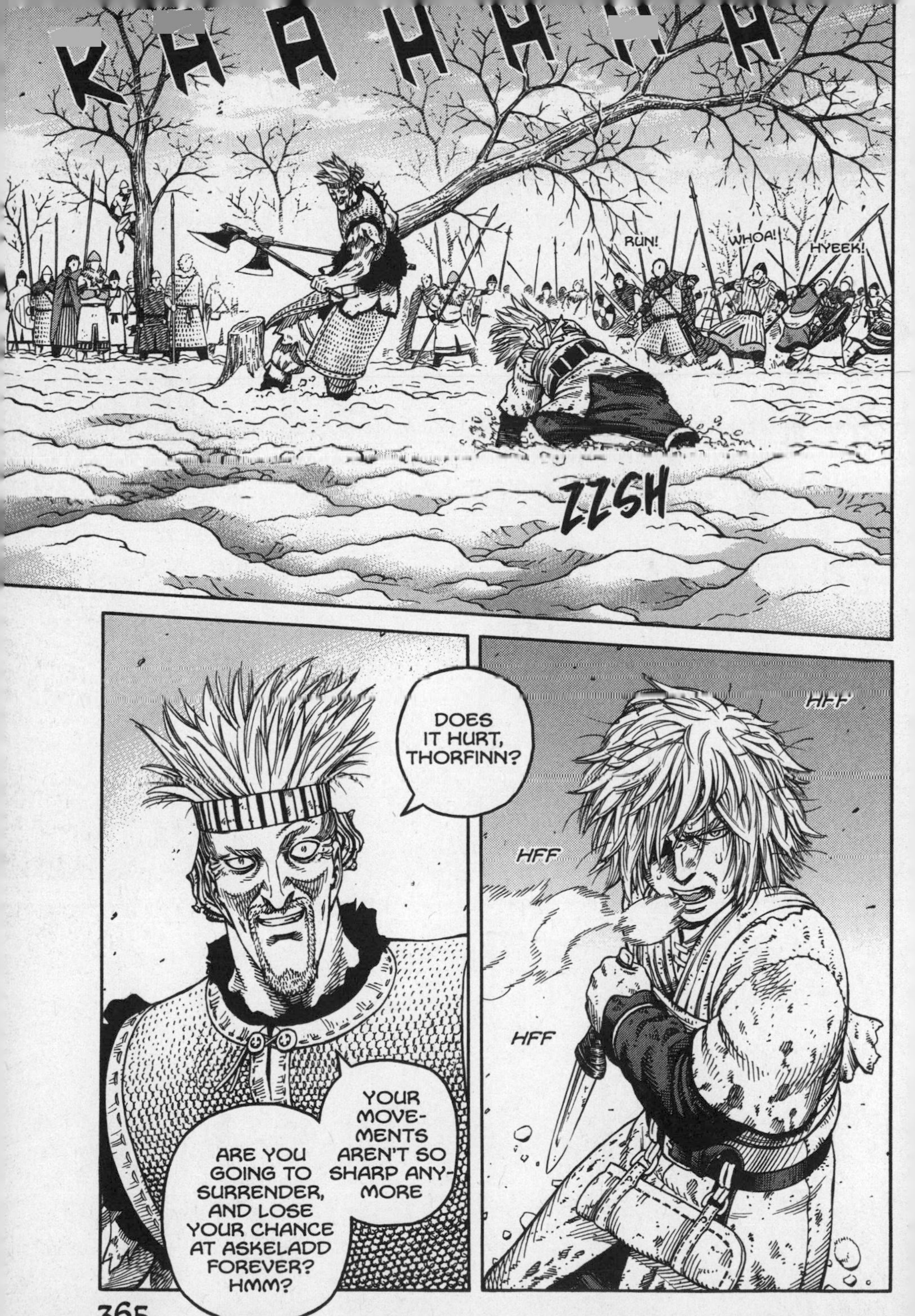
KAAHHHH
RUN!
WHOA!
HYEEK!
ZZSH
HFF
HFF
HFF
DOES IT HURT, THORFINN?
YOUR MOVEMENTS AREN'T SO SHARP ANYMORE
ARE YOU GOING TO SURRENDER, AND LOSE YOUR CHANCE AT ASKELADD FOREVER? HMM?

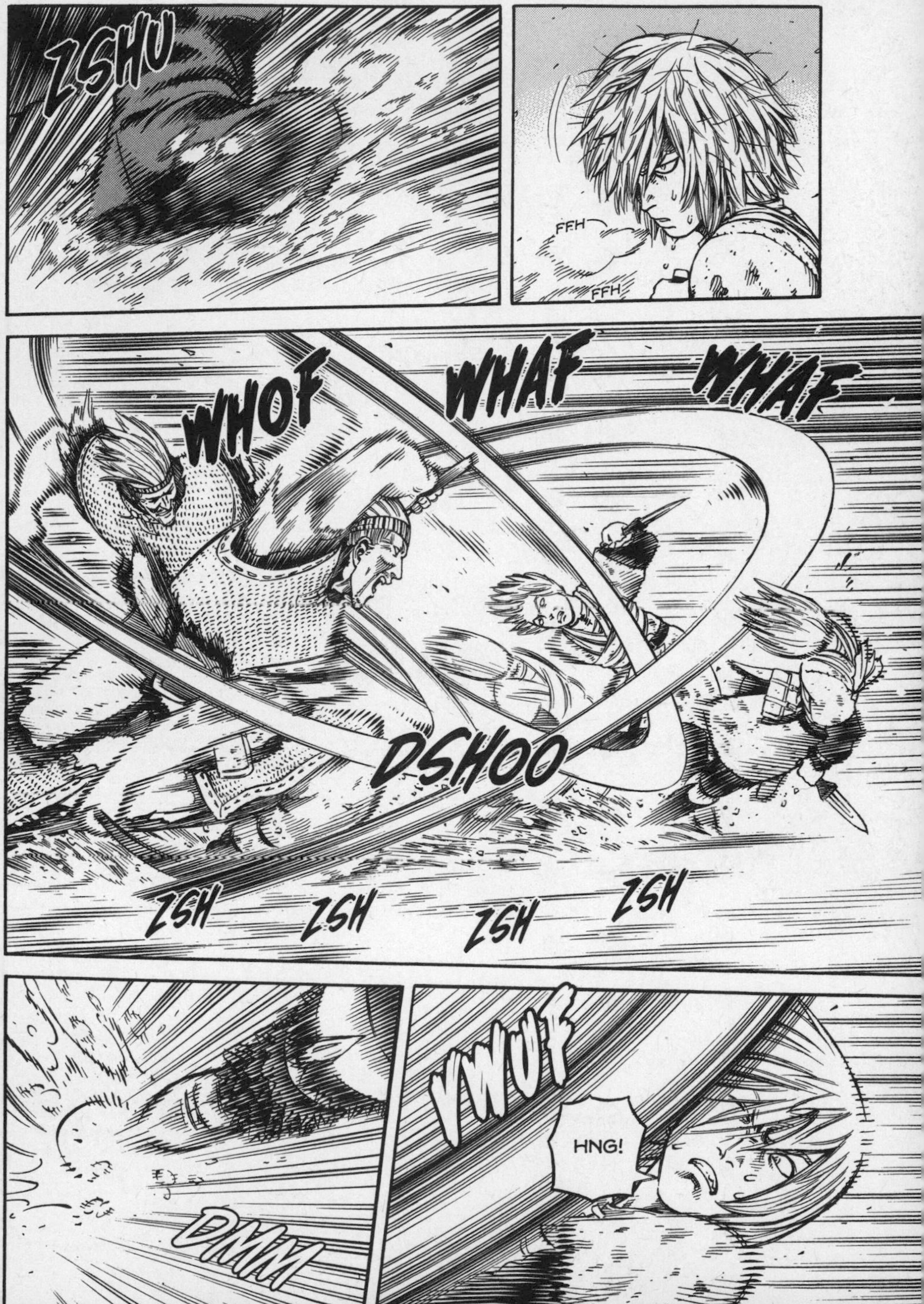
FFH
FFH
ZSHU
WHAF
WHAF
WHOF
DSHOO
ZSH
ZSH
ZSH
ZSH
VWUF
HNG!
DMM

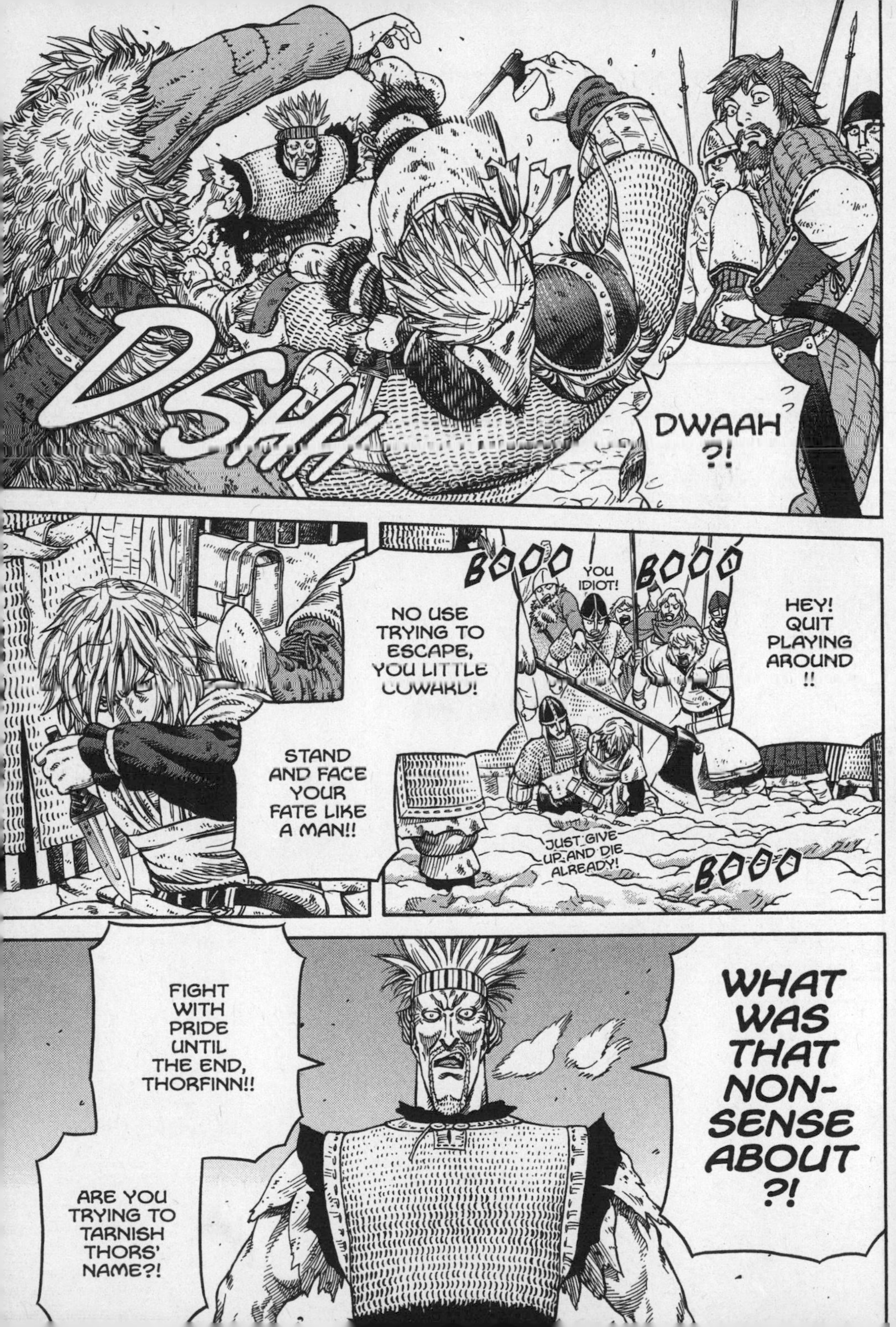
DSHH
DWAAH ?!
BOOO
BOOO
HEY! QUIT PLAYING AROUND !!
YOU IDIOT!
JUST GIVE UP AND DIE ALREADY!
BOOO
NO USE TRYING TO ESCAPE, YOU LITTLE COWARD!
STAND AND FACE YOUR FATE LIKE A MAN!!
WHAT WAS THAT NON-SENSE ABOUT ?!
FIGHT WITH PRIDE UNTIL THE END, THORFINN!!
ARE YOU TRYING TO TARNISH THORS' NAME?!

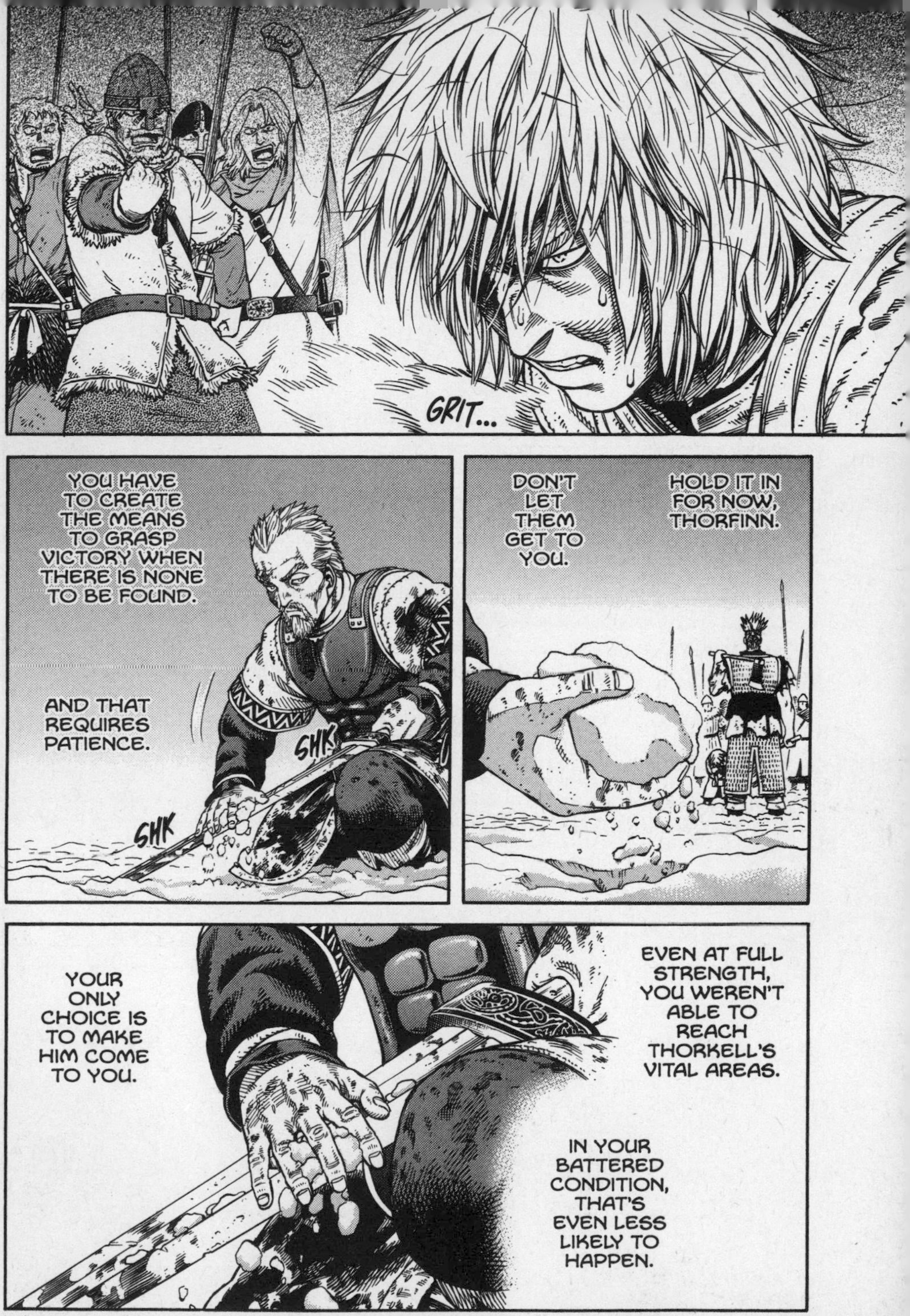
GRIT...
HOLD IT IN FOR NOW, THORFINN.
DON'T LET THEM GET TO YOU.
YOU HAVE TO CREATE THE MEANS TO GRASP VICTORY WHEN THERE IS NONE TO BE FOUND.
AND THAT REQUIRES PATIENCE.
SHK
SHK
EVEN AT FULL STRENGTH, YOU WEREN'T ABLE TO REACH THORKELL'S VITAL AREAS.
IN YOUR BATTERED CONDITION, THAT'S EVEN LESS LIKELY TO HAPPEN.
YOUR ONLY CHOICE IS TO MAKE HIM COME TO YOU.

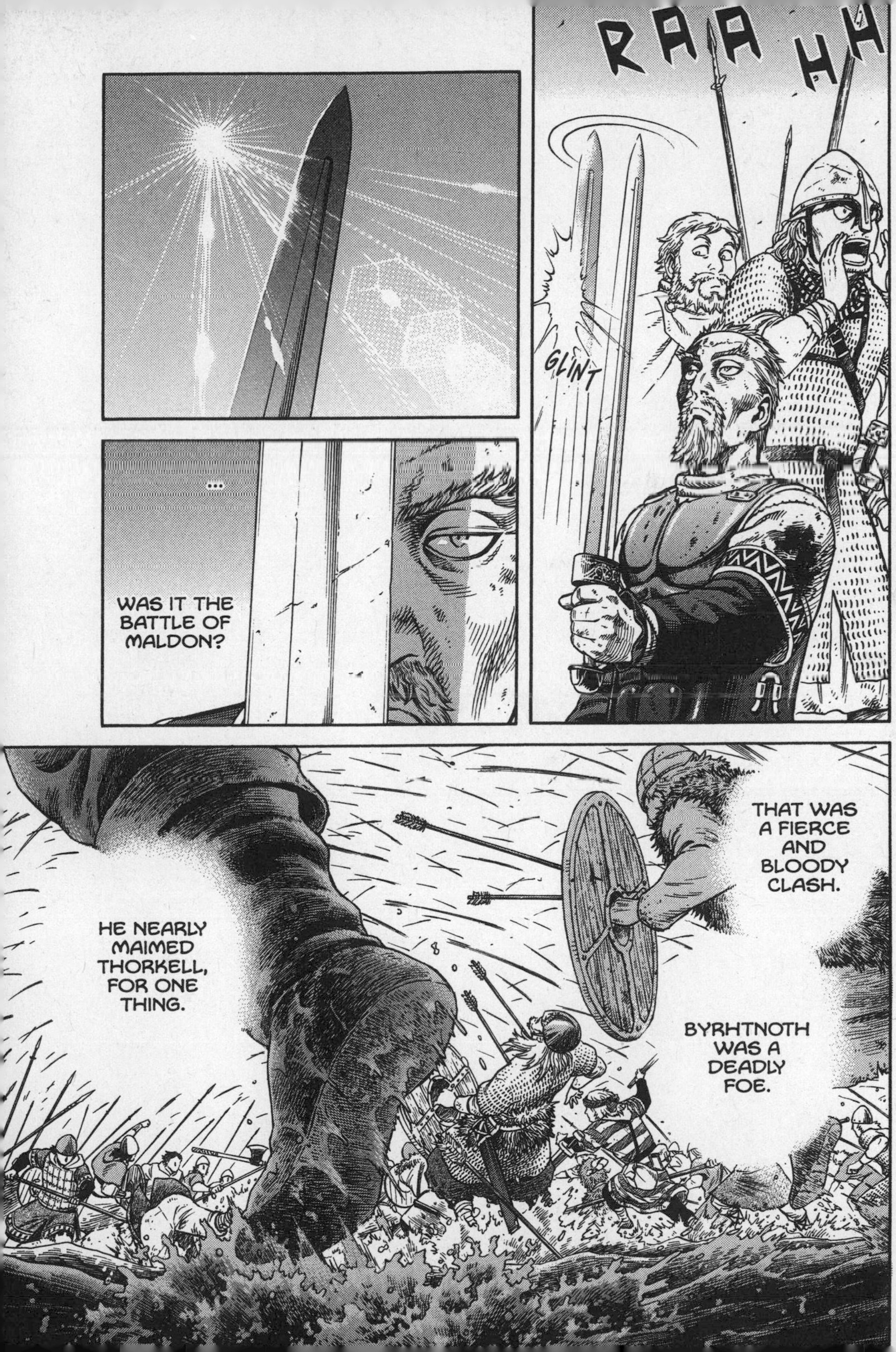
RAAHH
GLINT
...
WAS IT THE BATTLE OF MALDON?
THAT WAS A FIERCE AND BLOODY CLASH.
BYRHTNOTH WAS A DEADLY FOE.
HE NEARLY MAIMED THORKELL, FOR ONE THING.

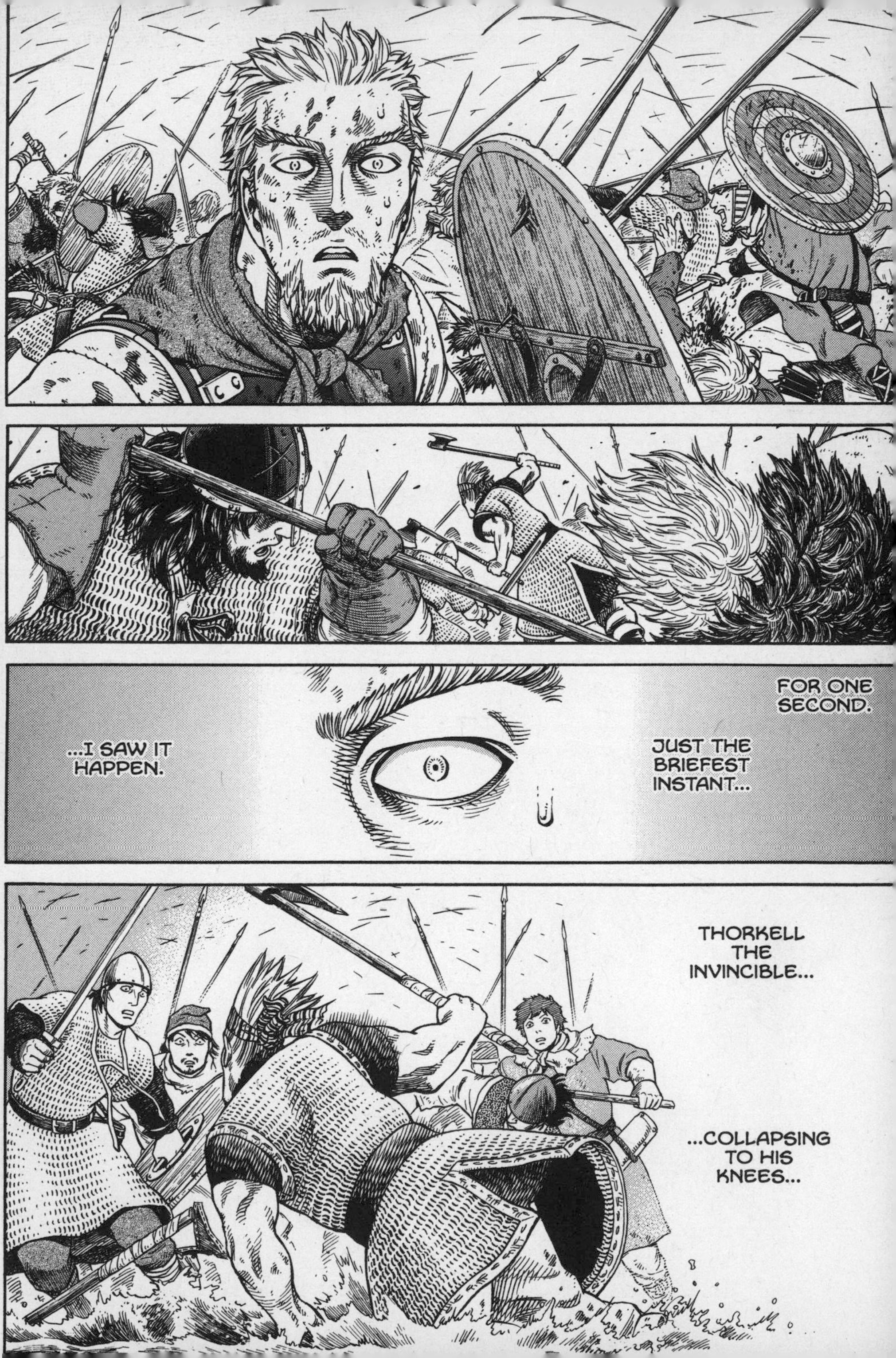
FOR ONE SECOND.
JUST THE BRIEFEST INSTANT...
...I SAW IT HAPPEN.
THORKELL THE INVINCIBLE...
...COLLAPSING TO HIS KNEES...

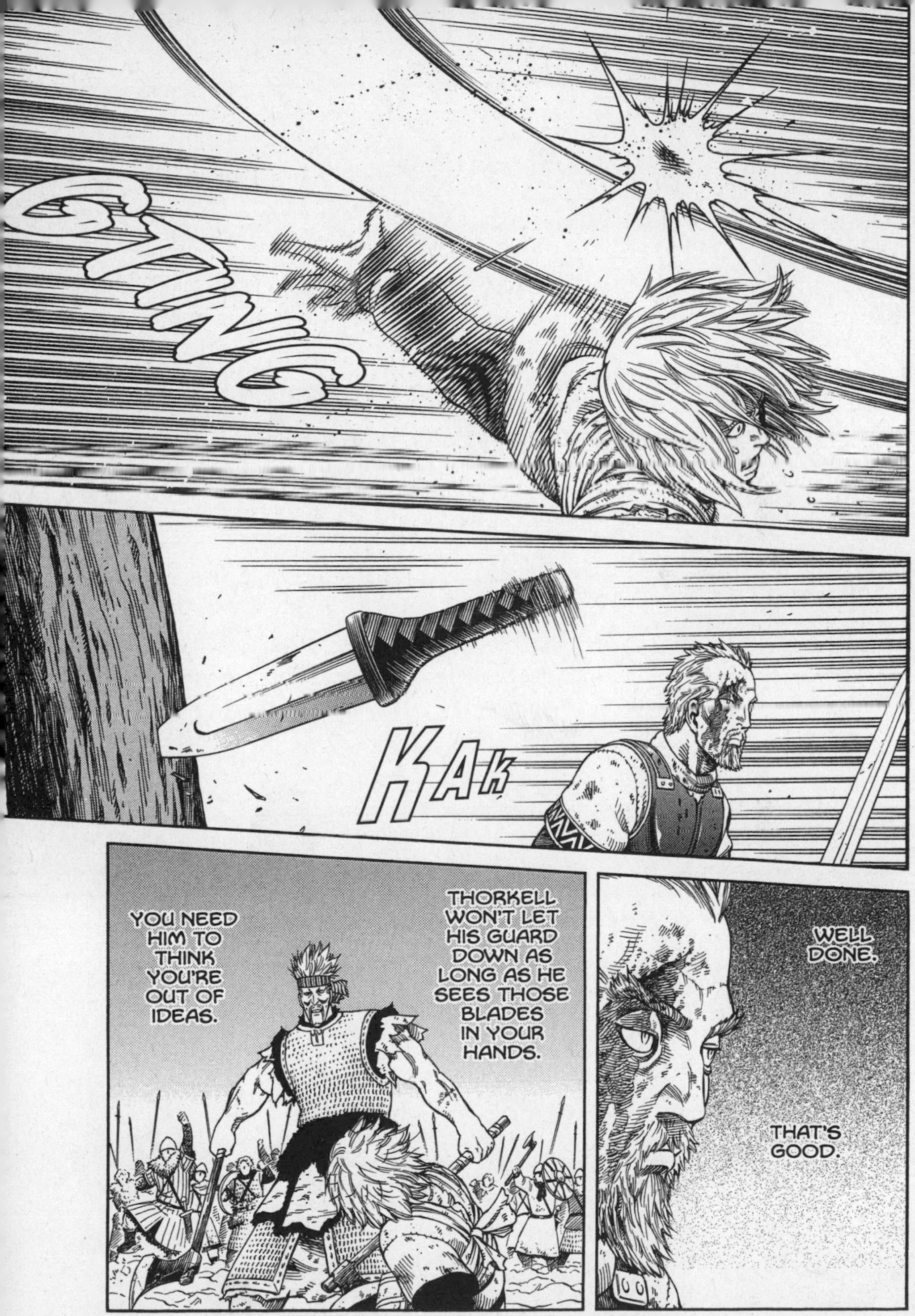
GYING
KAK
WELL DONE.
THAT'S GOOD.
THORKELL WON'T LET HIS GUARD DOWN AS LONG AS HE SEES THOSE BLADES IN YOUR HANDS.
YOU NEED HIM TO THINK YOU'RE OUT OF IDEAS.

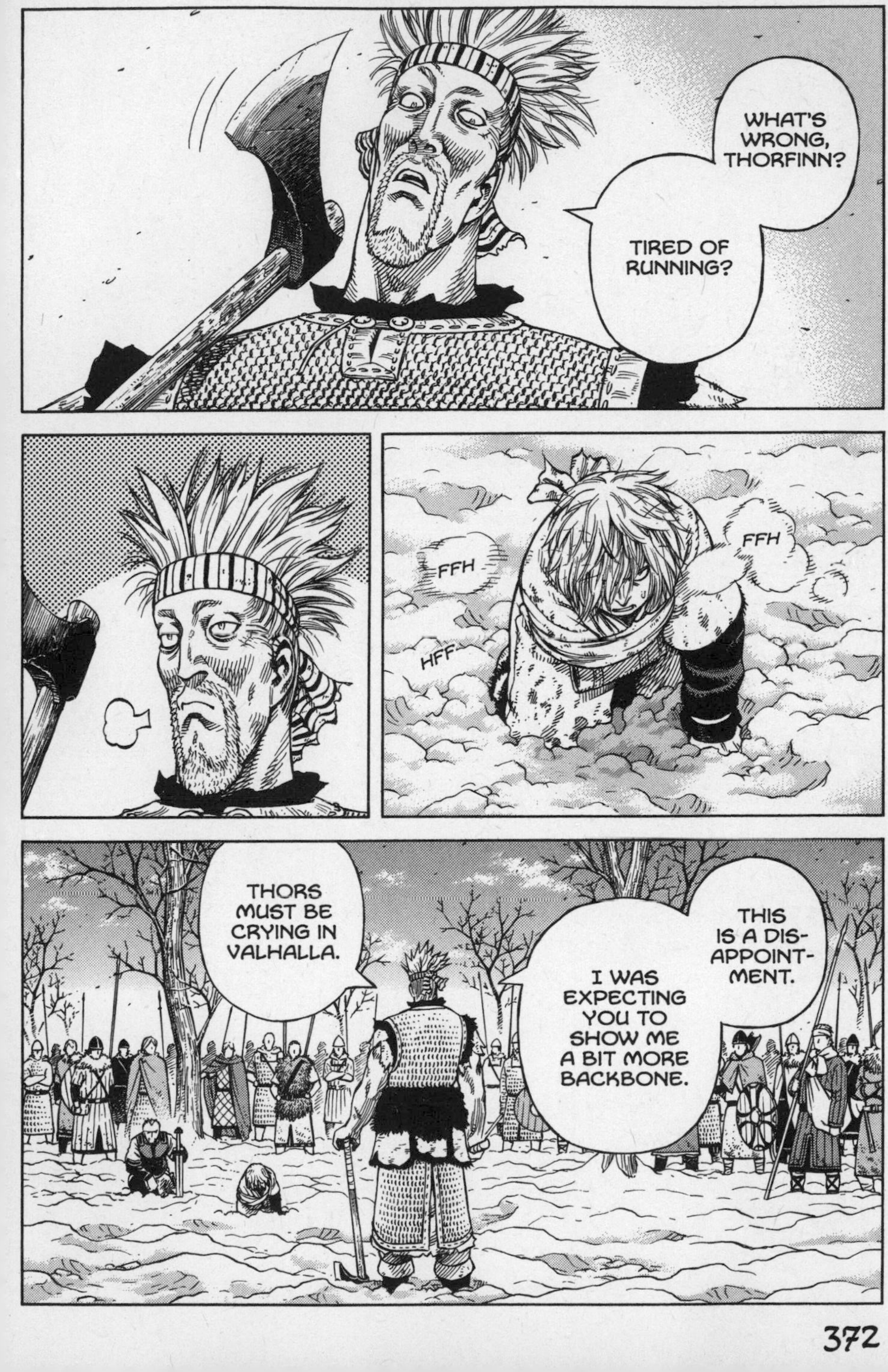
WHAT'S WRONG, THORFINN?
TIRED OF RUNNING?
FFH
FFH
HFF
THIS IS A DIS-APPOINT-MENT.
I WAS EXPECTING YOU TO SHOW ME A BIT MORE BACKBONE.
THORS MUST BE CRYING IN VALHALLA.

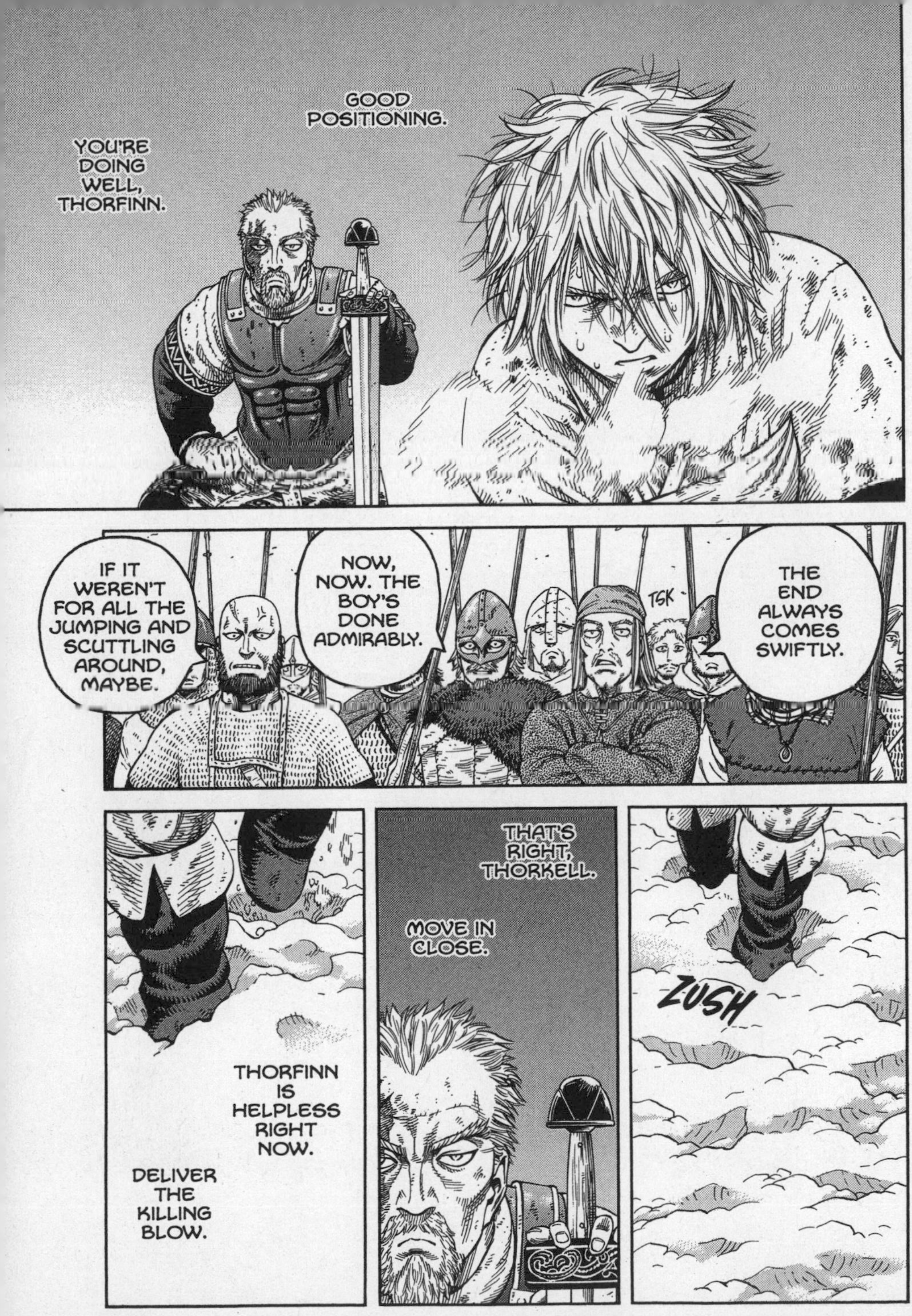
GOOD POSITIONING.
YOU'RE DOING WELL, THORFINN.
THE END ALWAYS COMES SWIFTLY.
TSK
NOW, NOW. THE BOY'S DONE ADMIRABLY.
IF IT WEREN'T FOR ALL THE JUMPING AND SCUTTLING AROUND, MAYBE.
ZUSH
THAT'S RIGHT, THORKELL.
MOVE IN CLOSE.
THORFINN IS HELPLESS RIGHT NOW.
DELIVER THE KILLING BLOW.

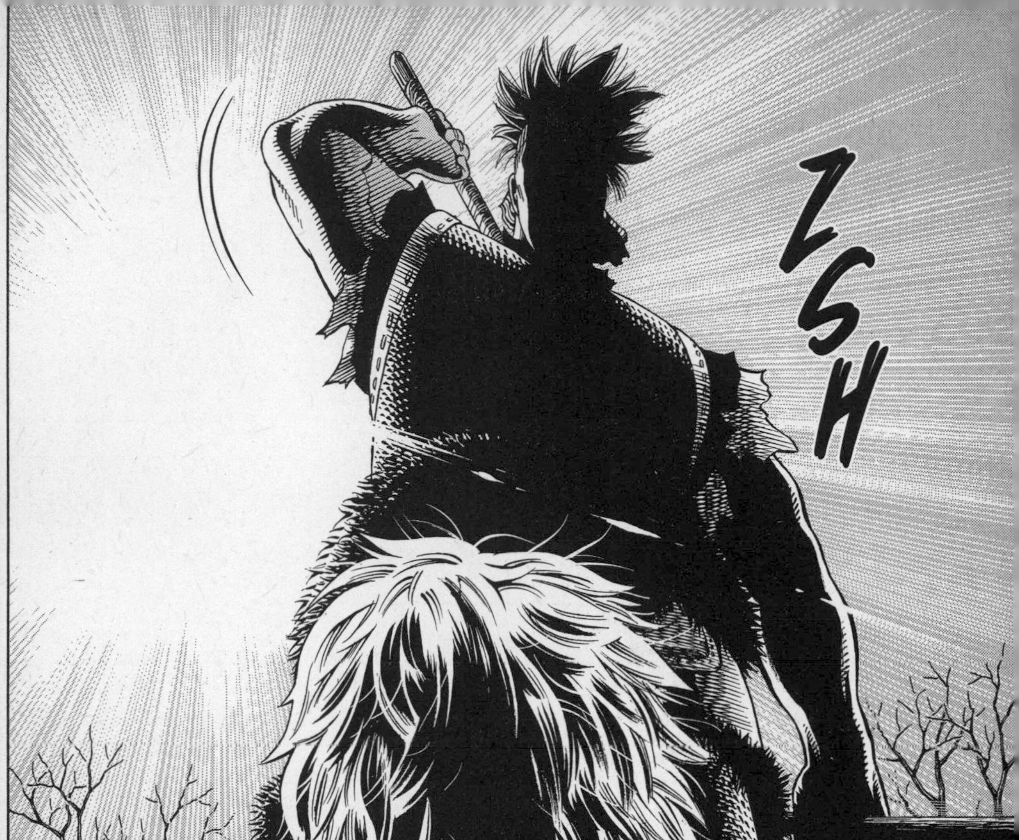
ZSH
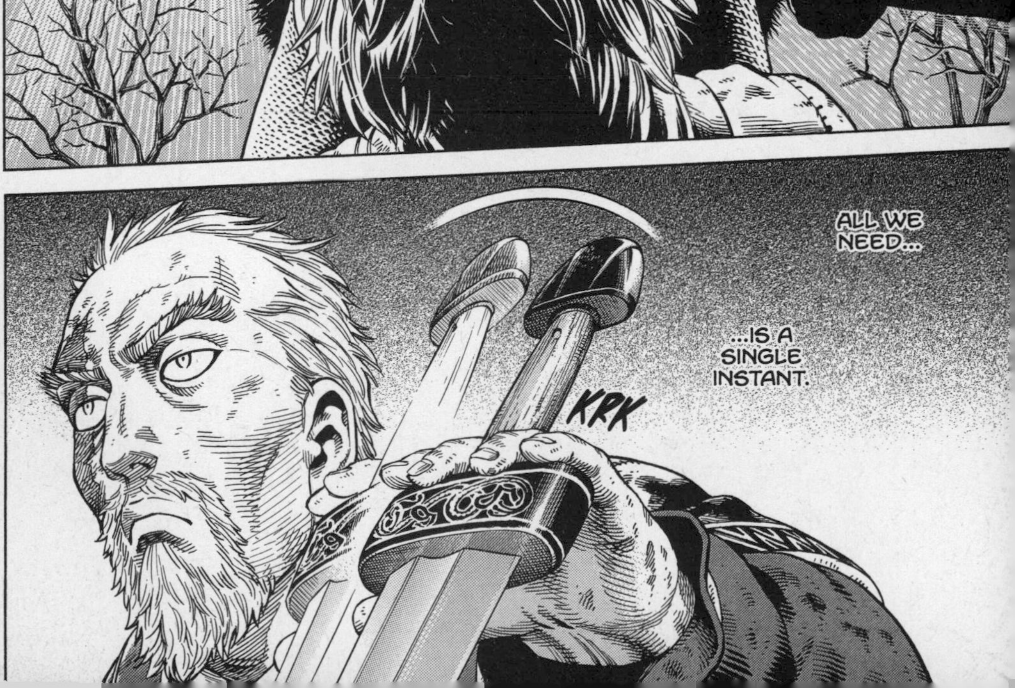
ALL WE NEED...
...IS A SINGLE INSTANT.
KRK

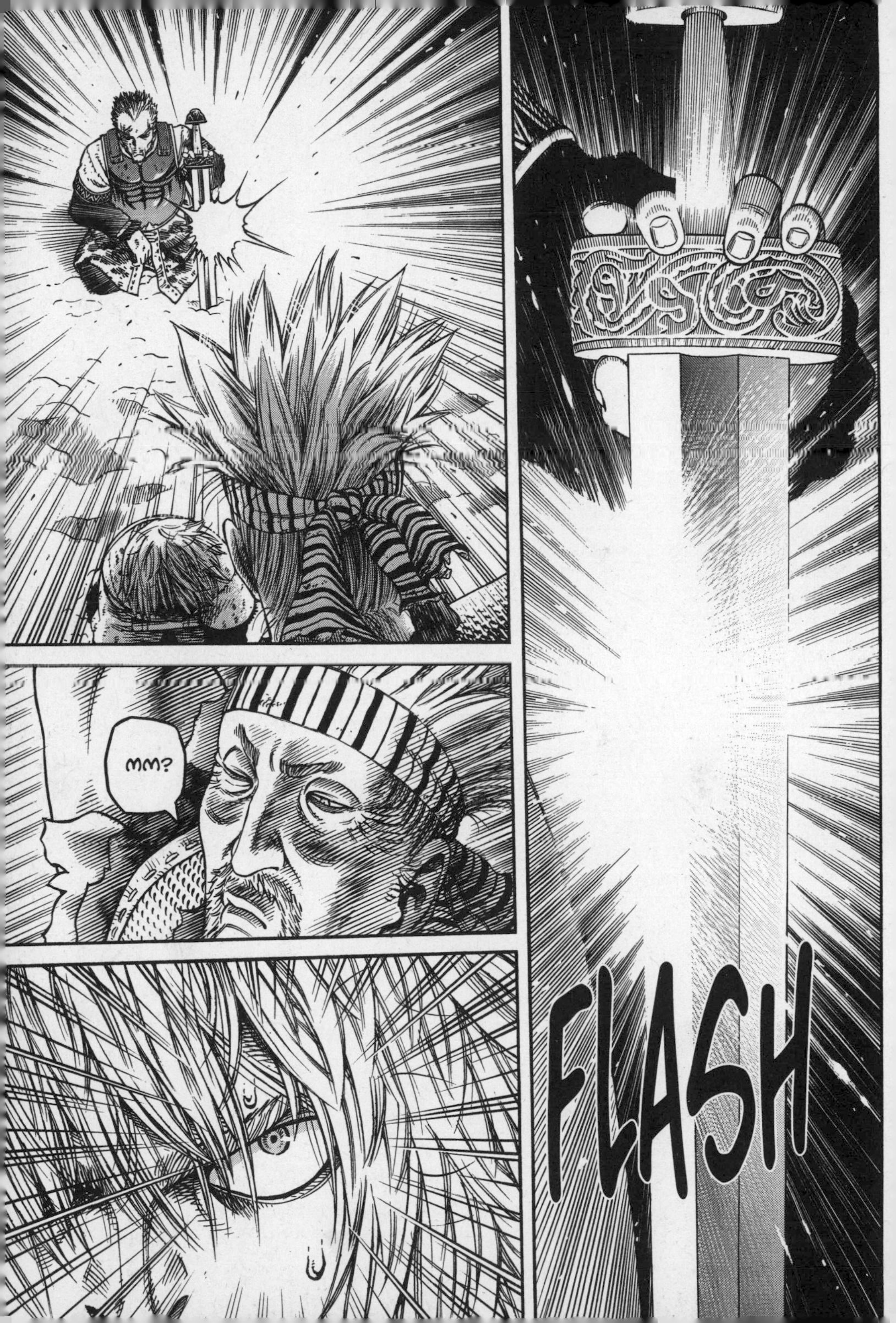
FLASH
MM?

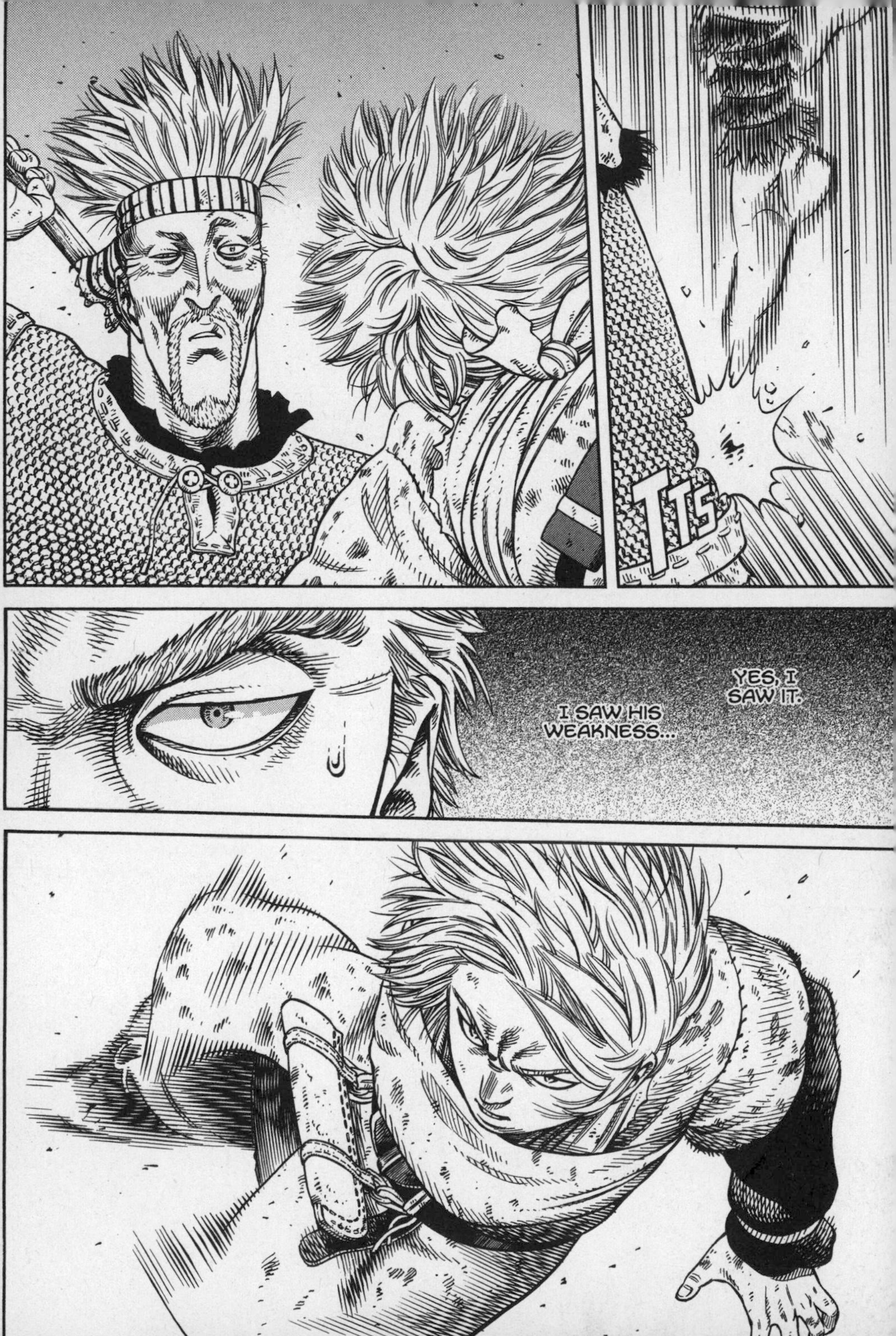
TTS
YES, I SAW IT.
I SAW HIS WEAKNESS...

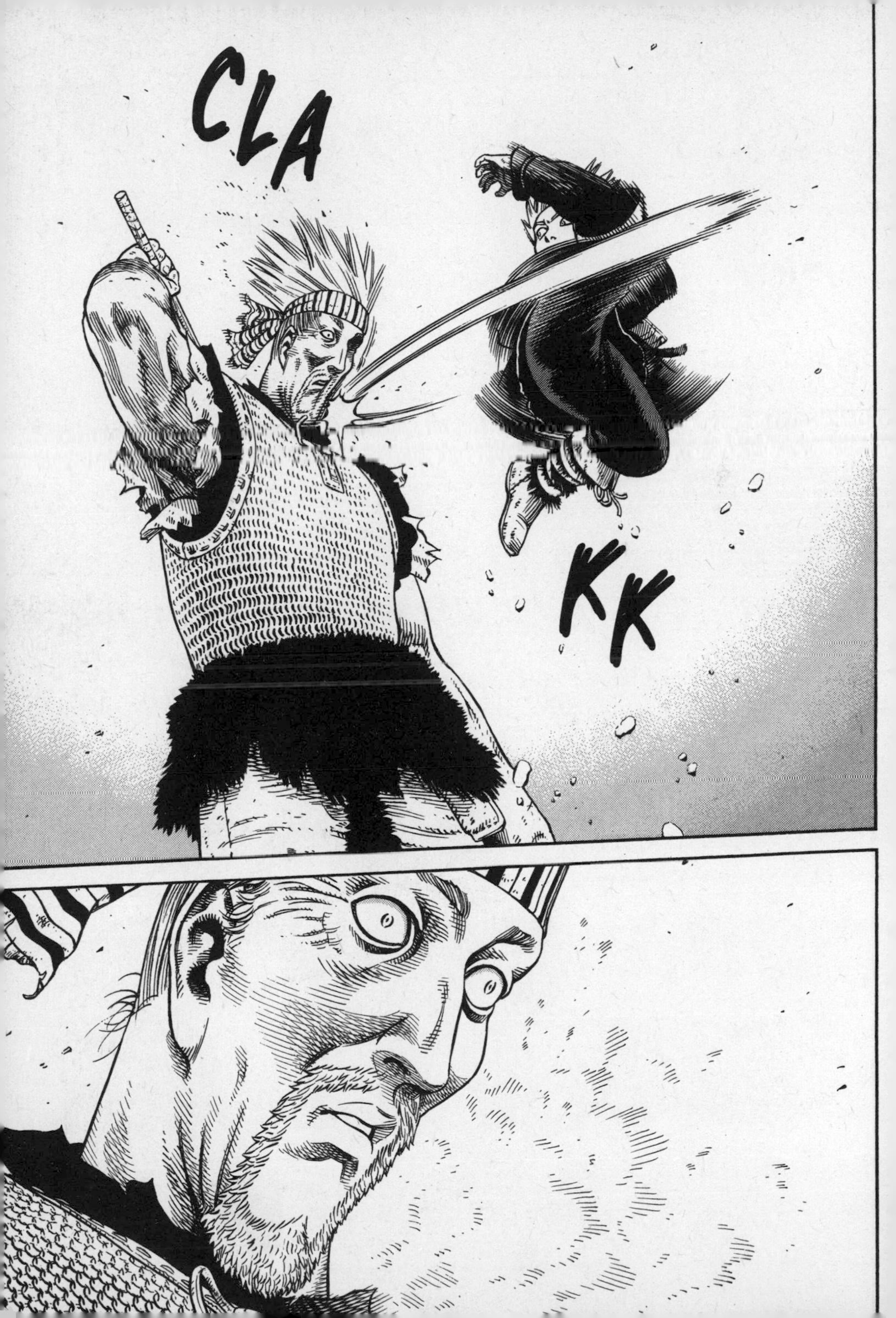
CLA
KK

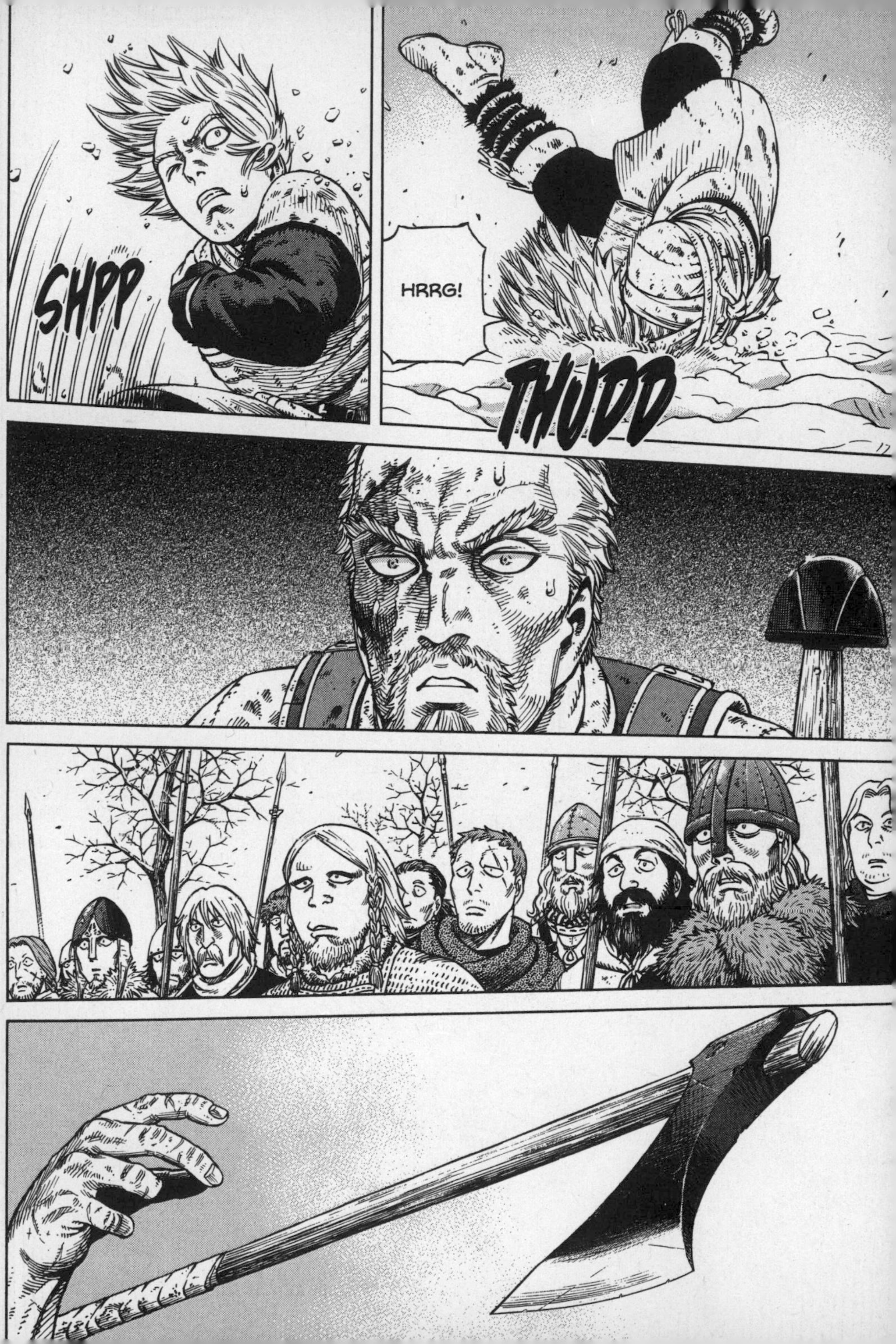
HRRG!
THUDD
SHPP

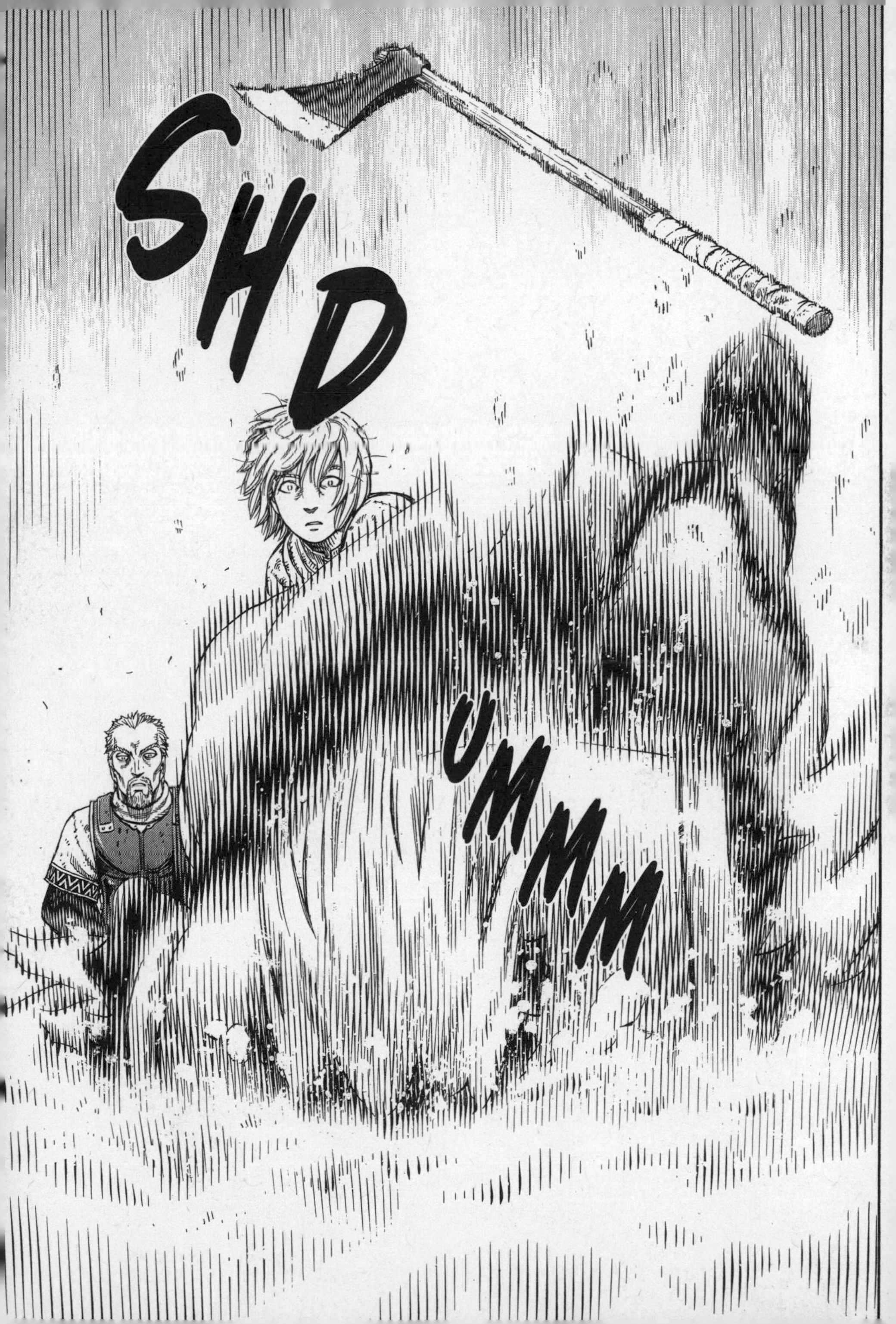
SHD
UMMM

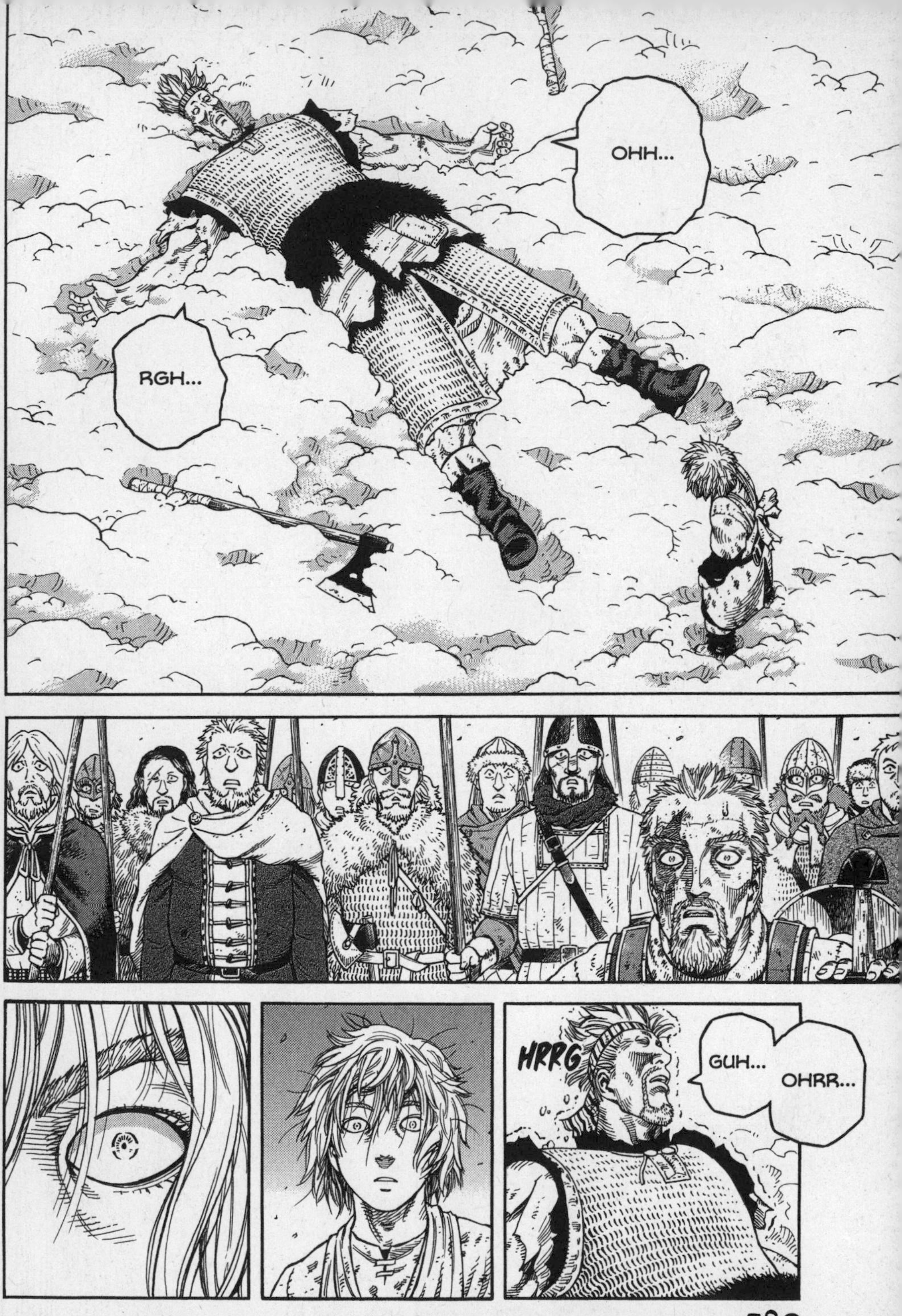
OHH...
RGH...
GUH...
OHRR...
HRRG

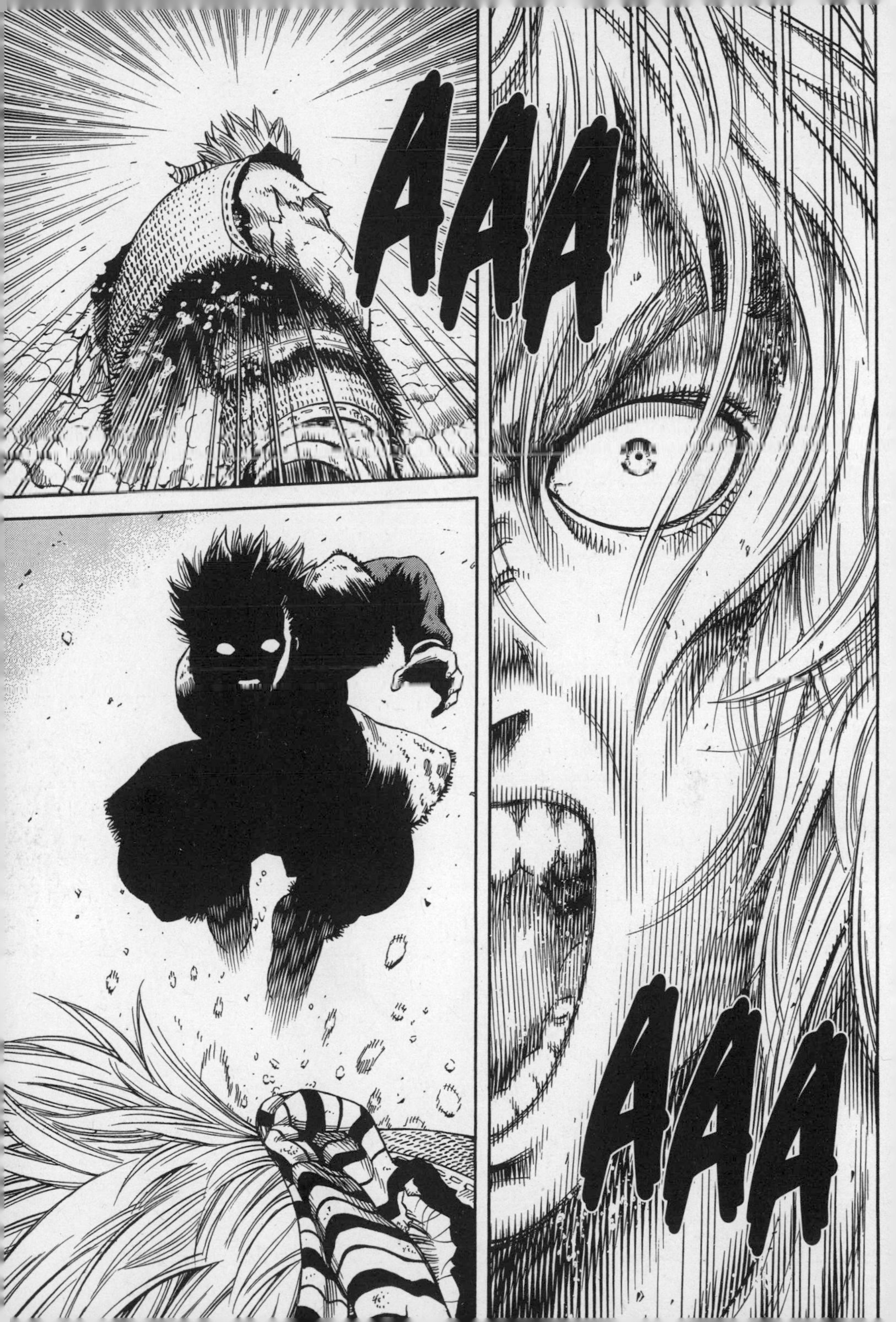
AAA
AAA

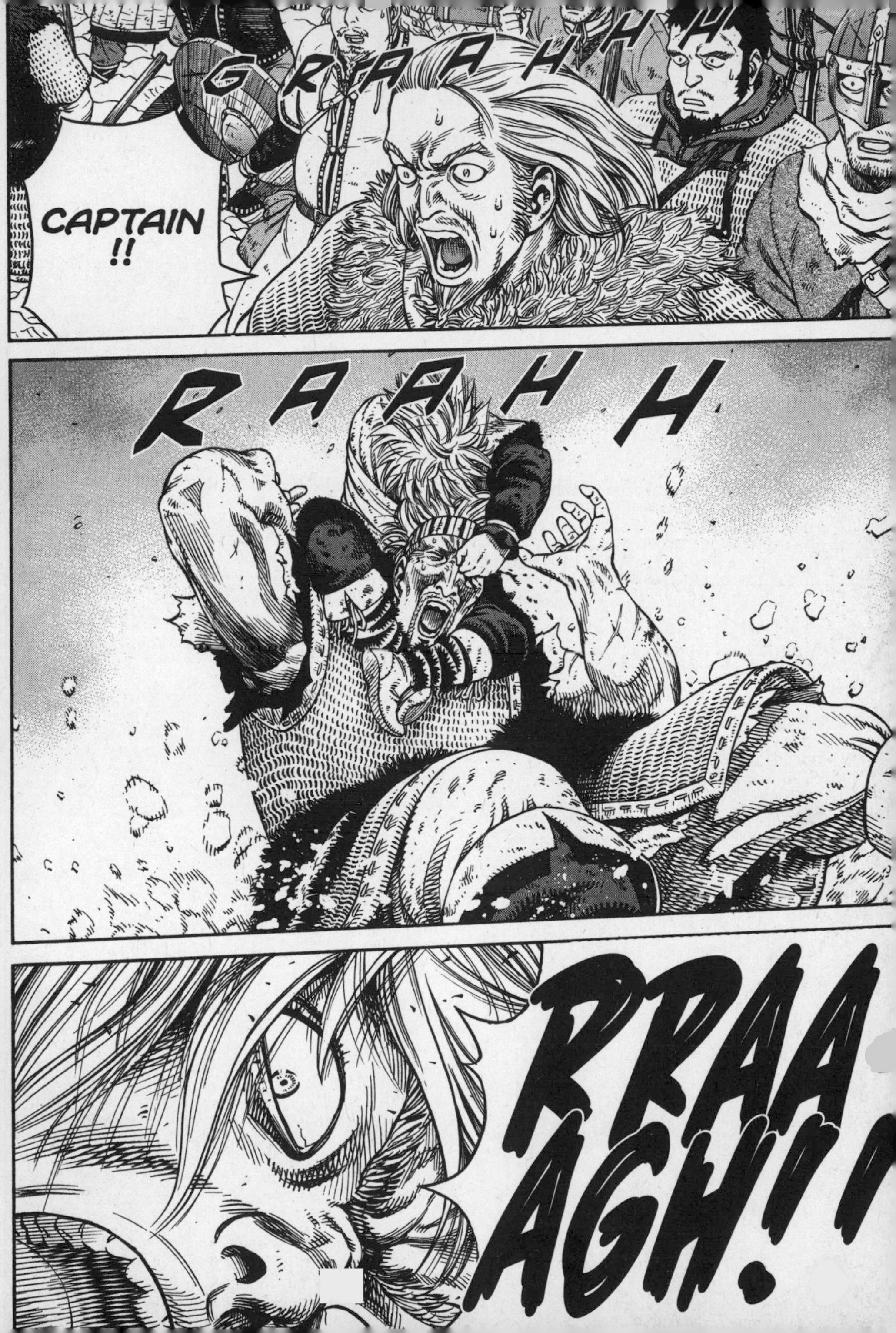
GRAAHHHH
CAPTAIN !!
RAAHH
PRAAAGH!!

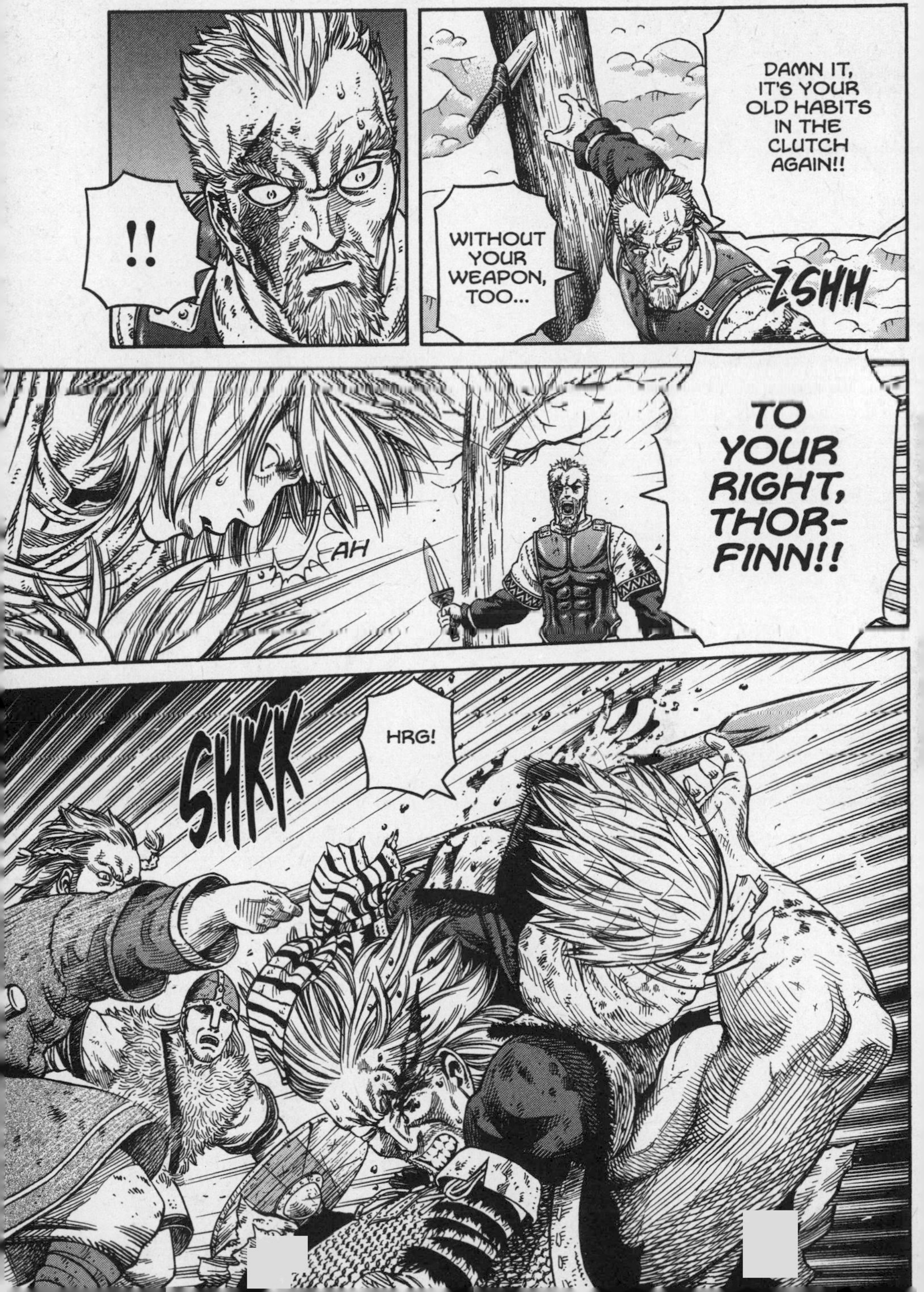
DAMN IT, IT'S YOUR OLD HABITS IN THE CLUTCH AGAIN!!
WITHOUT YOUR WEAPON, TOO...
ZSHH
!!
TO YOUR RIGHT, THOR-FINN!!
AH
SHKK
HRG!

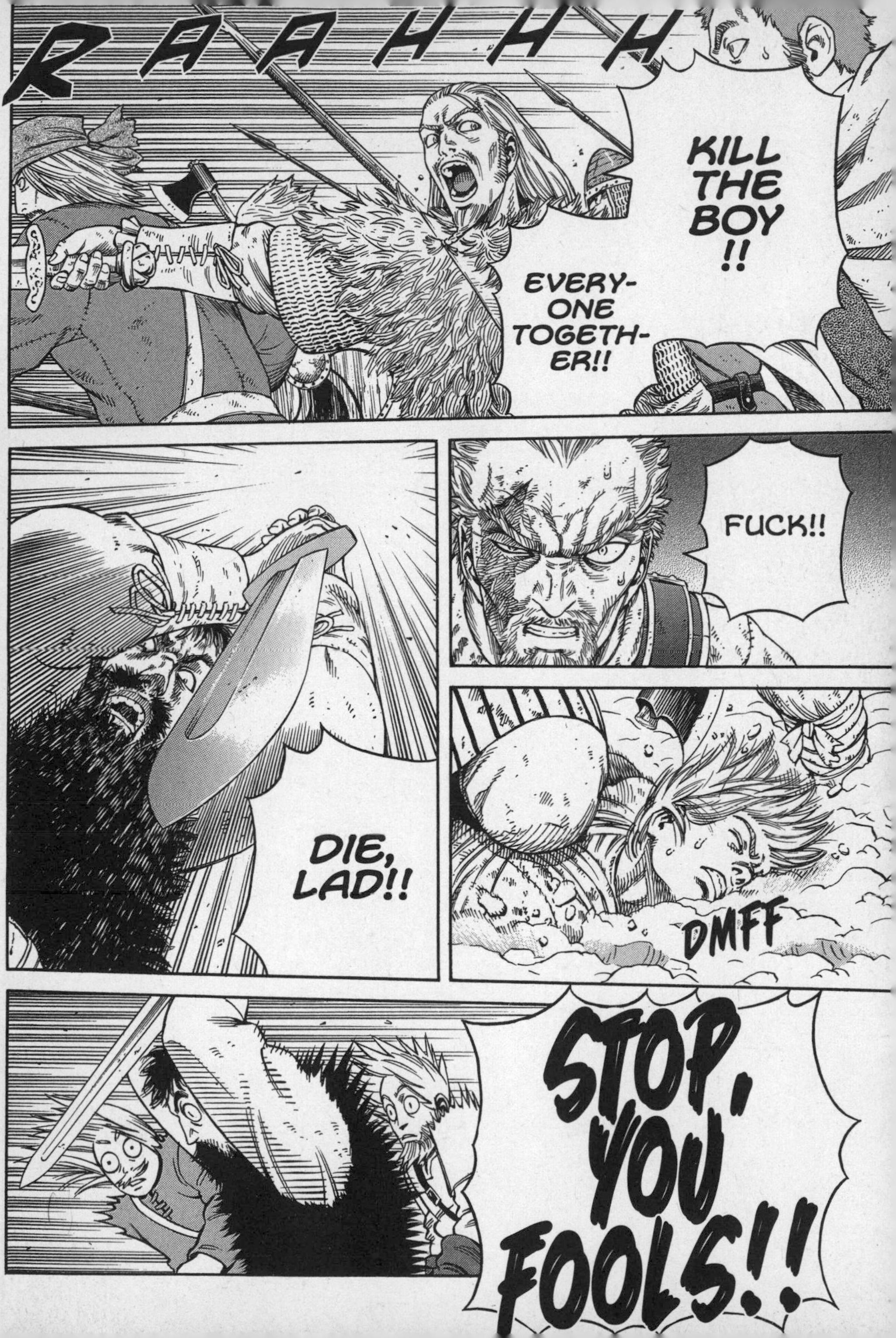
RAAHHH
KILL THE BOY!!
EVERY-ONE TOGETH-ER!!
FUCK!!
DMFF
DIE, LAD!!
STOP, YOU FOOLS!!

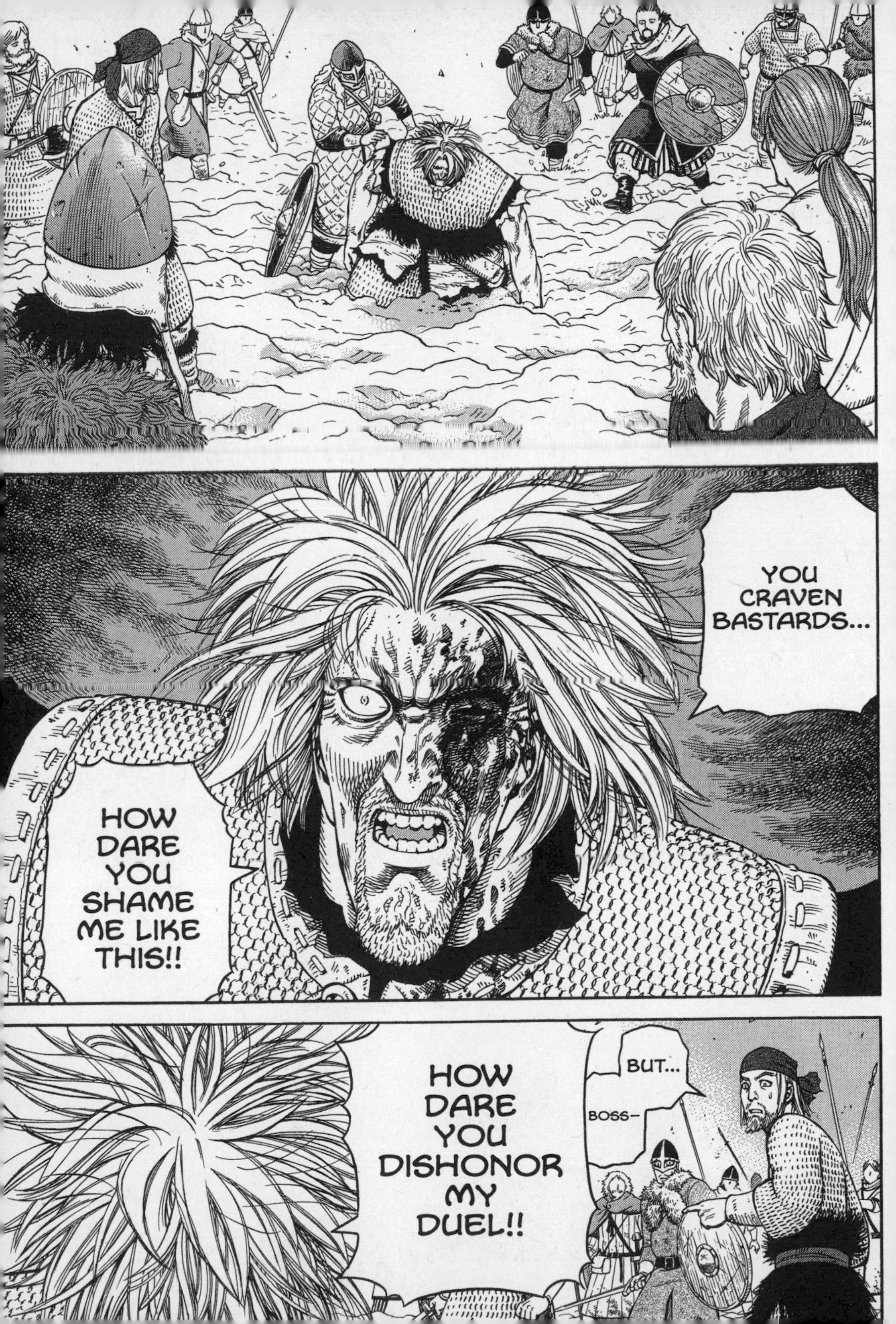
YOU CRAVEN BASTARDS...
HOW DARE YOU SHAME ME LIKE THIS!!
BUT...
BOSS–
HOW DARE YOU DISHONOR MY DUEL!!

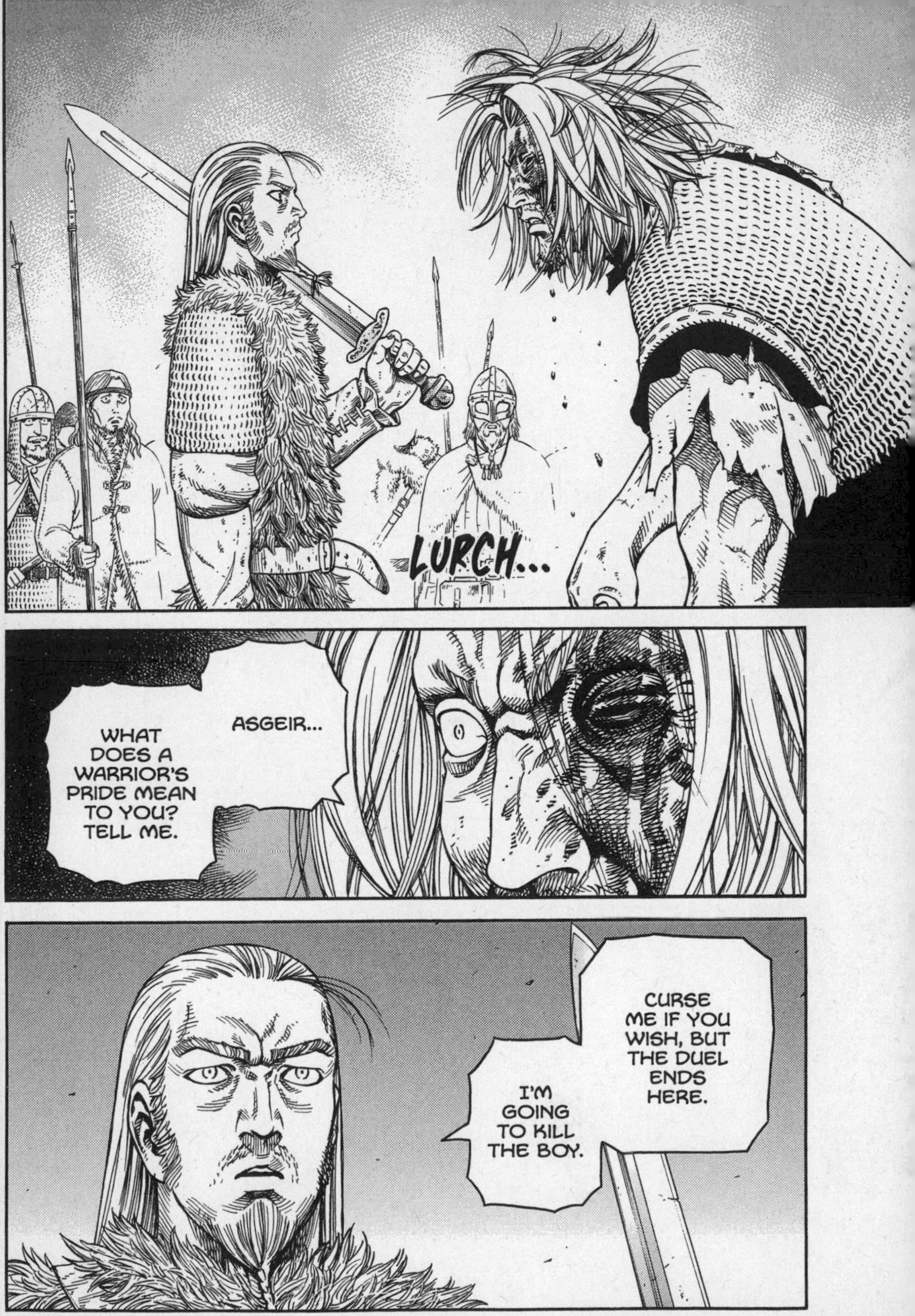
LURCH...
ASGEIR...
WHAT DOES A WARRIOR'S PRIDE MEAN TO YOU? TELL ME.
CURSE ME IF YOU WISH, BUT THE DUEL ENDS HERE.
I'M GOING TO KILL THE BOY.

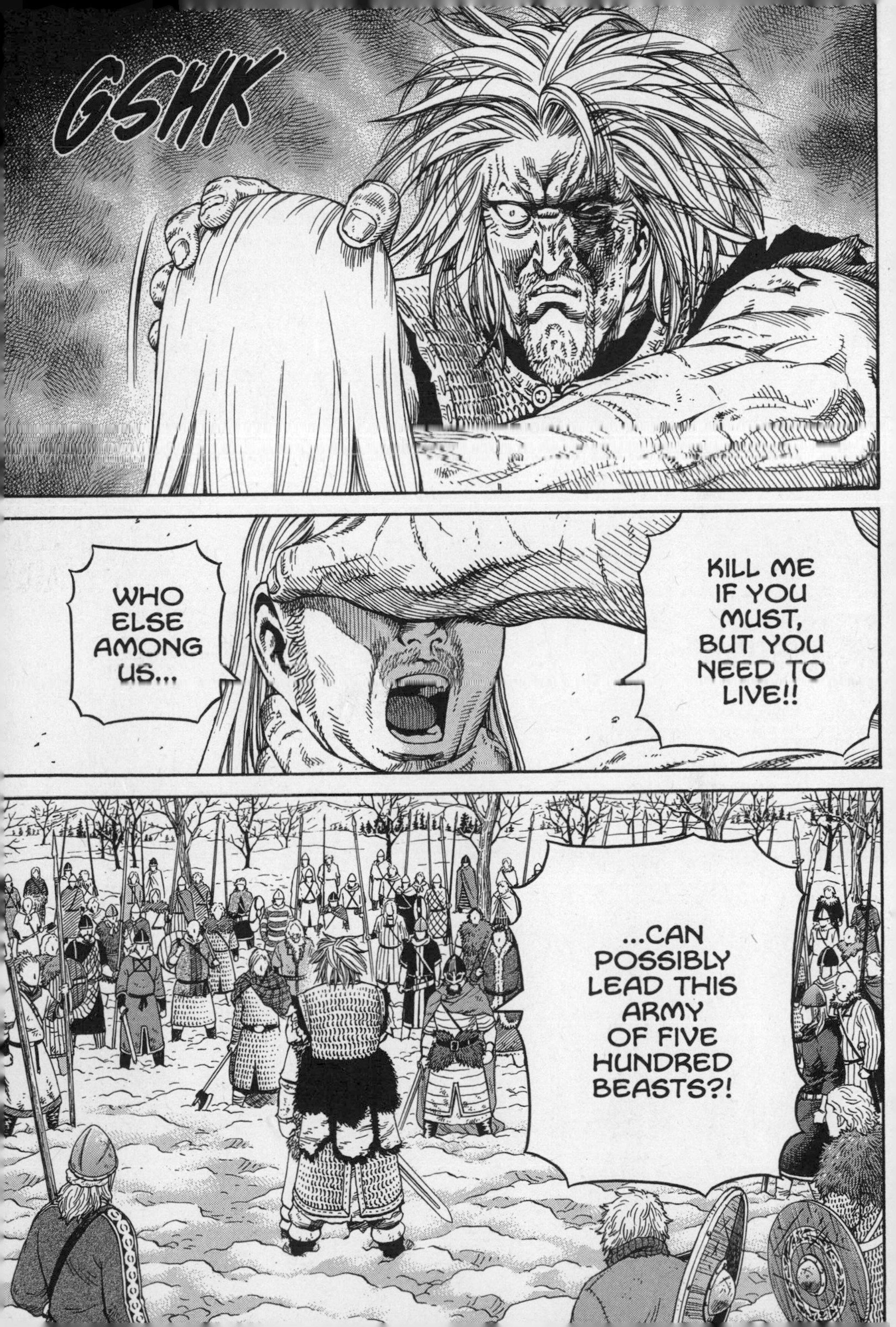
GSHK
KILL ME IF YOU MUST, BUT YOU NEED TO LIVE!!
WHO ELSE AMONG US...
...CAN POSSIBLY LEAD THIS ARMY OF FIVE HUNDRED BEASTS?!

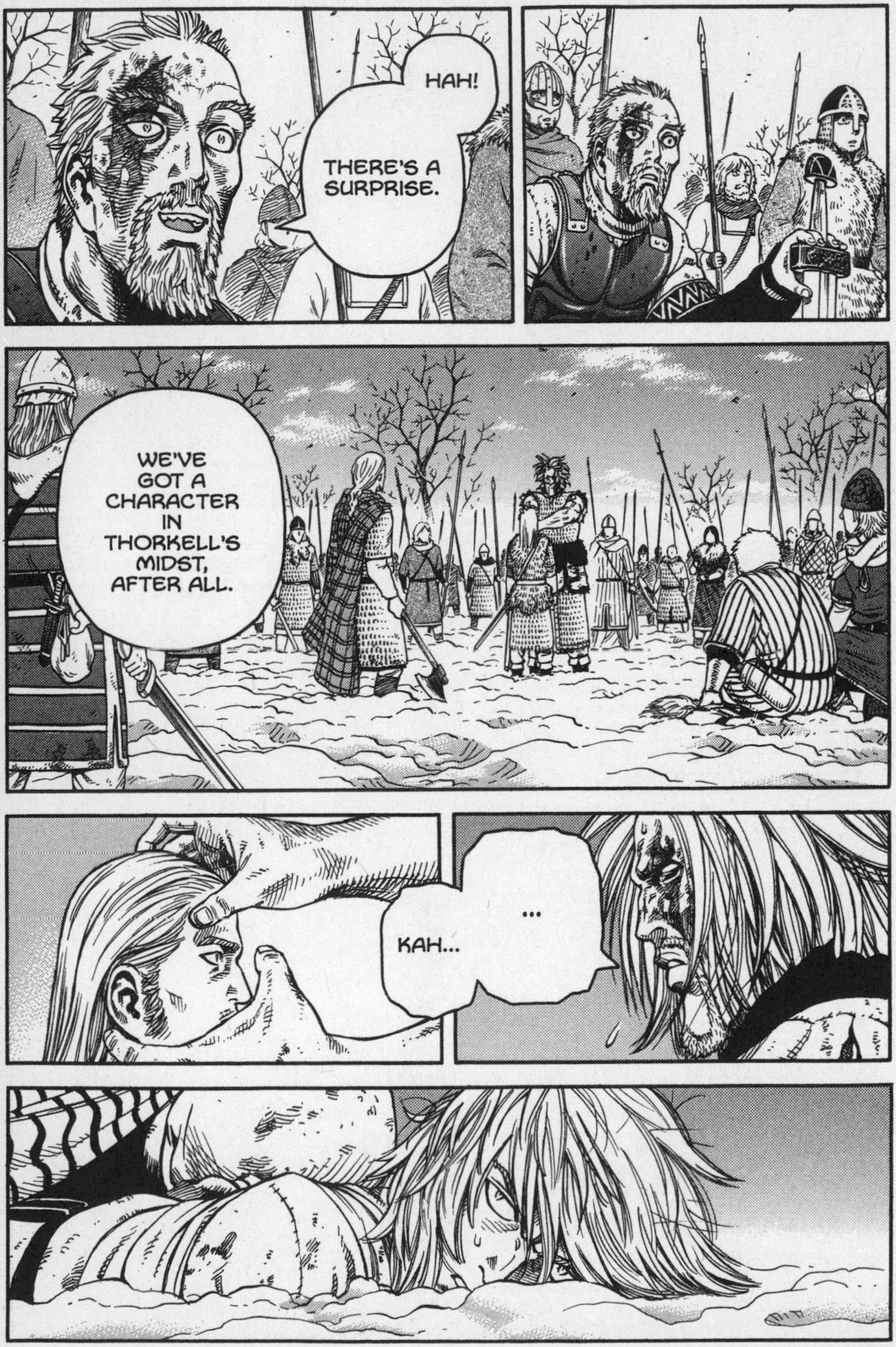
HAH!
THERE'S A SURPRISE.
WE'VE GOT A CHARACTER IN THORKELL'S MIDST, AFTER ALL.
...
KAH...

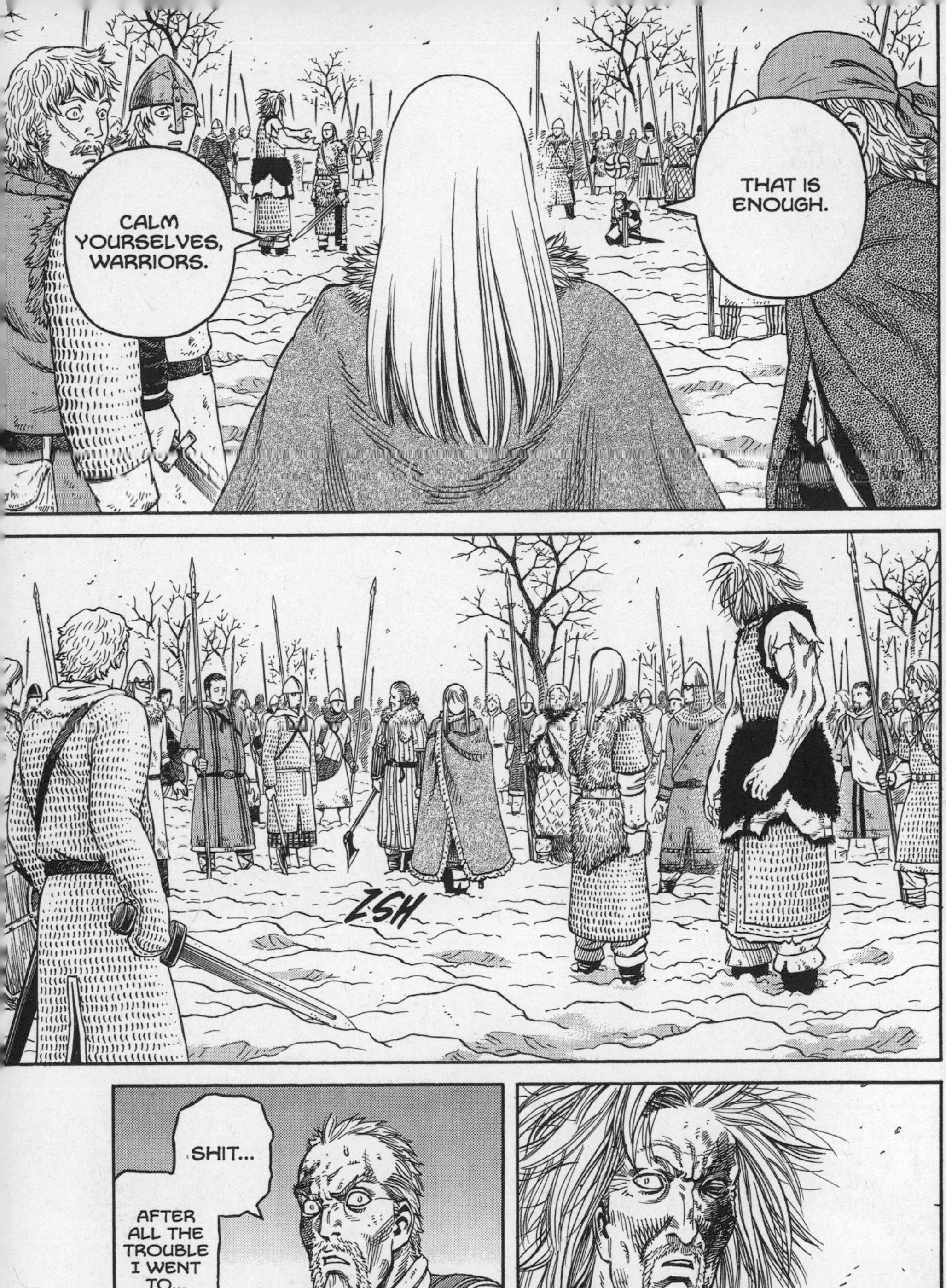
THAT IS ENOUGH.
CALM YOURSELVES, WARRIORS.
ZSH
SHIT...
AFTER ALL THE TROUBLE I WENT TO...

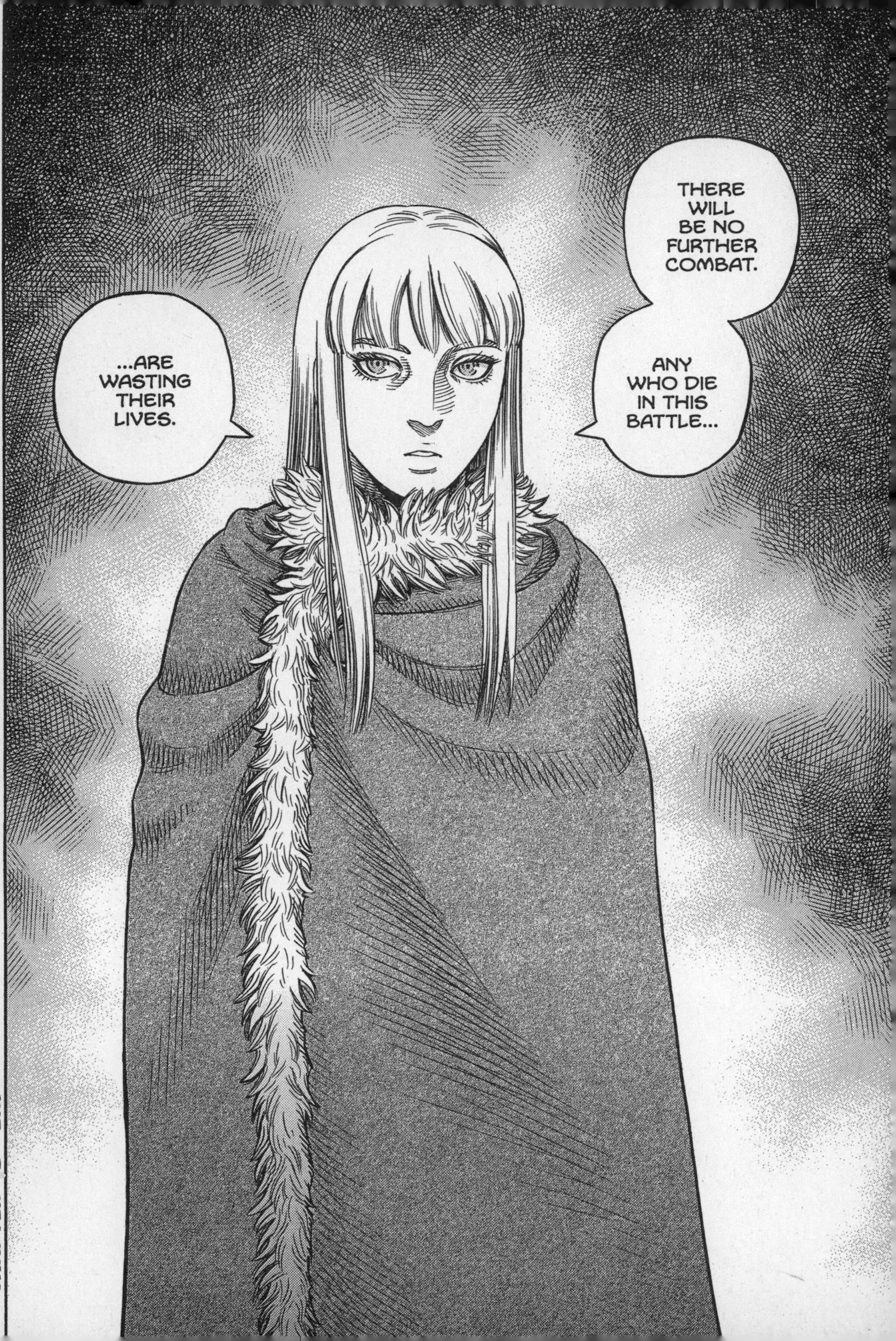
THERE WILL BE NO FURTHER COMBAT.
ANY WHO DIE IN THIS BATTLE...
...ARE WASTING THEIR LIVES.

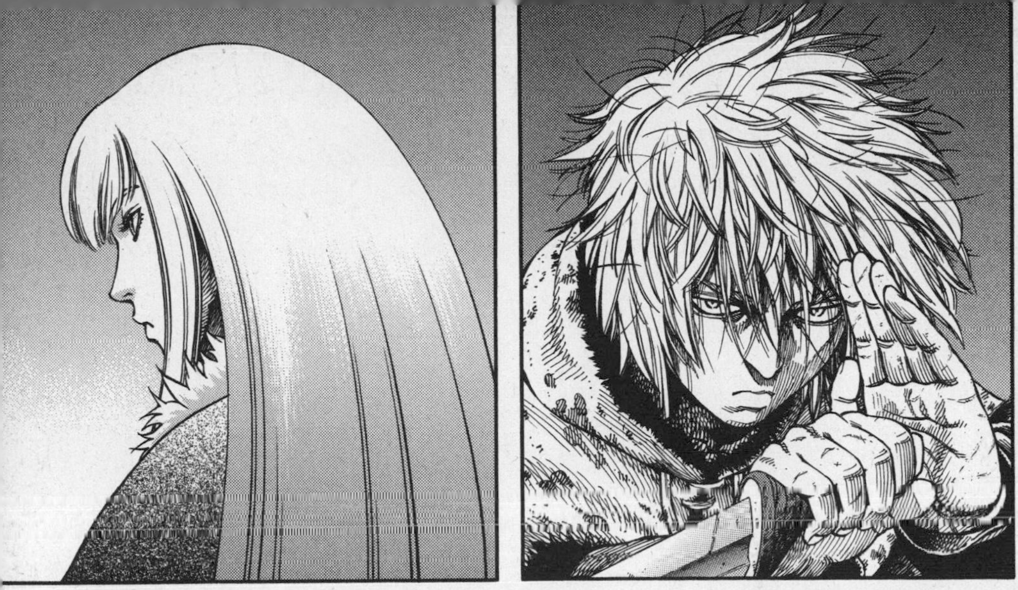

## CHAPTER 42: VERDICT

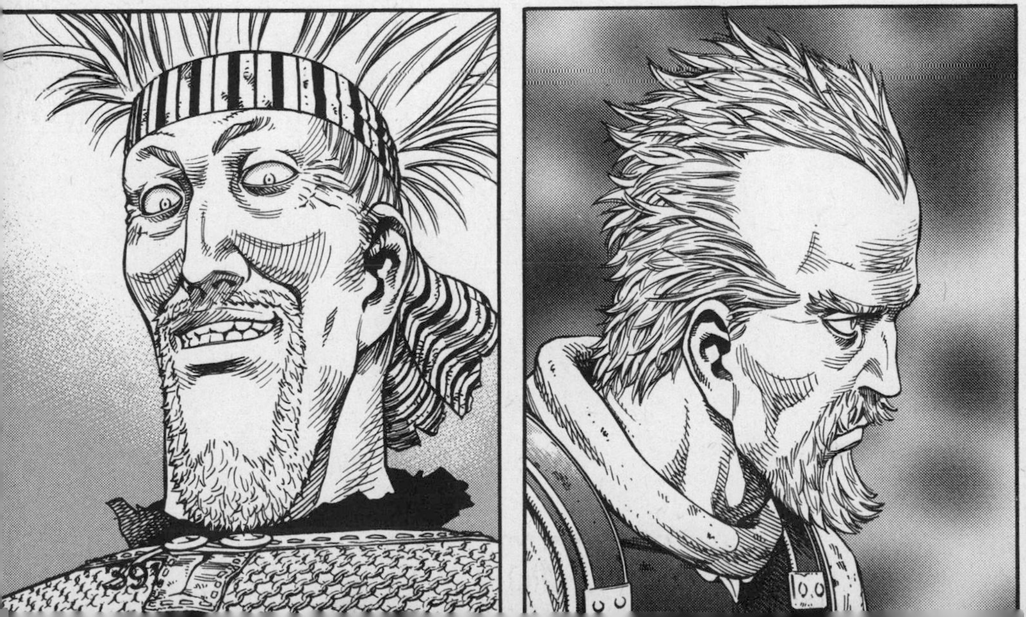

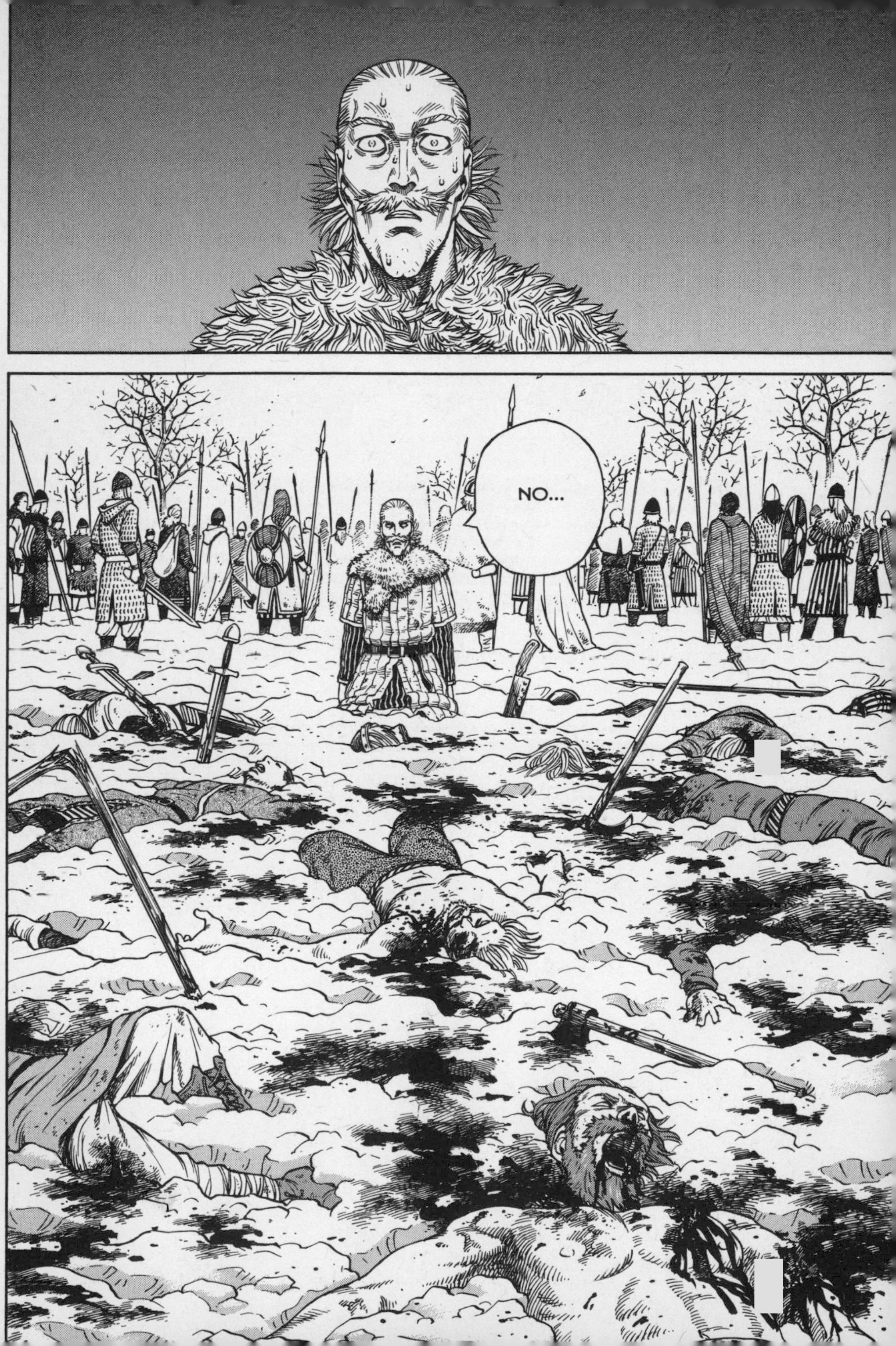
NO...

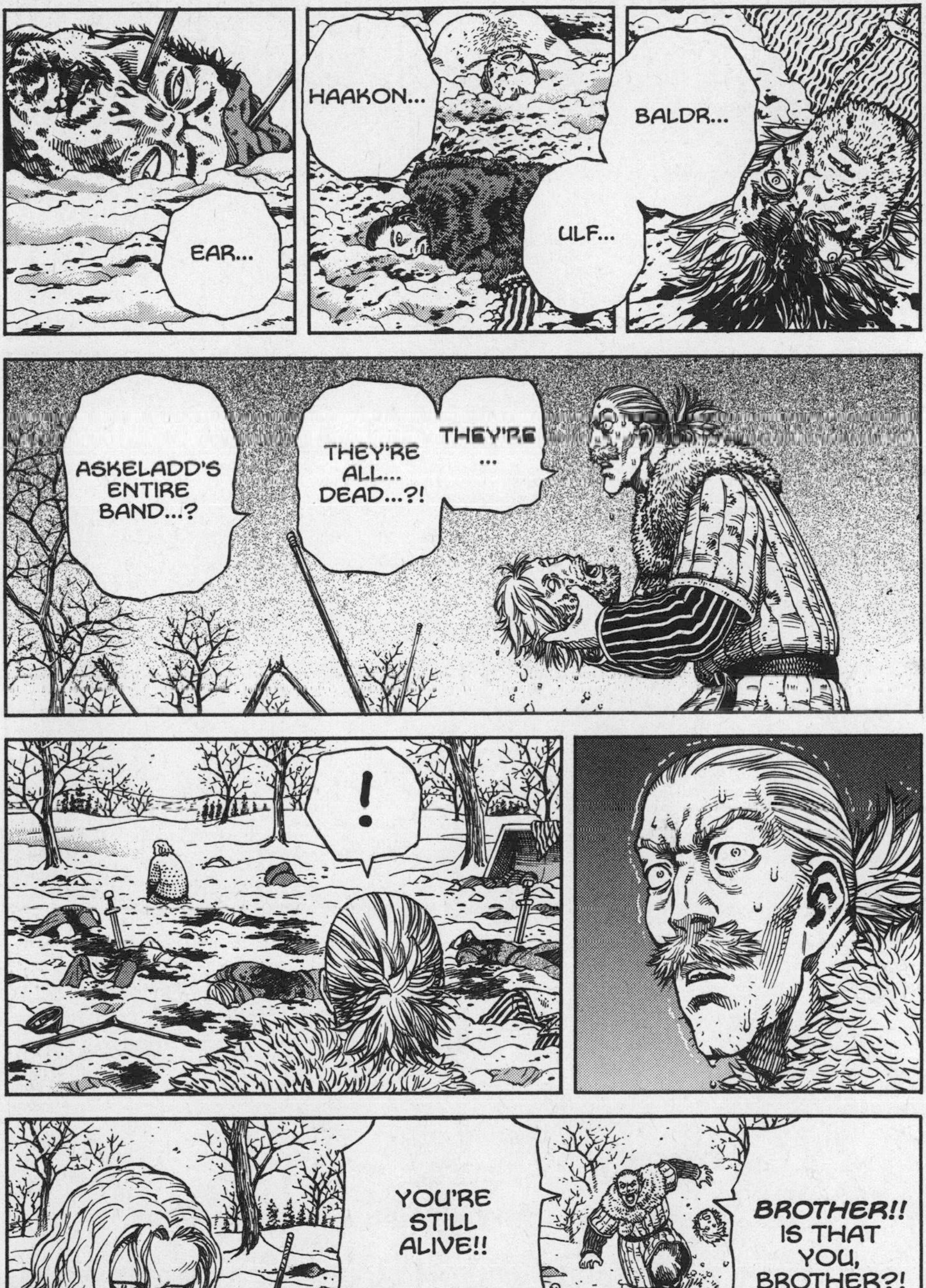
BALDR...
ULF...
HAAKON...
EAR...
THEY'RE ...
THEY'RE ALL... DEAD...?!
ASKELADD'S ENTIRE BAND...?
!
BROTHER!! IS THAT YOU, BROTHER?!
ZRSH
YOU'RE STILL ALIVE!!

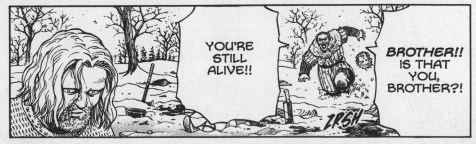

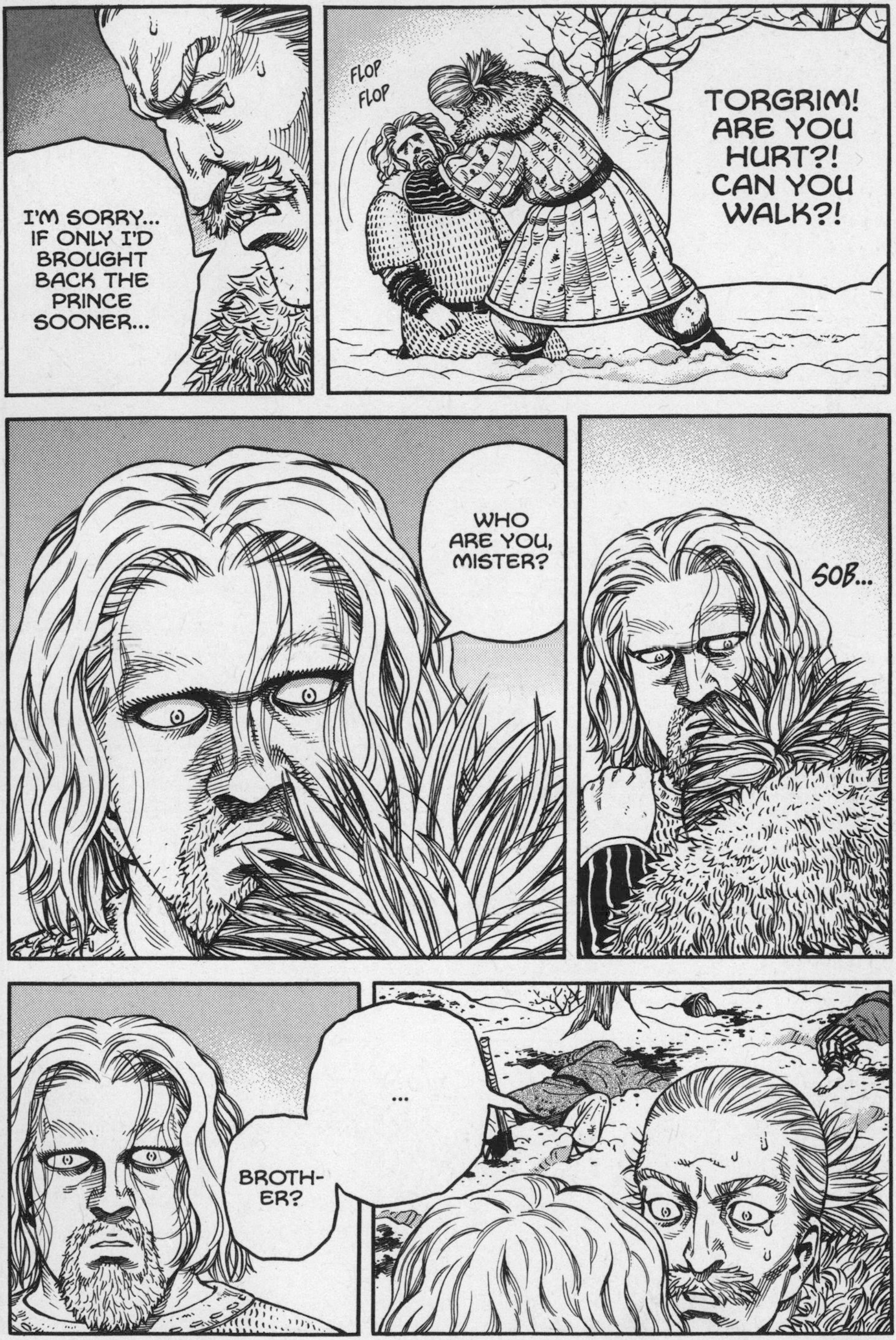

TORGRIM! ARE YOU HURT?! CAN YOU WALK?!
FLOP FLOP
I'M SORRY... IF ONLY I'D BROUGHT BACK THE PRINCE SOONER...
SOB...
WHO ARE YOU, MISTER?
...
BROTH-ER?

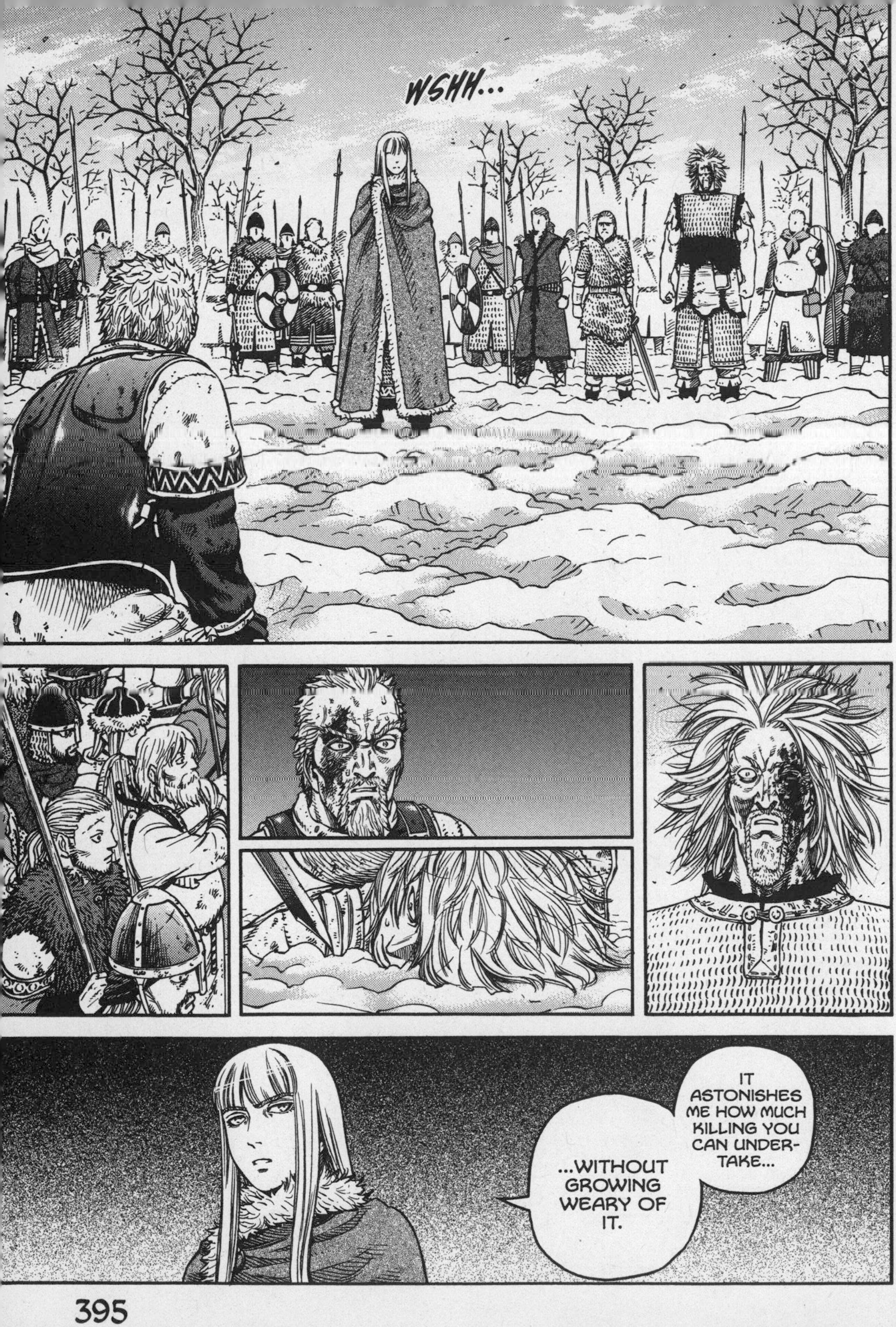
WSHH...
IT ASTONISHES ME HOW MUCH KILLING YOU CAN UNDER-TAKE...
...WITHOUT GROWING WEARY OF IT.

NO ONE HAS A RIGHT TO INTERFERE IN A DUEL. NOT KINGS, NOT GODS.

BEGONE, GIRL.

IT DOESN'T SEEM TO BE MUCH OF A DUEL ANYMORE.

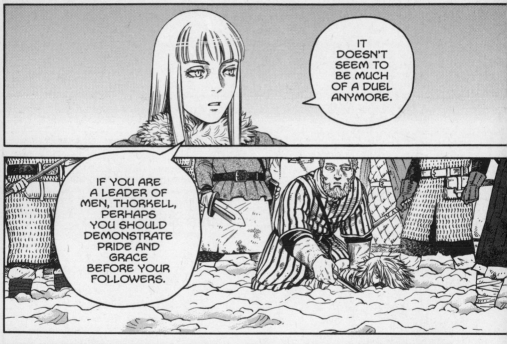

IF YOU ARE A LEADER OF MEN, THORKELL, PERHAPS YOU SHOULD DEMONSTRATE PRIDE AND GRACE BEFORE YOUR FOLLOWERS.

SCRATCH SCRATCH

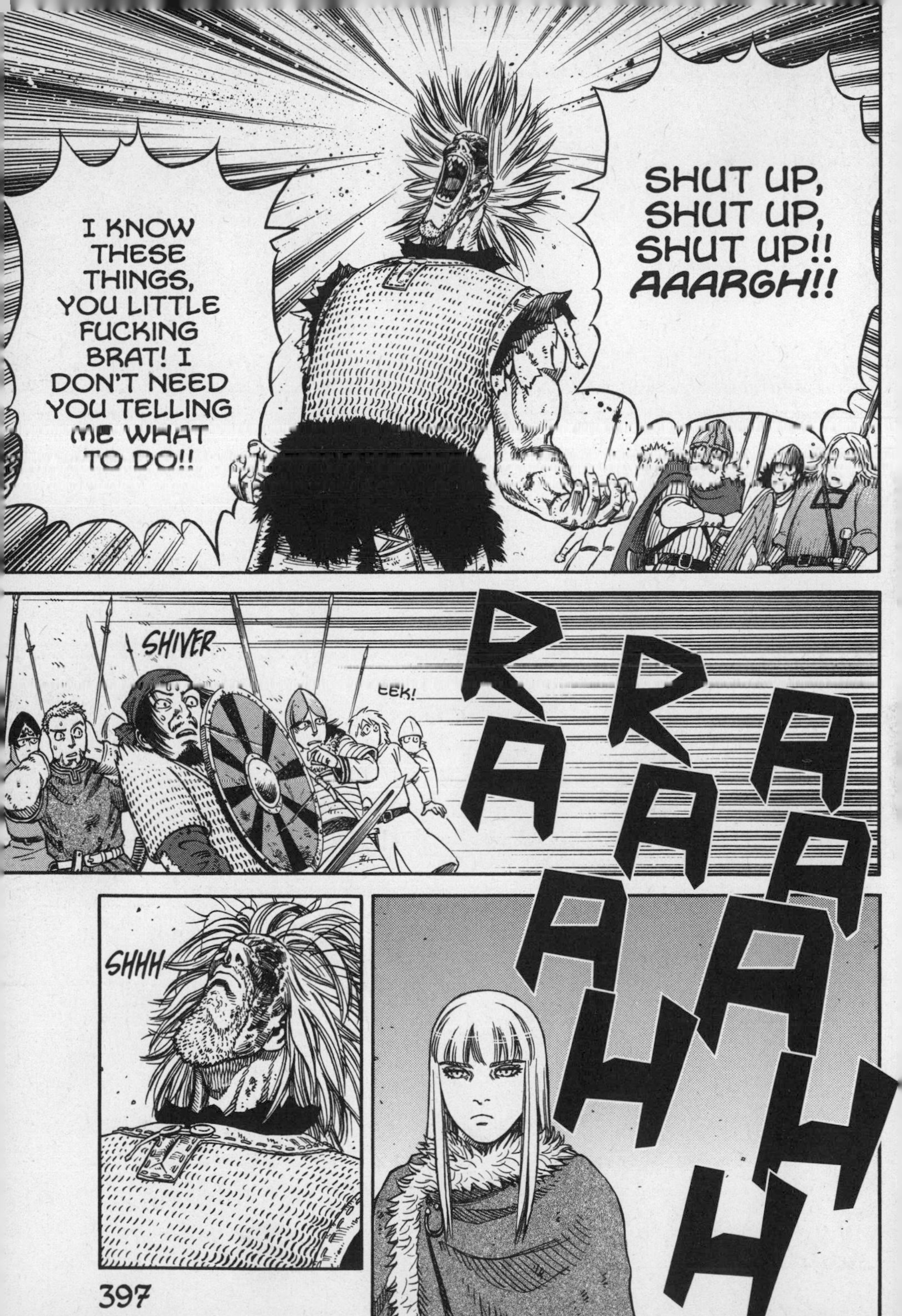
SHUT UP, SHUT UP, SHUT UP!! *AAARGH!!*
I KNOW THESE THINGS, YOU LITTLE FUCKING BRAT! I DON'T NEED YOU TELLING ME WHAT TO DO!!
RRAAAAAAAHHHHHH
tek!
SHIVER
SHHH

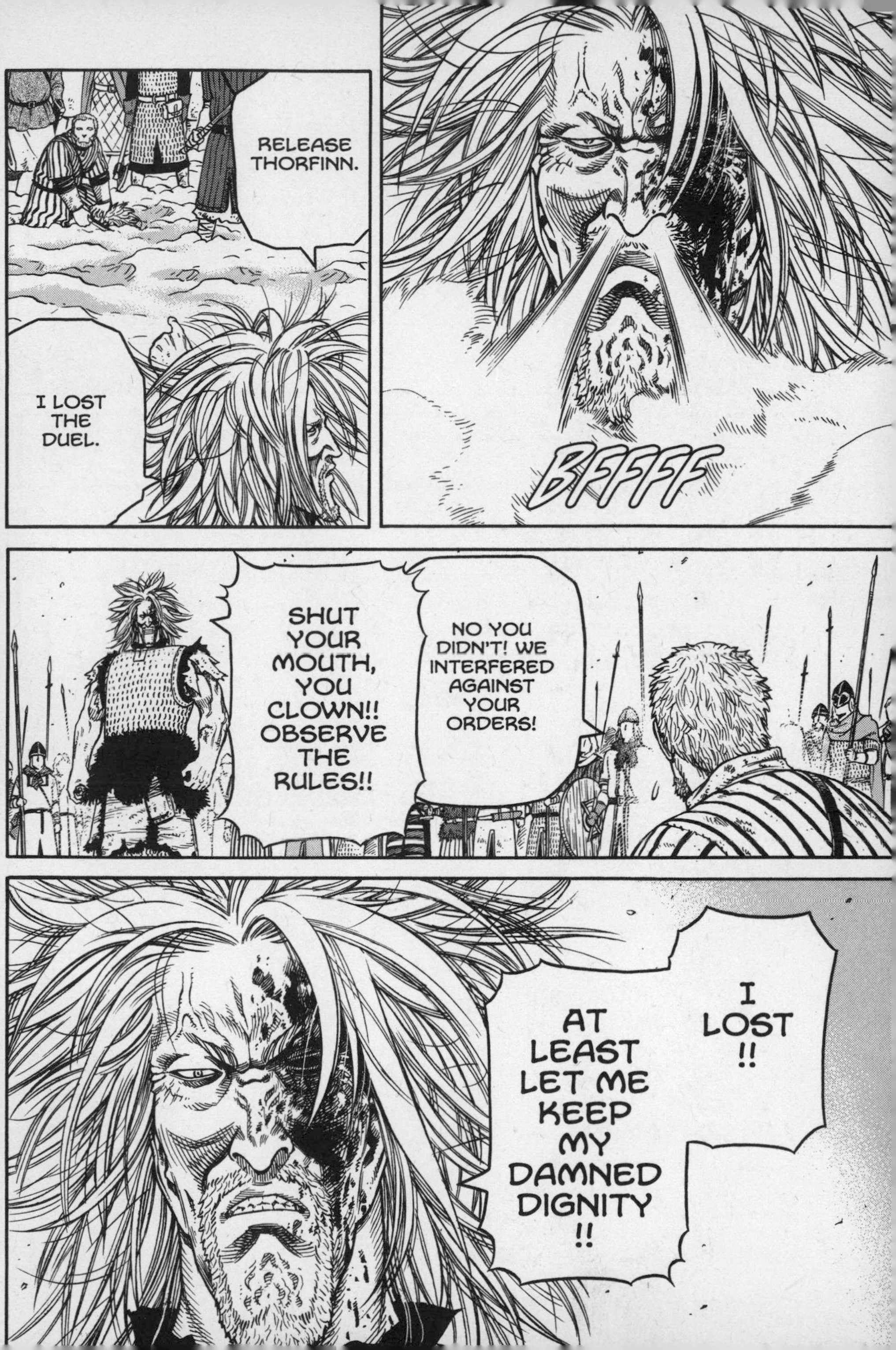
BFFFF
RELEASE THORFINN.
I LOST THE DUEL.
NO YOU DIDN'T! WE INTERFERED AGAINST YOUR ORDERS!
SHUT YOUR MOUTH, YOU CLOWN!! OBSERVE THE RULES!!
I LOST !!
AT LEAST LET ME KEEP MY DAMNED DIGNITY !!

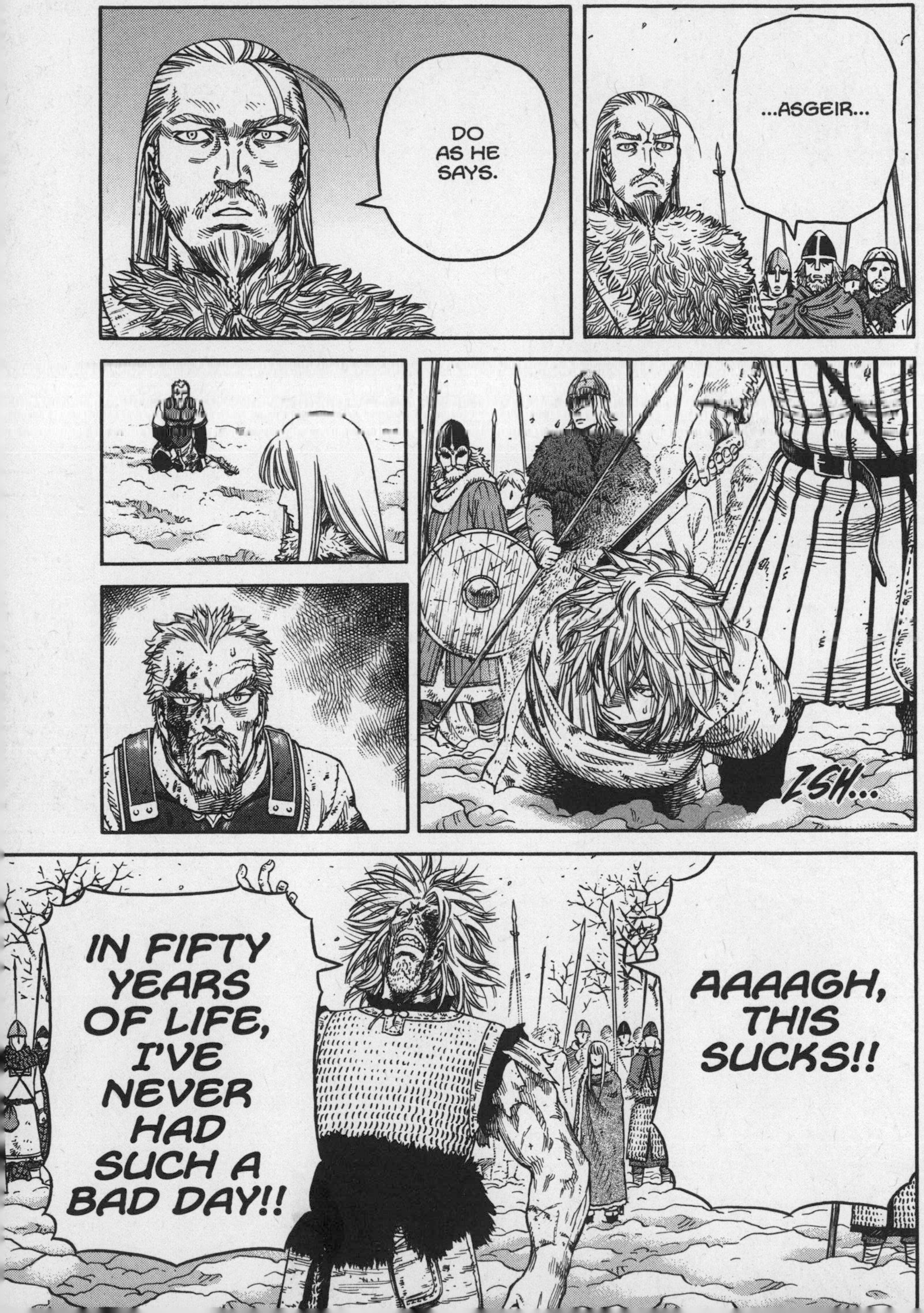
...ASGEIR...
DO AS HE SAYS.
ZSH...
AAAAGH, THIS SUCKS!!
IN FIFTY YEARS OF LIFE, I'VE NEVER HAD SUCH A BAD DAY!!

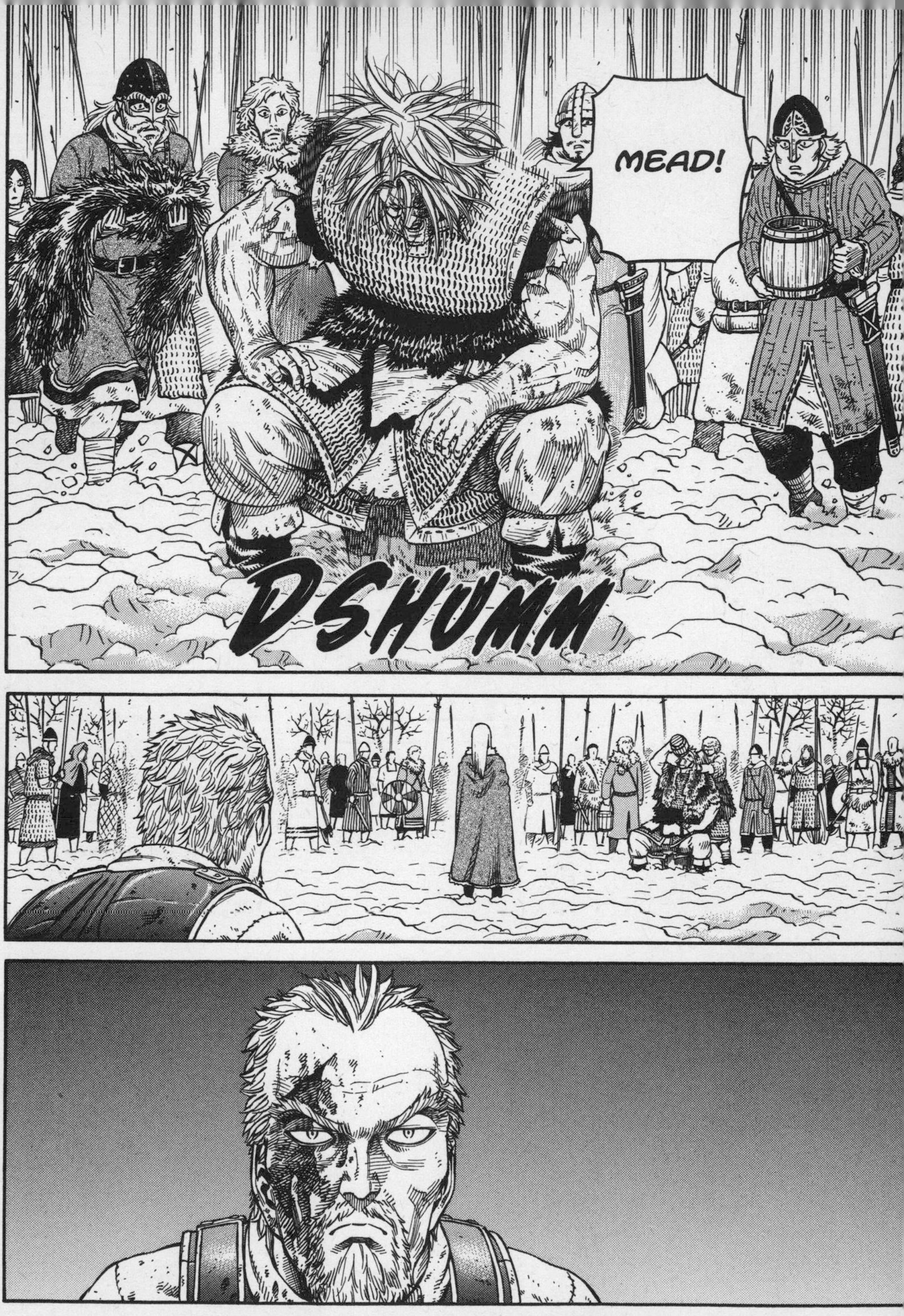
MEAD!
DSHUMM

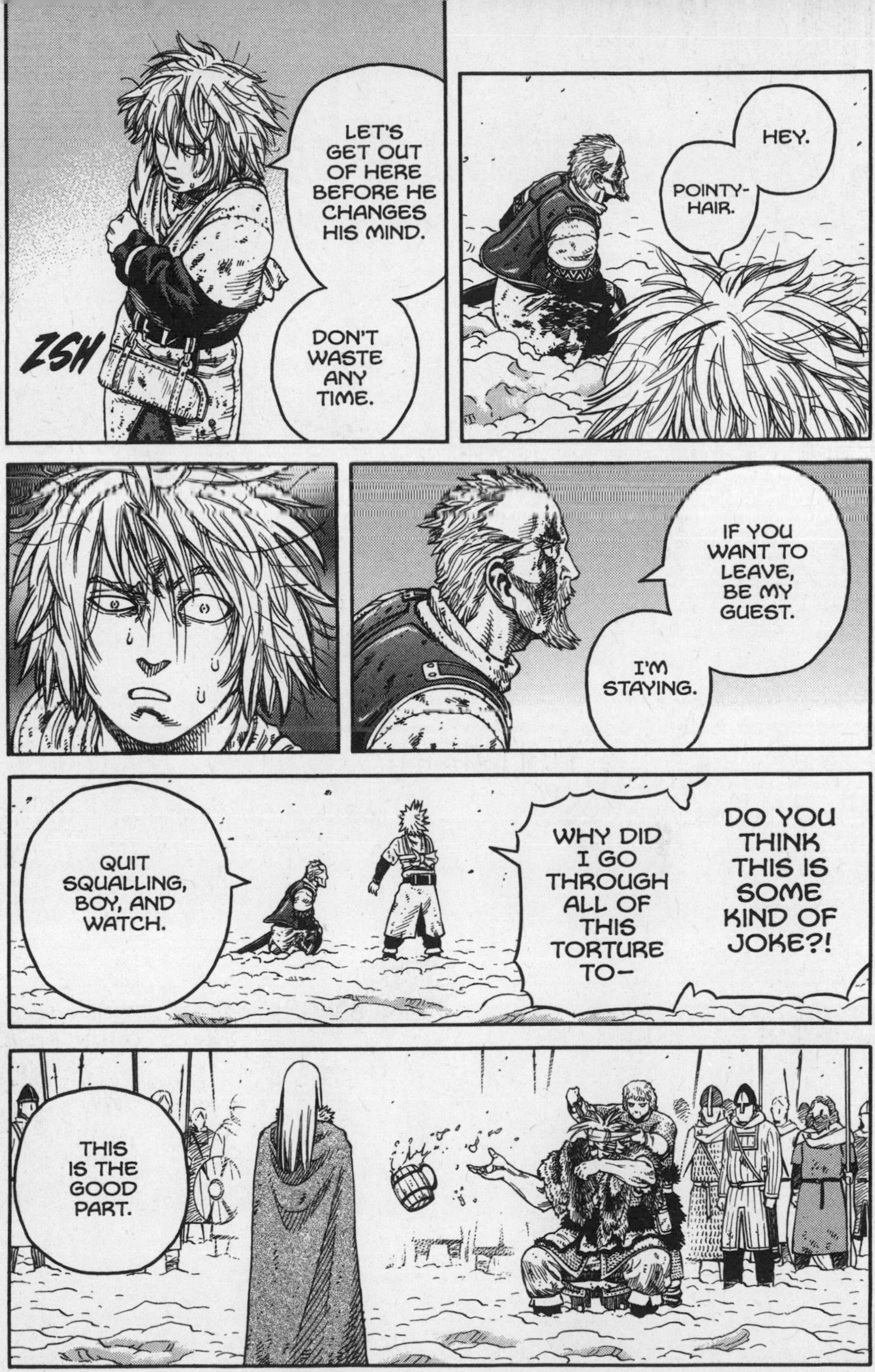
HEY.
POINTY-HAIR.
LET'S GET OUT OF HERE BEFORE HE CHANGES HIS MIND.
DON'T WASTE ANY TIME.
ZSH
IF YOU WANT TO LEAVE, BE MY GUEST.
I'M STAYING.
DO YOU THINK THIS IS SOME KIND OF JOKE?!
WHY DID I GO THROUGH ALL OF THIS TORTURE TO—
QUIT SQUALLING, BOY, AND WATCH.
THIS IS THE GOOD PART.

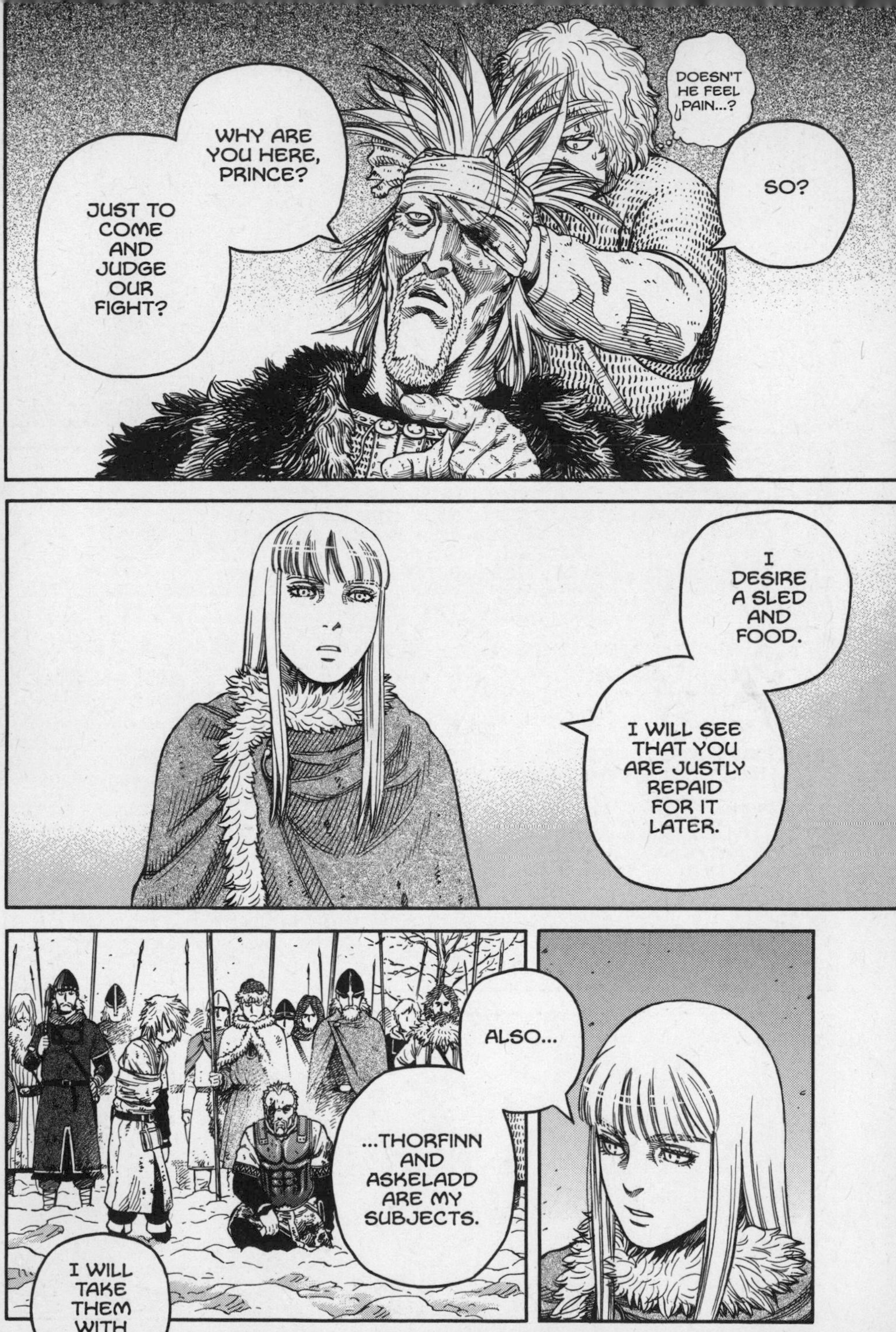
DOESN'T HE FEEL PAIN...?
SO?
WHY ARE YOU HERE, PRINCE?
JUST TO COME AND JUDGE OUR FIGHT?
I DESIRE A SLED AND FOOD.
I WILL SEE THAT YOU ARE JUSTLY REPAID FOR IT LATER.
ALSO...
...THORFINN AND ASKELADD ARE MY SUBJECTS.
I WILL TAKE THEM WITH ME.

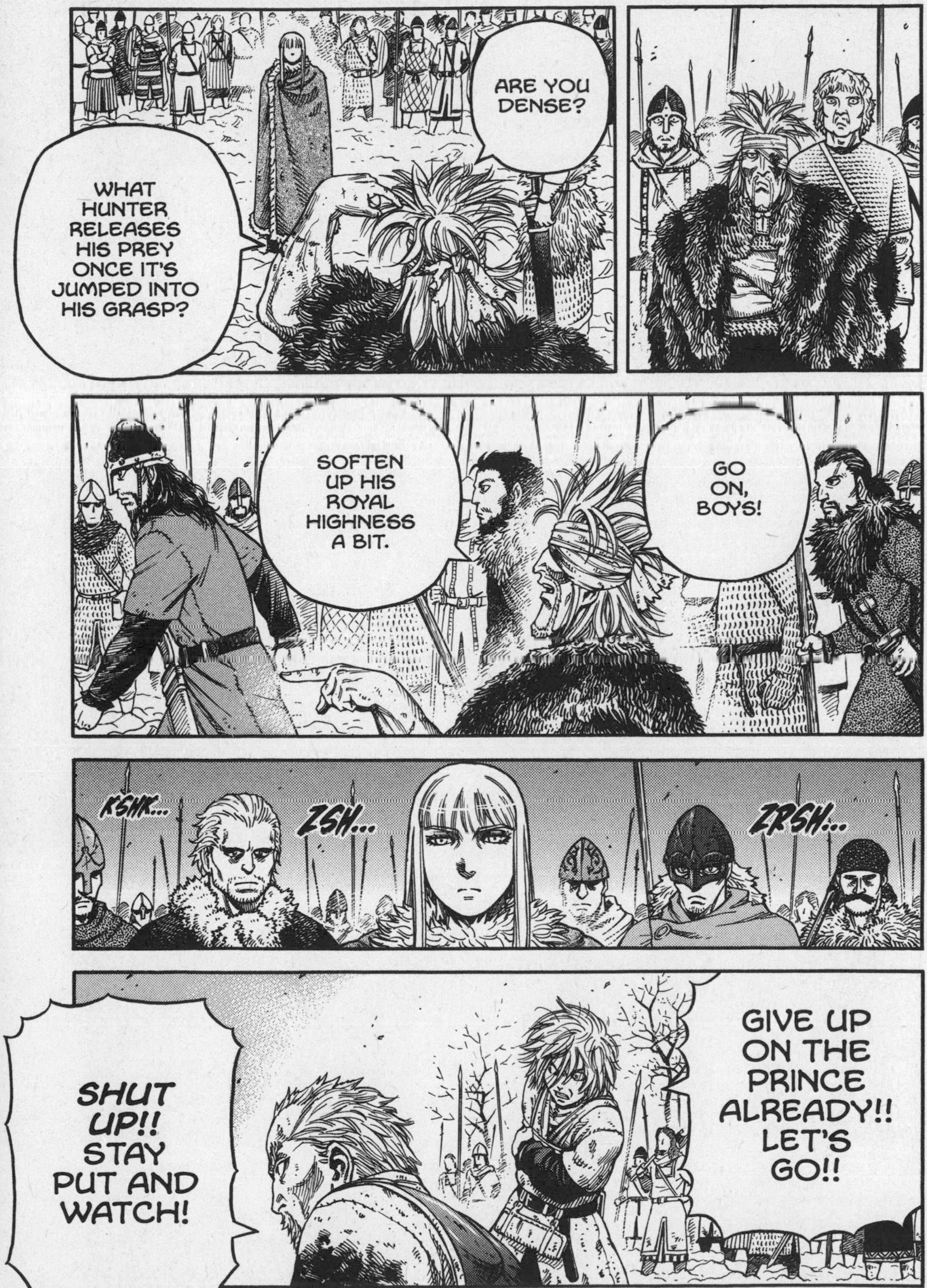
ARE YOU DENSE?
WHAT HUNTER RELEASES HIS PREY ONCE IT'S JUMPED INTO HIS GRASP?
GO ON, BOYS!
SOFTEN UP HIS ROYAL HIGHNESS A BIT.
ZRSH...
ZSH...
KSHK...
GIVE UP ON THE PRINCE ALREADY!! LET'S GO!!
SHUT UP!! STAY PUT AND WATCH!

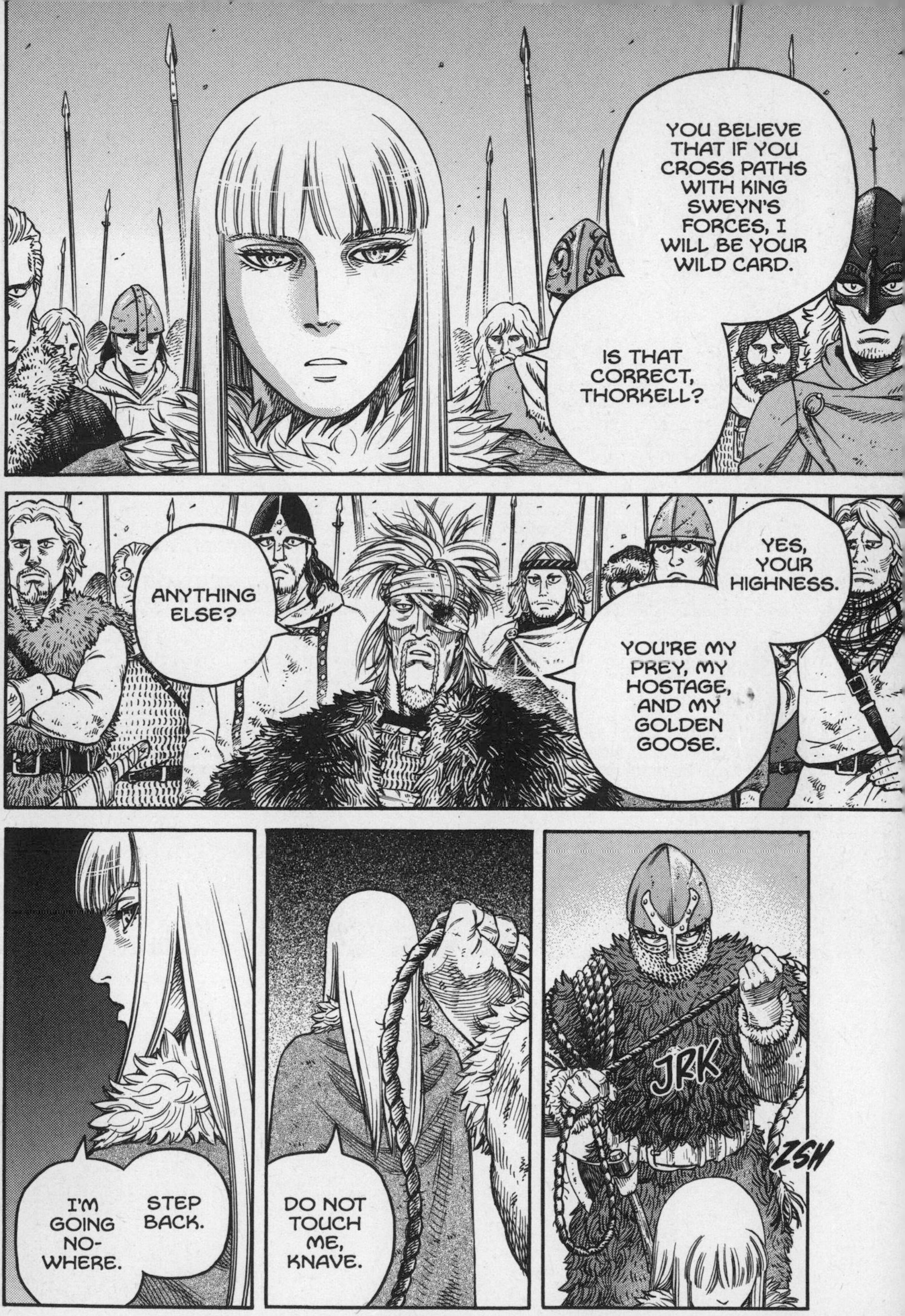
YOU BELIEVE THAT IF YOU CROSS PATHS WITH KING SWEYN'S FORCES, I WILL BE YOUR WILD CARD.
IS THAT CORRECT, THORKELL?
YES, YOUR HIGHNESS.
YOU'RE MY PREY, MY HOSTAGE, AND MY GOLDEN GOOSE.
ANYTHING ELSE?
JRK
ZSH
DO NOT TOUCH ME, KNAVE.
STEP BACK.
I'M GOING NO-WHERE.

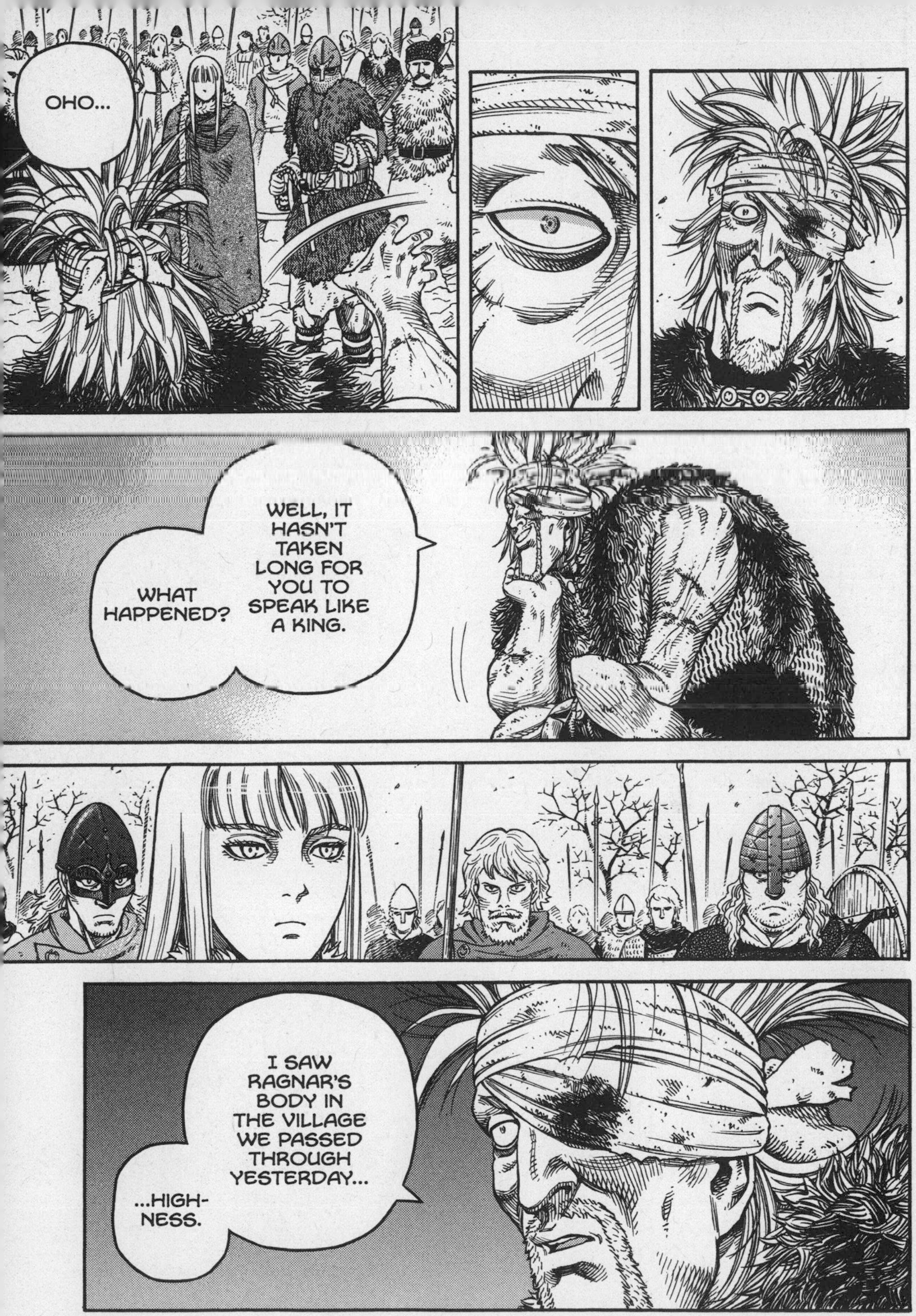
OHO...
WELL, IT HASN'T TAKEN LONG FOR YOU TO SPEAK LIKE A KING.
WHAT HAPPENED?
I SAW RAGNAR'S BODY IN THE VILLAGE WE PASSED THROUGH YESTERDAY...
...HIGH-NESS.

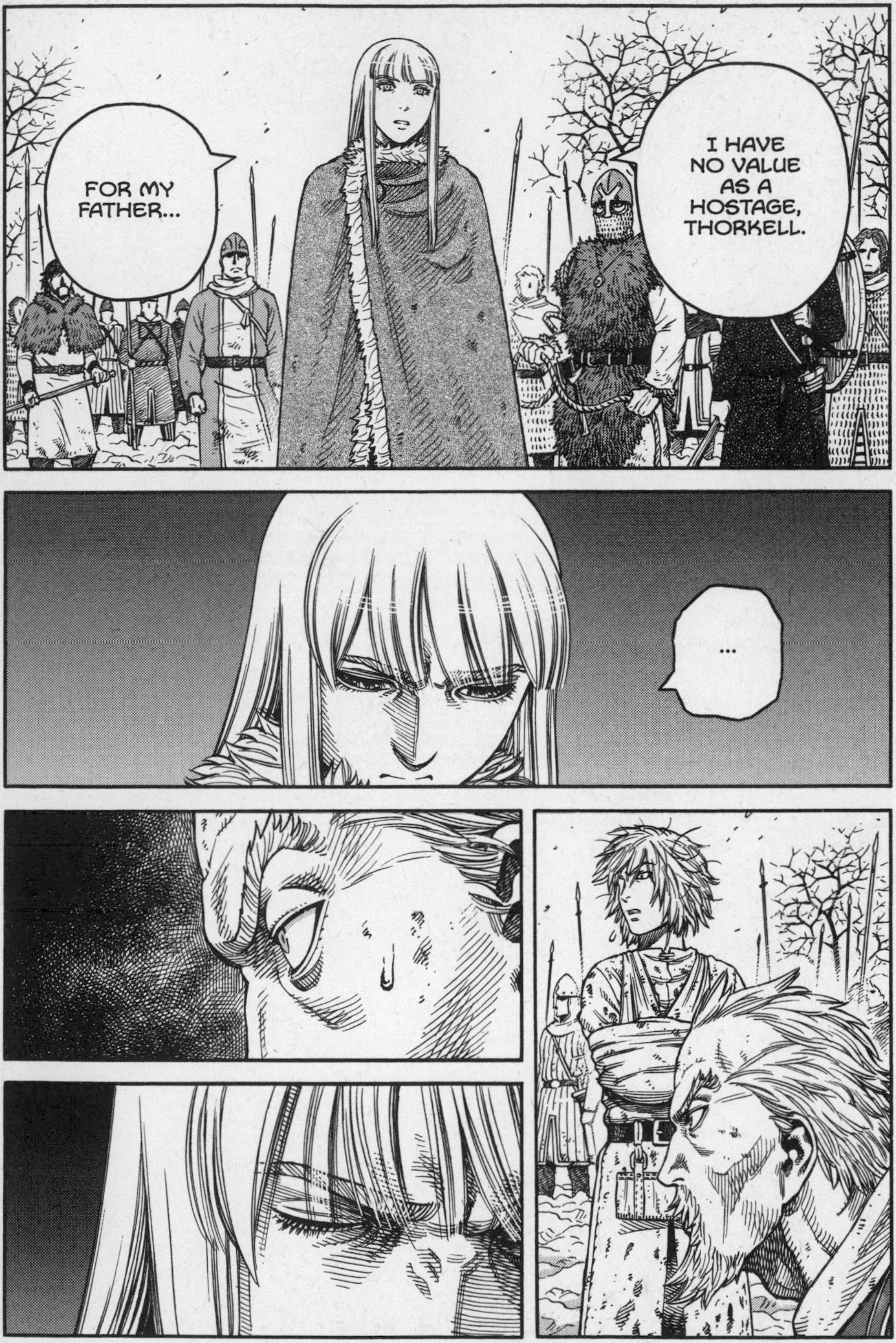
I HAVE NO VALUE AS A HOSTAGE, THORKELL.
FOR MY FATHER...
...

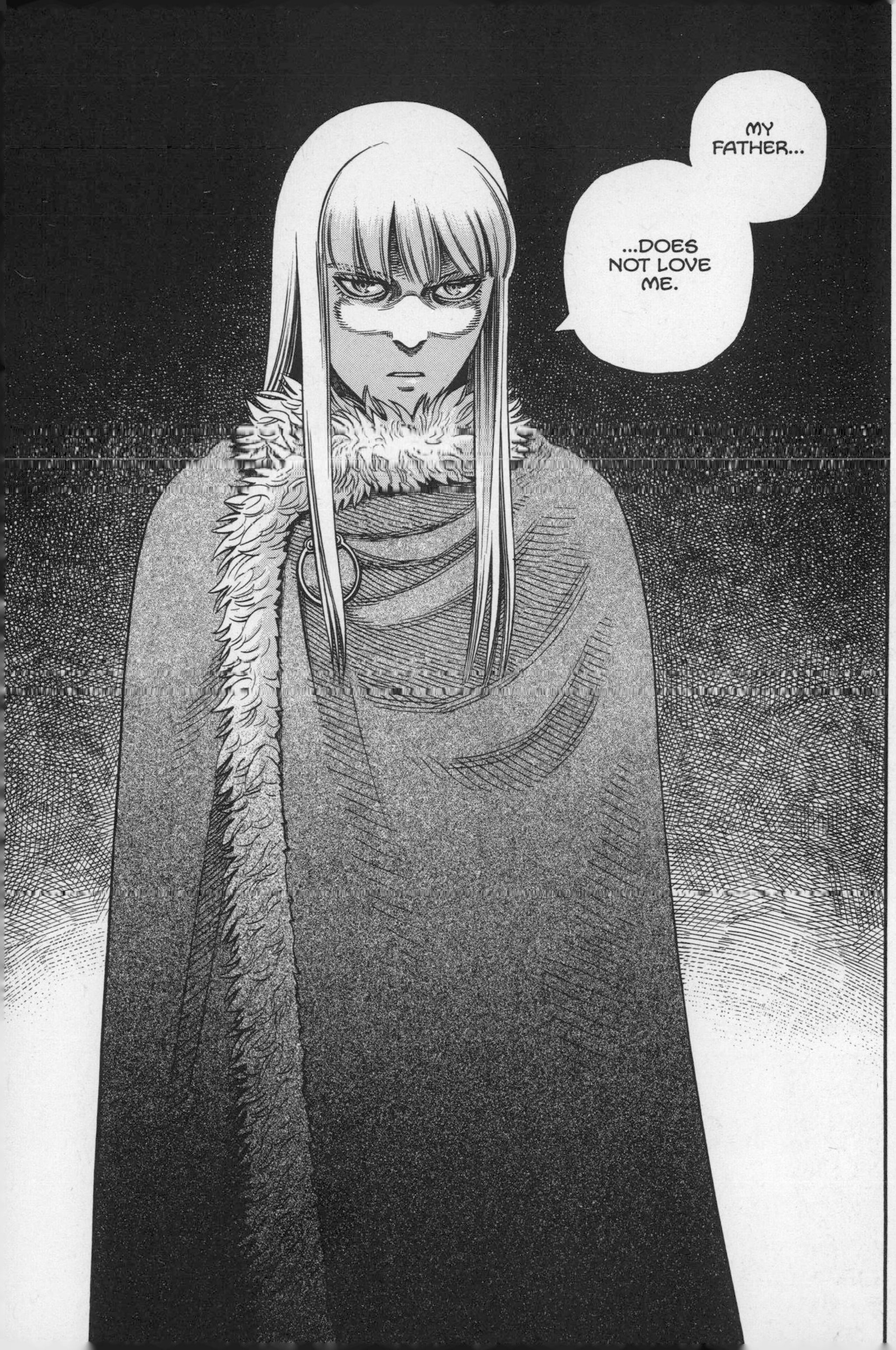
MY FATHER...
...DOES NOT LOVE ME.

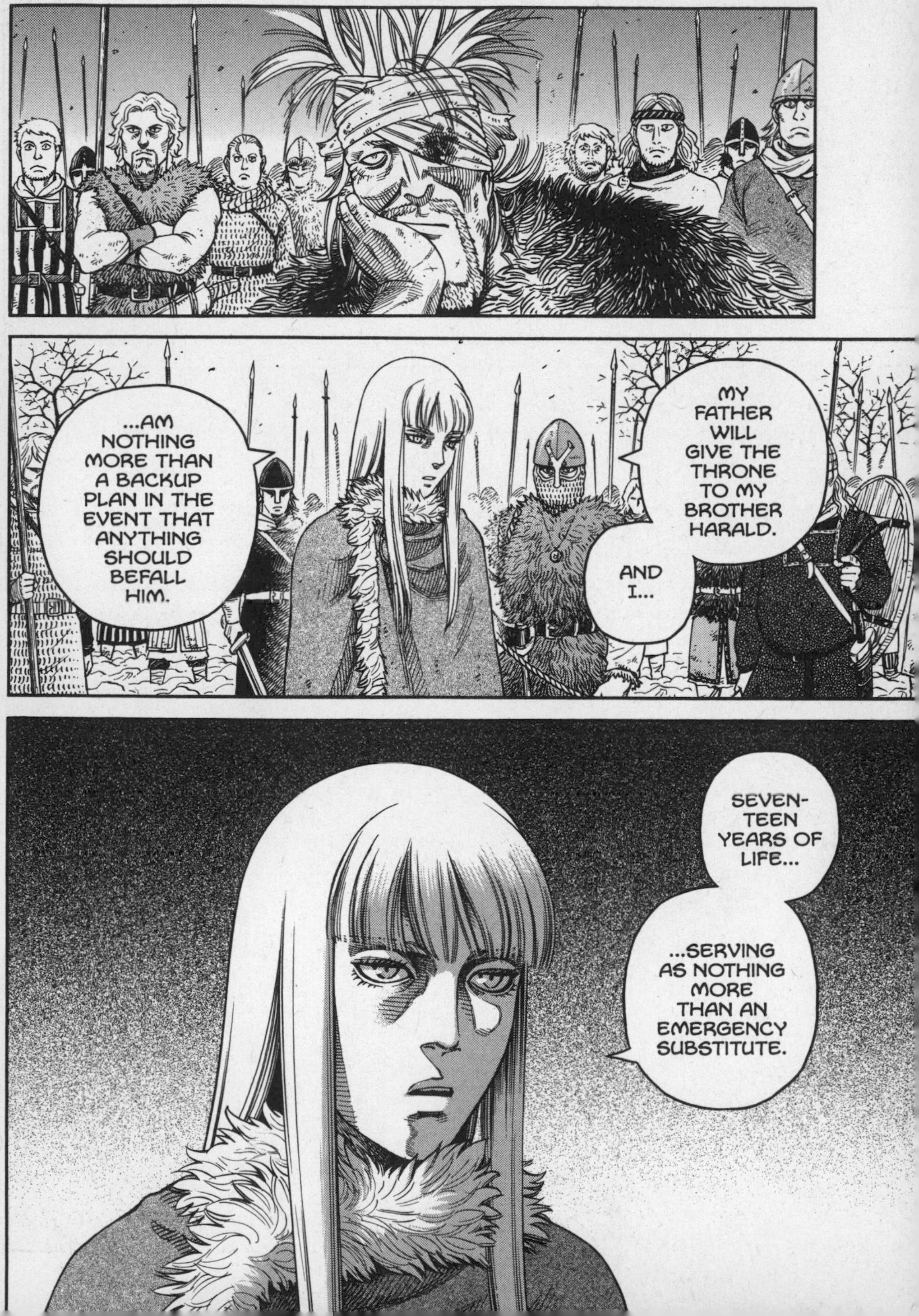
MY FATHER WILL GIVE THE THRONE TO MY BROTHER HARALD.
AND I...
...AM NOTHING MORE THAN A BACKUP PLAN IN THE EVENT THAT ANYTHING SHOULD BEFALL HIM.
SEVEN-TEEN YEARS OF LIFE...
...SERVING AS NOTHING MORE THAN AN EMERGENCY SUBSTITUTE.

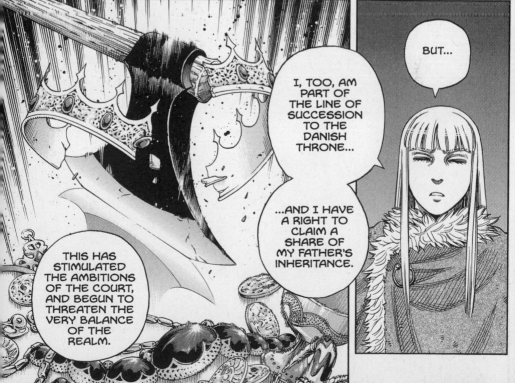

BUT...

I, TOO, AM PART OF THE LINE OF SUCCESSION TO THE DANISH THRONE...

...AND I HAVE A RIGHT TO CLAIM A SHARE OF MY FATHER'S INHERITANCE.

THIS HAS STIMULATED THE AMBITIONS OF THE COURT, AND BEGUN TO THREATEN THE VERY BALANCE OF THE REALM.

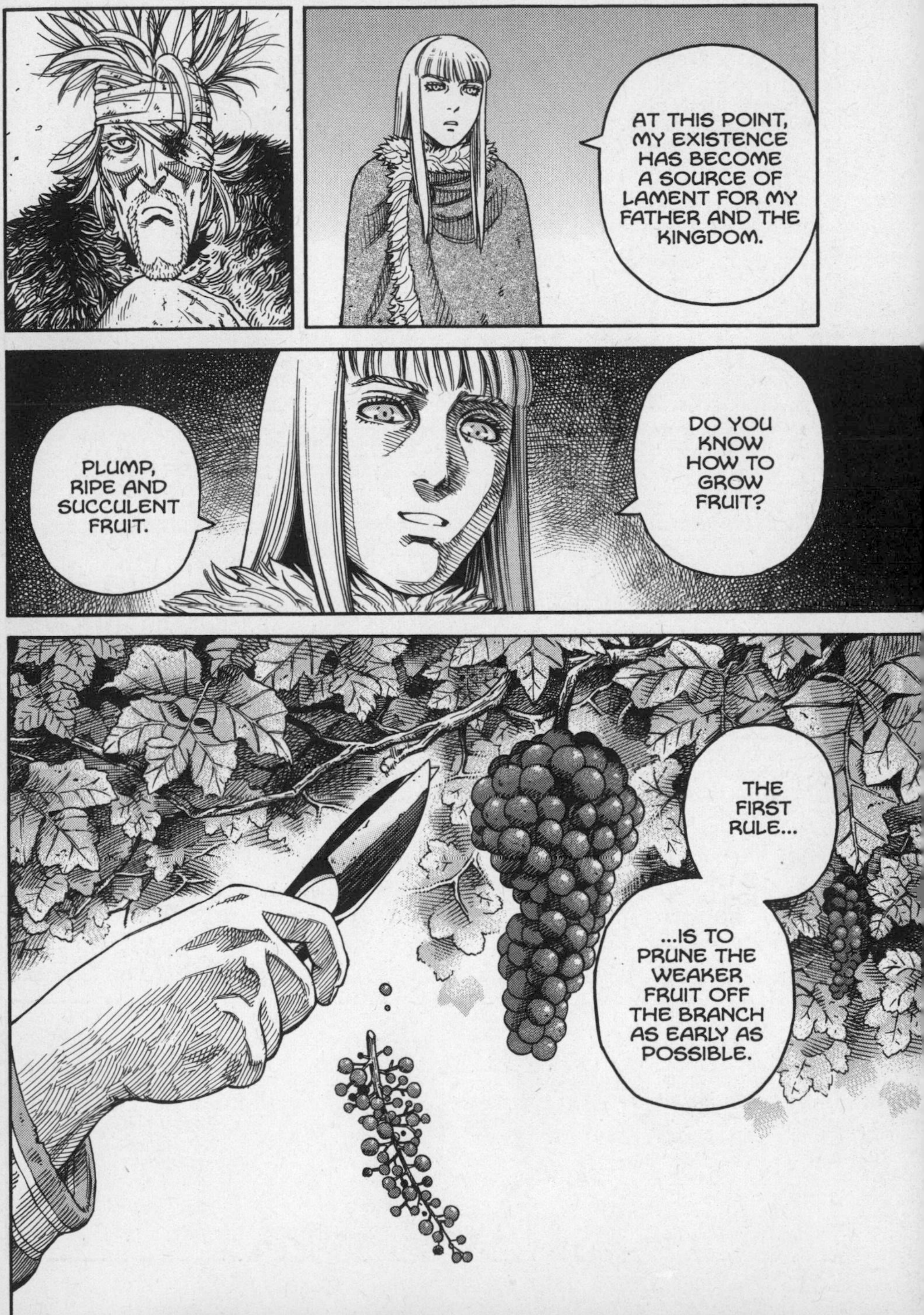
AT THIS POINT, MY EXISTENCE HAS BECOME A SOURCE OF LAMENT FOR MY FATHER AND THE KINGDOM.
DO YOU KNOW HOW TO GROW FRUIT?
PLUMP, RIPE AND SUCCULENT FRUIT.
THE FIRST RULE...
...IS TO PRUNE THE WEAKER FRUIT OFF THE BRANCH AS EARLY AS POSSIBLE.

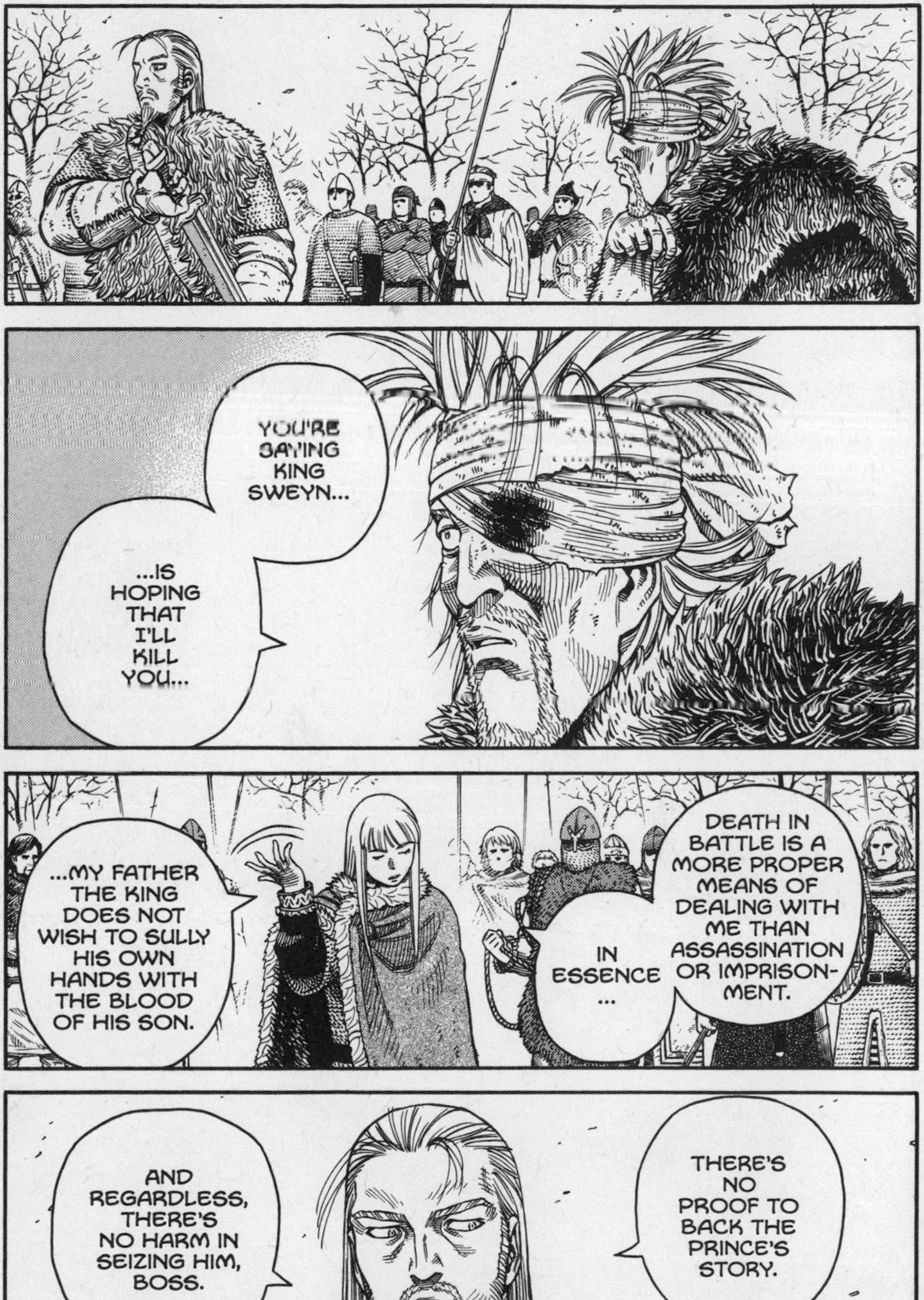
YOU'RE SAYING KING SWEYN...
...IS HOPING THAT I'LL KILL YOU...
DEATH IN BATTLE IS A MORE PROPER MEANS OF DEALING WITH ME THAN ASSASSINATION OR IMPRISON-MENT.
IN ESSENCE...
...MY FATHER THE KING DOES NOT WISH TO SULLY HIS OWN HANDS WITH THE BLOOD OF HIS SON.
THERE'S NO PROOF TO BACK THE PRINCE'S STORY.
AND REGARDLESS, THERE'S NO HARM IN SEIZING HIM, BOSS.

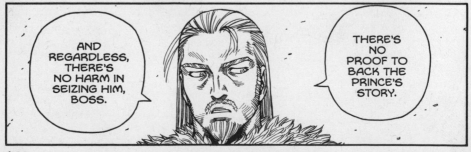

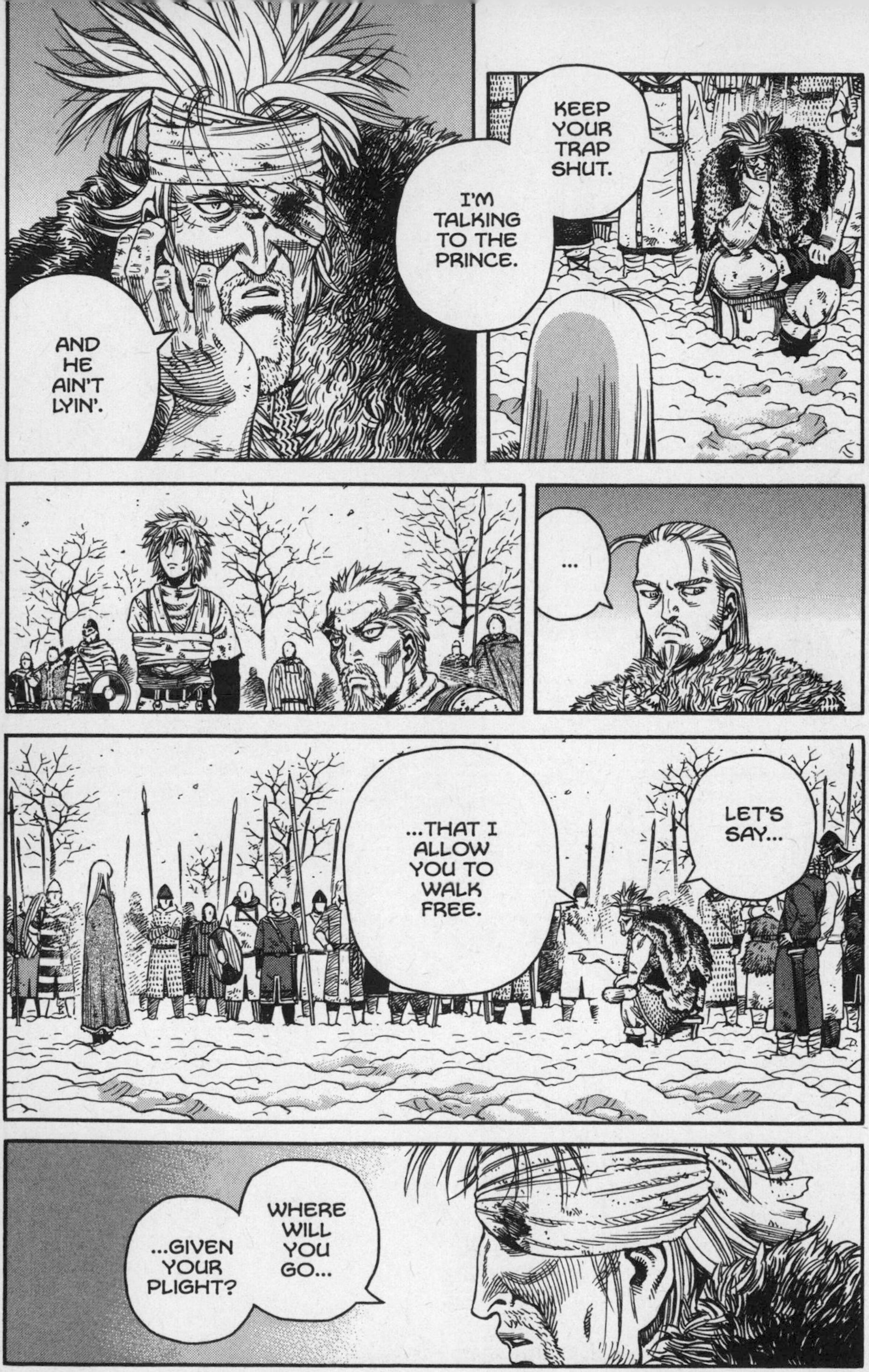
KEEP YOUR TRAP SHUT.
I'M TALKING TO THE PRINCE.
AND HE AIN'T LYIN'.
...
LET'S SAY...
...THAT I ALLOW YOU TO WALK FREE.
WHERE WILL YOU GO...
...GIVEN YOUR PLIGHT?

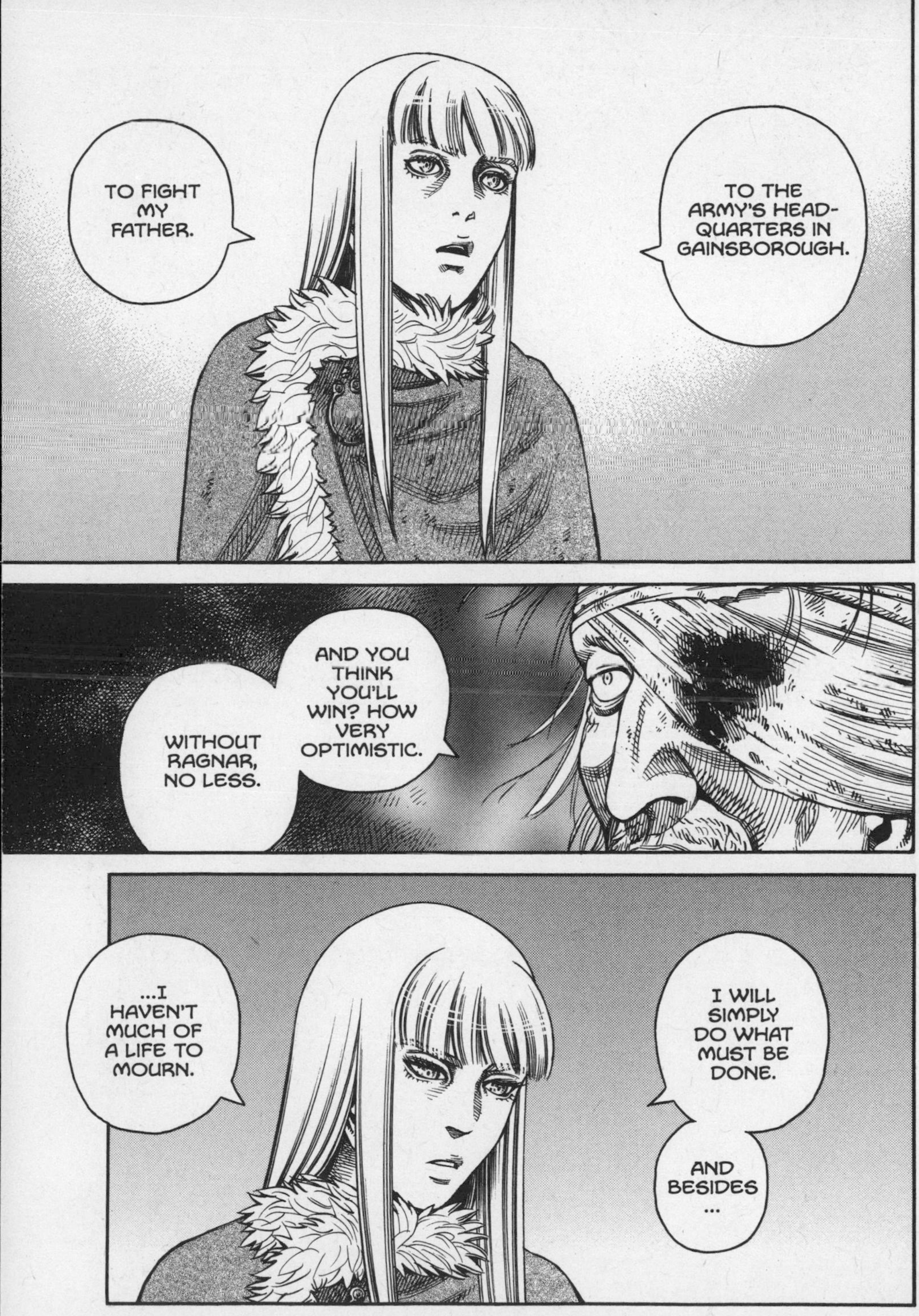
TO THE ARMY'S HEAD-QUARTERS IN GAINSBOROUGH.
TO FIGHT MY FATHER.
AND YOU THINK YOU'LL WIN? HOW VERY OPTIMISTIC.
WITHOUT RAGNAR, NO LESS.
I WILL SIMPLY DO WHAT MUST BE DONE.
AND BESIDES ...
...I HAVEN'T MUCH OF A LIFE TO MOURN.

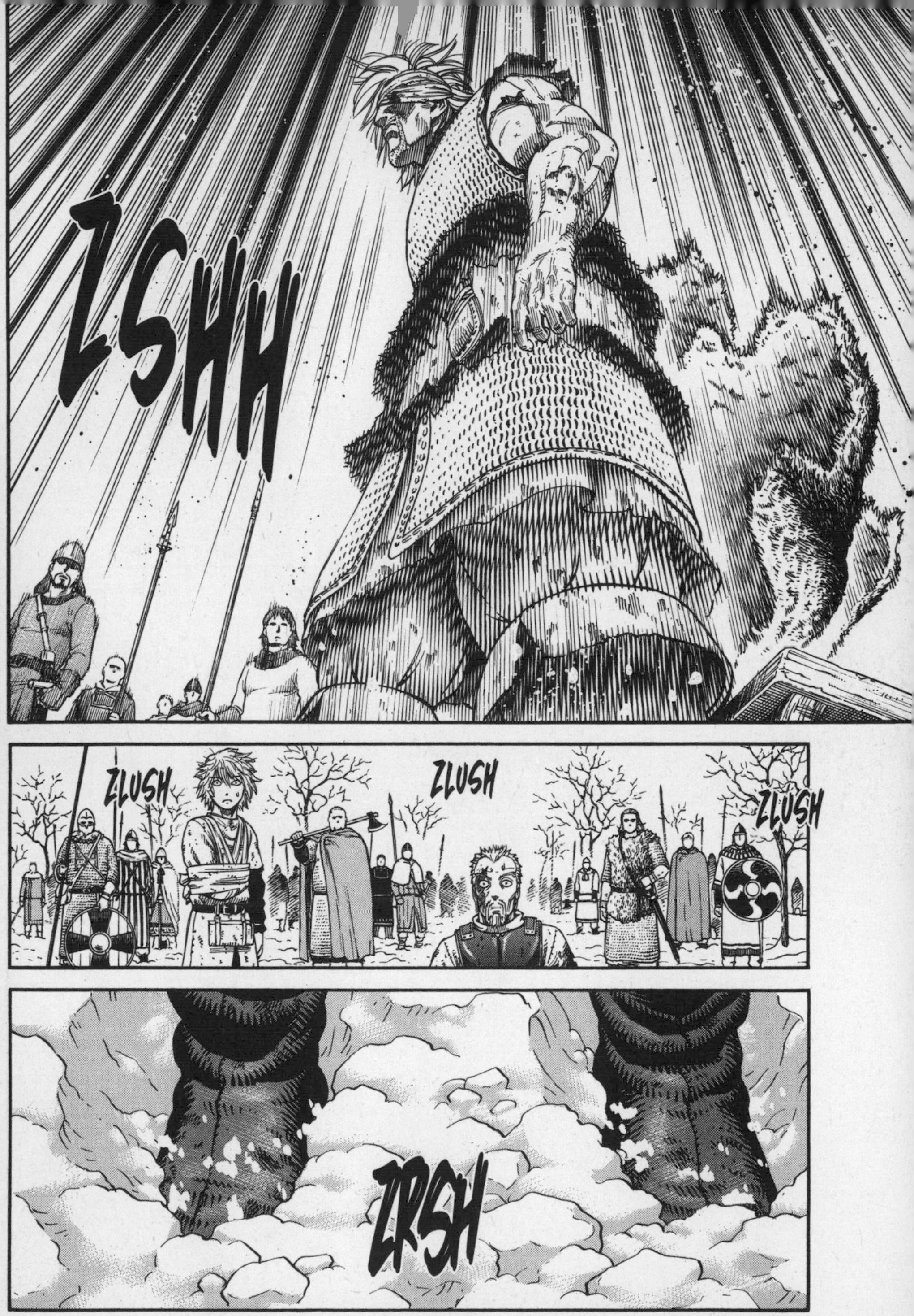
ZSHH
ZLUSH
ZLUSH
ZLUSH
ZRSH

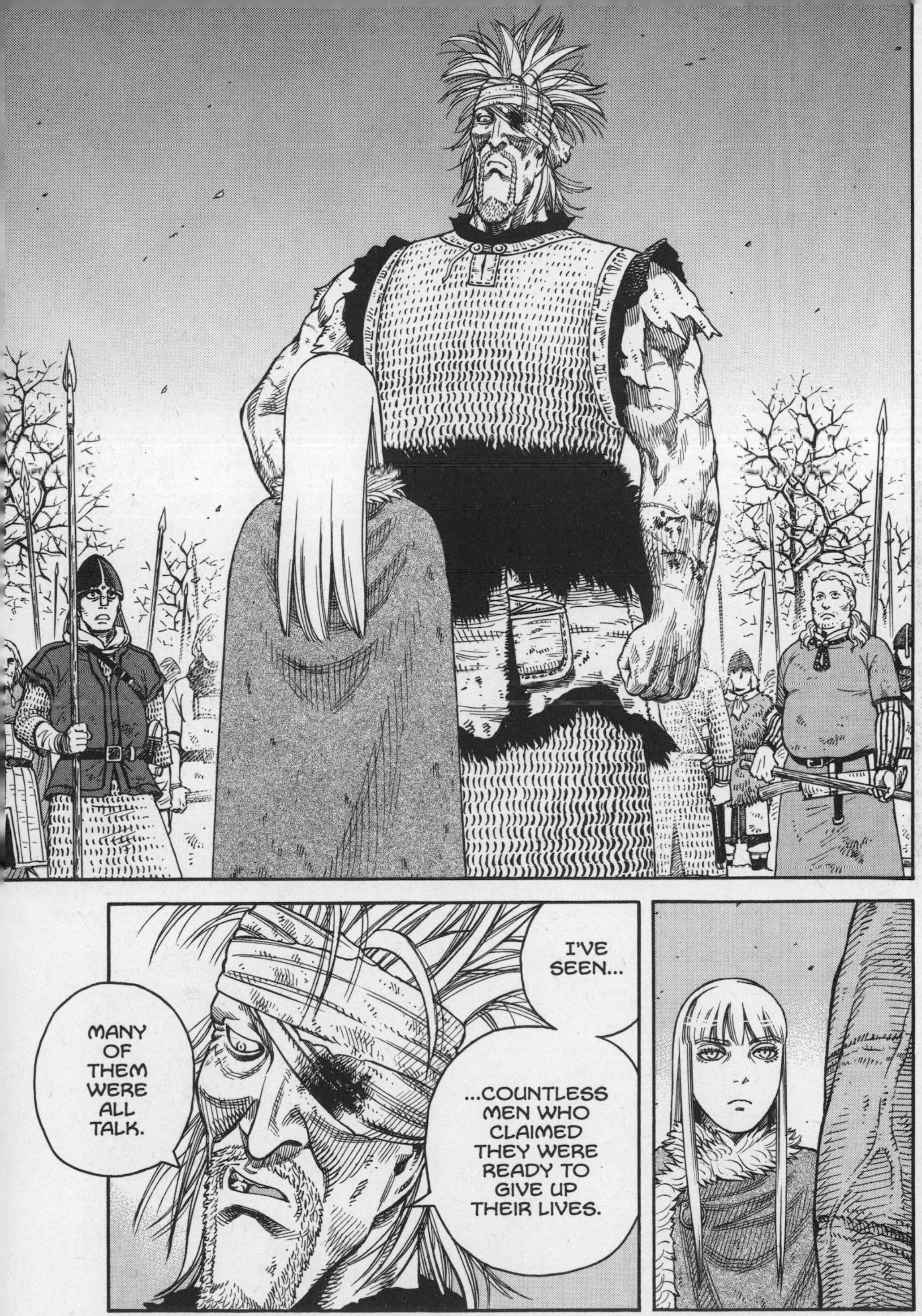
I'VE SEEN...
...COUNTLESS MEN WHO CLAIMED THEY WERE READY TO GIVE UP THEIR LIVES.
MANY OF THEM WERE ALL TALK.

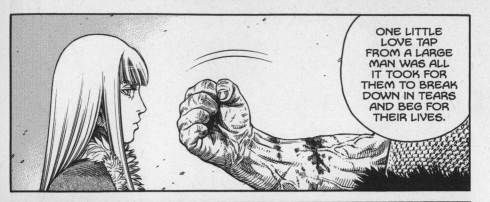

ONE LITTLE LOVE TAP FROM A LARGE MAN WAS ALL IT TOOK FOR THEM TO BREAK DOWN IN TEARS AND BEG FOR THEIR LIVES.

ARE YOU ONE OF THEM?

WELL?

HRRRG...

...!!

416

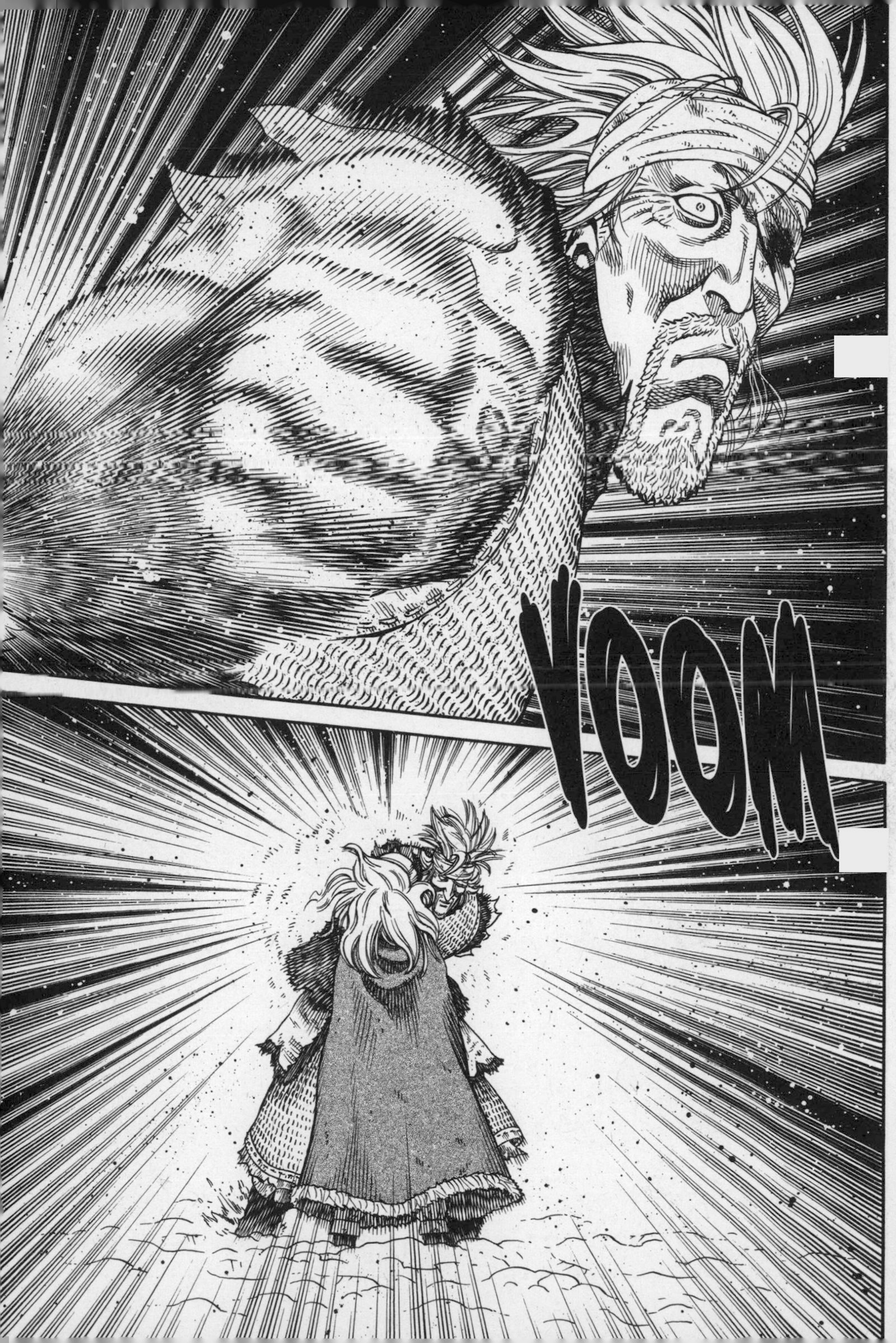
VOOM

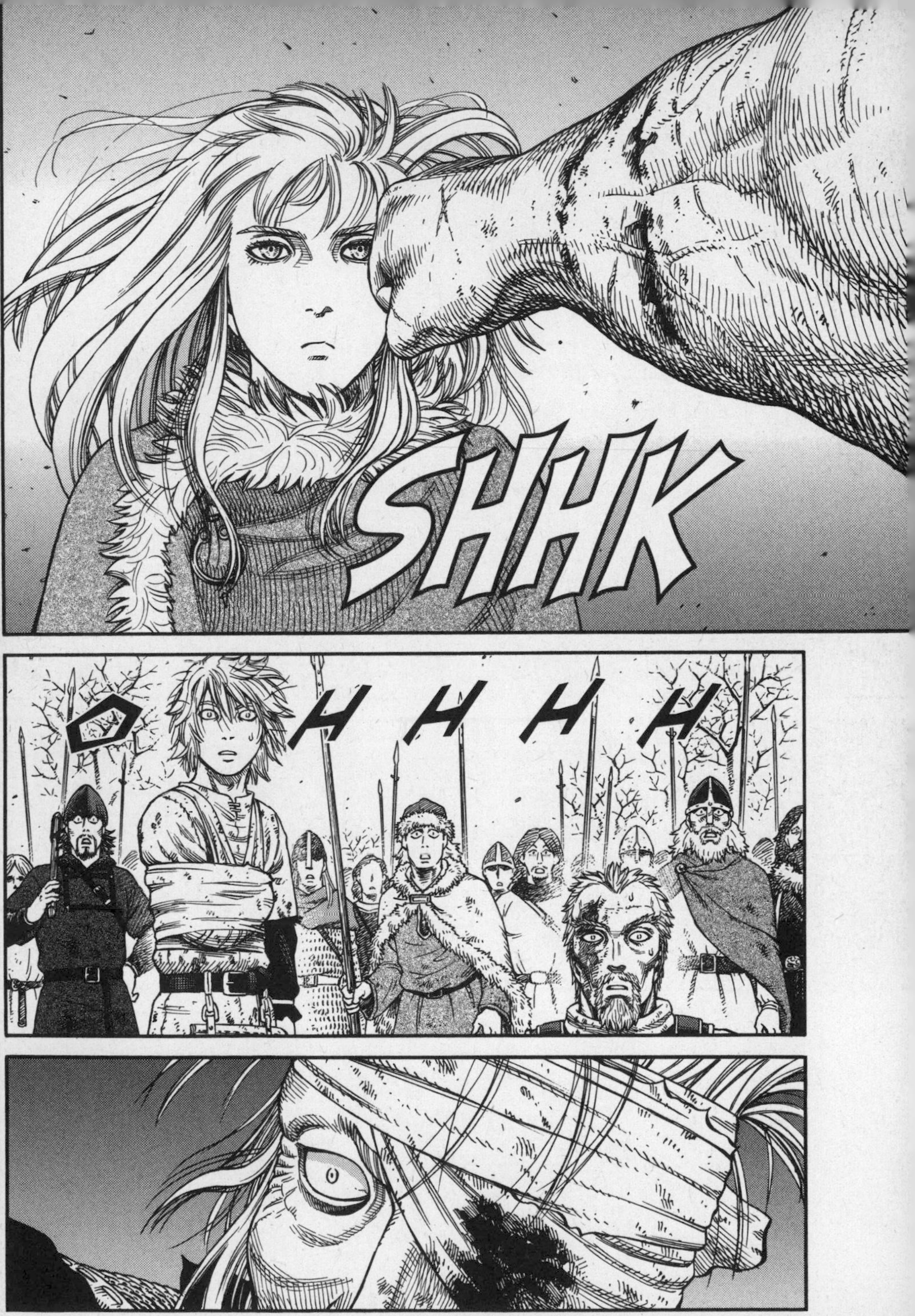
SHHK
OHHHH

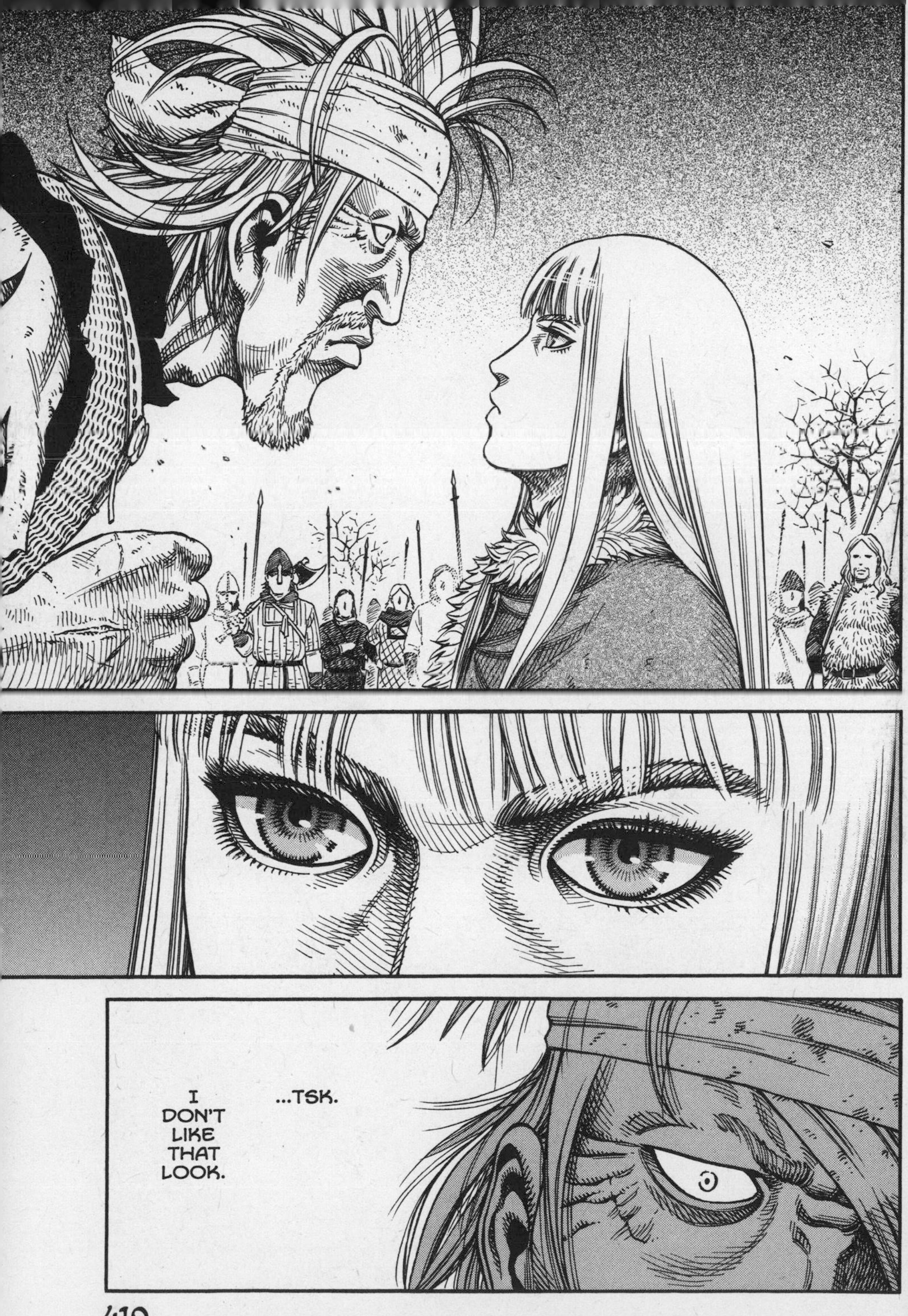
...TSK.
I DON'T LIKE THAT LOOK.

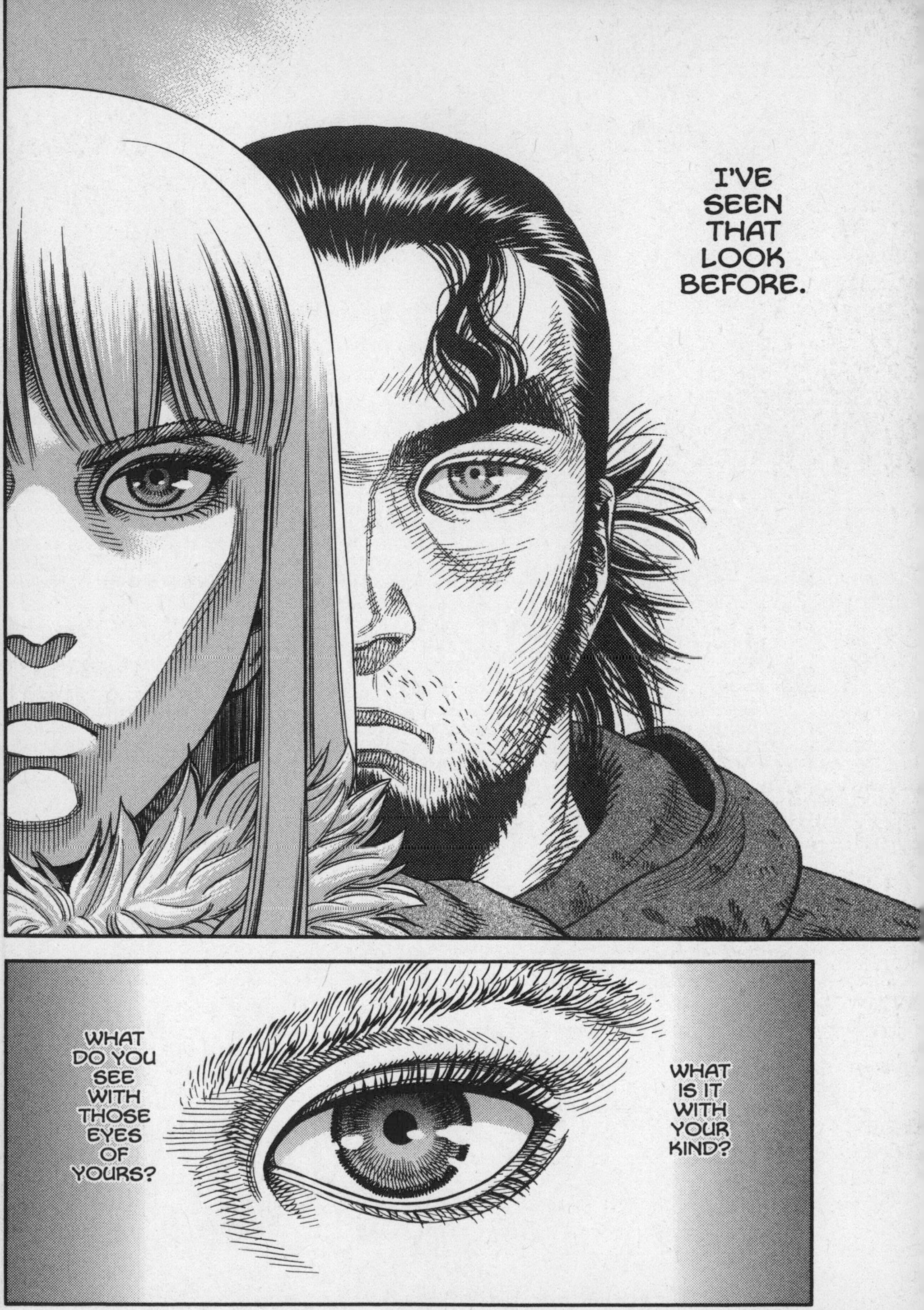
I'VE SEEN THAT LOOK BEFORE.
WHAT IS IT WITH YOUR KIND?
WHAT DO YOU SEE WITH THOSE EYES OF YOURS?

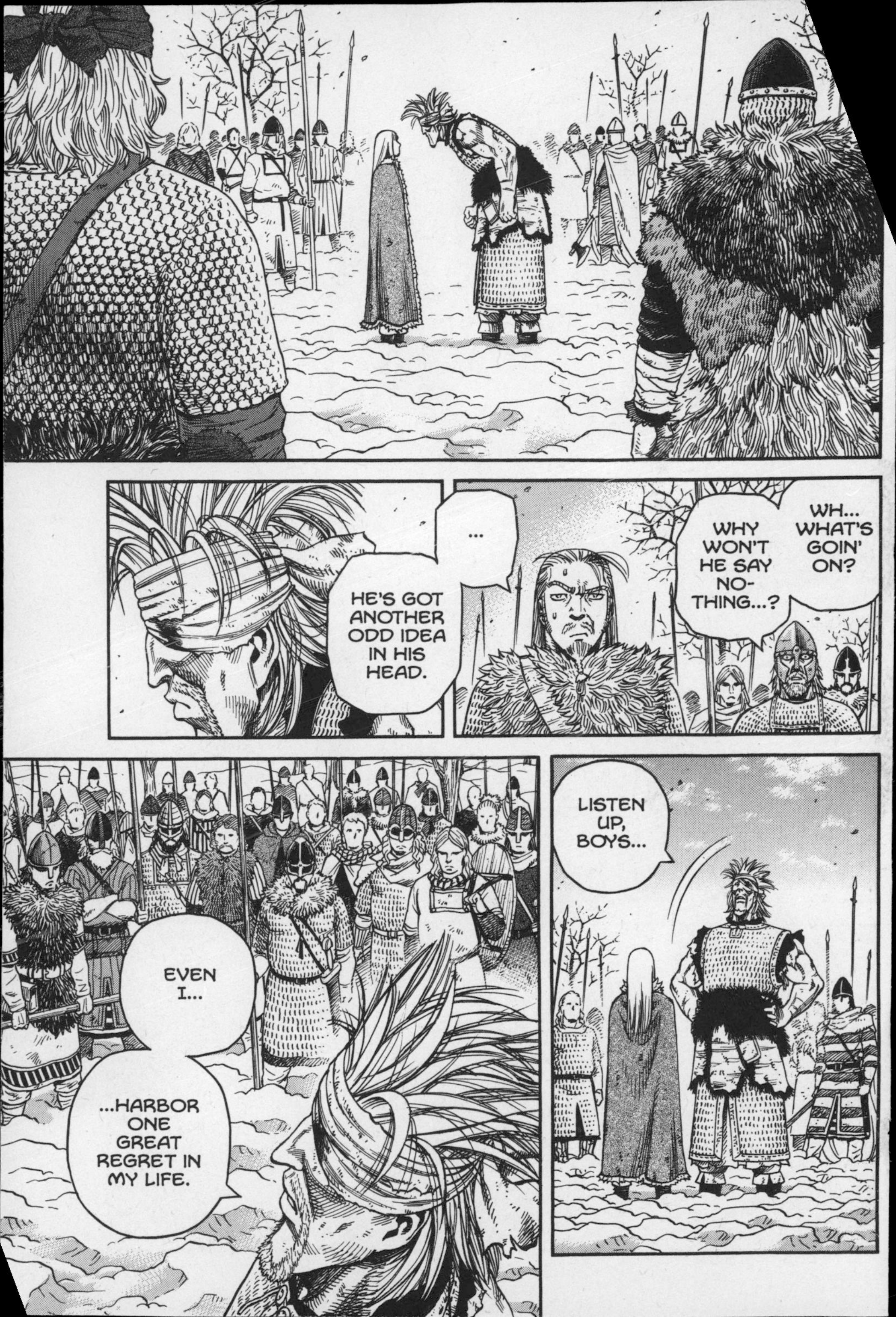
WH... WHAT'S GOIN' ON?
WHY WON'T HE SAY NO-THING...?
...
HE'S GOT ANOTHER ODD IDEA IN HIS HEAD.
LISTEN UP, BOYS...
EVEN I...
...HARBOR ONE GREAT REGRET IN MY LIFE.

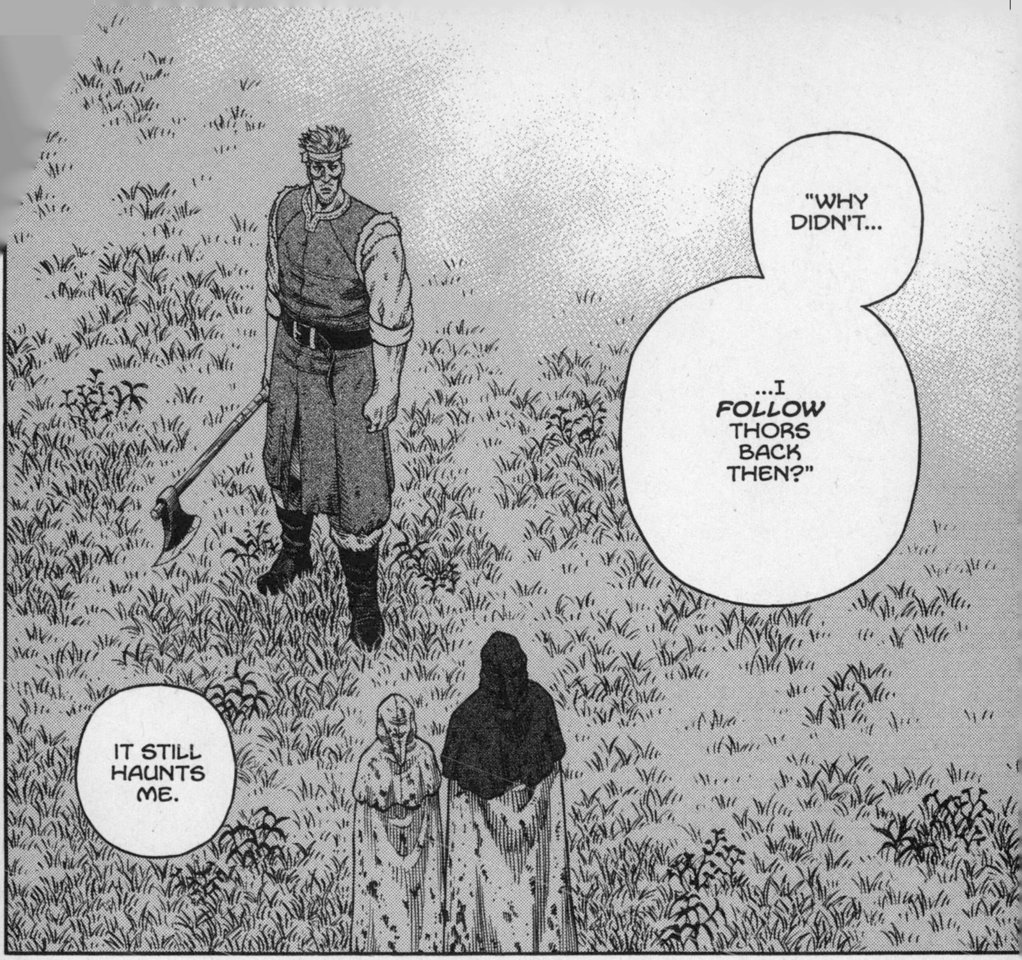
"WHY DIDN'T...
...I *FOLLOW* THORS BACK THEN?"
IT STILL HAUNTS ME.

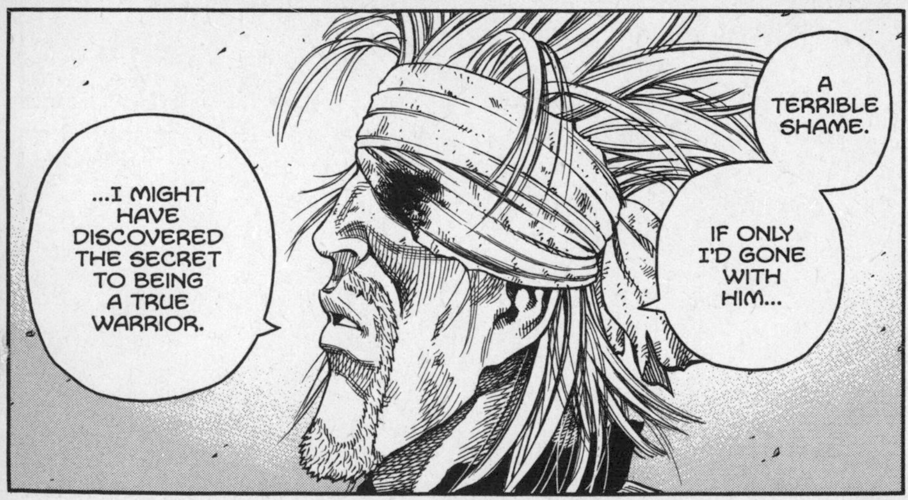
A TERRIBLE SHAME.
IF ONLY I'D GONE WITH HIM...
...I MIGHT HAVE DISCOVERED THE SECRET TO BEING A TRUE WARRIOR.

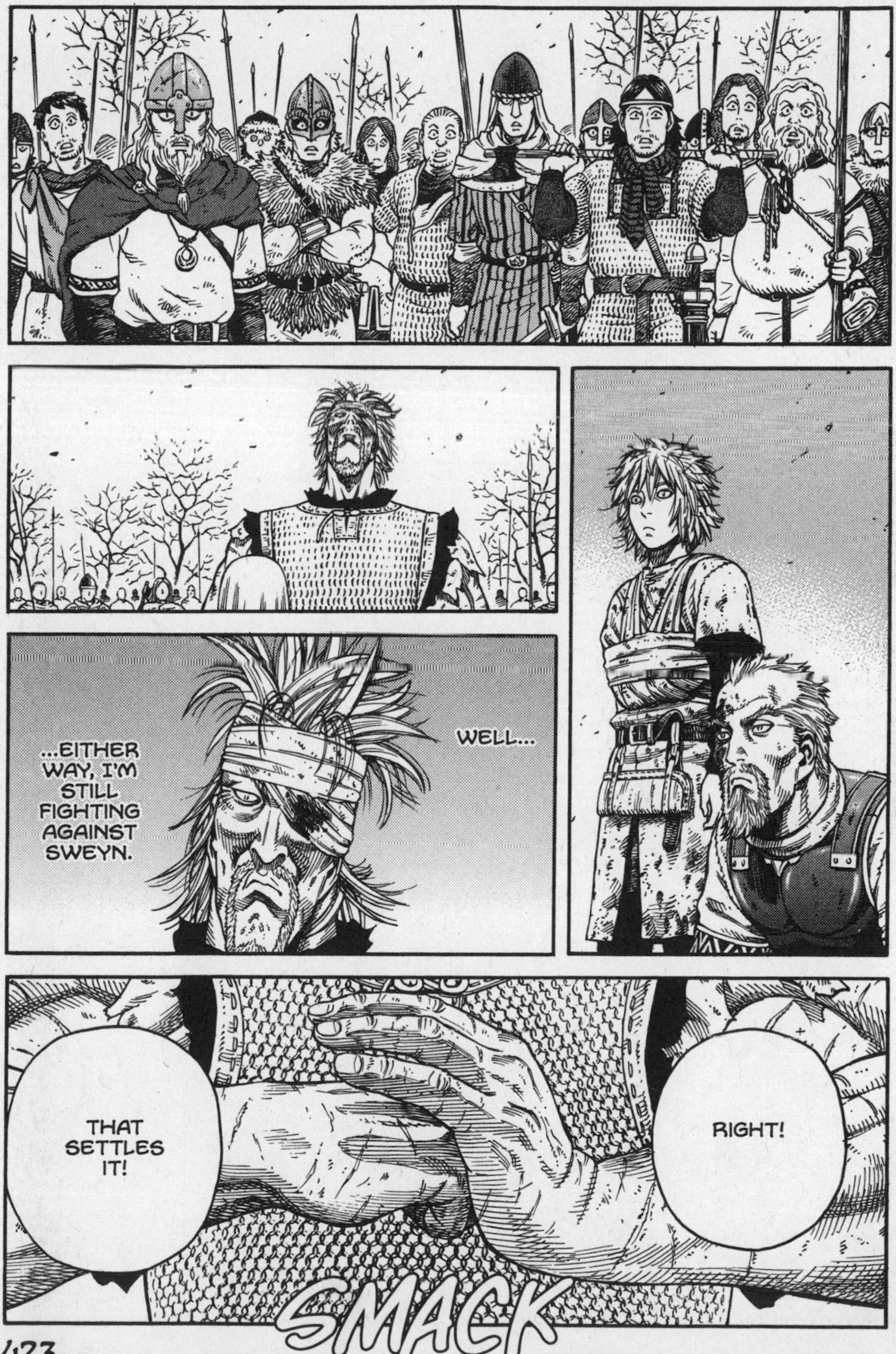
WELL...
...EITHER WAY, I'M STILL FIGHTING AGAINST SWEYN.
RIGHT!
THAT SETTLES IT!
SMACK

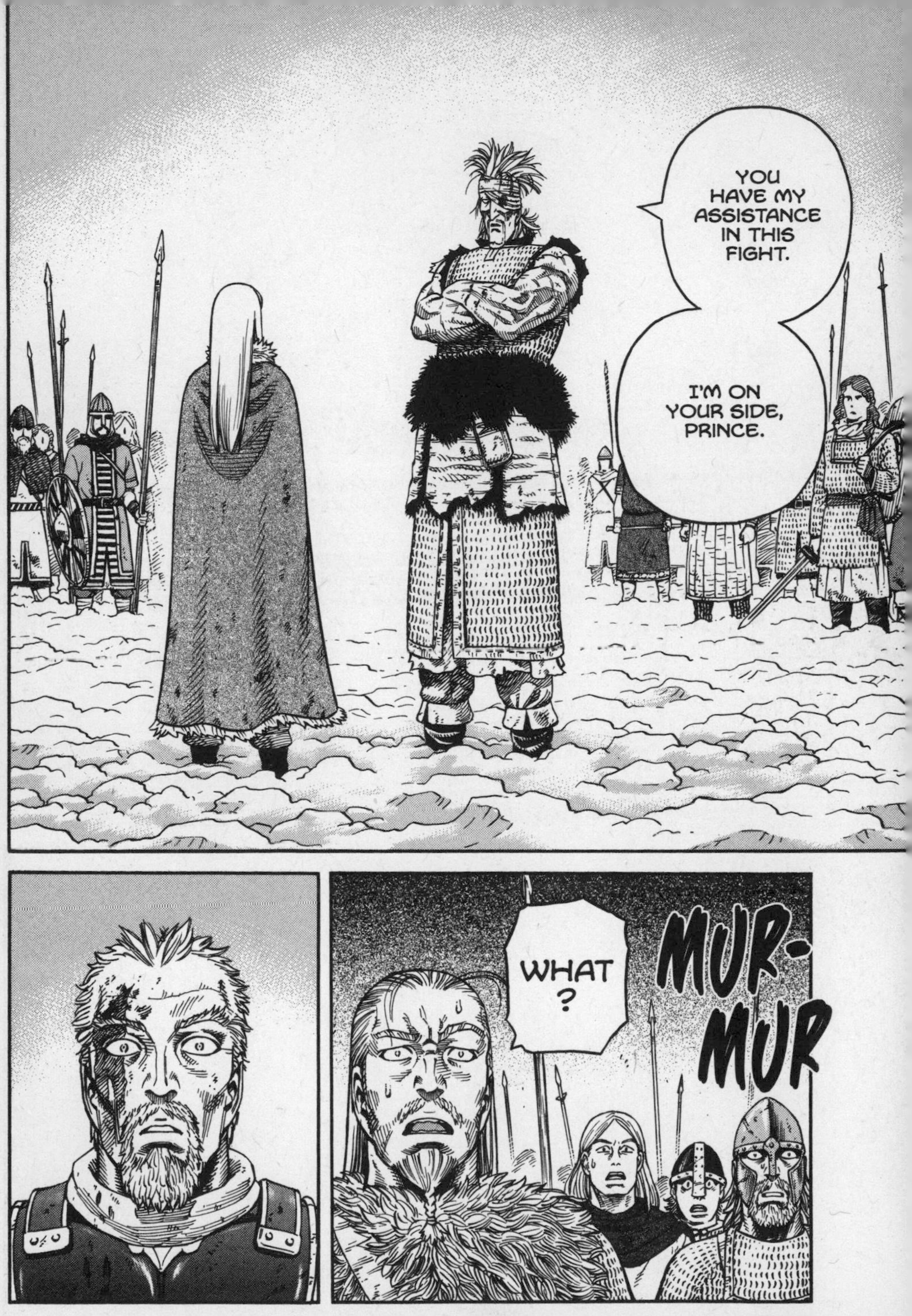
YOU HAVE MY ASSISTANCE IN THIS FIGHT.
I'M ON YOUR SIDE, PRINCE.
WHAT ?
MUR-MUR

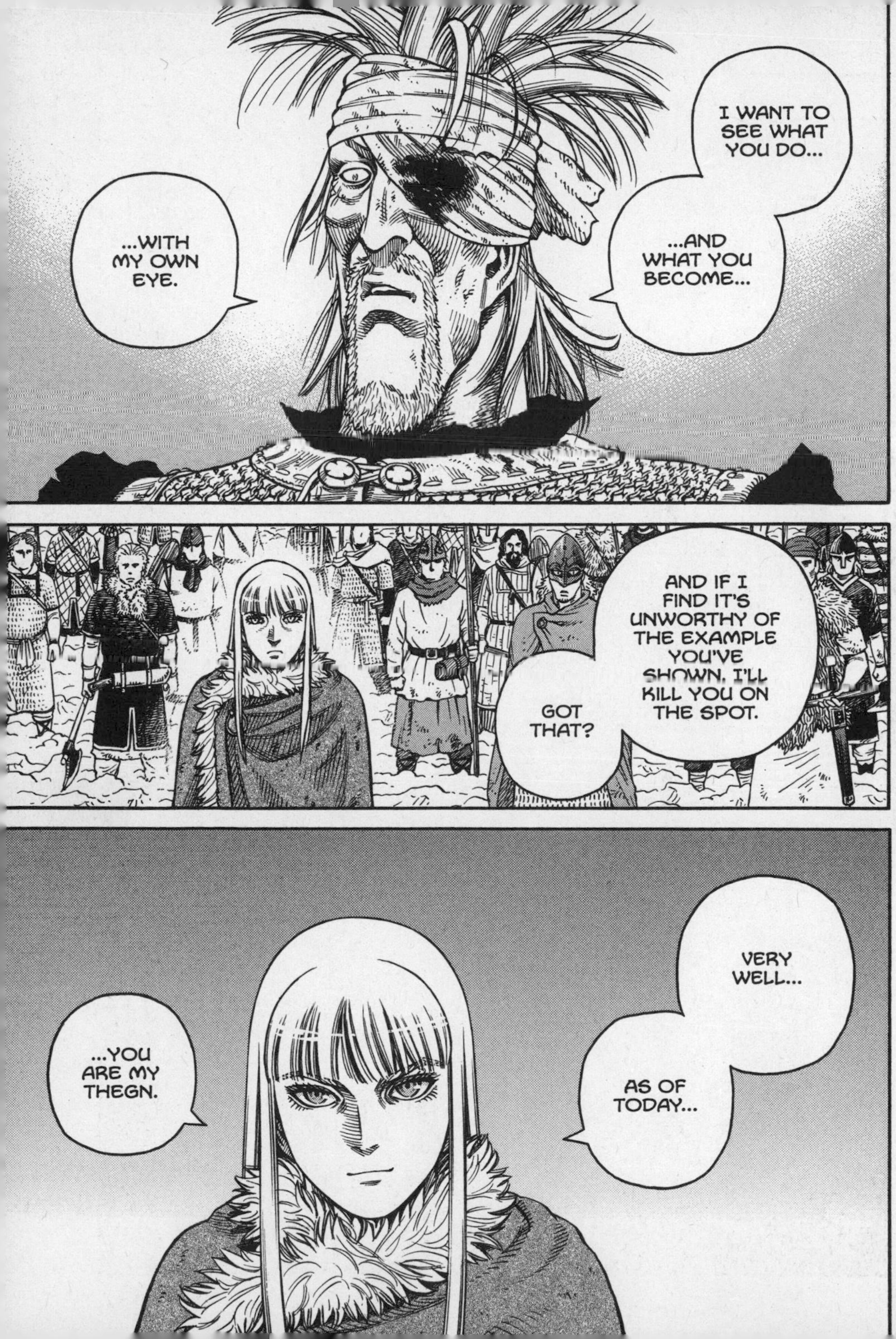
I WANT TO SEE WHAT YOU DO...
...AND WHAT YOU BECOME...
...WITH MY OWN EYE.
AND IF I FIND IT'S UNWORTHY OF THE EXAMPLE YOU'VE SHOWN, I'LL KILL YOU ON THE SPOT.
GOT THAT?
VERY WELL...
AS OF TODAY...
...YOU ARE MY THEGN.

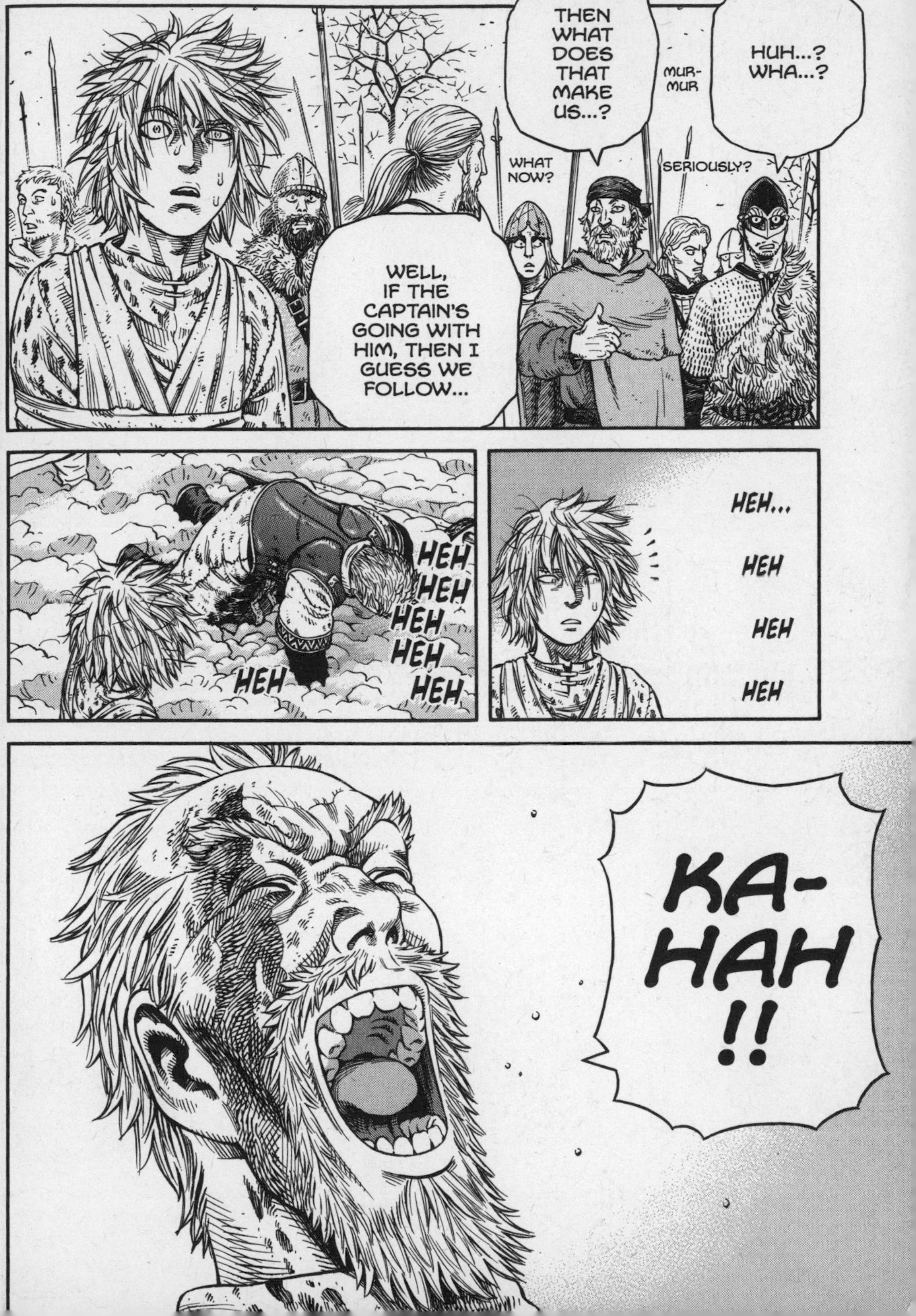
HUH...? WHA...?
SERIOUSLY?
MUR-MUR
THEN WHAT DOES THAT MAKE US...?
WHAT NOW?
WELL, IF THE CAPTAIN'S GOING WITH HIM, THEN I GUESS WE FOLLOW...
HEH... HEH HEH HEH
HEH HEH HEH HEH HEH HEH
KA-HAH!!

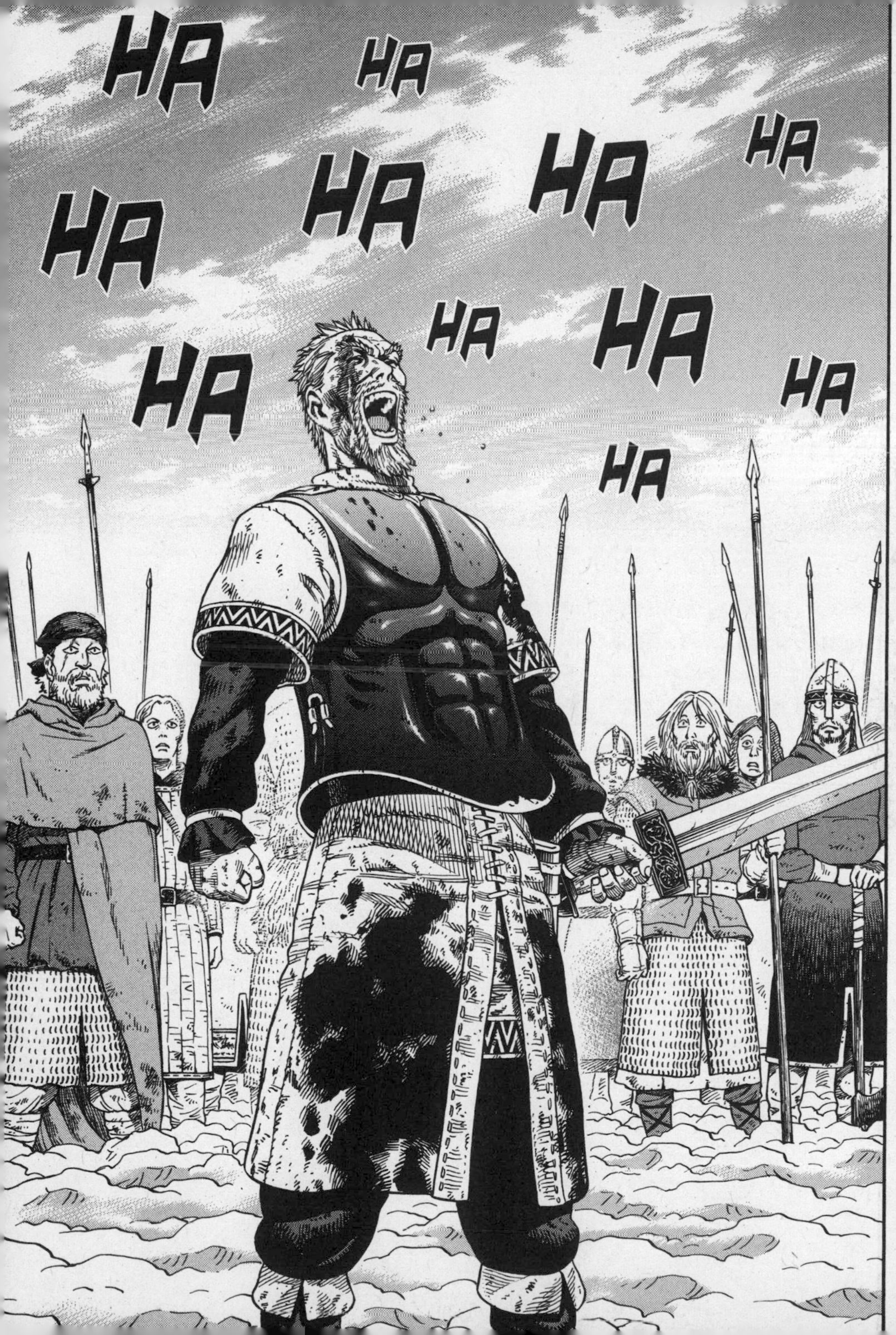
HA
HA
HA
HA
HA
HA
HA
HA
HA
HA
HA
HA

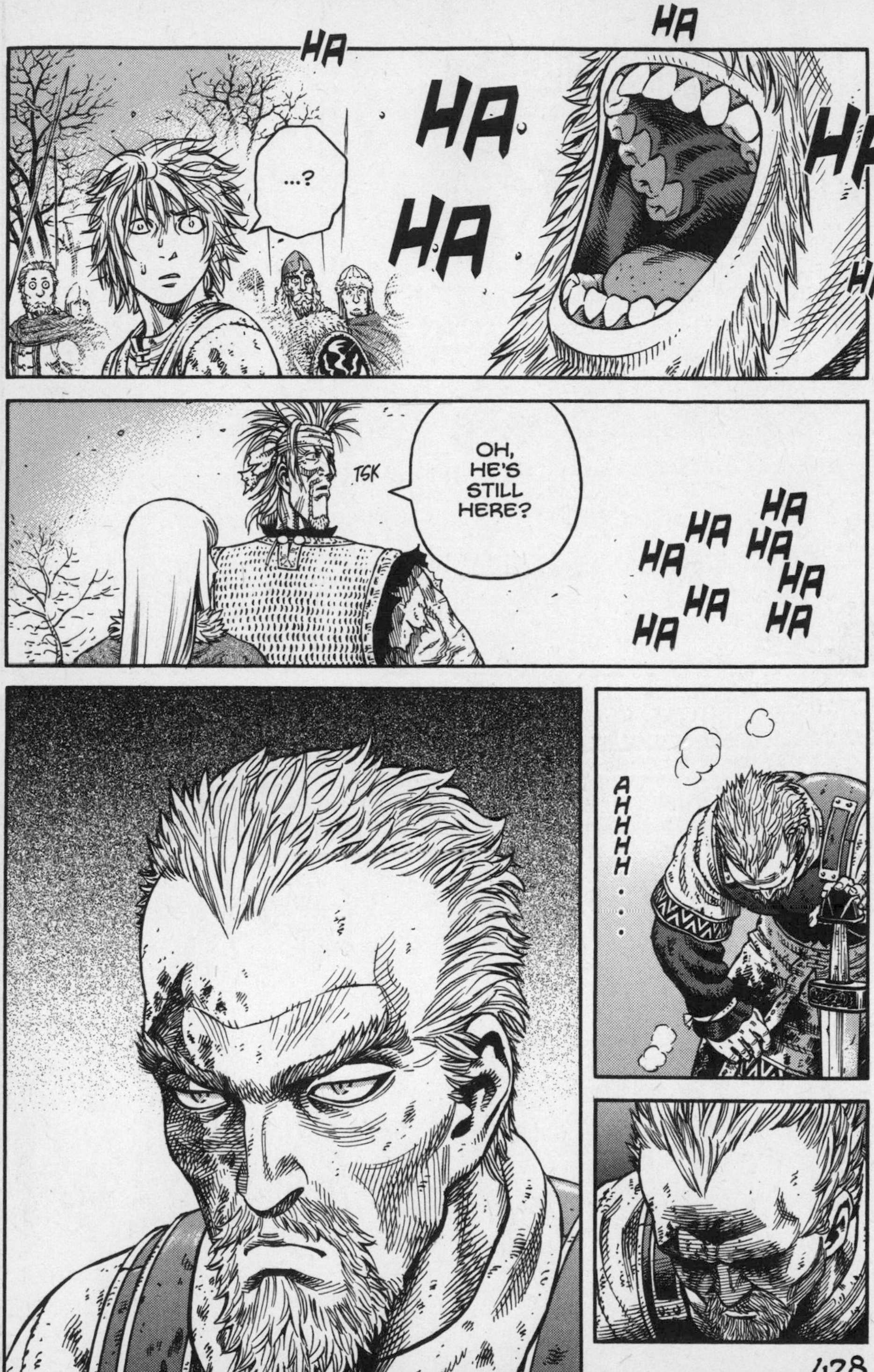
HA
HA
HAHA
HA
HA
...?
HA
HA
OH, HE'S STILL HERE?
TSK
HA
HA
HA
HA
HA
HA
HA
HA
AHHHH...

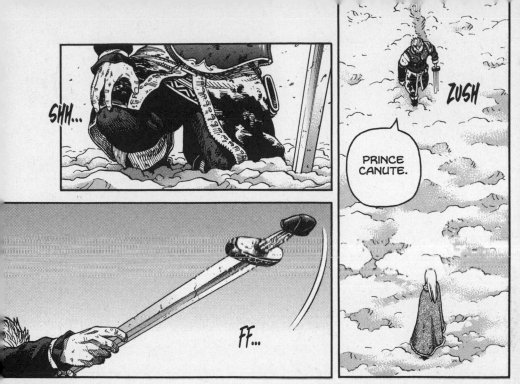

SHH...

ZUSH

PRINCE CANUTE.

FF...

IT WAS I WHO KILLED LORD RAGNAR.

STRIKE ME DOWN.

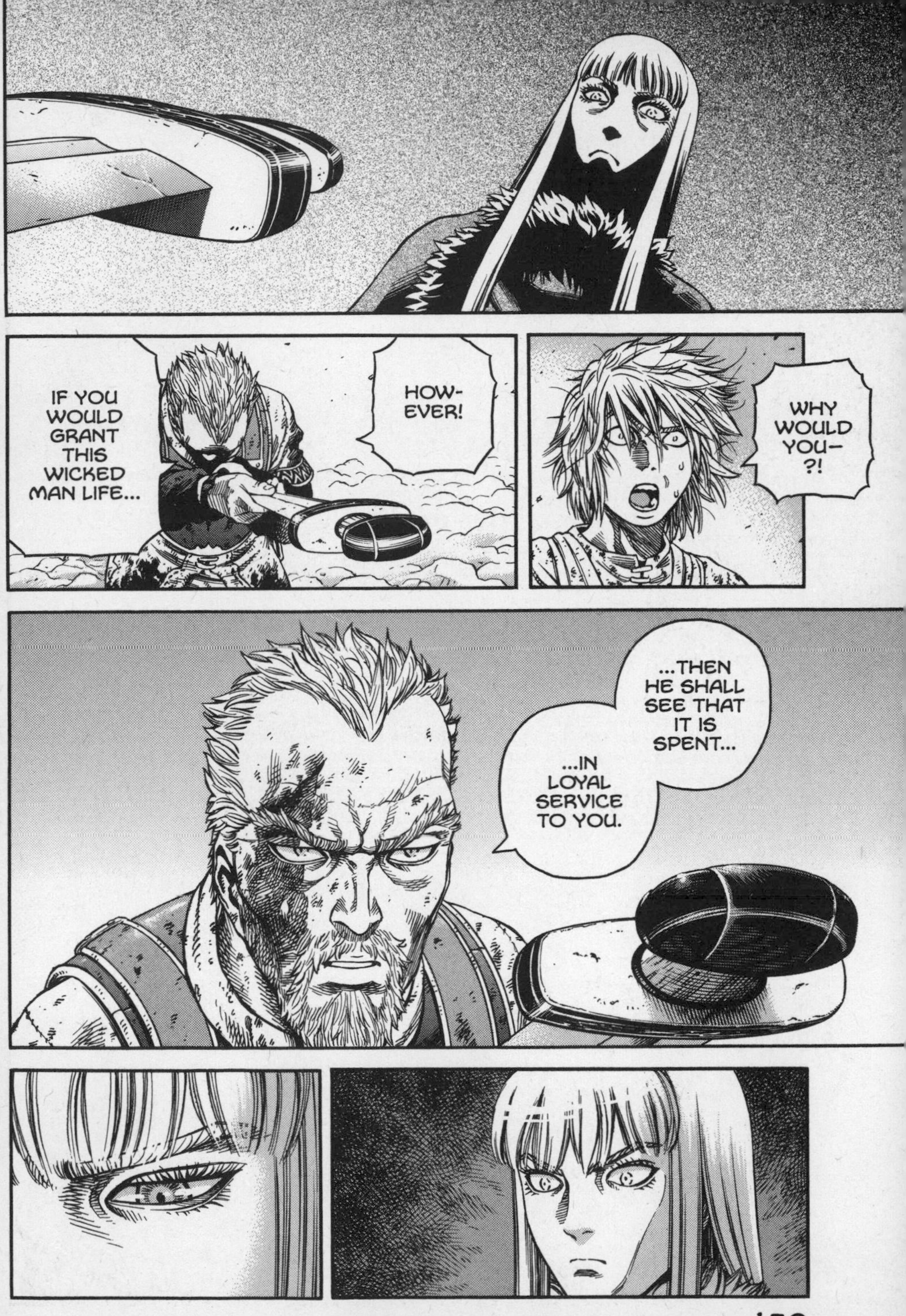
WHY WOULD YOU-?!
HOW-EVER!
IF YOU WOULD GRANT THIS WICKED MAN LIFE...
...THEN HE SHALL SEE THAT IT IS SPENT...
...IN LOYAL SERVICE TO YOU.

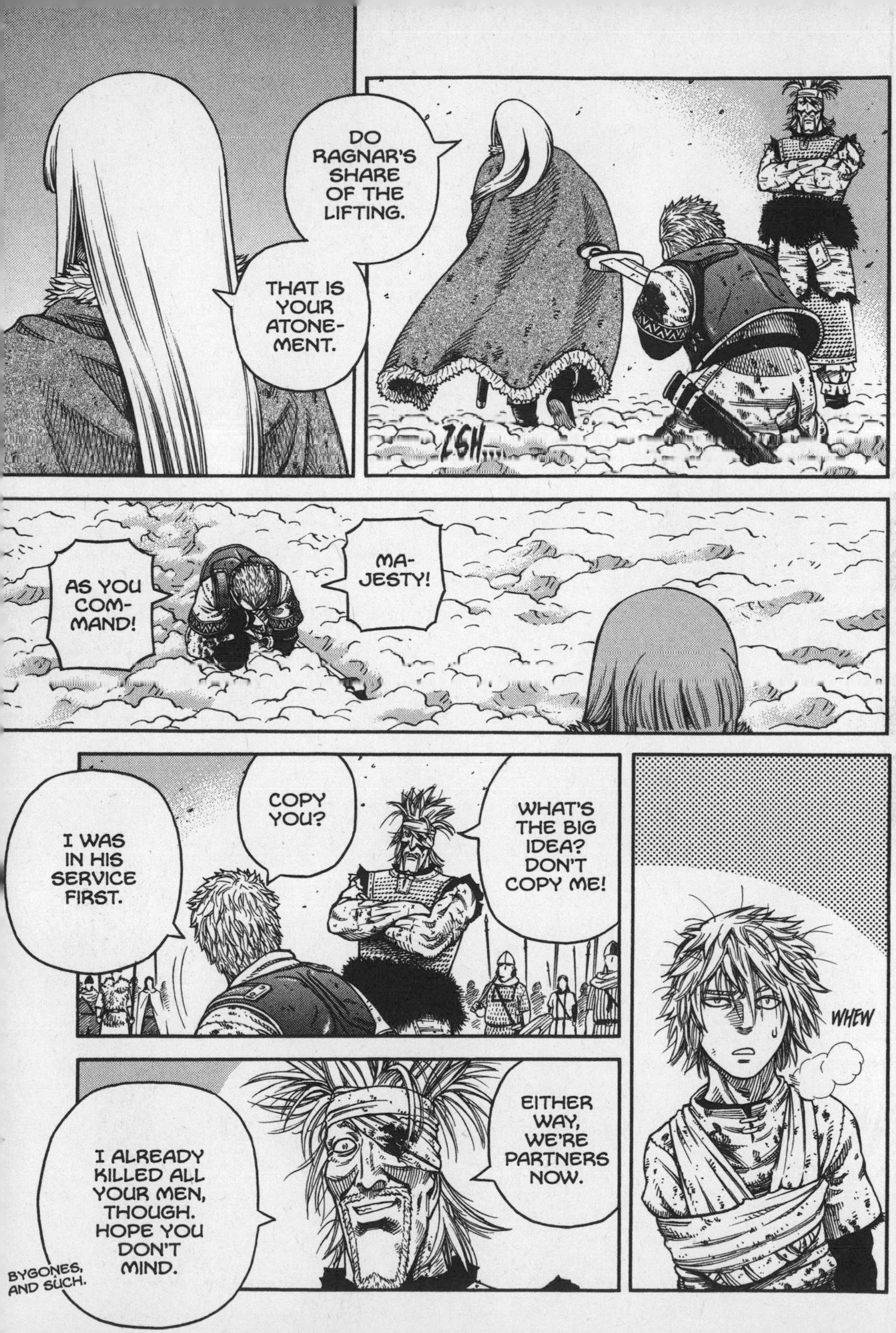
DO RAGNAR'S SHARE OF THE LIFTING.
THAT IS YOUR ATONEMENT.
ZSH...
MAJESTY!
AS YOU COMMAND!
WHEW
WHAT'S THE BIG IDEA? DON'T COPY ME!
COPY YOU?
I WAS IN HIS SERVICE FIRST.
EITHER WAY, WE'RE PARTNERS NOW.
I ALREADY KILLED ALL YOUR MEN, THOUGH. HOPE YOU DON'T MIND.
BYGONES, AND SUCH.

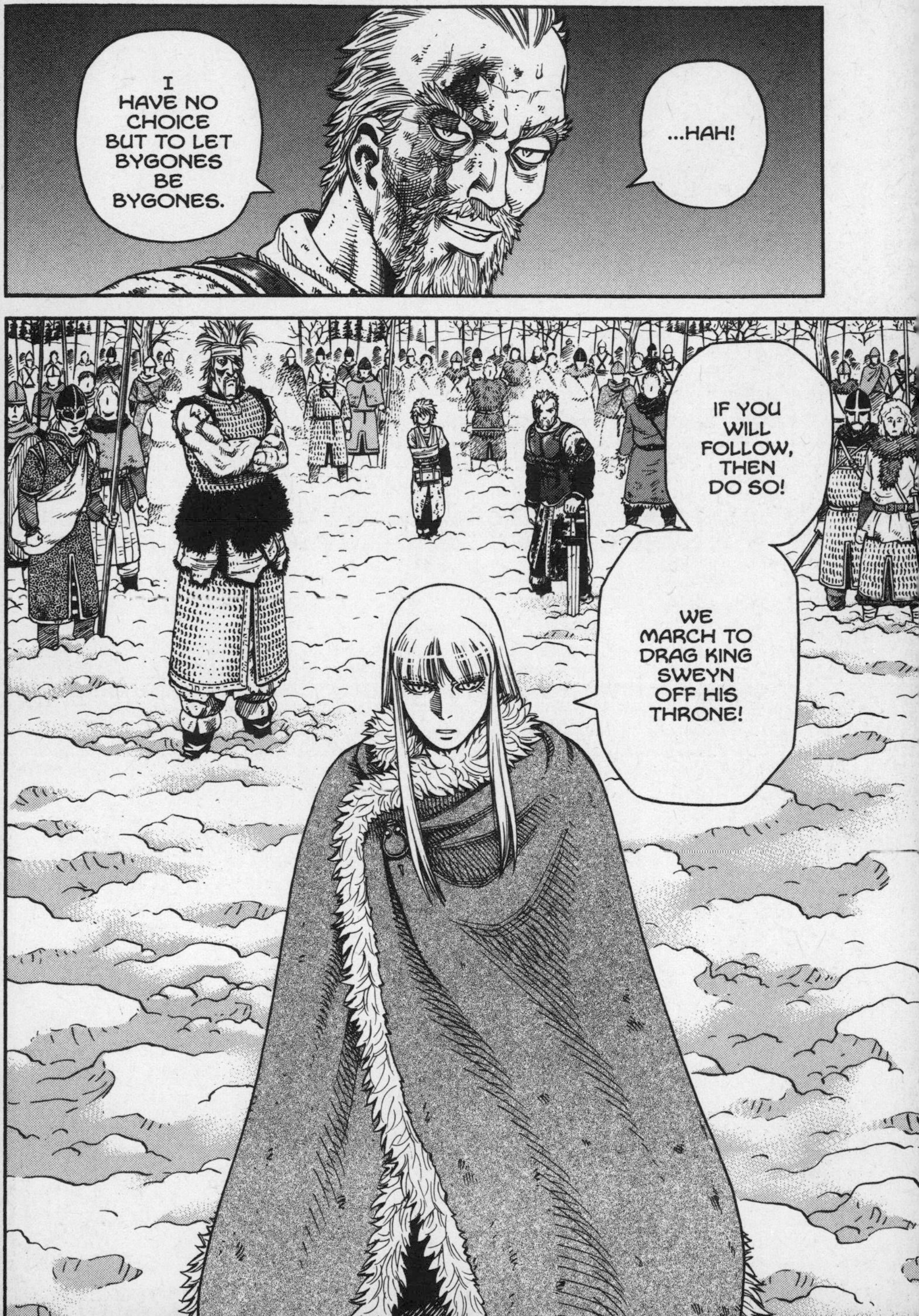
...HAH!
I HAVE NO CHOICE BUT TO LET BYGONES BE BYGONES.
IF YOU WILL FOLLOW, THEN DO SO!
WE MARCH TO DRAG KING SWEYN OFF HIS THRONE!

CHAPTER 42 - END

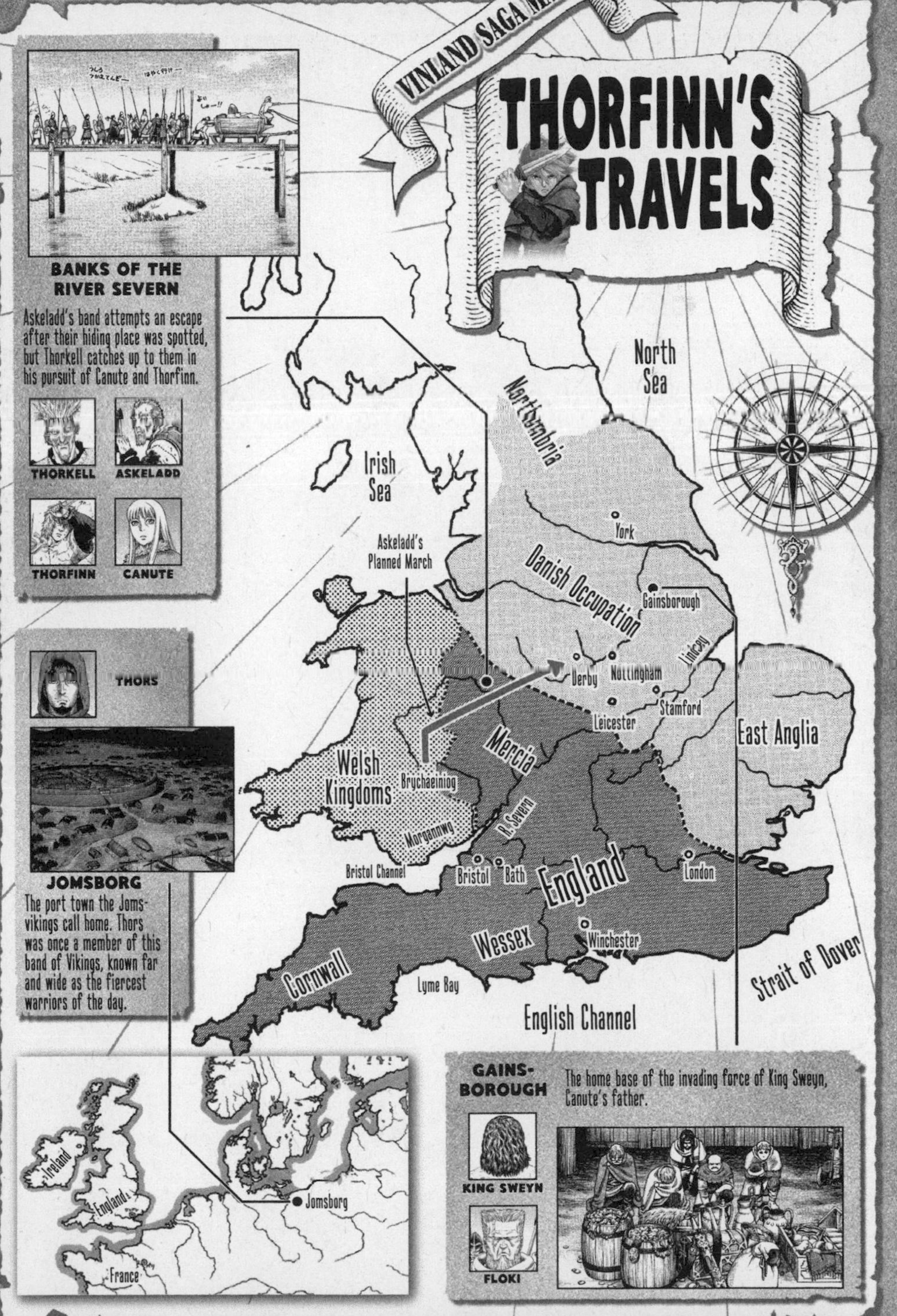
VINLAND SAGA MAP
THORFINN'S TRAVELS
BANKS OF THE RIVER SEVERN
Askeladd's band attempts an escape after their hiding place was spotted, but Thorkell catches up to them in his pursuit of Canute and Thorfinn.
THORKELL
ASKELADD
THORFINN
CANUTE
THORS
JOMSBORG
The port town the Jomsvikings call home. Thors was once a member of this band of Vikings, known far and wide as the fiercest warriors of the day.
North Sea
Northumbria
Irish Sea
York
Askeladd's Planned March
Danish Occupation
Gainsborough
Lindsey
Derby
Nottingham
Stamford
Leicester
East Anglia
Mercia
Welsh Kingdoms
Brychaeiniog
Morgannwg
R. Severn
Bristol Channel
Bristol
Bath
England
London
Wessex
Winchester
Cornwall
Lyme Bay
Strait of Dover
English Channel
Ireland
England
Jomsborg
France
GAINS-BOROUGH
The home base of the invading force of King Sweyn, Canute's father.
KING SWEYN
FLOKI

# DIMLY-REMEMBERED VINLAND SAGA

MEMORY 1

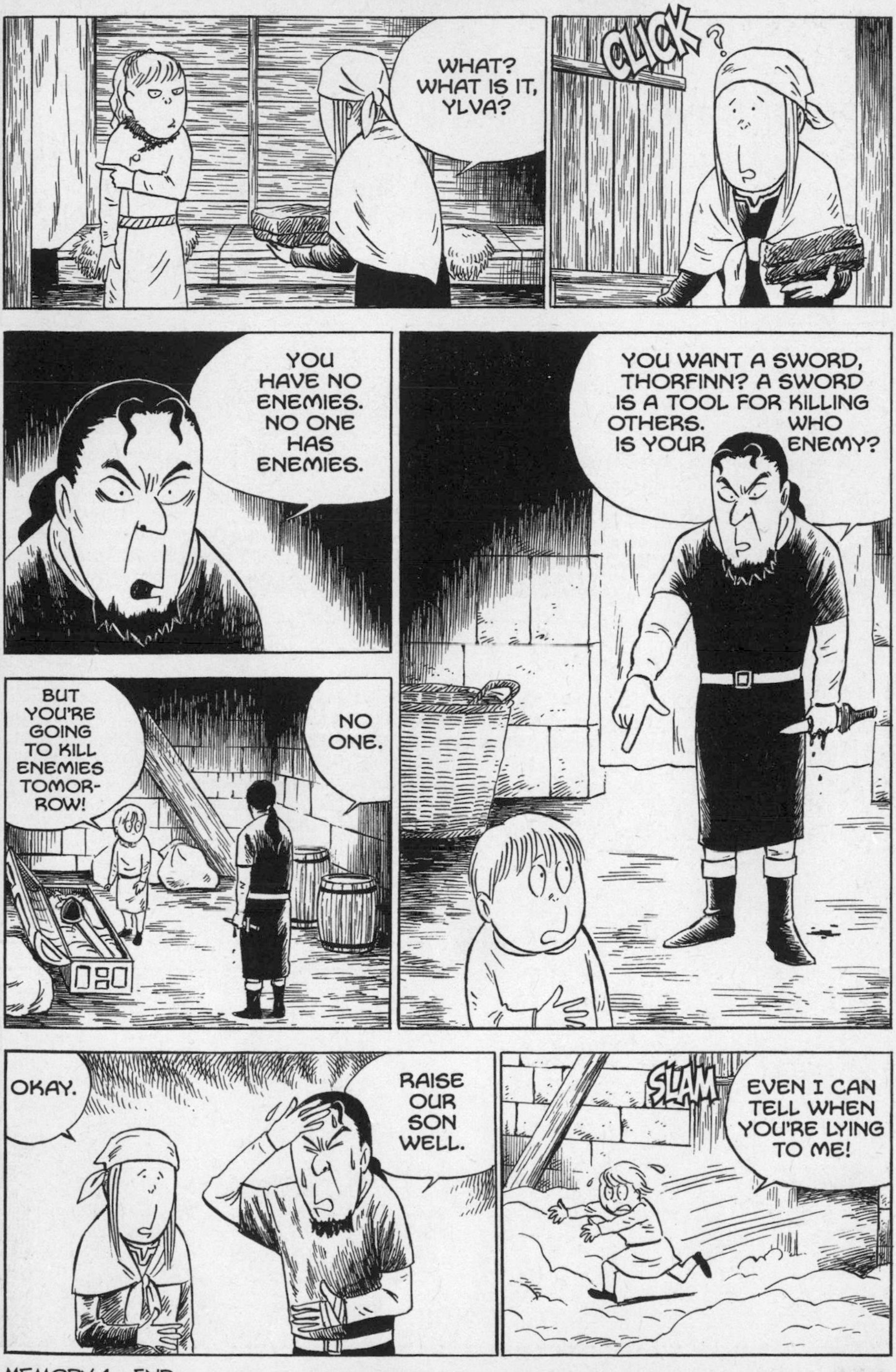

CLICK
?
WHAT? WHAT IS IT, YLVA?
YOU WANT A SWORD, THORFINN? A SWORD IS A TOOL FOR KILLING OTHERS. WHO IS YOUR ENEMY?
YOU HAVE NO ENEMIES. NO ONE HAS ENEMIES.
NO ONE.
BUT YOU'RE GOING TO KILL ENEMIES TOMORROW!
SLAM
EVEN I CAN TELL WHEN YOU'RE LYING TO ME!
RAISE OUR SON WELL.
OKAY.


*MANGA: HAITO KUMAGAI*

HAITO KUMAGAI PROFILE BY MAKOTO YUKIMURA: ONE OF THE TALENTED ASSISTANTS WHO HELPS CREATE THIS MANGA. HE'S INCREDIBLY VERSATILE. UM... ARE WE GOING TO YELLED AT FOR COPYING MIZUKI-SAN'S STYLE?

MEMORY 1 - END

MEMORY 2 **BONUS MANGA**

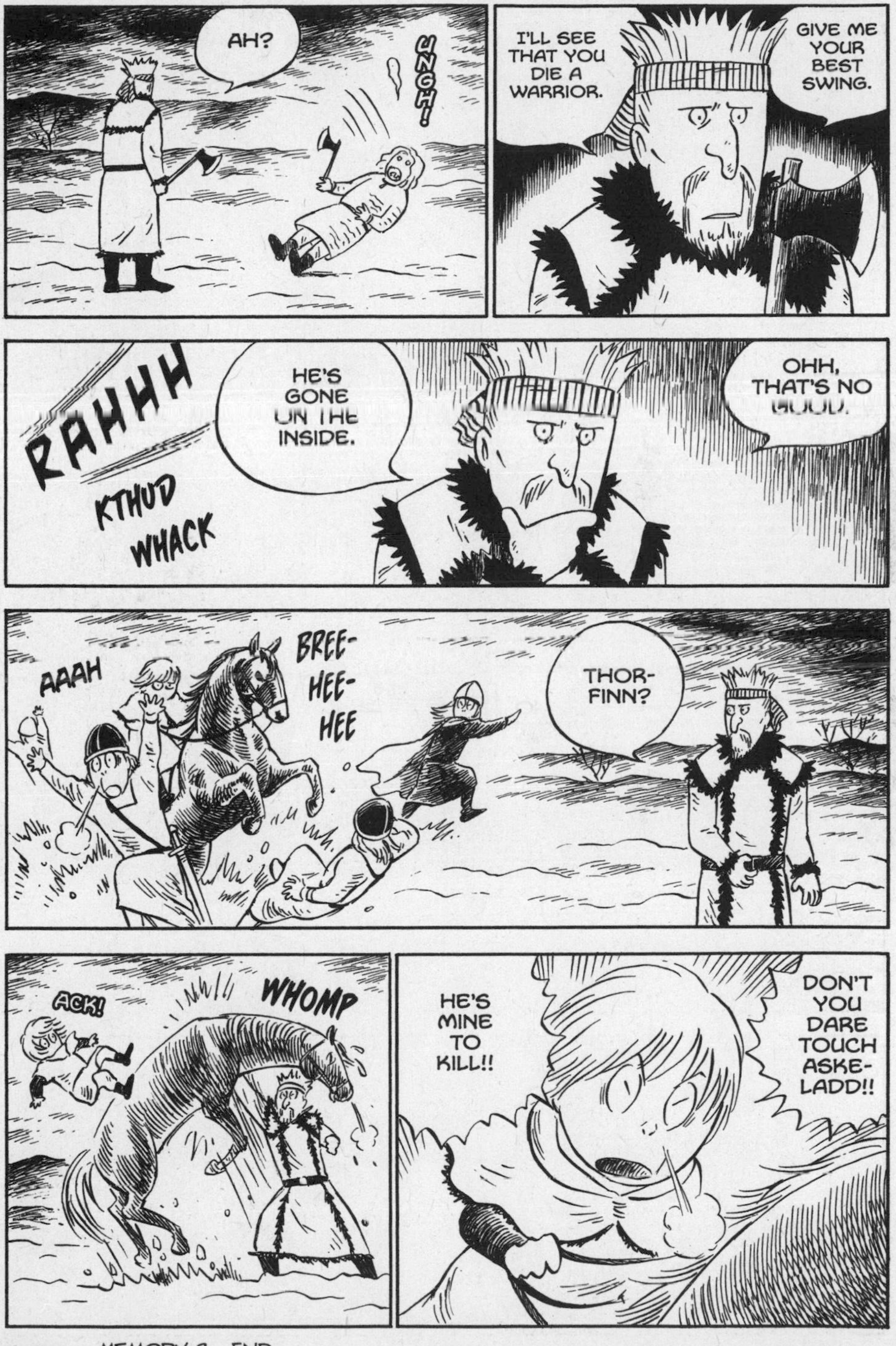
GIVE ME YOUR BEST SWING.
I'LL SEE THAT YOU DIE A WARRIOR.
UNGH!
AH?
OHH, THAT'S NO GOOD.
HE'S GONE ON THE INSIDE.
RAHHH
KTHUD
WHACK
THOR-FINN?
BREE-HEE-HEE
AAAH
DON'T YOU DARE TOUCH ASKE-LADD!!
HE'S MINE TO KILL!!
WHOMP
ACK!

 MEMORY 2 - END

My second son was born in 2008. The eldest is already two years old. Pretty soon he'll be able to read manga. So... what should I do? Frankly, this manga does not contain material that is suitable for children, what with the wanton murder and all. But despite that, I'd be happy if he read it. I want him to read it before he grows up. Even the smartest of children must learn something from those who came before, something they would never have discovered on their own. I will do my damnedest to draw what I've learned in this manga. Will you read it? It's actually rather entertaining. Should I slip in more jokes? What do you think, my sons?

**MAKOTO YUKIMURA**

VINLAND SAGA

# Translation Notes

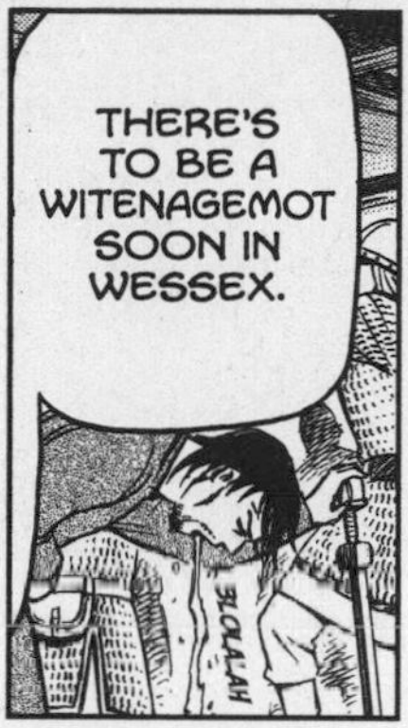
THERE'S TO BE A WITENAGEMOT SOON IN WESSEX.

## Witenagemot, page 14

A meeting of noblemen held in Anglo-Saxon culture meant to advise the king on various matters. In some ways a Witenagemot was similar to Parliament or the Althing of Iceland, but unlike the latter it was only called in service of the monarchy. In some cases, Witenagemots were summoned to assist in managing the kingdom during interregnum.

## Jelling, page 68

A village in Denmark that was once a significant seat for the Danish monarchy. It is most renowned today for the "Jelling stones," monuments erected in the 10th century by King Harald to mark his conquest of Denmark and Norway and the Christianization of his realm.

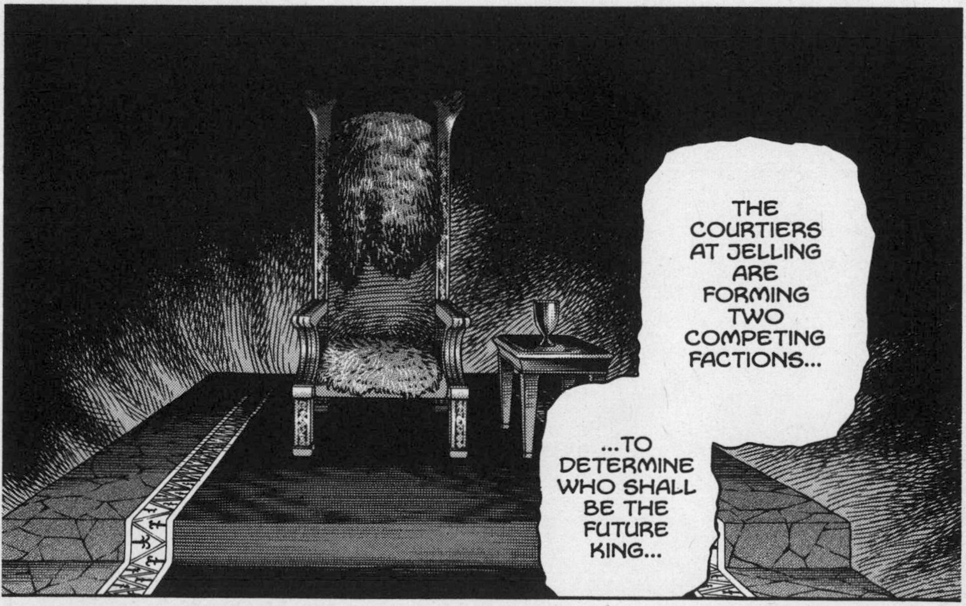
THE COURTIERS AT JELLING ARE FORMING TWO COMPETING FACTIONS...
...TO DETERMINE WHO SHALL BE THE FUTURE KING...

# Jarl, page 217

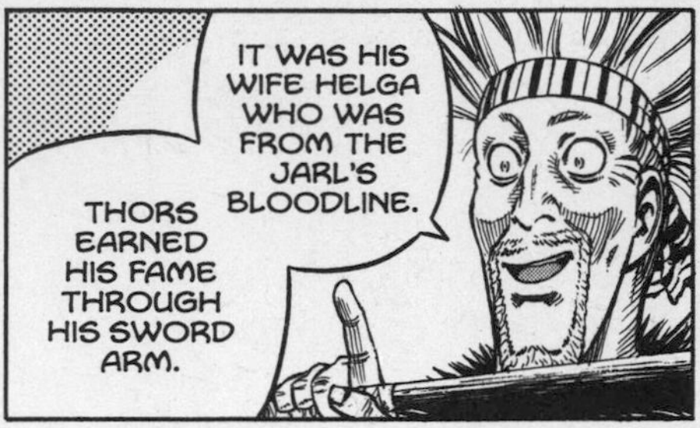
IT WAS HIS WIFE HELGA WHO WAS FROM THE JARL'S BLOODLINE.
THORS EARNED HIS FAME THROUGH HIS SWORD ARM.

A nobleman of medieval Scandinavia. The word jarl is the basis for the English "earl," and by most accounts, jarls were lords of their own regions, answering only to the king himself.

# Battle of Hjörungavágr, page 319

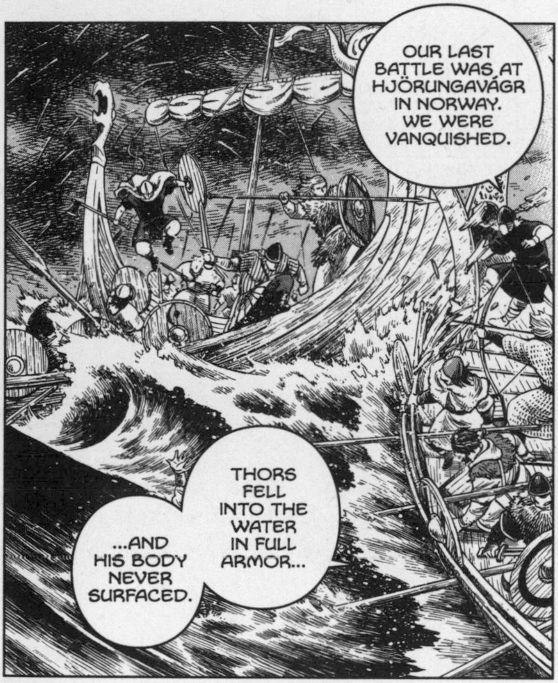
OUR LAST BATTLE WAS AT HJÖRUNGAVÁGR IN NORWAY. WE WERE VANQUISHED.
THORS FELL INTO THE WATER IN FULL ARMOR...
...AND HIS BODY NEVER SURFACED.

A naval battle estimated to have taken place around 986 A.D. between the Jomsvikings, acting on the behalf of King Harald of Denmark, and Haakon Sigurdsson of Norway. Until that point, Norway had been a vassal kingdom of Denmark, but Harald's conversion to Christianity and subsequent attempts to instate it throughout Scandinavia rankled the Norsemen. When Denmark struggled with the Holy Roman Empire to the south, Norway took thc opportunity to renounce its allegiance to Harald. In retaliation, he sent the Jomsvikings to invade Norway, but they were defeated by Haakon at Hjörungavágr, off the coast of Norway.

# Hnefatafl, page 355

A popular Viking Age board game played in Scandinavia. The suffix -tafl means "board." This board was attached to a variety of games originating in the region. Hnefatafl was a particularly popular game in which one side plays the forces of the king, who must move from the center of the board to the corners to escape. The other side plays the siege forces, who must capture the king. Although no concrete rules remain on record, hnefatafl is mentioned in several Viking sagas.

## Freya, page 360

The Norse goddess of fertility, love, beauty and war. Freya rules over Fólkvangr, a field in the afterlife that is the destination of those deceased who do not reach Valhalla.

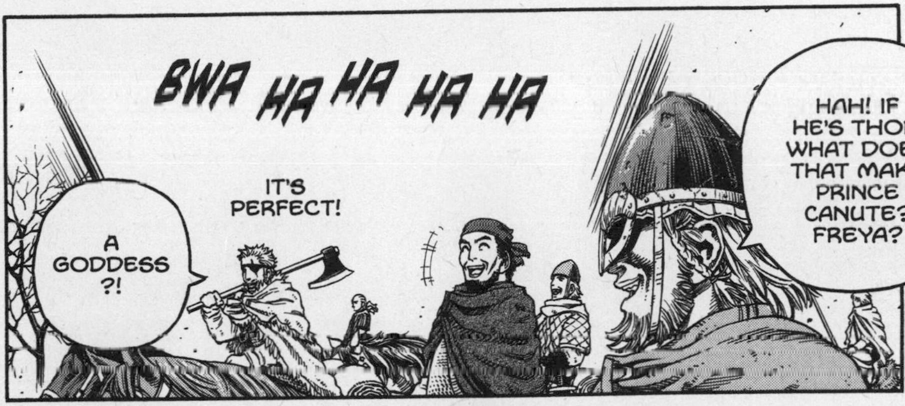
HAH! IF HE'S THOR, WHAT DOES THAT MAKE PRINCE CANUTE? FREYA?
BWA HA HA HA HA
IT'S PERFECT!
A GODDESS ?!

## Battle of Maldon, page 369

A battle between England and the invading Viking force in 991 A.D. Earl Byrhtnoth led a small force of Anglo-Saxons against the invaders and was routed. This defeat for the English led to the practice of Danegeld, a tribute paid in appeasement to the Danish invaders.

## Shigeru Mizuki, page 434

A manga artist, creator of the beloved *Gegege no Kitarô* series detailing a variety of yôkai, traditional Japanese monsters and spirits. Mizuki's artistic style is distinguished by its distinctive long faces and profile-view mouths, as well as his ability to combine the ghoulish with the cartoonish.

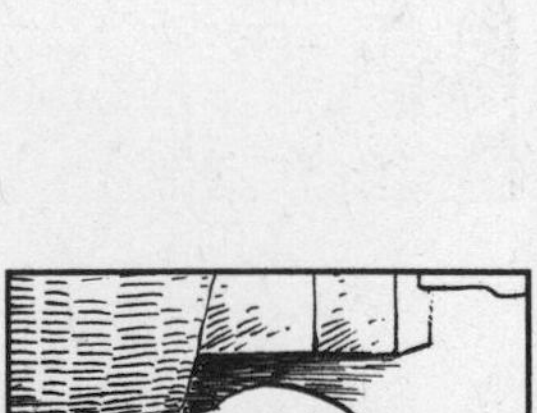

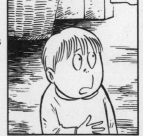

# For Our Farewell Is Near Part 3
## By Makoto Yukimura

# Introduction

At the end of the Edo Period, the arrival of the "black ships" from abroad spelled the end of 260 years of isolation enforced by the shogunate. In response to the shogunate's desire to open the country's borders, disgruntled regional forces loyal to the emperor, such as the Choshu Domain, planned a rebellion. The imperial loyalists massed in Kyoto, where the emperor lived, growing increasingly bold until the city became, in effect, a lawless area. In an effort to restore order, the shogunate recruited ronin (masterless samurai) in Edo (Tokyo) and sent them to Kyoto.

Among these men were Kondo Isami and Okita Soji, students at the Shieikan dojo in Tama. Upon reaching Kyoto, they formed the "Shinsengumi" under the orders of the daimyo of Aizu Domain, who had been charged with keeping the peace in the city. But, unable to reverse the tide of history, the shogunate lost power, and the Shinsengumi were defeated at the Battle of Toba-Fushimi. In 1868, Kondo and Okita had fled to Edo. Okita's body was already wracked with tuberculosis at this time.

To read Part 1 and 2 of the story, see *Vinland Saga* Book One and Book Two.

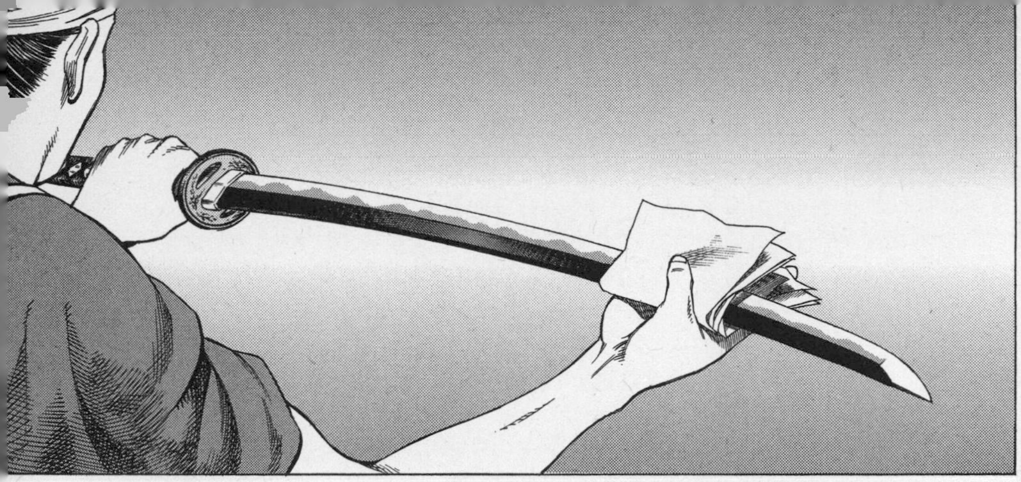

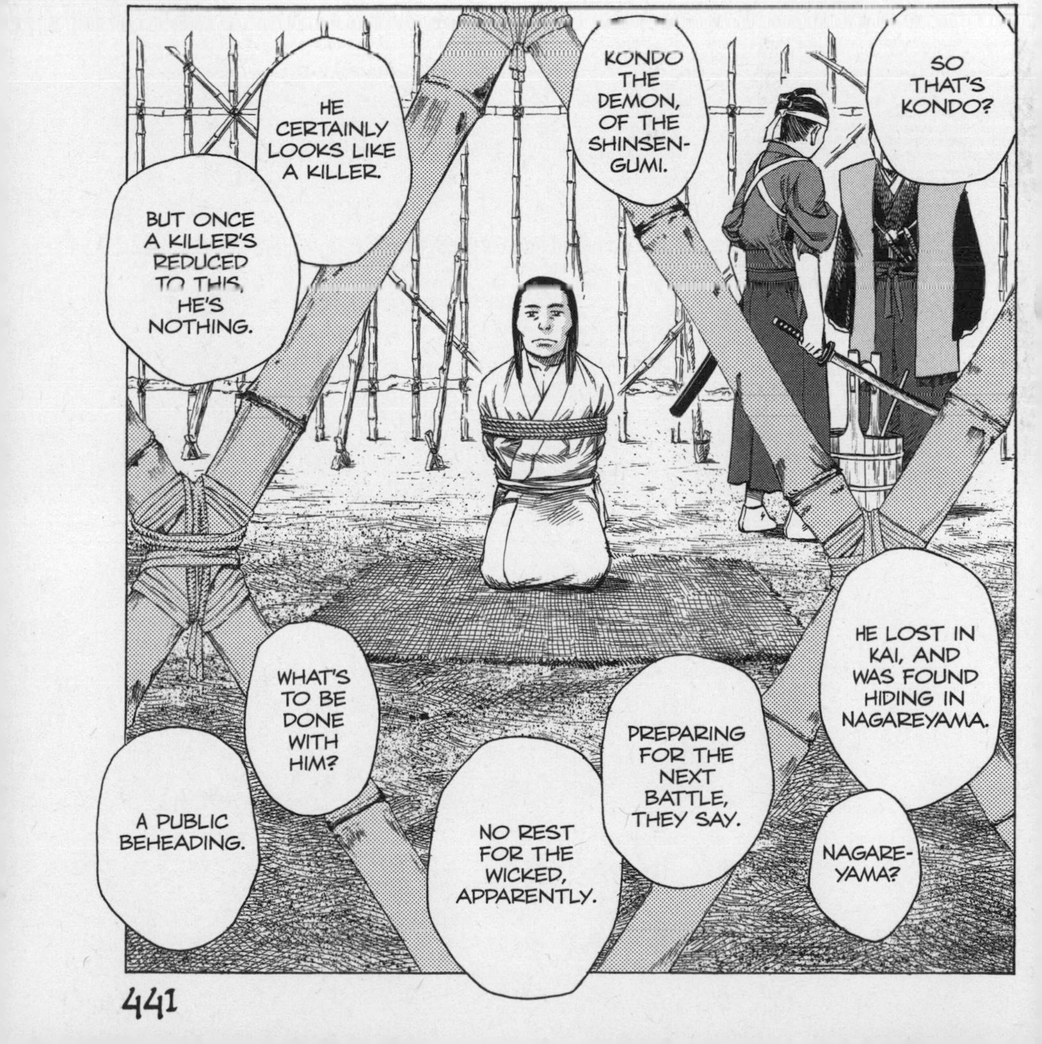
SO THAT'S KONDO?
KONDO THE DEMON, OF THE SHINSEN-GUMI.
HE CERTAINLY LOOKS LIKE A KILLER.
BUT ONCE A KILLER'S REDUCED TO THIS, HE'S NOTHING.
HE LOST IN KAI, AND WAS FOUND HIDING IN NAGAREYAMA.
NAGARE-YAMA?
PREPARING FOR THE NEXT BATTLE, THEY SAY.
NO REST FOR THE WICKED, APPARENTLY.
WHAT'S TO BE DONE WITH HIM?
A PUBLIC BEHEADING.

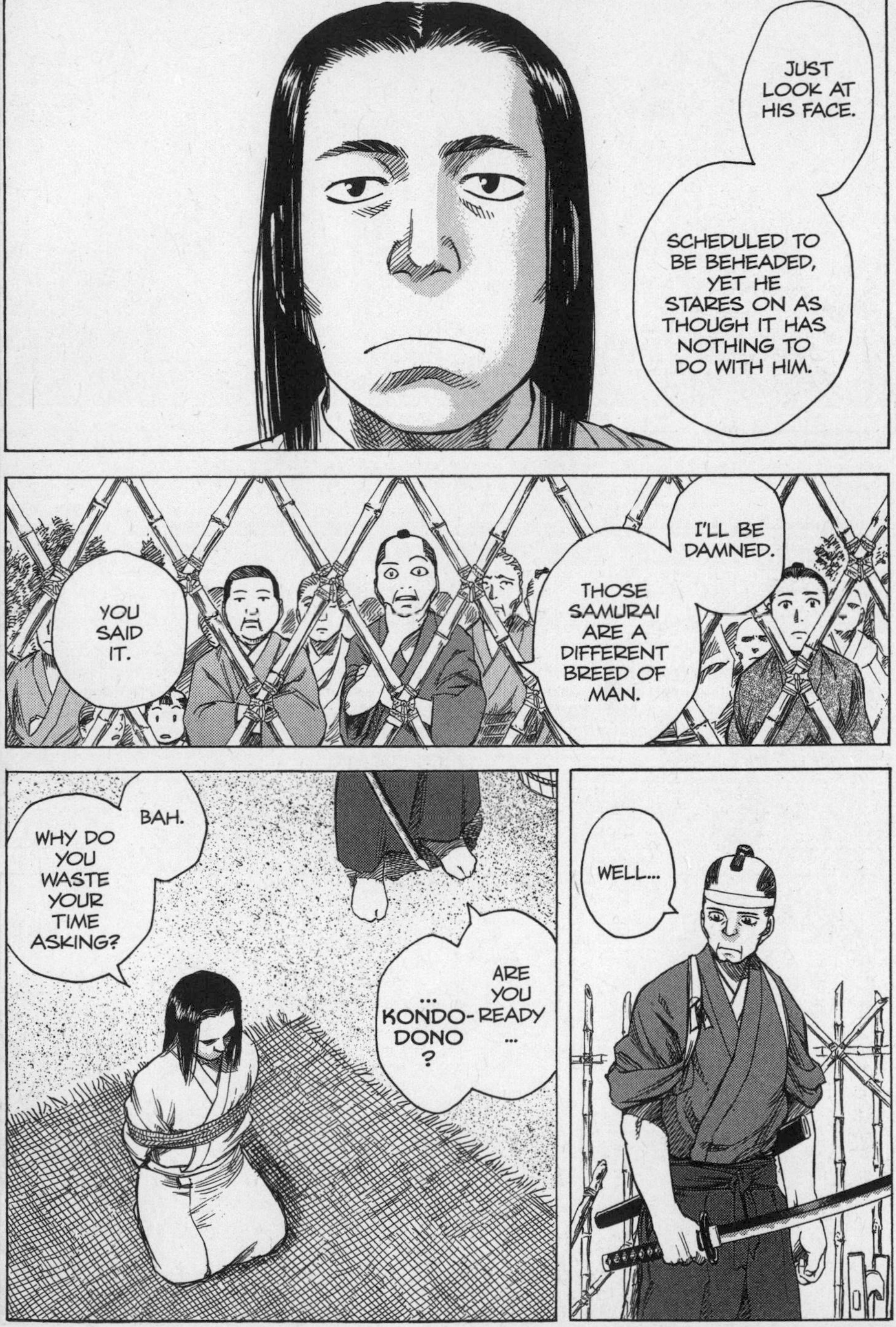
JUST LOOK AT HIS FACE.
SCHEDULED TO BE BEHEADED, YET HE STARES ON AS THOUGH IT HAS NOTHING TO DO WITH HIM.
I'LL BE DAMNED.
THOSE SAMURAI ARE A DIFFERENT BREED OF MAN.
YOU SAID IT.
WELL...
ARE YOU READY... ...KONDO-DONO?
BAH.
WHY DO YOU WASTE YOUR TIME ASKING?

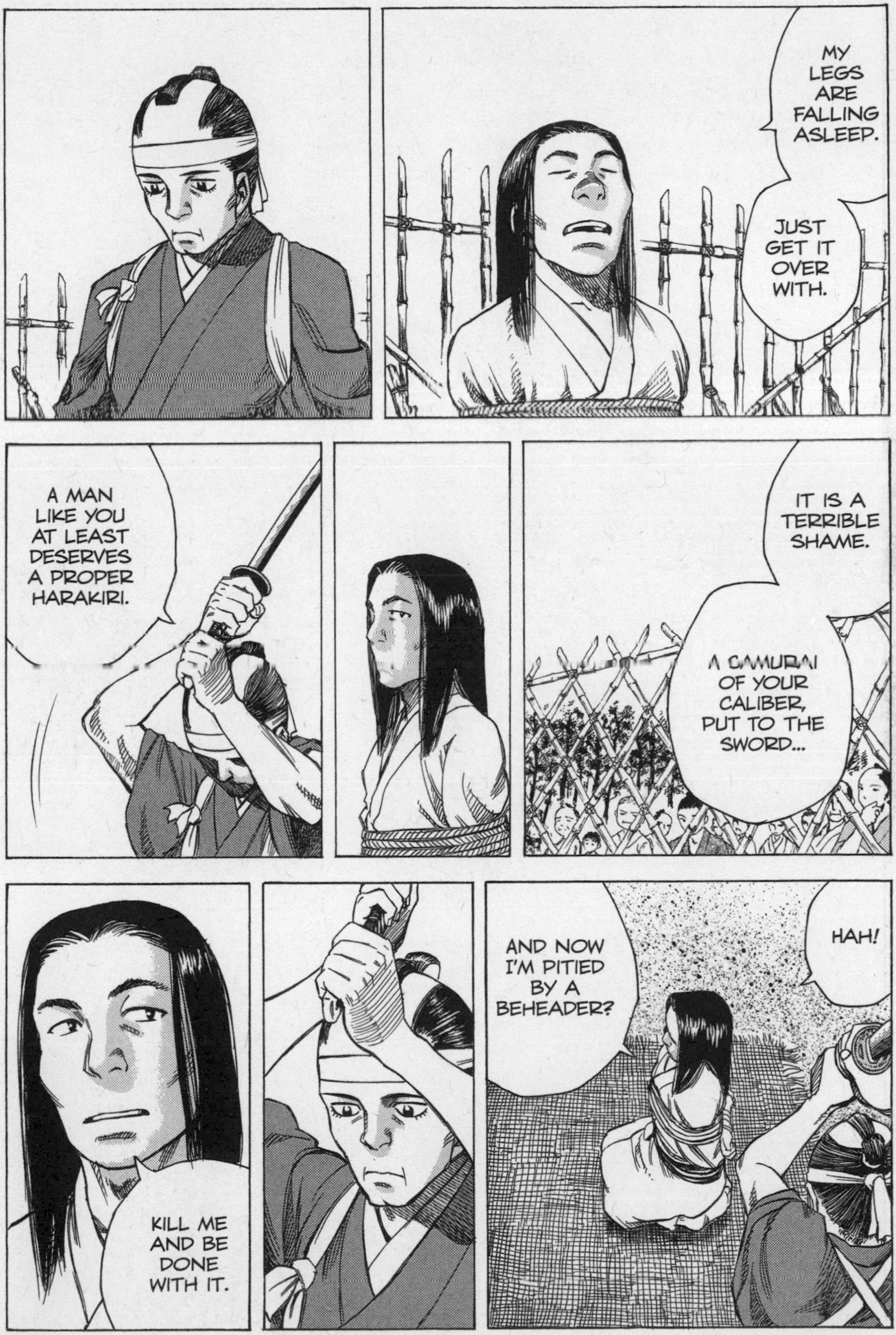
MY LEGS ARE FALLING ASLEEP.
JUST GET IT OVER WITH.
IT IS A TERRIBLE SHAME.
A SAMURAI OF YOUR CALIBER, PUT TO THE SWORD...
A MAN LIKE YOU AT LEAST DESERVES A PROPER HARAKIRI.
HAH!
AND NOW I'M PITIED BY A BEHEADER?
KILL ME AND BE DONE WITH IT.

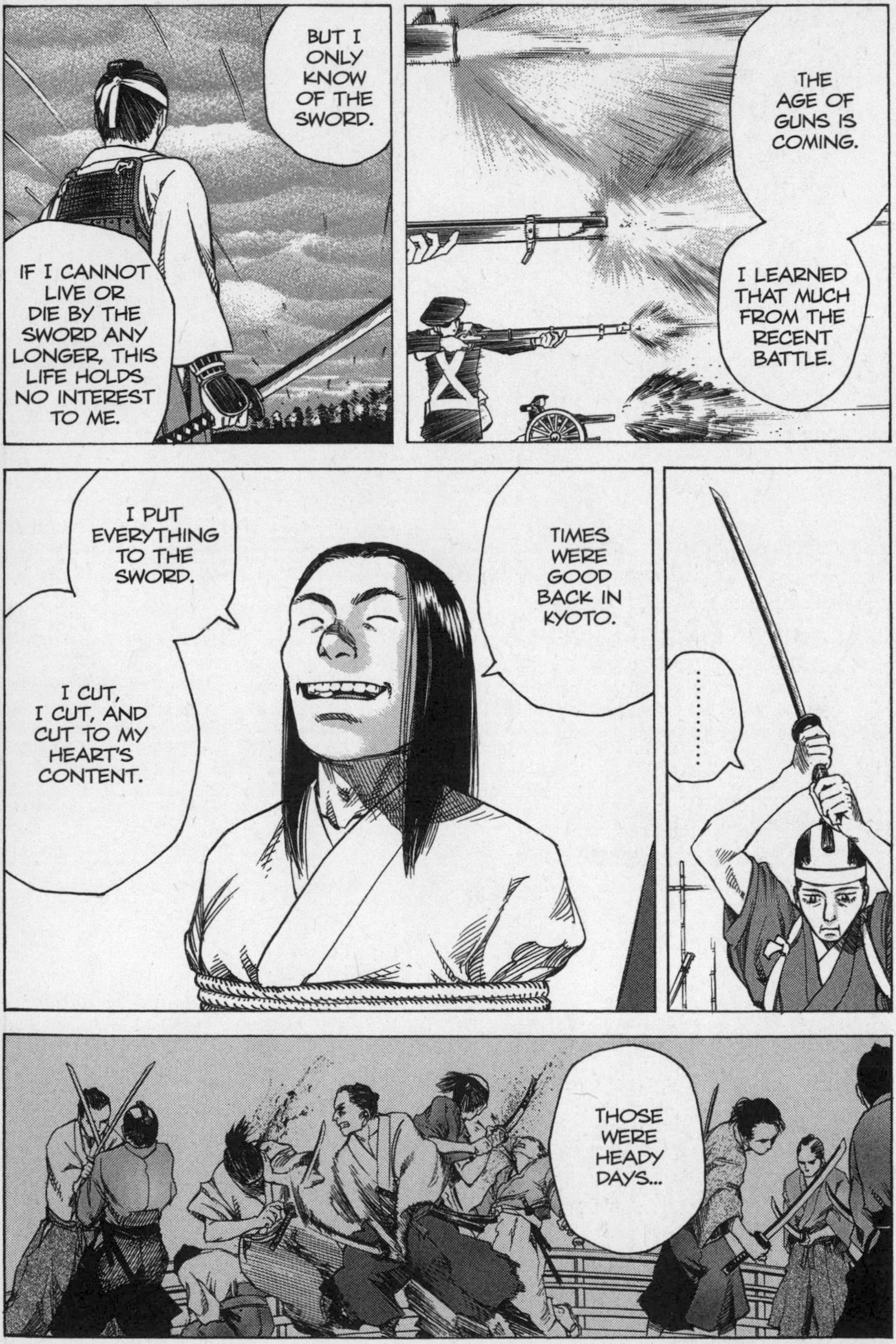
THE AGE OF GUNS IS COMING.
I LEARNED THAT MUCH FROM THE RECENT BATTLE.
BUT I ONLY KNOW OF THE SWORD.
IF I CANNOT LIVE OR DIE BY THE SWORD ANY LONGER, THIS LIFE HOLDS NO INTEREST TO ME.
......
TIMES WERE GOOD BACK IN KYOTO.
I PUT EVERYTHING TO THE SWORD.
I CUT, I CUT, AND CUT TO MY HEART'S CONTENT.
THOSE WERE HEADY DAYS...

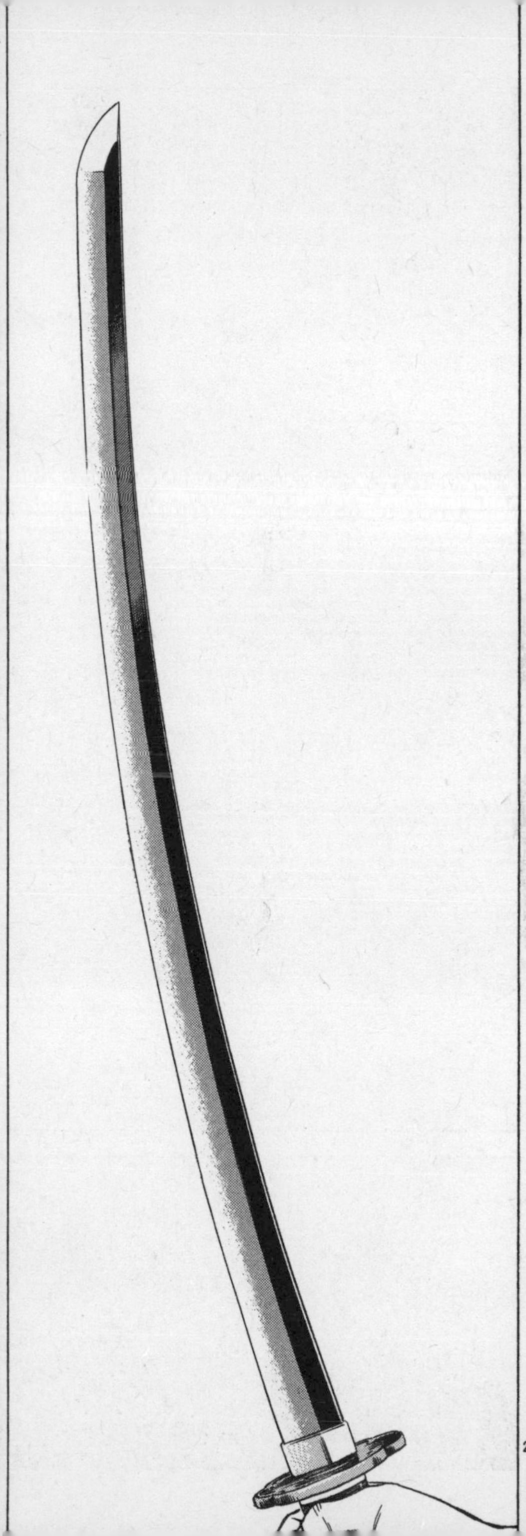

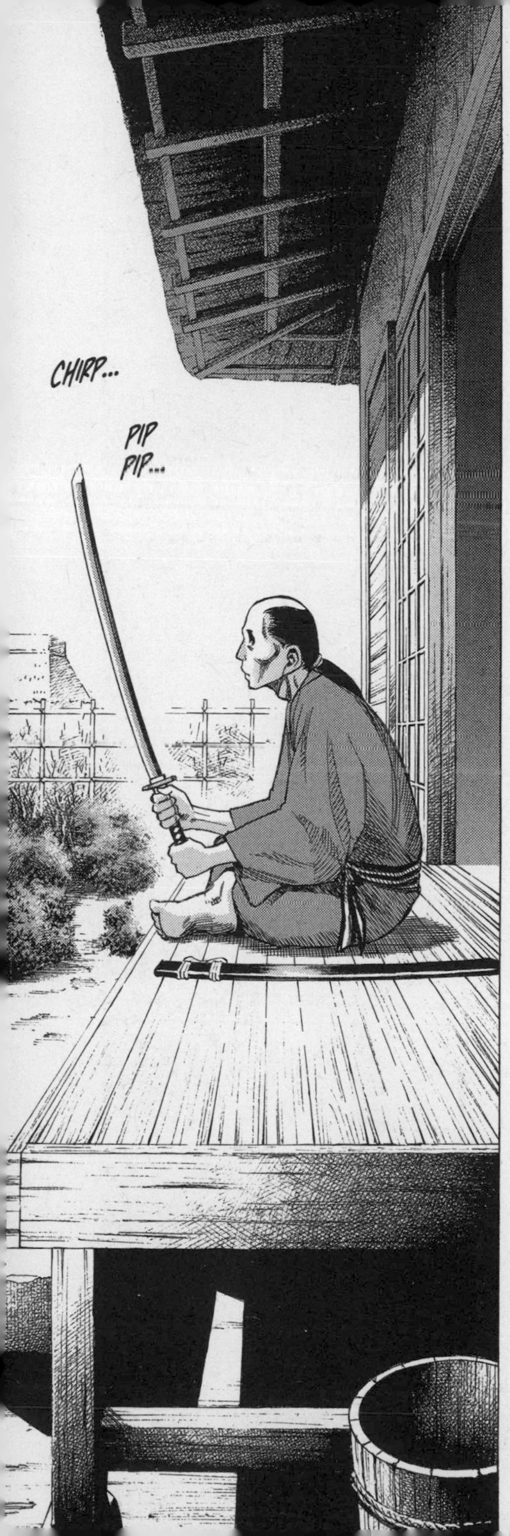
CHIRP...
PIP PIP...

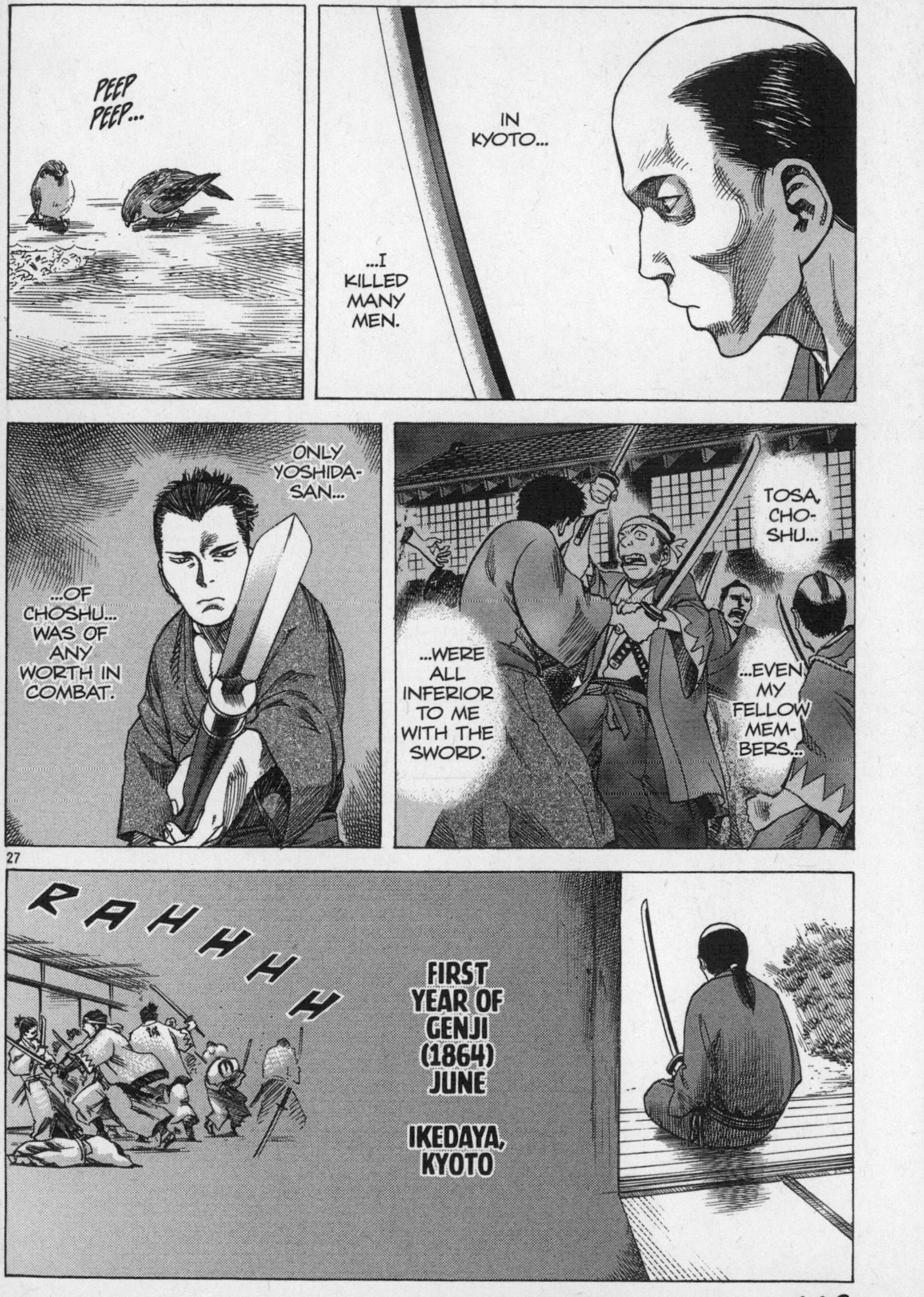
IN KYOTO...
...I KILLED MANY MEN.
PEEP PEEP...
TOSA, CHOSHU...
...EVEN MY FELLOW MEMBERS...
...WERE ALL INFERIOR TO ME WITH THE SWORD.
ONLY YOSHIDA-SAN...
...OF CHOSHU... WAS OF ANY WORTH IN COMBAT.
27
RAHHHHH
FIRST YEAR OF GENJI (1864) JUNE
IKEDAYA, KYOTO

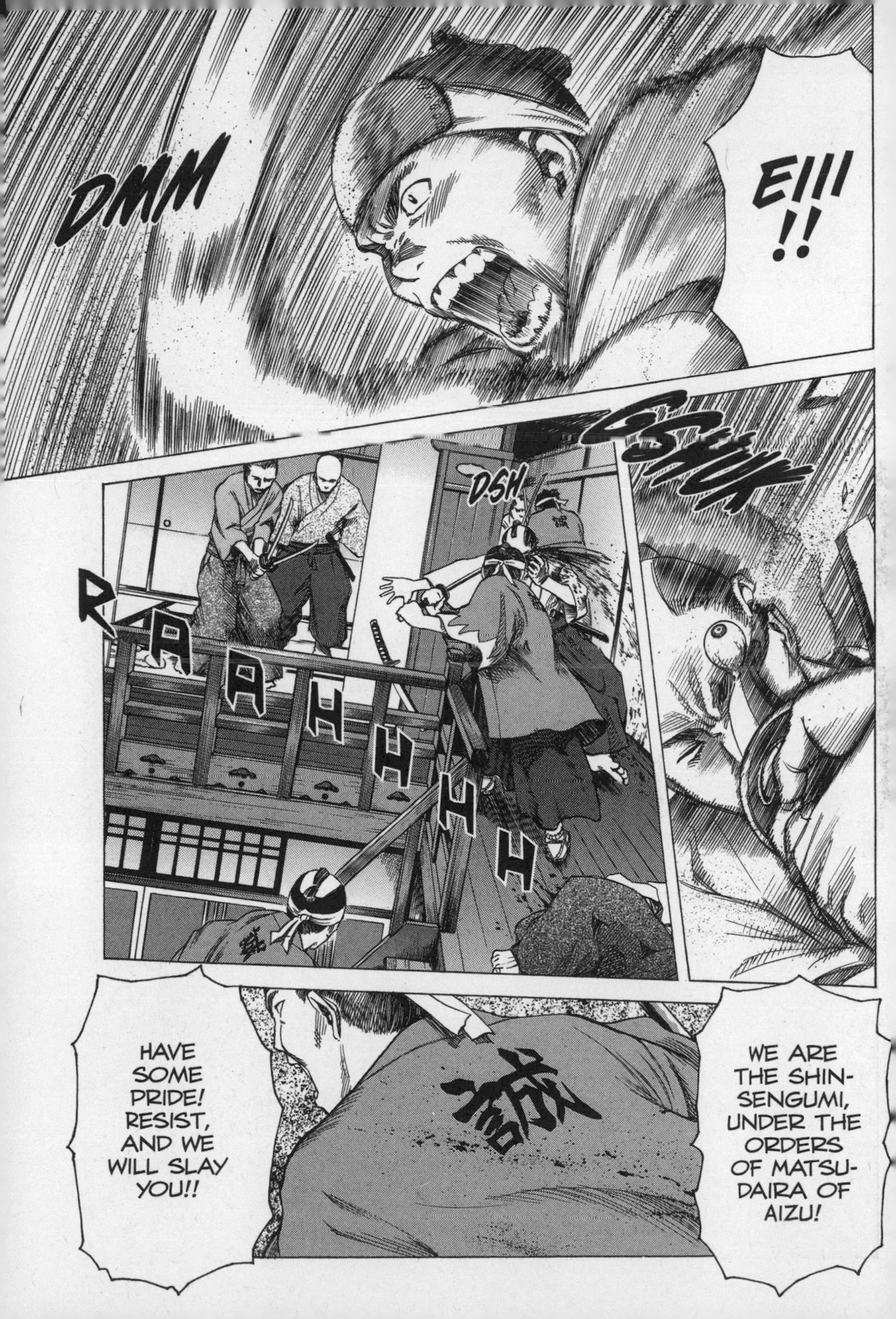
EIII
!!
DMM
GOSHUK
DSH
RAAAHHHHHH
WE ARE THE SHINSENGUMI, UNDER THE ORDERS OF MATSUDAIRA OF AIZU!
HAVE SOME PRIDE! RESIST, AND WE WILL SLAY YOU!!

STAMP

STOMP

STOMP

RAHH

AIEEE

HUFF

HUFF

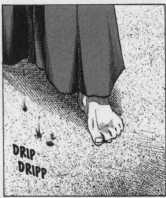

DRIP
DRIPP

YOUR SKILL WITH THE BLADE IS IMPRESSIVE.

I WOULD KNOW YOUR NAME.

COFF

COFF

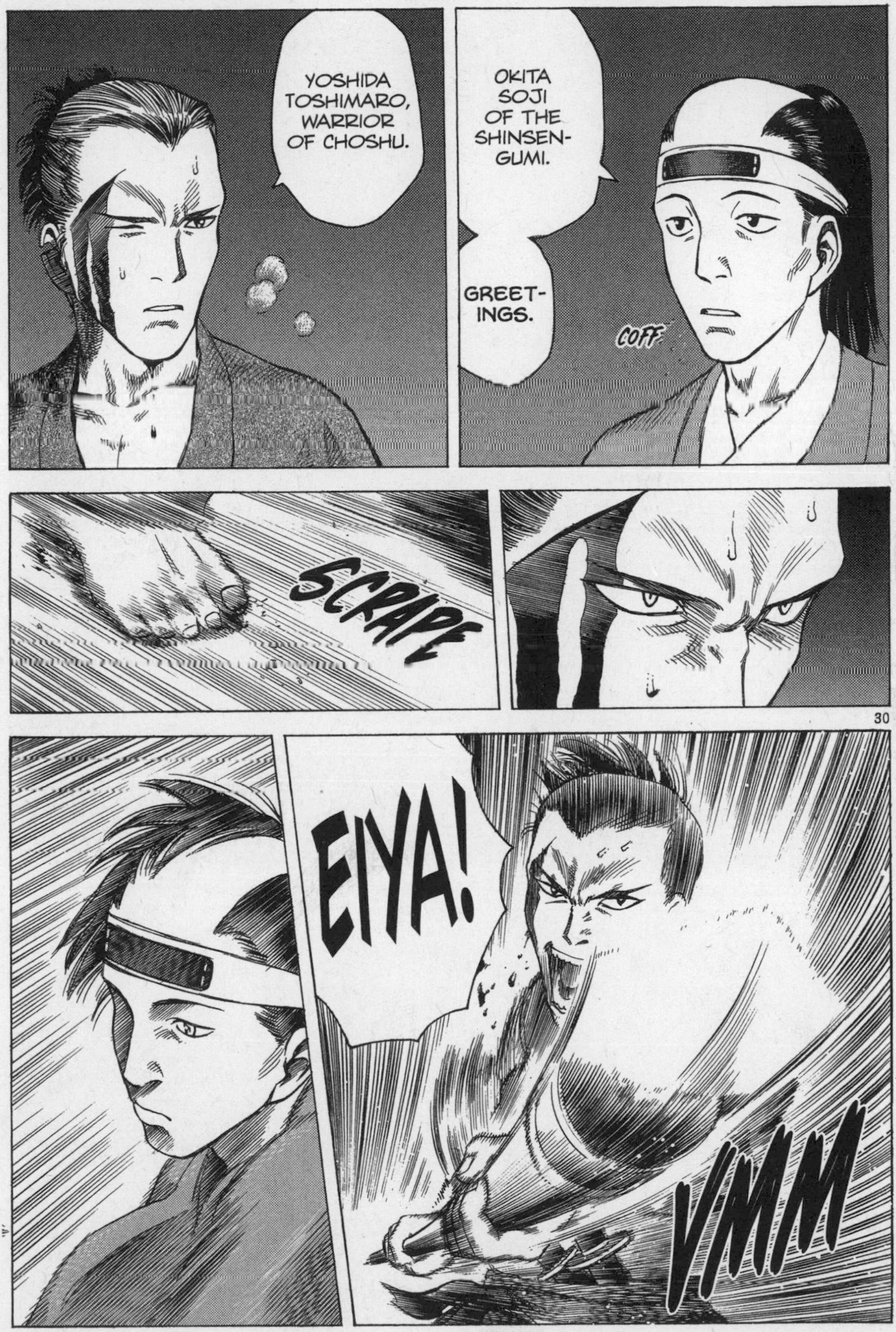
OKITA SOJI OF THE SHINSEN-GUMI.
GREET-INGS.
COFF
YOSHIDA TOSHIMARO, WARRIOR OF CHOSHU.
SCRAPE
30
EIYA!
VMMM

# ASK YUKIMURA

This exclusive Q&A with series creator Makoto Yukimura appears only in the U.S. edition of "Vinland Saga." Future volumes will include them, too, so if you have a question you'd like to ask Mr. Yukimura, please send it to kodanshacomics@randomhouse.com, or to:

Kodansha Comics
451 Park Ave. South, 7th floor
New York, NY 10016.

**Kodansha Comics:** *After your success with* Planetes, *what made you want to leave science fiction and write about Vikings instead?*

**Makoto Yukimura:** I decided that the Viking Age and its cultures were the most appropriate setting to explore violence, the theme I wanted to write about.

Relative to other manga artists, I don't get really hung up on genre. What's most important to me is how to communicate to the readers what I'm trying to say, what I'm trying to draw, in just the right way, without any misunderstandings. Certainly it's easiest to stay motivated if you just turn the motifs you like into manga, but the motifs I like aren't necessarily the best way to express these themes.

*You've obviously done a lot of research into Norse history and mythology. What surprised you most about Viking culture, and do you have a favorite Norse myth or tale?*

I forget the source, but the thing that surprised me most was about the Vikings' moral feelings about murder. Around the beginning of my research, I read in some book that, of course, they recognized that murder is a sin. But at a feast with drinking, if you killed the man next to you while under the influence of alcohol, the sin would be absolved because "the alcohol was sitting in the seat." I felt that a society that had feelings like that toward murder yet didn't collapse was very unique.

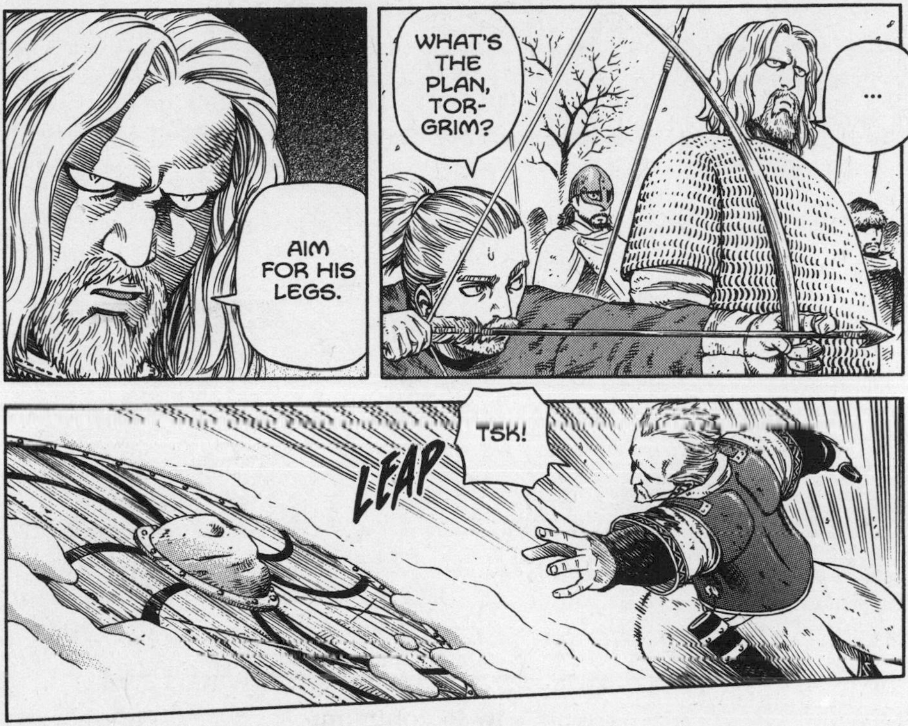
WHAT'S THE PLAN, TORGRIM?
...
AIM FOR HIS LEGS.
LEAP
TSK!

My favorite tale is Hænsa-Thorir's saga [Hænsa-Þóris saga]. As the name indicates, it's the story of a Viking farmer named Hænsa-Thorir. One day, a local big man named Ketil came to Thorir and suggested he sell some of his hay. But Thorir didn't want to sell. Thorir, who was born into a lower class and had no dependents or ability as a warrior, was despised and threatened by everyone living nearby, so no matter whom he sold to it wouldn't be a good deal for him. But Ketil pressured Thorir, using the social norm that he who has should give to those who have not. Ketil proposed deal after deal, but Thorir refused. Finally, Ketil said, "I have done everything I can to negotiate, but he has obstinately refused." Using that as a justification, he decided to take some of the hay without Thorir's consent. Thorir brought a claim against Ketil for seizing his hay, and the story gets complicated, but in the end Ketil was killed. When I read it, I realized that Vikings weren't mere anarchists. If there was something they wanted, they didn't immediately plunder it. In everyday life, they had negotiation procedures based on norms and laws. And it's easy for us living today to understand those norms and laws. This was the work that made me realize that the Vikings were people just like me. It made me see that they worried about the same things, fought over the same things, and had the same sense of right and wrong.

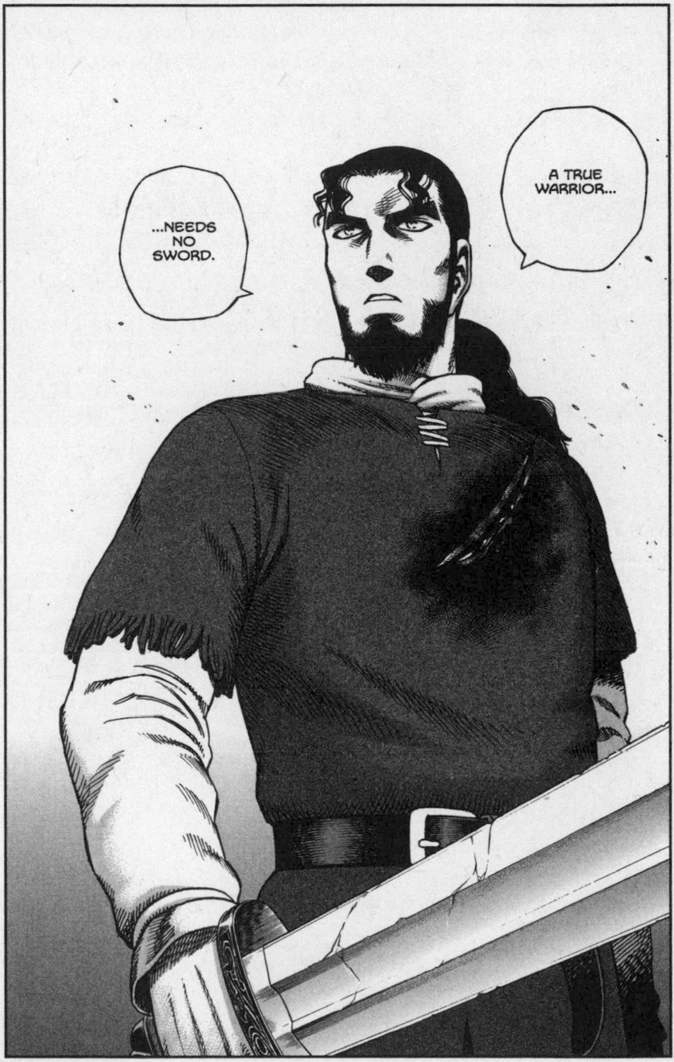
A TRUE WARRIOR...
...NEEDS NO SWORD.

*Do you have any message or advice for people reading the beginning of Vinland Saga in English for the first time?*

There is a message that I believe should be communicated to people if they aren't already aware of it. But I'm not confident that I can explain it in just a few sentences. My hope is that readers will understand this message through my work, by experiencing what my characters experience.

**SEE YOU IN BOOK FOUR, COMING JULY 2014!**

A Kodansha Comics Trade Paperback Original.

Published in the United States by Kodansha Comics, an imprint of
Kodansha USA Publishing, LLC, New York.

Publication rights for this English edition arranged through
Kodansha Ltd., Tokyo.

First published in Japan in 2007 and 2008 by Kodansha Ltd., Tokyo, as
*Vinland Saga*, volumes 5 and 6.

ISBN 978-1-61262-422-8

Printed in the United States of America.

www.kodanshacomics.com

9 8 7 6 5 4 3 2 1

Translation: Stephen Paul
Lettering: Scott O. Brown
Editing: Ben Applegate
Kodansha Comics edition cover & ownership tag design: Phil Balsman

Special thanks to Roderick Dale of the Centre for the Study of the Viking Age at the University of Nottingham for his assistance with the production of this book.

www.kodanshacomics.com/vinland

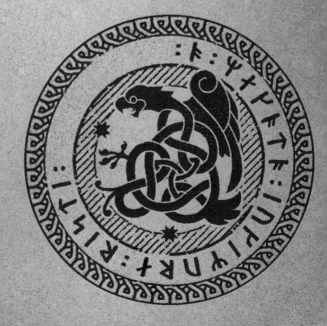